THE RISE OF THE BIGGEST LITTLE CITY

THE GAMBLING STUDIES SERIES

HAROLDS
ITY IN THE WORLD
LOANS
CAFE
SMOKES
Nevad
SPORTING GO

THE RISE OF THE

BIGGEST LITTLE CITY

AN ENCYCLOPEDIC HISTORY OF RENO GAMING, 1931–1981

Dwayne Kling

Foreword by Rollan Melton

University of Nevada Press, Reno & Las Vegas

Frontispiece: Virginia Street at Night, ca. 1950.
Courtesy Charlotte E. Heatherly.

The Gambling Studies Series
Series Editor: William R. Eadington

University of Nevada Press, Reno, Nevada USA
89557
Copyright © 2000 by University of Nevada Press
All rights reserved
Manufactured in the United States of America
Designed by Carrie Nelson House

Publication of this book has been assisted by a
generous grant from the John Ben Snow Memorial
Trust.

Library of Congress Cataloging-in-Publication Data
Kling, Dwayne, 1929–
The rise of the biggest little city : an encyclopedic
history of Reno gaming, 1931–1981 / Dwayne Kling;
foreword by Rollan Melton.
p. cm. — (The gambling studies series)
Includes bibliographical references and index.
ISBN 0-87417-340-x (cloth : alk. paper)
1. Gambling—Nevada—Reno—History.
2. Gambling—Economic aspects—Nevada—Reno.
3. Casinos—Nevada—Reno—History.
I. Title. II. Series.
HV6721.N45K58   1999   99-34609
795'.09793'55—dc21   CIP

The paper used in this book meets the require-
ments of American National Standard for Information Sciences—Permanence of Paper for
Printed Library Materials, ANSI Z39.48-1984.
Binding materials were selected for strength and
durability.

FIRST PRINTING
08 07 06 05 04 03 02 01 00
5 4 3 2 1

To my wife, Rose, who continually furnishes me support;

to my daughters, Michelle, Connie, and Debbie, who light up my life;

and to my grandchildren, Nic, Jennifer, Scott, Chad, and Allison,

who make me proud of them every day.

CONTENTS

ILLUSTRATIONS

FOREWORD

If made into a stage play and then taken on to Broadway, this epic gaming history might well be confused with fiction. Could what is between these covers pass as real, rather than make-believe? Is this work not a multifaceted literary stew, spiced by a writer's bizarre imagination?

Hardly! What author Dwayne Kling has done here is monumental, a factual atlas with an authenticity that is grounded in his incredibly painstaking fourteen-year research/writing effort. The book is powered by the presence of elements that have intrigued mankind through the ages: Riches/Poverty. Strength/Weakness. Mystery/Murder. Success/Failure. Challenge/Change.

Part of its magic are the revelations—for instance, that the dreams of industry giant William F. Harrah might well have perished in the 1930s and '40s, except for his friend Virgil Smith, who rushed in with eleventh-hour loans.

Kling introduces us to hundreds of people and gaming properties in Reno and Washoe in the fifty-year era from 1931 to 1981, in a manner that facilitates the reader's comprehension of chronology, place, and gaming principals. He uses an alphabetization format adeptly, sparing the lay reader, and the gaming researcher, the task of painstakingly tracking facts.

After I agreed to write this foreword, author Kling delivered the hefty manuscript, and I told myself, "Oh, Lord, this will be a formidable reading task." But I instantly accepted that hurry-up perusal wasn't possible. From cover to cover, each vignette, person, place, and statistic is compelling. From the first alphabetized entry, Nick Abelman, to the final entry, Zimba's Casino at 44 West Commercial Row, and what lies between, there is the reward of learning much that is new, and confirming much that we've known about the legalized enterprise that has made Reno internationally famous.

Illicit gambling had existed in Reno back rooms long before legislator Phil Tobin of Winnemucca introduced a proposal that Nevada legalize the practice. The Assembly acted first, voting 24–11 for approval. Eight days later, the State Senate voted 13–3 in favor. Governor Fred Balzar signed the measure into law on March 19, 1931, and Nevada was off on a long, arduous ride. It has been a journey that has taken owners from primitive hole-in-the-wall venues to the glitzy palaces so commonplace today.

The author weaves in flashbacks, affirming that long before legalization, gambling thrived in Goldfield and in Tonopah. It is in these settings that he introduces some of the famous and infamous who have appeared, and disappeared, including George Wingfield Sr., whose long green machine financed Nevada gamblers, politicians, and businesses for decades; and Jim McKay and William Graham, who owned the state's then-largest gambling hall, the Bank Club in

Reno. The McKay/Graham pairing had more than passing encounters with the notorious gangster Baby Face Nelson, and possibly with the Al Capone syndicate out of Chicago.

Dwayne Kling's lengthy search for documentation of licensing, good deeds, and misdeeds led him to examine newspapers, magazines, property transfers—in his most herculean effort, he plunged into microfilm, reading from cover to cover every issue of the *Nevada State Journal* published from 1931 to 1981. He spent so many years at the Nevada Historical Society in Reno, for instance, that the staff there came to think of him as a colleague. Prior to his retirement in 1995, he was, for forty-one years, an associate, then a top-ranked executive of several major gaming properties in Reno.

His daunting research has produced a blizzard of information, including the myriad reasons for gaming property closures. These included such elements as failure to pay taxes; ignoring subpoenas from the Nevada Gaming Commission; suspicious fires that smacked strongly of arson; narcotics possession among licensees; rubber checks; tampering with playing cards and roulette wheels; undisclosed partnership interests; dumping off the bankroll (an illegal practice wherein gaming employees conspire with nonemployee confederates to cheat the house); shootings; and murders that occurred both inside and outside gaming properties.

Kling ticks off forced closures, lists the reasons, and names licensees who were fingered by local and state enforcers of gaming standards.

As the years of legalization have lengthened, it is patently clear that Nevada's detailed screening of gaming license applicants and its increasingly tough controls and careful monitoring have dramatically reduced the number of forced closures and disciplined or barred licensees. The heavy regulation of the state's gaming industry has attracted the appreciation of other states, where legalized gaming is relatively new.

Gaming/entertainment long ago surpassed mining as Nevada's leading industry, and therein lies another major difference among leaders from the two enterprises. Historically, those who made their fortunes from Nevada mines left the state and spent their assets elsewhere. As Kling's research affirms, that hasn't been the case with the principals in the Nevada gaming community. Virtually every leader in the 1931–1981 period remained in the state, including the late Raymond I. "Pappy" Smith and his son, Harold Sr., of Harolds Club; the late Jessie Beck, who owned the Riverside Hotel; the late William F. Harrah and one of his top lieutenants, Rome Andreotti; the late Richard Graves, who sold his Nugget in Sparks to his executive colleague, John Ascuaga Sr., in 1960; the late Leon Nightingale, a Reno Cal-Neva principal who was a major philanthropist, especially to the University of Nevada, Reno; and other past figures, such as Virgil Smith, John Cavanaugh Sr., Newton Crumley, Ernest Primm, Lincoln Fitzgerald, George Wingfield Sr., Charles Mapes, and the incomparable Robert Ring, the left-hand man of Bill Harrah.

The living gaming principals remaining in Reno include Robert Cashell, the former Nevada lieutenant governor; Warren Nelson, retired major stockholder of Reno Cal-Neva; Harvard-educated George Drews, who did more than any other person to win the confidence of Wall Street in Harrah's transition to a publicly traded company; Lloyd Dyer of Harrah's, to whom Kling pays high tribute for his role in Harrah's physical expansion and in its going-public phase; Sil Petricciani, who was a second-generation owner/operator of the Palace Club, continues to live in Reno; and Robert Martin, a retired Harrah's senior vice-president, who lives at Glenbrook, Lake Tahoe, and in Las Vegas.

The mortality rate has been heavy among casinos that are now distant memories, and in recounting them, it is clear that the travail of closures in present-day Reno is nothing new. Challenge and change have been constant companions of the Reno gaming community, and not usually welcome, especially by associates who lost their jobs. Once upon a time, the Reno glitz was made brighter by the then-prominent enterprises. Kling's book lists 345 casinos licensed in the fifty-year period. He tells which no longer exist—which is nearly all. Among the most prominent firms that disappeared are the Club Fortune, where famed entertainers, including Lee Liberace and Sammy Davis Jr., starred; the aforementioned Bank Club; the famed nightspots the Willows, the Cedars, the Lancer, and the Country Club, all wiped out by fire; and the New York Club, which existed from 1931 to 1935, a glamorous enterprise at 224 North Center Street, and the first to exploit the magnetic combination of entertainment, dancing, drinking, and gambling. It was a common stamping ground for Hollywood stars and enjoyed the frequent presence of former world's heavyweight boxing champion Jack Dempsey. Gone, too, are the Tavern, the Cowshed, and the Dog House.

The author resurrects memories of the famed Harlem Club, which was at Lake Street and Commercial Row, and he ticks off famous visiting luminaries who assembled, played, and sang there: Louis "Satchmo" Armstrong, Pearl Bailey (a cousin of the owner), B.B. King, and Sammy Davis Jr.

As to the racial/ethnic mix, Reno was noted for it long before it became fashionable in other areas of the United States. Japanese-American Fred Aoyama of the Reno Club, which eventually was acquired by Bill Harrah, was the first Asian-American to acquire a gaming license in Nevada. That was in 1931, shortly after the passage of the legalization of gaming. Aoyama's partner, Fred Yamagishi, was also of Japanese descent. Over the first fifty years, licensees in Reno included Basques, Italians, African-Americans, Greeks, and Turks.

For the historic record, Dwayne Kling has ferreted out an elongated list of Nevada gaming "firsts." Most occurred in Reno. Here are some:

First legal gaming license: the Owl Club at 142 East Commercial Row.

First female keno writer: Ruth Beck.

First female hounded out of Nevada by federal Prohibition agents: Belle Livingstone. Not a single member of her family attended her funeral in New York City.

First full casino owned by Bill Harrah: opened in 1946 at 210 North Virginia Street.

First cheating case: the Dog House, in 1939.

First local scholarship donor for black students: Bill Fong of the New China Club.

First big-name entertainment in Northern Nevada: in 1941 Newt Crumley brought to Elko stars Ted Lewis, Sophie Tucker, Jimmy Dorsey, the Andrews Sisters, and the Paul Whiteman Orchestra.

Oldest continuously held gaming license in Nevada: Jack Douglass, who, as the Millennium drew near, remained active in ownership of the Comstock Hotel-Casino in Reno.

First female dealers: Harolds Club, late 1930s.

First Washoe licensee jailed for cheating: Shorty King, 1940.

First major casino to have the culinary union organize its food and beverage employees: Circus Circus, 1980.

First female security guard: Linda Wood, Harrah's Reno.

First female casino owner, Mildred Preston, 1932, Waldorf of Reno.

First gaming organization to go public: Harrah's, 1971.

Although William F. Harrah had the bigger name on the world stage, Dwayne Kling says the winner of the most-influential gaming leader competition would be Raymond I. "Pappy Smith," the general manager of Harolds Club. There are many provable reasons: Smith launched the incredible Harolds Club scholarship program in 1946, and in its lifetime the program awarded full-ride academic grants to some 250 young Nevadans, including the writer of this foreword. Smith was the first to employ females as floor managers. This marketing/promotion genius achieved a milestone in the late 1940s when he became the first person to advertise gaming on a national basis—his "Harolds Club, or Bust!" billboard signs were enormously successful. He was the first to implement five-dollar slot machines (1967). It was Pappy Smith who was instrumental in persuading political leaders to push successfully for the construction of Interstate 80 over the Sierra Nevada, and when that was done, circa 1960, Reno and Lake Tahoe became year-round entertainment meccas.

This Vermont native was a major philanthropist in a cultural sense as well, bringing great stars to Reno for civic concert performances. But the fabled Pappy leaves an influence sphere that extends to the conclusion of the Millennium, and will endure. The senior Smith set the memorable standard for the marketing of legitimate gaming; his example of innovation—the introduction of females into the gaming employee/executive stream may well have been his most significant—has influenced a generation of Reno and Las Vegas gamers, and those far beyond Nevada's borders. In Las Vegas, William Wilkerson, then Bugsy Siegel and others, tinkered with the notion that room accommodations offered as part and parcel of gaming provided the customers with creature comforts that compelled them to lengthen their visits—and gamble longer in the process. But that strategy was first hatched in Reno, at the Riverside Hotel, where owner George Wingfield Sr. possessed the happy combination of innovation, daring, and formidable personal wealth to carry out his schemes and dreams. Later, Mert Wertheimer brought big-league entertainment to the Riverside, helping to make Reno the entertainment capital of the country long before Las Vegas could even aspire toward that title.

That superb modern gaming executive William Harrah, who was keenly influenced by the "firsts" introduced by Raymond "Pappy" Smith, took all the usable ideas and combined them into a virtual entertainment/gaming art form. Steve Wynn, the contemporary gaming/entertainment whiz, has publicly declared how much Harrah's examples influenced how he has erected his own gaming/entertainment empire in Las Vegas.

Now, as the twentieth century nears its conclusion, Reno is confronted with the most formidable challenges of its legal gaming run. The city and other Northern Nevada points, especially Lake Tahoe, face the sternest competition ever—from sister city Las Vegas, from New Jersey, from the proliferation of other gaming states, and from neighboring California, where American Indian entrepreneurs edge closer to legal gaming.

As author Kling's research emphasizes, the 1931–1981 gaming operation closures did not occur because of economic travail. Not even the Great Depression was a factor in shutdowns. The proven culprits in business failure were the internal villains, thieves and/or arsonists. To its great credit, Nevada has sharply curtailed cheats. Effective safeguards against both internal and external wrongdoers are in place. Glory be to two Nevada governors, Charles H. Russell and Grant Sawyer, for creating the groundwork that subsequent administrations have built upon to thwart the undesirable owner candidates, licensed operators, employers, and customers.

To survive as a major gaming/entertainment center, what Reno must now do is reinvent itself as it bids to revitalize its reputation as an exciting destination city. Its campaign to modernize the inner city is gaining some momentum. Whether those efforts will be enough to reestablish Reno as the place that people are compelled to visit is yet to be determined.

The perfect solution would be the appearance of people who can, in their contemporary ways, match the attractive creative skills, the durability, and the financial power of the George Wingfields, the Norman Biltzes, the Raymond I. Smith family, and probably foremost, the leadership genius of William F. Harrah.

Dwayne Kling and his partner in this endeavor—the excellent publisher, University of Nevada Press—deserve warmest thanks for creating this vital gaming history. Kling has known many of those about whom he writes, and that association enables him to compose attractive word pictures, as few others could on this subject. He has marshaled thousands of facts beyond those mentioned in this foreword.

What he has given us is a grand, true account of a unique industry. For this, we shall remain ever grateful.

Rollan Melton
Reno Gazette-Journal

PREFACE

When I first came to Reno in 1947, I was immediately fascinated by the casinos and the individuals who owned, operated, and worked in them, and the fascination has never left me. This volume is the result of that fascination.

What started as a labor of love and an avocation soon began to approximate a vocation. I became almost obsessed with recording and preserving the names, dates, and places, which, although they were recent history, would be forgotten if not soon preserved.

The growth of gaming in Reno corresponded with the rise of the Biggest Little City—hence, the title of the book. In 1930 there were 18,494 people listed in the census, and the downtown area consisted of wooden buildings, most of them housing bars, cafes, small hotels, and even grocery stores. By 1940 Reno gaming was still in its infancy and the Reno census counted only 21,317 people.

By 1960 Reno's population had more than doubled, and by 1970, as gaming continued to grow, Reno's population was 72,863. By 1980 it had reached 100,756, more than five times larger than when gambling was legalized in 1931. The wooden buildings were gone, and the small hotels, bars, and cafes had been replaced by neon-lit gambling casinos and towering hotel-casinos.

The vast majority of data in this book was taken from magazine articles, newspaper accounts, and gaming records. The *Nevada State Journal* and the *Reno Evening Gazette* provided the foundation for this work. I read every issue of the *Nevada State Journal* from 1931 to 1985 from front page to back page during my fourteen years of research. The *New York Times* was also a valuable research tool in the history of Reno gambling in the 1930s. Magazines such as *Life, Collier's,* and the *Saturday Evening Post* also provided significant information. And firsthand observations, recollections, oral-history interviews, and conversations with gaming people furnished a wealth of information. All licensing dates, lists of games licensed, and, in most cases, addresses were taken from Harvey J. Fuller's *Index of Nevada Gambling Establishments.*

The year 1981 was selected as the cutoff date for several reasons. First, it marked the fiftieth anniversary of legal gaming in Nevada. Second, 1978 was marked by a tremendous explosion in the number of major hotel-casino properties in Reno, and by 1981 the new properties had become established, many former longtime casinos had gone out of business, and Reno casino properties remained somewhat static for the next several years. And third, the image of gambling had been improved because of the infusion of financing from outside sources, and several gaming properties had become publicly owned corporations. This, along with additional regulation of gaming, meant that more accurate records were being maintained and made available, which in turn will make it simpler for other historians to record the history of gaming in Reno after 1981.

One of the major purposes of this volume is to honor and salute the individuals who broke ground for the gaming industry and for those who kept it going and growing into what has become the dominant industry in the state of Nevada. On the fiftieth anniversary of gambling, in 1981, there were celebrations, festivities, and honors bestowed on the true giants of the industry—men and women such as Raymond I. Smith, Jessie Beck, Bill Harrah, and the like. However, little credit was given to the gaming employees who were there on the front lines, working with the public on a shift-by-shift basis and working Saturdays, Sundays, holidays, or any other days that the casinos needed staffing. Hundreds of these individuals are listed in this volume. Not forgotten either are some of the people who worked behind the scenes, away from the public, people who worked in finances, entertainment, and the restaurant and bar areas, and some employees who worked in the fields of advertising and public relations.

Also listed in this book are a few individuals who did harm to the gaming industry and who were forced to leave the industry.

There are many prominent individuals in the gaming industry today who are not listed in this work because they achieved their prominence after the cutoff date of 1981. Some of those prominent individuals who are not specifically mentioned in this work because of the time-line factor would include, but would not be limited to, the likes of Phil Satre; the Douglass brothers, William, John, David, and Dan; Phil Bryant; Jim Rogers; Bill McHugh; and Lou Phillips.

I regret any omissions, and I know there may be some. I found it nearly impossible to list everyone who contributed to Reno's gaming history, and I would welcome input from anyone who would care to contribute more data.

Finally, I would like to express my thanks to the people who helped me put this book into your hands. First and foremost, let me thank the late James A. Michener, who by letters and example encouraged me to continue my research.

Also, my thanks to Rollan Melton, who initially steered me in the direction of the University of Nevada Press, and to Dr. Eric Moody, Lee Brumbaugh, Phillip Earl, and Lee Mortenson of the Nevada Historical Society, who furnished answers to my many questions and helped me with my picture selections. A special thanks to William Pettite for his photographs and his information on Belle Livingstone.

Thanks also to Harvey Fuller for doing so much research pertaining to the licensing of the early-day casinos, and my special thanks to Neal Cobb, who gave me unlimited access to the fantastic photo collection compiled by his parents, Mr. and Mrs. Jerry Cobb, and Modern Studios.

A few important developments that occurred too late to be incorporated into the main text of the book have been covered in the addenda (p. 180). At the time of publication, Reno's gaming industry was in a state of flux, and it is likely that there will be more changes in the months and years to come. But they must be the subject of another book than this.

THE RISE OF THE BIGGEST LITTLE CITY

A

ABELMAN, NICK

Nick Abelman, one of the true pioneers of early gambling in Nevada, was born in Chicago on December 25, 1876. He came to Goldfield in 1906 and operated clubs and casinos there until moving to Tonopah in 1913. In Tonopah he owned and operated the Big Casino and the Tonopah Club. A list of his partners in the clubs included Charles "Shoshone" Brown, G. T. Osborne, Chet Carpenter, and the legendary Reno casino owner James McKay. While in Tonopah, Abelman had his first meeting with Bill Graham, who—in the 1930s, along with James McKay—became the most influential person in Reno. Nick Abelman gave Bill Graham his first job in Nevada gambling when he hired him as a pit boss at the Tonopah Club.

In 1927 Abelman, at the urging of George Wingfield, moved to Reno and became associated with Wingfield in many business ventures. In 1932, Abelman, Steve Pavlovich, and Bert Riddick opened the Ship and Bottle Club on North Center Street.

In 1935 they sold the Ship and Bottle Club and opened a casino in the Riverside Hotel, leasing the property from George Wingfield. They operated the casino, bar, and restaurant as the Riverside Buffet. In the early 1940s Abelman purchased Pavlovich's interests, and in 1949 he sold the casino to Mert Wertheimer.

Abelman also owned the Stateline Country Club on the South Shore of Lake Tahoe from 1933 to 1945 and was a part owner of the Christmas Tree Lodge on the Mount Rose Highway in the late 1940s.

In 1949 Abelman became a 75-percent partner in the Waldorf Club, taking over Howard Farris's percentage. Warren Nelson held the remaining 25 percent. Nelson soon left the Waldorf, but Abelman remained a licensee in the Waldorf Club until his death in 1951.

Shortly before his death, Abelman was named president, general manager, and licensee of the Sierra Investment Company, a company with partners who included Nick Sahati, Evelyn Barrett, and Charles O'Keefe. The plan was to open a casino at 232 North Virginia Street. Nick's death prevented the casino from opening.

Abelman, who was married to June Pettite Abelman, was prominently identified with Nevada's gambling industry for many years. He was also well known in the mining fraternity and was remembered as a big-hearted man who grubstaked hundreds of prospectors. He was generous with friends and employees, lending out thousands of dollars—most of it never repaid.

Abelman died on December 15, 1951.

Nev. St. Journal, 30 Mar. 49, 5 Apr. 49, 7 Sept. 51, 23 Oct. 51, 16 Dec. 51 (obit. and photo), 29 June 90.

Nick Abelman (l.) and Steve Pavlovich (r.) in front of the Riverside Hotel in 1933. Abelman and Pavlovich, along with Bert Riddick, leased the Riverside in the mid-1930s. Courtesy of William Pettite.

ACE OF SPADES

238 North Virginia Street; licensed from October to December 1934 for tango only.

The Ace of Spades was a small tango (bingo) parlor that was open for only a few months in the early days of legal gambling.

The former location of the Ace of Spades is today part of Harolds Club.

ACHUFF, JOHN

John Achuff was a co-owner with Gordon Rose and Jack Duffy of the Town House on First Street from April 1948 to November 1949. He later went to Las Vegas, where he was licensed as a shift manager at the Silver Slipper Casino in July 1970.

Warren Nelson called Achuff the finest roulette dealer he has ever seen.

Warren Nelson et al., *Always Bet on the Butcher: Warren Nelson and Casino Gaming, 1930s–1980s* (Reno: University of Nevada Oral History Program, 1994); *Nev. St. Journal,* 24 July 70.

ACME BAR

268 North Virginia Street; licensed from July 1, 1943, to January 10, 1944, for slots, 21, craps, and roulette.

The Acme Bar was located on the corner of Commercial Row and Virginia Street, under the Reno Arch. Today the former location of the Acme Bar is part of Harolds Club.

Nev. St. Journal, 15 Aug. 44 (adv.).

ADLER, SANFORD

Sanford Adler purchased the former Club Fortune property in 1947 and opened it as the Cal-Neva Club in Reno on November 20, 1948. He also owned the Cal-Neva Lodge at Lake Tahoe.

On November 12, 1955, the Cal-Neva Club was closed by the Internal Revenue Service. On November 16, 1955, Adler was permanently barred from the gaming industry by the State of Nevada for failure to pay taxes and for failing to respond to a subpoena from the Gaming Commission regarding the relicensing of the Cal-Neva Club.

Nev. St. Journal, 8 Feb. 55, 12 Nov. 55, 16 Nov. 55.

ALIBI CLUB

1695 South Virginia Street; licensed from April 1948 to 1954 for 21 only.

The Alibi was opened in 1948. In 1953 Robert Douglass was licensed for one 21 game at this location.

The Alibi closed in 1954 and later the same year reopened as Vario's. The business operated as Vario's, a fine restaurant, for many years.

The former location of the Alibi Club is currently occupied by Bricks Restaurant.

Nev. St. Journal, 24 Mar. 53.

ALLEY CLUB

10 East Douglas Alley; licensed from August to October 1938 for a pony-express race game (actually a type of slot machine).

The Alley Club was one of many bars licensed at this same address. Most of them were of short duration, and the Alley Club was no exception.

The former location of the Alley Club is today part of Harolds Club.

ALPINE CLUB

116 North Center Street; licensed from May to November 30, 1931, for slots and roulette.

The Alpine Club offered gambling for only a few months in the early days of legalized gaming; however, the club had operated as a bar since the early 1900s.

Eddie Vacchina originally opened the Alpine and continued as its proprietor for many years. The Alpine continued to operate as a bar, cabaret, and nightclub until it was sold to Andre Duque and Leon Indhart in 1939. They renamed it the 116 Club. It later became known as the Stein and was a popular local gathering place until it closed in 1985.

The former location of the Alpine Club is now part of the Cal-Neva parking garage on the east side of Center Street.

Nev. St. Journal, 29 Dec. 33 (adv.), 11 Aug. 34 (adv.).

ALTURAS BAR

139 East Second Street; licensed from April 15, 1944, to 1946 for 21 only.

The Alturas Bar was licensed by Ralph Henson in 1944 and 1945, by H. Fanucchi in April 1946, and by Al Figoni in October 1946. The site is now a parking lot.

ALTURAS CLUB

139 East Second Street; licensed intermittently from 1931 to 1936 for slots and 21.

The Alturas was a bar that sometimes leased space to a 21 game operator. It had several owners over the years. One of the early owners was Adolph Gianotti, who was given a beer license when Prohibition was repealed in 1933.

The former location of the Alturas is now a parking lot.

Nev. St. Journal, 8 Apr. 33.

AMANTE, CARL

Amante was licensed as a one-third owner of the Town House in July 1953. He later became sole owner of the club. When the Town House was destroyed by fire in 1959, Amante was accused but never convicted of arson.

Nev. St. Journal, 22 Dec. 59.

AMES COCKTAIL LOUNGE

218 Sierra Street; licensed from October 24, 1936, to 1938 for 21 and roulette.

The Ames was located in the Carlton Hotel. It was more a bar and cocktail lounge than a casino or club, with gaming available for hotel guests or whomever came in for a drink or entertainment.

The former location of the Ames Cocktail Lounge is now part of Eddie's Fabulous 50's.

ANDREOTTI, ROMANO "ROME"

Rome Andreotti was born in Reno on June 15, 1923. After serving in World War II as an interpreter in the army counterintelligence corps, he began his gaming career at the Frontier Club in 1946. In 1948 he joined Harrah's as a roulette check racker and a weekend 21 dealer. He soon began his almost meteoric climb up through the casino hierarchy.

Andreotti, a soft-spoken, affable man, loved the gaming industry. He was a behind-the-scenes stickler for detail who oversaw all of Harrah's departments at one

Left to right: Bob Ring, general manager of Harrah's; Gene Diullo, keno manager; and Rome Andreotti, operations manager, ca. 1976. Courtesy of Gene Diullo.

time or another during his career. In the 1960s and 1970s it was not unusual for him to work twelve to fourteen hours a day, six or seven days a week. He was a workaholic who didn't believe in passing work on if he could do it himself.

There were many individuals who played important roles in the success of Harrah's, but it would be impossible to leave out the name of Rome Andreotti if one were to make a list of Bill Harrah's key people.

Rome Andreotti died on April 3, 1984, while still acting as Harrah's vice-president and chief executive officer of operations.

Nev. St. Journal, 5 Sept. 66, 26 Feb. 77, 6 Apr. 84 (obit. and photo).

AOYAMA, FRED

Fred Aoyama was a co-owner of the Reno Club, a bingo parlor that opened in 1931. The Reno Club is thought to be the first licensed bingo parlor in the state, and Aoyama is believed to be one of the first persons of Asian origin licensed in the state for gaming.

ARENA CIGAR STORE

342 North Virginia Street; licensed from March to June 1931 for poker only.

The Arena Cigar Store sold tobacco products and sundry items. A poker game was licensed there during the first three months after gaming became legal in Nevada.

The Wild West Souvenir Shop is currently in business at this location.

ART'S DARTO DEN

14 East Commercial Row; licensed from June 18 to December 1937 for tango (bingo).

Art's Darto Den opened on June 19, 1937, with something new and different. The darto game was played exactly the same as bingo or tango, except that winning numbers were selected by patrons throwing darts at the numbers. The club went out of business in December 1937. Bill Harrah opened a bingo parlor at this location in 1938.

The former location of Art's Darto Den is now part of Harolds Club.

Nev. St. Journal, 19 June 37 (adv.).

ASCUAGA, JOHN

John Ascuaga was born in Notus, Idaho, in January 1925. He grew up on a farm, and after graduating from high school he entered the military service. When he returned home, Ascuaga heeded his father's advice to get an education and earned an economics degree from the University of Idaho. One year later, he added a degree in restaurant management from the University of Washington.

While working summers as a bellman in McCall, Idaho, he met his future boss, Dick Graves, who hired the young Ascuaga at his food operation in Coeur d'Alene. Graves had built a slot machine empire in Idaho, but when that state outlawed slot machines in 1953, Graves headed for Nevada and took Ascuaga with him.

Graves opened casinos in Yerington, Carson City, and Reno and named them all the Nugget. Ascuaga was put in charge of the food and beverage departments of all the Nuggets.

In March 1955 Graves opened the Sparks Nugget and named Ascuaga manager of the sixty-seat coffee shop, which opened with about fifty slot machines.

In May 1958 the Nugget moved across the street. The new property opened with a thirty-six-thousand-square-foot casino, five restaurants, two bars, and banquet rooms.

On October 1, 1960, Dick Graves sold the Sparks Nugget to John Ascuaga for $3.75 million. Terms of the contract called for no money down and twelve years to pay off the note—Ascuaga paid it off in seven!

Ascuaga has continuously expanded the Nugget. By 1997 his hotel-casino had twin hotel towers with almost two thousand hotel rooms, 75,000 square feet of casino space, eight restaurants, and a race and sports book. The facility also had a parking garage with 1,252 parking spaces.

John Ascuaga's Nugget is one of the most popular hotel-casinos in northern Nevada, and it is one of the few still owned by one person. The Nugget is a family-run operation with three of Ascuaga's four children—Michonne, John Jr., and Steven—working at the property.

Ascuaga lives in Jack's Valley and drives the forty-two miles to work every day. He has no plans to retire.

Nev. St. Journal, 30 Sept. 60, 10 Nov. 60; *Sacramento Bee,* 7 Jan. 90.

AUSTIN, JACK

Jack Austin was licensed as a co-owner of the Palace Club from December 1953 to April 1964.

In 1959 Austin was licensed at the El Morocco Club in Las Vegas, and in 1961 he was licensed, along with Henry and George Hornstein and Joe Padilla, at the Colony Club on North Virginia Street.

In 1964 the group sold the Colony Club to Harolds Club. In 1967 they opened the Colony Turf Club on North Center Street. Austin was licensed in 1974 for 70 percent of the Colony Turf Club. Later that year he became sole owner of the club and retained ownership until it closed in 1976.

Nev. St. Journal, 10 Nov. 53, 11 Dec. 53, 14 Apr. 64, 9 Dec. 64, 20 Jan. 67, 18 July 71, 18 Oct. 74.

AUSTIN, RALPH

Ralph Austin, along with Virgil Smith, was a co-owner of Colbrandt's Flamingo Club on North Virginia Street from 1940 to 1946.

BAILEY, WILLIAM "BILL"

Bill Bailey was born in South Dakota in 1903 and came to Reno in 1934. He worked for the WPA and helped build the Reno Golf Course (later known as the Washoe County Golf Course).

He entered the military service in 1940, and after his discharge in 1944 he returned to Reno and became a part owner of the Peavine Club in 1945. After operating for a little more than a year, the Peavine Club closed when the building was condemned and the property was turned into a parking lot. Bailey then opened the Harlem Club on the corner of Lake Street and Commercial Row in 1946. The Harlem Club was one of the few integrated clubs in Reno at that time. After their regular shows were over, many African American entertainers came to the Harlem for unscheduled jam sessions. It was common for Pearl Bailey (Bill Bailey's cousin), Louis Armstrong, Sammy Davis Jr., and B.B. King to play at the Harlem until dawn.

Bailey sold the Harlem Club in 1958; it later became known as the Soul Club. He was later a co-owner of the Happy Buddha Club and the China Mint Club.

Bailey is also remembered as a civil rights advocate, president of the Reno-Sparks NAACP, and the leader of many marches and demonstrations in the civil rights battles of the 1950s and early 1960s.

He retired to Edgemont, South Dakota, in the early 1970s and lived the remainder of his life on the 640-acre ranch that his father had homesteaded in 1903.

Nev. St. Journal, 8 Feb. 45, 28 Apr. 53, 26 Jan. 56, 22 July 58, 6 Oct. 80.

BAKER, FAY

Fay Baker, descendent of pioneer Nevadans, was born in Mina and came to Reno in 1930. He was long active in the ho-tel, bar, restaurant, cabaret, and gaming business.

When the Tavern on West Fourth Street opened in 1932, Baker was its first general manager. He was also associated with the Capitol Club, the Ship and Bottle, the Town House, and the Golden Hotel.

Baker died on June 22, 1972.

Nev. St. Journal, 8 Dec. 32, 16 Dec. 36, 24 June 72 (obit.).

BANK CLUB

239 North Center Street; licensed from March 30, 1931, until 1952 as a full casino. In 1952 it joined with the Golden Hotel and became known as the Golden-Bank Casino.

The Bank Club (originally licensed as the Bank Palace Club) was the second casino to be licensed in 1931 when gaming became legal (the Owl Club at 143 East Commercial Row was the first). The licensees at the Bank Club were Bill Graham, James McKay, and Ray Kindle.

The Bank Club had been operating illegally in a basement clubroom for several years, so shortly after the bill legalizing gambling was passed, the Bank Club was ready for action. Twenty-seven days after his workmen commenced enlarging and renovating the Bank Club, Frank Retmier, the building contractor, announced that the Bank Club would be opening for business in its new ground-floor quarters on April 25, 1931.

The casino had floor space of nearly 500 square feet, making it by far the largest gaming resort in the state. One of the outstanding features of the renovated club was its new electric keno (bingo) board. Controlled by five hundred switches and containing one thousand light bulbs, its installation cost thousands of dollars.

A new façade had been added to the building. The downstairs clubroom was abandoned, and the new ground floor housed two roulette tables, two craps games, two 21 games, three faro games, one hazard game, one keno (bingo) game, two pan games, one stud poker game, and one slot machine. The Bank Club was the state's leading producer of tax revenue under the new legal gaming law: its tax bill for one quarter (three months) for the gaming devices listed above totaled $1,875.00.

Within the next month, the Bank Club added a baseball book, a horse-race book, another craps game, and another roulette game.

On April 25, 1931, a full-page ad appeared in the local paper with the following message: "Grand opening today of the Bank Club, 239 North Center Street. The club has been greatly enlarged, however, management remains the same. They have an enviable reputation of 'square dealing.' This policy will be rigidly maintained."

The Bank Club was owned by Bill Graham, James McKay, and Ray Kindle. Kindle was an investor only, and Graham and McKay were the operators. Graham and McKay had met in Tonopah in the early teens, and they both came to Reno in the early 1920s. Graham and McKay were partners in several businesses, among them the Willows, the Rex Club, the Cal-Neva Lodge at Lake Tahoe, the Miner's Club, and others, including the Bank Club, which they had opened illegally in the late 1920s. Kindle became associated with the Bank Club in 1929, two years prior to the legalization of gaming.

Jack Sullivan, a longtime associate of Graham and McKay, came to Reno from Ely with Tex Hall in the 1920s. Shortly after their arrival, Sullivan and Hall both went to work for Graham and McKay in various locations around town. Eventually, Sullivan became manager of the Bank Club, and in 1939 he became a part owner of the club and was a "watchdog" for Graham and McKay while they were serving time in prison from 1939 to 1945. (Graham and McKay were convicted of embezzlement and mail fraud in 1938 and were sent to Leavenworth Prison in 1939.) Also, while Graham and McKay were in prison, Broderick "Rod" Perkins, the Bank Club's comptroller, was listed as a licensee.

Tex Hall worked at the Bank Club until 1935, when he was found guilty of conspiracy to harbor George "Baby Face" Nelson, one of America's most-wanted criminals. Hall served six months in jail, and shortly after being released he died of a heart attack at the age of fifty-eight.

Looking south on Center Street, ca. 1934. Courtesy Nevada Historical Society.

quors and the establishment that never closes."

In January 1937 the Bank Club installed a new bar said to be the "classiest bar this side of the Waldorf-Astoria." It cost an estimated $22,000 to $35,000 to install.

During the late 1930s and 1940s, the Bank Club was a popular late-night gathering spot where other club owners, casino bosses, and dealers met to discuss the evening's events and perhaps have a drink or two. One other reason the Bank Club was so popular in the late evening was that the owners also owned the Stockade, Reno's red-light district. Covering nearly a full city block, the Stockade was surrounded by a high board fence with a wide-open gate. After entering, visitors came into a large oblong space, faced on three sides by a large three-sided brick building divided into narrow rooms exactly like the rows of cells in a prison. Each cell had a door and window that were open all the time. There were one hundred cells, and each cell was occupied by a prostitute plying her trade. Each woman worked an eight-hour shift, so there were three hundred women working during a twenty-four-hour day.

The Stockade was owned by Acme Realty Company, whose majority stockholders were Bill Graham and James McKay. Every night between midnight and 2 A.M., the "girls" getting off work would come to the Bank Club, where they always attracted attention.

On the morning of October 31, 1944, there was a shooting in the Bank Club that was a commentary on what things could be like in Reno during the early years of gaming. The incident, which occurred in front of dozens of witnesses, involved Jack "Jelly" Blackman and James Lanigan. Blackman, thirty-two, one of the owners of the Town House, shot James Lanigan, a local hustler. Blackman said that Lanigan was trying "to shake him down." Blackman shot Lanigan only after Lanigan taunted him and then struck him in the face, knocking him down and breaking his nose. When Blackman fell to the floor, he pulled out a gun and shot six times. Three of the bullets hit Lanigan, who staggered out the door and died on the street. Lanigan was in the

Three other longtime employees of the Bank Club were Harry Bond, Walter Parman, and Elmer "Baldy" West. All of them were in charge of gaming at one time or another.

During the 1936 presidential election, the Bank Club accepted bets on the outcome of the election, and a total of $75,000 was posted on the betting board. President Roosevelt was a three-to-one favorite over Republican Alfred Landon.

On December 25, 1936, a large ad appeared in the local paper sending season's greetings "from the largest casino in the United States, the business that has Nevada's second largest payroll, the business that pays the most taxes to the state, the business that serves the finest li-

The Bank Club seen from the corner of Center Street and Douglas Alley. Courtesy of Neal Cobb and the Nevada Historical Society.

company of local gambler Swede Oleson and George Hilliard, former owner of the Coral Isle Club, when the incident occurred. A trial was held, and on April 17, 1945, after six days of testimony, the jury found Blackman not guilty of murder by reason of self-defense in the death of James Lanigan.

Bill Harrah was a regular visitor at the Bank Club during the wee small hours of the morning, until one day an off-duty bartender from the Bank Club stole one of Harrah's dollar slot machines out of his Blackout Bar. Bill Harrah reported the incident to the police, and that didn't sit well with Jack Sullivan, manager of the Bank Club. Sullivan told Harrah, "We don't need the police to settle things like this, you and I can work it out." But Bill Harrah didn't agree and testified against Sullivan's bartender, and the thief was sent to jail. Harrah was never again welcome in the Bank Club.

Many clubs made money during World War II and expanded their gaming licenses. The Bank Club was no exception, and in January 1945, when the gaming li-

censes were renewed, taxes were paid on twenty table games and ninety-one slot machines. (Note the ratio of table games to slot machines. Currently, for every twenty table games licensed by a casino, there might be as many as four hundred slot machines licensed.)

In October 1946 the Golden Hotel—the building where the Bank Club was located—was sold by George Wingfield for $1.5 million to a group consisting of John Mueller, Henry Bennett, Norman Biltz, and James Lloyd. The twenty-year lease to the Bank Club was not affected by the sale.

In June 1950 Jack Sullivan attempted to sell his one-third interest in the Bank Club to Joseph "Doc" Stacher, once a member of the Meyer Lansky–Bugsy Siegel gang who had been involved in bootlegging and illegal gambling with the notorious gambler Longy Zwillman. (Stacher was eventually deported to Israel in 1960.) The Gaming Commission was not receptive to the sale, and Sullivan sold his percentage back to Graham and McKay, who once again became sole licensees of the Bank Club.

Their partnership was dissolved in May

1952, and Bill Graham became the sole lessee of the Bank Club when he negotiated a twenty-year lease with the then-owner of the Golden Hotel, Frank Hofues. The casino area became known as the Golden-Bank Casino.

In March 1954 John Drew was licensed as 25-percent owner of the Golden-Bank Casino. In February 1954, Hofues had sold the Golden Hotel to James and William Tomerlin. However, Bill Graham's lease was not affected until November 1955. At that time, the Tomerlin brothers, along with twenty-five limited partners, bought the remaining seventeen years on the gaming lease from Graham and Drew for $425,000 and were licensed by the state, effective December 1, 1955, for 289 slots, two craps games, six 21 games, one roulette game, one poker game, and two pan games.

That licensing ended Bill Graham's career in Reno gaming. However, he remained in town and was frequently seen at boxing matches and sporting events. He died at his home on California Avenue on November 5, 1965. Graham's longtime partner and friend, James McKay, had passed away on June 19, 1962.

The Bank Club was destroyed by the fire that consumed the Golden Hotel on April 3, 1962. The hotel was later partially rebuilt by the Tomerlin brothers and sold to Harrah's in 1966. The former site of the Bank Club is located in the northernmost portion of Harrah's Hotel-Casino, fronting on Douglas Alley and Center Street.

Nev. St. Journal, 1 Apr. 31, 25 Apr. 31, 25 Apr. 31 (adv.), 8 Apr. 33, 19 July 34, 3 Nov. 36, 3 Nov. 36 (adv.), 25 Dec. 36 (adv.), 23 Jan. 37, 2 Sept. 40 (adv. and photo), 31 Oct. 44, 23 Jan. 45, 30 June 50, 7 July 50, 19 Sept. 50.

BARBOOT COFFEE HOUSE AND CASINO

560 East Fourth Street; licensed in November 1965 for a barbouti game.

On November 24, 1965, the game of barbouti was introduced to Reno gamblers at the Barboot Coffee House and Casino on Fourth Street. Matt Skender, co-owner of the new business, was in charge of operating the first barbouti game ever licensed in

Reno. Particularly popular among Greeks, Turks, Basques, and some other ethnic groups, barbouti is an ancient game that has been played for centuries in Europe and the Middle East.

The game is played on a table similar to a regulation craps table, although the layout was considerably different. The game is an even-money, no-limit game, and the house makes its money by taking a sliding percentage of between 3 and 5 percent of the money wagered. In essence, it is a game in which players can bet as much money as they can get covered by opposing players.

The game never caught on in Reno, and the Barboot closed its doors after just a few weeks. The short-lived club was co-owned by Matt Skender, his wife, Betty, and Martin Schwamb, president of Martin Iron Works.

The former site of the Barboot Coffee House and Casino is now the Earl Schieb Auto Paint Shop.

Nev. St. Journal, 26 Nov. 65.

BARN

207 North Center Street; licensed from 1941 to 1944 for slots, 21, and craps.

In December 1940 the Barn officially opened, but gambling wasn't licensed until January 1941. The Barn was located at the site where the famous Northern Club, operated by Felix Turillas Sr., had been in business since 1931.

Owners Jack Fugit and Walter Oswald completely remodeled the property in a rustic style. The club had a bar, gaming tables, pinball machines, and numerous other amusements.

In August 1941 Mike Micheletti, a well-known Reno gambler, took over the gambling operation and featured all types of poker and pan games as well as the established pit games.

Late in 1941 Jack Fugit and Walter Oswald sold their interests in the Barn to George Hilliard. Hilliard soon sold his interest to Irving Cowan. By August 1942, the Barn was under the management of Larry Brady, Mike Micheletti, and Irving Cowan.

In November 1942 Larry Brady got into an altercation in the Bank Club, drew a gun, and threatened to kill Harry Bond and Hugh Smithwick. Brady, who had recently sold his interest in the Barn, was given probation with the provision that he be out of Reno and in the merchant marine within forty-eight hours. He was also ordered never to return to Reno.

Brady's troubles weren't over. In April 1945, a few days before he was to have started serving a six-year term in a California penitentiary for transporting narcotics, Brady committed suicide.

The Barn was sold in 1944 to Wilbur Clark (who later gained fame at the Desert Inn in Las Vegas) and renamed the Bonanza. The Bonanza had several owners (*see* Bonanza Club) before becoming the Frisco Club in 1951 and Harrah's Bingo in 1953.

The former location of the Barn is currently part of Harrah's main casino on the west side of Center Street, between Second Street and Douglas Alley.

Nev. St. Journal, 24 Dec. 40, 8 Aug. 41 (adv.), 15 Aug. 42 (adv.), 15 Aug. 42, 17 Jan. 43, 17 Apr. 45.

BAR OF MUSIC

136 North Center Street; licensed from February 23, 1946, to October 21, 1951, for craps, 21, keno, and roulette.

The Bar of Music was one of several small clubs that featured dining, dancing, entertainment, and some gambling. It first opened in December 1945 with no gambling. The owners, Sam Erlich, Harry Short, and George Johnson, were granted a gaming license early in 1946. They instituted an active newspaper advertising campaign early in the year, and after a good business had been built, they sold the club in July to Harry Sherwood and Joseph Skoff of San Francisco, for $150,000.

In December 1946 Sherwood and Skoff traded the property to Denny and S. M. Wood and Fred Wilkins for a casino on the South Shore of Lake Tahoe called the Tahoe Village.

On September 17, 1947, Harry Sherwood was shot to death by his then-partner in the Tahoe Village, Louie Strauss. First accounts of the shooting in local newspapers treated it as just another local

The Reno Rodeo parade heading south on Center Street in the mid-1940s. Note the sign for the Barn. This location was the former site of the Northern Club. Courtesy of Neal Cobb.

homicide, until it was revealed that Sherwood was a one-time partner of Tony Stralla, a well-known West Coast gaming figure, and Strauss was the notorious "Russian Louie" of eastern gangland fame.

Meanwhile, M. L. "Harry" Brody had purchased the Bar of Music in April 1947 and had been granted a gaming license for one keno game, one 21 game, one craps game, one roulette game, and twenty slot machines.

In May 1948 Brody rented one room of the property to Walter Chinn and Silk Mar. They opened a restaurant called the Confucius Room. This operation was a failure, and Brody had to sue Chinn and Mar to get his rent money.

On January 18, 1949, Harry Brody was arrested for possession of narcotics. It was then revealed that Brody had an extensive criminal record. One week later, he withdrew his application to renew his gambling license, and the Bar of Music closed. On December 31, 1949, Harry Brody was sentenced to three years in prison. His good behavior resulted in his early (July 1951) release, but on November 28, 1951, he was again arrested for narcotics possession. He was again sentenced to prison, this time for five years.

In later years, many clubs operated at the Bar of Music's address, including Beery's, O'Brien's Corner, the Trade Winds, the Roaring Twenties, Buddy Baer's, and Freddy's Lair.

The Bar of Music seemed to put a curse on its owners. One of the first owners, Sam Erlich, killed himself on May 25, 1947. He was only forty-five years old but was reported to have been in ill health. And as previously mentioned, Harry Sherwood was shot and killed by "Russian Louie" Strauss, and Harry Brody was plagued by a narcotics addiction and served a great deal of his adult life in prison.

The former location of the Bar of Music is now a section of the Cal-Neva's parking garage on the east side of Center Street.

Nev. St. Journal, 29 Dec. 45 (adv.), 1 Jan. 46, 5 Dec. 47, 15 May 48 (adv.), 29 July 48, 25 Jan. 49, 26 Feb. 49, 29 Apr. 49, 15 Nov. 49, 24 Dec. 49, 31 Dec. 49, 28 Nov. 51.

BASIN STREET

246 Lake Street; licensed from June 15, 1964, to November 1, 1966, for slots and 21.

The Basin Street was more a nightclub and "girlie-girlie" club than a gambling casino. It was located in a section of Reno that was then considered sleazy. Prostitutes worked Lake Street, and there were other illegal activities in the area.

In August 1963 Harry Chon applied to the Nevada Gaming Control Board for permission to invest $15,000 to operate the Basin Street. The property, formerly known as the China Mint, had been closed since the previous April.

Chon had previously been licensed at the Old Cathay Club and the Lido Bar in Reno and at the Bank Club in Fallon. His license at the Old Cathay Club had been revoked in June 1957.

After four months of deferrals and hearings, Chon was granted a gaming license for eleven slots and two table games on December 17. Then it was discovered that the owner of the property, Al Figoni, had been okayed by the Reno City Council in November to operate a "bare bosom" show. On the day that Chon was granted a gaming license, the state discovered that the Basin Street had been closed two days earlier by Al Figoni.

The next day, the Gaming Commission decided to deny Chon a gaming license because of his allegedly questionable background. Rocco Stillian, manager of the Basin Street, said there had been some union problems but that the club was open and, according to Stillian, "it had never been closed."

Regardless of whether the club had been closed or not, Harry Chon was never licensed at the Basin Street, although Al Figoni was granted a license for two table games and fifteen slots on April 21, 1964. The Basin Street continued to operate as a striptease club and a cabaret with gaming until November 1966.

The Basin Street was located in an area that was razed in the 1970s and became a parking lot.

Nev. St. Journal, 6 Aug. 63, 10 Sept. 63, 24 Sept. 63, 25 Sept. 63, 13 Nov. 63, 17 Dec. 63, 18 Dec. 63, 31 Dec. 63 (adv.), 21 Apr. 64, 10 Apr. 66 (adv.), 28 Aug. 66 (adv.).

BEATRICE KAY GUEST RANCH

865 Peckham Lane; licensed from May to July 1956 for a 21 game only.

Beatrice Kay was a popular singer in the 1940s and 1950s. She was a nationally known Gay Nineties–style singer who appeared in showrooms around the United States. She was popular in Reno, was heard on nationally broadcast radio programs, and appeared in several movies.

She eventually made her home in Reno and, along with her personal manager, Sylvan Green, she opened the Beatrice Kay Guest Ranch. It catered mostly to women who came to Reno for the six-week divorce "cure," but it also did a great deal of local business.

A 21 game was opened there on Memorial Day Weekend in 1956, but it wasn't popular and was in operation for less than two months.

The former location of the Beatrice Kay Guest Ranch is today occupied by the Fat Cats Lounge.

BECK, FRED

Fred Beck, who was born in Sheboygan, Wisconsin, in 1892, leased the keno, horse-race book, poker, and pan games in Harolds Club from 1940 until his death in 1954. His first wife, Ruth, is said to have been the first woman keno writer in Reno.

Upon his death in January 1954, his second wife, Jessie Howard Beck, took over the lease and operated the keno game until Harolds Club was sold to the Hughes Corporation in 1970.

Nev. St. Journal, 10 Feb. 55, 28 Oct. 55; Raymond I. Sawyer, *Reno: Where the Gamblers Go* (Reno: Sawston Publishing Co., 1976).

BECK, JESSIE

Jessie Howard, a thirty-four-year-old divorced mother, came to Reno to work as a roulette dealer in Harolds Club in the late 1930s. While on vacation in Texas, Pappy Smith had offered Beck a job after he spotted her quick mathematical skills while she was working as a cashier. After coming to

A parade float sponsored and staffed by Harolds Club, ca. 1947. Left to right: Jessie Beck (of Riverside fame), Monita McKinley, Fluff Webster, Chuck Webster (as Uncle Sam), and Bessie Hoyt. Courtesy of Darl and Marj Voss.

work in Harolds Club, Beck soon rose through the casino ranks, building a reputation for friendliness and good business sense.

Her third husband, Fred Beck, owned and operated the keno, poker, pan, and horse-race book concessions at Harolds Club. Jessie took over the operation of these concessions when her husband died in January 1954. She lost the lease to the concessions in 1970 when Harolds Club was sold to the Hughes Corporation.

Jessie Beck bought the Riverside in 1971 for $3 million and hired a staff of former Harolds Club employees who had quit or been terminated by the Hughes Corporation. She spent most of her working hours roaming the casino floor, sometimes staying as late as 3 A.M. Frequently, she took over a 21 game and dealt for hours.

Beck, who was known as the Gambling Grandmother of Reno, spent untold thousands of hours and thousands of dollars

doing favors for servicemen in Vietnam and all over the world. The Award of Merit, the highest honor the Defense Department can give a civilian, was presented to her in 1968. In 1969 then-governor Paul Laxalt named her a Distinguished Nevadan.

On March 10, 1978, spokesmen for the Riverside Hotel and the Overland Hotel announced that Harrah's was purchasing the Riverside so it could trade it to Overland, Inc., for that firm's old hotel-casino site at Center Street and Commercial Row. Pick Hobson was licensed to operate the Riverside the following month. This transaction was favorable to all parties, because it allowed Jessie Beck to retire from gaming and Pick Hobson to get back into the gaming business, and it gave Bill Harrah the key piece of real estate he needed for the parking garage in his multimillion-dollar expansion on North Center Street.

Jessie Beck died on July 17, 1987, at the age of eighty-three. She was a lifetime

member of the St. Mary's Hospital Guild, the Washoe Medical Center League, and the VFW Auxiliary, and she was active in the Republican Party.

Shortly after her death, Harold Smith Jr. said of Mrs. Beck, "She was a credit to the gaming industry, to Reno, to the state of Nevada and to all concerned. We all held her in highest regard. Jessie was a lady." And Helen Mapes, wife of former casino owner Charles Mapes, described Mrs. Beck as "a very gracious person; a very loving, caring, generous person. And she was a very good businesswoman."

Reno Evening Gazette, 31 Mar. 71; *Nev. St. Journal,* 10 Mar. 78, 18 July 87 (obit. and photo).

BEERY'S NIGHT CLUB

136 North Center Street; never licensed.

Formerly the Bar of Music, Beery's Night Club was denied a gaming license in 1952. The applicants for the license were Sam Mintzner and Jack Lewis.

BELLE LIVINGSTONE'S COWSHED

2295 South Virginia Street; licensed from September 1931 to May 1937 for slots, 21, craps, and roulette.

Belle Livingstone was a New York City nightclub hostess who gained nationwide fame for her escapades during the late 1920s and early 1930s.

She left New York in July 1931 after frequently running into trouble with Prohibition agents. On July 18 she announced that she planned to open a nightclub one mile south of Reno on the Hall Ranch. She met with determined resistance from a group of neighboring farmers who declared that the club would be in a "farmer, residential district" and that some restrictions should apply. (This is the area directly across from Park Lane Mall on the west side of Virginia Street.)

Livingstone's notoriety was so great that when she was granted a gaming license, the news was reported in the July 19, 1931, issue of the *New York Times*: "By a 3–2 vote, the County License Board decided to issue a gambling license to Belle Livingstone, former New York night club hostess. The Board argued for thirty minutes before reaching their decision. There were 15 ranchers owning property adjoining the location who protested that the club would constitute a nuisance."

Belle Livingstone opened her resort (sometimes called Belle's Barn) on September 6, 1931. There was dining, dancing, entertainment, and of course, gambling. The opening revue featured an African American orchestra and a chorus line of African American girls.

Prohibition was still in effect nationwide in 1931, and in less than a month federal agents raided Livingstone's establishment and she was forced out of control of her club for a few days. But the *Nevada State Journal* of October 24, 1931, included the following advertisement: "All is forgiven. Belle is back in her Royal Box to greet her friends. You haven't seen Reno if you haven't seen Belle's Cowshed."

It wasn't long before Prohibition agents harassed Livingstone again, and in late November 1931 she left Reno. The business closed shortly after she left town but reopened in September 1932. During the next few years, it had several openings and closings. When it opened in May 1933, it was elaborately decorated and the different areas of the club were given names: the dining room was known as "The Haymow," the gambling games were located in "The Creamery," and the original cow barn, now the dance floor, was called "The Cowbarn."

In October 1936, Marcel and C. H. Freeman took over management of the Cowshed. They brought in Ray Wilson as their chef and hired the well-known Al Rae and his orchestra for entertainment. Gaming tables, including craps, 21, and roulette, were in evidence, as were twenty slot machines. However, this venture failed to become successful, and in May 1937 the Cowshed closed for the last time.

In August 1937 the business reopened as the Club Moderne, with famous Reno host Aldo Dinelli, known locally as "Maryootch," as manager. There was no gambling.

The Club Moderne lasted less than a year, and in September 1938 Carlan's Lakeside Inn opened at the former location of the Cowshed. A few years later, the Lakeside Inn was destroyed by fire.

The former location of the Cowshed is now a small shopping mall where the A. G. Edwards Company and the El Pollo Restaurant are located.

BIG HAT

3501 South Virginia Street; licensed from August 1947 to April 1954 for 21, roulette, and slots.

The Big Hat was actually more a dinner house than a gambling casino. It was one of those places where people went to have a nice dinner and perhaps enjoy a few drinks and a little gambling.

Over the years, several people had the gaming concession at the Big Hat. They included K. O. Cunningham in 1948; Joe LaDue and Fred Detore in 1948; Andre Simetys from 1950 to 1952; Miles Keogh in 1952; Godfrey Werner in 1953; and Josephine Parker, the last owner and licensee of the Big Hat, who was granted a restricted gaming license (slots only) in 1970.

The former location of the Big Hat is currently occupied by the La Vecchia Restaurant.

Nev. St. Journal, 15 Aug. 48, 24 Sept. 48, 16 Nov. 50, 30 Jan. 52, 18 June 52, 1 July 52, 18 June 53, 10 Sept. 70.

BILL'S CORNER BAR

150 Lake Street; licensed in August 1965 for two table games and three slots.

On August 6, 1965, William Campbell, principal owner of the Sonoma Inn in Winnemucca, applied to invest $5,000 to operate two table games and three slots at Bill's Corner Bar. His wife, Martha, and veteran gambler Birches Bird would be licensed as corporate officers without investment. On August 17, 1965, the Nevada Gaming Control Board recommended that Bill's Corner Bar be approved.

The former location of Bill's Corner Bar is now part of the Harrah's Club parking garage.

Nev. St. Journal, 6 Aug. 65, 17 Aug. 65.

BINGO CENTER

102 East Second Street; licensed in 1948 for bingo.

The Bingo Center, which was operated by Don Guilford, was located in the Profes-

The Big Hat, a popular restaurant, ca. 1950. The Big Hat had various owners over the years; at the time of this picture, it was owned by Andre Simetys. Courtesy of Neal Cobb and the Nevada Historical Society.

sional Building on Second Street. It opened in the summer of 1948 and closed early in 1949.

Currently located at the former site of the Bingo Center is a Japanese restaurant, the Imperial Palace.

Nev. St. Journal, 11 June 48, 18 July 48, 17 Nov. 48.

BITTNER, CLYDE

Clyde "Sugar Plum" Bittner was born in Great Falls, Montana, on September 27, 1913, and came to Reno in 1936. He was one of the men whom Francis Lyden brought to the Palace Club to open the first race-horse keno game, and he was also one of the first keno shift managers at the Palace Club. The other two keno shift managers were Warren "Swede" Nelson and Jack "MacTavish" Mullen.

Bittner later learned to deal table games, became a pit boss, and eventually worked as a shift manager at Harrah's Lake Tahoe and at the Club Cal-Neva in Reno.

Clyde Bittner was an energetic, witty, sharp person who was generally well liked by his associates. He died in April 1964, while employed at the Club Cal-Neva as a shift manager.

Nev. St. Journal, 1 Feb. 64, 26 Apr. 64 (obit. and photo); Warren Nelson et al., *Always Bet on the Butcher: Warren Nelson and Casino Gaming, 1930s–1980s* (Reno: University of Nevada Oral History Program, 1994).

BLACK DERBY

1410 East Fourth Street; licensed in April 1937, for only a few months, for 21, craps, and roulette.

The Black Derby was located in the same building where the Silver Slipper had previously operated. The Silver Slipper later reopened at the same location.

The Black Derby was a supper club managed by Caucasians but featuring African American musicians and entertainment. The manager was Harry Mayer, and the club was licensed for one roulette game, one 21 game, one craps game, and three slot machines.

It was located near the site where the Jim Jeffries–Jack Johnson championship heavyweight boxing match was held in 1910. The first club at this location was the

Idlewild, which later became the Silver Slipper, then the Black Derby, and finally the Sphynx in December 1941. On January 1, 1943, the building was destroyed by fire and never again opened as a club or casino.

There is a historical marker near the location indicating the site of the Jeffries-Johnson boxing match; however, the exact former location of the Black Derby is now the parking lot between the Ponderosa Lodge and the Los Compadres Restaurant.

Nev. St. Journal, 3 Apr. 37, 10 Apr. 37.

BLACKMAN, JACK "JELLY"

Jack Blackman was a co-owner, along with George "Frenchy" Perry, of the Town House on First Street from 1941 to 1945.

On October 31, 1944, at 3 A.M., Blackman, then thirty-two, shot James Lanigan while they were arguing at the bar in the Bank Club. Blackman claimed that Lanigan was "trying to shake him down" and that he shot Lanigan only after Lanigan had taunted him and then struck him in the face, knocking him down and breaking his nose. When Blackman reeled to the floor, he pulled out a gun and shot six times. Three of the bullets hit Lanigan, who staggered out the door and died in the street. Lanigan was in the company of Ed "Swede" Oleson and George Hilliard when the incident occurred.

In April 1945, after a six-day trial, Blackman was found not guilty of murder by reason of self-defense. He left Reno shortly after the conclusion of the trial.

Nev. St. Journal, 31 Oct. 44 (photo), 1 Nov. 44, 2 Nov. 44, 29 Nov. 44, 18 Apr. 45.

BLACKOUT BAR

230½ North Virginia Street (also listed at 231 Lincoln Alley); licensed from 1943 to 1946 for slots, craps, and 21.

When Bill Harrah leased the Reno Club at 232 North Virginia Street in 1942, the property was next door to Jacob's Clothing Store. When Phil Jacobs died, his son, Murray, turned the clothing store into a liquor store. Harrah leased the rear of the store and put in the Blackout Bar, so named because of the blackouts brought on by World War II. There was a back en-

trance to the bar at 231 Lincoln Alley and a side entrance from Harrah's Heart Tango Club.

Bill Harrah had leased the slots in the Heart Tango Club, but in the Blackout Bar, he put in his own slots, one 21 table, and a one-man craps table. This was Harrah's first real taste of any type of gambling other than bingo.

It was at the Blackout Bar that Bill Harrah hired his first entertainment—Jack McCarg, known professionally as "Jackson," who appeared there several times. In Bill Harrah's oral history, he recalls that "Jackson brought thousands of customers to the Blackout Bar."

When the lease expired, Murray Jacobs took the property back. The former location of the Blackout Bar is now a part of the Nevada Club.

William F. Harrah, "My Recollections" (1980); Robert A. Ring, "Recollections" (1973); *Nev. St. Journal,* Jan. 46 (adv.).

BLOCK N CLUB

210 North Virginia Street; licensed from 1931 to 1941 for roulette, keno, slots, a football pool, poker, and pan.

The Block N opened as a billiard parlor and soft-drink parlor in 1930. In 1931 it was licensed for one pan game and one stud poker game.

In April 1933, when Prohibition was repealed, Charles Evans, J. W. Ball, and Ed Rotholtz took over the operation.

On July 1, 1939, Howard Jones took over management of the Block N, and longtime gambler Swede Collet operated the cardroom. The club had been closed for several weeks for extensive remodeling. Eight booths and a cigar counter were located in the front of the building, with a bar, more booths, a gaming room, and a poolroom in the rear. The walls were finished in light colors, and the flooring was light-tan linoleum with red trim. The property was owned by the Rotholtz brothers.

In August 1939, the Block N, which already featured roulette, 21, pan, and poker, announced that it was opening a $5,000-limit racehorse keno game; in October it opened a football pool, which was oper-

Looking north on Virginia Street, ca. 1940. The Block N Club shown in this photo later became the site of Bill Harrah's first full casino. Courtesy of Neal Cobb and the Nevada Historical Society.

ated by Dick Kolbus and known as "Tricky Dick's."

In 1940 the Block N was taken over by Jake Hagenson, formerly of the Waldorf. In 1941 the lease was taken over by Dick Kolbus and Joe "Luke" Lukanish, and the club was given a new name—the Mint. Bill Harrah assumed the lease in 1946 and opened his first full casino at that location in June.

Today the former location of the Block N is part of Harrah's Club on North Virginia Street.

Nev. St. Journal, 6 Apr. 33, 1 July 39 (adv.), 1 July 39, 12 Aug. 39 (adv.), 1 Oct. 39 (adv.), 11 Nov. 39 (adv.), 5 Apr. 40 (adv.), 15 Aug. 40 (adv.).

BLONDY'S BAR

26 West Second Street; licensed from April 1944 to 1945 for one 21 game only.

Blondy's Bar opened in 1941, but it wasn't until 1944 that Sam Caruso was licensed there for a 21 game. The game was closed in the latter part of 1945. The location later became the Merry-Go-Round Bar and is now part of a downtown gift shop.

Nev. St. Journal, 20 May 41, 23 Jan. 45.

BLUE BIRD CLUB

10 West Commercial Row and 132 East Second Street; licensed from July 18, 1945, to April 2, 1949, for slots, 21, poker, and craps.

In June 1941 Peter Monticelli opened the Blue Bird Club (a bar) at 132 East Second Street. In July 1945 Monticelli opened the New Blue Bird Club at 10 West Commercial Row, at the former site of Sewell's Grocery Store. In the late 1940s, gaming was operated in the club on an irregular basis. In one instance, Monticelli's application for a license was denied, and in April 1949 the Blue Bird was closed by the health department for sanitary reasons. Four days later, Monticelli's check for $270—to pay for his Washoe County gaming license— bounced. The failure of the check to clear resulted in Monticelli's going to jail.

Two months later, in April 1949, a fire believed to have been caused by arson damaged the Blue Bird Club, which had been closed for a month.

The club remained closed until July 1951, when Gene Rovetti, John Hickok, and Doug Busey reopened the business and changed its name to the Haymarket Club.

The former location of the Blue Bird Club is now part of Fitzgeralds Casino-Hotel.

Nev. St. Journal, 26 June 41, 13 July 45 (adv.), 20 Jan. 48, 1 July 48, 25 Jan. 49, 2 Apr. 49, 6 Apr. 49, 7 June 49, 2 June 51, 15 June 51, 20 July 65.

BLUE CHIP CARD ROOM

21 East Douglas Alley; licensed from January 1958 to 1959 for poker only.

The Blue Chip Card Room was located at the former site of the Menlo Card Room. Several bars, small casinos, and poker rooms operated at this location over the years.

Currently the former location of the Blue Chip Card Room is part of Harolds Club.

Nev. St. Journal, 25 Jan. 58.

BOB'S COCKTAIL LOUNGE

325 South Virginia Street; licensed in January 1952 for one 21 game.

In January 1952 Robert Schmitt bought Charlie's Cocktail Lounge from Charlie Frisch and renamed the property Bob's Cocktail Lounge. The state of Nevada licensed Robert Schmitt for one 21 game on January 30, 1952, and the grand opening of Bob's Cocktail Lounge was held on February 8, 1952.

The former location of Bob's Cocktail Lounge is now part of the Bank of America Plaza.

Nev. St. Journal, 17 Jan. 52, 29 Jan. 52, 30 Jan. 52, 8 Feb. 52 (adv.).

BOB'S SALOON

19 East Douglas Alley; licensed from June 1965 to 1966 for poker only.

Bob's Saloon was one of several businesses licensed for poker at the same location during the 1950s, 1960s, and 1970s. The site is now part of Harolds Club.

BODIE MIKE'S

South Virginia Street (no address); licensed from December 8, 1948, to October 31, 1954, for slots and 21.

Bodie Mike's was owned by "Bodie Mike" Lazovich. Also granted licenses at the location were James McCallum and A. G. Scott.

Lazovich was later licensed at Bodie Mike's Branding Iron, located at 4700 North Virginia Street. He had previously been licensed in 1946 at Bodie Mike's Depot Bar on Commercial Row.

Nev. St. Journal, 6 Apr. 52, 14 Apr. 52, 7 Aug. 52, 27 Feb. 54, 2 July 54, 28 Sept. 61.

BONANZA CLUB

207 North Center Street; licensed from April 1944 to 1951 for craps, 21, roulette, and slots.

The Bonanza Club, formerly the Barn, was opened in 1944 by Wilbur Clark, who later gained fame as the proprietor of the Desert Inn in Las Vegas. It was considered by many to be the most beautiful club in Nevada. Decorated by Tom Douglas, designer of Ciro's and La Rue's, both famous Hollywood nightclubs, the bar had a Gay-Nineties motif. The ceiling was supported by eight-foot-tall plaster-of-Paris damsels, buxom and completely nude. They were a startling feature of the club. (One of them is on display in the Nevada State Museum in Carson City.) The Bonanza was also famous for its spectacular paintings.

In February 1945 the Bonanza was licensed by John Wilds for three 21 games, two roulette games, and one craps game. The property was owned by Larry Tripp, Thomas Hull, and Eunice Lewis. Before the year was out, Tom Hull sold his interest to Larry Tripp, Lou Wertheimer, Al Gersten, H. E. Calloway, and Myron Beck. Al Gersten was named manager of the club.

In its early days, the Bonanza was famous for its food, but in March 1945 the dining room was changed into a cocktail lounge, and dinners and lunches were discontinued for the duration of the war. In October 1945 the Bonanza reopened its dining room and hired Jackson (Jack McCarg) to entertain at the piano bar. Considered by Bill Harrah to be one of the top customer draws of the early 1940s, Jackson appeared both in the dining room and in the lounge.

In May 1946 the Bonanza closed temporarily for alterations but reopened on May 25 with "Sundown" Wells as manager and featuring great entertainment, a casino, and a large dinner menu.

In August 1947 Wertheimer, Tripp, H. E. Calloway, Gersten, and Beck sold the Bonanza. Mervyn Rosenthal, former manager of the club, later sued the partners for a percentage of the sale. He claimed that he had been told that if the club sold for over $75,000 he would receive 25 percent of the excess.

The new owners of the Bonanza were Andre Simetys and Ad Tolen. They went out of business in the summer of 1950, and the state filed suit against them for $479 in unemployment compensation. Later they, along with the previous owners, were sued by various wholesale establishments in Reno for many unpaid bills. As late as 1952 the case was not yet settled, and Tripp, Gersten, Calloway, and Beck sued Andre Simetys for $5,503. Simetys, who was food and beverage manager, was supposed to be solely responsible for all food and beverage bills, and they had never been paid.

In March 1951 a gaming license was granted to the S&K Corporation, doing business as the Bonanza Club. The two partners were William Sullivan and Dan Kilbride of Bozeman, Montana. In April 1951 the Bonanza was licensed for forty slots, one 21 game, one craps game, and one roulette game. Also added to the license were two more partners, Jack Sparkman and N. B. Ellis. Cap Ellis was named casino manager.

In August 1951 the Bonanza was renamed the Frisco Club, and "Back Line" Joe Snyder was named manager.

The S&K Corporation continued to operate the Bonanza/Frisco Club until 1952. The business was sold to Harrah's Club in 1952 and was opened as Harrah's Bingo in 1953.

The former location of the Bonanza Club is now part of Harrah's Club, on the west side of Center Street between Second Street and Douglas Alley.

Nev. St. Journal, 28 Sept. 44 (adv.), 10 Oct. 44 (adv.), 17 Mar. 45, 26 Apr. 45, 20 May 45, 1 Aug. 45, 26 Oct. 45, 7 May 46 (adv.), 25 May 46 (adv.), 11 Feb. 48, 25 Feb. 48, 16 July 48 (adv.), 23 Sept. 50, 1 Mar. 51, 24 Apr. 51, 15 June 51, 29 July 51, 4 Aug. 51, 24 Aug. 51 (adv.), 25 Aug. 51, 30 Aug. 51 (adv.), 14 Nov. 51, 27 Nov. 51, 10 Apr. 52, 13 May 52, 18 June 52, 11 Jan. 53; Reno City Directory (1946).

An interior view of the Bonanza Club. Pictured having dinner are (l.) Mr. and Mrs. Walt Mulcahy and (r.) Mr. and Mrs. Jerry Cobb. Mulcahy was a historian and Cobb a photographer and radio personality as well as a radio station owner. Courtesy of Neal Cobb and the Nevada Historical Society.

BONANZA SQUARE INN AND CASINO

4720 North Virginia Street; licensed since 1973 for slots, keno, 21, craps, and roulette.

In August 1973 Don Baldwin and Lou Benetti Jr. were licensed for 50 percent each of the thirty slots located in the Bonanza Square Inn and Casino. They opened the property the following month.

The Bonanza soon attracted a big local clientele, because it featured great food at reasonable prices. In January 1974 Robert McDonald and Robert Douglass each purchased one-third of the business, and Baldwin and Benetti eventually left the operation. In June 1975 Russ Sheltra was licensed as a 25-percent owner of the property and as comptroller of the company.

The casino continued to expand, and in August 1977 the Gaming Commission approved the use of hand-held decks in the Bonanza's 21 games. The pit at that time had six 21 games.

In January 1980 Pat Brady purchased 2 percent of the operation from Russ Sheltra and Robert McDonald.

Dean Hubbard, a former employee of Harolds Club and a prominent boxer in the 1950s, worked for many years as casino manager of the Bonanza.

The Bonanza has shown continual growth over the years. After completing a major expansion in 1989, the country-western-themed casino started another major expansion in 1994 that was completed in 1996. Plans are being finalized for the next expansion, a two-story, 105-room hotel.

Nev. St. Journal, 16 Aug. 73, 5 Oct. 73, 26 Jan. 74, 15 Aug. 74, 20 June 75, 19 Aug. 77, 17 Jan. 80, 16 Sept. 89.

BOOMTOWN CASINO

Seven miles west of Reno on I-80; licensed since October 27, 1967, as a full casino.

In November 1967 Robert Cashell of Longview, Texas, a salesman with the Humble Oil and Refining Company of Houston, was licensed to operate ninety slot machines at Bill and Effie's Cafe and Truck Stop in Verdi. Cashell had been in the Reno area for three years.

A few weeks later, it was announced that Bill and Effie Engel were selling their truck stop and the fourteen surrounding acres and going into retirement. The purchasing company was known as the Verdi Development Company and was headed by Robert Cashell. Cashell managed the casino, Jimmy Middaugh was owner and manager of the restaurant, and Bill Savage was owner and manager of the service station.

Cashell announced that his company planned to make $80,000 in improvements within the next six months. The improvements would include adding fifteen units to the ten-unit motel and construction of a swimming pool and sauna.

In March 1969 Cashell announced that George Alley, formerly of Harrah's, would be the new restaurant manager and that Bill and Effie's would spend $100,000 to modernize the restaurant and enlarge its seating capacity to two hundred.

In March 1970 the Gaming Commission approved the following reorganization of the corporation operating Bill and Effie's at the Boomtown location: new directors of the corporation were Robert Moore, Richard Kearney, Robert McDonald, and Donald Carano; and Robert Cashell was president of the corporation.

In 1972 the property dropped the name Bill and Effie's and was licensed under the name of Boomtown. The casino added one 21 game to its slot operation.

In September 1972 Bob Cashell initiated one of his greatest marketing ploys. To publicize his truck stop and casino, he offered all truckers in the United States a free full-course barbecue buffet with steaks, ribs, and beans. The only thing the truckers had to do was stop in, pick up a plate, and get in line. This was something unheard-of at the time, and it resulted in Boomtown becoming one of the most popular truck stops in the country.

By April 1976 Boomtown had grown to a property with 275 slots, nine 21 games, and one craps game. Cashell announced that he would remain as president and that Jack Renwick would become the general manager. He also announced that another expansion would begin shortly.

This $2-million expansion phase was completed in December 1976 and included new restaurants, more gaming facilities, additional parking, a children's game room, and a larger general store. In addition, a shell for an additional 102 hotel rooms was completed, with the rooms to be ready for occupancy early in 1977.

In February 1977 Boomtown opened a keno game and named Bill Twedt as its first keno manager.

On December 1, 1977, Washoe County Commissioner Dick Scott resigned his post to become vice-president and general manager of Boomtown. A few months later, in March 1978, construction began on a two-story, 124-room hotel, which was to be part of a $2.4-million expansion.

In April 1978 plans were unveiled for an eventual multimillion-dollar development. In May the County Commission approved rezoning plans that allowed Boomtown to continue its expansion program.

On October 20, 1978, Ed Allison, former editor of the *Carson City Appeal* and former press aide to Governor Paul Laxalt, became assistant general manager to Dick Scott. Allison had been in charge of marketing for the casino. Don Dixon was named administration manager, and Jerry Anderson was promoted from games manager to casino manager. In addition, on December 3, 1978, Jim Minor was put in charge of marketing, Jim Middaugh was named operations manager, and Jack Langston became games manager.

In December 1980 the owners of Boomtown purchased the two major gaming properties in Winnemucca—Winner's and the Model T Truck Stop.

In April 1988 Timothy Parrott and Kenneth Rainin from the San Francisco Bay area purchased Boomtown for $50 million. In 1989 Boomtown's expansion continued as 12,000 square feet were added to the existing 165,000 square feet of property. In October 1992 Boomtown became a publicly traded firm, and in 1993 it added a four-story hotel and a youth arcade. This increased the total casino area to 47,613 square feet.

Boomtown continues to grow and currently has gaming properties in both Las Vegas and Mississippi. In early 1997 Boomtown presented a plan to the Washoe County Commission calling for another major expansion at the Verdi property.

On November 12, 1997, the Washoe County Commission unanimously approved a controversial expansion that would transform the property into northern Nevada's largest gambling-entertainment complex. The expansion, which is slated to begin in the year 2000 and be completed in three years, includes a 2,100-room hotel tower, 100,000 square feet of casino space, an eighteen-hole golf course, and an outdoor entertainment area.

Nev. St. Journal, 27 Oct. 67, 14 Nov. 67, 16 Mar. 69, 20 Mar. 70, 19 Apr. 70 (photo), 18 May 72, 17 Sept. 72 (photo), 4 Apr. 76, 16 Sept. 76, 5 Dec. 76 (photo), 9 Dec. 76, 17 Dec. 76, 27 Feb. 77, 13 Nov. 77 (photo), 2 Mar. 78, 12 Apr. 78, 23 May 78, 20 Oct. 78 (photo), 3 Dec. 78 (photos), 28 July 79, 20 Dec. 80, 7 Apr. 88, 11 June 89, 22 Oct. 92.

BOTORFF, GLEN

Glen Botorff, a graduate of the University of Nevada, began his gaming career at Harolds Club in 1948. He rose through the ranks with the Smith family organization, working in many supervisory positions. He stayed with Harolds Club when it was sold to the Hughes Corporation in 1970, and in August 1978 he was named director of casino operations.

In the late 1980s Botorff left Harolds Club and was employed by the Eldorado Hotel-Casino. He finished his gaming career as a pit supervisor with the Carano-owned operation, retiring in 1993.

Nev. St. Journal, 7 Apr. 74, 27 Aug. 78 (photo).

BRADY, LARRY

Larry Brady, whose real name was Lawrence Burger, came to Reno from Nome, Alaska. He was the owner-operator of the Sphynx Club on East Fourth Street in late 1941 and early 1942. He was also co-owner of the Barn Club on North Center Street in 1942.

On November 17, 1942, while playing craps (and losing) at the Bank Club, Larry Brady drew a gun and threatened to kill Hugh Smithwick and Harry Bond, both employees of the Bank Club. On January

17, 1943, Brady pleaded nolo contendere to the charge of threatening Smithwick and Bond and was given probation, with the provision that he be out of Reno and in the merchant marine within forty-eight hours. He was also ordered never to return to Reno.

In April 1945, a few days before he was to have started serving a six-year term in a California penitentiary, Brady was found dead in his San Francisco hotel room. Near his body, police found twenty-four empty capsules, suggesting the possibility of suicide. He had been convicted of trafficking in narcotics.

Nev. St. Journal, 15 Aug. 42, 17 Jan. 43, 17 Apr. 45.

BRAFFORD, HARDY

Hardy Brafford was born in Christopher, Illinois, on July 7, 1922. In 1947 Brafford came to Reno and was employed at Harolds Club. He was a member of the famous Harolds Club baseball and softball teams, which toured the western section of the United States and were a publicity tool of the club. Brafford and several other team members remained in the gaming industry for their entire careers.

Brafford worked in Las Vegas and Elko in the early 1950s but returned to Reno in 1954 and was employed at the Bank Club until 1956. At that time he went to work at the Cal-Neva as a box man. He left the Cal-Neva in 1959 and worked at the Sparks (Ascuaga's) Nugget as a shift manager until 1964.

In 1964 Brafford was hired as a shift manager and assistant casino manager at the Primadonna Club. When the Primadonna was sold to the Del Webb Corporation, Brafford continued to work at the Primadonna. He later worked for the Eldorado Hotel-Casino before leaving Reno to work as a pit supervisor at Whiskey Pete's Casino in Jean, Nevada.

Brafford retired from the gaming business in 1987 and now resides in Fort Walton, Florida. His son, Hardy Brafford Jr., followed his father into the gaming business and is employed as a pit supervisor at the Club Cal-Neva.

Nev. St. Journal, 23 July 76.

BRANDING IRON

4700 North Virginia Street; licensed from March 1, 1952, to October 29, 1957, for slots, 21, and craps.

The Branding Iron was a small bar with a few slots, a 21 game, and a craps game. It was first licensed by Robert Douglass, Al Figoni, and James Lloyd. Ted Peterson was also licensed in the early days of operation.

In February 1954 the bar's name was changed to Bodie Mike's Branding Iron when Mike Lazovich purchased the property and was licensed for gambling. Norman Nicholson was also granted a gaming license in February 1954, and in July 1954 Giovanni Sciacca was licensed at the property.

For the next few years, the business was known both as Bodie Mike's Branding Iron and as simply the Branding Iron.

Elizabeth Hartwick was licensed from July 1 to September 22, 1955. At that time, Frank Weiland took over the license. On October 24, 1957, the Gaming Control Board closed Weiland's operation at the Branding Iron for "tampering with the playing cards."

The former location of the Branding Iron is incorporated into the recently remodeled and enlarged Bonanza Casino.

Nev. St. Journal, 1 Mar. 52, 27 Feb. 54, 2 July 54, 30 June 55, 22 Sept. 55, 24 Oct. 57.

BREVICK, JOHN

John Brevick was employed at the Club Cal-Neva in 1962. When the Cal-Neva purchased the Cal-Neva Lodge at Lake Tahoe in 1967, Brevick was appointed casino manager of the property. When the Cal-Neva Lodge was sold, he returned to work at the Cal-Neva in Reno. In January 1975 Brevick was appointed general manager of the Cal-Neva. He remained in that position until 1981.

In 1978 Brevick was licensed as a co-owner of the Comstock Hotel-Casino.

In May 1981 Brevick was named general manager of the Mapes Money Tree. He operated the property for about eighteen months and reportedly made a profit of $750,000, which was sent to the Mapes Hotel in an attempt to keep that property open. Shortly after Brevick was replaced as general manager of the Money Tree, the property was closed.

Brevick also worked as casino manager at Pick Hobson's Riverside Hotel-Casino in the early 1980s, before leaving Reno for Texas to work on offshore gambling boats. Brevick subsequently worked in casino gaming in Mississippi and at Si Redd's Oasis Resort in Mesquite, Nevada.

Nev. St. Journal, 12 Jan. 75 (photo).

BRIGHT SPOT

234 North Center Street; licensed from July 1961 to February 1965 for slots only.

The Bright Spot was a bar with several slot machines but no table games. The site is now part of Harrah's Casino on the east side of Center Street.

BRODSKY, MORRIS

Morris Brodsky was one of a four-person group that opened the original Cal-Neva in 1948. The other three members were Sanford Adler, Louis Mayberg, and Charles Resnick.

Brodsky was named general manager of the Cal-Neva in January 1951; however, in January 1952 he was removed from the Cal-Neva license, both as owner and as general manager.

Nev. St. Journal, 20 Nov. 48, 10 Jan. 51.

BRUECKNER, WILLI

Willi Gustav Brueckner was born in Hamburg, Germany, in 1903 and came to Reno from San Francisco in 1930.

Brueckner worked mostly in the food and beverage area of the gaming business. His first job in Reno was at the Willows, a nationally famous nightclub, when it was owned and operated by Bill Graham and James McKay. He also supervised the food operation at Graham and McKay's Cal-Neva Lodge at Lake Tahoe. When the Tavern opened on West Fourth Street in 1931, Brueckner went to work there in the dining area.

In 1941 Brueckner, Marcel Peters, and K. D. Dalrymple opened the 116 Club on North Center Street, and the club was licensed for slots, 21, and roulette. They operated the 116 Club until losing their lease in 1955.

After the 116 Club closed, Brueckner worked as a maitre d' at the Riverside and Mapes Hotels in the late 1950s and early 1960s. He left Reno in the late 1960s to work for the Sahara Hotel in Las Vegas. When he retired in the early 1970s, he returned to Reno, where he enthusiastically pursued his hobby of fishing.

Brueckner died on July 27, 1992.

Nev. St. Journal, 30 Apr. 52, 10 Aug. 54, 1 May 55, 29 July 92 (obit.).

BRUNET, BARRY

Barry Brunet was licensed as the chairman of the board of the MGM Hotel-Casino when the property opened in 1978. In April 1979 he was elected president and chief executive officer of the MGM Hotel-Casino. He replaced Jack Pieper, who had left the organization.

Brunet stayed on as general manager when the property was sold to the Bally's Corporation in 1986, but he left when the Hilton Corporation took possession of the hotel-casino in July 1992.

BRUNSWICK CLUB

227 North Center Street (located inside the Golden Hotel on the first floor); licensed from 1931 to 1946 for poker and pan only.

Opened in 1931 with one draw poker game, one stud poker game, and one pan game, the Brunswick during its entire operation was basically a cardroom and bar, not a casino.

Nick Adams was granted a beer license there when Prohibition was repealed in 1933. In the 1940 City Directory, Curtis and Ed Goldman were listed as owners. In 1945 Brunswick owner Curtis Goldman was issued a liquor license, and the same year J. W. Van Erman was granted a gaming license for pan and poker.

In 1946, when George Wingfield sold the Golden Hotel to a group of investors headed by James Lloyd, the Brunswick closed. It was later reopened as the Golden Gulch Casino.

The former location of the Brunswick Club is now part of Harrah's Club on the west side of Center Street, between Second Street and Douglas Alley.

Nev. St. Journal, 6 Apr. 33, 9 Jan. 45, 27 Nov. 45, 10 Jan. 46, 17 Jan. 46 (adv.).

BRUNZELL, EVERETT

Everett Brunzell first came to Reno from Los Angeles in 1955, when his company was awarded the contract to build the Holiday Hotel on Mill Street. He headed the Brunzell Construction Company and over the years built many hotels, casinos, offices, and homes in the Reno and Lake Tahoe area, including the Pioneer Coliseum, the King's Inn, the Onslow Hotel, the Silver Spur Casino, and the Horseshoe Club.

Brunzell invested in several casinos in Reno and Lake Tahoe. Although he was not a casino operator in the true sense of the word, he was active on management boards and served as president of the board for many of the casinos with which he was associated.

He was one of six owners of the Ponderosa Hotel on South Virginia Street when it opened in 1966. He sold his interest in 1969.

Brunzell was also a co-owner of the Silver Spur Casino from 1967 to 1981, a co-owner of the Onslow Hotel-Casino from 1977 to 1987, and is currently a co-owner of the Crystal Bay Club on the North Shore of Lake Tahoe.

Nev. St. Journal, 3 Nov. 66, 11 Dec. 69.

BUDDY BAER'S

136 North Center Street; licensed in 1950 for slots and 21.

Buddy Baer's was opened at the former location of the Bar of Music, which had closed in January 1949. The property remained closed until February 1950, when Fred Cullincini and former heavyweight boxer Jacob "Buddy" Baer took over the business.

The city granted a gaming license to Buddy Baer on March 1, 1950, and a grand opening was held on March 8.

On January 23, 1951, Fred Cullincini was granted a gaming license, and the name of the club was changed to Freddy's Lair.

The former site of Buddy Baer's is now part of the Cal-Neva's parking garage on the east side of Center Street.

Nev. St. Journal, 11 Feb. 50, 1 Mar. 50, 8 Mar. 50 (adv.), 23 Jan. 51.

BUDWEISER BAR

244 North Virginia Street; licensed from August 1936 to December 1936 for poker only.

The Bud (or Budweiser) Bar operated at two different locations, 244 and 268 North Virginia Street. It was licensed for poker only. The site is now part of Harolds Club.

BUNGALOW CLUB

220 North Virginia Street; licensed for roulette only from August to October 1931.

The Bungalow Club was licensed for a roulette table for a few months in the early days of legal gambling. The site was eventually taken over by Pick Hobson. It was the site of Pick's Club and later the Frontier Club.

Currently the address is part of Harrah's on Virginia Street.

BURNS, DAVID

David Burns is an Ely, Nevada, native who first came to Reno to attend the University of Nevada, then returned to eastern Nevada and lived in Winnemucca and Elko prior to returning to Reno in 1957.

Burns worked for Newton Crumley in Elko, and when Crumley opened the Holiday Hotel in Reno, Burns came to work for him. Burns was comptroller and general manager of the Holiday under Crumley, and in 1962, when Crumley was killed in a plane crash, Burns became, along with Carl Hicks, co-owner of the Holiday Hotel.

Burns and Hicks operated the Holiday Hotel under the corporate name of CARDA until they sold it in 1967 to Tom Moore, Austin Hemphill, and John Monfrey, all of Texas, for a price reported to be "in excess of $5 million dollars."

Nev. St. Journal, 27 July 67.

BUSEY, DOUG

Doug Busey was a Reno attorney who was licensed as a co-owner of several casinos in Reno in the 1950s and 1960s—the Blue Bird Club in 1949, the Picadilly Club in 1950, the Haymarket Club in 1951, the Tahoe Palace in 1960, and the Club Cal-Neva in 1962.

Nev. St. Journal, 22 Sept. 50.

Mrs. Newton (Frances) Crumley signing the agreement selling the Holiday Hotel-Casino to David Burns (l.) and Carl Hicks in 1962. Courtesy of the Nevada Historical Society.

C & M CLUB

220 North Virginia Street; licensed in July 1940 for poker and pan.

The C & M Club was named after its owners, Swede Collet and Frank McKeown. Its location was the future site of Pick's Club and the Frontier Club. Currently the site is part of Harrah's on Virginia Street.

Nev. St. Journal, 27 July 40 (adv.).

CALIFORNIA CLUB

238 North Center Street; licensed from June 10, 1931, to December 31, 1932, for slots, 21, craps, roulette, and a big-six wheel.

The California Club was located in the lobby of the Overland Hotel. It was open twenty-four hours a day and had entrances on Center Street and through the lobby entrance on Commercial Row.

In January 1933 the lease on the gaming rooms expired, and W. A. Sanders, proprietor of the club, moved his equipment to a warehouse. The gaming rooms were then once again used as a lobby.

The site of the California Club is now part of Harrah's parking garage on Center Street.

Nev. St. Journal, 21 June 31 (adv.), 4 Jan. 33.

CALIFORNIA CLUB

268 North Virginia Street; licensed from 1944 to 1946 for craps, 21, and roulette.

The California Club opened in 1944 as the California Bar, but in 1945 the City Council gave its permission to owner Monte Haight to change the name to the California Club and licensed him to operate one craps game, one roulette game, one 21 game, and four slot machines. In May 1946 Monte Haight entered into a partnership with Mac Mael and Dick Farlow. Jack Duffy was put in charge of gaming.

In October 1946 James Powers was granted a gaming license at the location,

and the name of the business was changed to the Colony Club.

The former California Club is now part of the Harolds Club property.

Nev. St. Journal, 28 Dec. 45, 4 May 46 (adv.), 3 Aug. 46, 29 Oct. 46.

CALIFORNIA CLUB

222 Lake Street; never licensed.

In May 1957 George Chinn applied for a gaming license at the California Club on Lake Street. His application was deferred. On June 27, the state denied Chinn's application for three games. Chinn had planned to invest $42,000 to operate one craps game, one 21 game, and one keno game. He would have leased the rear of the premises from Fred Down, who operated the bar. The location of the proposed new casino was the Old Cathay Club, which closed in May 1957 when Harry Chon lost his license.

Chinn was denied a license because he had earlier failed to disclose his secret interest in the Yukon Club. That failure to disclose had resulted in the closure of the Yukon Club in 1955.

The site of the California Club is now a parking lot.

Nev. St. Journal, 24 May 57, 27 June 57.

CAPITOL BAR

43 East Second Street; licensed from April 1931 to 1948 for slots, 21, and roulette.

The Capitol Bar was opened by Page Wade in April 1931 and was licensed for one roulette game, one 21 game, and six slot machines. It was purchased in 1934 by Jack Clark and Shorty King, who installed Jack Dunneback as their manager and were licensed for one roulette game and one 21 game.

In 1935 Clark and King sold the Capitol to Karl Jones, their bartender, and George Coppersmith. In 1938 Jones bought out Coppersmith and became the sole owner of the Capitol. He later added a craps table to the license to go along with his slots, 21 game, and roulette table.

Jones died unexpectedly at the age of forty-three in February 1947. Roy Propst took over the Capitol a few months later. In September Propst stated that "he [was]

the sole owner of the Capitol Bar and that Cliff Judd or no one else [was] associated with the operation." The reason for Propst's statement was that Cliff Judd, who had an unsavory reputation in the gaming industry, was claiming to be an owner of the Capitol and Propst did not want to be known as Judd's associate. The operation closed in 1948.

In January 1949 the property was remodeled and opened as Jacobs and Jacobs Clothiers. The Jacobses owned another clothing store on Virginia Street.

The former location of the Capitol Bar is now part of Harrah's on Second Street between Virginia and Center Streets.

Nev. St. Journal, 10 Feb. 34 (adv.), 2 July 35, 14 Dec. 35, 1 Apr. 38, 15 Feb. 46, 26 Feb. 47, 17 Sept. 47, 18 Sept. 47, 25 Jan. 49, 6 May 49.

CARANO, DON

Don Carano, who was born in 1933 and raised in Reno, graduated from the University of San Francisco Law School and came back home to practice law. However, little by little, the law was pushed aside by the business of gaming.

By 1967 Carano was a partner in the Boomtown Casino, along with Bob Cashell and Bob McDonald. A few years later, Carano sold his interests to Bob Cashell, and in 1972 he became a co-owner, along with Jerry Poncia and John Lazovich, of the Pioneer Inn on South Virginia Street.

In May 1973 Carano, along with five other partners, was licensed at the Eldorado Hotel-Casino. The Eldorado was the first major casino to open on Virginia Street on the north side of the railroad tracks. At the time, this was considered an extremely daring venture, but it ultimately changed the profile of Reno gaming.

In 1993 Carano and the Circus Circus Corporation announced a joint gaming venture operation called Project C. The project was later named the Silver Legacy, and the megacasino opened in July 1995.

Carano has surrounded himself with family in all of his casino operations. His wife, Rhonda, is director of advertising at the Eldorado, and his sons Glen, Greg, Gene, and Gary and daughter, Cindy, all have executive posts in either the Eldorado or the Silver Legacy. The Caranos also own the Ferrari-Carano Vineyards and Winery near Healdsburg, California, which spreads over five hundred acres of prime land in the Dry Creek–Alexander Valley region and includes property in Knight's Valley and the Carneros area at the south end of the Napa Valley.

Nev. St. Journal, 13 Apr. 72, 17 May 73, 28 May 89.

CARLTON BAR (AND/OR) HOTEL

218 Sierra Street; licensed from November 12, 1943, to 1952 for slots, 21, craps, roulette, and poker.

The Carlton Hotel was patronized mainly by transients and locals, not by tourists. During the life of the Carlton, many people ran small-scale gambling operations on the property for short periods. The Carlton had entrances on both Sierra Street and Fulton Alley. In the 1930s the Carlton had slot machines licensed at all times, but no owner ever had a full casino there. In fact, it wasn't until 1943 that there were any table games at the location.

In 1944 there were poker games in the back lobby, and advertisements stressed that "ladies were welcome." The most common types of gambling at the Carlton were poker games and 21.

In February 1945 Clarence Horsely was licensed for one 21 game, and in July 1945 the City Council granted a cabaret license and a gaming license (for a craps game and a 21 game) to Sam Delich, whose partners in the operation were his brother, George, and Fritz Gersich. For their cabaret, they hired a well-known local piano player, Fay Thomas. Miss Thomas, who was an African American, had a large following and attracted many locals.

The Delichs sold the business to Stan Hanson for $20,000 in June 1946, and he was licensed for one 21 game and one craps game.

In June 1953 Ralph Swearns was given a gaming license, and in November 1964 J. R. (Rodney) Knight was licensed and operated the games until December 1966.

In June 1972 the Coral Reef Lounge was opened in the Carlton; its feature attraction was a large display of tropical fish in several tanks. Gaming was not present.

The Carlton was demolished in 1976 to make room for the Money Tree expansion. The former site of the Carlton is now part of Eddie's Fabulous 50's Casino.

Nev. St. Journal, 1 July 44 (adv.), 27 June 45, 5 Mar. 46 (adv.), 21 May 46, 4 June 46, 4 July 46 (adv.), 16 Oct. 46, 27 Nov. 46, 23 Jan. 47, 22 Mar. 47, 30 Oct. 51, 14 Nov. 51, 27 Nov. 51, 18 June 53, 12 Nov. 64, 10 Jan. 66, 11 June 72.

CASHELL, ROBERT "BOB"

Bob Cashell, born in Longview, Texas, in 1939, was employed by the Humble Oil and Refining Company of Houston and was living in Reno when he and three partners purchased Bill and Effie's Cafe and Truck Stop in 1967 for a little over $1 million. Cashell operated the property as Bill and Effie's until 1972, when it was licensed as Boomtown. Over the years the Boomtown property grew at a tremendous pace, and in April 1988 Cashell sold the casino to Timothy Parrott and Kenneth Rainin for $50 million.

During the growth period of Boomtown, Cashell became active in politics. He was elected in 1982 to a four-year term as lieutenant governor of Nevada. He also served on the Board of Regents of the University of Nevada and helped many students financially. Largely because of his generous contributions, a field house at the University of Nevada, Reno, was constructed and named in his honor.

Cashell was instrumental in bringing youth soccer to Reno, and he has sponsored hundreds of children's soccer teams over the past thirty years.

During his long gaming career, Cashell has often been the man whom the gaming industry has called upon to fix its problems. He has managed Karl's Silver Club in Sparks, the Bourbon Street Casino in Las Vegas, and the Avi Hotel-Casino for the Avi Indian Tribe, and he has been a partner in the Carson Station Casino in Carson City, the Comstock Hotel-Casino in Reno, and the Holiday Casino in Las Vegas.

Besides being 100-percent owner of Boomtown, he has also individually owned the Winner's Inn, Star Casino, and Model T Truck Stop in Winnemucca, the Alamo Truck Stop in Sparks, and the Horseshoe Club in Reno.

In 1998 Cashell was actively involved in overseeing the expansion of his Alamo Truck Stop in Sparks and was heading a management team that was operating the financially troubled Ormsby House Hotel-Casino in Carson City.

Nev. St. Journal, 27 Oct. 67, 14 Nov. 67, 4 Apr. 76, 20 Dec. 80, 7 Apr. 88, 26 Apr. 89.

CASINO BAR

124 East Commercial Row; licensed in 1942 for six months for poker only.

The Casino Bar was open for several years before it was licensed for poker in May 1942. The license was not renewed in 1943. The business was owned by Angelo Matteucci and Joe Archio in the late 1930s and the early 1940s.

The former location of the Casino Bar is now part of Harrah's parking garage.

Nev. St. Journal, 23 July 35, 27 Aug. 35, 21 Dec. 35, 25 June 36 (adv.), 17 Apr. 40 (adv.).

CASINO CIGAR STORE

120 East Commercial Row; licensed from June 1931 to 1932 for poker only.

The Casino Cigar Store was at a location that housed several bars, cardrooms, and tobacco stores during the early years in Reno. Poker was licensed there during the early months of legalized gaming in 1931.

The site is now part of Harrah's parking garage.

CASINO CLUB

123½ East Douglas Alley and 120 East Commercial Row; licensed for a few months in 1931 for one 21 game.

The Casino Club was a bar with an entrance on East Commercial Row and one on East Douglas Alley. It was also known as the Casino Bar and the Casino Cigar Store. It was licensed for a 21 game in 1931, but like several other small clubs, it closed the game after a few months of operation.

The club, which was owned by Andy Anderson, Jack Dugan, and Victor and Joe

Belosky, was closed by Judge Norcross in April 1933 for liquor violations.

The former location of the Casino Club is now part of Harrah's parking garage.

Nev. St. Journal, 8 Apr. 33.

CAVANAUGH, JOHN JR.

John Cavanaugh Jr.'s father was a co-owner of the Club Cal-Neva, and John Jr. continued in his father's footsteps. He was licensed as the major owner of the Gold Dust East Casino on the corner of Second and Sierra Streets in June 1976, and he opened the casino on July 1, 1976. He closed the club in 1982.

Cavanaugh opened the Gold Dust West Casino at 444 Vine Street in July 1977. He remains the owner and operator of that popular Reno casino.

Nev. St. Journal, 28 June 76, 14 July 77.

CAVANAUGH, JOHN SR.

John Cavanaugh Sr. was born in Tecoma (now a ghost town), near Tonopah, in 1913. He built his financial base from an oil distribution business. He owned the Mizpah Hotel in Tonopah for eighteen years and was a Nye County assemblyman from 1945 to 1947.

In 1953 Cavanaugh moved to Reno and became active in the building industry. He was the major partner in the development of the Arlington Towers, the Renata Crest subdivision, and many other projects. He also acquired the El Cortez Hotel in 1966 and operated it through a lease agreement for one year.

In March 1962 he was licensed as one of the six original owners of the Club Cal-Neva, along with Warren Nelson, Jack Douglass, Ad Tolen, Leon Nightingale, and Howard Farris. In March 1969 Cavanaugh was licensed as a co-owner of the Cal-Neva Lodge at Lake Tahoe.

Cavanaugh was killed in an automobile crash on the Mount Rose Highway in October 1973.

His legacy in the gaming industry continues through his son, John Jr., who owns the Gold Dust West Casino, and through his daughter, Barbara Cavanaugh Thornton, who along with her husband, William

Thornton, is a major stockholder in the Club Cal-Neva in downtown Reno.

Nev. St. Journal, 29 Mar. 62, 21 Mar. 69, 7 Oct. 73 (obit.).

CEDARS

1585 South Virginia Street (actual location was on Lakeside Avenue at the west end of Walts Lane, south of Ardmore Street); licensed from 1932 to 1947 for slots, roulette, 21, and craps.

The Cedars, which opened in the late 1920s, was one of Reno's finest nightclubs and dinner houses for many years. Gambling was really more an adjunct than an integral part of the Cedars operation, although at various times it had as many as five table games and several slot machines.

In the 1930s and the 1940s, this location was considered out of town, and in fact as late as 1946 it was still outside the city limits.

Owners and managers changed almost yearly, and the interior decor changed almost as frequently. When the Cedars opened in 1932, Gene Rovetti was one of the principal owners, and he employed a western motif, playing on a rodeo and riding-stable theme. In 1933 well-known

Renoites Louis Rosasco and Cam Mattino took over and featured fine music and Italian cuisine. Both were gifted musicians, and they contributed much of their talent to help make the Cedars a success. Mattino and his band were the featured attractions of the floor show. In 1936 Pat Harrison and Ted Harkins—two well-known local bartenders—and Carl Gottschalk took over. They chose a decor that resembled a tank-town depot, and patrons were encouraged to carve their initials into the bar. Shortly thereafter, Ace Page became the manager, and in early 1937 Eddie Murphy was named manager. Murphy said that "the Cedars will be the only out-of-town nightclub with a western background. The walls will be heavy with harness, wagon wheels, saddles, and other western paraphernalia. Also on display will be a hangman's rope, said to be the rope that stretched the neck of a horse thief here in Reno a few generations ago."

In November 1937 the Cedars changed hands again. Gene Rovetti was back in place, and his two new partners were John Cadlini and Ernie Russell.

Between 1939 and 1945 the club had three different names, used interchange-

Lou Rosasco entertaining at the popular night spot, the Cedars. Courtesy of Jan Rosasco Savage.

ably—La Hacienda, the Cedars, and the Cedars La Hacienda.

In January 1946 Gene Rovetti was still in charge, but now his partner was Jack Alton. Rovetti kept the Cedars until October 1947, when he leased the property to George Stone and N. C. Ullin. Stone was granted a gaming license on October 5, 1947, but only twelve days later the Cedars was razed by fire. This landmark property could not be rebuilt as a club because the zoning laws at the time allowed for residences only at that location.

The former site of the Cedars is now occupied by a private residence.

Nev. St. Journal, 14 May 33 (adv.), 7 Nov. 33 (adv.), 8 Dec. 33 (adv.), 22 May 35, 8 Aug. 36, 15 Aug. 36, 5 Dec. 36, 6 Mar. 37 (adv.), 24 Apr. 37, 13 Nov. 37, 13 Apr. 38 (photo), 2 May 39 (adv.), 16 Feb. 44 (adv.), 13 Jan. 46 (adv.), 26 Jan. 46, 18 July 46 (adv.), 5 Oct. 47, 17 Oct. 47, 17 Feb. 64.

CENTER CLUB

190 North Center Street (corner of Center and Second Streets); licensed from June 1948 to 1949 for 21, craps, and roulette.

The Center Club opened on June 11, 1948, with gaming managed by Curtis Harwood, John Redican, Cletus Libby, and Ed Hughes. The club was licensed for one craps game, one 21 game, one roulette wheel, and fifteen slots.

In October 1948 Al Ferreira was named manager of the club. Also in that month the Center Club introduced a penny roulette game, which according to its advertisement in the *Nevada State Journal* was the only penny game in the state.

The Center Club closed in 1949. Now located at its former site is the Cameo Super Pawn Shop.

Nev. St. Journal, 11 June 48, 30 Oct. 48 (adv.).

CENTER CLUB

228 North Center Street; licensed for craps, pan, 21, and racehorse keno from April to June 1931.

The Center Club opened on April 1, 1931, and paid the following license fees: $150 each for a craps game, a 21 game, and a keno game. They also paid $75 for the licensing of a pan game. Only one month later, in May 1931, new owners stepped in

and changed the name of the club to the Central Club.

The former location of the Center Club is now part of Harrah's Casino on Center Street.

CENTRAL CLUB

228 North Center Street; licensed from May 1931 to 1932 for roulette, faro, and poker.

The Central Club took over the location of the Center Club in May 1931. It advertised faro as its featured game.

The former location of the Central Club is now part of Harrah's on the east side of Center Street.

Reno Personal Service Bureau Report (1931).

CHARLIE'S COCKTAIL LOUNGE

325 South Virginia Street; licensed from January 1, 1941, to 1950 for slots, 21, and roulette.

On December 28, 1940, Charlie Frisch opened Charlie's Cocktail Lounge at 325 South Virginia Street. In 1950 Frisch discontinued gambling at his lounge, and in January 1952 he sold the business to Robert Schmitt, who operated the establishment as Bob's Cocktail Lounge.

The former location of Charlie's Cocktail Lounge is now part of the Bank of America Plaza.

Nev. St. Journal, 28 Dec. 40 (adv.), 4 Nov. 41 (adv.), 17 Jan. 52.

CHEROKEE CLUB

19 East Douglas Alley and 20 East Commercial Row (two entrances); licensed from July 1947 to December 1948 for slots, 21, and craps.

The Cherokee Club was one of many small bars, cardrooms, and single-table casinos that dotted Douglas Alley and Commercial Row for years. Jack Douglass was licensed at the Cherokee in July 1947. In January 1948 J. W. Lawrence was licensed at the site for one 21 game and one craps game. The Cherokee was destroyed by fire in December 1948.

The former site of the Cherokee Club is now part of the Harolds Club property.

Nev. St. Journal, 15 July 47, 20 Dec. 48, 7 Jan. 49, 2 Oct. 49 (photo), 21 May 50.

CHINA MINT

246 Lake Street; licensed from October 1960 to April 1963 for slots, 21, and craps.

In June 1960 the Gaming Control Board recommended approval to move the Happy Buddha from 222 Lake Street to 246 Lake Street and to change its name to the China Mint, but only if the business supplied a written financial statement to the Gaming Control Board, and only if Joe Yip was not hired as casino manager or in any other capacity. The licensees recommended for approval were Andrew Young, Frank Chung, Henry Leong, and William Bailey. Bailey had recently been fired from his bartending job at the Happy Buddha and was "86ed" (barred from entering the property). He wanted to sell his percentage of the club, but his partners wouldn't buy him out.

The state refused to make an immediate decision on the licensing but finally relented, and the China Mint was given a gambling license in October 1960 and operated until April 1963.

Currently the site is a parking lot.

Nev. St. Journal, 9 June 60, 21 June 60.

CHRISTMAS TREE

23900 Mount Rose Highway; licensed sporadically from 1948 to 1978 for slots, 21, craps, and roulette.

John and Alice Ross built and opened the Christmas Tree as a bar in the winter of 1946. They added the restaurant in 1947.

Over the years, there were many owners and operators of the Christmas Tree, and in many cases the bar and restaurant owner leased out the gambling concession. Longtime Nevada gamblers Nick Abelman and Walter Parman were actively involved in the early days of the Christmas Tree. Well-known concessionaire Virgil Smith is believed to be the first person to lease the gaming.

John and Alice Ross sold the operation to Jim Jeffress in 1948, and in 1952 Jeffress sold "The Tree" to Guy Michael and Art Fisher. Michael and Fisher operated the gaming until December 1959, when the Nevada Gaming Control Board closed the Christmas Tree and accused the 21 dealer of "turning the deck." Michael insisted that "there must be a misunderstanding, we are basically a restaurant and we would do nothing to harm our reputation." He requested and was granted a hearing on the revocation; however, on January 21, 1960, the Christmas Tree was ordered to surrender its gaming license.

The gaming was leased to George Slovin in June 1960 and to Dan Skanovsky in 1961. Bob Peccole leased the gaming in 1962 and 1963. Peccole was a well-known and popular gaming figure in northern Nevada, and the Christmas Tree enjoyed great success in the early 1960s, with Michael and Peccole proving to be a good combination. In September 1963 Val Ruggerio was granted the gaming license and operated the gaming until February 1964.

In July 1966, with Art Woods and Guy Michael listed as licensees, the Christmas Tree was again closed by the Gaming Control Board when loaded dice were taken from the craps table.

In 1967 the Christmas Tree was destroyed by fire. The combination of a bout with cancer, the license revocation, and the destruction of the property led Guy Michael to sell the business to Al Kuckhoff, who rebuilt and reopened the Christmas Tree. The casino operators for Kuckhoff were Reno Menicucci and Ken Clever.

Kuckhoff leased the property to Peter Apostolos in 1969. The business was plagued by financial problems, and in 1972 the bank foreclosed on the popular restaurant-casino operation.

The business remained closed until 1976, when it was reopened by Gloria Michael. She leased the gaming to Don Gilfillian, who operated the casino from December 1976 to spring 1978. Longtime Lake Tahoe gambler Jerry Mesorobian was Gilfillian's casino manager.

The next owners of the Christmas Tree were David and Mary Ellen Houston. David Houston is a Reno attorney. His mother, Virginia Houston, a longtime Reno resident, was a dealer at Harolds Club for many years. The Houstons purchased the property in 1983. Gloria Michael Stein worked for them as their chef and helped to manage the restaurant until

they sold the property in August 1995 to Don, Lisa, and Dana Emerson.

In 1998 the property was operating as a restaurant but was not licensed for table games.

Nev. St. Journal, 6 Dec. 59, 24 Dec. 59, 21 Jan. 60, 2 Mar. 60, 27 May 60, 9 June 60, 20 July 66, 9 June 77, 16 Dec. 77; Bethel Holmes Van Tassel, *Wood Chips to Game Chips: Casinos and People at North Lake Tahoe* (N.p.: Bethel Holmes Van Tassel, 1985).

CIRCLE R-B LODGE

2205 West Fourth Street; licensed from 1951 to 1962 for slots, 21, craps, and roulette.

The Circle R-B Lodge was famous for its fine food, especially prime rib. It was opened by Cliff Kehl and Walter Parman in the fall of 1951. Kehl was well known in the Reno area as a food and beverage expert, and in later years he worked for Harrah's Lake Tahoe as maitre d' in the South Shore Room. Parman was noted for his gambling expertise, and he was the owner and/or manager of several gambling clubs during his long career.

Kehl and Parman operated the Circle R-B from 1951 to 1953. At that time, Parman bought the California Club in Las Vegas, and Kehl operated the club by himself until 1954. In June 1954 Parman's name was deleted from the gaming license and Cliff Kehl was listed as sole proprietor. A few months later, the property closed.

Late in 1955 the Circle R-B was reopened by Denzil "Denny" Sayers and Maurice and Warren Kiefert. They operated the property until 1962. The location later became the Chinese Pagoda Restaurant, operated by the famous Chinese chef, T. F. Gee. Various other restaurants have since operated at the Circle R-B Lodge's former location.

Currently the Mexican restaurant Mi Casa Too is in business at this address.

Nev. St. Journal, 29 July 51, 25 Aug. 51, 10 Oct. 51 (adv.), 27 Nov. 51, 25 June 52, 12 Nov. 53, 16 June 54, 4 Nov. 55 (adv.).

CIRCUS CIRCUS HOTEL-CASINO

500 North Sierra Street; licensed since July 1, 1978, as a full casino.

In July 1977 construction began on the multimillion-dollar Circus Circus Hotel-Casino on the former site of the Grey Reid Department Store. The project was scheduled to be completed in May 1978 and to open with 102 hotel rooms. The Circus Circus Corporation had requested permission to build more hotel rooms, but because of sewer capacity limitations, they were forced to open with only 102.

The marketing concept of Circus Circus was to combine a casino with a carnival midway and free circus acts. It shattered the adults-only concept and triggered a new emphasis on family tourism in Reno. The building was capped by a pink-and-white "big top" and featured a huge free-standing sign featuring the casino's mascot-logo, Topsy the Clown.

The property opened on July 1, 1978—the same date the Sahara Reno and the Money Tree expansion opened. The first casino manager was Don Herbert, who returned to Las Vegas in November 1979 and was replaced by Loyal Borden, who was a shift manager when the property opened.

In June 1980 ground was broken for a twenty-one-story, 625-room expansion. The project was expected to be completed in thirteen months, but it wasn't finished until late in September 1981. Upon completion of the expansion, the hotel had a total of 725 rooms.

Prior to the completion of the expansion program, a union election was held at the Circus Circus. Culinary Union No. 86 had waged a long campaign to organize the casino's food and beverage employees, and in October 1980 the union was certified at Circus Circus. It was the first successful union election for a sizable number of casino employees in Reno history.

Shortly after the results of the election were announced, Fred Sikorski, the general manager of the Circus Circus, resigned. He had been general manager since coming to Reno from Las Vegas in 1979. Sikorski was replaced by Rick Bannis.

In 1985 a twenty-eight-story sky tower was completed, bringing the total number of rooms to 1,625 and adding 17,000 square feet of gaming area.

In 1993 Circus Circus announced a joint

venture program with the Eldorado Hotel-Casino to construct a lavish new luxury resort-hotel, the Silver Legacy, which opened in July 1995.

In 1994 Circus Circus purchased several city blocks around its existing property to make space for possible future expansion. Two years later, Circus Circus began construction of a new 1,800-space state-of-the-art parking facility on some of this property located just north of the main casino. The garage was completed in early 1997 and gave Circus Circus a total of 3,719 parking spaces.

Also in 1996–1997 Circus Circus began a $15-million renovation and refurbishing program to upgrade the hotel rooms. However, by creating several luxury jacuzzi suites, it lowered the room count from 1,625 to 1,575. By 1998 Circus Circus had over seventeen hundred slot machines, more than sixty-five table games, and employed approximately two thousand people.

Nev. St. Journal, 15 June 77 (photo), 1 July 78, 25 Nov. 79 (photo), 18 June 80 (photo), 15 Oct. 80, 23 Nov. 80 (photo), 26 Sept. 81, 18 Aug. 88 (entertainment sect.).

CLADIANOS, PETER JR.

Peter Cladianos Jr. was born in Reno in 1930. His father, Peter Cladianos Sr., came to Reno in 1913 and operated several businesses, including a grocery store, the Economy Market, on East Commercial Row. In 1932 he purchased five slot machines and went into the bar and slot-machine route business. As a youngster, Peter Jr. swept floors in his father's businesses and collected coins from the slot machines.

When Cladianos graduated from the University of Nevada in 1953, he went to work in the family's growing motel and casino business. The family had opened the El Rancho Motel on South Virginia Street in 1941 and later built the El Rancho Motel on Fourth Street and Wells Avenue. In 1963 they began construction of the Sands Motor Inn.

Peter Cladianos Jr. opened the Sands Motor Inn in 1964. He kept expanding that property until 1985, when he took the company public and named it the Sands

Regency. After going public, the property grew at an even faster pace. Today the property consists of five buildings, including three hotel towers. It has 838 hotel rooms, 30,000 square feet of casino space, one thousand slots, twenty-four table games, and one thousand employees.

Cladianos Jr. and his sister, Katherene Cladianos Latham, always worked together in the company business, and their children were also involved. Peter Jr.'s son, Peter III, and his daughter, Antonia, along with Katherene's daughter, Deborah Lundgren, were also all active in the Sands Regency. The Claudianos family sold their 45 percent of the Sands Regency to Sapphire Gaming LLC, of the Hertz Group of Los Angeles, in May 1999.

Nev. St. Journal, 27 Oct. 91; *Reno Gazette-Journal,* 22 May 99.

CLARK, JACK

Jack Clark was born in Missouri on September 18, 1883. He arrived in Reno shortly after World War I and worked originally as an auto mechanic. He was married to Marguerite Gosse, daughter of the owner of the first modern Riverside Hotel.

Clark opened the Tavern on West Fourth Street in 1932 and operated it as a partnership with Shorty King, George Coppersmith, and George Nelson until 1936. The Tavern was one of the area's most popular casinos and featured some of Reno's first floor shows.

Clark was also a partner with Coppersmith in other gaming and bar interests, including the Capitol Bar on East Second Street.

Clark died in Carthage, Missouri, in 1969.

Nev. St. Journal, 10 Feb. 34, 4 Dec. 35, 7 Mar. 69 (obit.).

CLIFFORD, CHARLES "CHUCK"

Chuck Clifford was born and raised in the Reno-Sparks area and was employed by Harolds Club in 1953. He came up through the ranks and served as a floor manager at Harolds Club for many years.

Shortly after Harolds Club was sold to

the Hughes Corporation, Clifford resigned and went to work for Jessie Beck at the Riverside Hotel-Casino. In 1975, after the Riverside was sold to Pick Hobson, Clifford went to work at the Sundowner Hotel-Casino. In October 1976 he was licensed as casino manager and director of gaming at the Sundowner, a position he still holds. He was also a co-owner of the Virginian Hotel-Casino on South Virginia Street.

Nev. St. Journal, 14 Oct. 76.

CLOVER CLUB

202 North Center Street; licensed from February 1945 to April 1957 for 21 and craps.

The Clover Club opened at the former location of the Silver Dollar Club in January 1945. Its proprietors, Ed Vogliotti and John Cadlini, were granted a gaming license in February.

The club was destroyed by fire in April 1953, but it reopened in January 1954 and operated until April 1957.

The former location of the Clover Club is now part of Harrah's Casino on the northeast corner of Center and Second Streets.

Nev. St. Journal, 9 Jan. 45, 27 Jan. 45 (adv.), 24 Apr. 53.

CLUB CAL-NEVA

38 East Second Street; licensed as a full casino since 1948.

In September 1948 the Fordonia Building on the southwest corner of East Second and Center Streets, owned by Jack Sullivan and James McKay, was sold to Sanford Adler, Louis Mayberg, Morris Brodsky, and Charles Resnick for $250,000. Adler and his associates announced that they would open a gambling casino at the former location of the Club Fortune. Clayton Rambeau was named general manager of the club.

The Cal-Neva opened on November 20, 1948. Sanford Adler had spent over $500,000 to remodel and renovate the former Club Fortune. Licenses were granted for three 21 games, three craps games, two roulette games, one keno game, and 126 slot machines. The club had a decor of copper and redwood and was decorated throughout with pinecones. There were also several wall-panel color photographs of Lake Tahoe scenes (Adler also owned the Cal-Neva Lodge at Lake Tahoe).

The new club featured two floor shows nightly, along with continuous music and dancing. Opening night featured comedians Moore and Lessy, the Leonard Sues Orchestra, comedian "Think-A-Drink" Hoffman, and Johnny White and His Trio.

One of the most famous entertainers to perform at the Cal-Neva was the then little-known pianist Liberace. He made his first appearance at the Cal-Neva from January 13 to January 27, 1949. He was so popular that he was brought back on April 15, 1949, for another two-week appearance.

On February 16, 1949, legal history was made when, for the first time, gaming apparatus (a keno cage, keno balls, etc.) was brought into a courtroom. Leon Pierce was suing the Cal-Neva for nonpayment of a $5,000 keno ticket, and the Cal-Neva brought in the apparatus along with witnesses Edgar Jolley, Rudy Starich, and casino manager Sam Boyd (who later founded the Las Vegas gaming empire known as the Boyd Gaming Corporation, with properties such as Sam's Town, the California Hotel, and others). After two days of hearings, the Cal-Neva was declared the winner of the suit.

On December 3, 1951, the Cal-Neva closed and announced that it would not reopen until May 1952 because the winter months were financially unprofitable. Approximately one hundred people were put out of work. However, on January 3, 1952, the Cal-Neva opened three 21 games and paid the license fees for them, but it did not pay fees on any of the slot machines. On January 29, Sanford Adler announced that the club would open on a full-time basis in mid-February and that it would license fifty slots, one keno game, one craps game, two 21 games, and one roulette game—three fewer table games and sixty-nine fewer slots than when the club closed in December. The Reno City Council was upset with the Cal-Neva for closing, and that was the only reason Adler announced a partial opening when he did. The council

soon passed a law making it illegal for casinos to close during the slow winter months.

In an attempt to appease the City Council, Adler replaced Morris Brodsky on the gaming license, inferring that the closing was Brodsky's decision. Adler felt that if he did not replace Brodsky, the club would not be licensed. Brodsky, who was one of the original owners, had been acting as general manager since January 1951.

In March 1952 the Cal-Neva licensed thirty more slots, and in May it licensed two more 21 games and a roulette game. The operation never closed again during the winter months.

In October 1955 Adler and his partners were ordered to show cause for relicensing. Adler was rumored to have allowed "hidden interests" to buy into the Cal-Neva.

On November 5, 1955, a group headed by James Contratto bought the Cal-Neva building and the adjacent property (but not the business) for $550,000 from Bernard Howard, Caspar Van Cittar, and Saul Freedman.

On November 12, 1955, agents from the Internal Revenue Service closed the Cal-Neva and took $30,000 in cash from the slots, table games, and cashier's cage. The owners of the Cal-Neva—Sanford Adler, Julius Wilks, Charles Resnick, and Louis Mayberg—were several months behind in their tax payments. Two hundred and thirty employees were put out of work because of the closure. The next day, the IRS revealed that it had actually confiscated more than $50,000 in cash. The Adler corporation surrendered its lease to the group headed by James Contratto, who purchased the lease for $546,000.

On November 15, 1955, Adler and Contratto were subpoenaed to appear before the Gaming Control Board. Adler failed to appear and was never again licensed in Nevada.

On November 26, 1955, the state licensed the following men as owners of the Cal-Neva: Dr. Robert Franks, 22 percent for $61,600; Al Rogell, 18 percent for $45,000; Sam Levy, 17 percent for $47,000; Caspar Van Cittar, 5 percent for $15,000; Jim Contratto, 12 percent for $35,000; and John

Callas, 16 percent for $50,000. Saul Freedman was to receive 10 percent as a finder's fee after the loans had been paid off. Jim Contratto was also licensed as general manager. The Cal-Neva reopened on December 2, 1955. It was licensed for 150 slots, four 21 games, one craps game, one roulette game, and one keno game.

In January 1956 Leon Nightingale and Frank Harris bought 5 percent of the Cal-Neva for $25,000 each. In May the Cal-Neva added a craps game, a 21 game, and fifteen more slots to its license.

The Cal-Neva started a $50,000 remodeling project in October 1956 that included a new marquee, three sets of double glass doors, and a general face-lift. In January 1957 the casino installed a $15,000 wall-to-wall carpet.

The Cal-Neva closed on September 18, 1961, following a dispute over lease arrangements with the Nev-Cal Corporation, which owned the Cal-Neva building. Cal-Neva president James Contratto closed the club despite the fact that the rent had already been paid until the lease expiration date of March 1, 1962. The closing put two hundred employees out of work. Two days later, the City Council ruled that the closed Cal-Neva would stay closed forever unless Contratto reopened the club by October 1. Contratto did not reopen.

However, on April 1, 1962, the Cal-Neva did reopen after the Sierra Development Corporation, doing business as the Club Cal-Neva, was licensed for six 21 games, two craps games, one roulette game, one keno game, and 175 slot machines. The group had purchased the club and the gaming equipment for over $1 million and spent over $100,000 refurbishing the building. The casino kept the same floor layout as the old Cal-Neva.

Prior to the reopening, the Gaming Commission recommended that the new group buy the building on Second and Center Streets from its owners, Franks, Rogell, and Levy. The Gaming Commission indicated it did not want the former landlords connected in any way with the new operation.

The following are the owners who opened the Cal-Neva on April 1, 1962: Ad

Tolen (a former roulette dealer at the Club Fortune and a former co-owner of the Tahoe Plaza), 5.71 percent; Jack Douglass (a former co-owner of the Riverside Hotel and other casinos and a slot-route operator for over twenty-five years), 20 percent; John Cavanaugh (a native of Tonopah, making his first investment in a Reno gambling club), 20 percent; Leon Nightingale (an associate of Jim Contratto in the Cal-Neva from 1955 to 1958 and a co-owner of the Tahoe Plaza), 25.71 percent; and Howard Farris and Warren Nelson (both of whom formerly held interests in the Tahoe Plaza and in the Waldorf Club), 14.29 percent each. On June 19, 1962, Doug Busey, a local attorney, was licensed for 2.7 percent of the Club Cal-Neva.

On March 21, 1969, the state allowed the operators of Reno's Cal-Neva to purchase the Cal-Neva Lodge at Lake Tahoe. The purchase price was $1.4 million. In June 1969 it was announced that the Denny's restaurant chain had purchased both Cal-Neva clubs; however, between then and March 1970 Denny's gaming application was delayed, deferred, and finally withdrawn. Eventually, in August 1970, the Cal-Neva group sold the Cal-Neva Lodge at Lake Tahoe to a group of investors from Ohio.

The Cal-Neva in downtown Reno began expanding in August 1969 with a multimillion-dollar construction project, adding a larger restaurant, a bar, an enlarged casino, and a snack bar. It also installed an air curtain, which enabled the club to function without doors and allowed easier access to the property. Air curtains are now commonplace in Nevada casinos. The expansion was completed in October 1969. One hundred more employees were added to the payroll, giving the Cal-Neva a staff of over four hundred.

In February 1972 the Cal-Neva purchased a 3,200-square-foot space on Center Street, just south of the casino, formerly occupied by the Western Union office. The 23-by-138-foot building was used in a three-level expansion that opened in June 1972. The Cal-Neva added 8,000 square feet to the gaming area and to the Copper Ledge Restaurant.

In October 1973 one of the original owners, John Cavanaugh Sr., was killed in an automobile accident on the Mount Rose Highway. As a result of Cavanaugh's death, his daughter, Barbara Cavanaugh Thornton, and his widow, Margery, were licensed at the Cal-Neva.

In the following years, many members of the original owners' families were licensed, including Greg and Gail Nelson, Gene Tolen, Bill Thornton, Steve Nightingale, and others.

The Cal-Neva's ongoing expansion program continued in July 1979, when it purchased the Waldorf Restaurant and adjoining businesses. On July 31, 1980, the Cal-Neva unveiled its $10-million expansion at the corner of Second and Virginia Streets, which offered cabaret entertainment, a sports and race book, and a cabaret restaurant. The main floor was devoted to gambling but also included the "longest bar in Reno." The mezzanine level housed the Hof Brau restaurant and additional gambling. The third level, or top deck, featured a 220-seat cabaret (which was soon discontinued) and a sports and race book. The casino had thirty-four table games and more than six hundred slots. An additional six hundred new employees were added, bringing the Cal-Neva's total work force to more than fourteen hundred people. The opening ceremony was attended by approximately six thousand people. Governor Bob List and casino president Leon Nightingale officiated at the ribbon-cutting ceremony.

Also completed in 1996 on Center Street, between First and Second Streets, was a parking garage, known as the "parking stadium," with 743 spaces. A skywalk over Center Street connects the garage to the casino. The skywalk has 150 slots, a small pit, a keno game, and a snack bar.

Currently the Club Cal-Neva has more than 1,300 slot machines, over sixty table games, more than fourteen hundred employees, eight bars, six dining facilities, two keno games, and covers 29,001 square feet. Through their Sierra Development Company, the casino's owners hold almost an entire city block. The Cal-Neva has the enviable reputation of being the most pop-

ular downtown local casino and remains the largest northern Nevada casino without hotel rooms. *(See Addendum 3)*

Nev. St. Journal, 11 Sept. 48, 17 Nov. 48, 20 Nov. 48 (adv.), 13 Jan. 49 (adv.), 27 Jan. 49, 15 Apr. 49, 16 Feb. 50, 18 Feb. 50, 10 Jan. 51, 2 Dec. 51, 3 Jan. 52, 29 Jan. 52, 1 Mar. 52, 21 May 52, 18 June 53, 8 Feb. 55, 26 Oct. 55, 5 Nov. 55, 12 Nov. 55, 13 Nov. 55, 15 Nov. 55, 16 Nov. 55, 26 Nov. 55, 1 Dec. 55 (article and adv.), 26 Jan. 56, 16 May 56, 16 Oct. 56 (photo), 15 Jan. 57 (photo), 2 Aug. 57, 8 Sept. 60, 19 Sept. 61, 20 Sept. 61, 12 Dec. 61, 1 Feb. 62, 20 Mar. 62, 21 Mar. 62, 29 Mar. 62 (photos), 21 Sept. 68, 21 Mar. 69, 21 June 69, 24 June 69 (photos), 25 June 69, 31 Aug. 69 (photo), 31 Aug. 69, 17 Oct. 69, 13 Nov. 69, 11 Dec. 69, 17 Dec. 69, 12 Mar. 70, 20 Mar. 70, 13 Aug. 70, 5 Feb. 72, 4 June 72 (photo), 7 Oct. 73, 14 Dec. 73, 20 Dec. 74, 12 Jan. 75, 28 Mar. 75, 6 July 75 (photo), 12 May 77, 20 July 79, 14 Feb. 80, 31 July 80 (adv., article, and photo), 1 Aug. 80; Warren Nelson, *Always Bet on the Butcher: Warren Nelson and Casino Gaming, 1930s–1980s* (Reno: University of Nevada Oral History Program, 1994).

CLUB FORTUNE

38–40 East Second Street; licensed from May 28, 1937, to January 20, 1947, for tango (bingo), slots, roulette, 21, and craps.

The Club Fortune was one of the finest gambling clubs in downtown Reno. It featured superb dining, entertainment, a cocktail lounge, casino diversions, and a tango (bingo) salon. Its dining room was recommended by Duncan Hines, who in the 1930s and early 1940s was considered one of the foremost gourmets in the United States. To be recommended by Duncan Hines during those years was the ultimate compliment that a restaurant could receive.

The story of the Club Fortune began in October 1936 when James McKay and J. B. Scarlett (also known as Jack Sullivan) purchased the two-story Fordonia Building at the corner of Second and Center Streets for $85,000. The building had housed the Palace Dry Goods Store for many years and just prior to the sale had housed the National Dollar Store. The second floor contained offices.

In February 1937 Robert Feder of Los Angeles announced the completion of arrangements for the opening of what became (up to that time) one of Reno's larg-

The Club Fortune, located on East Second Street, ca. 1938. Courtesy of Neal Cobb and the Nevada Historical Society.

est clubs. Feder had taken a five-year lease on the Fordonia Building from McKay and Scarlett. The Club Fortune would feature tango, although other games would also be available.

After two months of construction, the palatial gaming and dining establishment opened on May 28, 1937. More than two hundred men had been employed in the construction and remodeling of the club, and over $175,000 were spent on construction, furnishings, and equipment. Two large, high-ceilinged rooms were built on the ground floor of the Fordonia Building to house various features of the Club Fortune. The room on the east side of the building was the tango salon, modern in all respects, with many innovations in electrically controlled equipment. The room on the west side held a continental lounge, an elaborate bar, and gaming tables. A cocktail lounge and the club's offices were located on the mezzanine floor.

The center of attraction in the tango parlor was a movable cart into which patrons threw baseballs while playing the popular game. The compartments into which the balls fell were wired to a large board that registered the number hit by each throw of the baseball. An operator sat in a control booth at one end of the room and called out the numbers and at the same time switched on lights in the register board at the other end of the room. The patrons throwing baseballs into the compartments added excitement to the game because customers felt that their skill in throwing the ball could influence the outcome of the game and help them win.

Most tango games in the early 1930s used common beans to mark the winning numbers. However, the Club Fortune ordered several thousand small composition markers to be used instead of beans or kernels of corn.

Decorations throughout the club were elaborate. The windows in the partition between the two main rooms featured handsome sandblasted silhouettes. The continental lounge, filling most of the west room, had a stylish moderne decor. In the dining area, patrons were seated at horseshoe-shaped tables and served by waiters working from a small counter (the kitchen was in the basement). Gaming tables were placed near the center partitions and were lighted by specially designed fixtures. The main bar in the club was constructed in the shape of a T, and several sets of neon tubing built into its edges furnished a novel lighting effect.

When the club opened, it employed approximately eighty people, and the payroll was around $15,000 a month.

Acting as official greeter on opening night was the club manager, Robert Feder. He estimated that at least five thousand people entered the premises that night. Formal dress predominated among the groups of first-nighters who dined in the continental lounge and on the mezzanine floor. Diners were entertained by Joey Lee, "the G-Man of the G-String and his Music." The most colorful scene was in the big tango room, where pretty girls attired in bright western outfits assisted the game operators.

The newspapers reported that even Reno's most avid homebodies were drawn out to join the thousands of habitual gamblers attracted from their usual haunts by the opening. Sidewalks outside the club were crowded for hours with curious onlookers who peered through the big windows when the endless stream of visitors created such congestion that no one else could enter.

In October 1937 Joe Zemansky replaced Robert Feder as owner of the property, and in July 1938 Sam Erlich was named manager of the operation.

In August 1939 the Rainbow Bingo Salon (also known as the Rainbow Club) opened its own bingo game, which resulted in a "bingo war" between the three top bingo clubs in town—the Club Fortune, the Rainbow Club, and Bill Harrah's Heart Tango Club. The three clubs kept raising the value of their prizes and lowering the price of their cards until all three were in danger of going out of business. At one point, the Club Fortune gave away $150 at its 11 P.M. nightly cash drawing—besides its regular game prizes. Harrah's and the Rainbow Club were giving away $100 at their nightly cash drawings. Eventually, the Rainbow Club backed out of the bingo war, and the games returned to normal.

In March 1940 the Club Fortune redecorated its dining room, added potted palm trees, called it the Palm Room, and hired the famous chef, Jean Sigg. The Palm Room became the most popular downtown eating place for the next several years. Jean Sigg left the Palm Room in 1942 to work for the Riverside Hotel and was replaced by Andre Simetys.

In 1944 Louis Rosasco, one of Reno's favorite musicians, hosts, and food and beverage managers, took over as managing director of the Club Fortune. He replaced Sam Erlich, who had left the club to enter the military service.

On July 27, 1944, Sammy Davis Jr. made his first appearance in Reno when he performed at the Club Fortune with the Will Mastin Trio.

Sam Erlich returned from the military service in April 1945 and reclaimed his job as manager. He retained that position until October 1946, when he left to open his own business, the Bar of Music. Matt Howard replaced him as manager.

In January 1945 the Club Fortune was licensed for fifteen slot machines, one craps game, and one roulette game.

On January 18, 1947, Joe Zemansky, sole owner of the club, announced that his lease had expired and that the club and all the facilities would close on January 20, except the bingo game, which would close one week later.

The Club Fortune during its almost ten-year existence employed several people who were well known in the gaming, entertainment, food, and beverage world of Reno in the 1930s and through the 1960s.

Men such as Ad Tolen, Brad Hewins, Matt Dromiack, Sam Erlich, Louis Rosasco, Jean Sigg, Andre Simetys, Ed Orrick, and Isadore Kreisler all worked there at one time or another.

During its tenure, the Club Fortune presented over three thousand acts and entertainers. Among the stars who appeared there were Liberace, Blossom Seely, the Will Mastin Trio with Sammy Davis Jr., and Joaquin Garay.

Joe Zemansky and his wife, Sadie, who took an active role in the operation, were well liked in Reno and active in civic affairs.

The Fordonia Building, in which the club was housed, was sold by James McKay and Jack Scarlett (Sullivan) for $250,000 in June 1948 to Sanford Adler and his associates. In November 1948 the Adler group opened the Club Cal-Neva at this location, and it has operated as such ever since.

Nev. St. Journal, 22 Oct. 36, 4 Feb. 37, 26 May 37 (adv.), 27 May 37, 28 May 37, 29 May 37, 30 Oct. 37 (adv.), 22 July 38, 26 Aug. 39, 8 Mar. 40, 16 Mar. 40, 29 May 41 (adv.), 29 Mar. 42, 28 May 42 (adv.), 28 May 44 (adv.), 27 July 44 (adv.), 23 Jan. 45, 24 Jan. 45 (photo), 14 June 45 (adv.), 8 Oct. 46, 14 Jan. 47, 17 Jan. 47, 18 Jan. 47 (adv. and photo), 7 July 71; Robert A. Ring, *Recollections of Life in California, Nevada Gaming and Lake Tahoe Civic Affairs* (Reno: University of Nevada Oral History Program, 1982).

CLUB OF ALL NATIONS
227 Lake Street; licensed from May 9 to July 1942 for craps and 21.

The Club of All Nations was licensed for one craps game and one 21 game in May 1942. The games were removed two months later.

The site of the Club of All Nations is now part of Harrah's Club.

Nev. St. Journal, 5 May 42.

COHEN, FRANK

Frank Cohen was one of thirteen persons licensed at the Palace Club in December 1953. He was licensed for 7 percent of the operation. The group operated the Palace Club until 1964. However, Cohen died early in 1957, and his widow, Clara, was the licensee until the group's lease expired.

Nev. St. Journal, 11 Dec. 57.

COLBRANDT'S FLAMINGO CLUB
Opened at 123 North Virginia Street (address changed to 147 North Virginia Street in 1937); licensed from 1937 to 1946 for 21, roulette, and slots; from 1954 to 1956 for 21, craps, roulette, and slots.

This casino was originally opened by Mae Colbrandt in the early 1930s as a cigar store. In 1937 Virgil Smith leased the gaming concession. Smith was well known for leasing gaming tables, especially roulette tables, at various locations in the Reno area. He leased the gaming at Colbrandt's until 1940, when he and Ralph Austin purchased the club from Mae Colbrandt. Investing along with Smith and Austin was their longtime associate Bill Williams.

The Flamingo was noted for its beautiful carpeting, plush atmosphere, and nude paintings on the walls.

Virgil Smith put a $20 "straight up" limit on the roulette table for any player and a $100 "straight up" limit for "high rollers" like Lavere Redfield, who was acknowledged to be one of the heaviest roulette players in Reno history. The high limits on

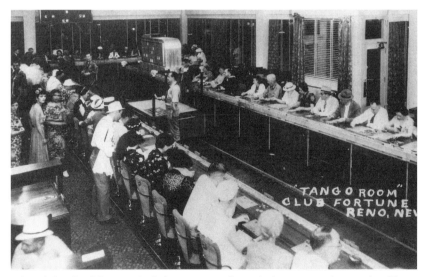

A busy shift at the Club Fortune in the late 1930s. Note the cart in the passageway between the tables. It has eighty compartments into which players threw baseballs to determine the winning numbers in the tango (bingo) game. Author's collection.

roulette proved to be an attraction, and all the facilities in the club benefited.

In October 1946 Smith and Austin sold the Flamingo to Floyd Anderson, who was licensed for one 21 game, one craps game, and one roulette game. In 1947 Anderson removed the gambling and operated the Flamingo as a bar only until 1954. In April 1954 A. G. Scott and William Burton were licensed as gaming partners with Anderson for three months. In July, Scott and Burton were removed from the li-

cense, and Anderson remained as the sole owner.

During the next few years, more gaming devices were added. By 1955 the Flamingo had fourteen slots, two 21 games, and a craps game.

In 1957 the Flamingo closed, and shortly thereafter the property was sold to Brick Jacobs, who operated a clothing store at this location for several years. From 1978 to 1989 the site was occupied by a store known as Leather and Lace. Currently

the site is the location of a Burger King Restaurant.

Nev. St. Journal, 7 June 44.

COLOMBO HOTEL/ COLOMBO CAFÉ

244 Lake Street/246 Lake Street; licensed from June 6, 1931, to July 1, 1943, as the Colombo Hotel, and as the Colombo Café from July 1943 to 1949 for slots, 21, craps, and roulette.

The Colombo location was more a nightclub, a supper club, and a cabaret than a gambling casino. Opened in the late 1920s, it was always well known for its good food and entertainment. There were usually a table game or two on the property and always a few slot machines.

First licensed in 1931 by Michael Di-Gioia, the Colombo was later owned by Phil Curti and Ed Vogliotti. One of the early managers was Aldo Dinelli, known more commonly by his nickname, "Maryootch." Pick Hobson, who later owned several major gaming properties in the Reno area, was licensed for gaming at the Colombo in the early 1930s.

In 1938 Curti and Vogliotti sold the property to Larry Siri, who reappointed Maryootch as manager. In March 1940 Curti and Vogliotti took over the Colombo once again and retained it until January 1944, when they sold it to Mike and Mario Gallo of Hawthorne. The property changed owners again in August 1944, when Joe Anselmo and Bob Schenone took over. Schenone was licensed for one 21 game, one roulette game, and one craps game. In November 1945 the Colombo was purchased by Art Conte and Ralph Festina. Conte was licensed from 1945 through 1947 for one 21 game and one craps game.

Appearing as master of ceremonies at the Colombo was well-known local singer Larry Semenza, who, when he retired from the entertainment business, was employed for many years as a pit floor manager at Harolds Club.

The Colombo Café and Hotel location was licensed as Ming's Café in 1954. The property was razed in the early 1960s, and the site is now a parking lot.

Nev. St. Journal, 13 Apr. 34, 29 May 35, 20 May 37,

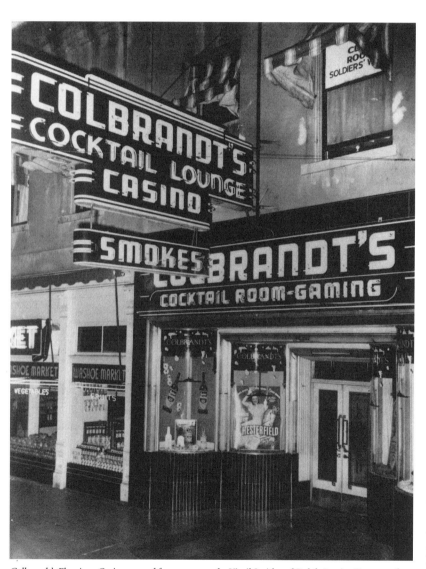

Colbrandt's Flamingo Casino, owned for many years by Virgil Smith and Ralph Austin. Courtesy of Mrs. Virgil (Nelva) Smith.

Co-owners of Colbrandt's Flamingo, Ralph Austin (standing, l.) and Virgil Smith (behind Austin), pictured near the roulette table. Note the exotic pictures on the wall of the dining area. Courtesy of Mrs. Virgil (Nelva) Smith.

1 June 37 (adv.), 1 Apr. 38, 20 Apr. 38 (adv.), 26 May 39, 14 Mar. 40, 27 Jan. 44, 16 and 17 Aug. 44 (adv.), 25 Nov. 45 (adv.), 27 Nov. 45, 19 Apr. 57, 23 July 57.

COLONIAL MOTOR INN

250 North Arlington; licensed since March 1978 for slots and/or 21 only.

In August 1966 the Colonial Motor Inn opened as a four-story, forty-five-unit structure. In November 1976 the owners announced that the Colonial would expand to a nine-story motor inn.

In May 1977 work began on the nine-story hotel-casino. The plans called for 168 rooms, a small casino, and a lounge. The principals, all local businessmen, were Charles Gadda, John and F. R. Hallahan, and Terrence McMullen. The project, which was completed in early 1978, was licensed for eighty slot machines in March 1978. In December 1978 a 21 game was added to the license, and in May 1979 another 21 game was added to the license.

The Colonial, which features an excellent restaurant specializing in prime rib, has never been a true hotel-casino. It has always been thought of more as a fine motor inn.

In 1998 it was licensed for slot machines only, and there are no table games currently operating on the property.

Nev. St. Journal, 7 Aug. 66 (photo), 11 Nov. 76, 4 May 77, 16 Mar. 78, 16 Dec. 78, 11 May 79.

COLONY CLUB

254 North Virginia Street from 1946 to 1964; 280 North Center Street from 1967 to 1971; licensed from 1946 to 1964 as a full casino; licensed from 1967 to 1971 for 21 and slots.

The Colony Club, formerly the California Club, was opened in 1946. Its first owners were James Powers, Jack Richards, and Bob Taffee. They participated in what was a common practice at the time—leasing areas of the club to various individuals, known as "leasing out the gambling concession." Vern Bell was licensed for five slot machines and two poker games in 1950, and later in the year Virgil Smith was licensed for the remainder of the slots in the club.

In early 1954 the Colony was closed for remodeling. It reopened in May. James Contratto had purchased 17 percent of the club for $100,000 on May 7. The other owners were James Powers and Jack Richards.

(In August 1955 Contratto sold his 17-percent interest for $150,000 and became a partner in the Cal-Neva.)

In July 1954 a keno game was added, and Joe Munley was named keno manager. A faro game was also added to the license. Faro, once one of the most popular games in Reno, was at that time licensed at only one other property in town, the Golden Hotel.

In July 1955 Lester Larson was licensed by the state for 50 percent of the keno game, and in October the Colony raised its keno limit from $10,000 to $25,000.

In 1956 some major changes were made in the ownership of the Colony Club. Jack Richards, Joe Padilla, Jack Austin, Morris Orloff, and Henry Hornstein applied for licensing. Richards, Padilla, Austin, and Hornstein were approved, but Orloff was denied. Jack Richards remained an owner until October 1964, when he sold his percentage of the Colony Club and bought a percentage of the Riverside Hotel.

The Colony operated until December 1964, when Harolds Club exercised its option to purchase the property. The Colony closed on December 7, and approximately forty employees were put out of work. The price of the 125-by-25-foot, two-story building was not disclosed, although it was rumored to be "in the neighborhood of one million dollars." Owners at the time of the sale were Henry Hornstein, Jack Austin, and Joe Padilla.

In January 1967 Henry and George Hornstein, Padilla, and Austin were licensed to open the new Colony Club at 280 North Center Street. The state licensed them for seven table games and one hundred slot machines; however, the licensing was subject to Reno's red-line gambling law (the "red line" limited casinos outside the central downtown area to only three 21 games and twenty slot machines). In June the Colony Club's owners decided they did not want to be hindered by the red-line law, and they withdrew their application. It wasn't until March 1969 that the Colony reopened with only a bar, a few slot machines, and a single 21 game.

In 1971 the Hornsteins and Austin changed the name of the Colony Club to

The Colombo Hotel on Lake Street in 1945. It was famous in the 1930s and 1940s for fine food and entertainment. Courtesy of Neal Cobb and the Nevada Historical Society.

67, 20 Jan. 67, 9 June 67, 29 Mar. 69, 18 July 71, 8 Aug. 73, 24 Aug. 73, 18 Oct. 74.

COLONY TURF CLUB
See Colony Club.

COMMERCIAL BAR
6 East Commercial Row; licensed in June 1944 for six months for 21 and craps only.

Located at an address that housed several bars, cardrooms, and small casinos in the 1930s and 1940s, this business had a short life during World War II.

The former location of the Commercial Bar is now part of the Harolds Club property.

COMMERCIAL HOTEL
207–209 North Center Street; licensed in 1933 for 21, craps, roulette, big-six, and faro.

The Commercial Hotel housed the Northern Club. The gambling operation was in the Northern Club, but both the gambling and the hotel were owned by Domingo "Felix" Turillas Sr.

Turillas licensed gaming in the hotel portion of the building in 1933 only. The Commercial Hotel was licensed for one roulette game, one craps game, one 21 game, and one faro game.

The former location of the Commercial Hotel is now part of Harrah's on the west side of Center Street.

Nev. St. Journal, 8 Apr. 33; listed in City Directory from 1933 to 1944.

COMSTOCK CLUB
226½ North Center Street; licensed from January 1, 1932, to 1935 for craps, 21, and roulette.

The Comstock was another of the downtown cabaret casinos that relied on entertainment as a draw to bring customers to the gaming tables. Local favorites such as Pat O'Brien and Matt Dromiack worked there at one time or another as owners, hosts, and general managers. In the 1930s and 1940s there were several local "personalities" who moved around from club to club, hoping to draw their following to the particular club where they were working at the time. Gaming was almost incidental, because managers knew that if customers came in to eat,

the Colony Turf Club. It operated as a race and sports book from that time until it closed in 1976. Two years before the closing of the Colony Turf Club, Jack Austin bought out the Hornstein brothers and became the sole owner.

The site of the original Colony Club at 254 North Virginia Street is now part of Harolds Club. The site of the second Colony Club/Colony Turf Club is now occupied by the Reno Turf Club.

Raymond Sawyer, *Reno: Where the Gamblers Go!* (Reno: Sawston Publishing Company, 1976); *Nev. St. Journal,* 27 Aug. 47, 5 Feb. 49, 1 Apr. 50, 12 Apr. 50, 7 May 54, 27 May 54 (adv.), 28 May 54 (adv.), 14 July 54, 28 July 54, 5 Dec. 54, 28 July 55, 29 Oct. 55, 20 Apr. 56, 20 June 56, 16 May 57, 28 May 57, 9 Dec. 64 (photo), 8 Jan. 65, 6 Jan.

drink, dance, or watch the entertainment, some of them would gamble.

The Comstock Club had a theme—silver mining in Virginia City. The entrance was made to resemble a mine tunnel, and the interior resembled a station in a Virginia City mine.

Bob Grignon and Bruce Sheehey owned the Comstock when it was sold to Vic Williams in May 1936. Williams remodeled and renamed the club the Inferno.

The site of the Comstock Club is now part of Harrah's on the east side of Center Street between Second Street and Commercial Row.

Nev. St. Journal, 7 Apr. 33, 11 Aug. 33 (adv.), 21 June 34, 20 Oct. 34 (adv.), 20 Mar. 35, 25 May 35 (adv.), 25 May 35, 30 May 36.

COMSTOCK HOTEL-CASINO

200 West Second Street; licensed since May 1978 as a full casino.

Construction of the Comstock Hotel began on May 16, 1977, during a boom period in Reno hotel construction—five other hotels were under construction at the same time,

resulting in a total of 2,074 new rooms. Forty-seven percent of the stock in the hotel was owned by the Fiesta Corporation, which was composed of the (then) owners of the Cal-Neva—Jack Douglass, Cal Kinney Jr., Leon Nightingale, John Douglass, Warren Nelson, William Thornton, Howard Farris, Ad Tolen, Greg Nelson, and Steven Nightingale. Another 47 percent of the stock was owned by the Comstock Land and Development Company, and the remainder was owned by several limited partners.

The Comstock opened in May 1978 with 160 hotel rooms, 325 slot machines, twenty table games, one keno game, one restaurant, and included 3,000 square feet of convention space. The hotel featured a decor reminiscent of Virginia City in the 1860s. The casino area was surrounded by false storefronts and a boardwalk typical of the silver-boom days on the Comstock, and the hotel rooms were decorated with authentic antiques, lace curtains, and enlarged photographs of historic early-Nevada scenes. Many of the employees were dressed in period costumes.

John Douglass was the first casino manager of the Comstock, and Chuck Tinder was the first operations manager.

In 1980 a second restaurant was added, and in 1983 the casino area was increased to 4,000 square feet. In 1984 the Comstock underwent a major expansion. An additional seven stories created a sixteen-story tower with 310 guest rooms, and the expanded casino area held a total of 750 slot machines, twenty table games, and two keno games.

In December 1986 an agreement was worked out between the owners of the Club Cal-Neva and the Jack Douglass family, whereby the Douglass family sold out of the Cal-Neva and the Cal-Neva owners sold out of the Fiesta Corporation. This gave the Douglass family controlling interest in the Fiesta Corporation and eventually controlling interest in the Comstock Land and Development Company, making them the major players in the Comstock Hotel-Casino.

In 1996 the Comstock Hotel-Casino added an exciting new display of lights to the exterior of its building. Even though it is out the downtown area, the Comstock is popular with locals and tourists alike. In May 1999 there was an announcement that the Comstock Hotel-Casino had been sold to the Hertz Corporation of Los Angeles for $5 million. The Douglass family took over the management of the 310-room hotel and leased the casino operation.

Nev. St. Journal, 18 May 77, 1 Feb. 78, 26 May 78, 27 May 78, 28 May 78, 9 May 91 (Fun and Gaming section); *Reno Gazette-Journal,* 7 May 99.

CONNELLY, HUGH

Hugh Connelly was born in Anaconda, Montana, in 1917. He was employed by Harrah's in 1946, and when the Cal-Neva opened in 1962, he went to work there as one of the original shift managers. He was serving as graveyard-shift manager at the Club Cal-Neva at the time of his death in December 1977.

Nev. St. Journal, 26 Dec. 77 (obit.).

CONTRATTO, JAMES "JIMMIE"

Jimmie Contratto operated illegal race books and cardrooms in Gardena, Califor-

A faro game being played in an unidentified casino in the 1940s. Courtesy of Neal Cobb and the Nevada Historical Society.

nia, in the 1930s and early 1940s, before coming to Reno in 1943.

In June 1943 Contratto, along with Ernie Primm, Joe Hall, Archie Sneed, and Baldy West, formed a partnership to operate the Palace Club. The following October, Contratto divested himself of his interest in the Palace Club. In 1944 he opened the Nevada Turf Club at 116 East Douglas Alley. It was a horse book only, with no other gambling on the premises.

In 1945 he left the Nevada Turf Club and moved to Las Vegas, where he worked at the El Rancho Hotel-Casino and the Flamingo Hotel-Casino. He returned to Reno in 1953, and in May 1954 he purchased 17 percent of the Colony Club for $100,000. His partners were James Powers and Jack Richards.

A little over a year later, in August 1955, Contratto sold his interest in the Colony Club for $150,000. He had been contacted by Dr. Robert Franks of Los Angeles, for his advice on buying the Club Cal-Neva from the Sanford Adler group. Contratto recommended the purchase, and in November 1955 a six-man group headed by Contratto and Franks was licensed for four 21 games, one craps game, one roulette game, one keno game, and 150 slot machines.

Contratto, who was also licensed as general manager of the Cal-Neva, purchased 12 percent of the stock for $35,000. His salary was $40 a day. Contratto was on the premises all day long, because he liked to control all facets of the business and was very much a "hands-on" manager. He was always well groomed and manicured, and he loved to smoke cigars. When he wasn't at the Cal-Neva, he could often be found shooting craps at one of the neighboring casinos.

After operating the Cal-Neva for almost six years, Contratto got into a dispute with the Nev-Cal Corporation, which owned the Cal-Neva building. Contratto closed the casino on September 18, 1961, putting two hundred employees out of work. The Cal-Neva was reopened in April 1962 by a six-man group headed by Leon Nightingale, but Contratto never returned to the casino business in Reno. He died of a heart attack shortly after he closed the Cal-Neva.

Mead Dixon, *Dealing the Cards That Are Dealt* (Reno: University of Nevada Oral History Program, 1992), 94–100; *Nev. St. Journal*, 22 Nov. 44 (adv.), 31 Oct. 51, 7 May 54, 28 May 54, 15 Nov. 55, 26 Nov. 55.

COPPER CLUB

1303 East Fourth Street; licensed in 1964 for slots and 21.

The Copper Club, formerly the Tux Club, operated as a bar with one 21 game and ten slot machines. Al Gaspar was the licensee. Through the years, several businesses operated at this location. They were all small bar and/or restaurant operations, and many of them had a 21 table and a few slots. However, none of them could be considered a casino.

A bar called Dilligas is currently operating at this location.

Nev. St. Journal, 28 June 64.

COPPERSMITH, GEORGE "SHORTY"

George Coppersmith was one of four partners in the Tavern, a nightclub and casino on West Highway 40 that operated from 1932 to 1935. He was also a co-owner, along with Jack Clark, in the Capitol Bar on East Second Street from 1935 to 1938.

In 1939 Coppersmith and George "Shorty" King were operating the games at the Dog House when the district attorney revoked their gaming license. They were accused of and pleaded guilty to operating a crooked roulette wheel. King was sentenced to six months in jail and a $1,000 fine. Coppersmith was fined $1,000 but was not sentenced to jail. The incident ended both men's gaming careers in Nevada.

Nev. St. Journal, 1 Apr. 38, 23 Aug. 39, 3 Apr. 40.

CORAL REEF

147 North Virginia Street; licensed in 1957 for slots.

On June 28, 1957, the Reno City Council granted a bar license and a gaming license for sixteen slots to John Ross (this was not the same John Ross who operated the Christmas Tree, Johnny's Open Door, and the 116 Club). The Coral Reef opened on July 1, 1957.

The Coral Reef was formerly known as Colbrandt's Flamingo and is not to be confused with the Coral Reef bar and cocktail lounge located in the Carlton Hotel on Sierra Street.

The former location of the Coral Reef is now a Burger King Restaurant.

Nev. St. Journal, 28 June 57.

CORN, J. G. "JAY"

Jay Corn was a true journeyman casino worker. He worked in just about every major casino during his career, which lasted from the mid-1940s to the early 1980s. He was a shift manager at the Mapes, the Riverside, Harolds Club, and the Holiday Hotel, among others, and casino manager at both the Holiday Hotel and the Mapes Hotel.

Nev. St. Journal, 28 July 74 (photo), 13 Apr. 78.

CORNER BAR

150 East Commercial Row (southwest corner of Commercial Row and Lake Street); licensed from 1937 to 1945 for slots only.

The Corner Bar was later known as Bill's Corner Bar. The site is now part of the Harrah's Club parking garage.

COSMO CLUB

140 East Commercial Row; licensed from September 1956 to 1974 for slots, 21, craps, and keno.

In September 1956 the city licensed Charles Chew for 10 percent and Phillip Fong for 90 percent of the Cosmo Club. They opened the club with one craps game, one keno game, and one 21 game.

In September 1958 the state licensed the father-son team of Eugene and Jay Hughes for 35 percent of the Cosmo. They invested $50,000 in the operation—$40,000 of it in remodeling. The Hugheses were in partnership with Charles Chew. Phillip Fong was bought out of the operation. In June 1959 the Hugheses sold their 35 percent of the business to James Eng.

Virgil Smith (l.) with his favorite pit boss, Jay Corn. Courtesy of Mrs. Virgil (Nelva) Smith.

rate ship. The cocktail room is an individual masterpiece with a circular bar and comfortable lounges. Off that room is the Bridge Room where the gaming tables are located. The circular porch provides a view of the entire countryside and at night huge floodlights play brilliant rays across the country club acres.

The opening was a great success, as the *Nevada State Journal* reported the next day:

> Hundreds attended the grand opening of the new Country Club. Guests from all over the state were present at the opening last night. The splendor around them held them partially spellbound. The exclusive Country Club floor show displayed talent seldom seen in Reno and the participants received thunderous applause.
>
> Architect Frederick Quandt has designed a resort that is far and above anything ever seen in Reno. The casino and bar room is built of walnut paneling throughout. At the far end of the room is an alcove featured by a throne and a grand piano. This is the throne room of the kings of song. Entertainers are grouped in the alcove during the evening. Around the alcove are seats, some high, others low, on which guests may rest while they listen. Richly draped in red silk velour, the throne has a canopy overhead draped in golden silks with a crown at the top.
>
> At the right of the room is the bar, built of prima vera antique wood. The back bar is made of birch, with a prima vera top, while above frosted glass—of an intricate pattern—extends to the ceiling. Opposite the bar are the "tables of fortune" [the gaming tables], in back of which John McQuarrie, foremost artist, has painted a picture of the ship "Fortune" coming into its home port.
>
> Several doors lead from the casino. One of them [goes] to the richly appointed women's powder room, one to the dining room and ball room[,] and others lead to the cocktail lounge . . . [or] outside to a large glassed in porch. There is also a second floor which has

When Charles Chew died in 1961, the state licensed his widow, Lai King Chew, for 50 percent of the operation.

In 1970 Pick Hobson purchased the Cosmo Club and was licensed for slots, 21, craps, and keno. The Cosmo closed in December 1974 to make room for future expansion of Hobson's Overland Hotel. The Overland never expanded but instead was sold to Harrah's Club in 1977 and was demolished soon after to make room for a parking garage.

The site of the Cosmo Club is now part of Harrah's parking garage.

Nev. St. Journal, 27 July 56, 24 Aug. 56, 27 Sept. 56, 28 June 57, 23 Sept. 58, 25 Sept. 58, 25 June 59, 8 June 61, 11 June 62, 24 July 70, 31 Dec. 74.

COUNTRY CLUB

On Plumas Avenue, adjoining the Washoe County Golf Course, two to three hundred yards north of Moana Lane; licensed from 1935 to 1936 for slots, roulette, craps, and 21.

The Country Club, although short-lived, was one of the most dazzling, exciting, and glamorous clubs ever opened in Reno.

In 1935 Charles Rennie, president of the corporation building the Country Club, announced that over $100,000 had already been spent on the club. The corporation was financed by Lewis Luckenback, a wealthy New York and San Francisco steamship-line executive. The club was built as a pleasure resort, with polo grounds, tennis courts, and other sporting areas. The total cost was expected to be near $175,000 by the time the club opened. Rennie also announced that longtime Reno gambler Baldy West would be in charge of the gaming.

On June 26, 1935, the *Nevada State Journal* reported that:

> Reno's $250,000 Country Club will open tonight. . . . The new club is one of the finest in the west and the opening will be spread out over three days to accommodate the hundreds of guests who have already made reservations.
>
> Five main rooms and a circular porch are included in the building with special dining rooms upstairs. The interior is done entirely of wood with heavy velour curtains forming the walls. The orchestra is situated in the dining room, which, without a doubt, is the beauty spot of the club. The main bar room is directly off the entrance hallway and over the bar is a huge mural depicting the landing of a pi-

private dining rooms as well as a polo equipment room and dressing rooms for the entertainers.

On July 31 Charles Rennie handed over the general manager's job to Dan Jensen and returned to the Town House to devote his full time to the management of that property.

And then came the big surprise—on August 18 the Country Club closed. H. A. Stafford, secretary of the corporation, announced on August 24 that the club would reopen in two weeks under new management. He also assured creditors that there was sufficient money to pay all bills. The business reopened in September with a new slogan—Reno's Ace of Clubs—and a new manager, James Merrell.

The club seemed to do well. For the next several months, George Hart, formerly of the Willows and probably the most beloved entertainer in Reno during the 1930s and early 1940s, appeared there nightly. The Country Club featured deluxe dinners for $2, and every Tuesday night its big-band radio broadcast was heard from coast to coast. The crowds were coming, and the gambling was going well. On April 19, 1936, twenty local businesses took out a full-page ad in the *Nevada State Journal* "thanking the management of the Country Club, Reno's Ace of Clubs, for the liquidation of its old indebtedness—in full."

Then, on May 15, 1936, the Country Club was leveled by a fire that started in the kitchen at 3:40 A.M. Within two hours, the club was turned into a twisted mass of wreckage. Fire Chief Lee Hawcroft said, "From all indications it was a set fire." But no evidence of foul play was ever discovered. Manager James Merrell put the loss at $225,000 and said that insurance covered only $100,000. He promised that the club would be rebuilt as soon as possible, but in less than two weeks Merrell was working as manager of the State Line Country Club at Lake Tahoe.

The remains of the Country Club, the twisted metal and the concrete building blocks, remained as they were for almost fifty years. In the late 1980s, the property was taken over by the Hyatt Corporation.

The site is now occupied by the Hyatt Classic Residence retirement complex.

Nev. St. Journal, 22 Feb. 35, 5 May 35, 23 June 35, 26 June 35, 27 June 35 (photo), 31 July 35, 20 Aug. 35, 20 Sept. 35 (adv.), 4 Apr. 36, 19 Apr. 36 (adv.), 16 May 36, 30 May 36.

COX, ELBERT "EBE"

Ebe Cox was born in Corpus Christi, Texas, on August 20, 1919. He was active in real-estate development in the Corpus Christi area for many years before coming to Reno in 1968.

In 1968 Cox purchased one-third of the Holiday Hotel-Casino on Mill Street from John Monfrey. His partners were Tom Moore and Austin Hemphill. Cox was more an investor than an operator, and Charles Kelly acted as his personal representative in the casino.

In May 1970 Cox sold his percentage of the Holiday Hotel-Casino, and in February 1971 he purchased the Bonanza Club in Virginia City from Joe Hobson for $200,000. Cox operated the Bonanza until 1972, when he sold it and purchased 50 percent of the Town Club in a partnership with Cy Lopp. He bought out Lopp's share in 1973 and changed the name of the Town Club to the Old Reno Club. Cox still owns and operates the Old Reno Club, assisted by his son, Paul Cox.

Nev. St. Journal, 2 Apr. 70, 19 Feb. 71, 14 Dec. 72.

CRANE'S, J. B. (ALSO KNOWN AS THE PUBLIC CLUB)

233 Lake Street; licensed in 1933 for craps, poker, and keno.

J. B. Crane was the owner and operator of the Public Club from 1932 to 1933. However, when he relicensed the property in 1933 it was under the name J. B. Crane's.

In 1933 Woo Sing tried to get licensed for a Chinese lottery game and was denied because, according to the gaming law of 1931, Chinese lottery was illegal.

In 1935 J. B. Crane's was once again licensed as the Public Club, and Woo Sing was the licensee.

The former site of J. B. Crane's is now the Santa Fe Restaurant.

CRUMLEY, NEWTON "NEWT"

Newt Crumley was born on February 3, 1911, in Tonopah, Nevada. He came to Reno to attend the University of Nevada and graduated in 1932. (He later served on the university's Board of Regents from 1950 to 1954.)

Crumley and his father owned the Ranch Inn and the Commercial Hotel in Elko from the 1930s until the early 1950s. They are remembered for inaugurating big-name entertainment in northern Nevada. Ted Lewis and Sophie Tucker were two of the major stars who first appeared in Elko in 1941. The Crumleys paid Ted Lewis $12,000 for his eight-day appearance there. Other well-known entertainers who appeared at the Commercial Hotel included Jimmy Dorsey, the Andrews Sisters, and Paul Whiteman. Crumley's contracts with his entertainers included a clause that required them to give a free community performance during each stand.

After meritorious service in the Air Force during World War II, Crumley returned to Elko, where he continued to operate the family hotel business and served as state senator from Elko County. After his father died in 1955, Crumley sold his Elko interests. In 1957 he headed a group of investors who purchased the newly built Holiday Hotel-Casino on Mill Street in Reno from the Norman Biltz group, for over $5 million. The Holiday offered no gambling (other than a few slot machines) at that time, so the first thing Crumley did was open full-scale gaming and make the Holiday "the place to go in Reno."

In February 1962 Newt Crumley, along with his good friend and associate E. J. Questa, president of the First National Bank of Nevada, was killed in a private plane crash near Tonopah.

Nevada Magazine 14, no. 2 (Mar./Apr. 1981): 38; *Nev. St. Journal*, 10 July 57, 14 Feb. 62 (obit.).

CURTI, PHIL

Phil Curti owned and operated several nightclubs and entertainment centers in Reno from the 1920s to the 1960s. He was more often the landlord for gambling facilities than an operator. In most instances, he leased out the gaming areas in the properties he owned—which included the Corner Bar, the Colombo Hotel, the Dog House, the Tropics, the Town and Country Bar, and the Town and Country Bowl.

A sixty-year Reno resident, Curti died on October 18, 1961, at the age of sixty-nine.

Nev. St. Journal, 29 May 35, 27 Jan. 44, 18 Jan. 47, 19 Oct. 61 (obit.).

CURTIS, MARK

Mark Curtis was born in Oklahoma City on September 19, 1921. He served in the Air Force from 1942 to 1945, and upon receiving his discharge he came to Reno to attend the University of Nevada. After Curtis graduated in 1951, he worked as a newspaper columnist and a radio broadcaster, and he ran his own advertising and public relations firm from 1952 to 1957.

In 1957 Curtis was hired by Harrah's Club as director of advertising and press relations. In that position, he was instrumental in publicizing the opening of the South Shore Room at Harrah's Lake Tahoe in December 1959 and Harrah's participation in the 1960 Winter Olympics in Squaw Valley. He left Harrah's in 1962 to become a partner and vice-president of the Tyson, Curtis, Wilson advertising company of Reno and Las Vegas. He returned to Harrah's in 1970 and was named director of press relations. In 1972 he was named director of advertising and public relations, and in 1976 he was named vice-president of public relations and advertising. He remained in that position until retiring in 1986.

Curtis was the driving force in keeping the image of Harrah's—especially its entertainment—in the public eye. He was instrumental in helping Harrah's build its tremendous customer base.

Curtis received many honors and awards during his career, including the R. I. Smith Civic Leader of the Year Award in 1987, and the President's Medal from the University of Nevada in 1994. He was also involved in community affairs, including serving on the board of directors of the Reno Philharmonic Orchestra, co-founding the William F. Harrah Lecture Series, and serving as chairman of the William F. Harrah Foundation of the National Automobile Museum.

Mark Curtis died in Reno on June 24, 1998.

Mark Curtis interview (March 1997); *Reno Gazette-Journal,* 26 June 1998 (obit.).

Mark Curtis (second from r.), pictured with Russ "Candy" Hall (l.), Harrah's entertainment director; Keely Smith, entertainer; and Pat France, general manager, at Harrah's Tahoe, 1958. Courtesy of Mrs. Mark (Ruth) Curtis.

DANDOLOS, NICK
"THE GREEK"

Nick Dandolos, who claimed to have won and lost over $500 million in a half-century career as a high-rolling gambler, died in Los Angeles on December 25, 1966. He claimed to be sixty-four or sixty-five years of age, but hospital records listed him as eighty, and some friends said he was born in 1883, which would have made him eighty-three years old.

Dandolos, a philosophical man known to some as the "Aristotle of the don't-pass line," was probably the highest-rolling professional gambler in American history. He was suave and soft-spoken, and in the gaming world he will always be remembered for playing the back line (don't pass) on the dice table. However, his favorite game was faro, and he would travel hundreds of miles to find an honest faro game.

Dandolos was a regular visitor to Reno in the late 1940s and 1950s, playing faro and the back line at Harrah's, the Bank Club, and Harolds Club. Harold Smith Sr. recalled, "I saw Carl Laemmle, the famous movie producer, stake Nick the Greek to three months of faro play in Reno and they lost it all."

By his own estimate, Dandolos went from rags to riches seventy-three times in his life. Often he played for days without sleep. It is said that once in Little Rock, he played for eight days and nights without sleep and won $530,000.

One of Nick the Greek's most famous sayings was, "The next best thing to playing and winning is playing and losing."

Nev. St. Journal, 27 Dec. 66 (obit.).

DAVIS, TOM

Tom Davis was born in Arkansas in 1932 and came to Reno in 1953. He was first employed by Harolds Club as a construction worker in one of the club's expansion programs and later played on the Harolds Club softball team. In 1954 Davis worked as a "key man" in the slot department for a short while before learning to deal the table games. He worked his way up through the ranks to become first a floor manager and eventually assistant shift manager.

He left Reno in 1971 with Harold Smith Jr. to open and operate a casino that Smith owned in Yugoslavia. After the Yugoslavian casino closed, Davis returned to Reno and worked as casino manager at the King's Inn and the Ponderosa Hotel-Casino and as a pit supervisor at the Pioneer Inn.

Davis was working at the Pioneer Inn when he died in 1984. His widow, Yvonne Todd Davis, who also worked at Harolds Club, is currently a pit supervisor at the Pioneer Inn.

DEAUVILLE

43 West First Street (corner of First and Sierra Streets); licensed from 1931 to 1933 for craps, roulette, 21, big-six, faro, and hazard.

The Deauville was the first casino whose owners came up with the idea of forming a corporation and selling shares in the operation. Several advertisements in the *Nevada State Journal* in the spring of 1931 announced that shares in the newly formed Deauville Corporation were for sale. Then, on May 9, 1931, the newspaper included an announcement that "the Deauville, a casino cabaret, is scheduled to open in one month at the corner of First and Sierra Streets with A. C. Langan as general manager."

The Deauville Casino Cabaret opened on July 31. Named for the famous French resort town at the mouth of the Seine, the casino was called a "new palace of pleasure that is declared to be the most beautiful and luxurious in the west." The decor, in green, gold, and red, was opulent and elegant. Floors were richly carpeted, except for the ebony-finished oval dance floor. From the high lobby inside the First Street entrance, a stairway lighted by massive chandeliers led to the lounge with its rich drapes and furnishings, an art display, and the well-known Sybil Huntington painting, *Her Day of Freedom.* Draped arches led from the lounge to the casino and cabaret. The Deauville featured fine dining and was open all night for dancing and gambling.

Interior of the ornately decorated Deauville Club. Note the chandeliers, floral arrangements, French-layout craps table, and big-six wheel. Courtesy of the Nevada Historical Society.

The ten gaming layouts in the casino, all of the latest deluxe construction, included a handsome inlaid roulette wheel, a French double roulette table, a chemin-de-fer table, an English hazard wheel, a big-six wheel, a faro game, a craps game, and two 21 tables. French plate mirrors covered the casino walls, surmounted by rich drapes in deep shades of green. In both large rooms, the plaster reliefs on the walls and ceiling were noteworthy for their beauty. The casino was declared to be equal in luxury to any club or gambling establishment in this country or in Mexico.

The president of the Deauville Corporation and general manager of the operation was Arthur Langan. It was he who conceived the plan of a first-class dining, dancing, and gaming resort in Reno, and he directed every detail of the design and construction. Langan was widely known in Nevada, having spent many years participating in the Tonopah and Goldfield booms. Later he was a mining broker in Rawhide and Reno. He was a close friend of the famous "plunger" Riley Grannon, was associated with Tex Rickard in the promotion of championship boxing events, and accompanied Rickard on excursions to South America. He was also involved in motion-picture productions with Thomas Ince, was second in command of the Scott Antarctic polar expedition of 1912, and had crossed the Atlantic Ocean more than twenty times.

Frank Cody was in charge of gambling at the Deauville. He was known from Miami and Havana to Aguascalientes, Mexico, as a successful casino operator, a "square shooter," and a friend of notables all over the country. Ray Holbrook, the casino cashier, had held a similar position under Tex Rickard and Kid Highley in the famous Northern Casino in Goldfield.

A torrential downpour in August flooded the Deauville and inflicted so much damage that it was necessary to close the club for over a week. Perhaps the flood contributed to the demise of the Deauville, or perhaps Reno was not yet ready for such an elegant club. Whatever the reason, the beautiful casino was in financial trouble as early as September 1931. A petition of bankruptcy was heard on September 30, and the Deauville closed a short time later.

It reopened briefly in June 1933. Shortly after it closed for the last time, the property was incorporated into an adjoining business, the Town House.

The location was razed by fire in 1955. After the fire, the J.C. Penney Company built and operated a retail store on the property for many years. Today the site of the Deauville is part of the Town Center Mall.

Nev. St. Journal, 9 May 31, 17 July 31 (adv.), 29 July 31, 1 Aug. 31, 6 Aug. 31, 20 Aug. 31, 2 Sept. 31, 30 Sept. 31, 29 June 33 (adv.), 14 July 33 (adv.), 17 July 33 (adv.).

DEER HEAD LODGE

2600 South Virginia Street; licensed from February 15, 1944, to July 1951 for slots, 21, and craps.

The Deer Head Lodge opened in October 1943 as a bar and restaurant. It wasn't until February 1944 that it was granted a gaming license. In July 1944 George Stone and Howard McMullen took over the Deer Head Lodge and operated it until 1950, when they sold the property to George Richter.

In July 1951 the Deer Head Lodge closed, and an advertisement in the *Nevada State Journal* stated that "the Deer Head Lodge was for sale for $2,500—lock, stock and barrel."

The property reopened as the Jolly Jolly Club in 1953. The site is now occupied by Friend's Liquor Store.

Nev. St. Journal, 30 Oct. 43 (adv.), 30 July 44, 1 Oct. 46, 19 July 47, 8 May 51, 1 July 51.

DELANO CLUB

6 East Commercial Row; licensed from May 6, 1945, to 1946 for slots, 21, roulette, pan, and poker.

The Delano was one of many bars, small casinos, and cardrooms that operated at this address. Robert Smalley was licensed for one pan game and one poker game in May 1945.

This short-lived casino was owned by Joe Delano and Paula Collins. Today the site is part of Harolds Club.

Nev. St. Journal, 6 Apr. 45 (adv.).

DELAUER, LEE

Lee DeLauer was born in Oakland, California, in 1925. After graduating from Oakland High School, he enlisted in the Marine Corps and participated in the invasions of Guam and Okinawa. He came to Reno in 1946 to attend the University of Nevada. After graduating with a degree in accounting, he was hired by the accounting firm of Semenza and Kottinger. Part of his job was to audit casinos, and while auditing Harrah's Club in 1955 he was offered a position as office manager at Harrah's Lake Tahoe Club. He later worked in the cashier's cage and the credit office before transferring to the public relations department of Harrah's Lake Tahoe, where he was instrumental in developing and instituting the first Harrah's Club golf tournaments in Reno and Lake Tahoe.

DeLauer resigned from Harrah's in 1963, and in 1964 he headed the group of investors who operated the Riverside Hotel. He was a 25-percent owner and general manager of the operation until it was sold in 1965. Next, he went to work at Harvey's Wagon Wheel at Lake Tahoe. He remained there until 1970, when he returned to Harrah's as a casino manager at Harrah's Reno operation.

Leaving Harrah's for the second time in the mid-1970s, DeLauer was later associated with the King's Castle at North Lake Tahoe, the development of the never-opened Florentine Hotel, the never-opened Player's Casino, the Shenandoah Hotel in Las Vegas (which became the Maxim), the Old Reno Club, and the Virginian Hotel-Casino.

DeLauer is currently retired and living in Reno.

Nev. St. Journal, 17 June 64.

DEL MONTE CLUB

6405 South Virginia Street; licensed from February to May 1936 for slots and roulette.

The Del Monte Club (previously known as the Heidelburg Club) was a supper club with dancing, entertainment, and fine food. The few slots and the roulette wheel were there for the amusement of the customers.

The former site of the Del Monte Club is now a small mall with two sandwich shops and a Chinese restaurant, the Great Wall of China.

Nev. St. Journal, 11 Apr. 36, 9 May 36.

DEMARIS, WARREN

Warren DeMaris was born in Hellgate, Montana, and came to Reno in the 1930s. A skilled keno man, he managed the first successful keno game in Harolds Club. The keno concession was owned by Fred Beck. DeMaris worked at Harolds Club until 1961, when he moved to the South Shore of Lake Tahoe.

During his tenure on the South Shore, he worked for Harrah's and was later the keno manager at Barney's Club.

DeMaris died in Minden, Nevada, on August 31, 1974, at the age of sixty-four.

Nev. St. Journal, 1 Sept. 74 (obit.).

DEN

21 East Douglas Alley and 22 East Commercial Row (two entrances); licensed from June 1947 to January 1950 for slots, 21, craps, and roulette.

The Den, previously known as the Louvre, was one of many cardrooms and bars that operated in Douglas Alley and Commercial Row. They were usually short-lived, because the licenses and proprietors changed frequently.

The Den was licensed by Robert Douglass for one 21 game and one roulette game in June 1947, and Nevada Novelty was licensed for sixteen slots. In March 1949 D. A. Bentley was licensed for one 21 game. His partners were John Hope and Robert Callahan.

Bentley's license was revoked on January 1, 1950, after a shooting incident involving Bentley and Lloyd McCrorey. When he attempted to renew his gaming license on January 24, he was denied and the club was shut down. A few hours after it closed, the Den was destroyed by fire. Arson was suspected but never proved.

In April 1950 Jack Douglass (Robert Douglass's brother) and Lou Benetti sued Bentley, Hope, and Callahan for $6,500. The following month, Douglass filed suit to regain possession of the Den, contending that when Bentley and his partners lost their gaming and liquor licenses they ne-

gated the $550-a-month lease signed in January 1949. Douglass took possession of the Den in June, and in July Douglass and Benetti were awarded $3,905 in their collection suit against Hope, Callahan, and Bentley for debts and back payments.

The Den never reopened, but over the years a number of other bars and cardrooms operated at the same location. Today the site is part of the Harolds Club property.

Nev. St. Journal, 5 June 47, 16 Mar. 49, 22 Mar. 49, 24 Jan. 50, 25 Jan. 50, 22 Apr. 50, 7 May 50, 2 June 50, 13 July 50.

DEPOT BAR

124 East Commercial Row; licensed from July to December 1947 for 21, craps, and roulette.

The Depot Bar, sometimes known as the Depot Club, was located in what was considered by some to be Reno's "skid row" during the 1930s and 1940s, and it had several owners through the years. It was licensed for about six months in 1944. Both the Depot Club and the Depot Bar usually had licensed and unlicensed poker games going on somewhere in the building. Among the owners in the 1940s were Cliff Judd and Blanche Dupuis, R. H. Owens, Joe Archio, Mike Lazovich, J. M. Lepp, and Ralph Pardini.

The site of the Depot Bar is now part of Harrah's parking garage.

Nev. St. Journal, 1 Mar. 46; Reno Telephone Directory advertisements, 1944, 1945, 1946.

DEPOT CLUB

128 East Commercial Row; licensed from April 6, 1931, to 1935 for stud and draw poker.

This business was sometimes called the Depot Bar and sometimes the Depot Club. It was a bar as well as a poker room.

Today the former location of the Depot Club is part of the Harrah's Club parking garage.

DESERT CLUB

140 and later 196 Airport Road (now Gentry Way); licensed from October 1, 1953, to 1954 for 21, slots, and craps.

The Desert Club, previously known as the Normandy Club, was one of those out-of-

downtown clubs that many casino employees and local rounders patronized. It was more a club for entertainment and drinking than for gambling. It was licensed by Tony Gallerani and Jerome Cornell in 1953. Their drawing card was a "girlie-girlie" show.

The "girls" must not have been a success, because in April 1954 Paul Tyler, Tony Hopper, and Mike Batsael were listed as owners but were denied a gaming license. In July they were granted a cabaret license, and in October Batsael, Merl Tanner, and Lois Behmer were licensed for gaming.

The site is now occupied by Tiger Tom's Bar.

Nev. St. Journal, 22 Sept. 53, 30 Sept. 53 (adv.), 2 Apr. 54, 1 July 54, 26 Sept. 54.

DESIMONE, ANDREW "ANDY"

Andy Desimone was born in Amalfi, Italy, in 1899 and came to America as a young man. In the late 1930s, he met Elmer "Bones" Remmer and went to work for him in the 1940s at the Cal-Neva Lodge in North Lake Tahoe as a pit floor man.

From 1955 to 1959, Desimone was licensed as a co-owner of the seasonally operated Bal Tabarin on the North Shore of Lake Tahoe. He was also employed as a floor man at the Golden Bank Casino during Lake Tahoe's off-season. He was licensed as a co-owner of the Horseshoe Club on Virginia Street from 1956 to 1964. From 1964 to 1967 he was licensed as a co-owner of the Riverside Hotel-Casino, but he lost his license when the casino was closed for cheating.

Desimone died on January 29, 1985.

Nev. St. Journal, 2 Mar. 55, 7 Dec. 55, 24 Aug. 56, 18 Nov. 64.

DIXIE'S LOG CABIN (ALSO KNOWN AS THE LOG CABIN AND AS DIXIE'S CLUB)

596 Airport Road (now Gentry Way); licensed as the Log Cabin from October 11, 1943, to June 30, 1947; as Dixie's Club and Dixie's Log Cabin from November 4, 1949, to May 1, 1954, for slots, craps, and 21.

Dixie's Log Cabin was a bar and cabaret that catered to local rounders and late-night partygoers. Joyce Mosely, Tony Gallerani, and Jerome Cornell were among those licensed at the location.

On January 13, 1953, local club owner Lee Maury shot and killed Bud Dutcher, former manager of the West Indies, in the parking lot of Dixie's Log Cabin. Maury was later found guilty of second-degree murder, and the shooting indirectly resulted in Joyce Mosely losing her gaming license in June 1953.

The site is now occupied by a used car lot.

Nev. St. Journal, 2 Dec. 52, 13 Jan. 53, 24 Jan. 53, 28 Mar. 53, 18 June 53, 22 Sept. 53.

DIXIE'S SOCIAL CLUB
218 East Douglas Alley; licensed from 1943 to 1949 for poker, 21, slots, and craps.

Opened in 1943 by William "Bill" Bailey, Dixie's Social Club served the African American and Asian trade. It was located at an address that was home to several bars and cardrooms over the years.

In February 1945 proprietor Bailey ejected a customer, James Bagby, from the club. A short time later, Bagby returned with a knife and attacked Bailey. Bailey was severely injured and was given only a 50-50 chance of survival, but he did recover.

In June 1948 the city of Reno granted a 21 license to Elmo Butler. He was licensed again the following January. The club closed later in the year.

The former site of Dixie's Social Club is now part of Harrah's parking garage.

Nev. St. Journal, 8 Feb. 45, 15 June 48.

DIXON, DEERING "DIX"
Dix Dixon was born in Reno on October 16, 1915. He attended local schools, including the University of Nevada, prior to going to work at the Waldorf Club in 1938. He worked there from 1938 to 1941 and became proficient at dealing all pit games.

After World War II, Deering went to work at the Cal-Neva Club when it was owned by the Charles Resnick and Sanford Adler group. In the years ahead, Dixon, like many journeymen dealers and pit bosses, moved around according to where the "good money" was and to where he

had "juice." During his career he worked at all job levels as a dealer, pit boss, shift manager, and casino manager. Some of the casinos he worked for included the Ponderosa, the Golden Hotel (as a dealer and pit boss), the Mapes (as a dealer and shift manager), the Money Tree (as a shift manager and casino manager), Harrah's, the Horseshoe, the Frontier Club, and the Holiday Hotel-Casino. One of his last jobs was as a pit boss and dealer at the Ponderosa Hotel-Casino when it was "The World's First Non-Smoking Casino."

Dixon retired in Reno.

Nev. St. Journal, 11 Oct. 74.

DIXON, MEAD
Mead Dixon was born in Springfield, Illinois, on September 9, 1919. After serving in the military in World War II, he entered law school. He began practicing law in Reno in 1950 and soon became counsel for casinos in Lake Tahoe, Reno, and Las Vegas.

In 1957 Dixon became Bill Harrah's principal attorney, and in 1960 he was named to the board of directors of Harrah's. Following Bill Harrah's death in 1978, Dixon was named executor of Harrah's estate, and soon thereafter, chairman of Harrah's board of directors. Dixon was the initiator and driving force behind the 1980 merger of Harrah's with Holiday Inns. He was also instrumental in the expansion of Harrah's and Holiday Inns into Atlantic City.

He resigned from Harrah's in 1986 and returned to the board of directors of the Showboat Casino (he had previously served on that board from 1968 to 1978). Dixon's expertise and knowledge of New Jersey gaming regulations were important factors in the Showboat being granted a gaming license in Atlantic City.

Dixon died after a lengthy illness on January 12, 1993. He is considered by some authorities to have been one of the first Nevada casino executives to anticipate the spread of casino gambling across the country.

Nev. St. Journal, 18 Mar. 79 (photos), 13 Jan. 93 (obit.).

DOG HOUSE
130 North Center Street; licensed from June 1935 to 1944 for slots, 21, craps, roulette, and keno.

The Dog House was a combination dance hall, entertainment center, casino, and restaurant, named in honor of a wire-haired terrier named Poochy. It was opened in June 1935 by Al Hoffman, who spent more than $12,000 in decorating the club.

During the late 1930s and early 1940s, the Dog House was one of Reno's most heavily patronized clubs. One of its slogans was "The Divorcee's Haven." In its early years, the Dog House had twenty-eight hostesses and offered continuous, twenty-four-hour entertainment. Proprietor Al Hoffman led the house orchestra. Charlie Dennis, formerly of San Francisco and Sacramento, opened the club as master of ceremonies and director of entertainment.

The club seated more than 250 people and was decorated in a modernistic style. A mural of typical Sierra Nevada scenery was painted on the north wall. There was a dance floor and stage, and a large bar along one side of the building.

The club featured a wide range of entertainers, including torch dancers, hula dancers, jazz dancers, Oriental fan dancers, tap dancers, striptease dancers, vocalists, and magicians. Among the acts were Joan Morrow, "the Lady of the Fans"; the Holiday Revue; Nan Bittner; Pauline Lewis; and hundreds more.

A short time after the Dog House opened, Al Hoffman took in two partners—Vic Williams, who was also club manager, and Phil Curti. In April 1938 Curti announced that the Dog House would close on January 1, 1939. The building was to be demolished and a brand-new club would be built on the site.

The owners spent $80,000 building the new Dog House. When the business reopened on April 1, 1939, it featured a western theme. From decorations to employee costumes, the spirit of the Old West was captured by the lively nightclub. All the musicians, bartenders, dealers, and waitresses wore colorful cowboy or cowgirl outfits.

Al Hoffman claimed to have the largest nightclub in Nevada. He had the greatest

Looking north on Center Street in the mid-1930s. Note the train in the background, the Bank Club (upper l.), and the Dog House (lower r.). Courtesy of the Nevada Historical Society.

number of entertainers, hostesses, waitresses, and musicians ever gathered in any cabaret in the state up to that time.

The outside of the building presented a striking appearance. The exterior had been completely renovated, a new sidewalk laid, and beautiful new neon signs erected. Neon lighting throughout the Dog House interior accentuated scenes from the covered-wagon days and the colorful lives of the prospectors. On the walls were pictures of ranch life and Latin American scenes formed from rock inlay work in multicolored stones, laid by William Hemstalk of Quincy, California. The walls behind the huge bar held murals depicting typical Nevada desert scenery. Neon logs "burned" on the musicians' stands, and the band instruments and piano were reconditioned, as was the gambling equipment. Some of the

dining tables were in a rustic style that resembled split tree trunks. Eight dozen new chairs were put in, and ranch house-style dining booths with mahogany tops lined the walls. More than fourteen thousand feet of knotty pine, cedar, and red fir were used in the interior. Neat tilework was featured in the new restrooms. Meals were served twenty-four hours a day, and the popular chef T. F. Gee featured Chinese specialties in his restaurant. A new master of ceremonies, Jerry Owens, was hired to preside over the continuous floor show, which featured over a dozen acts.

In August 1939 the district attorney revoked the Dog House's gaming license, which had covered ten slots, one roulette game, one craps game, and one 21 game. Shorty King and George "Shorty" Coppersmith were operating the gambling and

pled guilty to operating a crooked wheel. Phil Curti and Al Hoffman, the owners, immediately started action to have the license restored, claiming that the crooked wheel was being operated without their knowledge. King and Coppersmith were both found guilty. Coppersmith was fined $1,000, and King was fined $1,000 and sentenced to six months in jail.

Gaming reopened in January 1940. The tables and the slots were leased to the Block N Club, and Dick Kolbus operated the games there for a short time. Gaming continued until 1944. All during the early 1940s, the Dog House was noted for its fine entertainment, Chinese food, dancing, and gaming.

In April 1944 Al Hoffman and Phil Curti closed the Dog House. They completely renovated the building, and when they reopened in May 1944 they also changed the style of operation and the name—it became the Tropics. Later, the building housed a bowling alley, a nightclub, Harrah's employment office, a restaurant, and eventually part of the Cal-Neva's personnel office.

Late in 1994 the building was razed. The site is now part of the Cal-Neva's parking garage on the east side of Center Street.

Nev. St. Journal, 26 June 35 (adv.), 27 June 35, 8 Dec. 36, 2 Jan. 37 (adv.), 28 Nov. 37, 26 Feb. 38, 1 Apr. 38, 30 Dec. 38, 5 Apr. 39 (adv., article, photo), 7 Apr. 39 (photo), 23 Aug. 39, 25 Aug. 39, 5 Sept. 39, 3 Apr. 40 (adv.), 8 May 40 (adv.), 29 June 40 (adv.), 10 May 44; *Reno Gazette-Journal,* 7 July 93 (Ty Cobb's column), 21 July 93 (Ty Cobb's column).

DOLL HOUSE

2250 South Virginia Street; licensed from April 1955 to 1960 for slots and 21.

The Doll House was a small bar south of town. It was a local hangout that was busiest late in the evenings and in the early morning hours.

In December 1959, the Nevada Gaming Control Board closed the Doll House on cheating charges, accusing the dealer of "dealing seconds" and "turning the deck." The licensees initially made no comment, but later in the month, when represented by their attorney, Gordon Rice, they stated that they did not admit the facts alleged by the Gaming Control Board and demanded that a hearing be held.

In the hearing on March 16, 1960, card expert Robert Driscoll testified for the state that on September 11–12 and November 25, 1959, he saw dealers William Murphy and Sharon Griffith "dealing seconds," peeking, and stacking the deck. The license was revoked, and the Doll House never opened again.

Currently located at the former site of the Doll House is the Scott Motor Company used car lot.

Nev. St. Journal, 6 Dec. 59, 23 Dec. 59, 17 Mar. 60, 18 May 60, 9 June 60.

DON LEE CLUB

111 Lake Street; licensed from October to December 1931 for craps only.

The Don Lee Club was a small bar that was licensed for a craps game in 1931. The site is now occupied by the Oxford Motel.

DOUGLASS, JACK

Jack Douglass, noted as the holder of the oldest continual gaming license in the state of Nevada, was born in Tonopah in 1910. He came to Reno to attend the University of Nevada in 1929, but his father died shortly afterward, and the resultant shortage of money forced him to drop out of school and seek employment.

In the early 1930s, Douglass started a pinball-machine route, and a short time later he added jukeboxes. By 1934 he had added a few slot machines to the route. In 1935 he formed a partnership in a slot route with Lou Benetti. They named their new company the Nevada Novelty Company, and over the next few years the company expanded as the partners placed their machines in numerous locations around the state, not only in Reno but also in outlying towns such as Fallon, Lovelock, Tonopah, Goldfield, and Carson City. By the beginning of World War II in 1941, they had slot machines in dozens of bars and restaurants throughout northern Nevada.

Late in 1943, Douglass was inducted into the U.S. Army, and Benetti operated the business alone for the duration of the war. After Douglass was discharged, the company slot route continued to expand, and the partners were licensed for several more locations in the Reno area. Among the businesses leasing Nevada Novelty Company slot machines were the Cherokee Club, the Den, and the Montana Bar in Douglas Alley; the Turf Club on South Virginia Street; and the Picadilly Club on Virginia Street.

The Benetti-Douglass partnership in Nevada Novelty dissolved in 1959, and Douglass began investing in real estate around the Reno area. His partner in many transactions was John Cavanaugh Sr., who later became Douglass's partner in the Club Cal-Neva.

In January 1960 Douglass purchased 20 percent of the Riverside Hotel, but before the year was over he had sold his percentage. In 1962 Douglass, along with John Cavanaugh, Leon Nightingale, Ad Tolen,

Howard Farris, and Warren Nelson, purchased and began operating the Club Cal-Neva in downtown Reno. In 1969 the same group bought the Cal-Neva Lodge at Lake Tahoe—and sold it to a group of real-estate investors from Ohio in 1970.

In 1977 Jack Douglass was licensed as an investor in the Maxim Hotel in Las Vegas, but his group soon sold the Maxim to Jack Anderson.

In May 1978, Douglass, along with several partners, opened the Comstock Hotel in Reno. Many of the owners were also partners in the Club Cal-Neva. In the mid-1980s, serious differences arose among the partners in the Club Cal-Neva, and Douglass felt that it would be in everyone's best interest if he and his family sold their interests in that operation. As part of the transaction, the other owners of the Club Cal-Neva sold their percentages in the Comstock Hotel. Currently, the Douglass family owns approximately 75 percent of the Comstock.

In 1987, Douglass bought the property formerly known as the Gold Dust East Casino, formed a corporation known as the Carnival Corporation, and opened the Riverboat Hotel-Casino on the site in 1988. The Riverboat closed late in 1998.

Douglass's four sons—William (a professor at the University of Nevada, Reno), John, Dan, and David—are all active in the gaming industry in Reno as well as in Colorado. Jack Douglass remains active in the operation of the Comstock and goes there almost daily.

Nev. St. Journal, 14 Dec. 50, 29 Mar. 62, 2 Mar. 69, 26 Apr. 77, 1 Feb. 78; Jack Douglass, *Tap Dancing on Ice: The Life and Times of a Nevada Gaming Pioneer* (Reno: University of Nevada Oral History Program, 1996).

DOUGLASS, ROBERT

Robert Douglass, the brother of Jack Douglass, was licensed at the Den in 1947, the Alibi Club in 1948, and the Doll House in 1959. He was also one of the original owners of the Branding Iron, which later became the Bonanza Casino.

Robert Douglass is best remembered as the originator of a plan to develop a $12-

million hotel-casino in the air space over the I-80 freeway near the junction of I-80 and North Virginia Street. The idea was presented to the Nevada Highway Commission in June 1964 and later approved. When the freeway opened in 1978, a platform was built and plans were made to begin construction of the hotel-casino. However, the developers could not find sufficient financing to support the project, and the hotel was never built. The platform is still in place.

Robert Douglass passed away on November 5, 1997. He was eighty-three years old at the time of his death.

Nev. St. Journal, 24 Dec. 59.

DOUVILLE CLUB

21 East Douglas Alley; licensed from May 18, 1931, to September 19, 1933, for 21, craps, and roulette.

The Douville Club was located in Douglas Alley at a site that was home to several small casinos, bars, and cardrooms over the years. The site is now part of Harolds Club.

DREW, JOHN

In June 1953 John Drew applied to be licensed for 25 percent of the Golden Bank Club. The Golden Bank was owned by Frank Hofues, but Bill Graham held the lease on the casino. Graham wanted David High as his partner in the Golden Bank, but the State of Nevada refused to license High and in fact forced his resignation from the casino. This denial of High resulted in Drew's request to be licensed. He was questioned extensively regarding his association with the Al Capone syndicate, and he withdrew his application.

In January 1954 Drew again applied for a license. His application was deferred until the state could investigate him further. When the investigation was completed, John Drew was licensed for 25 percent of the Golden Bank Casino in April 1954.

In hearings held in December 1954, the State Tax Commission directed its investigators to "look into" reports that the Capone mob had taken control of the Golden Bank Club. Crime expert Virgil Peterson said that Lester Kruse, a former Al Capone mobster, had been brought to the Golden Bank by John Drew and put to work as a pit boss. No further action came out of the investigation, and John Drew and Bill Graham held the gaming lease at the Golden Bank until December 1, 1955.

At that time, Bill and Jim Tomerlin paid $425,000 for the remaining seventeen years of the lease. In May 1958 John Drew was licensed for 5 percent of the Stardust Hotel in Las Vegas.

Nev. St. Journal, 3 Apr. 54, 3 Dec. 54, 1 Dec. 55, 24 May 58.

DREWS, J. GEORGE

George Drews was born in Wilmington, Delaware, on February 22, 1930. He spent his early years in the New York City area and graduated from the U.S. Coast Guard Academy in 1952 with a B.S. in engineering. After serving three years in the Coast Guard, Drews was discharged and enrolled in the Harvard Graduate School of Business. He received a master's degree in business administration in 1957.

Drews worked in various top management positions in the United States and Europe before he was hired as controller of Harrah's Club in 1971. He later became executive vice-president of finance and administration. He helped take Harrah's public in 1971 and was instrumental in Harrah's Club being listed on the New York Stock Exchange in 1973. Drews also personally obtained for Harrah's Club the first "A" bond rating in the gaming industry and is considered by many to have been the first gaming industry executive to gain the confidence of the financial institutions on Wall Street. He, along with other Harrah's people like Lloyd Dyer, Mark Curtis, M. F. Sheppard, and of course Bill Harrah, was instrumental in changing the image of Nevada gamblers from shady characters in back rooms with questionable reputations to corporate executives who were a conservative, well-dressed, highly respected part of the American business world.

Forced to resign from Harrah's Club in March 1980 when the company was taken over by Holiday Inns, Inc., Drews was immediately hired by the Sircoma Company, which later became International Gaming Technology (IGT). He served as president, CEO, and director of the company from

Pictured at the New York Stock Exchange in 1973 when Harrah's was first traded on the "Big Board" are (l. to r.) J. George Drews, Harrah's controller; Lloyd Dyer, Harrah's vice-president; William Harrah; Maurice Sheppard, president of Harrah's; Charles Franklin, Harrah's counsel; and David Shuldiner, New York financial advisor. Courtesy of Lloyd and Joan Dyer.

1980 to 1986. During that time, he renamed the company and brought it public in 1981.

Currently Drews is associated with Bally Gaming International, Inc., and is an advisor and consultant for its Australian corporation.

DROMIACK, MATT

Matt Dromiack was a lifelong resident of Reno. His father built and operated the Overland Hotel, and after his father's death, Dromiack operated the hotel for several years before selling it.

After the Overland was sold, Dromiack held a variety of jobs. In 1934 he was general manager of the Comstock Club on Center Street. He worked at the Cal-Vada Club at Lake Tahoe in 1937, then the Cal-Neva Lodge at Lake Tahoe, the Northern Club on Center Street, and the Ship and Bottle Club on Center Street. He also worked as manager of the Club Fortune in 1940, and as manager of the Merry-Go-Round Bar in 1952.

Dromiack died in February 1965 at seventy-two. He was working at the Holiday Hotel at the time of his death.

Nev. St. Journal, 17 June 33, 21 June 34, 28 May 37, 30 July 37, 28 Aug. 37, 31 Dec. 37, 18 Jan. 47, 27 May 52, 17 Feb. 65 (obit.).

DUFFY, JACK

Jack Duffy worked at the Bonanza Club, the Palace Club, and the Bank Club as a dealer and pit boss. In 1948 and most of 1949 he was the co-owner of the Town House on First Street. His partners were John Achuff and Gordon Rose.

In 1949 Duffy moved to Las Vegas and finished his gaming career in that southern Nevada city.

Nev. St. Journal, 2 Nov. 49.

DUNES

222 North Center Street; never licensed.

On January 23, 1948, the Dunes Casino, owned by F. J. Esswein, was denied a gaming license. This was the first ruling made by Robbins Cahill, head of the newly created State Tax Board.

The site of the Dunes is now part of Harrah's Casino on the east side of Center Street between Second Street and Commercial Row.

Nev. St. Journal, 24 Jan. 48.

DUTCH GARDEN (ORIGINALLY KNOWN AS STENGLER'S DUTCH GARDEN)

565 West Moana Lane; licensed from May 1945 to 1948 for 21 and craps.

Stengler's Dutch Garden was opened by Fred Stengler in May 1945 as a fine dining house. The menu featured full-course steak and chicken dinners. Lou Levitt, the longtime Reno musician, and his orchestra were the opening night entertainment.

Early in 1946, Stengler sold the Dutch Garden to Mr. and Mrs. John Oleson, who hired Bill Bush as their manager. However, in July the Olesons (who had renamed the Dutch Garden the Great Dane and operated the property as a smorgasbord restaurant) sued Stengler for $23,660 for misrepresenting the earning power of the Dutch Garden. They wanted to give the property back to Stengler.

In turn, the Olesons were sued for $1,677 that they owed to their suppliers. The Olesons claimed that the club was only worth $55,000, but that they had paid $92,400 for it because they had been told that it grossed $17,000 and netted $4,500 a month.

The case was settled out of court, and the property reopened in September 1946 with Catherine Hemsing as owner and manager. However, the restaurant closed again in June 1947 because of financial problems. Fred Stengler took back the club and reopened it on August 29, 1947. He acted as the host and manager.

In March 1948 card-cheating charges were filed against Cliff Sikes, a fifty-one-year-old dealer at the Dutch Garden. A trial was held in June 1948, and Sikes was found guilty of cheating and sentenced to six months in jail and a $1,000 fine. This was only the second case of cheating in Washoe County (the first was at the Dog House in 1939).

The property was never again licensed for gambling. It later reopened as the Sharon House, a successful operation for many years. The site is currently occupied by Yen Ching, a Chinese restaurant.

Nev. St. Journal, 12 May 45 (photo and adv.), 17 Mar. 46 (adv.), 22 May 46 (adv.), 18 July 46, 22 Sept. 46, 25 Dec. 46 (adv.), 7 June 47, 29 Aug. 47, 7 Mar. 48, 31 Mar. 48, 11 June 48, 12 June 48, 15 June 48.

DYER, LLOYD

Lloyd Dyer, who was born in Pittsford, New York, in 1927, graduated from the University of Utah with a degree in banking and financing. He had previously attended the University of Denver and Brigham Young University. He went to work for Harrah's at Lake Tahoe in 1957 as a cashier. This was meant to be only a summer job, but it turned out to be the beginning of his lifelong career.

Dyer initiated several of Harrah's real-estate transactions, including the purchase of the Golden Hotel, the Overland Hotel, and the Palace Club. He was also instrumental in bringing Harrah's public, first as an over-the-counter stock, then to the American Stock Exchange, and finally a listing on the New York Stock Exchange.

Dyer was skilled, able, and thoroughly

Lloyd Dyer, employed by Harrah's for over twenty years, was president of Harrah's from 1975 to 1980. Courtesy of Lloyd and Joan Dyer.

indoctrinated in the right way (the Harrah's way) of doing things. Bill Harrah always expected things to be done the right way and the best way.

In 1975, after serving in several management positions at Harrah's, including employee counselor, scheduling supervisor, assistant slot manager, director of community affairs, vice-president of real estate and financing, and executive vice-president of finance and administration, Dyer was appointed president of Harrah's. He served as president of the corporation until March 1, 1980, when Harrah's sale to Holiday Inns was completed and Dyer was replaced by Richard Goeglein. He continued with the organization as a senior advisor for one year.

After leaving Harrah's, Dyer served on the boards of directors of Harvey's Resort Hotel, the Security National Bank, Southwest Gas, and other corporations. He currently serves on the board of directors of the William F. Harrah Trust.

Lloyd Dyer and his wife, Joan, live in Reno and are active in many civic, charitable, and community-oriented organizations.

Nev. St. Journal, 11 June 75, 5 Mar. 80 (photo).

ECHO'S CLUB

9825 South Virginia Street; licensed in May 1951 for 21 and slots.

Echo's Club was a dinner house located approximately seven miles south of downtown Reno. Other restaurants had been located there, and the Sunflower Club had operated there just prior to the opening of Echo's Club. The licensees at Echo's Club were Echo Leonetti and Phillip and Lorraine Kinzel.

Today the former site of Echo's Club is a sales office for mobile homes.

Nev. St. Journal, 8 May 51.

EINSTOSS, BERNIE

Bernie Einstoss came to Reno in 1947 from Los Angeles. When the Mapes Hotel opened in 1947, Einstoss, along with Leo Kind, Frank Grannis, and Lou Wertheimer, leased the casino from Charles Mapes. Rent was 50 percent of the casino's profits.

In 1955 Einstoss and Grannis were licensed for gaming at the Cal-Vada Club (which would become the Bal Tabarin). Charles Mapes objected because he felt that it would be a conflict of interest for Einstoss to operate both the Lake Tahoe club and the Mapes. The state refused to deny the Einstoss-Grannis application, so Mapes offered to buy out the remainder of their casino lease, which was scheduled to expire on January 1, 1958. After negotiations, Einstoss sold the remainder of the lease to Mapes for $125,000.

Einstoss and his partners operated the Bal Tabarin on a seasonal basis until 1959, when they sold the property to Lincoln Fitzgerald.

In 1956 Einstoss and several other investors, including Baldy West and Brad Hewins, opened the Horseshoe Club on North Virginia Street. Einstoss sold his portion of the Horseshoe Club in August

1964, and in November, with Jack Richards and Andy Desimone, he bought 75 percent of the Riverside Hotel.

In February 1966 Einstoss divested himself of his interests in the Riverside Hotel when he sold his percentage to James Lloyd. A month later, he became a minority stockholder in Caesars Palace in Las Vegas. It was in the Beverly Hills office of Caesars Palace that Einstoss died of an apparent heart attack on May 27, 1966. He was fifty-three.

Nev. St. Journal, 2 Mar. 55, 24 Aug. 56, 30 Oct. 59, 18 Aug. 64, 18 Nov. 64, 28 May 66 (obit.); Warren Nelson, "Gaming from the Old Days to Computers," unpublished oral history, University of Nevada Oral History Program, 1978.

EL CORTEZ HOTEL

239 West Second Street; licensed intermittently since October 1934.

Construction began on the El Cortez Hotel in 1930, and the grand opening of the six-story, sixty-room hotel took place on March 21, 1931, and featured the orchestra of Charles Kaley. The hotel was built and owned by Abe Zetooney, a native of Syria, who came to Reno shortly after World War I. In 1931 Zetooney leased the hotel to the Bulasky brothers, Joseph, Solomon, and Louis.

The first gaming license at the El Cortez was granted to W. H. Rutledge in 1934. In January 1936 W. W. Miller was licensed for gaming at the El Cortez and remained on the license until 1940.

The El Cortez proved to be a profitable venture, and in 1941 an extensive remodeling and expansion project was completed. There were now a total of 114 rooms and a new entertainment center known as the Trocadero. The "Troc," as it soon became known, was opened with Lee Herzoff and his orchestra appearing in what was advertised as "one of the most modern and beautiful nightclubs and cocktail rooms on the Pacific Coast." Charles Rennie and Jack Greer were in charge of the lounge. The adjacent gaming room, under the direction of George Hagenson, had two roulette tables, one craps table, and seventeen slot machines.

Gaming action at the El Cortez Hotel in 1944. In the center in a dark suit is longtime Reno gaming man Bill Williams. Courtesy of Neal Cobb.

In the middle and late 1940s, R. J. Miller managed the El Cortez and the Trocadero nightclub and was licensed for roulette, 21, and a craps game.

During World War II, many nationally known entertainers appeared at the El Cortez. In January 1944, Sophie Tucker, billed as "The Last of the Red Hot Mamas," appeared at the El Cortez. During her engagement, she also appeared at the Bank Club and the Club Fortune as part of a war-bond drive. Other famous performers who appeared at the Trocadero in the 1940s were Chico Marx, Victor Borge, Rubinoff and his violin, and Donald Novis.

In February 1966 the Alta Corporation, headed by John Cavanaugh Sr. and including John Cavanaugh Jr., William Thornton, and E. T. Redman, purchased the lease on the El Cortez from the Bulasky brothers' Nathan Realty Company, which had operated the hotel since 1931. The Alta Corporation operated the El Cortez until December 30, 1966, when it closed the property and returned physical custody of the hotel to the trustees for the property owners, the Zetooney family and its heirs.

In 1972 Bill Fong, formerly of the New China Club, opened a bar and a Chinese restaurant at the El Cortez. The Bally Distributing Company was licensed to operate slot machines in the bar and restaurant area (there have been no table games in the El Cortez since 1948). Fong operated the restaurant and the bar until his death in 1982.

The El Cortez is still open for business at its original location.

Nev. St. Journal, 21 Mar. 31, 14 May 41, 17 May 41, 28 Jan. 44, 7 Nov. 44 (adv.), 1 Jan. 46 (adv.), 1 Jan. 66, 3 Feb. 66, 30 Dec. 66, 18 Oct. 73, 10 Feb. 77.

ELDORADO HOTEL-CASINO

345 North Virginia Street; licensed since May 1, 1973, as a full casino.

In July 1972 plans were announced for a new Reno luxury hotel to be called the Eldorado. The principals in the eleven-story hotel were William Carano, George Siri, George Yori, Richard Stringham, Jerry Poncia, and Don Carano. Construction of the new hotel was to begin immediately, and tentative plans called for the facility to open in May 1973. The entire 300 block of

North Virginia Street was razed to make room for the new property. The businesses closed included Welsh's Bakery, the Little Waldorf, the Ace Coin Shop, Silver State Camera, the Reno Hotel, and Leo's Den.

In April 1973 the owners announced that George Siri would be the hotel manager and Richard Stringham his assistant. On May 16 the Nevada Gaming Commission approved Eldorado Associates—a limited partnership consisting of William Carano, Don Carano, George Siri, Richard Stringham, George Yori, and Jerry Poncia—for a gaming license. Herbert McCloskey was licensed as general manager of the hotel-casino, and Bob Goode was licensed as casino manager.

The Eldorado opened on May 24, 1973. A private reception for local dignitaries preceded the public opening. It had taken ten months to build the hotel-casino, and the cost was estimated to be about $6 million. Many experts predicted that the operation would fail because it was located north of the railroad tracks and away from the other downtown casinos.

The decor of the hotel was Spanish, with a gold, black, and brown color scheme carried throughout the property. The casino opened with two hundred slots, one keno game, and fifteen table games. Other amenities included a twenty-four-hour coffee shop seating 150 people and a dinner house seating 80 people. The hotel had 272 guest rooms and six suites. The opening entertainment at the stage bar was Lisa Dimio.

In August 1973 William DiCristina was named hotel manager. He had previously managed the Holiday Hotel, the Arlington Plaza, and since 1971, the Mapes Hotel. DiCristina stayed with the Eldorado until 1978, and in 1989 he returned as an executive hotel host. He remained in that position until his death in March 1995.

Also in August 1973 several changes were made in the ownership of the Eldorado. George Siri and George Yori sold their percentages, and Lud Corraro and Hubert McCloskey became owners. Richard Stringham sold his shares soon afterward.

In 1978 the Eldorado expanded to include 411 hotel rooms, thirty-one table games, five hundred slot machines, and two keno games.

Also in 1978 Al Lazzarone was named casino manager of the Eldorado. He had previously worked for Harolds Club for twenty-nine years. Prior to Lazzarone's appointment, several other former Harolds Club employees had been hired by the Eldorado. They included Danny Hill, Bob Coonradt, Don Lunceford, Mike Rowe, Ron Bissette, and Jorge Valdez. All of them served in key positions at the Eldorado in the 1970s and 1980s. They were joined in the 1980s by Jerry Sicka and Glen Botorff, two more longtime Harolds Club employees.

Another major management change occurred in April 1979, when Homer Pope was named slot manager. Pope had worked for Harolds Club for twenty-nine years and was a slot manager at the MGM Hotel-Casino when it opened in 1978.

History was made in September 1980 when the Eldorado paid Reno's first $50,000 keno ticket. The Nugget in Sparks had previously paid two $50,000 tickets, but the Eldorado's was the first paid in Reno.

In August 1985 the Eldorado opened a $30-million expansion. The new 20,000-square-foot casino designed by architect Jerry Poncia doubled the Eldorado's gaming area and created a block-long casino. Another keno lounge, five hundred more slot machines, and thirty more table games were added. The expansion had dark oak beamed-and-mirrored ceilings that blended with the existing casino. New escalators led up to a 350-seat buffet, the Market Place, which was brightly decorated with four giant skylights and sixty-one photographs of marketplaces around the world. A million-dollar stainless-steel kitchen supplied the buffet. (In 1995 the Market Place was replaced by a new six-hundred-seat buffet, the Chef's Pavilion.)

When the expansion was completed in 1985, the Eldorado had fifty table games, one thousand slots, and three keno lounges. A race and sports book also opened. A new hotel tower gave the Eldorado a total of 811 hotel rooms.

In 1993 the Eldorado opened a new ten-story, seven-hundred-space parking garage and announced a joint venture with Circus Circus called Project C. A contest held in 1994 produced the name of the new facility—the Silver Legacy—which opened on July 28, 1995. Skyways connecting the Silver Legacy with Circus Circus to the north and the Eldorado to the south make the three casinos seem like one giant property. In May 1997 the five-hundred-seat Eldorado showroom opened, featuring the Broadway musical *Smokey Joe's Cafe*.

Currently the Eldorado covers a full city block from North Virginia Street to Sierra Street between Third and Fourth Streets. The hotel has risen to twenty-five stories and has 817 rooms or suites, eight restaurants, 81,000 square feet of casino space, two thousand slot machines, and ninety table games.

Nev. St. Journal, 18 July 72 (photos), 29 Apr. 73, 17 May 73, 24 May 73 (photo), 25 May 73, 2 Aug. 73 (photo), 16 Aug. 73, 27 Aug. 74, 27 Aug. 78 (photo), 29 Apr. 79, 10 Sept. 80.

ELITE CIGAR STORE
2 East Commercial Row; licensed from May 5 to December 1931 for poker, craps, and 21.

The Elite Cigar Store opened a stud poker game on May 5, 1931, a craps game on May 22, and a 21 game on May 25. The licenses were not renewed in 1932.

The site of the Elite Cigar Store is now part of Harolds Club.

ELITE CLUB
219 East Douglas Alley; licensed from May 13, 1949, to June 24, 1952, for craps, keno, and poker.

The Elite Club was more a bar than a casino. Various licensees had games and slots in the club during its three-year history. The first person licensed was Ed Jackson for a craps game in May 1949, and a few weeks later Loren Buechler was licensed for seven slot machines. In December 1950 Buechler was joined on the license by Willie Clark and James Taylor. In 1951 Buechler was licensed for one craps game, seven slot machines, and one poker game.

In June 1952 the business was destroyed by fire. Buechler applied for a license at another location, but it was never granted.

The site of the Elite Club is now part of Harrah's parking garage.

Nev. St. Journal, 12 Apr. 49, 27 Apr. 49, 25 May 49, 14 Dec. 50, 28 Mar. 51, 23 Oct. 51, 14 Nov. 51, 24 June 52.

ELITE TANGO CLUB
238 North Virginia Street; licensed from January 6 to April 1, 1935, for tango only.

The Elite Tango Club was licensed for tango (bingo) only early in 1935. Other bingo games were operated at the same location during the latter 1930s. The site is now part of Harolds Club.

ELITE TURF CLUB
208 North Center Street; licensed from December 3, 1957, to May 2, 1961, for a race book.

Opened in December 1957, the Elite Turf Club was owned by Carl Dowler and managed by Harry Eccles. It was sold to A. L. Cohen and Phil Rosenburg in 1960. On May 4, 1961, the club was closed because it had been accepting bets from outside of the club (a violation of Nevada state law). The site is now part of Harrah's Club on the west side of Center Street.

Nev. St. Journal, 26 Dec. 57 (adv.), 4 May 61.

EL MOROCCO
2999 South Virginia Street; licensed for six months in 1947 for a craps game and a 21 game.

The El Morocco was a bar with entertainment and dancing, and was considered one of the "hot spots" of Reno. It was owned by Joe and Sue Harris.

The site is currently occupied by the European Fitness Center.

Nev. St. Journal, 8 May 46, 4 July 46 (adv.), 19 Jan. 47.

EL RANCHO BAR
3310 South Virginia Street; licensed from September 17, 1954, to August 1956 for slots and 21.

The El Rancho was a bar located in what were the outskirts of town in the 1950s. The club had a piano bar and featured small entertainment groups. Harold W. Smith (no relation to the Smiths of Harolds Club) was the licensee. The site is now occupied by Carl's Bar.

Nev. St. Journal, 30 June 55.

ERLICH, SAM
Sam Erlich managed the Club Fortune in the late 1930s and early 1940s. After serving in World War II, he returned to Reno in 1945 and again became manager of the Club Fortune. He was licensed in January 1946, along with George Johnson and Harry Short, at the Bar of Music on North Center Street. Six months later, in July 1946, they sold the Bar of Music to Joseph Skoff for $150,000.

Sam Erlich committed suicide in May

Riverside Hotel casino employees in 1938. Left to right: Eddie Gersich, unknown, Clarence Ehmke, Sam Erlich. Courtesy of William Pettite.

1947, after a long illness. He was forty-five years old at the time of his death.

Nev. St. Journal, 16 Jan. 46, 11 July 46, 25 May 47 (obit.).

ESQUIRE CLUB

16 West Second Street; licensed in 1951 and 1952 for thirty-five slots and one 21 game.

The Esquire Club was primarily a bar, a local "watering hole" popular with casino workers and sports fans. This location was formerly occupied by John's Bar and the Stork Club.

Tom Lawson was granted a cabaret license and a gaming license for thirty-five slots on July 25, 1951, and the Esquire opened the next afternoon. In August 1951 Lawson added a 21 game to his license. His partners in the operation were Roy White and Eddie Gersich.

The site of the Esquire Club is now part of the Pioneer Gift Shop.

Nev. St. Journal, 25 July 51, 26 July 51, 30 Aug. 51, 24 July 52, 27 Dec. 52.

EUGENE'S

2955 South Virginia Street; licensed from June 26, 1944, to 1953 for slots, 21, and roulette.

Eugene's was one of Reno's finest restaurants for many years. Gaming was added to the property to entertain the customers. The business was long owned by Joe Patrucco and Gilbert Yasserot. Another longtime owner and operator was Walter Zahnd, whose wife, Pauline, was a dealer at Harolds Club for many years.

In December 1995 the building that had housed Eugene's for so many years and was later operated as the Hacienda Del Sol was sold to the Peppermill Casino. The building was razed, and the land where the building stood became part of the Peppermill parking lot.

Nev. St. Journal, 30 June 46.

FAGAN, VINCE

Vince Fagan, a native of New York City, came to Reno in 1946. He was a pit boss and shift manager at several casinos, among them the Palace, the Cal-Neva, the Primadonna, and the Mapes.

Dan Fagan, Vince's brother, also came from New York and was employed at the Nevada Club for almost forty years.

Nev. St. Journal, 26 June 76 (obit.).

FAN TAN CLUB

143 West Third Street; licensed in 1967 for slots, 21, keno, pan, fan-tan, and pai-gow.

In May 1967 the State of Nevada licensed Harold Wyatt, formerly associated with San Francisco nightclubs, and John Burton, a Menlo Park securities trader, to operate the Fan Tan Club. The club was licensed for one keno game, two pai-gow games, one fan-tan game, and twenty slots.

The club opened on June 5, 1967, but closed shortly thereafter. The site is now a vacant building.

Nev. St. Journal, 24 May 67, 5 June 67.

FARRIS, HOWARD

Howard Farris was born in Minneapolis in 1902. He moved to Casper, Wyoming, at an early age and came to Reno in the 1930s. His first employer was the Palace Club.

After World War II, Farris worked at the Bonanza Club and Harrah's before being licensed in 1948 and 1949 as a co-owner, along with Warren Nelson, at the Waldorf Club.

In 1953 Howard Farris and twelve other people leased the Palace Club for ten years. Farris, Harry Weitz, and Jack Guffey were licensed as co-owners and shift managers of the casino. About the same time, Farris was also licensed as a co-owner of the Nevada Turf Club. He became a co-owner of the Tahoe Palace in 1956.

In 1962 Farris was licensed with Leon Nightingale, Warren Nelson, Jack Douglass, Ad Tolen, and John Cavanaugh as a co-owner of the Club Cal-Neva. In February 1978 Farris was licensed as a co-owner of the Comstock Hotel-Casino.

Howard Farris died on July 17, 1985. He was still a co-owner of the Club Cal-Neva at the time of his death.

Nev. St. Journal, 11 Dec. 53, 20 June 56, 29 June 56, 29 Mar. 62, 21 Mar. 69, 1 Feb. 78.

FASCINATION CLUB

230 North Virginia Street; licensed from June 24 to September 24, 1935, for keno (bingo) only.

The Fascination was a small club that featured bingo for a few months in 1935. The location later became known as Murray's Club. The site is now part of the Nevada Club.

FITZGERALD, LINCOLN

Lincoln Fitzgerald was born on October 21, 1892. He came to Reno in 1945 from Macomb County, Michigan, with his longtime partner, Dan Sullivan. Before coming to Reno, the two men had operated a large gambling club in Macomb County, just outside Detroit, where the famed Purple Gang was centered.

In Reno, Fitzgerald, Sullivan, Ruby Mathis, and Mert Wertheimer entered a partnership with Harry and Ed Robbins, who were operating a club called Robbin's Nevada Club. In March 1946 the name was shortened to the Nevada Club.

In August 1946 Sullivan and Fitzgerald were named in a fugitive-from-justice case, charged with bribing public officials in Michigan on several dates between August 1, 1940, and August 1, 1946. They were sent to Michigan in August 1948 to face the illegal gambling charge (the bribery charges had been dropped). They were found guilty and fined $52,000. After paying the fine, they were released and returned to Reno to continue operating the Nevada Club. Sullivan acted as general manager and Fitzgerald was the casino manager. When Sullivan died in 1956, Fitzgerald became sole owner of the club.

On November 19, 1949, Fitzgerald was ambushed and shot twice with a shotgun at his residence on 123 Mark Twain Drive. "Fitz," who was fifty-seven when he was shot, was very close to death and did not fully recover until April 1950. The attack left him slightly crippled, and he walked with a limp for the rest of his life. He also suffered damage to his liver and one kidney. His assailant(s) were never found, and it was said that Fitzgerald requested that investigations into his ambush be curtailed.

After the ambush, Fitzgerald made the Nevada Club his residence. For many years, he seldom left the club, and it was only in the last years of his life that he made many appearances outside of the Nevada Club. His actions were—by choice and design—the complete opposite of his next-door neighbor, "Pappy" Smith. Only their style of dress was somewhat similar. "Fitz," like "Pappy," almost always wore a white shirt, necktie, and suspenders, and his curly hair and gold-rimmed glasses gave him an almost cherubic image. Robbins Cahill, chairman of Nevada's first Tax Board, said that Fitzgerald "was an individual character all his own. He knew the gaming business and he ran a good gaming operation."

Fitzgerald was the image of an old-time casino boss. He ruled the Nevada Club like a lord, with his strong-willed—yet often compassionate—wife, Meta, by his side. He believed in a hands-on management style, and for many years, no one was hired at the Nevada Club without being personally interviewed by "The Boss" himself. Known as a strict, demanding employer, Fitzgerald quickly expressed his displeasure with poor service or food. His abhorrence of stale pastries made the Nevada Club's dessert shelves among the freshest in town. However, his employees apparently respected him. A porter at the club was quoted as saying, "It's different at his club. All the help works together."

In 1970 Fitzgerald was singled out by Nevada Gaming Control Board member Keith Campbell, who commented that "the Nevada Club and the Nevada Lodge had incurred no control violations in over 25 years and they were both well run operations."

In 1957 Fitzgerald purchased the Biltmore Lodge at North Lake Tahoe. He renamed it the Nevada Lodge and operated it until his death. From 1969 to 1974, he also owned the Silver Dollar Club, which later became part of Fitzgeralds Casino-Hotel.

In December 1974 Fitzgerald began construction of his "monument," Fitzgeralds Casino-Hotel. The property was opened for business on Memorial Day weekend, 1976.

Fitzgerald was named to the Nevada Gambler's Hall of Fame during the fiftieth anniversary of legalized gambling in 1981. He was unable to attend the ceremonies because of poor health.

Lincoln Fitzgerald died on April 18, 1981, in a Reno hospital. He had been in declining health for some time and had been hospitalized since March 31. He was eighty-eight years old at the time of his death.

Nev. St. Journal, 15 Feb. 62, 10 Sept. 70, 30 Apr. 76.

FITZGERALDS CASINO-HOTEL

255 North Virginia Street (corner of South Virginia and Commercial Row); licensed since May 1976 as a full casino.

In early 1964 Lincoln Fitzgerald started purchasing property on the half block bounded by Commercial Row, Sierra Street, Douglas Alley, and Virginia Street. Some of the businesses he purchased were the Blue Bird Hotel at 12 West Commercial Row, Cannan's Drug Store at 14 West Commercial Row, the Stag Inn at 265 North Virginia Street, and the Silver Dollar Club at 261 North Virginia Street. Fitzgerald operated the Silver Dollar Club as a casino from 1965 until 1974, when the building was razed. In December 1974 Fitzgerald broke ground at Commercial Row and Virginia Street and announced plans for a $12-million hotel-casino. He said the sixteen-story, 347-room hotel would be completed by June 1976. By January 1976 the outer shell of the building was completed, and the McKenzie Construction Company started on the interior of the building and the furnishings.

In April 1976 the Gaming Commission licensed Fitzgeralds Casino-Hotel for thirty-five table games, two keno games, and one thousand slot machines. The structure was tentatively scheduled to open on May 24. Lincoln Fitzgerald and his wife, Meta, would own 99.9 percent, and Carlton Konarske, Mrs. Fitzgerald's brother, would own the remainder.

Fitzgerald, who was known in the industry for his high standards, knew exactly what he wanted. His assistant hotel manager, Jim Mack, stated before the opening, "We're going to have one hell of a hotel and casino, and it's going to be first class. Mr. Fitzgerald wants it done right, and by God we're going to do it right." The same standards were applied to employees for the new facility. According to Mack, "Fitzgerald has been in the business long enough that he knows what he wants. He will look for people in the tradition he wants to start at the new hotel. He looks for dependabil-

Fitzgeralds Casino-Hotel towering over Virginia Street, 1982. Author's collection.

ity and honesty, of course." Fitzgerald intended his new operation to become a major attraction in Reno. "We intend to go nose to nose with Harrah's from the time we open our doors," Mack said.

On May 27, with no fanfare, Fitzgeralds Casino-Hotel opened. Actually, only the restaurant, Molly's Garden, and the casino were fully open, along with a few of the hotel rooms. The rest of the facility opened within a few months. Fitzgerald paid all the building costs of the $16-million structure out of his cash reserve.

After Fitzgerald's death in 1981, the property was operated by Meta Fitzgerald and Carlton Konarske until April 1, 1985. At that time, the Lincoln Management Corporation, headed by Phil Griffith, took over. Along with the management contract, the corporation obtained an option to buy the property from Meta Fitzgerald. It exercised the option on December 31, 1986. Records on file at the Washoe County Assessor's office showed a purchase price of $26.25 million. The property was appraised at $25.96 million. The records also indicated a down payment of only $750,000.

The property is currently operating at the same location with the same owners and is firmly established as one of the showplace hotel-casinos in the Reno area.

Nev. St. Journal, 11 Dec. 74, 14 Dec. 74 (photo), 2 Jan. 76 (photo), 15 Apr. 76, 20 Apr. 76, 24 Apr. 76, 29 May 76, 16 Mar. 87.

FLAMINGO HILTON
255 North Sierra Street; licensed since January 1, 1982, as a full casino.

The property originally opened as the Sahara Reno on July 1, 1978. The Sahara Reno was sold to the Hilton Corporation on December 29, 1981, and became known as the Reno Hilton at that time. The property, twenty-one stories high and 604 rooms, became known as the Flamingo Hilton on July 1, 1989. The property is still operating as the Flamingo Hilton.

FLORENTINE HOTEL-CASINO
Corner of West Fifth and North Sierra Streets; never licensed.

The Florentine was a dream that started in 1976. During an unprecedented period of hotel-casino growth in Reno, Lee DeLauer announced plans in November 1976 for a 112-room hotel-casino. After the initial groundbreaking and the beginning of construction, a legal problem over the exchange of land with the Drake Taxi Cab Corporation stalled the project. Construction did not resume until August 1977. Revised plans called for the property to have 192 rooms.

In November 1977 DeLauer announced that plans for the project had been scrapped and the site would be turned into a high-rise one-thousand-space parking garage for the Circus Circus Hotel-Casino.

Nev. St. Journal, 11 Nov. 76, 21 Aug. 77 (photo), 10 Nov. 77.

FONG, BEW "BILL"
Bill Fong was born on August 30, 1920, in Canton, China, and came to the United States in the late 1930s. In 1952 he came to Reno from Oakland. He purchased the old Palm Cafe at the corner of Lake Street and Commercial Row and reopened it as the New China Club, operating it for almost twenty years, from August 1952 to December 31, 1971.

Fong's New China Club served African American and Asian customers. Fong operated the first legal fan-tan and pai-gow games in the state. He also established the first local scholarships for African American students. He sent several students to the University of Nevada, including then national high-jump champion Otis Burrell. Fong also sponsored golf tournaments and other events that attracted several nationally known black athletes, including Jesse Owens and Joe Louis.

One year after closing the New China Club, Bill Fong opened a Chinese restaurant in the El Cortez Hotel. There were slot machines on the property but no table games.

Fong, a high-profile extrovert, was very active in promoting gaming in the entire Reno area, rather than only at the New China Club. He also founded and served as the first president of the Nevada Casino Association. He loved to gamble, and in his earlier days in Reno he was often seen betting the table limits in various casinos around town.

Bill Fong died in a local hospital on April 11, 1982, after a long illness.

Nev. St. Journal, 6 Aug. 52, 7 Aug. 52, 12 Jan. 72, 3 Dec. 72.

FONTANA, AL
Al Fontana was born in Imlay, Nevada, and moved to Lovelock at an early age. He was a professional boxer in his youth.

Fontana came to Reno in the middle 1930s. His first job was at Colbrandt's Flamingo, where he worked for another Lovelock man, Virgil Smith. After World War II, he went to work at Harrah's Club as a shift manager and later became club manager. He closed out his gaming career at Harolds Club in the late 1960s.

Fontana died on December 14, 1971. He was fifty-seven.

Nev. St. Journal, 25 Dec. 71 (obit.).

FRANCE (FRANCELLINI), PAT
Pat France was born in Clairton, Pennsylvania, on March 27, 1921. He came to Reno in 1946 to play football for the University of Nevada, and after his college days were over he stayed in the Reno–Lake Tahoe area and spent a lifetime in the gaming industry.

France's first job in gaming was at Harrah's Club in Reno, but he transferred to Harrah's Lake Tahoe when Bill Harrah opened his club there. France's early expertise was in the cashier's cage and in finances, but he worked his way up through the ranks and eventually served as club manager of Harrah's Tahoe. Later, France was appointed vice-president of entertainment, a position he filled for six years before resigning in 1971 to become entertainment director of the Sahara Tahoe. He served in this role for ten years and was instrumental in attracting many big-name acts to the Lake Tahoe area.

When he was cashier manager, France hired and trained many young men who went on to become club managers and chief executive officers of Harrah's Club and other casinos. Among them were Lloyd

Dyer, Holmes Hendricksen, Lowell Hendricksen, Dennis Small, and Doyle Mathia. Pat France died on May 22, 1996.

Nev. St. Journal, 1 Sept. 68, 11 Aug. 71.

FRANKOVICH, LEE

Lee Frankovich came to Reno from the Commercial Hotel in Elko in 1956 to become general manager of the Riverside Hotel. Over the next several years, he worked as general manager and/or hotel manager at the Riverside Hotel (twice), the Holiday Hotel (twice), the Bal Tabarin at Lake Tahoe, the Sparks Nugget, and the Eldorado Hotel and Casino. He was also a co-owner of the Holiday Hotel on two different occasions and was employed by Harrah's in the late 1950s.

In 1969 Frankovich owned and operated Lee's Hofbrau House at 136 North Virginia Street. He was licensed for twenty slot machines, but when he applied to be licensed for table games he was denied—not as a reflection on him or his operation but because Reno's red-line law prohibited the operation of a casino with fewer than one hundred hotel rooms outside an imaginary red line drawn around the heart of downtown Reno.

Frankovich is retired and living in Reno.

Nev. St. Journal, 3 Jan. 56, 21 July 57, 10 May 60, 1 June 60, 12 Aug. 62, 16 Aug. 67, 27 Oct. 67, 12 Jan. 68, 14 June 69, 24 June 69.

FRANKS, DR. ROBERT

Dr. Robert Franks headed a seven-man group, including James Contratto, who purchased the Cal-Neva from the Sanford Adler group in November 1955. The Franks group operated the Cal-Neva until September 1961.

In December 1959 Franks began buying into the Riverside Hotel. He became majority owner in 1960 when he purchased Virgil Smith's percentage. Franks eventually owned 64 percent of the Riverside. He sold all but 5 percent of his interest in November 1960, and in 1961 he completely divested himself of his holdings in the Riverside. He was never licensed in Reno again.

Nev. St. Journal, 26 Nov. 55, 20 Apr. 60.

FREDDY'S LAIR

136 North Center Street; licensed by the City of Reno, but never licensed by the state.

Freddy's Lair was previously known as the Bar of Music and Buddy Baer's. Buddy Baer, former heavyweight boxer, and Fred Cullincini purchased the Bar of Music from Cliff Judd in 1950. The property was granted a city gaming license in March 1950 and opened as Buddy Baer's. In January 1951 Fred Cullincini was granted a city gaming license and named the property Freddy's Lair, but the club did not open. In February 1951 Cullincini sued Herman and Marge Lilienthal for failure to pay their share ($12,000) of the $18,500 purchase price.

In July 1951, and again in October, the state denied George "Frenchy" Perry a gaming license at Freddy's Lair. The property remained closed until September 1952, when it was opened as O'Brien's Corner, owned and operated by Sam O'Brien.

The former location of Freddy's Lair is now part of the Cal-Neva parking garage on the east side of Center Street.

Nev. St. Journal, 23 Jan. 51, 28 Feb. 51, 29 July 51, 19 Oct. 51, 30 Nov. 52.

FRISCO CLUB

207 North Center Street; licensed from May 13, 1951, to November 30, 1952, for slots, 21, craps, and roulette.

In March 1951 the S&K Corporation (doing business as the Bonanza Club) was granted a gaming license by the state. The S&K Corporation's partners were William Sullivan and Dan Kilbride from Bozeman, Montana. In the next few months, Jack Sparkman and N. B. Ellis became stockholders in the corporation. The S&K Corporation took over the Bonanza Club, which had been closed since late 1950. It was licensed for forty slots, one 21 game, one craps game, and one roulette game in April 1951.

The club was closed for a short time, and almost $5,000 were spent remodeling and redecorating the premises. On August 30, 1951, the Frisco Club, "The Golden Gate of Reno," opened with well-known Reno gambler "Back Line Joe" Snyder as manager.

The club had only been open for two weeks when it drew the wrath of the Nevada Gaming Commission. At a hearing attended by Joe Snyder, who stated that he was the manager and a small percentage owner, the Frisco Club was fined $750 for operating four games instead of the three that it was licensed for. The major owners, William Sullivan and Dan Kilbride, did not attend the hearing.

On October 30, 1951, Charles Stebbins and Eliza Tracy were licensed as stockholders of the S&K Corporation and named as operators of the Frisco Club. Joe Snyder was terminated.

In the spring of 1952, the Frisco Club opened the Bonanza Room. Paul Dano, formerly of the Palmer House in Chicago and the Riverside Hotel in Reno, was named the chef. The "three friendly bartenders" at the stage bar were well-known local favorites Jim McGowan, Bill Bostwick, and Sam Francovich.

In May 1952 the S&K Corporation filed for reorganization with J. W. Russell as licensee and Eliza Tracy as co-owner. They were licensed for twenty slot machines, one pan game, and two 21 games.

The Frisco Club was closed in November 1952. In February 1953 Harrah's Club purchased the property and reopened it as Harrah's Bingo Parlor. It operated as a bingo parlor until it was destroyed by the Golden Hotel fire in 1962.

The former location of the Frisco Club is now part of Harrah's on the west side of Center Street, between Second Street and Douglas Alley.

Nev. St. Journal, 24 Aug. 51 (adv.), 25 Aug. 51, 30 Aug. 51 (adv.), 14 Sept. 51, 30 Oct. 51, 14 Nov. 51, 7 Mar. 52 (adv.), 6 Apr. 52, 1 July 52, 30 Nov. 52, 9 Jan. 53.

FRONTIER CLUB

220 North Virginia Street; licensed from February 1946 to November 1956 as a full casino.

The Frontier Club was licensed for eleven table games and thirty slot machines in February 1946. In May 1946 a grand opening was held for "Reno's newest and finest casino and bar—featuring race horse keno. Also featuring a horse book managed by

Jerry Poncia." Partners in the Frontier Club were the Hobson brothers, Joe and Pick, Marion Hicks, Dub McClanahan, George Sedlow, Dave Callahan, and Cliff Jones. The Hobsons took over complete ownership of the operation in 1947 when Hicks moved to Las Vegas to take over the Thunderbird Hotel operation. The logo of the Frontier Club was a cowboy on a bucking red bronco, and one of its slogans was "Look for the Frontier Club at the sign of the pitching red horse." The bucking red bronco was also featured on the reels of the club's slot machines.

In July 1946 Fred Murrill, a nightclub operator from Dallas, came to the Frontier to play dice. The manager on duty, Dave Callahan, gave Murrill unprecedented high limits on the craps table. On the point of four, Callahan okayed Murrill for a flat bet of $23,000 with $46,000 odds. The total payoff on the winning wager was $115,000. Murrill played for several hours and had several other winning wagers, but the $115,000 payoff was the largest of the evening. Murrill gave the dealers over $24,000 in tips. The Frontier did not have the cash to pay Murrill his winnings that night, so in August F. L. (Dub) McClanahan flew to Dallas and paid Murrill $141,375, which was the balance owed to him from his July winning streak.

When the Frontier was opened in 1946, it had an elaborate and expensive glass-brick front. In 1948 the Frontier closed briefly, and the glass brick was removed and replaced by several doors. The Frontier also installed a slot-machine arcade with thirty slot machines. Virgil Smith, a longtime Reno gambler, was licensed for the slot machines, and he operated them on a lease (or concession) basis. In July 1948 the Frontier opened a bingo salon, and for the next six years the Frontier's gaming consisted mainly of slots and bingo.

In 1954 Pick Hobson was licensed for a keno game at the Frontier, and James Brady was named keno manager.

On November 29, 1956, Harrah's purchased the Frontier Club for a rumored price of over $500,000. The club closed, putting 150 employees out of work. When the wall separating the two clubs was re-moved, Harrah's nearly doubled its former size.

When the Frontier closed, it had two craps tables, four 21 games, one roulette table, one keno game, and 172 slot machines. One of the conditions of the sale was that Pick Hobson was not allowed to open another gambling casino for at least seven years. This stipulation was intended to prevent any of Hobson's many loyal customers from following him to a new location.

The site of the Frontier Club is on the north end of Harrah's Casino on the east side of Virginia Street, between Second Street and Douglas Alley.

Nev. St. Journal, 15 Feb. 46, 29 May 46 (adv.), 25 June 46, 12 July 46, 1 Aug. 46, 13 Feb. 48, 25 Feb. 48, 3 July 48 (adv.), 14 July 54, 18 Dec. 54 (adv.), 1 July 55, 29 Nov. 56.

FRONTIER SALOON

Located in Lincoln Alley; licensed from November 15, 1950, to May 31, 1952, for slots and 21.

The Frontier Saloon was a section of the Frontier Club that was licensed separately for a short time in the early 1950s. The site is now part of Harrah's Club.

G

GASTANAGA, EUGENE, JAKE, AND JOSE

The Gastanagas were three of the investors in the original Ponderosa Hotel-Casino in 1966. They were also the owners of the Eagle Thrifty drug and grocery chain and operated a slot-machine route for many years in Reno. They later sold the Eagle Thrifty stores to the Raley's grocery chain.

Eugene and Segundo "Jake" were brothers, and Jose was their nephew. They were investors more than operators, but they worked actively with their management teams. Jake died shortly after the Gastanagas sold out of the Ponderosa in 1969. Jose was a licensed co-owner of the Silver Spur Casino as well as the Ponderosa. Eugene was a licensed co-owner of the Onslow Hotel-Casino and is currently (1999) licensed as a co-owner of the Crystal Bay Club and the Tahoe Biltmore.

Nev. St. Journal, 3 Nov. 66, 20 June 68, 11 Dec. 69, 9 June 77.

GEE, T. F.

Known simply as "Mr. Gee" to thousands of Renoites, he was one of the most famous chefs in early Reno gaming history, and his name alone would guarantee business in a casino or restaurant. A graduate of the University of California at Berkeley, Gee turned from engineering to cookery. He started his Reno career at the Dog House in 1937, and over the years he owned and/or worked at the Tropics, the Dog House, the Town House, the Monaco, and the Chinese Pagoda in Sparks and in Reno.

Nev. St. Journal, 29 Apr. 49, 20 Dec. 62.

GEM

275 North Virginia Street; licensed for slots and a race book from 1977 to 1978; licensed for slots and 21 in 1987 and 1988.

The Gem, located at the former site of a casino known as Poor Pete's, was granted a nonrestricted slot license in February 1977. Richard Drake was the licensee. In August 1977 John Thompson was licensed as sportsbook manager, and Frank Mendietta was licensed as general manager.

The former location of the Gem is currently the site of Fitzgeralds personnel office.

Nev. St. Journal, 19 Feb. 77, 14 Aug. 77.

GOLD DUST EAST CASINO (SOMETIMES CALLED THE GOLD DUST, DOWNTOWN)

34 West Second Street (corner of Sierra and Second Streets); licensed as a full casino from July 1, 1976, to 1983.

In March 1976 John Cavanaugh Jr. applied for and was granted a city gaming license. In 1976 the City of Reno was still enforcing the red-line law (an ordinance requiring a gaming casino to have 100 hotel rooms), and in order for Cavanaugh to be granted a gaming license he had to combine the Royal Hotel and the Parkway Hotel. This combination gave him a total of 101 hotel rooms, which made him eligible for unlimited gaming. At the time, many local businessmen claimed that some of the 101 rooms were only spaces with flimsy walls erected for the sole purpose of beating the red-line law. True or not, Cavanaugh was licensed by the city, and in May 1976 the state granted a gaming license to the Gold Dust Corporation.

The corporation consisted of John Cavanaugh Jr. as president and director, Robert Hall as vice-president, and Margery Cavanaugh as secretary-treasurer. Frank Sorce was approved as general manager and casino manager with 4 percent of the annual net income, less debt service.

The Gold Dust opened on July 1, 1976. The casino had two levels and featured four hundred slot machines, twelve table games, a keno game, and a twenty-four-hour food and beverage operation. The exterior combined outdoor illumination with sculptured steel, and the exterior walls, down to street level, were tiled in antique gold.

During its short existence, the Gold Dust frequently changed the layout of the casino as well as its upper-level management. Some of the general managers were Al Gomes in 1977, Dennis Small in 1979, and Darl Voss in 1980. Some of the casino managers were John McClure in 1977 and Ted Kelty in 1979.

The Gold Dust had two major expansions, one in 1978 and another in 1979. After the 1979 expansion, the casino offered live entertainment and the only Mexican restaurant in downtown Reno, El Sombrero.

The Gold Dust closed in 1982, and in 1987 the Riverboat Corporation bought the property. The casino was torn down in November 1987 and the site cleared for construction of the Riverboat Hotel-Casino. The Riverboat was licensed in April 1988 with the Douglass brothers, William, David, Daniel, and John, as co-owners and executives of the new company and Ralph Albright as co-owner and general manager.

The Riverboat Hotel-Casino operated at the former location of the Gold Dust East until late 1998. *(See Addendum 2)*

Nev. St. Journal, 11 Mar. 76, 21 May 76, 28 June 76, 12 May 77, 25 Dec. 77 (photo), 30 June 78, 27 May 79 (photo), 10 Aug. 79, 20 Apr. 80, 25 Nov. 87, 7 Apr. 88.

GOLD DUST WEST CASINO

444 North Vine Street (corner of Vine and Fourth Streets); licensed in July 1977 for a full casino; currently operating as a slots-only casino.

In March 1976 John Cavanaugh Jr. announced his plans for a casino complex in northwest Reno. The property involved was bounded by Vine and Washington Streets between Fourth and Fifth Streets. On July 21, 1977, the Gaming Commission licensed the Gold Dust West for operation with John Cavanaugh Jr. as 100-percent owner, Robert Hall as vice-president, Tim Cope as controller, and Robert Heller as casino manager.

When the Gold Dust West opened in late July, the entertainment featured the well-known singing group the Mike Curb Congregation.

In 1981 Chuck Kruse was appointed general manager and Dick Piper was named casino manager.

In 1999, the property is brightly painted in shades of orange, red, yellow, and blue. The casino is a popular local slot-machine establishment specializing in video poker slots. Lynne Keller, the casino's executive vice-president, has been with the Gold Dust West since it opened. For the last several years, Cavanaugh, in a show of good will and generosity, has offered free dinners to all local senior citizens on major holidays such as Christmas and Thanksgiving.

Nev. St. Journal, 25 May 76, 14 July 77.

GOLDEN GATE CLUB
241 North Virginia Street; never licensed.

On October 1, 1951, Ernie Primm began evicting tenants from 241 North Virginia Street. The building had formerly housed the Victory Coffee Shop, and at this time Morgan Smith Jewelers and the Lincoln Apartments were located on the property.

Primm, who had paid $100,000 for the building, applied to the Reno City Council for a gaming license for thirty slot machines, two roulette wheels, two craps games, and four 21 games. The gaming application was filed under the name Golden Gate Club. The City Council denied the application because it wanted no gambling on the west side of Virginia Street between the railroad tracks and the Truckee River. In February 1952 Primm sued the city because of the license denial. In March he applied for a $35,000 building permit on the property, and in May he opened the Cafe Primadonna. He still had no gaming license.

In August Primm applied to the state for a gaming license, but the state deferred action on the application. In January 1953 the state supreme court ruled against Primm and stated that the City Council had the right to deny him a gaming license because of the location of his property.

It wasn't until July 1, 1955, that Primm was finally granted a gaming license. At that time he opened the Primadonna Club at this location.

The site is now part of the Reno Flamingo Hilton on the west side of Virginia Street.

Nev. St. Journal, 30 Sept. 51, 9 Oct. 51, 19 Oct. 51, 23 Oct. 51, 8 Feb. 52, 8 Mar. 52, 21 May 52, 7 Aug. 52, 5 Sept. 52, 21 Jan. 53.

GOLDEN GULCH
34 East Second Street; licensed in 1964 for slots, chuck-a-luck, and wheel of fortune.

John Hickok was licensed by the City of Reno for eighteen slots, one wheel of fortune, and one chuck-a-luck game on April 23, 1964. The site of Hickok's Golden Gulch is now part of the Club Cal-Neva.

Nev. St. Journal, 10 Sept. 69.

GOLDEN GULCH
219 North Center Street; licensed from June 1947 to July 1948 for a full casino plus a horse race book and a bingo game.

In October 1946, when the Wingfield family sold the Golden Hotel to a group consisting of John Mueller, James Lloyd Sr., Norman Biltz, and Henry Bennett, the hotel had a gaming area that was then leased to the Brunswick Club. Early in 1947, James Lloyd Sr., managing director of the Golden Hotel, bought out the lease of the Brunswick Club, and on June 27, 1947, he opened the Golden Gulch Casino. The Golden Gulch was licensed for a bingo parlor, forty-seven slot machines, a keno game, and a horse race book. A roulette table was leased to and operated by Virgil Smith. The Golden Gulch also featured a bar, a restaurant, and showroom entertainment.

In June 1948 the Lloyd group sold the Golden Hotel and the Golden Gulch to Thomas Hull, who in turn leased it to his own corporation, the El Rancho Reno. Hull soon declared bankruptcy and was never licensed. The Lloyd group took the property back in January 1949. Lloyd retained the gaming license under the name of the Golden Hotel until the hotel was sold to Frank Hofues in 1952.

The former location of the Golden Gulch is now part of Harrah's Club on the west side of Center Street between Second Street and Douglas Alley.

GOLDEN HOTEL-CASINO/ GOLDEN BANK CASINO
219 North Center Street; licensed from 1935 to 1966 for a variety of games.

The Golden Hotel was built in 1906 by Frank Golden Sr., a Tonopah banking and mining man, as competition for the Riverside Hotel. The Wingfield bank chain was the lending company for the Golden Hotel, and when Frank Golden died in 1914, the Wingfield family took over ownership and operation of the Golden Hotel and thereby went into competition with themselves as owners of Reno's only other major hotel, the Riverside.

The Golden Hotel did not have a casino of its own until 1947. Prior to that date, certain areas of the hotel were leased out for gambling, and gamblers such as Virgil Smith, Bill Williams, Wayne Martin, and others operated table games and slot machines in the hotel's Golden Bar area in the middle and late 1930s. The bar was operated by Vic Patroni, and Del Hammond was licensed for gambling from June 26, 1935, to July 1, 1947.

In 1946 the Wingfield family decided to sell the Golden Hotel in order to finance the remodeling of the Riverside. The purchasers of the Golden Hotel, who paid $1.5 million in October 1946, were Norman Biltz, James Lloyd Sr., John Mueller, and Henry Bennett. In November 1946 Lloyd was named managing director of the Golden. His group was in charge of the hotel rooms only, because the first floor of the building was leased to the Brunswick Club and the Bank Club.

Early in 1947, Lloyd bought out the lease of the Brunswick Club, and in June he opened the Golden Gulch Casino at that location. It featured a bingo parlor, forty-seven slot machines, a keno game, a roulette table, a horse race book, and showroom entertainment.

In June 1948 the Golden Hotel was sold to Thomas Hull, a widely known hotel man, who in turn leased it to his own organization, the El Rancho Reno. Hull began an extensive remodeling program in July. In October the Golden Hotel opened its Golden Club Theater Restaurant, which featured red-and-white checkered tablecloths and a stage surrounded with old-time gilt-framed pictures and red plush curtains. The cost of the remodeling exceeded $300,000. By January 1949 Hull was gone from the Golden Hotel and the Lloyd group was back in control.

In February 1949 the Hull Hotel Corporation declared bankruptcy, but to Hull's credit he paid off all the creditors.

The Lloyd group continued to operate the Golden Hotel and to manage the showroom for the next three years. Some of the entertainers who appeared there included Hilo Hattie in January 1949, Liberace in December 1949, and Max Baer, Tennessee Ernie Ford, Guy Mitchell, and Cab Calloway in 1950 and 1951.

In February 1952 the Golden Hotel closed, and in March 1952 the Golden Hotel and the Bank Club were sold to Frank Hofues for "between five and six million dollars." Bill Graham, no longer in partnership with Jim McKay, negotiated a twenty-year lease with Frank Hofues for the newly created Golden Bank Casino. Graham and David High applied for the gaming license; Graham was okayed in April 1952, but High was deferred and later denied a gaming license. The sale of the Golden Bank was completed on May 3. Hofues paid $6 million, on terms that provided for $1.5 million down; promissory notes to Bill Graham and Jim McKay totaling $3.5 million; and promissory notes of $500,000 each to James Lloyd Sr. and David High.

On May 26, 1952, Bill Graham was licensed at the Bank Club for 272 slot machines, nine craps tables, four roulette wheels, eighteen 21 games, two faro games, one keno game, one pan game, and one cabaret. This licensing was slightly different from his original application in April 1952.

Hofues had spent $350,000 remodeling the Golden during the eleven weeks the hotel was closed. The entire appearance of the hotel was changed, and the Bank Club was refurbished and expanded to make it the largest casino in the world at that time, so far as floor space—40,000 square feet—on one level was concerned. Harolds Club had more total floor space, but it was on three floors. The Golden Bank Hotel-Casino had four hundred employees and the largest payroll in downtown Reno.

Opening the showroom on May 27,

1952, was well-known band leader Cab Calloway.

In January 1953 David High, who had never been granted a gaming license, withdrew from any association with the Golden Hotel.

In June 1953 John Drew applied for 25 percent of the Golden Bank for an investment of $100,000. He was said to have been an associate of Al Capone. After extensive questioning, he withdrew his application in September 1953. He reapplied in January 1954, and on April 2, 1954, he was licensed for 25 percent of the Golden Bank.

On February 6, 1954, Frank Hofues sold the Golden Hotel to James and William Tomerlin for $3.5 million. He had paid $6 million for the hotel only two years earlier. The sale had no effect on the gambling lease held by Bill Graham.

On June 28, 1954, the Golden Bank was licensed for twenty-nine table games (including two of the five faro games then operating in the state) and 360 slot machines—an increase of almost 100 slot machines from the original licensing two years earlier.

In December 1954 the state held hearings to look into reports that the Al Capone mob had taken control of the Golden Bank Club. Crime expert Virgil Peterson said that Lester Kruse, a former Al Capone mobster, was brought to the Golden Bank Club by John Drew and was employed there as a pit boss. However, the investigation was inconclusive and no further action was taken.

On December 1, 1955, William and James Tomerlin were granted a gaming license. They had bought the remaining seventeen years on the gaming lease from Bill Graham and John Drew for $425,000. This transaction effectively ended Graham's long Reno gaming career. The Tomerlins, along with twenty-five limited partners, were licensed for four bars, 289 slot machines, two craps games, one roulette game, six 21 games, one poker game, and two pan games. George Smilanick, longtime Reno gambler, was licensed as casino manager, and his pit floor managers included Dick Mackinaw, Ed Hughes, Ed "Swede" Oleson, Dom Stillian,

Jack Hoge, Andy Desimone, Sam Goodman, and Doc Ledford. Joe Munley was keno manager, and Percy Kelly was slot manager. During the change of ownership, the property was closed for seven days, from December 1 to December 7. It reopened with 250 employees.

One year later, on December 12, 1956, Dom Stillian was licensed as casino manager. A few months later, in April 1957, the Golden began a major remodeling program, which involved tearing down the brick wall on the west side of the hotel and replacing it with a forty-four-foot fully glassed entrance area topped by a large marquee.

In April 1959 the Tomerlin brothers proudly announced the opening of the Mardi Gras Show Lounge, which included the first sunken bar in Reno. In February 1961 they opened the Gay 90's Saloon and Gambling Hall, located at the corner of Lincoln and Douglas Alleys and featuring gaming as well as a bar.

Tragedy struck the Golden Hotel on April 3, 1962, when a disastrous fire completely destroyed the building. Six people died in the fire.

On May 25, 1962, the Tomerlins announced that construction of a new twenty-four-story hotel would begin the following week. William and James Tomerlin were licensed for 48 percent each, Dom Stillian was licensed for 4 percent, and Charles Welch was licensed as a corporate officer with no investment. The first phase of the new Golden opened on July 3, 1963, with a four-hundred-seat showroom, a two-hundred-seat show lounge, three bars, a casino, and a three-level garage, but no hotel rooms. Opening the Carnival Room was popular singer Buddy Greco. One year later, on July 1, 1964, the Golden opened its new five-hundred-seat Mardi Gras Theater Restaurant with a Barry Ashton production, *Playmates in Paris*. That opening concluded the first phase of the Golden's reconstruction.

The second phase was to have included a multistory hotel, a swimming pool, a cabana, and a convention hall, but before the second phase was completed, the Tomerlins ran into financial problems and halted construction. Bill Harrah was quick to see the opportunity to purchase the property, and on March 29, 1966, Harrah's Club took possession. The Golden Hotel closed the same day, and three hundred employees were put out of work.

Harrah's reopened the property on June 20, 1966. The former location of the Golden Hotel is now part of Harrah's Hotel-Casino on the west side of Center Street between Second Street and Douglas Alley.

Nev. St. Journal, 8 Oct. 46, 16 Nov. 46, 15 June 47, 17 June 47, 27 June 47, 15 July 47, 15 Oct. 47, 19 June 48, 20 June 48, 22 June 48, 16 July 48, 18 July 48, 1 Oct. 48, 8 Oct. 48 (adv.), 13 Jan. 49 (adv.), 14 Jan. 49, 8 Feb. 49, 4 Dec. 49 (adv.), 5 Jan. 52, 6 Jan. 52 (photo), 23 Feb. 52, 11 Mar. 52, 5 Apr. 52, 8 Apr. 52, 15 Apr. 52, 4 May 52, 13 May 52, 20 May 52 (photos), 27 May 52, 28 May 52, 1 June 52, 5 Sept. 52, 24 Jan. 53, 13 June 53, 17 Sept. 53, 18 Sept. 53, 21 Oct. 53 (adv.), 19 Jan. 54, 20 Jan. 54, 6 Feb. 54, 3 Apr. 54, 29 June 54, 2 Dec. 54, 3 Dec. 54, 5 Dec. 54, 27 Apr. 55, 26 July 55, 9 Aug. 55, 26 Aug. 55, 16 Nov. 55, 26 Nov. 55, 1 Dec. 55, 3 Dec. 55 (photo), 7 Dec. 55 (adv. and photos), 9 Dec. 55 (photo), 20 Jan. 56, 13 Dec. 56, 14 Apr. 57, 27 June 57, 16 Aug. 57 (adv.), 16 Jan. 59, 12 Apr. 59 (photos), 3 Feb. 61, 12 Apr. 61, 14 May 61, 9 Feb. 62, 3 Apr. 62, 4 Apr. 62 (photos), 25 May 62, 6 June 63, 19 June 63, 3 July 63, 4 July 63 (photo), 16 Apr. 64, 1 July 64, 29 Mar. 66, 30 Mar. 66.

GOLDEN RESORT HOTEL AND CASINO

567 West Fourth Street; licensed from July 1, 1980, to May 29, 1981, for slots and 21.

The Golden Resort Hotel and Casino was located at the site of what was formerly the Reef Hotel. In April 1980 Carl Corzan was licensed as the operator of the Golden Resort Hotel and Casino, and on July 11, 1980, the business was licensed for slots and a 21 game.

The site of the Golden Resort Hotel and Casino later became known as Cheers and subsequently the Ramada Inn. It is now Howard Johnson's Great American Hotel-Casino. There are slot machines but no table games on the property.

Nev. St. Journal, 25 Apr. 80.

GOLDEN ROAD

3800 South Virginia Street; licensed in the 1970s and 1980s for slots only.

Originally opened as a motel called the Golden Door, the property became known as the Golden Road in 1972.

In August 1973 the Gaming Commission allowed the Bally Distributing Company to install twenty slot machines at the Golden Road, which was owned by John Farahi. In July 1975 Kathy Tripp was licensed to operate twenty-five slot machines at the Golden Road, on a lease basis. Farahi retained ownership of the property.

The location is now the site of the Atlantis Hotel. The Atlantis, formerly the Clarion, is owned by the Monarch Corporation. Monarch's majority owner is John Farahi, who is also Monarch's president and general manager.

Nev. St. Journal, 16 Aug. 73, 26 July 75.

GOLD TRAIL BAR

8 West Commercial Row; licensed from February to September 1956 for poker only.

The Gold Trail Bar was a bar licensed for a poker game in 1956. In 1957 the Sourdough Club was licensed at this location. The site is now part of Fitzgeralds Casino-Hotel.

GRADY, CLIFF

Cliff Grady came to Reno in the early 1930s. He worked at the Rex Club and the Bank Club and was manager of the Ship and Bottle Club on Center Street in 1936. He was one of thirteen people licensed as a co-owner of the Palace Club in 1953, and in 1956 he was licensed as a co-owner of the Tahoe Palace (Plaza).

Grady died in the early 1960s.

Nev. St. Journal, 8 Apr. 33, 14 Mar. 36, 11 Dec. 53, 20 June 56.

GRAHAM, BILL

Bill Graham was born in San Francisco in 1891. He came to Tonopah in the early days of the mining boom and became involved in gambling clubs and in mining. He worked in Tonopah's famous Big Casino, where he met Nick Abelman, the future operator of the Riverside Hotel, as well as his own long-time partner, James McKay. Graham and McKay came to Reno in the early 1920s and were major figures in the days of Prohibition, liberal divorce laws, prostitution, and gambling in and around Reno.

They operated the Willows, the Rex Club, and the Bank Club long before gaming was legalized in 1931. When gaming became legal, they were fully prepared and ready for action. Some have said that Graham and McKay were the invisible driving force behind the legalization of gambling, because it was easier for operators like them to have their business legalized than to continue making payoffs to remain open when gambling was illegal.

Graham was an avid sportsman and boxing fan. In 1931 he and McKay entered a partnership with Jack Dempsey to promote boxing matches, and they also built a large outdoor arena at the Reno Race Track—now the Washoe County Fairgrounds—on North Wells Avenue. It was there that the Max Baer–Paulino Uzcuduno fight was held in 1931 and where the Max Baer–Kingfish Levinsky fight was held in 1932.

On June 4, 1931, Bill Graham shot and killed Blackie McCracken in the Haymarket Club, a bootlegging establishment in Douglas Alley. Graham and McCracken had engaged in a fistfight before the shooting, and McCracken's face was badly battered. He left the club, went to his room at the Pickett Hotel, and returned with a .45-caliber automatic pistol. As he entered the second barred door of the club, he fired a shot at Graham but missed. His second shot creased Graham's arm, then the pistol jammed when the empty cartridge was not ejected and McCracken was unable to fire again. Graham fired three shots, the third striking McCracken in the heart and killing him instantly. A coroner's jury, convened the same day, returned a verdict that Graham had fired in self-defense. He was exonerated of all blame.

In February 1934 Graham and McKay were arraigned on charges of using the mail to defraud. On March 23, Roy Frisch, a key witness for the prosecution, disappeared. In one of Reno's most famous unsolved mysteries, neither Frisch nor his body was ever found. Many stories circulated about what had happened to Frisch, one of them that gangster Baby Face Nelson had kidnapped and killed Frisch and later buried him in the Nevada desert.

Graham and McKay's first trial started on July 5, 1934, and resulted in a hung jury. Over the next few years, two more trials were held, during the course of which it was established that Graham and McKay were the major owners of the Stockade, the main area of prostitution in Reno, and that they had interests in several clubs in and around Reno. Their third trial ended on February 12, 1938, when they were found guilty of operating a swindling ring and of mail fraud and were sentenced to nine years in a federal prison and fined $11,000. After two appeals and many delays, they reported to prison officials on August 4, 1939. On November 11 they entered Leavenworth Penitentiary.

While Graham and McKay were in prison, Jack Sullivan, a one-third owner of the Bank Club, protected their interests.

Graham and McKay returned to Reno on October 30, 1945. They had served six years of their nine-year sentence. In 1950 Senator Pat McCarran interceded with President Truman, and both men were given full pardons.

In 1950 they purchased Jack Sullivan's interest in the Bank Club and continued to operate the business as partners until 1952. Bill Graham became the sole lessee in May 1952 when he negotiated a twenty-year lease with Frank Hofues. Graham took in John Drew as a 25-percent partner in 1954.

Also in 1954 Hofues sold the Golden Hotel to William and James Tomerlin; however, Graham's lease was not affected until November 1955. At that time, the Tomerlins paid Graham and Drew $425,000 for the seventeen years remaining on their lease.

That was the end of Bill Graham's career in Reno gaming, but he remained in town and was frequently seen at boxing matches and other sporting events. He died at his home on California Avenue on November 5, 1965. He was seventy-four years old.

Nev. St. Journal, 5 June 31 (photos), 4 June 31, 5 June 31, 6 June 31, 20 July 34, 28 Oct. 45, 31 Oct. 45, 19 Sept. 50, 8 Apr. 52, 6 Nov. 65 (obit.).

GRAND BUFFET

31 East Second Street; licensed for three months in 1935 for 21 only; from 1951 to 1960 for a pan game.

The Grand Buffet was in the Grand Café owned by the Petronovich family. The pan game was licensed to Swede Collet, a local gambler who operated card games at several locations in Reno.

The site is now part of Harrah's Club on Second Street between Center and Virginia Streets.

GRANNIS, FRANK

Frank Grannis, along with Bernie Einstoss, Leo Kind, and Lou Wertheimer, was licensed at the Mapes Hotel from 1947 to 1955. Grannis, along with Einstoss, Tom Gerun, and Andrew Desimone, was licensed at the Bal Tabarin (formerly the Cal-Vada) from 1955 to 1959. He was also licensed, along with Einstoss, Baldy West, and ten others, at the Horseshoe Club in 1957. Grannis was a licensee at the Horseshoe until it was sold to the Mason Corporation in 1967.

Nev. St. Journal, 2 Mar. 55, 24 Aug. 56.

GRAVES, RICHARD "DICK"

Dick Graves was born on August 23, 1912, in Boise, Idaho. He owned several restaurants and resorts in Idaho. At that time, it was legal in some areas of Idaho to operate slot machines. Graves took advantage of the situation and had hundreds of slot machines operating around the state.

In 1954 Idaho declared slot machines illegal in the entire state, a ruling that forced Graves to transfer his operation to Nevada. He opened his first casino in Yerington and named it the Nugget. He later opened three more casinos—the Carson City Nugget, the Reno Nugget, and the Sparks Nugget.

Graves's practice was to open a casino, sell it, then move to another town. His partner in the Reno Nugget, which opened in 1954, was Jim Kelly. When Graves wanted to move to Sparks, he and Kelly broke up their partnership. Kelly kept the Nugget in Reno, and Graves went to Sparks without him. However, he did take along his food and beverage manager, John Ascuaga. Ascuaga was named manager of the new Sparks Nugget, which opened on March 17, 1955, with fifty slot machines and a sixty-stool coffee shop.

Graves was a marketing genius who put on many promotions to publicize his casino. One of his most famous was when he hired "Happy" Bill Howard on August 4, 1955, to sit on a six-foot-wide platform sixty feet above the Nugget parking lot. Howard had set the flagpole-sitting record two years previously when he stayed on his perch for 196 days. This time, Howard stayed on his perch for 204 days, and when he came down Graves paid him $5,000.

In 1958 Graves tried another gimmick, putting a fifteen-pound gold statuette of a rooster on display to publicize his Golden Rooster Room restaurant. The federal government seized the rooster, citing a law that a private citizen could not possess more than fifty ounces of gold. After almost four years of legal wrangling, a jury decided that it was legal for the Nugget to own and display the statuette.

In 1960 Graves purchased a sixteen-year-old elephant from a circus in Baraboo, Wisconsin. He named the elephant Bertha, and she eventually became the star performer in the Nugget's Circus Room Theater Restaurant (later the Celebrity Room) and the de facto mascot of the Nugget.

In 1960 Graves decided that he did not want to be the "richest man in the cemetery," and he sold the Nugget to his general manager, John Ascuaga, for $3.75 million. The terms of the agreement called for no down payment and the note to be paid off in twelve years. Ascuaga took only seven years to pay off the note.

Graves died on January 13, 1990, in a Carson City hospital.

Nev. St. Journal, 20 Jan. 54, 30 Sept. 60, 10 Nov. 60, 14 Jan. 90 (obit.).

GREAT DANE

565 West Moana Lane

See Dutch Garden and Stengler's Dutch Garden.

GREEN LANTERN

Corner of Spokane and River Streets; licensed in 1931 for a craps game.

The Green Lantern was better known as a bar and a house of prostitution than it was for its gaming. It was destroyed by fire in November 1945.

Nev. St. Journal, 15 Nov. 65.

GRELLMAN, HERB

Herb Grellman was born in San Francisco on April 1, 1913. He came to Reno in 1935 and went to work at the Bank Club. In 1936 he married the daughter of Jack Sullivan, the longtime Reno gaming manager and part owner of the Bank Club. Grellman's career was interrupted by World War II. After the war he returned to the Bank Club but soon left to join the Harrah's organization shortly after the casino opened in 1946.

Grellman also worked at the Frontier Club, the Nevada Club, and the Nevada Lodge. He was vice-president of the Primadonna in 1970, casino manager of the Mapes in 1976, and at the time of his death on February 5, 1981, he was casino manager of the Pioneer Inn.

Nev. St. Journal, 18 July 36, 15 Oct. 70, 23 July 76, 7 Feb. 81 (obit.).

GRID IRON CLUB

222 North Center Street; licensed in March 1947.

On March 11, 1947, A. K. Sekt was licensed by the City of Reno at the Grid Iron Club, which was located at the former site of the La Fiesta and the 222 Clubs. The Grid Iron Club never opened, and the 222 Club reopened there in June 1947.

The site is now occupied by Harrah's Club on east side of Center Street between Second Street and Douglas Alley.

Nev. St. Journal, 11 Mar. 47.

GRIFFITH, PHIL

Phil Griffith was born in Kansas City, Missouri, and came to Reno by way of Las Vegas. Griffith, who graduated from Wichita State University, was employed by the Summa Corporation in Las Vegas when he was named controller of Harolds Club in August 1973.

Griffith advanced rapidly through the Harolds Club organization, and in February 1979 he was named president of Harolds Club, replacing J. C. Jordan. He later divided his time between Reno and Las Vegas, where he helped operate the Summa Corporation's Sands Hotel-Casino.

In the mid-1980s, Griffith left the Summa Corporation and formed the Lincoln Management Group, later known as the Fitzgerald Gaming Corporation. The group purchased Fitzgeralds Casino-Hotel, Harolds Club, and the Nevada Club. At the time of publication in 1999, Griffith was president, chief executive officer, and director of the Fitzgerald Gaming Corporation.

Nev. St. Journal, 5 Aug. 73, 2 Nov. 75 (photo), 25 Feb. 79.

GROTTO BAR

361 North Virginia Street; licensed for a poker game only in 1954.

The Grotto Bar, which was owned by Ray Pollman, was licensed by the state on January 20, 1954, for one poker game. The business later became known as Leo's Den. The site is now part of the Eldorado Hotel-Casino

Nev. St. Journal, 20 Jan. 54, 26 Jan. 54.

GUFFEY, JACK

Jack Guffey was one of thirteen people licensed at the Palace Club from 1953 to 1964. He was personally licensed for 5 percent of the club and as one of the shift managers. Guffey was also licensed as a co-owner of the Tahoe Palace (Plaza) in 1956.

Nev. St. Journal, 25 July 56.

GUY'S RANCHO BAR

140 Airport Road (now Gentry Way); licensed from March 17 to September 1, 1955, for 21 only.

Guy's Rancho Bar was basically a local bar that was licensed for a 21 game for a few months in 1955. An automobile repair mall is now located at the site.

HALF WAY HOUSE

1601 East Fourth Street; licensed from December 1, 1944, to 1946 for 21 only.

The Half Way House has always operated as a bar and restaurant, not as a casino. It is called the Half Way House because it is located approximately halfway between Reno and Sparks. In the 1950s, '60s, and '70s, it was operated by "Steamboat" Stempeck and was a favorite hangout for many locals. Stempeck was active in youth activities and was a dominant force in Reno's early days of youth-oriented baseball as a supporter of the Babe Ruth League and the Little League.

At the time of publication, the business is being operated by Stempeck's widow, Inez, as Casale's Half Way House and features home-style Italian cooking. There is currently no gambling at the location.

Nev. St. Journal, 10 Jan. 46.

HALL, HENRY "TEX"

Tex Hall was born in Texas in 1878, and when he was a young man he worked as a cowboy. He came to the Goldfield-Tonopah area in 1901. From there, he moved to Ely, then came to Reno with Jack Sullivan in the early 1920s. He was first associated with the Social Club, which stood on the site of the present post office on Virginia Street.

Hall soon went to work with Bill Graham, James McKay, and Jack Sullivan in various clubs and casinos in the Reno area. Most of the clubs he worked in either had illegal gambling or were illegal speakeasies, or both. He had an active interest in the Cal-Neva Lodge at Lake Tahoe, where he acted as manager, and he also worked in and managed the Willows, the Rex, and the Bank Club.

On January 13, 1935, Tex Hall was arrested by federal agents. According to the *Nevada State Journal* of January 14, 1935, Hall was "assertedly beaten during an eight hour questioning period." He was later returned to the U.S. Commissioner in Reno and released on $25,000 bail posted by Ray Kindle and J. B. Scarlett (also known as Jack Sullivan). Hall was accused of harboring the nation's number-one criminal, George "Baby Face" Nelson. On March 21, 1935, Hall was identified as an accomplice of Nelson's and was ordered to stand trial. On April 6 he was found guilty of conspiracy to harbor a criminal (Nelson) and was sentenced to one year in jail and a $2,000 fine.

Hall was released in October after serving only six months of his sentence and went back to work at the Bank Club. He died of a heart attack at his home on Gordon Avenue on June 12, 1936.

Kansas City Star, 26 Apr. 31; Nev. St. Journal, 14 Jan. 35, 15 Jan. 35, 6 Apr. 35, 5 Oct. 35, 13 June 36 (obit.); Reno Evening Gazette, 12 June 36 (obit.).

HALL, JOE

Joe Hall was one of five persons licensed as a co-owner of the Palace Club in June 1943. He was from Southern California and was not involved in the operation of the club. In 1951 Baldy West and Archie Sneed bought out his interest.

HANNIFAN, PHILLIP

Phil Hannifan was born in Butte, Montana, on October 3, 1934. He attended Bishop Manogue High School in Reno and graduated from the University of Nevada. He worked his way through the University by working as a keno writer in the Palace Club. In his early career, he was the founding director of Wittenburg Hall and supervisor of the Job Corps Youth Center.

Hannifan served as chairman of the Gaming Control Board from 1971 to 1977. Six weeks after resigning from the Control Board, he was named director of Howard Hughes's Summa Corporation, a position that entailed oversight of six Las Vegas casinos and one Reno casino (Harolds Club). He stayed with Summa Corporation until 1984, when he was appointed president of Harrah's West with authority over operations at Harrah's Reno, Harrah's Tahoe, and Harrah's Holiday Inn in Las Vegas. Hannifan lost this position when Harrah's West was eliminated during a corporate restructuring in 1986.

In 1987 Hannifan was named vice-president and general manager of Fitzgeralds Casino-Hotel and the Nevada Club. In 1990 he was named executive vice-president of the Fitzgerald Group (formerly the Lincoln Management Group).

Nev. St. Journal, 1 Sept. 77, 10 Feb. 78, 26 Mar. 79 (photo), 14 July 87, 28 Dec. 90.

HAPPY BUDDHA CLUB

222 and 246 Lake Street; licensed from August 1958 through October 1964 for 21, craps, poker, and keno.

The Happy Buddha Club was located at the former site of the Old Cathay Club. Licensed in July 1958 as owners of the Happy Buddha were Andrew Young, Henry Leong Jr., Frank Chung, and William Bailey. Their license was contingent on Moon Wyatt having no part of the operation.

The club opened in August 1958 at 222 Lake Street and operated at that address until October 1960. On that date, the club was moved to 246 Lake Street, and the name was changed to the China Mint. The licensees at the China Mint were the same individuals who owned the Happy Buddha—Young, Chung, Leong, and Bailey. From this time until the club closed in December 1964, many people were confused about its name—some still called the club the Happy Buddha, and others knew it as the China Mint.

The club catered primarily to Asian customers. The property was very small and was as much a bar and hangout for local Asians as it was a casino.

The former location of the Happy Buddha (and China Mint) is now a parking lot.

Nev. St. Journal, 22 July 58, 5 Apr. 60, 9 June 60, 21 June 60, 7 July 60, 21 Sept. 60, 17 Dec. 64.

HARLEM CLUB

221 East Douglas Alley; licensed from 1948 to 1968 for slots, poker, 21, craps, pan, and chuck-a-luck.

The Harlem Club was patronized mainly by African Americans. It had a bar and at various times a craps table, slots, 21, and other gambling games. It was opened in 1946 by William Bailey, and in 1948 Eddy Jackson, who was well known in the entertainment field and had a large local following, was named manager of the property. In 1956 William Bailey took in Norval Embry as a 40-percent partner of the operation.

The Harlem Club, which was located in what was known at that time as the skid row of Reno, was a rough place, and there were frequent fights and disturbances. In the early years, William Bailey was shot one night when he was dealing craps. Indeed, there were so many reports of disturbances at the Harlem Club that in 1956 it was placed off-limits to military personnel for almost an entire year (the Reno Air Base—Stead Air Base—was active at this time, and there was a large contingent of air force personnel stationed in Reno). During the life of the club, there were shootings and knifings; the owner, William Bailey, was arrested for operating an unlicensed game; one of the club's pit bosses was arrested at the New China Club for cheating; the club was required to deal out of a shoe (a dealing device that makes it difficult to cheat a customer or the house); and the City Council threatened to close the club because of several health and fire violations.

In 1958 Norval Embry bought out Bailey and took over as sole proprietor of the Harlem Club. Embry operated the club until 1968. At that time, it was renamed the Soul Club and operated as such until 1977.

The former location of the Harlem Club is now part of Harrah's parking garage.

Nev. St. Journal, 10 Oct. 46, 23 Mar. 48, 2 and 3 Apr. 48 (adv.), 15 June 48, 28 Apr. 53, 2 Apr. 54, 16 June 54, 26 Jan. 56, 17 Feb. 56, 26 Feb. 56, 2 Mar. 56, 27 Sept. 56, 11 Oct. 56, 20 Oct. 60, 21 May 63, 24 Mar. 64.

HAROLDS CLUB
236 North Virginia Street; licensed from February 1935 until March 31, 1995, as a full casino.

Harold Smith Sr. borrowed $500 from his father, Raymond I. "Pappy" Smith, to start Harolds Club on February 23, 1935. Coin-cidentally, that date was Harold Smith's twenty-fifth birthday. Harold and his brother, Raymond A. Smith, opened the doors with only themselves and their wives as employees. The club opened with a single penny roulette game. It was an eight-foot wheel—sometimes called a flasher wheel—mounted vertically on the wall in front of a large mirror, and it had forty-three layouts. In a short time, the wheel became busy enough to require six clerks to sell chips and service the layouts. The club also opened with two slot machines—one nickel and one dime machine.

The *Nevada State Journal* of June 30, 1935—in what is believed to be the first ad for Harolds Club—carried the following copy: "Harolds Club, 236 North Virginia Street. Open at twelve noon. There is a big surprise in store for you."

Shortly after the "store," as Harold liked to call his club, opened, the two men's father, Raymond I., came to work for them as general manager. The "store" was only 25 feet wide and 150 feet deep.

In the fall of 1935, a 21 game was added, and shortly after that a klondike game, fan-tan, craps, and a red-dog game. Gross receipts for the first year were $25,000, but the operation lost $2,000. By 1938, Harolds Club had eight employees on the payroll; by 1939 there were almost forty people on the payroll.

In May 1938 Harolds Club introduced mouse roulette to Reno. Contrary to common belief, mouse roulette was not popular, and it was not offered for long. An article in the *Nevada State Journal* of May 15, 1938, tells of the short-lived gambling experiment but fails to mention Harolds Club. Evidently daunted by the failure of mouse roulette, Pappy Smith waited almost twenty-five years before he "hired" more mice. On April 18, 1962—to celebrate his seventy-fifth birthday (he actually was born on April 30, 1887)—he introduced "mice dice." This experiment was also short-lived, but it garnered untold thousands of dollars' worth of advertising, and that of course was what Pappy was looking for.

In May 1938 Harolds Club tried its first racehorse keno game. The first keno game didn't succeed, but the owners soon tried again. In September 1940 they leased out the racehorse keno game and the horse-race book to Fred Beck. Pappy had known Beck since they had both operated games of chance on the boardwalk in San Francisco. He asked Beck to lease the game as a favor to him, and when Beck hesitated, Pappy loaned him $2,500 to get started. Beck also had a lease for pan and poker games during his long association with the Smith family. The association proved to be beneficial for both parties. For many years after Fred Beck's death, his widow, Jessie Howard Beck, continued to operate the keno game in Harolds Club. In fact, she kept the keno game until she was forced out when Harolds Club was purchased by the Summa Corporation in 1970.

Harolds Club continued to grow at a rapid pace, and by 1941 the club advertised that it never closed and featured "games of every description." Jim Hunter was named the graveyard-shift manager, while Raymond A. Smith ran the day shift and Harold Smith Sr. was in charge of the swing shift. Also in 1941 Harolds Club leased the property next door and increased its gaming to twenty-six slot machines, four craps tables, one pan game, one big-six wheel, one poker game, two roulette games, and five 21 games.

On the Fourth of July, the club opened its first bar. It took over the Rex Club at the corner of Douglas Alley and Lincoln Alley and extended its "hole-in-the-wall" to form an *L.* Leo Schwarz was hired as the first bar manager. Pappy Smith was the owner of the first bar, and he maintained separate ownership of all the bars through the years. Sometimes the separation of the bar and the gaming caused hard feelings between the Smiths, especially when Harold announced that drinks were on the house. The added space, gaming devices, and facilities required a staff of eighty employees.

From November 1941 to December 1942 Harolds Club carried on an intense advertising campaign, running 3-by-5-inch advertisements almost daily. The ads had some variation in verbiage but always this line: "Complete Line of Amusements—We

Never Close—The Friendly Club." By the end of 1942, Harolds Club had grown to include 140 employees and was offering $500 limits on its table games.

In the late 1930s Harolds Club defied precedent by introducing female dealers to the gaming business. The first women working in the club were members of the Smith family, but by the early 1940s and during World War II, nine employees out of every ten were women.

In September 1941 the Washoe County Commissioners and the district attorney's office warned clubs that they would no longer be permitted to use female dealers at gaming tables located near the windows and doorways of their clubs. Local residents had allegedly complained that Virginia Street had come to look like a "Hollywood carnival." At a hearing in the commissioners' office, Harold Smith said that he had introduced female dealers in Reno to give his club "added refinement." He further stated that "my idea has always been that as long as gambling in Nevada is open, it should be open for everyone to see." He said that he had started a $25,000 advertising campaign to place

Bessie Hoyt, a 21 dealer at Harolds Club for many years, is shown here dealing to live action in the late 1940s. Courtesy of Darl and Marj Voss.

Dorothy (Mrs. Harold Sr.) Smith with a family friend, Joe Brown, in 1938. Courtesy of Neal Cobb.

signs throughout the nation advertising his club and Reno.

Dorothy Smith (wife of Harold Smith Sr.) and Dora Mae Pigeon Smith (first wife of Raymond I. Smith, and Harold's mother) were the first female dealers in Harolds Club. They saw the long hours that Harold, his brother Raymond A., and Harold's father, Raymond I., were working, and they came to the club to give them breaks. Male dealers from the Palace Club and the Bank Club came in to play at their tables and gave them tips on becoming better dealers.

Soon they were as skilled at dealing craps, roulette, and 21 as anyone in town. As business grew, they taught other women to deal and then retired, although they still took over the tables in emergencies.

It is uncertain who was the first non-family female dealer in Harolds Club, but it is almost certain that it was either Ruby Nash, who had worked with Pappy on the boardwalk in San Francisco and is said to be the person who gave Raymond I. Smith the nickname "Pappy"; Ruth Linderman, a tall, Junoesque redhead, also called Lindy

Ray or "Big Ruth," who came to Reno from San Francisco with Smith in 1935; or Elsie Young. Mrs. Young and her husband, Grover, who also worked at the club, had also come to Reno in 1935 with Pappy Smith and had worked with him on the boardwalk in San Francisco.

Other early female dealers include Mabel Chastain, who was married to Pappy in 1938 and whose sister, Jessie Howard Brown Beck, was the first female dice dealer in Harolds Club and one of the first female supervisors; Ethel Blake, who had worked with Pappy in San Francisco; Mildred Holland, who came to Reno from Montana; Paula Motley, who was an experienced poker dealer from Texas when she

was hired at Harolds Club; Doris Rose, who was Ruby Nash's daughter; Rae Scurlock, said to be as good a dice dealer as any man in Reno; Aileen Murphy, who later became a pit supervisor; Diamond Lil Brooks, another talented dice dealer; and Ruth Fuller, who also became a pit supervisor during the war years.

During World War II, when the shortage of male dealers hit its peak in 1943, Harolds Club ran the following want-ad on August 3 and continued the ad daily for several weeks: "Help wanted: Harolds Club wants lady clerks, between the age of 21 and 35, capable of learning to deal games. Many of our present dealers who started this way are now earning $60 a week. Men please do

not apply." The ad was changed on November 2 to read, "Many of our dealers are making $90 a week" and "Please, no men except disabled veterans of this war, need apply."

In August 1943 Pappy Smith married a roulette dealer, Iola Hutchins, and in June 1944 they became the parents of twins, George and Betty.

On Christmas Day 1943 Harolds Club took out a full-page ad in the *Nevada State Journal* to wish everyone a Merry Christmas and to mention that its payroll was then over $12,000 a week.

The club continued to grow during the war years. In March 1945, a hearing held in the state legislature regarding a 10-percent tax on gross gaming revenue recorded that

The World War II years were busy ones in Reno, as this picture of the interior of Harolds Club, taken on June 21, 1944, illustrates. Note the 21 games along the right wall and the keno game along the left wall. Also note the race book in the rear of the building. Courtesy of the Neal Cobb Collection and the Nevada Historical Society.

A group of Harolds Club dealers are pictured on this Reno Rodeo parade float, ca. 1947. Standing tall in the center of the float is "Big Ruth" Linderman. To her immediate left is "Little Ruth" Fuller. Both were gaming supervisors at Harolds Club during the war years of the 1940s. Courtesy of Darl and Marj Voss.

Harolds Club had at that time twenty-one table games and thirty-eight slot machines. By year's end, they were licensed for twenty-eight table games and fifty-four slots. This was the first year the original forty-three-layout flasher wheel was not licensed.

In May 1947 Harolds Club expanded again—this time to the north, taking over the property formerly leased to the Giant Shop and Harrah's Bingo at 242 North Virginia Street. On June 12, 1948, the Smiths opened their Covered Wagon Room, which boasted the first escalator in Nevada and featured thousands of dollars' worth of colored glass, animated wall maps, whiskey waterfalls, and copies of western art. An electric-eye counting device clocked 3,365 people up the motorized stairs during the first two hours of operation—and then the rate increased. The escalator had been rated to handle 3,000 people per hour, but there were several twenty-minute periods when the stairs exceeded capacity with two people riding on each step.

The Covered Wagon Room featured the Silver Dollar Bar, an elaborate curved bar with an orange plastic railing and 2,141 silver dollars set flush in the clear plastic top of the bar. Lights shone upward through the top and left the dollars in sharp relief. The coins proved to be a temptation to more than one gambler down on his luck, but they were set in so securely that none was ever lost.

On opening night there was a waterfall of Old Forrester whiskey streaming down the rocks and splashing into a pool surrounded by rustic scenery. A short time later, water had to be substituted for the whiskey because the fumes became so powerful that it was unpleasant to be in the bar area. To the left of the bar was a large colored map of Nevada with incidents from pioneer history painted at various locations around the state. All major highways were shown, and they would repeatedly light up, a red streak gliding out the highway from Reno, stopping at the site of each incident. Farther left of the bar, two of the largest full-color photo transparencies in the

world featured views of Lake Tahoe on sheets of plastic more than twelve feet wide and reaching from floor to ceiling. They were illuminated from behind to replicate the full cycle of the day. Automatically the lighting changed from dawn to noon, to afternoon, then a storm came up with clouds and a sudden shower. Lightning flashed, then the storm cleared away into a magnificent colored sunset. Evening came with moonlight beaming on the lake. The cycle repeated itself on a continual basis.

Carpeting on the floor had been specially created with a covered-wagon design, and other artwork from Harolds Club highway signs was woven into the fabric.

The cost of the Covered Wagon Room was not made public, but it was estimated to have run into hundreds of thousands of dollars. The carpeting alone cost $45,000, and the club had ordered two sets—one as a spare.

In August 1948, about two months after the opening of the Covered Wagon Room, the Smiths announced that they now had five hundred people on their payroll. They had 210 slot machines, and in the previous week they had paid 10,707 jackpots.

In January 1949 the club announced another huge expansion program. The Virginia Hotel, located at 240 North Virginia Street, was to be demolished to allow for a $200,000 expansion of the second floor of Harolds Club. This expansion became known as the Roaring Camp Room and was filled with western memorabilia, most of which came from Raymond Stagg's Roaring Camp located on Lake Street and purchased by Raymond I. Smith in 1949. The collection included hundreds of firearms, including flintlock muskets, dueling pistols, Civil War weapons, Winchester rifles, Colt revolvers, Gatling guns, a fourteenth-century Chinese cannon, prairie schooners, Concord stages, other types of pioneer transportation, and amusement devices, including cards, dice, faro, and mechanical orchestras, along with phonographs, letters, documents, posters, newspapers, and other items relating to early Nevada.

Harolds Club established special family viewing hours so children could see and learn about early pioneer days in the West.

The exhibit attracted hundreds of thousands of viewers and remained on display in the Roaring Camp Room through the 1960s. After Harolds Club was sold, the collection was neglected, and finally, in May 1994, it was sold at auction by the Butterfield and Butterfield Auction Company in San Francisco, and the once-famous collection was no more.

Also in 1949, the Smith family commissioned Theodore McFall to create a mural thirty-five feet high and seventy-five feet wide to commemorate Nevada pioneers and settlers. The mural, which spread over the Virginia Street entrance, was made of 220 separate porcelain mosaic panels and was said to be the largest such project ever undertaken. It cost $60,000, took four months to complete, and became a widely photographed Reno landmark. The words above the mural read, "Dedicated in All Humility to Those Who Blazed the Trail."

By 1950 the club had doubled in size and was operating 531 slot machines, forty-six table games, chuck-a-luck, and keno. In December 1950, the Smiths purchased one of Reno's oldest business properties, the Ritz Hotel at 8 East Commercial Row, for approximately $135,000. A few months later, in February 1951, growth continued when the Smiths purchased a building at 232 North Virginia for $200,000. This was the former location of one of Reno's first bingo parlors, and the Reno Club still held a long-term lease on the property. It wasn't until 1954 that Harolds Club was able to expand into the new property.

In July 1952 Harolds Club reported that 19,136 people had passed through its electric-eye counting device on July 4. Two months later, the management reported that over Labor Day weekend, on Saturday, Sunday, and Monday, 44,206 people had passed through the doors.

There were many reasons for the continued growth and success of Harolds Club, but none was so important as Pappy Smith's decision to advertise his business. No one had ever done that before. Gaming's first advertising campaign was launched by Harolds Club in the 1940s, and soon there were outdoor billboards as far away as the North Pole. Harolds Club eventually had more than 2,300 billboards around the United States and at selected locations throughout the world. Most of the billboards featured cartoon characters headed for Harolds Club by various comical means, including holding on to the tail of a bear and fording a river on a raft. The message was simple, "Harolds Club or Bust."

The first signs were erected in California, but eventually they could be seen in forty-five other states. More than five hundred signs were located in California alone, while the smallest showings, two billboards each, were in Maine, Connecticut, and Rhode Island. Only four states—Vermont, New Hampshire, New Jersey, and Massachusetts—had none at all. It was said that a motorist in the United States was never farther than eight hours' drive away from a Harolds Club sign.

The advertising campaign was not restricted to roadways in the United States. Military personnel stationed abroad wrote requesting signs for their military posts, and soon "Harolds Club or Bust" signs were found all over the world.

Most of the signs had to be dismantled in 1965 when the Federal Highway Beautification Act became effective.

In 1946 Pappy Smith made another major marketing move when he hired one of Reno's first advertising specialists, Thomas C. Wilson, to create a new advertising campaign for Harolds Club. Wilson's campaign began with a series of newspaper advertisements that depicted forgotten incidents in early-day Nevada history. During the early 1950s, the sums spent annually to publicize Harolds Club were said to exceed the advertising budgets of all other casinos combined. That heavy investment made Harolds Club the best-known gambling resort in Nevada during the 1950s. It was also the largest casino. In July 1951 Harolds Club was licensed for ten craps games, ten roulette games, twenty-eight 21 games, and 616 slot machines.

Harolds Club and the Smith family contributed generously to many local churches, the Boy Scouts and Girl Scouts, hospitals, day-care centers, and other charitable causes. By far the most notable and costly benefactions were the celebrated Harolds Club Scholarships, which were established shortly after the end of World War II. Through the scholarships, graduates of some forty Nevada high schools—one each year from the larger schools, one in alter-

"Fran" dealing a twenty-five-cent minimum table at Harolds Club, ca. 1952. Note the varied expressions on the players' faces. Courtesy of Neal Cobb.

nate years from the smaller schools—were annually awarded grants-in-aid that financed full four-year courses at the University of Nevada. The scholarships totaled $4,000 each and were paid in installments of $250 at the beginning of each quarter throughout the holder's college career. The scholarships, which cost the club $160,000 a year, were a blessing to hundreds of students who would not otherwise have been able to obtain a college education. During the time the scholarship program was in operation, 250 graduates benefited, and the total cost to Harolds Club was $1 million.

Another practice unique to Harolds Club was what was called the "Once Only Book." That book (which actually became a card file) contained the names and addresses of players who had gone broke at Harolds Club and had had money lent to them. The purpose of "the book" was to make sure that no one had to leave Harolds Club with empty pockets. If a player lost all his money, he could approach one of the Smiths or a floor boss and request a loan to help him get home. If he repaid the loan, he could borrow again; if the loan was not repaid, the player was never eligible for another. (Like many rules at Harolds Club, this rule was bent quite frequently. If a regular longtime customer lost his money and hadn't repaid his previous loan, he could almost always get more money.)

In the 1950s a new rule came into being. Anyone was eligible for a maximum loan of $50 a year, whether or not the previous year's loan had been repaid. Needless to say, the main desk where the money was doled out was very busy during the first few days of each new year. The loan was meant to help losers get home, but it was not uncommon for the customer to take the loan to a neighboring casino and attempt to "run it up."

Many customers played in Harolds Club because of the "Once Only Book." They enjoyed the comfort of knowing that as long as they kept their credit current, they could never go broke in Harolds Club.

Harolds Club's continued success led to more expansion. In October 1953 the Smiths announced that they would soon begin

Dwayne Kling and Fran Sheehan dealing a twenty-five-cent dice game in Harolds Club in 1955. Author's collection.

construction of a "seven or eight story addition." Construction began in 1954—the same year that Harolds Club opened its "pigeon hole" parking garage, located to the north of the club, just across the railroad tracks and west of Virginia Street. The facility utilized a forklift mechanism that raised a car up to a space, unloaded it in that space, then returned to ground level.

In 1955 Harolds Club opened its first restaurant, located on the third floor. Also in 1955 the seventh floor was opened. Initially, the seventh floor had no entertainment, but it offered high-limit gaming and a bar that featured a tiny model-railroad train that the bartender sometimes used to deliver drinks to the patrons. The train sta-

tion was modeled after the train station in Pappy's hometown of Vergennes, Vermont.

Big-name entertainment was introduced in the new seventh-floor showroom on June 19, 1957. The opening acts were Betty Reilly and the Jodimars. One month later, Helen Forrest, a well-known female vocalist who performed with big bands such as Harry James and Tommy Dorsey, opened as the second act to appear in the Fun Room, as the showroom was called.

In November 1947 two young medical students from the University of Chicago gained national fame and publicity when they won $8,000 playing roulette in Reno. Albert Hibbs and Roy Walford started playing at the Palace Club with a $300 bankroll. By spelling each other in eight-hour shifts, they played for forty straight hours and were $6,000 ahead when the Palace Club decided to change the roulette wheel. The young men then moved across the alley to Harolds Club.

After the move to Harolds Club, they clocked the wheel for seven days before they began playing. Daily news bulletins went out over the national wire systems reporting their winnings, and they were featured in Billy Rose's column. They were also featured in *Life* magazine's "Picture of the Week." After sixty hours of play, they had won $7,000 from Harolds Club, to make them $13,000 winners.

Their system, which consisted of betting the number nine with various amounts of money, started to fail when they reached $13,000. They lost steadily the last sixteen hours they played, betting $19 on each spin of the wheel. They finally cashed in, having won a total of $8,000 between the Palace Club and Harolds Club. Harold Smith advised the young men that "his club would let them win a million dollars if their system would do it," but he suggested they quit while they were still ahead of the game.

Ten years later, a similar incident occurred. On June 1, 1956, after recording every winning number on a roulette table for several days, two young men began betting nickel chips. Originally the two men did all the betting, but after a short time they added two more men to their group, and later others joined to make a group of seven. At least one member of the group was at the wheel twenty-four hours each day until the wheel was taken out seven weeks later. The size of the bets increased as their winnings increased, and ultimately they were betting as much as $25 on each of eight numbers. At the conclusion of their play on July 24, 1956, the group was said to have won a total of $96,000.

An interesting sidelight was that one of the gamblers, Bruce Jones, became romantically involved with one of the roulette dealers, and the two were later married.

After the wheel was taken out and examined, it was determined that some of the frets (the small metal divisions separating the numbered slots into which the ball falls) were loose. It is very probable that this irregularity caused certain numbers to come up more frequently than they should have. A similar situation had occurred at another casino a few months earlier, so the Smiths were aware of what could happen when frets were loose. Some people wondered if the wily Smith family, always looking for a way to publicize their club, weren't aware that there was an irregularity on the wheel and allowed the game to go on nonetheless, figuring that $96,000 was a small price to pay for the amount of publicity that the club had enjoyed.

In January 1960 Harolds Club opened Room 25, commemorating the casino's twenty-fifth anniversary. The room, formerly known as the Music Room because of the many mechanical music devices exhibited there, also was opened to celebrate the 8th Olympic Winter Games being held at Squaw Valley. Room 25 featured the internationally popular game of baccarat—Harolds Club was the first casino in Reno to offer baccarat.

In March 1956 it had been announced that Harolds Club had been sold to the Morgan and Agostini Corporation of San Francisco, headed by Jules Agostini. The sale never materialized, and in August 1957 Harolds Club was awarded $500,000 from Agostini when the sale fell through. A similar situation arose in December 1960, when daily reports and rumors surfaced about the sale of Harolds Club to Oliver Kahle and Ben Jaffe. For about ten days there were denials one day and affirmations the next. Finally, on January 1, 1961, Raymond I. Smith announced that the sale was off. The club was to have been sold to a group of Seattle investors for a reported $17 million, and the gaming was to have been leased to Kahle and Jaffe, but the group failed to meet the December 30, 1960, deadline for a deposit. Pappy Smith stated that he was glad the deal was off and that the club would not be sold in the future unless the sale included a lease-back agreement so that the Smiths could continue to control the gambling.

In June 1962 the Smiths did sell their property and buildings for $16 million to a New York investment firm, the Webbel Corporation, but then they leased back the casino. The corporate structure was changed, and the following ownership percentages were announced: Raymond I. Smith, from 33 percent to 48 percent; Raymond A. Smith, from 33 percent to 4 percent; and Harold Smith, from 33 percent to 48 percent.

On December 9, 1964, Harolds Club purchased the Colony Club, which was located at 254 North Virginia Street. The following March, a $300,000 remodeling project was started to convert the Colony Club into the latest part of Harolds Club's continual expansion. Opening day for the addition was July 1, 1965. Named the Arch Lounge, it contained gaming and lounge entertainment on the main floor and executive offices on the second floor. The bar area was decorated in dark English oak with melon-colored trim and was backed by a picture of the Reno arch. The opening-day entertainment was furnished by vocalist Johnny Prophet, banjo player Freddy Morgan, and pianist Freddy Henshaw. The relief group was known as the Winners and featured Cork Proctor. The addition was licensed for sixty-three slot machines, one craps game, one roulette game, three 21 games, and one keno game.

On May 24, 1967, the driving force behind Harolds Club, Raymond I. "Pappy" Smith—who had started as the general manager of the club and later became an owner as well as the general manager—died of cancer in St. Mary's Hospital. He was eighty years old. At the time of his death, Harolds Club was the largest casino in Nevada.

Smith's funeral was held on May 27, 1967, but his passing went unnoticed by the thousands of tourists who crowded into Harolds Club. The club remained open during that Memorial Day Saturday while five hundred persons gathered at Reno's largest Catholic church to pay their last respects. Mourners represented every walk of life, from congressmen to cleaning women, and many Harolds Club employees were there dressed in their western-style uniforms. The graveyard-shift floor managers worked overtime so that the day-shift floor managers could attend the funeral. Active pallbearers included longtime employees Chuck Webster, Roy Powers, Lee Crawford, Tom Frias, Russell Nerase, Robert Klaich, and Jim Hunter.

Business at Harolds Club continued as usual, and on December 23, 1967, Harolds Club introduced two five-dollar slot machines, the first in the state. Harolds' slot department had converted two one-dollar machines to the new denomination. Governor Paul Laxalt, Mayor Roy Bankofier, and Gaming Control Board chairman Frank Johnson were among the fifty invited guests at the introduction "party," which was hosted by longtime Harolds Club employee James Hunter, the director of public relations.

A headline story in the *Nevada State Journal* of May 17, 1970, reported that Howard Hughes had purchased Harolds Club, subject to the Gaming Commission's approval. No sale price was announced, but $11 million was the estimated price. The Gaming Commission approved the deal on June 19, 1970.

On June 11 Jessie Beck was notified that because of the sale to the Hughes Corporation, her lease on the keno game would be terminated on June 30. The Beck Corporation had operated the keno and pan games for almost thirty years. Fred Beck had opened the keno game in 1940, and Jessie assumed control after Beck's death early in 1954.

Edith Grishman, credit manager and a licensed staff member for twenty-nine years, was also terminated. Dan Orlich, casino manager, continued in that position during the interim period.

As the Hughes Corporation became more familiar with the new operation, it made several changes in personnel and in many of the procedures and policies that had been so successful for so many years. Shift managers Chuck Webster, Steve Derrivan, and Don McDonnell were among the first longtime employees to leave the club. The Hughes Corporation brought some new gaming supervisors into Harolds Club, including Richard Balkanny, Paul Paxton, Jay Corn, and others, but several longtime employees, including Al Lazzarone, Glen Botorff, Jerry Sicka, Bob Don-

nelly, Stan Gazutis, and Clarence "Cous" Couslouskie, stayed in the organization and soon became top-level executives in the new management structure.

For the first time in the history of the club, the tables were arranged into pits, supervisors' wives were terminated from employment at the club, and dealers were forced to pool their tips instead of keeping their own. The Hughes Corporation believed that by not allowing husbands and wives to work together, they would eliminate the possibility of collusion and/or favoritism.

The site of the former children's theater was turned into a children's amusement arcade. This in-casino movie theater had been in operation since the early 1950s and was visited by more than sixty thousand children annually, with highs of three thousand a week in summer months. The theater showed mostly old westerns and children's films, and customers of Harolds Club were encouraged to leave their children there, free of charge, while they were playing in the casino. It was an ideal situation for parents with younger children because it gave them a chance to enjoy Harolds Club and not worry about their children's whereabouts. This was the first attempt by a casino to provide entertainment for children and make the casino a suitable destination for the entire family.

The seventh-floor Fun Room was closed on January 3, 1971, and reopened in February as a prime-rib dinner house. The Fun Room had opened in June 1957 and had featured some of the leading names in the entertainment business, including Louis Armstrong, Harry James, Petula Clark, Brenda Lee, and Trini Lopez, to name just a few. Jackie DeShannon, who headlined from December 16 to January 2, was the last act to appear in the Fun Room. The Arch Lounge was also closed temporarily for remodeling.

In 1970, Jack Pieper, then fifty-two, was appointed manager of Harolds Club, and in June Dan Orlich and Bob Klaich resigned for "personal reasons." Orlich and Klaich had combined careers of thirty-two years at Harolds Club. Orlich had been ca-

sino manager, among other job titles, for many years, and Klaich had been longtime comptroller of the club.

In June 1972 the Howard Hughes Corporation announced that Jack Pieper was being transferred to the Frontier Club in Las Vegas and that J. C. Jordan, a casino executive and a former co-owner of the North Shore Club, would become general manager of Harolds Club. In August 1973 Jordan named Phil Griffith controller. Griffith, a twenty-eight-year-old former senior accountant with Haskins and Sells, had been in Las Vegas since 1970, coming from Kansas City, Missouri. He graduated from Wichita State in 1967 with a degree in business administration. Griffith would later be named secretary-treasurer of Harolds Club (in 1975), and in February 1979, when J. C. Jordan retired, he was named president.

In May 1977 Harolds Club executives announced plans for a three-story expansion of their property on the northeast end of the casino and asked the City Council for air rights over Douglas Alley. They planned to spend $10 million to acquire property on Commercial Row between Virginia Street and the site of the Palace Club, and $10 million more for construction. Plans also included a makeover for the seventh-floor Prime Rib Room, which was closed on Saturday, November 4, 1978, at midnight. It would reopen in May 1979 and be known as the Presidential Dining Car.

On February 15, 1979, the four-story, $20-million expansion opened to the public. The addition, which made ample use of brick and oak, was aimed at accentuating the "good old days" at the turn of the century.

The longtime favorite bar in Harolds Club, the Silver Dollar, was closed in September 1980. Opened originally as a bar in 1948, the area had been enlarged into a lounge in 1964. A small, intimate area, it was a gathering place for Harolds Club employees, neighboring casino employees, and quite frequently, Harold Smith Sr. and Harold Smith Jr. Big-name entertainers like Herb Jeffries, Sonny King, and Helen Forrest often appeared there, but more often it was the Winners, Freddy Henshaw, or the Rudy Rodarte Trio.

In 1985, the year that Harolds Club celebrated its fiftieth birthday, Harold Smith Sr. died. In contrast to his carousing early years, Smith had spent much of his final decade in solitude. During the casino's Smith era, Pappy was the tough-minded, shrewd genius who carefully planned the club's growth and eagerly promoted Reno through the "Harolds Club or Bust" billboard campaign, and he was most often given all the credit for the success of Harolds Club. Harold Sr., who became better known for drinking, gambling, and cavorting around the casino, was seldom given the credit he deserved, although he was the most knowledgeable family member when it came to operating, protecting, and managing the table games. But his father's death had a profound effect on Harold Sr. Shortly after he sold the club to the Hughes Corporation in 1971, he was quoted as saying, "My Pappy and I were partners, and when I lost my Daddy, I couldn't run Harolds Club."

By its fiftieth year of operation, the club had expanded to 1,525 slot machines, sixty-one table games, three keno counters, two restaurants, five bars, and over 1,500 employees.

Three years later, on June 1, 1988, Harolds Club was taken over by the Lincoln Management Group. Four members of the Lincoln Group, later known as the Fitzgerald Group, were former executives of Harolds Club.

Harolds Club, when it was owned by the Smith family, was unique in the gaming industry. The employees were treated like family, and it was common for employees to spend their entire career at the club. Twenty-, thirty-, and even forty-year employees were not unusual. To list all the longtime employees would be impossible, but a partial list of floor managers would include Jim Wilbur, Norman Maushardt, Joe Speicher, Dale Roper, Bill Parga, Cornel Fagetan, Dave Cable, Bob Donnelly, Jerry Sicka, Dean Rittenmeyer, Keith Jones, Walt Robinson, Connie Paris, Joe Fontaine, Harry Burke, Clark Brown, Steve Derrivan, Tom Davis, Larry Semenza, Bob Dodson, Al Lazzarone, Skip Vinson, Jim Rogers, Jack Shaver, Dutch Vandervort, Chuck Clifford, and George Wilson. Shift managers Chuck Webster, Darl Voss, and Don McDonnell also worked twenty-five or more years at Harolds Club. Executives Dan Orlich, Jim Hunter, and Bob Klaich also worked many years for Harolds Club.

Longtime dealers were even more numerous than floor managers, and the list could be endless. Nevertheless, the following names should be mentioned: Lou Cardella, Bessie Hoyt, Annie (Lund) Delaplane, Esther DeRosa, Agnes Skillen, Liz Depathy, Mary Casey, Patti Cable, Jean Peterson, Betty Sayers, Anne Marie Bamberger, Lucille Vinson, Jean (Roper) Poland, Cleo Chiatovich, Marion Markowitz, Louise Jones, Lois Bates, Jean Pinkerton, Jean Sales, Marj Voss, Winona Webster, Jo Schellin, Betty Harling, Mary Kalinski, Claire Vandervort, Rosalie Beasley, Ruth Cantrell, Betty Downs, Fran Sheehan, Ronnie O'Bryan, Florence Signalness, Ruby Collins, Midge Hogan, Arline Harper, and Edna Corban.

There were other employees who never worked in the gaming part of Harolds Club but who contributed heavily to the success of the operation. Included in that list, not necessarily in the order of their importance, were the following:

Edith Grishman, who came to work in 1939 and stayed until terminated by the Summa Corporation in 1970. She was the credit manager and was instrumental in the development of a central credit system for first the Reno casinos and eventually all Nevada casinos.

Roy Powers, who was in charge of the publicity department from 1958 to 1973. He was the promoter of such events as the Reno Air Races, and he helped to create images of Reno that brought tens of thousands of tourists to town.

Guy Lent, whom Pappy considered a financial genius, came to work in 1944 and stayed with the Smiths until his death in 1964. Pappy considered Lent his right-hand man when it came to finances.

Russ Nerase, who was hired as a bartender in 1944. He soon became bar manager and stayed with Harolds Club for over twenty-five years.

And Elsie Clifford, who was hired in 1943 as the "pay-roll lady" and remained in that department for over twenty-five years. Mrs. Clifford in later years was also in charge of the club's group insurance.

Also working in the offices upstairs were Esther Marino, hired in 1945, and Mercedes Hoover. Both women worked as secretaries and receptionists, as well as performed other duties required in the twenty-four-hour-a-day operation. They were invaluable to the Smiths because of their loyalty and integrity. Dave Reichmann and Diane Tucker were two of the early restaurant managers. Their joint efforts were instrumental in the success of the Harolds Club restaurant that opened in 1955.

In a special job category of longtime employees was LaVerl Kimpton. Kimpton went to work at Harolds Club in 1953 and was soon assigned to the "catwalk" (the overhead area in old casinos where men crawled on narrow boards or beams, watching casino activities through one-way mirrors and reporting cheating and unusual behavior to owners and/or bosses). Kimpton worked on the catwalk at Harolds Club for almost twenty years. He later worked as a pit supervisor at the Silver Spur, the Onslow Hotel, the Riverside, and other area casinos.

Twice-annual reunions of former Harolds Club employees are still held, and the turnouts are large. An organization known as the Harolds Club Pioneers meets monthly, and along with planning "fun events," members contribute time and money to worthwhile causes in the Reno-Sparks area. No other casino has ever seen groups of former employees continue to maintain organized contact and friendships, or to participate as an organization in civic activities.

Another example of the loyalty that was developed at Harolds Club reflects the customer base that was built when the Smiths owned the club. During the Forties, Fifties, and Sixties, there were tens of thousands of customers who never went to another casino when they were in Reno. Harolds

Club employees knew about their customers' families, their illnesses, their children and grandchildren, and often the customers felt like they were part of the employees' families.

Another unique part of Harolds Club was that dealers were assigned to a specific table, sometimes for years at a time. Many customers had a favorite dealer, and when they came to the club they usually knew right where to find that dealer.

Customers also felt like they knew the Smith family. Pappy especially endeared himself to hundreds of thousands of customers as he wandered through the club wearing his wrinkled slacks, a white shirt, an Indian-bead tie, and red suspenders, and doubling customers' bets or dealing them what he called "the poor bastard's hand" at the 21 table (referring to the unlucky customer as a "poor bastard"). With his method of dealing, he made it impossible for the "poor bastard" to lose. He would even hit twenty and go broke just to ensure a winning hand for the customer.

It was also Pappy's custom to introduce his dealers to the players at their table. He was a great believer in memory association, but sometimes it failed him. A favorite story of many old Renoites concerns two Harolds Club dice dealers named Barbara Maxwell and Dwayne Kling. When Pappy came by the table to introduce them, he associated Kling with cling peaches and Maxwell with Maxwell House coffee. The next time he came by to introduce them, the following occurred: "Ladies and gentlemen, I would like you to meet Dwayne Bartlett and Barbara Sanborn." Bartlett, of course, being bartlett pears—instead of peaches—and Sanborn from Chase and Sanborn coffee—instead of Maxwell House.

Harold Sr. was often very visible and audible. He even rode his horse, Bobby Sox, into the club on occasion. Quite frequently, he would get on the club's loudspeaker system to make announcements or sometimes just to talk to customers and employees.

In the early days of gaming, club owners were allowed to gamble in their own clubs, and both Harold Sr. and Harold Jr. won and lost sizable amounts of money on occasion. Harold Sr. often gambled with younger, newer dealers so he could observe their abilities and determine whether they were going to become good dealers or to see if they were progressing well enough to be moved to higher-limit tables.

It has often been said that Harolds Club (when operated by the Smith family) was unique and that there never had been and never would be another casino like it. Truer words have never been spoken.

On December 6, 1994, Phil Griffith, president and chief executive officer of the Fitzgerald Gaming Corporation, then owner of Harolds Club, announced that the corporation had entered into an agreement to sell the casino to a New Jersey gaming company called Gamma International Ltd. Griffith explained that "we acquired Harold Club . . . with the intent of turning the 55 year old casino into Reno's premier hotel-casino. However, with the tightening of the financial markets, we have been unable to obtain the capital required to build hotel rooms." On March 31, 1995, Harolds Club was closed, and sixty-nine employees were put out of work. The previous December, when the sale was announced, there was a workforce of over four hundred people.

The purchasing firm, American Gaming and Entertainment Ltd. of Atlantic City, paid $8.9 million for the property and announced plans to spend $15 to $20 million to transform the exterior and interior of Harolds Club to an Australian theme. The club was to be known as Harolds Club Down Under. The planned sale was called off early in 1996, and the property remains closed. *(See Addendum 1)*

Nev. St. Journal, 30 June 35 (adv.), 11 May 38, 15 May 38 (adv.), 30 July 39 (adv.), 26 Sept. 40 (adv.), 6 Sept. 41, 13 Oct. 41 (adv.), 16 Oct. 41 (adv.), 23 Dec. 42, 17 June 43 (adv.), 3 Aug. 43 (classified adv.), 2 Nov. 43 (classified adv.), 25 Dec. 43 (adv.), 23 Jan. 45, 14 Mar. 45, 9 Jan. 46 (adv.), 2 May 47, 13 June 48, 6 Aug. 48 (adv.), 7 Jan. 49, 7 Feb. 51, 4 July 52, 3 Sept. 52, 18 Oct. 53, 2 July 54, 30 July 54 (photo), 27 Apr. 55, 26 May 55, 19 Oct. 55 (adv.), 2 Mar. 56, 16 May 56, 25 July 56, 19 June 57, 17 July 57, 17 Aug. 57, 24 Dec. 59, 24 Jan. 60, 22 Dec. 60, 24 Dec. 60–1 Jan. 61, 18 Apr. 62, 8 June 62, 30 Sept. 62 (photos), 9 Dec. 64 (photo), 22 Mar. 65 (photo), 2 July 65, 20 Dec. 66, 23 Dec. 67, 1 May 68, 29 June 69, 8 Aug. 69, 10 Aug. 69, 6 May 70, 17 May 70, 11 June 70, 19 June 70, 1 July 70, 6 Oct. 70, 4 Dec. 70, 7 Feb. 71 (photo), 30 June 71, 24 June 72, 29 June 73, 5 Aug. 73 (photo), 7 Apr. 74, 2 Nov. 75 (photo), 3 Dec. 75, 11 Dec. 75, 19 Mar. 76, 27 Aug. 76, 10 Feb. 77, 14 May 77, 17 July 77 (photo), 31 July 77, 11 Nov. 77 (photo), 27 Aug. 78 (photo), 27 Aug. 78, 3 Nov. 78, 11 Feb. 79 (photo), 15 Feb. 79, 16 Feb. 79, 25 Feb. 79, 3 May 79 (adv.), 18 Sept. 80, 26 Mar. 88, 20 Aug. 89, 17 Oct. 90; *Reno Gazette-Journal*, 29 May 94; Roger Butterfield, "Harold's Club," *Life*, 15 Oct. 1945, 116–31.

HAROLDS GUN CLUB

Located on Pyramid Lake Highway; licensed intermittently from the 1940s to 1979 for slots, 21, craps, and roulette.

Harolds Gun Club was owned and operated by the Smith family, and when gambling was conducted there, employees from the downtown club were taken off their regular schedule and assigned to work at the gun club. The property was opened as a trap and skeet-shooting club in the 1940s, and it had a bar and restaurant but no lodging facilities.

Several Harolds Club employees were shooters, and all employees were given discounts on club fees and shotgun shells. The champion shooter in the United States for many years, Dan Orlich, worked for Harolds Club for over twenty-five years in various capacities. Another longtime Harolds Club employee, Joe Devers, was often Orlich's main competition. Frequently, Devers and Orlich finished first and second in the United States, with Devers winning almost as often as Orlich.

The gun club was open several days a week for shooting, but gaming was available only when major trap shoots were held there, which was about four to six times a year. Depending on the size of the shoot, there would be one or two dice tables, three to six 21 games, one roulette game, and fifty to sixty slot machines. The gaming would open early in the morning and stay open until there was no more play, often lasting fourteen to sixteen hours a day. The action was heavy, and the limits were high. The shooters had almost unlimited credit, and $500 and $1,000 wagers were common. Hundreds of thousands of dollars in chips and currency were transported between Harolds Club downtown

Harolds Gun Club in the early 1950s. Left to right: unknown, Al Lazzarone, unknown, Bernice Turkovich, Gloria Affleck, Doris Rose, Jim Hunter, Fran Slaughter. Courtesy of Al Lazzarone.

and the gun club every day of the shoots—which usually lasted three to five days.

Off-duty Washoe County deputy sheriffs were hired to stay with the money at all times. The money was transported to and from the gun club in a convoy with the bosses and the money in one car, and the deputies riding shotgun in front of and behind the "cash car." There was never an incident of any sort or any breach of security during the many years that gambling was conducted at the out-of-the-way location.

To be selected to work at the gun club was an honor and a much-sought-after job. Cash bonuses were given to the employees, and the long hours meant lots of overtime pay, plus the tips received from the players, which sometimes amounted to hundreds of dollars a day.

The employees at the gun club were selected for their honesty, friendliness, and dependability. Many dealers, such as Joyce Carrigan, Esther DeRosa, Dell Hoover, Marjorie Norcross, Bobbie Patterson, Laura Ambler, Gloria Affleck, Fran Slaughter, Chuck Adams, Jorge Valdez, and Jean Jefferson Callahan, worked the shoots for years. Some of the bosses who worked the shoots included Jim Wilbur, Joe Speicher,

Dwayne Kling, Jerry Sicka, Darl Voss, Bob Donnelly, and Glen Botorff. Botorff, who originally worked at the gun club as a key man in the slots, then as a dealer, and later as the gaming boss, worked at that location longer than anyone else.

When Harolds Club was sold to the Summa Corporation in 1970, the gun club property was included in the transaction. The former location of Harolds Gun Club is now the site of the Spanish Springs Recreational Area on the Pyramid Lake Highway.

HARRAH, JOHN

John Harrah, father of Bill Harrah, was born in Iowa in 1883. He studied at Iowa State University and Drake University and earned a degree in law. In 1919 he moved to Venice, California, and became involved in real estate while practicing law. He was mayor of Venice from 1922 to 1924.

He moved to Reno in the late 1930s, shortly after his son, Bill, came to Reno. He was active in the management of Harrah's Club in the early years of the casino on Virginia Street, especially during the years when Bill Harrah was drinking and gambling heavily. After Bill Harrah quit drink-

ing in 1952, John Harrah became less active in the club.

John Harrah was a tall, taciturn man who, like his son, did not have a lot to say. He didn't smoke or drink and seldom gambled. "Never really cared for it myself," he said. "I find it gets monotonous."

John Harrah died in Phoenix, Arizona, on May 1, 1969.

Meyer Berger, "The Gay Gamblers of Reno," *Saturday Evening Post*, 10 July 48, 26; *Nev. St. Journal*, 2 May 69 (obit. and photo).

HARRAH, WILLIAM FISK "BILL"

Bill Harrah was born on September 2, 1911, in Pasadena, California. He came to Reno to open his first bingo parlor in October 1937. Although it stayed open only two weeks, from that humble beginning Harrah went on to build the largest gaming empire in the world.

William Eadington, an important authority on gambling in Nevada, in the prologue to Leon Mandel's book *William Fisk Harrah* states: "William Fisk Harrah . . . had greater impact upon the development of the casino gaming industry in northern Nevada, and indeed, in Nevada, than any other single individual."

After Harrah's initial venture failed, he tried again with a bingo parlor on Commercial Row. Soon after, he moved to Virginia Street, where he took over the Heart Tango Club. In 1942 he leased the Reno Club, and in 1943 he opened the Blackout Bar, which contained slot machines, a craps table, and a 21 game.

After a nine-year series of moves, Harrah finally opened his first full casino. In June 1946 he opened Harrah's Club at the former location of the Mint Club, at 210–214 North Virginia Street.

Nine years later, he bought George's Gateway Club on the South Shore of Lake Tahoe, and in 1958 he purchased the property across the highway (Sahati's Stateline Country Club) and began an extensive remodeling and refurbishing program. In December 1959 Harrah opened the new South Shore Room in the Stateline Club, with Red Skelton appearing as the first headliner.

John Harrah watching the table drop boxes being transported into Harrah's counting room in 1948. Courtesy of Scherry Harrah.

Meanwhile, he was continuing to expand in Reno as he took over the locations of the Bonanza Club, the Frontier Club, the Golden Hotel, the Overland Hotel, the Palace Club, and the Greyhound bus depot.

In 1962 Harrah opened his automobile museum, and by 1970 one million visitors had been through the museum. Harrah's automobile collection, which included as many as fourteen hundred cars at one point, was the largest such collection in the world. *Motor Trend* magazine said, "Henry Ford built the car; Bill Harrah built its monument."

Harrah began construction of his Reno hotel in 1968 and opened the 24-story, 365-room hotel in 1969.

In 1971 Harrah's went public with an over-the-counter stock offering. In 1972 Harrah's was listed on the American Stock Exchange, and in 1973 Harrah's was listed on the New York Stock Exchange. It was the first business that derived most of its revenues from gaming to appear on the New York Stock Exchange.

In 1972 the ground floor of Harrah's Tahoe Hotel opened. This addition, adjoining the existing casino, made Harrah's Tahoe the largest single casino in the state of Nevada. In November 1973 Bill Harrah officially opened 250 rooms in his Tahoe hotel.

Bill Harrah's success was not a chance happening. He was meticulous in every detail. He was a quiet person who delegated authority and sought the advice of others. He demanded perfection, and two of his philosophies in life were: "Treat people like you would like to be treated yourself," and "Do the impossible, please everyone." His development of the best-run, and possibly the most profitable, casino of his era was the result of careful planning and attention to detail.

Harrah feared federal intervention in the gaming industry and was a consistent supporter of tight state legislative controls on gambling. To this end, he put all his influence behind the 1955 measure to create a state Gaming Control Board and the 1959 successor establishing the Nevada Gaming Commission.

Harrah was married to six women during his lifetime (to one of them, Scherry, twice). His first marriage in the late 1930s was to Thelma Batchelor, from his hometown of Venice, California. His longest marriage was to Scherry Teague. Harrah met her when she was dealing in Harolds Club, and their marriage lasted (off and on) for twenty years. They adopted two sons, John and Tony. Harrah later had three short marriages—one to Bobbie Gentry, then Mary Burger, and later Roxanna Carlson. In 1974 he married Verna Frank Harrison and remained married to her until his death.

Harrah's treatment of the stars who appeared at his casinos was legendary. As one entertainer put it, "There's places to work and then there is Harrah's." Harrah was a shrewd judge of entertainment, and he had a knack for picking a performer at just the right time (or the ability to listen to the advice of his entertainment executive). Just when a new entertainer would be "busting on the scene," he or she would be appearing at Harrah's Club. Harrah formed many lifelong friendships with people who appeared in his club. Stars such as John Denver, Bill Cosby, Frank Sinatra, Sammy Davis Jr., Jim Nabors, and a host of others were more than just stars appearing at Harrahs's—they were true friends.

In June 1978 Bill Harrah went to the Mayo Clinic in Rochester, Minnesota, to have surgery for an aortal aneurysm (a weakening of the heart's main artery). It was his second operation for the same problem, the first having been performed in 1972. Two days after undergoing surgery—on June 30, 1978—Bill Harrah died. He was two months short of his sixty-seventh birthday when he passed away.

Harrah's funeral was held on July 5, 1978, at St. John's Presbyterian Church on Plumb Lane. The church was filled to overflowing with hundreds of people from all walks of life. John Denver sang "Singing Skies and Dancing Waters," and George Vargas, one of Harrah's attorneys, delivered the eulogy. Seventy-six people were named as honorary pallbearers.

William Fisk Harrah, who in 1972 had been designated a Distinguished Nevadan

Bill and Scherry Harrah in one of their classic antique automobiles. Courtesy of Scherry Harrah.

price reported to be in excess of $500,000. The wall separating the two clubs was taken down, and Harrah's doubled its size overnight. The expansion resulted in the licensing of ten more table games and two hundred and fifteen more slots.

In June 1957 Harrah's made nationwide news when it installed the first air curtain in Nevada, making the entrance accessible and inviting in all weather. The air curtain was part of the remodeling and expansion resulting from the purchase of the Frontier Club.

Another "first" resulting from the expansion was the construction of a revolving stage. Located behind a thirty-six-stool bar, the stage revolved and allowed for continuous entertainment with no intermissions necessary. Whenever one act completed its sct, the stage revolved to present a second act. The total elapsed "down time" between acts was perhaps forty-five to sixty seconds.

by the Board of Regents of the University of Nevada for his "outstanding social, cultural and economic contributions to Nevada," was buried in Hailey, Idaho, on July 19, 1978.

Leon Mandel, *William Fisk Harrah* (Garden City, N.Y.: Doubleday and Company, 1982); Robert A. Ring, "Recollections of Life in California, Nevada Gaming, and Reno and Lake Tahoe Civic Affairs" (unpublished oral history, University of Nevada Oral History Program, 1973); *Nev. St. Journal,* 31 July 47, 26 Apr. 72 (photo), 12 May 72, 1 July 78 (obit. and photos), 2 July 78, 5 July 78, 6 July 78 (photos), 19 July 78.

HARRAH'S

210 North Virginia Street; licensed since June 20, 1946, as a full casino.

William Harrah operated bingo games and the Blackout Bar in the late 1930s and early 1940s, but Harrah's Club, which started at 210 North Virginia Street and eventually spread across Virginia Street to Center Street, was his first full casino.

Harrah's Club opened on June 20, 1946. It was advertised as "Nevada's most beautiful casino, a full casino plus horse race bet-

ting, two bars and an all-male staff." The casino originally had 35 front feet on Virginia and was 140 feet deep, reaching into Lincoln Alley. It was licensed for a keno game, a faro bank, two roulette games, six 21 games, three craps games, forty slot machines, and a horse-race book.

Bob Ring's oral history states that "originally we put in rubber tile, inlaid square flooring and all our fixtures were either real fine oak or a mahogany, but since Harrah was advertising the new place as 'The Casino to See,' the rubber tiles and inlaid squares didn't quite cut it with Mr. Harrah. We had to put in Terrazzo tile and carpeting."

In July 1952 Harrah's bought the property where the club was located from Joe and Victor Saturno for a total price of $302,450. The terms were $62,450 down and $40,000 or more annually. In January 1953 Harrah's purchased the former Frisco Club at 207 North Center Street and opened it the following April as Harrah's Bingo Parlor.

In November 1956 Harrah's purchased the Frontier Club, which was located to the immediate north of Harrah's Club, for a

Bill Harrah and his father, John Harrah, pictured in front of one of their bingo parlors. Courtesy of Lloyd and Joan Dyer.

Scherry Teague (Harrah) dealing 21 in Harrah's Club in 1948, a few months prior to marrying Bill Harrah. In the background are Warren Nelson, Bill Harrah, and Bob Ring. Courtesy of Scherry Harrah.

Crowds thronged to Harrah's to see the new air curtain and the revolving stage. Both innovations were firsts for the Reno area.

Two other innovations received less publicity but had an equally significant impact on the gaming industry. It was Harrah who introduced bells and lights on slot machines and thereby gave the interior of casinos their now-customary carnival atmosphere. Harrah is also credited with creating "the eye in the sky"—a crawl space beneath the upstairs offices equipped with one-way glass to allow him or his managers to observe the activity in the casino. This is the first known instance of casino surveillance, another casino device that has become commonplace.

In January 1962 Harrah's announced plans for a four-level casino restaurant on the corner of Second and Center Streets. The site was formerly occupied by the Grand Hotel and Grand Cafe.

Owner Bill Harrah opened his personal automobile collection to the public in February 1962. The collection, which was housed in Sparks, eventually became the world's largest. It is now housed in the National Automobile Museum near downtown Reno.

In April 1962 the Golden Hotel was destroyed by fire, and as a result, Harrah's Bingo Parlor was closed. It reopened on May 29, 1962, at a new location, 136 North Center Street, on a limited basis, and opened full time on July 27, 1962. The new operation included bingo, a restaurant, a $25,000-limit keno game, and slot machines.

On June 14, 1963, after a full year of construction, Harrah's opened its new casino-restaurant on the northwest corner of Second and Center Streets. The building contained 9,520 square feet of casino space with 430 slot machines, three craps games, twelve 21 games, one roulette game, one pari-mutuel wheel, and an eight-station keno game. A 165-seat restaurant called the Terrace Room opened on the second floor. Five hundred and forty new employees were hired to staff the facility.

On June 27, 1965, Harrah's Club opened its Grand Buffet on Second Street at the former site of the Grand Cafe, which had been owned and operated by the Petrono-

vich family for more than fifty years. The buffet was located in the basement and seated 264 people. The decor was red brick and oak and included several ornate chandeliers. Buffet prices were $1.50 for lunch, $2.95 for dinner, and $2.00 for Sunday brunch.

On March 29, 1966, Harrah's Club leased the partially rebuilt Golden Hotel for five years, with an option to renew. After a hurried and extensive remodeling of the property, Harrah's opened a four-hundred-seat theater-restaurant on June 20, 1966. The showroom, later called the Headliner Room, was located in the former Golden Hotel casino. Eddie Fisher was the first entertainer to appear there. The opening coincided with the twentieth anniversary of Harrah's original downtown opening.

Other facilities that opened on June 20 included a 250-seat theater-lounge, the Blackout Bar, a coffee shop, a steak house, and two other bars. Gaming devices added included 450 slot machines and twenty-four table games. More than four hundred new employees were hired for the facility.

In January 1968 Harrah's announced plans to build a twenty-four-story hotel, and in April the casino announced that William Callahan would be the hotel's first general manager. Work on the hotel started the first week of May, and the hotel was topped out in November 1968. A Christmas tree and a U.S. flag were attached to the final beam of the hotel on the penthouse roof. This was actually the twenty-eighth level of the full Harrah's structure. The 326-room, $6-million hotel was scheduled to open in the fall of 1969.

The hotel opened as scheduled on October 11, 1969. Officiating at the ribbon-cutting ceremony, along with William Harrah, were entertainers Pat Paulsen, Mitzi Gaynor, and Flip Wilson. Lou La-Bonte of Auburn, California, was the first person to register as a guest at the hotel. When the hotel opened, it was only 60-percent complete, but it was totally completed by November. The hotel added 150 more people to Harrah's payroll.

At the official grand opening and dedication in November, among the several invited dignitaries attending were Danny

Thomas, Jim Nabors, Rock Hudson, Danny Kaye, and Carol Burnett.

Also in 1969, Bob Ring, who had been with Harrah's for over thirty years and had been president since 1966, was promoted to vice-chairman of Harrah's. Maurice Sheppard, first employed by Harrah's in 1946 as an accountant, was named president.

In May 1970, Bob Martin, vice-president of planning, announced the opening of Harrah's 30,000-square-foot convention center. Also in 1970 the one-millionth customer visited Harrah's Automobile Collection.

In September 1971 Harrah's made financial history when it became the first casino operation to become a publicly traded company. The Nevada Gaming Control Board approved the transaction that allowed Harrah to sell 13 percent of its 3,460,000 shares of stock. Willam Harrah retained 87 percent of the company. Harrah's stock was first offered as an over-the-counter stock, then it was listed on the American Stock Exchange in 1972. In 1973 it became the first business listed on the New York Stock Exchange to derive most of its revenue from gaming.

Money from the sale of stock was used

to begin construction of the Harrah's Hotel on the South Shore of Lake Tahoe. The hotel was completed in 1973.

In June 1973 Linda Woods was hired by Harrah's as a security guard. She is believed to be the first female security guard in Northern Nevada's gaming industry.

In September 1973 Harrah's announced that it would take over the Greyhound Bus Station property on North Center Street. Harrah's then purchased property for the Greyhound Corporation on Stevenson Street between West First and West Second Streets, and a new bus station was built there.

On June 11, 1975, Maurice Sheppard resigned as president of Harrah's and was replaced by longtime Harrah's employee Lloyd Dyer, who served as president until the company was sold to Holiday Inns, Inc., in 1980. Dyer, who was hired by Harrah's in 1957, had served as vice-president under Sheppard and was instrumental in many of Harrah's real-estate transactions over the years.

Harrah's opened its Sports Casino at the former site of the Greyhound Bus Station on June 20, 1975. The casino had 11,000

square feet of gaming area and was licensed for fourteen table games, a $25,000-limit keno game, and 150 slot machines.

On March 31, 1977, Harrah's leased the Overland Hotel-Casino, and that longtime gaming property at the corner of North Center Street and Commercial Row was closed down. In June the property was demolished and construction of a 450-space parking garage began. In July 1977 the Reno City Council approved Harrah's plan to build a three-story skyway over Center Street, connecting Harrah's existing hotel-casino with its planned facility on Center Street (final completion was not expected until early 1980). A year later, in March 1978, Harrah's purchased the Riverside Hotel so it could trade it to Pick Hobson for the Overland site. Hobson was licensed at the Riverside in April 1978. With the sale of the Riverside, Jessie Beck retired from the gaming business.

On June 30, 1978, Bill Harrah died. In a period of a little over forty years (1937–1978), Harrah had built the largest gaming empire in the world. But he had not done it alone, as he would be the first to admit. Bill Harrah was a firm believer in delegating responsibility, and he was fortunate and perceptive enough to surround himself with an organization of loyal, devoted, hardworking, talented, and creative executives and managers. Many were tested and fell by the wayside, but those who survived helped to create the Harrah empire.

First and foremost was his alter ego, Bob Ring. Ring came to Reno in 1938 to manage Harrah's first bingo parlor and was with Harrah for more than forty years. Ring was Bill Harrah's best man in every sense of the word. Not only was he Harrah's general manager for years, he was also Harrah's best man at his wedding to Scherry and was one of his best friends.

Without a doubt, the second most valuable man in Harrah's organization during the 1950s and 1960s was Rome Andreotti. He had an eye for detail and was largely responsible for procedures used in all areas of Harrah's operation, including the near perfection of the gaming operation. He was directly responsible for all pit procedures, and it was through his direction

Bill Harrah and his wife, Scherry, pictured standing near the front of his cabin cruiser, the Thunderbird. *Standing on the stern of the boat is longtime Harrah's employee Lloyd Dyer. Courtesy of Lloyd and Joan Dyer.*

that Harrah's pit became one of the most efficient in Nevada. Every aspect of the Harrah's operation was dictated by carefully spelled-out procedures, and there were more than fifty operations manuals written by company executives covering everything from window-washing policy to business decorum. Andreotti was so loyal to Bill Harrah and so devoted to him that Harrah once said, "If I say, 'Rome, go that way,' he'll keep right on going that way, even if he walks straight through a wall."

Some of the other very early associates of Bill Harrah included William "Bill" Goupil, William "Bull" Demarco, Eldon Campbell, Ed Crume, Vance Beatty, Bill Ames, Fred Brady, and Bill Jackson.

Athletes also played a large role in the early days of Harrah's, and there were many athletes who came to Reno—most of them to attend the University of Nevada—who were hired by Harrah. Many of them stayed to help create the Harrah's empire, including several who became part of Harrah's management team—Andy Marcinko, Pat France, Joe Sheeketski, Lee DeLauer, Bob Martin, and Carmel Caruso.

Another contributor to the early success of Harrah's was Bill Harrah's friend Virgil Smith. Bill Harrah and Virgil Smith spent many hours together in the 1930s and 1940s. Smith, along with helping Bill Harrah financially on occasion, introduced him to two of his early-day club managers—who just happened to be from Virgil Smith's hometown, Lovelock, Nevada—Wayne Martin and Al Fontana.

Yet another important contributor was Maurice Sheppard, who first went to work for Bill Harrah in 1946 and served him faithfully for over thirty years, including six years as president of the company.

Lloyd Dyer, who replaced Sheppard as president, was the leader in the many complicated real-estate transactions that Harrah was continually involved in, as well as in helping to take Harrah's public. Dyer's personality and management style, along with his ability to work with everyone in the organization, made him an integral part of Harrah's successful operation.

Another individual who contributed immensely to the success of Harrah's was

Mark Curtis Sr. His efforts in advertising and public relations kept the name and the image of Harrah's in the public eye for decades.

In later years, young men such as Holmes Hendricksen, George Drews, Doyle Mathia, Dennis Small, and Mert Smith took on positions of importance in the organization and helped to make it grow. Hendricksen was particularly important. He was named vice-president of entertainment in 1971, and it was under his direction that Harrah's became synonymous with top entertainment. He also helped to make Harrah's the number-one venue where most entertainers wanted to appear. Because entertainment was one of the major reasons for Harrah's success, it follows that Hendricksen's role in the development of the entertainment department was a highly significant one in the overall picture of Harrah's growth and success.

Of equal importance to the success of Harrah's was the addition in 1971 of financial expert George Drews, who helped make Harrah's a public company and who, along with Lloyd Dyer and Maurice Sheppard, was instrumental in the listing of Harrah's on the New York Stock Exchange.

Also joining the Harrah's management team in 1971 was Joe Fanelli. He had been employed for many years by the Kahler Corporation, a hotel complex associated with the Mayo Clinic in Rochester, Minnesota. He became acquainted with Bill Harrah and some of Harrah's top executives while they were at the Mayo Clinic undergoing physical exams. Fanelli's contributions to the food and beverage department were an important part of helping Harrah's achieve the reputation of having the finest cuisine in Northern Nevada casinos.

There were so many middle-management and front-line employees who gave years of loyal service to Harrah's that it would be impossible to list them all. However, the following is a short list: Bud Garaventa, Tom Yturbide, Major Inch, John Gianotti, Bill Jones, Ed Posey, Bob Contois, Ed Wessel, Gene Diullo, Harley Green, Dean Gloster, Mando Rueda, Lee Jellison, Clyde Wade, Bob Hudgens, Bessie Peter-

son (one of the first female pit supervisors), Winnie Connor (who dealt 21 for more than twenty-five years), George Haskell (a pit supervisor for over thirty years), and maitre d's Cliff Kehl, Leon Harbert, and John Maniscalco.

Although Bill Harrah died in 1978, Harrah's Club continued to live and grow. Largely because of the tireless efforts of Mead Dixon, Harrah's Club and Holiday Inns reached an agreement on a merger in September 1979. Also in September it was announced that after many months of negotiations, Harrah's had purchased the Palace Club, located at the northwest corner of Center Street and Commercial Row.

On December 17, 1979, Phillip Satre became vice-president, general counsel, and secretary of Harrah's. The joint-venture merger agreement between Harrah's and Holiday Inns, Inc., was given final approval by the Gaming Commission on December 17, but it wasn't until March 1, 1980, that the transaction was actually completed. On that date, Harrah's was officially purchased by Holiday Inns, Inc., for $300 million.

Shortly after the sale, on March 4, 1980, Lloyd Dyer was replaced as president of Harrah's by Richard Goeglein, and at the same time George Drews, Harrah's chief financial officer, was asked to resign.

In August 1980 Harrah's opened a 12,000-square-foot expansion on Center Street. The expansion included a 250-seat cabaret, an expanded race and sports book, an eighty-seat lounge, and a pedestrian skyway linking the Virginia Street and Center Street casinos. Licenses were granted for an additional seven hundred slot machines, twenty-seven 21 games, four craps games, two roulette games, five poker games, a keno game, and a baccarat game. With the new expansion, Harrah's employees numbered over 3,700.

In September 1980 a second-floor restaurant offering buffet dining was opened, and an 870-space parking garage was completed.

Through the 1980s and the 1990s, as legalized gambling spread beyond the boundaries of Nevada, Harrah's continued to expand its operations throughout the United States. It is still growing in every part of the gaming world. From its humble beginnings in 1937, Harrah's became one of the largest and most respected gaming organizations in the world. *(See Addendum 1)*

Leon Mandel, *William Fisk Harrah: The Life and Times of a Gambling Magnate* (Garden City, N.Y.: Doubleday and Company, 1982); Robert A. Ring, "Recollections of Life in California, Nevada Gaming, and Reno and Lake Tahoe Civic Affairs" (unpublished oral history, University of Nevada Oral History Program, 1973); *Nev. St. Journal,* 28 Oct. 37 (adv.).

HARRAH'S CLUB BINGO

124 North Center Street; licensed from October 29 to November 15, 1937, for bingo only.

When Bill Harrah opened his first bingo parlor in Reno, the following advertisement appeared in the *Nevada State Journal* of October 28, 1937. It was the first ever printed in a Reno newspaper by Bill Harrah: "Grand opening of Harrah's Club Bingo, 124 North Center Street. Free inside parking at the Reno Garage. First game is Saturday, October 30, at 7:00 P.M. Free favors, special games, bingo and tango."

The business was very short-lived—it closed only two weeks later. Harrah later realized that the location was too far from "the action." He had received a good deal on the lease price, and he soon understood why the price was so low. His next move was to Commercial Row, but not until July 1938, and not until he had sent for his friend Bob Ring to help him operate his next bingo parlor.

The former location of Harrah's Club Bingo is now part of the Cal-Neva parking garage on the east side of Virginia Street.

Nev. St. Journal, 28 Oct. 37 (adv.), 29 Oct. 37 (adv.); Robert A. Ring, "Recollections of Life in California, Nevada Gaming, and Reno and Lake Tahoe Civic Affairs" (unpublished oral history, University of Nevada Oral History Program, 1973).

HARRAH'S HEART TANGO CLUB (ALSO KNOWN AS HARRAH'S BINGO)

242 North Virginia Street; licensed from November 1938 to 1945 for bingo (tango) only.

Harrah's Heart Tango was the third bingo parlor that Bill Harrah owned in Reno. He bought the lease of the Heart Tango Club in 1938 from Ed Howe for $3,000. Tom Smith was the manager of the Heart Tango, and Harrah retained his services. Smith remained working for Bill Harrah until Harrah's death in 1978.

A large advertisement in the *Nevada State Journal* of November 4, 1938, announcing the opening stated that Harrah's Heart Tango Club would open at 2 P.M. on Saturday, November 5. Two cards cost only five cents, and the prize for each game would be at least $4. In 1944 the' club became known as Harrah's Bingo. In May of that year, Harrah's Bingo advertised: "Two cards for ten cents—six cards for fifty cents."

Harrah's bingo operation was located next door to Harolds Club, with a door between to allow drinks from the Harolds Club bar to be served in the bingo club. A similar arrangement prevailed in Harrah's Reno Club, which was located on the other side of Harolds Club.

When Harrah's lease expired in 1945, the property became part of Harolds Club.

William F. Harrah, "My Recollections of the Hotel-Casino Industry, and as an Auto Collecting Enthusiast" (unpublished oral history, University of Nevada Oral History Program, 1980); *Nev. St. Journal,* 4 Nov. 38 (adv.), 26 Aug. 39, 6 May 44 (adv.), 2 May 47; Robert A. Ring, "Recollections of Life in California, Nevada Gaming, and Reno and Lake Tahoe Civic Affairs" (unpublished oral history, University of Nevada Oral History Program, 1973).

HARRAH'S PLAZA TANGO

14 East Commercial Row; licensed from July 1 to September 1, 1938, for tango (bingo) only.

The Plaza Tango was the second tango (bingo) parlor opened by Bill Harrah in Reno. Tango was the name given to what we now know as bingo. The Plaza Tango was located at 14 East Commercial Row, next door to a well-known Reno restaurant, the Wine House.

The club had two entrances, one at 14 East Commercial Row and the other one at 15 East Douglas Alley.

Harrah held his grand opening on July 1, 1938. The club opened with six employees. Fred Brady was one of the original em-ployees, and he stayed with Bill Harrah until retiring in 1973. Bob Ring, who was to become Harrah's alter ego, came to Reno on August 5 to take over management of the club.

On July 8 Harrah ran an ad in the *Nevada State Journal* that said: "Bring this ad in for six free games at the 8:30 P.M. game on July 9th. The $25 game at 9:30 P.M. is five cents a card."

Harrah's main competition was from the Heart Tango Club, just north of Harolds Club at 242 North Virginia Street. Harrah eliminated his competition by buying the lease from owner Ed Howe in September 1938. He then closed the Plaza Tango and began operation of the Heart Tango Club.

The former location of the Plaza Tango is now part of the Harolds Club property.

Nev. St. Journal, 29 June 38 (adv.), 30 June 38 (adv.), 1 July 38 (adv.), 8 July 38 (adv.); Ring, "Recollections."

HARRAH'S RENO CLUB

232 North Virginia Street; licensed from 1942 to 1948 for bingo only.

Bill Harrah took over the lease on the Reno Club from Fred Yamagishi and Fred Aoyama early in 1942. When the U.S. entered WW II in December 1941, the Japanese owners were forced to sell their business.

Harrah operated the establishment as a bingo parlor until 1948, when the court ruled that the lease he had signed in 1942 was null and void and that he must vacate the premises. The property was owned by Harolds Club and eventually became a part of the Harolds Club operation.

Nev. St. Journal, 12 Feb. 48, 14 Feb. 48, 17 Feb. 48, 25 May 52.

HAYMARKET CLUB

10 West Commercial Row; licensed from July 1951 to May 1953 for slots, 21, and craps.

In July 1951 Gene Rovetti, Doug Busey, and John Hickok reopened the Blue Bird Club under the name of the Haymarket Club. The property had been closed since May 1949 when a fire, believed to have been caused by arson, severely damaged the club.

The Haymarket, like so many other small clubs, was more a bar than a casino. Occasionally the Haymarket offered entertainment on its small stage. The Tony Pecetti Orchestra—one of early Reno's favorite groups—sometimes appeared there.

In March 1952 Clifford Quinlisk was added to the license as a new partner, but he remained only until November 1952. At that time, both Hickok and Quinlisk were deleted from the license.

In March 1953 C. J. Gaertner and F. W. Barrett were granted a gaming license at the Haymarket for a 21 game and a craps game. The property was closed a few months later.

The former location of the Haymarket Club is now part of Fitzgeralds Casino-Hotel.

Nev. St. Journal, 2 June 51, 15 June 51, 20 July 51 (adv.), 25 July 51, 25 Jan. 52, 1 Mar. 52, 24 June 52, 22 Aug. 52 (adv.), 26 Nov. 52 (adv.), 2 Dec. 52, 10 Mar. 53.

HEART TANGO CLUB
216 North Virginia, 220 North Virginia, and 242 North Virginia Street; licensed from May 1932 to September 1938 for tango (bingo) only.

On May 18, 1932, the Heart Tango Club opened at 220 North Virginia Street. The grand opening was held at 7 P.M. The following day the club opened from 1 to 7 P.M. It offered nickel tango (an early name for bingo—which was also sometimes called keno) and "large pots."

On June 18, 1932, the club moved to 216 North Virginia Street, where it featured two tango cards for a nickel.

As a forerunner of things to come in the gaming business, the Heart Tango Club gave away a new Chevrolet as a prize in a drawing held on November 11, 1934. This event was part of an advertising campaign to make known the club's newest location at 242 North Virginia Street.

In September 1938 Bill Harrah bought the lease from Ed Howe and operated the club as Harrah's Heart Tango until 1945. At that time, the property was taken over by Harolds Club. It remains part of the Harolds Club property.

Nev. St. Journal, 18 May 32 (adv.), 18 June 32 (adv.), 9 Apr. 33 (adv.), 3 Nov. 34, 24 June 37.

HEIDELBURG CLUB
6405 South Virginia Street; licensed from September 1931 to September 1935 for craps and 21.

The Heidelburg Club was a nightclub and dinner house located in an area then considered out of town. The gaming was leased to Swede Collet and Swede Oleson. Virgil Smith later operated the gaming there for a short while.

Some of Reno's most popular musicians played there. Louis Rosasco and his orchestra performed frequently, as did Della Quadri and his orchestra. Louis Marymount, a well-known Reno personality in the entertainment field, managed the club from 1934 to 1936.

The Heidelburg Club closed in 1936 and reopened as the Del Monte Club. The site is now occupied by the One Stop Burger Shop.

Nev. St. Journal, 21 Jan. 33, 28 Apr. 33, 1 Aug. 34, 2 Aug. 34 (adv.), 1 Apr. 36 (adv.).

HEMPHILL, AUSTIN
Austin Hemphill purchased 30 percent of the Holiday Hotel on Mill Street in June 1967. His partners were John Monfrey and Tom Moore. Hemphill, who was from Texas, as were Moore and Monfrey, was an investor rather than an operator.

Hemphill and his associates sold the Holiday Hotel in 1970 to William Bradley, John Squire Drendel, Al Ferrarri, and Len McIntosh.

Nev. St. Journal, 23 June 67, 2 Apr. 70.

HENDRICKSEN, HOLMES
Holmes Hendricksen was born in Holyoke, Colorado, on April 22, 1933. He and his family soon moved to Idaho, and Holmes grew up in Gooding. He first came to Harrah's Lake Tahoe in the summer of 1956 and worked as a busboy. In the fall of 1956 he returned to the University of Utah, where he received a B.S. degree in physical education in 1957. He then returned to Harrah's Lake Tahoe and was employed as a cashier. In 1958 he was named cashier and credit manager. He served in that position for nearly five years. In 1963 he became a relief shift manager, then shift manager, and in May

1965 he was named assistant club manager. In 1967 he was named club manager of Harrah's Lake Tahoe.

In February 1971 Hendricksen was named vice-president of entertainment and was soon named executive vice-president of entertainment and advertising. Hendricksen headed up the entertainment department of Harrah's until his retirement in 1995. To a large degree, the tremendous success of the entire Harrah's operation was due to the great success of its entertainment department, which was under Hendricksen's direction for so many years.

Holmes Hendricksen is currently living in Reno.

HENRY CLUB
133 Lake Street; licensed from April 1931 to 1932 for slots, 21, craps, keno, and fan-tan.

The Henry Club was owned and operated by Woo Sing. One of the first casinos licensed in Reno (April 6, 1931), it opened with one 21 game, poker, and a craps game. Later, slots and a keno game were added. Sing also wanted to operate a Chinese lottery, but this was not a legal game under the 1931 gaming law. (Chinese lottery later evolved into what we currently know as keno.)

Currently the former site of the Henry Club is a parking lot.

Nev. St. Journal, 27 May 31.

HENRY'S CLUB
211 North Virginia Street; licensed from June to September 1945 for bingo only.

Henry's Club operated a short-lived bingo game at a site that later became the location of the Mapes Money Tree.

Currently the former location of Henry's Club is the site of the Thrifty Gambler.

Nev. St. Journal, 2 June 45 (adv.).

HEWINS, BRAD
Brad Hewins was born in Randolph, Massachusetts, in 1903. In his early twenties he went to the Philippine Islands to work in the hotel and restaurant business. After five years he returned to the United States and came to Reno, where he went to work at the Wine House in 1931.

Hewins was employed at the Club Fortune from the early 1940s until it closed in January 1948. In the late 1940s and early 1950s, he was one of the managers of the Bank Club. In July 1953 he leased the Palace Club, but after only four months he sold the lease to a group of thirteen people headed by Howard Farris and Harry Weitz. In August 1956, Hewins was one of thirteen people licensed at the Horseshoe Club on North Virginia Street. When the Horseshoe was sold to the Mason family in 1967, Hewins stayed on with the new organization as president and general manager.

Brad Hewins died in a San Francisco hospital on February 8, 1972.

Nev. St. Journal, 18 Jan. 47, 26 May 53, 19 July 53, 24 Aug. 56, 10 Feb. 72 (obit. and photo).

HICKOK, JOHN

John Hickok was a prominent realtor and land developer who was associated with many clubs and casinos in Reno. He also founded Home Savings and Loan and the Reno Realty Company.

In 1950 he, along with Doug Busey, Jack Douglass, and others, was licensed at the Picadilly Club on North Virginia Street. In 1951 he was licensed at the Blue Bird Club, later renamed the Haymarket Club. In 1953 he was licensed as a 35-percent owner of the Nugget, formerly the Picadilly Club. In 1964 Hickok was licensed as the owner of Hickok's Golden Gulch Casino on East Second Street.

John Hickok passed away on October 29, 1975, at seventy-three years of age.

Nev. St. Journal, 22 Sept. 50, 15 June 51, 19 Aug. 53, 14 Apr. 64, 30 Oct. 75 (obit. and photo).

HICKS, CARL

Carl Hicks was born in Palisade, Colorado, on July 16, 1913. He was a real-estate broker when he moved from Los Angeles to Reno in 1957. Shortly after arriving in Reno, he and his wife won first prize in a promotional contest held by the Holiday Hotel— a trip around the world. Less than a year later, Hicks was licensed as a 7.6-percent owner of the Holiday Hotel.

In 1962, after the death of majority owner Newt Crumley, Carl Hicks and David Burns purchased the Holiday. Hicks became a 73-percent owner, and Burns owned the remaining 27 percent. In July 1967 Hicks and Burns sold the Holiday Hotel to three men from Texas—Austin Hemphill, Tom Moore, and John Monfrey.

After selling the Holiday Hotel, Hicks remained active in the real-estate business for several years. He died on November 3, 1997.

Nev. St. Journal, 23 Sept. 58, 27 Jan. 59, 27 July 67, 5 Nov. 97 (obit. and photo).

HIGH, DAVID

David High was born in New Jersey in 1912 and came to Reno in 1950 at the request of Joseph "Doc" Stacher, who was attempting to buy a percentage of the Golden Hotel Casino and wanted High as his advisor.

Stacher was denied a license at the Golden, but in 1952 High, who had been appointed managing director of the hotel, applied for 25 percent of the Golden Hotel Casino. In March 1952 High was questioned intensely by the state tax commission (the predecessor of the Gaming Commission) about his association with Stacher and with the Anastasia brothers, notorious mob figures. He was also questioned about where he was getting the money to buy a percentage of the Golden. High stated that he had put up no money for his 25 percent but was given the percentage by Bill Graham because of his managing ability and as repayment for his efforts in rebuilding the Golden Bank Hotel-Casino to its status as a paying property.

The state kept deferring High's application until September, when he withdrew it. In January 1953 he resigned as manager of the Golden.

In 1959 High applied for licensing of the landlord company of the Club Cal-Neva. Although the Control Board recommended approval, the Gaming Commission denied his application.

In April 1960 it was rumored that High was to enter an association with the owner of the Riverside Hotel, Robert Franks, and in November it was rumored that High might go to work for William Miller, who had purchased the Riverside from Franks.

In both cases, the Gaming Commission emphatically stated that High was not to be connected with the management of the Riverside in any way.

High was never granted a gaming license.

Nev. St. Journal, 19 June 52, 4 Sept. 52, 24 Jan. 53, 4 Oct. 59, 15 Oct. 59, 3 Feb. 60, 20 Apr. 60, 22 Nov. 60.

HILL, BERNARD "BENNY"

Benny Hill was born Bernard Hilsenteger in Odessa, Russia, on March 8, 1906, and came to Reno in 1938. He was a supervisor of gaming in various establishments, including the Palace Club, Harrah's, the Bank Club, and the Mapes Hotel, and he was one of the thirteen original owners of the Horseshoe Club on North Virginia Street. He remained a co-owner until the club was sold to the Mason family in 1967.

In 1972 the Gaming Commission, at the request of 30-percent owner Paul Richards, appointed Hill as casino manager of Zimba's Casino when it was put into receivership. He worked there as casino manager until the club was closed a few months later.

Hill retired after his stint at Zimba's and devoted his energy to playing golf. He died in Reno on January 4, 1997.

Nev. St. Journal, 24 Aug. 56, 11 Aug. 72, 25 May 73, 6 Jan. 97 (obit. and photo).

HOBSON, JOSEPH "JOE"

Joe Hobson was a co-owner, along with Pick Hobson, his brother, and others, of the Frontier Club from 1946 to 1956. He was also a co-owner, again with his brother Pick, of the Overland Hotel from 1960 to 1977. Hobson was also licensed for the gaming at the Bonanza Club in Virginia City from April 1968 to February 1971.

Nev. St. Journal, 4 Apr. 68, 19 Feb. 71.

HOBSON, RICHARD "PICK"

Pick Hobson, who was honored in 1981 at the gaming industry's fiftieth-anniversary celebration at the MGM Hotel-Casino, was the only honoree who had actually been in gaming for the entire half century. Hobson was born in Illinois on May 15, 1911, and moved to Corning, California, as a child. He didn't remember how he got the nickname, only that when he was growing up he was always called "Pick." He left home in 1929 when his father died, and his wanderings led him to Reno and the world of wide-open gambling.

Hobson worked as a dealer and pit boss at the Palace Club in his early years, but it wasn't long until he became the operator of the games at the Colombo Club on Lake Street. Hobson owned and operated ten clubs in the Reno-Sparks area during his fifty-year career. He also owned, along with his brother Joe, a gambling casino in Hawthorne during the early years of World War II.

In 1943 he opened Pick's Club, located at 220 North Virginia Street. He operated it alone until 1945, then took in several partners, including his brother Joe, closed Pick's Club, and reopened the property as the Frontier Club in 1946.

Hobson operated the Frontier Club from 1946 until November 1956, when he sold it to Harrah's Club. Conditions of the sale prevented Hobson from opening another casino for the next three years.

Pick's next casino was the Overland Hotel, where he was licensed from 1960 to 1977. In May 1977 Bill Harrah leased the property from Hobson. In March 1978 Harrah purchased the Riverside Hotel from Jessie Beck and traded it to Hobson for the Overland. The acquisition of the Overland was a key move in Bill Harrah's plan to expand his own gaming operation, because this property eventually became the site of the multistory garage that Harrah so badly needed for his hotel and customer parking. During the period that Hobson owned the Overland Hotel, he also owned the Cosmo Club (1970 to 1974), the Gold Club in Sparks (1974 to 1980), and the Topaz Lodge (1974 to 1985).

Hobson was licensed at the Riverside Hotel-Casino from April 1978 until November 1986. The casino was closed in December 1986, but Hobson continued to operate the hotel portion of the Riverside until November 1987.

Hobson was extremely well liked by his employees, and whenever he opened a casino, people who had worked for him in the past at one of his other casinos almost always "came back to Pick." When beset by financial difficulties, he always made certain that his employees were paid in full for their services, even when he was forced into closures.

Hobson, who spent the last few years of his life living near Portola, California, passed away on August 19, 1996.

Nev. St. Journal, 6 Apr. 60, 24 July 70, 19 July 74, 13 Oct. 74, 31 Dec. 74, 10 Mar. 78, 13 Apr. 78, 4 Jan. 80, 21 Aug. 96 (obit. and photos).

HOFFMAN, AL

Al Hoffman was a large, gravel-voiced man who was usually seen wearing a cowboy hat. He was co-owner, along with Phil Curti, of the Dog House from 1935 to 1940. He was also co-owner of the La Fiesta Club on North Center Street in 1946 and co-owner of the Tropics on North Center Street from 1944 to 1947.

Al Hoffman died of throat cancer in the early 1950s.

HOLIDAY HOTEL

111 Mill Street (corner of South Center and Mill Streets); licensed as a full casino from August 1957 to November 1998.

In June 1955 it was announced that construction would begin on the Holiday Hotel. Partners in the operation were Norman Biltz, John Mueller, Marsh Johnson, and the Stanley Dollars, Sr. and Jr. The contractor was Everett Brunzell.

The eight-story, two-hundred-room hotel was scheduled to open without gambling, and there was much conjecture at the time as to whether such a large hotel could succeed without gambling. However, on December 12, 1956, five days before the hotel was to be opened, the owners announced that the A-1 Supply Corporation would operate fifty slot machines in the hotel but that there would be no table games.

On December 16, 1956, the hotel held a pre–grand-opening night, and the Holiday officially opened for business on December 17.

The Holiday operated without table games until 1957, when in July it was announced that Newton Crumley, who had operated the Commercial Hotel in Elko for several years before selling out in 1955, would buy the hotel for a reported $5 million. Crumley and his six associates stated that they would put in gambling and take over operation of the property on August 1.

On July 23 the state approved the Crumley group for licensing at the Holiday. They had a two-year lease with an option to buy. Their rent was $21,363 per month. If the group did not purchase the property after two years, the rent was to go up to between $30,000 and $35,000 a month.

In the license application, Crumley stated that they had already invested $600,000. Of the total amount, $200,000 was for remodeling, $100,000 for gambling equipment, and $300,000 for the bankroll.

The Holiday opened with fifty slot machines and seven table games (two craps games, four 21 games, and one roulette game). Fifty more slot machines were added a month later. The licensees were Newt Crumley, 45 percent for $275,000; John Richards, 8 percent for $50,000; Joe McCarthy, 4 percent for $25,000; John Berger, 12 percent for $75,000; Lee Brack, 16 percent for $100,000; L. A. Eldridge, 8 percent for $50,000; William Hawkins, 4 percent for $25,000; and Lee Frankovich, who had been manager of the Riverside Hotel for the last one and a half years, as manager, with no investment.

The Holiday opened on August 1, 1957. What was to have been a one-night public opening turned into an event that lasted for an entire week. The opening was highlighted by a free buffet, surprise gifts and drawings, and entertainment furnished by six different musical groups. Cash drawings, mink coats, and even a round-the-world trip were some of the inducements offered to entice both locals and tourists to visit the Holiday.

George Hayes was the first casino manager of the Holiday Hotel-Casino, and his three shift managers were John Sanford, Roy Nelson, and Jim Metrovich. Frenchy Dupuoy was the bar manager.

Carl Hicks, a real-estate investor from Los Angeles, won the round-the-world

Ready to tee off at a Harolds Club–sponsored golf tournament are (l. to r.) David Burns, co-owner of the Holiday Hotel Casino; Dow Gayle; Jim Wilbur, Harolds Club pit supervisor; James Slattery, Republican senator from Storey County; and Harold Smith Jr. of Harolds Club. Courtesy of Jim Wilbur.

trip in November 1957, and in September 1958 he purchased 7 percent of the Holiday for $50,000.

In May 1958 Bill Williams, a resident of the Reno area for over thirty years, was named casino manager; however, a few months later, in September 1958, Walter Parman was named casino manager and George Hayes was named his assistant.

In January 1959 Lee Frankovich resigned as general manager. He was replaced by David Burns, with Carl Hicks as his assistant.

In July 1960 five of the original investors in the Holiday—John Berger, William Hawkins, John Richards, Lee Brack, and Joe McCarthy—representing 26.07 percent of the stock, sold their interests back to Crumley Hotels, Inc., for $250,000. This left four stockholders—Newt Crumley, Loyal Eldridge, Carl Hicks, and Lee Frankovich.

In February 1962 Newt Crumley, along with E. J. Questa, was killed in an airplane crash near Elko. Crumley's widow, Frances Crumley, took over as president of the Holiday and said that there would be no

changes in policy or personnel. David Burns stayed on as vice-president, and John Sanford, who had replaced Walter Parman, stayed on as casino manager. However, in less than four months, Mrs. Crumley and her associates sold the Holiday to the newly formed CARDA Corporation for a price in excess of $1 million. Carl Hicks, former vice-president of the Holiday, held 73 percent of the new corporation, and David Burns, comptroller and executive assistant, owned the remaining 27 percent. (The name CARDA was derived from the two first names of Hicks and Burns, Carl and David.)

In what was a news-making event, the Holiday unveiled the first electronic 21 game in February 1963. The new device caused a great deal of speculation as to the future of "real" 21 dealers.

In June 1963 Jack Walker, who had been prominent in the management of various gaming operations since coming to Reno in 1955, was named casino manager of the Holiday. Walker, whose son Wayne was a professional football player, helped con-

tinue the Holiday's marketing program relating to professional and amateur sports.

For many years the Holiday sponsored the Mug Hunt, a golf tournament that invited famous athletes to compete not only in golf but in gaming as well. High-rolling customers of the Holiday were also invited, and the celebrities and gaming customers brought many dollars to the gaming tables.

In July 1967 the Holiday was sold to Tom Moore, John Monfrey, and Austin Hemphill for $5 million. The three new licensees were all from San Antonio, Texas. A few months later, Lee Frankovich resigned from John Ascuaga's Nugget to become general manager and a 2.5-percent owner of the Holiday. In less than six months Frankovich left his post as general manager as a result of the termination of public relations director Bob Dill. His percentage of ownership was transferred to the other owners.

From 1967 to 1970 there were other partners in the Holiday. The most prominent of them was Elbert Cox, who is still active in Reno gaming. Also licensed as partners were Felton McCorquodale, a poker supervisor at the Holiday; Philip Wilborn; and Bessie Aldridge, a San Antonio schoolteacher.

The hotel-casino was known as "Tom Moore's Holiday" during Moore's regime, and many consider that era the most exciting in the Holiday's history. Moore brought in high-rolling customers from Texas and other parts of the Southwest, and during that time there was probably more high-limit action at the Holiday than in any other casino in town.

In May 1970 a group of four local men purchased 75 percent of the Holiday. John Squire Drendel, a local attorney who purchased 12.5 percent, would act as secretary. William Bradley, also a local attorney, bought 12.5 percent and was named treasurer. Al Ferrarri, a dairy firm executive, purchased 25 percent and was named president and general manager. Len McIntosh purchased 25 percent and became the vice-president. Tom Moore retained 25 percent of the operation but did not take an active role in the management of the new company.

The new group of owners had a very

short association. In September 1970 John Squire Drendel, William Bradley, and Tom Moore sold their percentages, and McIntosh and Ferrarri became sole owners.

In 1979 Jack Pieper, president of Reno's MGM Hotel-Casino, announced that he was resigning to become president and general manager of the Holiday. He also stated that he would acquire a financial interest in the hotel-casino. In August 1980 Pieper left the Holiday and said he was returning to Las Vegas.

In May 1995 Al Ferrarri and Len McIntosh announced that they had sold the Holiday—pending state approval—to Eric Specter of Carlsbad, California, for $7.5 million in cash. Specter announced plans to refurbish and expand the property and add a 350-room hotel tower, a parking garage, retail space, and a thirty-lane bowling facility. However, in March 1996 Anne Mudd, general manager of the Holiday, announced that Specter had failed to obtain financing for the property and had pulled out of the deal.

On July 10, 1996, Ferrarri and McIntosh announced that the Holiday was not for sale and that they had appointed a new general manager, Dick Piper. Piper, a forty-five-year veteran of the gaming industry, planned to make the Holiday a first-class property once again.

However, a downturn in the Reno gaming economy and the eighteen-month closure of the Center Street bridge combined to force the Holiday to shut down its operation. On September 21, 1998, the Holiday announced that it would close at the end of November, but said it was negotiating a possible sale. Five days later, Lawrence Denig, president of Diamond Resorts International, Inc., of Klamath Falls, Oregon, announced that he was buying the Holiday, renovating it, and reopening it as a time-share hotel-casino. On October 29, 1998, general manager Dick Piper said that the hotel-casino would close on November 1, 1998, and that the deal to sell it appeared shaky. The closure of the 193-room hotel resulted in the termination of 175 employees.

The Holiday was sold at a public auction held on January 22, 1999, to an unnamed Los Angeles developer for the minimum bid of $2.5 million. The developer then sold it to the Capital Salvage Company, a San Leandro–based investment company headed by Barney Ng. On February 20, 1999, Peter Wilday, a Reno architect and also an executive in the Gaming Entertainment Management Company, announced preliminary plans to begin work on a $14- to $20-million remodeling project.

Nev. St. Journal, 17 June 55, 22 June 55 (photo), 12 Dec. 56, 15 Dec. 56 (adv.), 10 July 57, 21 July 57, 23 July 57, 30 July 57, 3 Aug. 57 (photo), 20 Aug. 57 (adv.), 21 Nov. 57, 16 May 58, 30 July 58 (adv.), 11 Sept. 58, 23 Sept. 58, 25 Sept. 58, 27 Jan. 59, 11 Feb. 59, 14 July 59, 20 Oct. 59, 27 Oct. 59, 28 Oct. 59, 7 July 60, 9 Feb. 62, 11 Feb. 62, 20 Feb. 62, 12 June 62, 19 Jan. 63, 21 Feb. 63, 16 Mar. 63 (photo), 23 June 67, 27 July 67, 28 July 67, 16 Aug. 67, 27 Oct. 67, 11 Jan. 68, 12 Jan. 68, 23 May 68, 22 June 68, 20 Nov. 68, 11 Feb. 69, 2 Apr. 70, 14 May 70, 23 May 70, 12 July 70 (photo), 21 Aug. 70 (photo), 10 Sept. 70, 18 Oct. 70 (photo), 14 Dec. 72, 28 July 74 (photo), 12 Jan. 79, 30 Aug. 80 (photo), 31 Aug. 80 (photo), 23 Jan. 99, 21 Feb. 99.

HOLIDAY LODGE

9400 West Fourth Street (five miles west of Reno on old Highway 40); licensed from July 1963 to June 1968 for slots, 21, craps, and roulette.

The Holiday Lodge was just one of many names given the property located at 9400 West Fourth Street. For many years it was known as Lawton's (or Laughton's) Hot Springs. Thousands of Renoites and tourists alike visited the swimming pool and hot mineral baths on the property.

By July 1962 the property was known as the Holiday Lodge and consisted of twenty-eight deluxe motel units. In May 1963 four men—George Ruppert of Reno, Clarence Crandall of Auburn, Stan Simmons of Stateline, and Ralph Roberts—applied for a gaming license at the property. The four men, operating under the corporate name of River Luck, Inc., sought a license for four table games and fifty slot machines. They were granted a license and operated the gambling from July 1963 to March 1964. At that time Warren Hancock of Casper, Wyoming, purchased 50 percent of the operation for $50,000. Ralph Roberts bought the other 50 percent and became the casino manager. Stan Simmons, Clarence Crandell, and George Ruppert sold their interests.

In May 1965 Muriel Geddes of Millbrae, California, was licensed at the Holiday Lodge. She invested $365,000 for the privilege of operating the lodge, three table games, and twenty-five slot machines.

In March 1966 ownership of the Holiday Lodge reverted back to Mark Yori, and in May, David and Mark Yori reopened the Holiday Lodge.

The rapid progression of licensees continued. In August 1967 Robert Van Vleet was licensed to operate one dice game and two 21 games. Less than a year later, in June 1968, Paul Richards was licensed for forty slot machines. Later the same month, the Holiday Lodge was sold for $800,000 to the Interstate Mutual Investment Corporation of Reno. The corporation was composed of Reno attorneys Paul Richards, A. D. Demetras, and David Cook. In March 1969 Richards, Demetras, and Cook sold the Holiday Lodge to the Pig 'n Whistle restaurant chain of Elgin, Illinois. The Holiday Lodge was operated by the Pig 'n Whistle Corporation for a little over a year and then was closed from May until September 1970. At that time, the Rodeway Inn (doing business as the Holiday Lodge) was licensed for gaming with George Ruppert as president and 50-percent owner; Francis Friedman, vice-president and 25-percent owner; and Charles Schlegel, treasurer and 25-percent owner. Roy Rosenthal was general manager. In 1971 the name was changed to the Holiday Spa Casino, and the new gaming licensees were Norman David, Eddie Gassman, and Clifford Sanford.

The property has been closed since 1982. George Benny, who owned the property, went bankrupt after spending $16 million remodeling the facility that he had named the River Palace.

Nev. St. Journal, 30 June 62 (adv.), 15 May 63, 3 July 63, 17 July 63, 16 Mar. 64, 17 May 65, 17 Mar. 66, 6 May 66, 17 Aug. 67, 20 June 68, 22 June 68, 22 Mar. 69, 19 June 70, 26 June 70.

HOLIDAY SPA

9400 West Fourth Street (five miles west of Reno on old Highway 40); licensed from April 1971 to November 1978 for slots, 21, craps, poker, and bingo.

The Holiday Spa was the name of one of several casinos located on the property operated as Laughton's (Lawton's) Hot Springs for many years. The site was famous for its large swimming pool and hot mineral baths.

In April 1971, Norman David, Clifford Sanford, and Eddie Gassman were licensed for gaming at the Holiday Spa Casino operating in the Rodeway Inn Motel. The three were bought out by Emmett O'Neil in May 1972. O'Neil was a graduate of St. Mary's College of California, a member of St. Mary's Hall of Fame, and a former professional baseball player for the Boston Red Sox. He was licensed for 100 percent of the gaming on May 18, 1972, and operated the casino until November 1, 1978.

In 1972 the property's name was changed from the Rodeway Inn to the River Inn; however, the gaming license remained under the name of Holiday Spa, Inc.

The River Inn, owned at that time by the Leisure Time Corporation, ended up in bankruptcy court in March 1978. A bankruptcy auction was scheduled for May 7, 1979, but on May 5 a public auction was avoided when George Benny bought the property for $2,070,000. Benny announced that the property would henceforth be known as the River Palace and that he would soon begin an extensive remodeling and renovation program.

Benny, a real-estate developer and speculator who had once owned the Double Diamond Ranch property, instituted a lavish spending program that, along with many other problems, eventually caused him to file for bankruptcy. He owed his creditors approximately $16 million when the project was finally called to a halt. The building was boarded up in 1982. The property remains closed, and there are no plans for its reopening.

Nev. St. Journal, 10 Sept. 70, 1 Nov. 70 (article and adv.), 23 Apr. 71, 18 May 72.

HOLLYWOOD CLUB

29½ East Douglas Alley; licensed from June 19 to September 19, 1931, for poker and pan.

The Hollywood Club was a bar that licensed a poker and a pan game for a few months in the early days of legalized gaming. The site is now part of Harolds Club.

HORNSTEIN, JOE, GEORGE, AND HENRY

The Hornstein brothers came to Reno from Colorado in the mid-1930s. During the next thirty years, they were all involved in various casinos as well as in race and sports books.

Joe was a leading figure in Nevada bookmaking for many years and was licensed at the Nevada Turf Club from 1946 to 1955. From 1953 to 1964 he was a partner in the Palace Club, and from 1959 to 1962 he was licensed as a co-owner of the El Morocco Club in Las Vegas. He was also one of the backers of Harold Smith Jr.'s ill-fated gambling venture in Yugoslavia in 1971.

Henry Hornstein was licensed as a 48-percent owner of the Colony Club on North Virginia Street from 1956 to 1964. He was also an owner of the El Morocco Club in Las Vegas from 1959 to 1962.

George and Henry Hornstein were licensed at the Colony Club on North Center Street (later known as the Colony Turf Club) from 1967 to 1974.

The Hornstein brothers severed their last connection with gaming in Reno in 1974 when they sold their interests in the Colony Club to Jack Austin. Joe Hornstein moved to Stockton, California, where he passed away on October 21, 1975, and Henry and George Hornstein resided in San Francisco until their deaths in the late 1970s.

Nev. St. Journal, 11 Dec. 53, 20 June 56, 6 Feb. 59, 6 Dec. 62, 13 Aug. 63 (photo), 15 Dec. 63 (photo), 9 Dec. 64, 20 Jan. 67, 18 July 71, 18 Oct. 74, 24 Oct. 75 (obit. and photo of Joe Hornstein).

HORSESHOE CLUB

229 North Virginia Street; licensed intermittently from October 1956 until September 1995 as a full casino.

The Horseshoe Club opened in October 1956. Over the years, there were five different owner/management teams, but other than two occasions when the Horseshoe was closed because of bankruptcies, the business operated as a gambling casino at the same location for almost forty years.

The Horseshoe was the second casino to open on the west side of Virginia Street (the Primadonna Club opened there in 1955). Prior to 1955 gambling was not permitted on that side of the street.

In March 1956 Elmer "Baldy" West, Bernie Einstoss, and Brad Hewins began negotiating for the purchase of Patterson's Clothier's and the Monarch Cafe. Negotiations were soon completed, and in June 1956 construction began on the Horseshoe.

The Horseshoe was tentatively scheduled to open on Labor Day weekend, and on August 24 the casino was approved for licensing by the state. The licensees and their percentages were: Elmer West, 31 percent of the $600,000 casino; Bernie Einstoss, 16 percent; Brad Hewins, 8 percent; Tom Beko, 8 percent; Frank Grannis, 7 percent; Jim Powers, 6 percent; Ben Hill, 5 percent; Irene Marich, 5 percent; Gerald Cooper, 5 percent; Andrew Desimone, 4 percent; William Rogers, 2 percent; Fred Cavendish, 2 percent; and Pat Kelly, bar manager, 1 percent. The Horseshoe was licensed for 176 slot machines, one roulette game, two craps games, and six 21 games.

The Horseshoe actually opened on October 25, 1956. The president of the corporation was Elmer West. Bernie Einstoss was vice-president, and Brad Hewins was secretary-treasurer. The club's motto was "Fun, Food and Fortune." The interior decor was based on a horseshoe theme, and the carpeting was designed with thousands of red horseshoes scattered on a black background.

In December 1956 William Pappas, long-time Reno gambling figure, purchased 6.9 percent of the Horseshoe for $48,000. In January 1957 Eugene Sullivan bought 6.9 percent of the club, and in May 1957 Pat Mooney purchased 3.4 percent.

In 1957 the Horseshoe introduced two new marketing ploys to attract customers.

The Silver Spur and the Horseshoe, two popular small casinos no longer in existence, pictured in 1970. Author's collection.

The first was a bingo game that featured a "bonus bingo," which paid $50,000 if a player covered the entire card by the time the first fifty numbers were called. The only other bingo games in town at the time were at Harrah's Club, Dick Graves's Nugget, and the Primadonna. Needless to say, the $50,000 prize was never paid, considering the odds against a customer filling an entire card in such a short time. The closest they came was on June 19, when "Reno's Lucky Horseshoe Club" paid a $5,000 bonus to a lucky winner.

The second marketing ploy was one that was common at the time—and is still used by most casinos—inexpensive food. Prime-rib dinners were $1.18 on Wednesdays, chicken dinners were $1.15 on Sundays, and holiday dinners, such as Thanksgiving and Christmas, featuring turkey, duck, ham, or trout, were $1.23.

In December 1958 Elmer West sold his remaining 22.9 percent of the Horseshoe to his other partners for $215,000. Also selling their percentages were Pat Kelly and William "Spike" Rogers. The remaining stockholders were Bernie Einstoss, Brad Hewins, Frank Grannis, Pat Mooney, William Pappas, Eugene Sullivan, Ben Hill, Gerald Cooper, Tom Beko, James Powers, Irene Marich, and Fred Cavendish.

In January 1959 Ruby Mathis purchased 11.2 percent of the Horseshoe.

In October 1960 the Horseshoe initiated a remodeling and expansion program that, when completed in May 1961, cost over $1 million and added 2,800 square feet to the ground level, as well as a new second level. The club took over the space formerly occupied by the Reno Jewelry Store. A restaurant, a bar, and a keno game were added on the second floor. The expansion resulted in the hiring of an additional 80 employees, bringing the total workforce to 250 people.

In March 1962 Bernie Einstoss sold 3 percent of his holdings to Ben Hill, Fred Cavendish, and Frank Grannis, for $17,000 a point. In September 1963 he sold 3 percent to Clarence "Jack" Hoyt for $67,500 and 2 percent to Morrie Mandell for $45,000. In August 1964 Einstoss completely divested himself of his Horseshoe holdings when he sold his remaining 19 percent to the corporation and shareholders for $475,000. Later in 1964 Bernie Einstoss bought controlling interest of the Riverside Hotel.

In August 1967 the Horseshoe was sold to the Taylor International Construction Corporation, which leased the property to the 229 Corporation, composed of Stuart and Walter "Wally" Mason, Brad Hewins,

Ned Turner, and Francis Breen. The Mason brothers were both associated with Taylor International as well as being principals in the proposed new club operation. Brad Hewins was a partner in the Horseshoe and had been in the casino business in Reno for more than forty years. Ned Turner was a former member of the Nevada Gaming Control Board who had retired only a few months previously. Francis Breen was a Reno attorney who served as a director of the 229 Corporation but had no financial interest in the corporation.

Taylor International, the landlord, had built many noted hotels, among them the Fountainebleau, the Eden Roc, and the Deauville Hotels, all in Miami Beach; the Riviera and the Tropicana Hotels in Las Vegas; the Denver Hilton; and the El San Juan and La Concha Hotels in San Juan, Puerto Rico. (Taylor International continued in the building business and later built Caesars Palace; the original MGM Hotel—which became Bally's Hotel—in Las Vegas; the MGM in Reno—now the Reno Hilton; the second MGM Hotel in Las Vegas, completed in 1993; and the addition to the Flamingo Hilton in Las Vegas.)

In early November the Gaming Control Board turned down Taylor International as a landlord because of previous financial difficulties, and the entire deal had to be restructured. The problems were resolved, and the Horseshoe was taken over by the 229 Corporation—Stuart Mason, Walter "Wally" Mason, Ned Turner, Brad Hewins, and Francis Breen—on November 28, 1967.

In June 1970 the Masons announced that Sam Silverberg, a fourteen-year veteran of the gaming industry, would take over as general manager of the operation. In October 1971 Silverberg sued the Horseshoe for "wrongful termination." He claimed that he had signed a five-year contract that allegedly provided that in addition to his salary he would be paid 10 percent of the yearly profits. After a dispute over terms of the contract, Silverberg had been terminated in July 1971. The suit was settled in August 1975, with Silverberg being awarded $112,000.

In January 1977 Tom Mullis, a co-owner of the Silver Spur and a Reno physician, and Jess Hinkel, former head of Del Webb's gaming operations, applied to the Gaming Commission to buy the Horseshoe Club for an undisclosed price. Mullis, who would own 75 percent, and Hinkel, who would own 25 percent, applied for licenses for twenty-one table games and 355 slots.

Mullis and Hinkel were licensed effective April 1, 1977, and immediately initiated a $1-million remodeling program. The project lasted almost the entire summer of their first year of operation and included the development of a casino, a lounge, a keno game, and a restaurant on the second floor, along with a gourmet dining room. The entertainment on the second floor included belly dancers from Greece and Turkey.

Mullis, who had a penchant for fine art, commissioned several oil-painting masters to help decorate the gaming facility. The club's decor was in the Louis XIV style, with original artworks accentuated by museum-type lighting and elaborate chandeliers. Many of the paintings depicted explicit nudes, and their "exposure" created much conversation and many negative comments in the Reno gaming community.

In August 1977 Vic Leonardi, a twenty-year veteran of the gaming industry, was named assistant general manager and casino manager of the Horseshoe.

On January 8, 1980, newspapers announced that the Horseshoe had closed at 5 P.M. on Sunday, January 6, after its owners had filed for bankruptcy. Bob Brodie, the general manager, said that most of the club's 310 employees had been laid off and would receive their final check that day. Some local observers said that the disruption of business during the remodeling project had led to the failure of the casino.

On January 16, Jess Hinkel, 25-percent owner of the Horseshoe, filed a lawsuit against principal owner Tom Mullis and general manager Bob Brodie, alleging fraud, collusion, mismanagement, and misappropriation of funds. Hinkel, who had served as general manager until terminated in June 1978, said that he was in a state of shock about the casino closing. The suit was never resolved.

In February 1981 Sil Petricciani, who had recently been appointed general manager of the Horseshoe Club, said he planned to reopen the casino on the first of April. Petricciani, who had owned the Palace Club for many years, said that the owners, Maury and Stuart Mason, had filed an application with the Gaming Commission to reopen the Horseshoe. The Masons were hoping to get the application on the Commission's March agenda.

The Horseshoe reopened on April 1 at 1:30 P.M. The club had a small lounge in the basement with a small band, and the second floor had an expanded restaurant and bar area. The first floor, minus the nude pictures, looked the same as when it was closed in January 1980. The club opened with nine table games and 270 slot machines.

At midnight on December 31, 1981, the Horseshoe, owned by the Mason Corporation, completed the purchase of the adjoining Silver Spur Casino. On January 1, 1982, at 12:01 A.M., the two casinos became one entity and the property was called the Horseshoe–Silver Spur for a short time. Eventually the Silver Spur portion of the name was dropped and the property was once again known as the Horseshoe Club.

Dwayne Kling, former co-owner and general manager of the Silver Spur, took over as general manager of the combined properties. Most of the management team from the Silver Spur remained in place when the two casinos merged in 1982. Don Dennis and Bob Higgins from the Horseshoe pit department were joined by Kent Buchanan, Steve Gerlach, and Danny Troye from the Silver Spur pit. Chuck Thomas, Rod Jones, Gordon Drendel, Neil Lyden, and Cliff Hogan operated the keno game, and Reuben "Sandy" Sanderson was named slot manager. Joining the management team later were Gordon Allison, Frank Holmes, and Jason Prater. Supervising the restaurant was executive chef Bill Behymer, and overseeing the bar department was longtime Silver Spur employee James "Waco Jim" Horn.

Dwayne Kling resigned as general manager in 1983 but stayed on as an advisor to the new general manager, Mike Hessling. After Hessling resigned, Kling stayed on to work with general managers Jerry Raasch and Bob Brodie until leaving in 1988 to open the Ponderosa Hotel, "The World's First Non-Smoking Hotel-Casino."

On December 14, 1988, the Horseshoe once again closed its doors. Actually, the club itself was doing well. The financial problems were coming from the parent company, the Mason Corporation. Problems from the corporation's other investments forced the Horseshoe to keep sending money to the Las Vegas headquarters, and in doing so, the Horseshoe became so strapped for cash that it was unable to pay gaming taxes and other required bills and was forced to close. The club had already closed the keno game and most of the pit in an effort to cut the payroll. None of these drastic measures worked, and when the club finally closed there were only one hundred employees still working. The closing was conducted in an orderly fashion as state gaming officials and casino workers attended to the necessary closing procedures.

In May 1989 the Horseshoe, like the legendary phoenix, rose again from the ashes. Bob Cashell, former lieutenant governor of Nevada and former owner of Boomtown, opened the Horseshoe Club and the neighboring Silver Spur Casino as one establishment. Cashell had obtained a thirty-two-year lease on the Silver Spur property from an investment group composed of Everett Brunzell, Conrad Priess, Dwayne Kling, James Parker, John Gojack, Jose Gastanaga, and Charles Stepro. He also acquired the Horseshoe Club from the Mason family, which was facing an involuntary bankruptcy petition from creditors. The petitioners included suppliers seeking more than $110,000 in money allegedly owed them by the Masons.

Bob Cashell's Horseshoe Club had its grand opening on May 25, 1989. The club, which Robert Cashell Jr. helped to operate, opened with 525 slot machines, a keno game, eight 21 games, one craps game, and a 150-seat restaurant.

The club cost Cashell $3 million. It was decorated in a burgundy and green motif, and the upstairs restaurant, called Grandma's, was redesigned so people could sit by the windows and look out on the activities on Virginia Street.

In September 1995 Bob Cashell closed the Horseshoe operation. He blamed the deterioration of the downtown area, citing such problems as the abandoned Mapes and Riverside Hotels, the shuttered Harolds Club, the increase of crime, and increasing problems from panhandlers and homeless people as his reason for closing.

Currently the former site of the Horseshoe is occupied by the Horseshoe Jewelry and Loan Store.

Nev. St. Journal, 31 Mar. 56, 3 May 56 (photo), 22 June 56 (photo), 24 July 56, 15 Aug. 56, 24 Aug. 56, 23 Oct. 56 (adv.), 25 Oct. 56 (adv.), 27 Oct. 56 (photo), 18 Nov. 56 (adv.), 28 Nov. 56, 18 Dec. 56, 24 Jan. 57, 3 Apr. 57 (adv.), 24 May 57, 28 May 57, 25 June 57 (adv.), 13 Nov. 57 (adv.), 16 Nov. 57 (adv.), 3 Jan. 58, 28 Dec. 58 (adv.), 21 Jan. 59, 3 Jan. 60 (adv.), 21 Oct. 60, 4 Dec. 60, 9 May 62, 15 Apr. 63 (photo), 7 Sept. 63, 23 Oct. 63, 11 July 64, 18 Aug. 64, 19 Aug. 64, 22 Dec. 65, 17 Aug. 67, 27 Sept. 67, 17 Nov. 67, 28 Nov. 67, 30 July 69 (adv.), 14 June 70 (photo), 10 Dec. 70 (adv.), 24 Oct. 71, 15 June 72, 27 Dec. 73 (photo), 6 Aug. 75, 25 Jan. 77, 29 Mar. 77, 23 June 77 (photo), 7 Aug. 77 (photo), 8 Jan. 80, 16 Jan. 80, 17 Feb. 81, 1 Apr. 81, 2 Apr. 81 (photo), 15 Jan. 82, 21 Oct. 88, 14 Dec. 88, 26 Apr. 89, 11 May 89, 26 May 89 (photo).

HOYT, CLARENCE "JACK"

Jack Hoyt was a co-owner of the Wheel Club, along with John Coffee, from February 1944 to November 1945. He was also a 3-percent owner of the Horseshoe Club on North Virginia Street from October 1963 to November 1967.

Nev. St. Journal, 15 Feb. 44, 7 Sept. 63.

HUB

142 South Virginia Street (located in Number 9 of the Arcade Building); licensed for a few months in 1932 for one roulette game.

The former site of the Hub is now part of the Virginian Hotel-Casino.

HUNTER, JAMES "JIM"

Jim Hunter was hired by Harolds Club in 1939. His first job was as a lookout on the roulette table, where his responsibilities consisted of watching the players to see that they did not add money to their wagers after the wheel had stopped. He soon became a dice dealer, and in 1941, when

Jim Hunter (l.), longtime Harolds Club manager, and Raymond I. Smith (r.). Courtesy of Neal Cobb and the Nevada Historical Society.

Harolds Club first stayed open for twenty-four hours, he was named graveyard-shift manager. Harold Smith Sr. was swing-shift manager, and Raymond A. Smith was day-shift manager. In 1945 Hunter was appointed assistant general manager. He later worked as casino manager. He was for many years the most powerful and influential person, outside the Smith family, in the Harolds Club operation.

In 1970, after Harolds Club was sold to the Hughes Corporation, Hunter resigned to work for the Mapes Money Tree. In 1971, when his longtime friend and associate Jessie Beck opened the Riverside Hotel-Casino, Hunter was appointed the Riverside's publicity director. He stayed with the Riverside until Jessie Beck sold the hotel to Pick Hobson in 1978.

Nev. St. Journal, 15 Feb. 71.

HUTTON'S HUT (ALSO CALLED THE RENO CHICKEN HUT; ALSO CALLED THE CHICKEN HUT)

4245 West Fourth Street; licensed for a few months in 1931 and licensed from May 1945 to April 1946 for 21, craps, and roulette.

Mr. and Mrs. Hutton operated a restaurant at this location that was famous for steak and chicken dinners. They also had a small bar, a dance floor, and a clubroom. They leased out the three gaming tables—one roulette game, one 21 game, and one craps game. After a short time, they eliminated the gaming, but the restaurant operated for many years.

The property opened as the Villa Sierra in 1944 and operated under that name for a year. Then from May 1945 to April 1946 it operated under the name of Reno's Chicken Hut. Bill Dixon was the owner and operator of the business and the gaming, and Ted Percovich was the chef. They featured "chicken in the rough"—fried chicken served in a basket and surrounded by french-fried potatoes.

In 1946 the property once again became known as the Villa Sierra and operated under that name until 1952. It is currently operating as a fine Italian restaurant known as Johnny's Little Italy.

Nev. St. Journal, 19 June 31, 16 May 45; Reno telephone directory, 1945.

IACOMETTI, LOUIS

Lou Iacometti was born in Trecate, Italy, and came to the United States in 1919. From 1953 to 1964, he was licensed as one of thirteen partners in the Palace Club, where he was in charge of the slot department.

Iacometti was also licensed at the Tahoe Palace (Plaza) at Lake Tahoe from 1956 to 1961.

Lou Iacometti died on May 19, 1979, in a Reno hospital. He was sixty-six years old.

Nev. St. Journal, 11 Dec. 53, 20 June 56, 21 May 79 (obit.).

IDLEWILD CLUB

1410 East Fourth Street

The Idlewild Club had gambling and drinking in the 1920s, when neither form of entertainment was legal. It was located near the site where the Jack Johnson–Jim Jeffries heavyweight title fight was held on July 4, 1910.

When gambling was legalized in 1931, the property was operated by Felix Turillas and was called the Silver Slipper.

Currently near the former location of the Idlewild is a monument marking the site of the 1910 heavyweight championship fight. However, the actual location of the club is now the parking lot between the Ponderosa Lodge and the Los Compadres Restaurant.

INFERNO CLUB

226½ North Center Street and 124 East Commercial Row; licensed from June 1936 to 1945 for slots, 21, and craps.

In May 1936 Vic Williams purchased the Comstock Club from Bob Grignon. Williams, who had operated other cabarets in Reno, renamed the cabaret the Inferno and decorated the club to look like Dante's Inferno.

The deluxe equipment and decorations included a sheet of flame over the orchestra stands, red devils on black walls, and new chromium furnishings. Imitation stone walls looked like part of an infernal region with a colorful and novel rainbow waterfall in the background. The entire aura of the club was uniquely different, and it offered something unusual for Reno nightclub patrons to check out when they were making their rounds of the local night life. The Inferno was a popular spot in Reno all through the years of World War II.

In January 1945 Marie Quintel was licensed for one 21 game and one craps game at the Inferno. Warren Wilson was also an owner of the Inferno in the 1940s.

In June 1945 Ralph Owens became the owner of the Inferno and hired Jimmie Curley as his casino manager. Owens brought in an entirely new type of entertainment—his show featured Juanita Rhea, "Queen of the Strip Tease Artists."

In August 1945 the Inferno closed because of the expansion of the Greyhound bus depot into its location. Ralph Owens requested and was granted permission to move his gaming license to the site of the Depot Bar at 124 East Commercial Row.

The Inferno lasted only a few months at its new location. In March 1946 the Depot Bar, under the ownership of "Bodie Mike" Lazovich and Ralph Pardini, reopened at 124 East Commercial Row.

The first location of the Inferno (226½ North Center Street) is part of Harrah's on the east side of Center Street, and the 124 East Commercial Row address is now part of Harrah's parking garage.

Nev. St. Journal, 30 May 36, 13 June 36, 29 Apr. 38, 23 Jan. 45, 21 June 45 (adv.), 28 Aug. 45, 22 Nov. 45 (adv.), 1 Mar. 46.

JACKPOT ARCADE

231 and 204 North Center Street; licensed from 1945 to 1951 for slots only.

William Huffman was licensed for three slot machines at the Jackpot Arcade, a business that operated in the Golden Hotel building until the James Lloyd Sr. group purchased the Golden Hotel and took over Huffman's lease. At that time, the business moved across the street to 204 North Center Street, where it operated at that address until 1951. The club was licensed for slots only.

Currently both former locations of the Jackpot Arcade on Center Street are parts of Harrah's Club.

Nev. St. Journal, 3 July 47, 2 Apr. 48, 4 Feb. 50, 15 May 51.

JACKSON, JOSEPH

Joe Jackson was born in Glendale, California, on December 13, 1929. After dividing his early years between California, Reno, and Las Vegas, he settled permanently in Reno in 1971.

Jackson, who was sometimes called the "guru" of keno in the 1970s and the 1980s, was highly respected by his employers. Terry Oliver, president of the Fitzgerald Group, who worked with Jackson for eleven years, said, "Whenever the state had questions or issues about the game of keno, they consulted Joe Jackson. Whenever virtually any innovations were being done to the game of keno, Joe Jackson was involved."

Jackson was a gaming executive for Hughes and Summa Corporation and Harolds Club for twenty-two years. He was instrumental in raising keno limits from $25,000 to $50,000, and he developed the first electronic keno hand calculator. He also lobbied for the approval of keno games with progressive jackpots.

The U.S. Navy veteran died in Gilpin, Colorado, on September 13, 1992.

Nev. St. Journal, 16 Sept. 92 (obit.).

JACOBS, MURRAY

Murray Jacobs was born in Reno on August 25, 1906. Both his father and his grandfather were clothiers in Reno, and Murray continued the family tradition until 1942.

In 1942 Jacobs turned his clothing store into a liquor store, and soon afterward into a bar. He called his property Murray's Club, and he eventually licensed sixty slot machines and three table games at the location.

His club fronted on North Virginia Street, and its rear (east) entrance was located on Lincoln Alley. In 1944 he leased the eastern half of the property to Bill Harrah, who opened a club called the Blackout Bar. One year later, the lease expired, and Jacobs again operated the entire property.

In 1952 he sold the business to the Nevada Club for $50,000 and leased the property to the Nevada Club for $25,000 a year for the first five years. The owners of the Nevada Club renewed the lease at five-year intervals until Jacobs sold them the property in 1996.

Jacobs currently (1999) spends six months a year in Arizona and six months in Reno.

Nev. St. Journal, 16 Apr. 52.

JARRARD'S

2400 South Virginia Street; licensed from January 1960 to November 1960 for slots and 21.

Jarrard's operated for less than a year. Mac's Club had been at the location since 1950, and in December 1959 "Mac" (Howard McMullen) leased the club to his "singing host," Al Jarrard. Jarrard changed the name of the club to Jarrard's, and in January 1960 he was licensed for one 21 game and three slot machines.

On November 7, 1960, the State of Nevada closed Jarrard's for alleged cheating on its 21 game. On November 24 Howard McMullen returned to Mac's Club (Jarrard's) as owner, manager, and operator. By November 30 Mac's Club (Jarrard's)

had failed to post a notice of defense against the cheating charges, and the state revoked the license of former operator Al Jarrard without a hearing.

The club operated as Mac's Club until 1963, when McMullen's lease expired.

The former location of Jarrard's is now occupied by Heidi's Family Restaurant.

Nev. St. Journal, 31 Dec. 59 (adv.), 21 Jan. 60, 8 Nov. 60, 30 Nov. 60.

JELLISON, LEE

In 1957 Lee Jellison, with the assistance of Fred Howell (both employed by Harrah's Club), designed and constructed the first keno blower. The idea for the keno blower was developed by Gene Diullo, longtime keno manager of Harrah's.

This device made it possible—for the first time—for keno balls to be selected without being touched by human hands. The invention is a large plastic bubble in which the eighty keno balls are placed. A blower mixes the balls (which are actually Ping-Pong balls) and allows one ball at a time to be selected as a winning number. The selected balls pass upward one ball at a time into the two arm sections (commonly called the "rabbit ears") of the machine. When ten balls have entered one section of the machine, that section is automatically closed off and ten more balls are allowed to fill the other section of the "rabbit ears." This invention, which is currently used by almost all casinos in Nevada, took a great deal of suspicion out of the game and helped both owners and customers to feel more comfortable about the honesty of the game.

Jellison was employed by Harrah's for twenty years and retired in October 1973. He spent much of his twenty years with Harrah's working in Harrah's Automobile Collection.

Nev. St. Journal, 7 Mar. 57.

JIM'S BAR

135 East Second Street; licensed from July 1, 1948, to April 1, 1949, for 21 only.

Jim's Bar was owned by James Gallardo, who operated one 21 game for a short time in 1948 and 1949. The site is now a parking lot.

Nev. St. Journal, 15 June 48.

JOHN'S BAR

16 West Second Street; licensed from 1937 to February 1947 for slots, roulette, and 21.

John "Mohair" Etchebarren opened John's Bar, sometimes called John's Place, in July 1937. He operated it as a bar and slots-only establishment until October 1940. At that time, he was granted a license for a football pool to go along with the slots.

In January 1946 Wayne Martin was granted a gaming license for a roulette game and a 21 game. His partners in the business were Bill Harrah, Virgil Smith, and Bill Williams. In October 1946 Bill Harrah and Wayne Martin sold their half-interest to Howard McMullen. Virgil Smith and Bill Williams retained their interests until February 1947, when the establishment was sold to Bill Dixon and Bill Wirts, who changed the name to the Stork Club.

The former location of John's Bar is now part of the Pioneer Gift Shop.

Nev. St. Journal, 3 Apr. 43 (adv.), 29 Jan. 46, 9 Mar. 46 (adv.), 1 Oct. 46, 28 Feb. 47.

JOHNNY'S OPEN DOOR

See Open Door.

JOKERENO CLUB

130 North Center Street; licensed from December 1931 to September 1932 for slots and keno (bingo) only.

The Jokereno Club opened on December 19, 1931. The Nevada Holding and Trust Company and W. F. Bolte of New Jersey were co-owners, and William Hackett of Boston was the manager. The special guest on opening night was Reno's mayor, E. E. Roberts, who started the first bingo game.

No expense was spared to make the club one of the most attractive in the state. Chairs were upholstered in Spanish morocco leather to harmonize with the window draperies. Deep rugs covered the floor, and specially made lighting fixtures displayed the word JOKERENO on the paneling. Among the interesting features of

the club was the original brass cashier's grill from the Comstock Bank of Virginia City, through which millions of dollars of silver had passed.

The club opened daily at 1 P.M. and remained open as long as there was anyone to play.

The Jokereno Club closed in 1932, and the location later became known as the Dog House. The site is now part of Cal-Neva's parking garage on the east side of Center Street.

Nev. St. Journal, 19 Dec. 31 (article and adv.).

JOLLY JOLLY CLUB

2600 South Virginia Street; licensed from May 1953 to July 1954 for 21 only.

This business was known as the Deer Head Lodge prior to its being taken over by G. W. Kendall and Al Johnson. They operated it as a bar with one 21 game until June 1954. At that time it became known as the PJ Club, and there was no gaming.

Currently the site of the Jolly Jolly Club is occupied by the Friends Liquor Store.

Nev. St. Journal, 2 Apr. 54, 30 June 54.

JONES, KARL

Karl Jones, who was born in Pennsylvania, came to Reno as a young man. He was a bartender at the Capitol Bar on East Second Street in 1935, when he purchased a percentage of the club from Jack Clark and Shorty King. In 1938 he purchased controlling interest of the Capitol Bar from George Coppersmith.

Jones died of a heart attack on March 25, 1947. He was forty-three years old.

Nev. St. Journal, 1 Apr. 38, 15 Dec. 46, 26 Mar. 47 (obit.).

JORDAN, J. C.

J. C. Jordan began his gaming career working on a gambling boat in which his father held an interest. He came to Las Vegas in 1939 and later moved to Lake Tahoe. He was a co-owner and manager of the North Shore Club at Crystal Bay, Nevada, from 1949 to 1971, spending the winters when the Tahoe club was closed supervising

craps tables in the Bahamas. In 1971 he sold his interest in the North Shore Club and was named casino manager of Harolds Club; in 1972 he was named general manager, replacing Jack Pieper, who was transferred to Las Vegas. In 1975 Jordan was appointed vice-president and director of Harolds Club and director of the Landmark Hotel in Las Vegas.

On February 28, 1979, Jordan retired from his post as president of Harolds Club, a position he had held since 1978. He had been employed by Harolds Club and Summa Corporation for eight years.

Jordan passed away on June 18, 1981, at seventy years of age.

Nev. St. Journal, 24 June 72, 11 Dec. 75, 16 Feb. 79 (photo).

JUBILEE CLUB

23005 South Virginia Street (Highway 395 South); licensed intermittently from 1953 to 1978 for slots, 21, craps, and poker.

The Jubilee Club was owned by the Pagni brothers, William, Roy, Relio, Al, and Elio. The club was opened as a bar and dinner house, featuring steak and fine Italian dinners. The five brothers all worked in and around the club, tending bar, helping to cook, dealing games, and doing just about everything to make the business a success.

The Pagnis were first licensed for gaming in September 1953. They closed the club in 1960 when the State of Nevada passed an entertainment-tax law that forced many small clubs out of business. In 1967 a law was passed that exempted small clubs from paying that entertainment tax, and the Jubilee reopened on April 21 of that year with three table games and five slot machines.

The club closed forever on November 12, 1978. The building has been razed, and there is currently a vacant lot at the former site of the Jubilee Club.

Nev. St. Journal, 22 Sept. 53, 18 Dec. 58, 20 Apr. 67, 15 Nov. 78.

JUDD, CLIFF
"THE GALLOPER"

Cliff Judd was a club and bar owner in the late 1940s and 1950s who seemed to be continually in trouble with the law. In March 1945 he was operating the Depot Club on Commercial Row when he and Frank Sheley (Shealey), a former owner of the Silver Dollar Club, were arrested and charged with illegally transporting eighteen cases of whiskey across the state border of Utah for resale. Two weeks later, on April 16, 1945, he was arrested again, this time for operating a craps game and a 21 game at the Depot Club without a license.

Two months later, on June 8, 1945, he and Frank Sheeley (Sheeley) were charged with threatening bodily harm to a San Francisco bartender, Lee Halliman, if he testified against them in their upcoming trial. Judd was sentenced to six months in jail for threatening Hallihan. While serving his time in prison, his bar license at the Depot Club was revoked.

On October 24, 1945, Judd was acquitted of transporting liquor across the state line, and two days later he was acquitted of selling liquor without a license.

In September 1947 Judd was licensed as part owner of the Capitol Bar on East Second Street.

In February 1949 Judd was convicted of "drilling" (an illegal method of obtaining money from a slot machine) in Las Vegas. In his trial, he stated that he was part owner of the Bar of Music Club on North Center Street. The State of Nevada said it had no record of any connection between Judd and the Bar of Music.

In March 1952 Cliff Judd was booked for disturbing the peace, and in June 1952 he was booked for destruction of property when he was accused of pouring acid on the layout of a 21 table at the Frisco Club. He was later released on the charge of destruction of property.

Judd was never granted a gaming license after 1949, although he did make Nevada his residence for several more years.

Nev. St. Journal, 17 May 44 (photo), 30 Mar. 45, 17 Apr. 45, 8 June 45, 27 June 45, 24 Oct. 45, 26 Oct. 45, 17 Sept. 47, 27 Feb. 49, 18 Mar. 52 (photo), 15 June 52, 19 June 52.

KARADANIS FAMILY

George Karadanis, originally from Pittsburg, California, came to Reno via Lake Tahoe in 1974. His construction company built the Sundowner Hotel, and Karadanis has owned and operated the Sundowner since being licensed in 1975. When the Sundowner opened, it was the largest hotel under one roof in Reno.

Karadanis, along with his partner, Bob Maloff, purchased the closed Mapes Hotel in June 1988 but did not open or operate the property. They sold it to the City of Reno in August 1996.

Matt Karadanis, the youngest son of George Karadanis, was employed at the Sundowner as assistant general manager and slot manager before being licensed as co-owner—along with his brothers Mitch and Marty—and general manager of the Virginian Hotel-Casino on South Virginia Street in November 1988.

KELLY, JIM

Jim Kelly came to Nevada from Idaho with Dick Graves in 1953, and they purchased the Reno Nugget in 1954. When Graves opened the Sparks (now Ascuaga's) Nugget, Kelly became the sole owner of the Reno Nugget and renamed it Kelly's Nugget.

In 1962 Kelly purchased the Sierra Lodge at Crystal Bay, Nevada, and renamed it the Tahoe Nugget. He sold Kelly's Nugget to Jackpot Enterprises in 1990, but he retained the Tahoe Nugget.

Jim Kelly died in 1993.

Nev. St. Journal, 20 Jan. 54, 19 June 62.

KELLY'S NUGGET

233 North Virginia Street; licensed from March 1954 to 1990 for slots, 21, craps, and roulette.

This property operated as the Picadilly Club from 1946 to 1952. At that time, it was sold to a group headed by realtor John Hickok and was renamed the Nugget.

Dick Graves and Jim Kelly purchased the property late in 1953. They closed the club for remodeling and reopened on March 1, 1954. They were licensed for forty-five slots, one 21 game, and one craps game. One of their first employees was John Ascuaga, who later established a name for himself at a casino in Sparks—Ascuaga's Nugget.

The Nugget soon became famous for its fine food and reasonable prices. It advertised daily in the local paper, promoting such features as "Hard Likker and Good Grub." Its restaurant introduced the "Awful-Awful" sandwich (a hamburger with lots of meat and lots of condiments), which was "awful" good and "awful" big. Over forty years later, this is still a popular menu item, both at the current Nugget location and at John Ascuaga's Nugget.

The Nugget also placed a daily ad in the paper naming a local personage as the "Nugget's Guest of the Day." This entitled "the guest" to a free lunch at the Nugget and generated lots of publicity and gaming activity for the club.

In later years, the Nugget became famous for its prime-rib dinners, which featured the best selection of prime rib at the best prices. The chef, Jimmie Hughes, supervised the restaurant for over twenty years.

In 1955 the Graves-Kelly partnership was dissolved. Dick Graves wanted to move on to bigger things, and Kelly was happy to stay where he was. It was a friendly parting, and they were both immensely successful in their own casinos.

Adam Miltenberger worked with Kelly for many years and served in many capacities in the Nugget during the lifetime of the casino. Another longtime Kelly employee was Fran Cannon, who also wore many hats in the Nugget.

Over the years there were many changes in the makeup of the casino. In the early years there was a craps game and one or more 21 games and always lots of slot machines. Kelly strongly believed that if he could get people into the club to eat or drink, he could get them to "invest" in his slot machines or table games. As the years went by, the casino became more and more slot-machine oriented, and in the

last years of operation there was only one 21 game to go along with the slots. For a while, the casino operated with slot machines only.

An opinion frequently expressed around Reno by people "in the know" was that Kelly's Nugget (35 feet by 140 feet) made as much money per square inch as any casino in Reno.

Jim Kelly sold his Nugget to Jackpot Enterprises in 1990. In 1999 the Nugget was owned by Eric "Rick" Heaney and was operating at the same location.

Nev. St. Journal, 9 Mar. 54 (adv.), 26 Jan. 55, 26 Aug. 55, 11 Mar. 58 (adv.), 8 June 62, 18 May 72.

KENO CLUB

232 North Virginia Street; licensed from August to December 1931 for roulette, craps, 21, and keno (bingo).

The Keno Club, which occupied the former site of the Flagg Furniture Store, was opened at 6:30 P.M. on October 7, 1931, by Thomas O'Brien. The club was decorated in an Oriental motif using a skillful combination of brilliant Chinese reds and greens.

After opening with only a keno (bingo) game, O'Brien soon added table games.

O'Brien closed the Keno Club in December 1931. It reopened with new owners as the New Keno Club in August 1932 with keno (bingo) only. Later in the year it closed again and was subsequently opened as the Reno Club.

The former site of the Keno Club is now part of Harolds Club.

Nev. St. Journal, 7 Oct. 31 (article and adv.), 20 July 32, 21 July 32, 28 July 32, 29 July 32 (adv.).

KINDLE, RAY

Ray Kindle was born in Colorado in 1870. He came to Reno in 1908 and was always associated with the nightclub and bar business. He became associated with Bill Graham and James McKay in the 1920s and was a 25-percent partner in many of their enterprises, including the Bank Club.

Kindle died in Tucson, Arizona, on April 9, 1937.

Nev. St. Journal, 17 Sept. 35, 10 Apr. 37 (obit.).

KING, GEORGE "SHORTY"

Shorty King was one of the original owners and operators of the nationally known Tavern on West Fourth Street. He, along with George Coppersmith, George Nelson, and Jack Clark, opened the Tavern in 1932 and operated it until 1934.

In 1934 Shorty King and Jack Clark opened the Capitol Bar on East Second Street. In 1935 King and George Coppersmith leased the gaming concession at the Dog House on North Center Street.

In August 1939 King and Coppersmith pleaded guilty to operating a crooked roulette wheel at the Dog House. The wheel was wired so it could be stopped on a number selected by the dealer. In April 1940 King was fined $1,000 and sentenced to six months in jail. He was the first man in Washoe County to be given a jail sentence for "operating a cheating and thieving gambling game."

Nev. St. Journal, 10 Feb. 34, 4 Dec. 35, 23 Aug. 39, 3 Apr. 40.

KING'S CAFE

246 Lake Street; never licensed.

King's Cafe was located at the former site of Ming's Cafe. The location was a bar, burlesque house, and "girlie-girlie" property, both before and after the existence of King's Cafe.

In November 1956 Robert and Denise Crowley's application for a gaming license was deferred, then denied in December.

In August 1957 King's Cafe was put off limits by the Air Force when a bouncer assaulted an Air Force man from Reno Air Base (later Stead Air Base). A few days later, the Reno City Council closed the club.

It reopened as the Mint Club in 1958. The site of King's Cafe is now a parking lot.

Nev. St. Journal, 28 Nov. 56, 18 Dec. 56, 23 Aug. 57.

KING'S INN HOTEL-CASINO

303 West Street (corner of West and Third Streets); licensed from August 21, 1975, to May 1982 as a full casino.

In September 1973 the Brunzell Construction Company began construction of a $3-million, seven-story, 167-room hotel on the corner of West and Third Streets. Project designer Ed Kinney announced that the hotel would be owned by three local businessmen, Matthew Chotas, Joe Fischer, and Bob Scoggins.

In March 1974 the local newspaper announced that the hotel costs had risen to $6.5 million and that it was expected that the hotel would open by July 1. The original plans had been changed, making the hotel eight stories high instead of seven. The room count remained at 167, and the casino had plans for ten table games, one keno game, and 240 slot machines. The facility would include a gaming area with a circular bar, a lounge with an open fire pit, two levels of underground parking, and a swimming pool on the third floor.

Applying for gaming licenses were Mr. and Mrs. Harold Spivock, Monroe Spivock, Mr. and Mrs. Marshall Davis, and Mr. and Mrs. Val Ruggerio.

The hotel opened in September 1974, without gambling. In December, Allen Bergendahl purchased controlling interest in the hotel-casino, but the original owners retained small interests.

In January, still with no gambling on the property, Allen Bergendahl applied for a gaming license for 150 slot machines and twelve table games. He would be the general manager and principal stockholder. Other applicants were Val Ruggerio, casino manager, 5 percent; Lilio Marcucci, food and beverage manager, 2 percent; William Moller, 1 percent; and Otis Scog-

Dwayne Kling dealing a twenty-five-cent dice game in Harolds Club in 1955. Author's collection.

gins, 5 percent. The King's Inn was finally given a gaming license in August 1975, for the requested 150 slot machines and twelve table games.

The club had several casino managers in the next few years, including Tom Davis, A. R. Robbins, Gerald Cumpton, and Roy Rosenthal.

In June 1981 the owners filed for a Chapter 11 reorganization bankruptcy when they were threatened with foreclosure on a $3.4-million construction loan. The bankruptcy order was lifted in May 1982, and Bergendahl became sole owner of the property in a foreclosure auction. The casino closed in 1982, and the hotel closed in 1986 after the sprinkler, heating, and ventilation systems failed to meet fire-code regulations.

In 1999 the property remained closed.

Nev. St. Journal, 18 Sept. 73 (photo), 31 Mar. 74, 15 Nov. 74 (adv.), 6 Dec. 74 (photo), 4 Jan. 75, 15 Aug. 75, 22 Aug. 75 (photo), 11 Dec. 75, 23 Nov. 80 (photo), 13 May 89.

Dick Kolbus (l.), co-owner of the Mint Club, photographed with an unidentified roulette dealer, 1942. Courtesy of the Joe "Luke" Lukanish family.

KIT CARSON HOTEL-CASINO

133 North Virginia Street; never licensed as the Kit Carson.

In November 1975 Reno newspapers announced that five investors had joined together in a second try to build a multimillion-dollar hotel-casino on the site of the old Hilp's Drug Store. Construction of the sixteen-story, 182-room facility named the Kit Carson was scheduled to start in January 1976 and be completed in a year. It was to employ four hundred people. Two of the five investors, Conrad Priess and Eugene Gastanaga, had originally announced construction plans in 1973. The other investors were Everett Brunzell, Jose Gastanaga, and Tania Maloff.

Groundbreaking ceremonies for the Kit Carson were scheduled in May 1976, but a few days before the ceremonies, the name was changed from the Kit Carson to the Onslow to honor longtime Reno resident Onslow Dodd. Informed sources said that the owners were given a sizable discount on the price of the property when they agreed to rename their facility in Dodd's memory.

The hotel-casino opened as the Onslow in September 1977 and operated as such until September 30, 1989. The Riverboat Hotel-Casino purchased the property in 1992; it operated the ground floor as a retail store and used the hotel rooms as an adjunct to its main hotel. After the closing of the Riverboat in late 1998, this property also closed. In June 1999 the Club Cal-Neva leased and reopened the hotel portion of the property.

Nev. St. Journal, 27 Nov. 75 (photo), 4 May 76.

KLAICH, ROBERT "BOB"

Bob Klaich was born in East Ely, Nevada, on November 30, 1929. He came to Reno in the 1960s and was employed as the comptroller of Harolds Club. He resigned from Harolds Club for personal reasons in 1971 after Harolds Club was purchased by the Hughes Corporation.

In 1975 Klaich was licensed, along with John Tillis, Don Eamelli, and Lou Benetti, as a co-owner of the Monte Carlo Casino, located in the Holiday Hotel on East Sixth Street.

Klaich was still a co-owner of the Monte Carlo when he died in April 1994.

Nev. St. Journal, 30 June 71, 2 Apr. 76, 27 Apr. 94 (obit.).

KLING, DWAYNE

Dwayne Kling was born in Turlock, California, on September 4, 1929. He first came to Reno in the summers of 1947 and 1948 to play semiprofessional baseball for the Harrah's Club team. After graduating from St. Mary's College in California in 1950, Kling played professional baseball and served in the military prior to returning to Reno in 1954.

Kling worked in Harolds Club from 1954 to 1956. In 1957 he was employed at Harrahs Club, Lake Tahoe, as a pit boss, shift manager, and pit manager. He left Harrah's Club in 1963 and returned to Harolds Club. He left Harolds Club in 1971, shortly after the Hughes Corporation purchased the casino.

In 1971 Kling was hired by the Silver Spur Casino on North Virginia Street as a shift manager. He later became casino manager, general manager, and eventually a co-owner of the Silver Spur. When the Silver Spur was sold to the Horseshoe Club in 1981, Kling was named general manager of the combined properties and served in that capacity until 1988. At that time, he was named general manager of the soon-to-be-reopened Ponderosa Hotel-Casino, "The World's First Non-Smoking Casino."

After the Ponderosa was "up and running," Kling left and was employed by the Peppermill Casino from 1991 to 1992. In 1992 he was named casino manager of the Virginian Hotel-Casino, a position he held until September 1995. At that time, after forty-one years in the gaming industry, he retired.

Currently Kling lives in Reno and works with the University of Nevada Oral History Program as an interviewer for oral history projects relating to casino gaming in Nevada. He is also associated on an advisory basis with the Desert Hills Surveillance Company.

Nev. St. Journal, 19 Aug. 79, 2 Mar. 89.

KOLBUS, RICHARD "DICK"

Dick Kolbus came to Reno in the mid-1930s to attend the University of Nevada, where he was a star basketball player and captain of the team in his senior year.

In 1939 he was employed at the Block N Club and operated a sports book there. He was also involved in gaming at the Dog House in 1940.

In 1941 Kolbus and Joe Lukanish leased the Mint Club from Victor and Joe Saturno, and in 1942 they subleased the property to Bill Harrah. The Mint was located at 214 North Virginia Street and later became the site of Harrah's Club.

Nev. St. Journal, 18 May 67, 15 May 69.

L & A CLUB

6 East Commercial Row; licensed from June 6, 1931, to 1932 for roulette, 21, craps, poker, and a big-six wheel.

The L & A Club packed a lot of games into a fairly small casino-bar in the early days of gaming. However, the business only lasted about eighteen months.

Over the years there were several small bars and casinos at the same location. The site is now part of Harolds Club.

Nev. St. Journal, 4 July 31 (adv.).

LA FIESTA

222 North Center Street; licensed from October 1944 to 1947 for slots, 21, and craps.

The property at 222 North Center Street was home to many nightclubs from the 1930s to the 1950s. Prior to the opening of La Fiesta, the location was occupied by the 222 Club.

La Fiesta was opened in October 1944 by Al Hoffman, formerly with the Dog House, and Frank Mercer, formerly associated with the Cal-Vada Lodge in Lake Tahoe, and was managed by Mack McPherson. The club had a Latin-American decor, and the entertainment featured Mexican dancers and singers performing in gala floor shows.

In 1947 La Fiesta was sold to William Barrett and was reopened as the 222 Club. The property is now part of Harrah's Club on Center Street.

Nev. St. Journal, 27 Oct. 44 (adv.), 3 Feb. 46, 9 July 46, 22 July 48, 23 July 48, 2 Nov. 64.

LANCER

Located on the Mount Rose Highway; licensed from July 14, 1959, to August 2, 1971, for slots and 21.

The Lancer Restaurant, previously known as the Mesa, was one of the most elegant restaurants in the Reno–Lake Tahoe area from the late 1950s to the early 1970s. It featured gourmet dining, cocktails, and dancing.

The property was owned by Roy Crummer and was opened on July 1, 1959. Crummer, who owned the Riverside Hotel for a time, selected Bill Nitschke as manager of the Lancer and Denny Sayers, a longtime Reno resident, as a host and greeter. In September 1959 Roy Bell and Bill Nitschke were approved for a gaming license for slot machines and two 21 games.

The popular restaurant was perched on a hill overlooking Reno and the Truckee Meadows, and the view was spectacular. Many regular customers had their own cocktail and wineglasses kept for them at the bar, and the Lancer was famous for its spinach salad and its side dish of white seedless grapes. On an average weeknight, as many as three hundred dinners were served, and on a busy Saturday night, as many as five hundred people had dinner there.

The Lancer was destroyed by fire, believed to have started in the kitchen, on the night of August 1, 1971, and was never rebuilt. At the time of the fire, the property was owned by Walter McCarrell and leased to Frank Sebastian and Arthur Allen.

Nev. St. Journal, 4 July 59 (photo), 5 Sept. 59; Denny Sayers, interview with the author.

LANGLEY'S TANGO PARLOR

224 North Virginia Street; licensed from March 15, 1940, to October 1, 1940, for tango (bingo) only.

C. L. Langley opened his tango (bingo) parlor at the former location of the Snooker Club in March 1940. After operating for only a few months, the business was taken over by the Robbins family. Harry and Ed Robbins opened Robbin's Nevada Club at that location in 1941.

The site of Langley's Tango Parlor is now part of the Nevada Club.

Reno City Directory, 1941; *Nev. St. Journal,* 14 Mar. 40.

LA RUE CLUB

244 North Virginia Street; licensed from March 23 to June 23, 1935, for roulette.

The La Rue Club was one of many small locations, usually with a bar, that obtained a license for a few months when gaming was first legalized. Roulette was a popular game in the early 1930s, and many bar owners were either licensed for a game or leased space to an operator.

The site of the La Rue Club is now part of Harolds Club.

LAUGHTON'S (LAWTON'S) HOT SPRINGS

9400 West Fourth Street (about five miles west of town on old Highway 40); originally licensed on April 7, 1931, for slots, craps, roulette, and 21, the property was licensed sporadically under various names and owners and for different types of gaming devices until 1978.

Lawton's Hot Springs was actually supposed to be called "Laughton's" after the property's original owner, Sumner Laughton. The first signs made for the resort (in the 1880s) were misspelled, and rather than order new signs, Laughton allowed his hot springs resort to be known as "Lawton's Hot Springs."

From the 1920s to 1957, the resort was in the hands of the Mark Yori family, whose Italian ancestors were among Reno's first settlers. During this thirty-year period, the resort became famous for its large outdoor swimming pool and tree-filled park area. It was the training camp in the early 1930s for Max Baer, who later became the world heavyweight boxing champion.

During the 1930s, Yori leased the facilities to various people. In 1931 Felix Turillas and John Etchebarren operated the resort. When Lawton's was first licensed in April 1931 by Turillas and Etchebarren, the casino had one 21 game, one craps game, one roulette wheel, and seven slot machines. An Olympic-size swimming pool that cost $65,000 to build was also opened in 1931.

Gene Rovetti operated the Club Lawton in 1936 and 1937. In 1938 greyhound dog-racing was introduced. There was a ten-cent admission charged to view the races, and there were eight races nightly.

In 1939 John Hickok opened a bar, club, and dining room at the resort.

The resort was often closed during the winter months. The bars, restaurants, and gaming areas were operated on a sporadic basis, but the swimming pool was always open during the summer months, except for a short period during World War II.

In January 1942 Mark Yori went into partnership with Frank Herman. Yori operated the bar, and Herman took care of the gaming. The club was called the River House from 1942 to 1943, and for most of the time that it was open it featured the entertainment of the Duncan Sisters, Topsy and Eva.

In May 1944 the club was leased to Bob Neeman, who named it Bob Neeman's Reno Rancho. The gaming was operated by "Smiling" Jesse Zilliox, who was licensed for craps, 21, slots, and roulette. Neeman's Reno Rancho naturally featured lots of western music, and in June 1944 the management proudly announced that Don Sworder, composer of the nation's top tune, "Deep in the Heart of Texas," would appear in the showroom. Evidently Sworder wasn't a big enough name to draw many customers, because the Reno Rancho closed in July 1944.

The resort continued to operate for the next several years as a bar and restaurant, and it remained a popular spot for locals, especially in the summertime, when its huge swimming pool and picnic area attracted customers.

For a short period in 1951, Mark Yori was partners with Roy Nelson and Harold Walters on the gaming license. In 1956 Al Figoni and Mark Yori were gambling partners, and in 1957 Mark Yori and Edgar Jolley each had 50 percent of the Lawton Hot Springs gaming operation.

In October 1957 Mark Yori sold the property to four California investors—Irwin "Bob" Siegel, Carl Long, Stewart Garey, and Robert Clarke Jr.—for $227,878, and in January 1958 Siegel was licensed for one 21 game and became manager of the resort. The following November, Paul Kessinger and Bill Smith purchased the property, and in 1959 Bill and Audrey Smith were licensed as 50-percent owners of Lawton's. In 1962 the property was sold to George Ruppert, Clarence Crandall, Stan Simmons, and Ralph Roberts and was renamed the Holiday Lodge.

The property has been closed since 1982. George Benny, who owned it at that time, went bankrupt after spending $16 million remodeling the facility, which he had renamed the River Palace.

Nev. St. Journal, 14 June 31 (adv.), 4 July 31, 5 July 31 (adv.), 31 Dec. 34 (adv.), 4 May 34 (adv.), 4 July 36, 16 Dec. 36, 26 June 38 (adv.), 8 Apr. 39, 4 May 46 (adv.), 8 May 51, 20 June 56, 19 Apr. 57,

22 Oct. 57, 25 Jan. 58, 28 Feb. 58 (adv.), 8 Nov. 58 (adv.), 3 Dec. 59, 25 Feb. 61 (adv.), 4 May 61 (adv.), 30 June 62 (adv.); William F. Harrah, "My Recollections of the Hotel-Casino Industry, and as an Auto Collecting Enthusiast" (unpublished oral history, University of Nevada Oral History Program, 1980).

LAYNE, GERALD

In December 1960 William Miller, owner of the Riverside Hotel-Casino, appointed Gerald Layne of Las Vegas as his new casino manager. On January 4, 1961, Layne applied for licensing as casino manager and 5-percent owner of the Riverside. His application was deferred.

A few days later, on January 10, Layne, who had several thousand dollars on him when he headed for a high-stakes poker game in Placerville, California, disappeared, and foul play was suspected. His car was later found abandoned in Harrah's Tahoe parking lot.

Ironically, the Gaming Commission denied Layne's applications for co-owner and casino manager the same day he was reported missing. The Commission disclosed that Layne had been arrested two years earlier in Tulsa, Oklahoma, in a car loaded with crooked dice and cards. He had been carrying a loaded pistol when he was arrested.

The search for Gerald Layne continued for several months, but neither Layne nor his body was ever found.

Nev. St. Journal, 28 Dec. 60, 4 Jan. 61, 5 Jan. 61, 10 Jan. 61, 17 Feb. 61 (photo).

LAZZARONE, AL

Al Lazzarone, who graduated from the University of Nevada with a degree in economics, came to Reno from Sacramento in 1947 to play for the Harolds Club softball team. During a three-week tour of California cities, another team player, who was also a Harolds Club employee, taught Lazzarone how to deal 21, and when the tour was over he began working at Harolds Club.

He worked his way through the ranks and served as a floor manager for several years. In 1973 he was named shift manager and casino executive at Harolds Club and remained in that position until 1978.

The River House in 1942. Bill Harrah (center) with a female companion, and two of his friends and their spouses, Wayne Martin (l.) and Virgil Smith (r.). Courtesy of Mrs. Virgil (Nelva) Smith.

The Harolds Club 1947 state championship softball team. Al Lazzarone is in the middle row on the far right. Other players are (back row, l. to r.) Harold "Lefty" Riordan, unknown, Glen Neely, Chuck Morris, Bill Riordan. Middle row, Babe Nygren, Wes Priest, unknown, Lazzarone. Front row, Pat Peeples, Les Haney, Raymond A. Smith (sponsor), Bill Bletcher, Hardy Brafford. Courtesy of Al Lazzarone.

In 1978, after working for Harolds Club for twenty-nine years, Lazzarone resigned in order to accept the position of casino manager of the Eldorado Hotel-Casino. Lazzarone's gaming knowledge and knowledge of people contributed a great deal to the Eldorado's success in the 1980s.

After stepping down as casino manager in the late 1980s, he stayed with the Eldorado as a casino host and tournament host and director, a position he still holds.

Nev. St. Journal, 7 Oct. 73, 26 Feb. 77, 27 Aug. 78 (photo).

LEE'S HOFBRAU HOUSE
136 North Virginia Street; never licensed for table games.

In June 1969 Lee Frankovich of Lee's Hofbrau House applied for a gaming license to test the red-line law. At the date of the application (June 14), there were twenty slot machines on the property, but Frankovich wanted to add table games and eighty more slot machines.

On June 17 the Reno City Council opted to take no action on the application, then, on June 24, the governing body denied Frankovich's application for one roulette game, one craps game, four 21 games, one keno game, and one hundred slot machines. The Council was quick to state that the denial was based on the city's red-line law and was no reflection on Frankovich or his operation.

The former location of Lee's Hofbrau House is now part of the Club Cal-Neva.

Nev. St. Journal, 14 June 69, 17 June 69, 24 June 69.

LEO'S DEN
361 North Virginia Street; no record of gaming.

No records were found of Leo's Den being licensed for gaming. However, George Ar-

dans and Chester Sealund were licensed as owners, and they were both associated with the gaming business, so one would suppose that there may have been some form of gaming at the location. Previously, the Grotto Bar (at the same address) was licensed for poker.

Leo's Den was closed when the owners of the Eldorado Hotel-Casino bought the entire 300 block of North Virginia Street and began construction of the hotel. The site is now part of the Eldorado Hotel-Casino.

Nev. St. Journal, 10 Sept. 70.

LEON & EDDIE'S
12 East Second Street; licensed from April 15, 1938, to December 15, 1957, for slots and 21.

Leon & Eddie's was formerly known as Louie's Rendevous. In October 1935 Leon Harbert and Ed Harris took over the property and renamed it Leon & Eddie's. Harbert had previously worked at the Cedars and the Grand Buffet, and at this time, he was employed at Louie's Rendevous. Harris had also formerly worked at the Cedars. Harbert and Harris operated the club together until April 1938, when they dissolved the partnership and Eddie Harris became the sole owner.

In August 1943 Harry Brody took over the management of Leon & Eddie's. In March 1947 Leon Nightingale and Ed Silva took over the business. They were licensed for one craps game, one 21 game, and three slot machines. Leon Nightingale sold the club in the early 1950s.

Leon & Eddie's featured entertainment in its small lounge, and in December 1947 a local favorite, Patsy Hogue, appeared there. Another popular favorite at the organ, Ray Sawyer, frequently appeared at Leon & Eddie's.

In the 1940s and 1950s there were several people who operated Leon & Eddie's, and various persons were licensed for the gaming. Included among the licensees were Virgil Smith, Denny Wood, Perry Griffith, Len Trusklaski, Carroll Swearingen, Art Frederickson, and J. P. Gabrielli. The licensees leased the games and the slot machines but did not own the property.

Virgil Smith brushing up on his dealing techniques at his 21 table in Leon & Eddie's. Courtesy of Mrs. Virgil (Nelva) Smith.

In October 1954 Luther Cochran was licensed for one 21 game and four slot machines, but in July 1956 the State of Nevada cited Leon & Eddie's to show cause why their license should not be revoked for improper operation of a 21 game. Cochran surrendered his gaming license but denied any knowledge of cheating. The state accepted the surrender of Cochran's gaming license (with prejudice) in August and revoked his slot license also.

Leon & Eddie's was purchased by Chester Young and Bud Ittner the following November. Young had been bar manager at the Hotel Golden for ten years. Ittner had been bar manager at several clubs around town and was employed as bar manager at Leon & Eddie's when he and Young purchased the club. Ugo Ceccarelli was licensed to operate three slot machines on the property in December 1956, and in January 1957 Chester Young was licensed for three slots.

In November 1958 Leon & Eddie's was sold to Jack Williams. The Club Cal-Neva purchased the property in the 1970s. The site is now part of the Club Cal-Neva.

Nev. St. Journal, 16 Apr. 38, 14 Aug. 43 (adv.), 26 Mar. 47 (adv.), 26 Mar. 47, 7 Dec. 47 (adv.), 15 Dec. 49 (adv.), 7 Aug. 52, 27 Aug. 52, 10 May 53, 18 June 53, 19 Aug. 53, 26 Oct. 54, 7 July 56, 1 Aug. 56, 2 Dec. 56, 18 Dec. 56, 16 Jan. 57, 19 Nov. 58 (adv.).

LIBERTY BELLE

4250 South Virginia Street; licensed since November 28, 1958.

The Liberty Belle opened in November 1958 at the former location of the Li'l Red Barn. Licensed for one 21 game were Frank Fey and Marshal Fey, and licensed for ten slots were Edmond Fey Sr. and Marshal Fey.

The Liberty Belle soon became a popular steak and prime-rib restaurant. Heavily patronized by locals, it was (and still is) well known for its collection of antique slot machines, music boxes, western memorabilia, and great food.

The Liberty Belle is still a popular dining spot for locals and tourists alike. There are slot machines at the location, but no gaming tables.

Nev. St. Journal, 22 Nov. 58 (adv.), 25 Nov. 58.

LIDO CLUB

222–224 Lake Street; licensed from June to December 31, 1956, and from March 1962 to April 1964 for slots, 21, craps, keno, and roulette.

The Lido Club was located at an address on Lake Street that housed several small casinos and bars over the years. Many of them catered to Asian customers.

When the Lido Club first opened, it was an exception to this pattern. Owners Walt Sanderson and John Caruso operated the Lido Club as a cabaret that featured western and popular music. In April 1955 Margaret Smith joined the partnership.

In December 1955 a group of Chinese businessmen took over management of the Lido. Horace (Yat Ming) Fong applied for a gaming license but was denied because of an unsuitable background. In 1956 Harry Chon applied for a keno license. After being deferred for several months, he was granted a license for keno in June 1956. In July, Horace Fong once again applied for and was denied a gaming license. However, the State of Nevada licensed Harry Chon for one craps game, one 21 game, and slots in August, and in October the City of Reno did the same.

There was no gaming at the Lido from 1957 until March 1962, when John Alarcon was licensed to operate a poker game. The

Lido was licensed for poker until April 1964.

The building was razed in the middle 1960s, and the site is currently a parking lot.

Nev. St. Journal, 7 May 54, 25 May 54 (adv.), 16 June 54, 27 Apr. 55, 21 Dec. 55, 18 May 56, 20 June 56, 27 July 56, 24 Aug. 56, 28 Aug. 56, 9 Oct. 56, 20 Mar. 62.

LI'L RED BARN

4250 South Virginia Street; licensed from December 1953 to June 1956 for 21 and roulette.

The Li'l Red Barn opened on December 9, 1953, as a bar and restaurant. The chef was the well-known and popular T. F. Gee of Dog House fame. Licensed for gaming were Leo Lien, Francis Licini, and Charles Rivara.

Gaming was closed in 1956, but the Li'l Red Barn operated until 1958, when it became the Liberty Belle. In 1999 the business was still operating as the Liberty Belle.

Nev. St. Journal, 9 Dec. 53, 11 Dec. 53, 31 July 58 (adv.).

LIVINGSTONE, BELLE (ALSO SPELLED LIVINGSTON)

Belle Livingstone was a New York City nightclub hostess, actress, showgirl, and speakeasy hostess who had many brushes with Prohibition agents in and around New York before coming to Reno in July 1931 to open a "swanky club." Livingstone, who was a friend, rival, and contemporary of Texas Guinan, another famous nightclub hostess, had billed herself in her early showgirl days in the 1890s as the "Kansas Sunshine Baby." But those days were long past. She was now in her sixties. She was six feet tall and weighed about one hundred and seventy-five pounds.

Upon arriving in Reno, she announced that she had come "in search of freedom" and proclaimed herself the "Empress of the Nevada Desert." In January 1931 she had served thirty days in a New York jail for violation of the Volstead Act (the Prohibition act), and she thought she would not be bothered in Reno.

Livingstone, a nationally known personality, garnered untold amounts of publicity for the recently legalized gaming. Her experiences in Reno with then-mayor E. E. Roberts were mentioned frequently in the *New York Times* and other well-known newspapers throughout the country.

In September 1931, after meeting vigorous opposition from adjoining ranchers, Livingstone was granted a gaming license to open one of the most unusual night spots in Reno. The club, called the Cowshed (or sometimes Belle's Barn), was located at 2295 South Virginia Street and featured African American musicians and a female African American chorus line.

Prohibition agents closed the club shortly after its opening, but Livingstone was allowed to open it again in late October. However, in November she left Reno for Texas. She later surfaced in San Francisco, where she again encountered trouble with Prohibition agents.

Her time in Reno was short but fiery. During her brief sojourn—which coincided with the first year of legalized gaming—the celebrated New Yorker helped to let the world know that gambling was legal in Nevada.

During 1930 and 1931 Livingstone achieved national notoriety. She was in the newspapers week after week as federal agents raided her saloons. Rounds of court appearances followed, but soon Livingstone appeared in another location. The story of her early years as it appeared in *Belle of Bohemia*, an alleged autobiography later serialized in *Cosmopolitan* magazine, was a press agent's dream.

Livingstone returned to New York in 1932, and the remainder of her life was relatively free of publicity. She died in a New York City nursing home on February 7, 1957. Her age at the time of death, according to her son, was eighty-four, but the hospital gave her age as ninety-two. She was survived by her daughter, Solange Graham; her son, Edward Mohler; and three grandchildren. None of her family was among the one hundred persons present at the nondenominational funeral services held at St. John's Lutheran Church in New York City.

LLOYD, JAMES SR.

Jim Lloyd was born in Youngstown, Ohio, on July 2, 1902. He was associated with hotels in California and Hawaii before he came to Reno shortly after World War II. He was active in the mining industry, especially in the Dayton, Nevada, area.

In 1946 Lloyd was one of a five-man group, including Norman Biltz, John Mueller, Harold Harris, and Henry Bennett, that purchased the Golden Hotel from George Wingfield for $1.5 million. The Lloyd group was in charge of the hotel rooms only. The first floor was rented to the Brunswick Club, the Bank Club Casino, and a few other small businesses. In 1947 Lloyd closed the Brunswick Club and opened a bingo parlor, a racehorse book, slots, and a penny roulette table.

In 1948 the Lloyd group sold 51 percent of the Golden to Thomas Hull. However, after only six months Hull filed for bankruptcy, and the Lloyd group with Jim Lloyd as manager resumed control of the Golden. Gaming was continued as the casino area was first named the Golden Gulch and later became known simply as the Golden Casino. Jim Lloyd continued as general manager of the Golden Hotel until 1952, when it was sold to Frank Hofues.

In January 1965 Lloyd purchased 12.5 percent of the Riverside Hotel-Casino, and in February 1966 he purchased Bernie Einstoss's stock, giving him control of 51 percent of the Riverside. He also became president of the corporation.

In 1967, when the Riverside was closed for cheating, Jim Lloyd was listed as a licensee, along with Bernie Richter and Andrew Desimone. All three lost their license at the Riverside. However, Lloyd kept his license for his slot-route company, the A-1 Novelty Company.

Lloyd, who was one of the original investors in Reno's first shopping mall, Park Lane Mall, and an original member of Reno's Prospector's Club, died on July 20, 1974, after a long illness.

Nev. St. Journal, 8 Oct. 46, 16 Nov. 46, 17 June 47, 15 July 47, 4 May 52, 19 Jan. 65, 16 Feb. 66, 16 Sept. 67, 29 Dec. 67, 21 July 74 (obit.).

LOG CABIN

596 Airport Road (now Gentry Way); licensed from October 1943 to June 1947 for 21 and craps.

The Log Cabin was located out of town and was a bar and nightclub patronized by late-night local casino workers and "rounders."

The Log Cabin was purchased by Joyce Mosely in 1949 and renamed Dixie's Log Cabin. The site is currently a used-car lot.

LOUIE'S RENDEVOUS

12 East Second Street; licensed from February 15, 1935, to April 1938 for 21 only.

Louie's Rendevous was owned by Louis Marymount. He opened the bar and lounge in December 1934 and was licensed for a 21 game in February 1935. The following October, Ed Harris and Leon Harbert took over the establishment and named their new club Leon & Eddie's. Louis Marymount left Louie's Rendevous to operate the Heidelburg Club.

The site is now part of the Club Cal-Neva.

Nev. St. Journal, 20 Dec. 34, 12 Oct. 35.

LOUVRE

22 East Commercial Row; licensed from July 1931 to December 1939 for craps, roulette, faro, a big-six wheel, pan, slots, and hazard.

Shortly after gaming was legalized in March 1931, the Louvre was licensed for one 21 game, one big-six wheel, one craps game, one hazard game, two roulette games, two pan games, two stud poker games, and three slot machines. The licensees in the operation were Joe Elcano and John Petricciani.

In April 1933, when the sale of beer became legal, W. E. Creps was given a beer license at the Louvre. In September 1935 the Louvre was taken over by Shorty Masini and Fred Santina.

On May 5, 1936, the "new" Louvre Club opened under the management of W. F. Normandy and his son Frank. They spent approximately $10,000 on remodeling. As a feature of their opening, they dispensed eight-year-old whiskey. They employed forty men to work the three shifts, and they were licensed for faro, 21, poker, pan, craps, and slots. Normandy came from Wyoming and Utah, where he had managed and owned clubs. He had been connected with the Becker Brewing Company for thirty years.

In less than six months, the club closed, but it reopened on December 31, 1936, with Phil Blume as proprietor. The club closed again in December 1939 and reopened as Martin's Bar in May 1940.

The former location of the Louvre is now part of Harolds Club.

Nev. St. Journal, 6 Apr. 33, 20 Sept. 35 (adv.), 5 May 36 (article and adv.), 31 Dec. 36.

LUCKY CLUB

125 East Second Street from 1931 to 1936; 121 East Second Street from 1936 to 1944; licensed from June 1931 to November 1944 for craps, 21, and slots.

The Lucky Club was first licensed in June 1931 for one craps game, one 21 game, one chuck-a-luck game, and one roulette game. In July a stud poker game and a fan-tan game were added to the license. In April 1933 Fred Santina was given a liquor license at the Lucky Club.

In February 1936 the Lucky Club moved from 125 East Second Street to 121 East Second Street, and Ugo Angeli was named manager of the club.

In 1942 Alfred Rooney, a 21 dealer at the Lucky Club, was convicted of "dumping off the bankroll" (allowing a player to win illegally) to a confederate. He was sentenced to six months in the county jail.

On November 5, 1944, city attorney Emerson Wilson conducted an investigation into another alleged cheating incident at the Lucky Club. His investigation determined that a dealer, Bob Thomas, had switched dice on the craps table. When some customers accused Thomas of cheating, he pulled a revolver from the drawer of a 21 table and threatened to shoot them. On November 6 Wilson revoked the Lucky Club's license and stated that the licensees, Lewis and Elsie Cates, were never to be licensed again.

The site is currently occupied by Doc Holiday's Saloon.

Nev. St. Journal, 24 Nov. 31, 8 Apr. 33, 25 May 40, 5 Nov. 44, 7 Nov. 44.

LYDEN, FRANCIS

Francis Lyden, who was originally from Montana, was working in the Palace Club as a pit boss in 1936. He is credited with convincing the owner, John Petricciani, to install a keno game and to bring Warren Nelson, Clyde Bittner, and several other Montana keno men to Reno to set up the first racehorse keno game in Nevada.

MAC'S CLUB

*2400 South Virginia Street; licensed from
October 1950 to November 1960 for slots, 21, and
craps.*

Mac's Club opened in November 1950. It was owned by Howard McMullen. In September 1951 the gaming license at Mac's Club was revoked when the State of Nevada cited the club "for operating a 21 game improperly." McMullen was licensed again in April 1952. Initially, he was denied an unrestricted license but was licensed for slots; in August he was given an unrestricted gaming license. In June 1954 Mac's Club was licensed for eight slot machines, two 21 games, and one craps game.

Mac's Club was a popular local hangout and featured western entertainment as well as dancing and gaming.

In 1959 Howard McMullen leased the business to Howard Jarrard, who named the club Jarrard's. Jarrard was licensed for one 21 game and three slot machines in January 1960. On November 7, 1960, the Gaming Control Board closed Jarrard's when gaming agents charged that the 21 game was being operated improperly. The agents said the dealers were "dealing seconds."

On November 23, 1960, Howard McMullen reopened the property as Mac's Club. His ad announced that "Mac is back at Mac's Club. After a one year absence, Howard McMullen is returning as manager, owner and operator. Dancing nightly 10 P.M. to 4 A.M. on a new dance floor."

McMullen's lease expired in 1963, and Mac's Club closed in November 1963. The site of Mac's Club is now part of the parking lot of Heidi's Family Restaurant.

Nev. St. Journal, 7 Sept. 51, 9 Apr. 52, 1 July 52 (adv.), 7 Aug. 52, 29 Mar. 53, 30 June 54, 30 Nov. 54, 6 Nov. 57 (adv.), 8 Dec. 58, 21 Dec. 59 (adv.), 21 Jan. 60, 8 Nov. 60, 24 Nov. 60 (adv.), 30 Nov. 60, 13 Dec. 60, 29 Dec. 60, 4 Jan. 61, 1 Aug. 63, 10 Sept. 63.

MAJESTIC CLUB

*116 North Center Street; licensed from July 16,
1931, to 1932 for 21 and craps.*

The Majestic Club opened in July 1931 and was licensed for one 21 game. On July 3, 1931, the club ran an ad in the paper wishing Jack Dempsey well in his promotion of the Max Baer–Paulino Uzcuduno heavyweight fight that would take place the next day.

In January 1932 a craps game was added to the license. Later that year the Majestic closed, and the property, which had previously operated as the Alpine Club, reopened once again as the Alpine Club operated by Eddie Vacchina. In later years the property housed the 116 Club and later the Stein.

The site is now part of the Club Cal-Neva parking garage on the east side of Center Street.

Nev. St. Journal, 3 July 31 (adv.).

MAPES, CHARLES

Charles Mapes was born in Reno, Nevada, on June 30, 1920. He grew up in Reno and attended Reno High School, where he was state tennis champion and led his debating team to a state championship. He graduated from the University of Nevada, where he was student-body president, was listed in *Who's Who of College Students,* and was named outstanding student debater in the state of Nevada. During World War II, Mapes served in the Naval Air Transport Service in Alaska and was discharged as a lieutenant, senior grade.

In 1945 he began construction of the Mapes Hotel-Casino, which was the first high-rise hotel built in the United States after World War II. When completed in 1947, it was at that time the tallest building in the state of Nevada.

The Mapes Hotel opened on December 17, 1947, and closed on December 17, 1982.

Charles Mapes was also the owner of the Mapes Money Tree, located at 211 North Virginia Street. The Money Tree first opened in 1969, and in 1978 it expanded across Fulton Alley and took over the corner of Second and Sierra Streets. It closed in 1980 but opened again in May

1981, only to close permanently on December 17, 1982.

Mapes created much animosity in the community, especially in the gaming community, when he closed both the Mapes Hotel and the Money Tree unannounced and failed to pay his employees for the last days they worked.

Mr. Mapes died in a San Diego hospital on May 12, 1999.

Nev. St. Journal, 31 Dec. 74; *Reno Gazette-Journal,* 15 May 99 (obit. and photo).

MAPES HOTEL-CASINO

*Located on the corner of East First and South
Virginia Streets; licensed from December 17,
1947, to December 17, 1982, as a full casino.*

Shortly after the conclusion of World War II, in November 1945, Mrs. Charles Mapes Sr. and her son, Charles Mapes Jr., announced their plans to build a ten-story, 250-room hotel at the corner of First and Virginia Streets. Ground was broken on December 1, 1945, and the Mapes became the first high-rise hotel to be built in the United States after World War II.

The Mapes opened on December 17, 1947, with three hundred hotel rooms in a twelve-story building. When the Mapes opened, it contained one of the first nightclubs in Reno within a hotel. The Trocadero in the El Cortez Hotel had introduced entertainment shortly before, and the Golden Hotel and the Riverside Hotel soon followed with their own big-name entertainment.

Charles Mapes leased the gaming to Lou Wertheimer, Leo Kind, Bernie Einstoss, and Frank Grannis. They were licensed for three craps games, three roulette games, six 21 games, and sixty-six slot machines.

On December 17 at 7:00 A.M., the 180-seat coffee shop on the ground floor opened for business—the first stage of a gala day-long opening celebration. At 10:00 A.M. the ground-floor cocktail lounge and casino opened. The informal and widely anticipated opening of the Sky Room took place at 4:30 P.M. At 7:30 P.M. a buffet supper for $3.00 a plate was served in the banquet room on the mezzanine level, and the crowds were so large that the buffet lasted until midnight. From 8:00 P.M. until 2:00 A.M. there was dancing in the Sky Room to the music of Joe Reichman and his orchestra.

Huge crowds of people massed around the elevators as they tried to get up to the Sky Room, one of the main attractions of the hotel. The room was beautifully appointed for dancing and dining, and the wait proved to be more than worthwhile once patrons reached the top floor. Around the bar, which took up the west and south portions of the Sky Room, there were so many people that the view from the large windows was mostly obscured. However, people who did gain a glimpse out the windows were thrilled by the sight of thousands of city lights twinkling below. The Sky Room's muted blue and green lights blended with the rest of the decor, and the people in the room were impressed by the beauty of their surroundings.

On the ground level, throngs of people crowded the lobby and the downstairs bar. The casino areas were also crowded, and the games were heavily played. Adding Hollywood color and excitement to the casino area was Hollywood's Tarzan, Johnny Weissmuller, complete with long hair, dark glasses, and his unmistakable physique.

The Mapes Hotel and the Sky Room were by far the most exciting attractions in Reno up to that time. The Mapes immediately became the showplace of Reno and a venue for the most famous entertainers in show business. The Riverside and the Golden soon entered the competition, and in the late 1940s and 1950s Reno was considered the entertainment capital of the world. In its heyday, the Mapes featured most of the top names in show business. Liberace made his first appearance there in December 1950, and in January 1951 he was followed by the Will Mastin Trio, featuring Sammy Davis Jr. Other major stars who appeared at the Mapes included Mae West, Judy Garland, Milton Berle, Gypsy Rose Lee, Lili St. Cyr, Ann-Margret, and many more. During the filming of *The Misfits*, the Mapes was headquarters for the movie production company, and the female lead, Marilyn Monroe, stayed in a suite on the sixth floor.

In March 1955 Bernie Einstoss and Frank Grannis, who still had almost three years left on their gaming lease at the Mapes, became licensed at the Cal-Vada Club at Lake Tahoe. Charles Mapes objected because the payment on the Mapes gaming lease was 50 percent of casino profits, and he felt that the Cal-Vada (later known as the Bal Tabarin) would represent a conflict of interest for Einstoss and Grannis. Mapes demanded that their license be revoked, but the state refused. Mapes then declared that he wanted to buy up the remainder of the lease, which was to expire on January 1, 1958, for the fair value of the gaming equipment plus the bankroll. Einstoss responded that he wanted $425,000 for the lease.

During this same period, the state questioned Mapes about the status of one of his employees, Bill Pechart. Pechart had been in trouble with the state previously because of his past history, and in 1952 he had been denied a gaming license at the Palace Club. Mapes stated that Pechart was "watching" his money for $35 a day, plus a suite in the hotel and $1,000 a month for expenses.

In May 1955 the state transferred the gaming license of the Mapes Hotel to Charles Mapes only. Mapes was ordered to have Pechart off the property by July 1 and to pay Einstoss $125,000 for the balance of the lease.

Mapes complied with the order about Bill Pechart in an abstract manner. Pechart no longer came into the casino or even on the property, but he did station himself in a parked automobile on the street just outside of the hotel. Any pit matter of importance was presented to him by a runner. Pechart made his decision, and the runner was sent back into the casino with Pechart's instructions, which were followed by the staff. Pechart also maintained full authority over hiring or firing. This arrangement lasted for several months until it was finally stopped by the state.

One month after he took over the gaming license, Mapes opened up the ground floor of the Mapes with six thousand square feet of casino space, ten gaming tables, and 124 slot machines. One month later, in July 1955, the Mapes was licensed for three more 21 games.

In 1957 Glen Thorne was named casino manager. The casino had added two more 21 games to its license and now had fifteen table games.

Also in 1957 Charles Mapes announced plans for a 125-seat restaurant that would extend along the south side of the building facing the Truckee River. The restaurant, called the Coach Room, opened in February 1958.

In September 1958 the Mapes discontinued entertainment in the Sky Room, which was henceforth to be used only for private parties and banquets. (There was still entertainment in the lounge on the first floor.) This policy lasted until June 11, 1959, when Mapes reopened the Sky Room. The opening act was Ken Murray's Blackouts, featuring Marie Wilson.

In July 1960 Mapes petitioned the Gaming Control Board to allow him to rehire Bill Pechart. The Board agreed but stipulated that Pechart was not to be allowed in the pit area or in the counting rooms.

In June 1961 Mapes expanded the ground-floor lounge and initiated a stronger entertainment policy.

The Gaming Control Board finally ended its restrictions on Bill Pechart in March 1963, stating that restriction "no longer served any purpose." Pechart was at that time employed as a credit manager for the hotel. This ruling allowed him to go anywhere in the casino. (In September 1965, while on duty as casino manager in the Mapes Hotel, Bill Pechart suffered a heart attack and died. He was seventy-three years old.)

On October 1, 1965, shortly after Pechart's death, Mapes announced the following appointments: Harold Baker, hotel manager; Jack Sommer, assistant hotel manager and host; and Ray Smith, casino manager.

In September 1968, as a result of a trial that lasted for several weeks, Charles Mapes was awarded $56,400. He contended that his employees had stolen $431,000 from him by manipulating the credit system of the Mapes. The insurance company had refused to pay the claim, and the award from the insurance company came only after a lengthy trial.

The year 1969 ushered in the beginning of big jackpots and the accompanying publicity. The Mapes was one of the first to capitalize on the excitement. On October 31, 1969, the Mapes announced that it had paid what was at that time the world's record jackpot: $9,261.70 on a three-reel, five-coin, dollar slot machine.

In 1973 Julius Pozzi was named casino manager, a position he held until 1976, when Herb Grellman was appointed to that position.

Charles Mapes and the Mapes Corporation began to get in financial trouble in 1979. In 1969 Mapes, along with his sister, Gloria Mapes Walker, opened a small casino, the Money Tree. The casino did a good business, and everything went so well that in 1977 construction was begun on an expansion of the Money Tree. The expansion extended across Fulton Alley all the way to Sierra Street. The two-story addition contained 43,500 square feet of casino space and opened on July 1, 1978—the same date that Circus Circus and the Sahara Reno opened, and the same year that the MGM and the Comstock opened.

So many new hotel-casinos resulted in Reno being overbuilt as far as gaming was concerned. The proliferation of casinos was a major problem for the Money Tree (as well as for many other properties), but when that situation was compounded by soaring interest rates, a lack of parking space, and the absence of hotel rooms, the Money Tree expansion was doomed. That led to a shortage of cash for the Mapes Corporation and of course for the Mapes Hotel.

In January 1980 the Money Tree addition was closed. The following July, the First Interstate Bank announced that it intended to foreclose on several loans that listed the Mapes Hotel and the Money Tree Casino as collateral. The loans totaled $9.36 million of principal and $1.5 million in back payments. Mapes had thirty-five days to make the payments on the loans. When he could not come up with the necessary cash, the First Interstate Bank agreed to provide $1.4 million in operating funds to the Mapes Corporation if a management-consulting firm was brought in to operate

the business. Jaeger Industries, a Southern California consulting firm, was hired to operate the property and did so from September 1980 to October 1981.

On November 14, 1980, amid the bank's threats of foreclosure for back payments on loan principals, Mapes filed a Chapter 11 bankruptcy plan to allow payments to the corporation's 710 creditors over an extended period of time.

In January 1981 Jaeger hired Ron Erickson, former general manager of the Onslow Hotel, as general manager of the Mapes. Erickson was terminated in April 1981 and replaced by William Dougall.

All during 1981 and most of 1982, legal maneuvering, threats of foreclosure, public auctions, and foreclosure deadlines came and went, and still the First Interstate Bank continued to give Mapes more time to come up with refinancing or to sell the properties. But it was to no avail. Finally, on December 17, 1982, exactly thirty-five years after it opened, the Mapes ran out of operating cash and closed its doors. The sister casino, the Money Tree, closed the same day. At the time of closure, the banks were owed about $16 million, administration expenses totaled $2 million, unsecured creditors were owed about $880,000, and between five hundred and six hundred employees were owed about $73,000 in back wages.

Sil Petricciani, general manager of the Mapes and the Money Tree, announced to the employees shortly after 5 P.M. that the properties were closing. The announcement at the Money Tree resulted in angry shouting and near rioting. At the Mapes, however, things were quite different. Long-time employees felt sorrow, not just over losing their jobs but over the loss of the Mapes Hotel. The employees loved the Mapes, which was like a second home for many of them, and there was much crying, hugging, and sadness.

The First Interstate Bank obtained title in January 1983, when no one countered its initial $6-million bid at the foreclosure sale. Because the properties owed the bank about $15 million in past-due loans, no money changed hands.

On June 1, 1988, George Karadanis and

Robert Maloff, partners in the Sundowner Hotel and other ventures, bought the Mapes Hotel from the First Interstate Bank for an undisclosed sum. They put the Mapes up for sale three weeks later. Through the years there were many prospective buyers and many near sales, but it wasn't until August 1996 that the Mapes Hotel was once again sold. This time the purchaser was the City of Reno. On August 20 the Reno City Council finalized the purchase of the Mapes Hotel from Maloff and Karadanis for a purchase price of $4 million.

On September 24, 1998, the City of Reno announced a $46.6-million plan to convert the Mapes into time-share units. San Diego developer Oliver McMillan is negotiating an agreement with QM Resorts of Sparks. The plan calls for turning the twelve-story hotel into eighty-eight time-share apartments. *(See Addendum 3)*

Nev. St. Journal, 22 Nov. 45, 2 Dec. 45, 17 July 46, 15 Oct. 47, 30 Nov. 47, 3 Dec. 47, 7 Dec. 47, 9 Dec. 47, 16 Dec. 47, 17 Dec. 47, 1 Aug. 48, 28 Dec. 50, 25 Jan. 51, 4 Feb. 55, 2 Mar. 55, 24 May 55, 30 June 55, 12 July 55, 16 Dec. 56 (photo), 11 June 57, 23 Oct. 57, 10 Nov. 57, 17 Dec. 57, 26 Feb. 58, 28 Sept. 58, 2 June 59, 26 July 60, 9 Apr. 61, 29 June 61, 20 Mar. 63, 15 June 63, 28 May 64, 26 Sept. 65 (obit.), 1 Oct. 65, 7 Sept. 68, 2 July 69, 31 Oct. 69, 18 Oct. 73, 31 Dec. 74, 23 July 76, 19 Nov. 76, 20 Oct. 78, 8 July 80, 9 July 80, 6 Aug. 80, 12 Aug. 80, 22 Sept. 80, 2 Oct. 80, 23 Oct. 80, 18 Nov. 80, 18 Nov. 80, 22 Jan. 81 (photo), 17 Feb. 81, 9 Apr. 81, 17 Apr. 81, 18 Dec. 82, 3 June 88.

MARTIN, ROBERT "BOB"

Bob Martin was a student at the University of Nevada and working his way through college when he was first hired at Harrah's as a security guard in 1952. He later became a craps dealer, then worked in purchasing, construction, and the food department.

In 1966 he was named administrative assistant to the executive vice-president and assistant to the general manager. In 1968 he was appointed general manager of the construction of Harrah's Hotel, and in October 1969 he was promoted to vice-president of planning. In May 1980 Martin was appointed vice-president and general manager of Harrah's Reno.

Martin retired from Harrah's in the

mid-1980s and is currently dividing his time between homes in Las Vegas and in Glenbrook, at Lake Tahoe.

Nev. St. Journal, 5 Sept. 66, 19 Oct. 69, 3 May 80.

MARTIN, WAYNE

Wayne Martin was born in Lovelock, Nevada, where he was an outstanding athlete at Pershing County High School. In 1936 he moved to Reno to work with his friend Virgil Smith. He was a partner with Smith in several operations around Reno, including the roulette wheel at the Golden Hotel, the table games at Colbrandt's Flamingo, the table games at the Villa Sierra, and the poker games at the Palace Club.

In 1943, Martin also became a partner, along with Virgil Smith, Bill Harrah, and Bill Williams, in John's Bar on West Second Street. In June 1946, when Bill Harrah opened his first full casino on Virginia Street, Martin became the first club manager. When Martin died in October 1964, he was working for Harrah's Club as a department manager and had recently com-

pleted his eighteenth year of employment with the club.

Nev. St. Journal, 3 Oct. 64 (obit.).

MARTIN'S BAR

22 East Commercial Row; licensed from May 8 to December 31, 1940, for poker only.

This location was formerly known as the Louvre Casino and is now part of Harolds Club.

MASON FAMILY

The Mason family was originally in the construction business. They owned the Taylor International Construction Company and built hotels such as the Fontainebleau in Miami, Caesars Palace in Las Vegas, the MGM Hotels in Reno and Las Vegas, the Riviera in Las Vegas, and many others.

Maury Mason received his first gaming license in 1955 after his company had completed construction of the Riviera Hotel in Las Vegas. He took a percentage of the casino in lieu of payment. Shortly after the

Riviera opened, Mason divested himself of his interest in the hotel, and it wasn't until 1967 that a Mason family member was again licensed.

In 1967 Maury Mason's two sons, Stuart and Walter "Wally," were licensed, along with Brad Hewins, at the Horseshoe Club on North Virginia Street. They operated the Horseshoe until 1977, when they sold it to Dr. Tom Mullis and Jesse Hinkel.

After selling the Horseshoe Club, Walter and Stuart Mason owned and operated the Shy Clown Casino in Sparks from 1979 to 1981. They closed the Shy Clown when the City of Sparks refused to allow them to build hotel rooms on the property.

In 1980 the Mullis-Hinkle operation went bankrupt, and the Mason family took back the property. On the license when the Horseshoe was reopened in April 1981 were the names of Maury Mason and Stuart Mason.

In December 1981 the Mason-owned Horseshoe Club purchased the adjoining Silver Spur Casino and merged it into the Horseshoe. Maury and Stuart Mason operated the Horseshoe Club until they were forced into bankruptcy in 1988.

No member of the Mason family is currently licensed as a casino owner.

MATHIA, DOYLE

Doyle Mathia, who graduated from Washburne University in Topeka, Kansas, was hired by Harrah's Tahoe in 1957 as a cashier. He worked for the Harrah's organization for twenty years and reached the position of president and general manager of Harrah's Tahoe. He was later named vice-president and general manager of Harrah's Automobile Collection.

In 1977 Mathia resigned his position as executive vice-president of administration for Harrah's to accept the position of vice-president and general manager of the Sahara Reno, which opened on July 1, 1978.

Nev. St. Journal, 28 June 73, 11 Oct. 77 (photo).

MATHIS, RAYMOND "RUBY"

Ruby Mathis was born in Detroit, Michigan, in 1899. He came to Reno in 1946 and

Wayne Martin (r.) in the counting room of Harrah's in 1948, with Warren Nelson (l.) and Bob Ring (center). Courtesy of Scherry Harrah.

entered into a partnership with Mert Wert-heimer, Lincoln Fitzgerald, Dan Sullivan, and Harry and Ed Robbins at the Nevada Club on North Virginia Street.

In 1949 Mathis, along with Mert Wert-heimer and Baldy West, took over management of the Riverside Hotel, including the gambling, for the hotel owner, George Wingfield. In December 1955 Mathis, the Wertheimer brothers, Lou and Mert, and Baldy West purchased the Riverside from Wingfield. The Wertheimer group sold the Riverside to the Crummer Corporation in January 1958. However, they took a ten-year lease on the casino, bars, restaurants, and entertainment.

Shortly after they sold the Riverside to the Crummer Corporation, both Lou and Mert Wertheimer died. Baldy West had left the group earlier, so Ruby Mathis was the only surviving partner. In August 1958 he sold the lease to Virgil Smith.

In January 1959 Ruby Mathis bought 11 percent of the Horseshoe Club on North Virginia Street. He maintained his ownership until the Horseshoe was sold to the Mason family in 1967.

Ruby Mathis died in Reno in March 1986.

Nev. St. Journal, 17 Dec. 55, 21 Jan. 58, March 86 (obit.).

MAURY, OSCAR "LEE"

Lee Maury operated the gaming in the 222 Club on North Center Street in 1948. However, in 1949 he was denied a gaming license because his wife, Alice, had been arrested for possession of narcotics and sentenced to two years in jail.

In January 1953 Maury shot and fatally wounded Bud Dutcher, manager of the West Indies nightclub, in the parking lot of Dixie's Log Cabin on Gentry Way. In March 1953 he was found guilty of second-degree murder and was sentenced to prison.

Nev. St. Journal, 13 Jan. 53, 24 Jan. 53, 28 Mar. 53.

MAVERICK

19 East Douglas Alley; licensed for slots, poker, 21, and pan from November 1961 to March 1965.

The Maverick, formerly known as Roy's

Cocktail Lounge, was a local bar and hang-out seldom patronized by tourists. It was closed in 1965 and reopened as the Ring-side. The site is now part of Harolds Club.

Nev. St. Journal, 27 Sept. 62.

MCCALL, CLELLAND

Clelland McCall was born in Kansas in 1903. He came to Reno in 1944, where his first job was with Lawton's Casino on West Fourth Street.

He had worked in several illegal clubs in and around Kansas and Missouri before coming to Reno, and he was skilled in all the "tricks of the gaming trade." In the 1930s, '40s, and '50s, casino workers had to know the games from the "outside" as well as the "inside" if they were to protect their games from "crossroaders." McCall was one of the best.

McCall leased the gaming at the California Club on North Virginia Street in the mid-1940s. He also worked at the Palace Club for Baldy West, the Horseshoe Club for Brad Hewins in the late 1950s, the Holiday Hotel-Casino in the early 1960s, and he was a shift manager at the Golden Bank Club and the Primadonna Club.

In an interview shortly before his death, he said, "I'm glad I had a good time when I was young, because growing old can be hell." He was eighty-five when he died.

MCCLOSKEY, HUBERT "MAC"

Mac McCloskey was born in Terre Haute, Indiana, on August 28, 1900. He came to the Reno–Lake Tahoe area in 1932.

He was an owner-operator of the Crystal Bay Club in Crystal Bay, Nevada, from 1960 to 1968. In 1970 McCloskey and Ray Plunkett were named managers of the Crystal Bay Club for an investment group from Ohio.

In 1973 Mac was licensed as general manager of the Eldorado Hotel-Casino in Reno, and in August 1974 he was licensed as a co-owner.

McCloskey died on May 5, 1979.

Nev. St. Journal, 13 Aug. 70, 25 May 73, 27 Aug. 74, 8 May 79 (obit. and photo).

MCCLURE, ROBERT "BUSTER"

Robert McClure, a native of Dardanelles, Arkansas, came to Reno in 1944 to attend the University of Nevada. He was an outstanding college football player for the Wolf Pack, was chosen for several All-Coast and All-American football teams, and was picked to play in the prestigious East-West Shriner's football games in 1945 and 1946. Upon graduation, he signed a contract with the Boston Yankees football team and played professional football for several years.

After retiring from football, McClure was employed by the Riverside Hotel during the 1950s. In 1960 he was named night manager of the Holiday Hotel-Casino and remained in that position until 1967. He left the casinos to work as sales manager of Anderson Dairy from 1967 to 1970 but returned to the gaming business in 1970 when he was named assistant manager of the Holiday Hotel-Casino.

McClure remained at the Holiday and worked there in various managerial posi-

Robert "Buster" McClure (l.), hotel manager of the Riverside Hotel, pictured in 1959 with Riverside owner-operator Virgil Smith. Courtesy of Mrs. Virgil (Nelva) Smith.

tions until his retirement in the late 1980s. He died of a heart attack on April 17, 1999.

His son, Willie McClure, followed his father's footsteps and is currently employed as a casino executive at the Club Cal-Neva in Reno.

Nev. St. Journal, 21 Aug. 70 (photo), 13 Apr. 78.

MCDONNELL, DON

Don McDonnell was born in Minot, North Dakota, on February 13, 1913. After serving in the army in World War II, he came to Reno in 1945.

He was hired by Harolds Club in 1945 and remained there until 1971. McDonnell worked as a shift manager for many years and was a casino manager during the last few years of his employment there.

In 1971, after Harolds Club was sold to the Hughes Corporation, McDonnell was terminated by the new owners. A few months later, he was named casino manager of the newly opened Riverside Hotel by the hotel's new owner, Jessie Beck. McDonnell stayed with Jessie Beck's Riverside Hotel-Casino until it was sold to Pick Hobson in 1978.

He passed away on December 20, 1994.

Nev. St. Journal, 30 Mar. 71.

MCKAY, JAMES "CINCH"

Jim McKay was born in Virginia City, Nevada, on September 14, 1888. He became acquainted with Bill Graham in Tonopah during the early days of the mining boom there, and they developed a lifelong partnership. In fact, the names Graham and McKay became almost synonymous for the rest of their lives.

In the 1920s McKay came to Reno and became involved in a number of illegal businesses involving nightclubs and gambling. Included among these properties were the Willows, the Cal-Neva at Lake Tahoe, the Bank Club, the Miner's Club, and the "Stockade," an area of prostitution located just a few blocks from downtown. In 1931, when gaming became legal, McKay and Graham simply opened their businesses to the public. They had already been in operation illegally for years, so it was easy for them to "get into action."

McKay was especially interested in sports and horse racing, and he was active in promoting professional boxing matches in Reno. He was also involved with Graham and Jack Dempsey, former heavyweight boxing champion, in promoting horse races at the old Reno Race Track—now the Washoe County Fairgrounds—on North Wells Avenue.

McKay and Graham's Bank Club on Center Street was the premier gambling casino in the early 1930s and was considered the largest casino in the world for many years.

In 1934 McKay and Graham were arrested for mail fraud. The subsequent disappearance of a key witness for the prosecution, Roy Frisch, and the three-week trial generated nationwide headlines. The trial resulted in a hung jury. Another trial, held in 1935, also resulted in a hung jury. It wasn't until a third trial, held in January and February 1938, that McKay and Graham were convicted and sentenced to nine years in a federal prison and fined $11,000. After numerous delays and appeals, Graham and McKay entered Leavenworth Prison in November 1939. They remained there until their release in October 1945. They had served just under six years. In 1950 Nevada senator Pat McCarran interceded with President Harry Truman, and Graham and McKay were both given full pardons.

Shortly after their return to Reno, they were once again active in the Bank Club. In 1950 they bought back from Jack Sullivan the one-third percentage of the Bank Club that they had sold him before they went to prison.

In 1952 James McKay and Bill Graham's partnership in the Bank Club and the Golden Hotel was dissolved.

On June 19, 1962, James McKay died in a Reno hospital after a long illness.

Nev. St. Journal, 3 Dec. 31, 1 Feb. 34, 2 Feb. 34, 24 Mar. 34, 5–19 July 34, 21 July 34, 25 July 34, 27 July 34, 10 Sept. 35, 17 Sept. 35, 21 Sept. 35, 29 May 37 (photo), 24 Jan. 38, 8 Feb. 38, 13 Feb. 38, 30 Mar. 38, 5 Oct. 38, 7 Mar. 39, 1 Aug. 39, 4 Aug. 39, 17 Nov. 39, 9 Sept. 42, 28 Oct. 45 (photos), 31 Oct. 45, 1 Apr. 50, 19 Sept. 50, 21 June 62 (obit.).

MCMULLEN, HOWARD "MAC"

Howard McMullen was born in Joplin, Missouri, on August 30, 1908. In 1939 he came to Reno, where he attended and graduated from the University of Nevada.

In July 1944 McMullen, along with George Stone, purchased the Deer Head Lodge on South Virginia Street. They sold it in 1951.

In 1946 McMullen added to his holdings when he purchased a 50-percent interest in John's Bar on West Second Street from Bill Harrah and Wayne Martin. The remaining 50 percent was owned by Virgil Smith and Bill Williams. John's Bar was sold in February 1947 to Bill Dixon and Bill Wirts, who renamed the property the Stork Club.

In October 1950 McMullen was licensed for a 21 game and a craps game at Mac's Club, located at 2400 South Virginia Street. He operated the club until 1963. Mac's Club lost its gaming license once for improper gaming procedures and a second time for serving liquor to minors, but Mac always bounced back and managed to get back in action. He was finally put out of business at Mac's Club when the lease expired in September 1963.

McMullen passed away on September 28, 1979.

Nev. St. Journal, 1 Oct. 46, 19 July 47, 7 Sept. 51, 9 Apr. 52, 7 Aug. 52, 30 June 54, 30 Nov. 54, 24 Nov. 60, 1 Oct. 79 (obit.).

MENLO CARD ROOM

21 East Douglas Alley; licensed from July 8, 1957, through 1958 for faro only.

The Menlo Card Room was one of those businesses along Douglas Alley whose names and proprietors changed frequently. Two of the licensees at the Menlo Card Room were a Mr. Bortolini and a Mr. Disney. The site is now part of Harolds Club.

Nev. St. Journal, 25 Jan. 58.

MERRY-GO-ROUND BAR

26 West Second Street; licensed from March 1946 to August 1956 for slots, craps, 21, and roulette.

The Merry-Go-Round Bar was located at the former site of Blondy's Bar. The bar was actually set on a carousel mechanism that when activated caused the bar stools to revolve around the center part of the bar.

During its ten-year existence, the Merry-Go-Round Bar had many owners. Allen Roberts was granted the first gaming license in March 1946 for one craps game, one roulette game, and two 21 games, plus twelve slot machines. Over the years, the following people were some of the other licensees: Ad Tolen in the late 1940s; Herman Smith in 1950 and 1951 for one craps game, one 21 game, one roulette game, and twenty slot machines; Vivian Gattis in 1951; Matt Dromiack and Dan Gordon in 1952 and 1953, for one craps game, one 21 game, and ten slot machines; and finally the last licensee, Lonnie Logsdon. Logsdon was licensed in August 1953 and for a short time had Bruce Gandy as his partner; however, in July 1956, when Logsdon was cited by the state to show cause why his license should not be revoked for improper operation of a 21 game, he was the sole licensee.

On July 31, 1956, the Gaming Control Board recommended revocation of the slot and gaming license, and on August 1, 1956, the State Gaming Commission concurred.

The former location of the Merry-Go-Round Bar is now part of the Pioneer Gift Shop.

Nev. St. Journal, 13 Mar. 46, 22 Aug. 46 (adv.), 26 July 50, 9 Sept. 50, 27 Nov. 51, 4 Dec. 51, 30 Jan. 52, 27 May 52, 24 June 52, 6 Aug. 52, 19 Aug. 53, 2 July 54, 14 July 54, 26 Nov. 55, 1 Dec. 55, 21 Dec. 55, 31 July 56, 1 Aug. 56.

MESA

Located a few miles up the Mount Rose Highway; licensed from July 1948 to June 1959 for slots, 21, and roulette.

The Mesa was actually a fine dining house that people frequented more for dining and dancing than for gambling. However, when people in Reno went out for dinner, they often wanted to gamble, and the proprietors of the Mesa were always ready to accommodate them.

One of the owners of the Mesa was Arthur Allen, who was also a hotel manager at the Riverside Hotel for many years. Another owner was Guy Michael, who also owned the Christmas Tree Restaurant.

Over the years the gaming was leased out to various concessionaires, some of whom included Brownie Paretti, Benny Petronzi, and J. J. Coffee Jr.

In 1959 the Mesa Restaurant was sold to the Crummer Corporation and renamed the Lancer.

Currently there are no buildings on the property. The Lancer Restaurant was completely destroyed by fire on August 3, 1971.

Nev. St. Journal, 8 May 51, 8 Mar. 58.

METROVICH, JAMES "JIM"

Jim Metrovich, a native of Manhattan, Kansas, attended St. Mary's College in California, where he was an outstanding athlete. When he finished college, he pursued a career in professional baseball. He was also a renowned golfer and won the national left-handers' championship in 1955.

Metrovich was a co-owner of the table-games concession in the Town House on First Street from 1949 to 1951. When Newt Crumley opened gambling at the Holiday Hotel in 1957, Metrovich was one of the first shift managers. He was later employed in executive positions at the Mapes, the Cal-Neva, and other casinos, and he also operated the Reno Golf Driving Range.

On September 30, 1970, Metrovich collapsed and died on a Bahamian golf course. He had been a gambling inspector in the Bahamas since 1967.

Nev. St. Journal, 2 Nov. 49, 1 Oct. 70 (obit.).

MGM HOTEL-CASINO

2500 East Second Street; licensed from May 3, 1978, to April 1986 for a full casino.

In October 1975 the MGM Corporation announced plans to build a one-thousand-room hotel in Reno. The tentative site was said to be a sixty-acre parcel two miles west of downtown Reno, adjacent to Interstate 80. MGM had purchased a lease option on the property, although Frank Rosenfelt, president of MGM, said that no final site selection had yet been made. Then, on November 7, MGM announced that it was looking at fifteen or twenty different parcels in the Reno area and that no definite decision had yet been made.

On November 18, MGM chose a lease site with an option to buy on 110 acres of land between Second and Mill Streets, east of the Reno-Sparks Indian Colony, and dropped its bid on the parcel west of town. Four days later, MGM announced that it was definitely going to build at the Second and Mill Street location.

Construction started on the hotel-casino early in 1976, and in July Barry Brunet, chairman of the board, and Jack Pieper, president of MGM Reno, were licensed by the Gaming Commission. The MGM management team took out a full-page in the *Reno Gazette-Journal* on December 25, 1977, to wish everyone a "Merry Christmas from MGM." Included in the ad were Barry Brunet, chairman of the board; Jack Pieper, president; Glen Neely, casino manager; Mike Clay, slot manager; and Gordon Fulton, keno manager.

On March 24, 1978, the Gaming Commission licensed the MGM for 141 table games, two thousand slot machines, and one jai alai game.

The MGM opened officially on May 3, 1978, at twelve noon. There were 1,900 invited guests, including celebrities from the entertainment world, politicians, gaming executives, and well-known personalities from all over the United States. An estimated 10,000 other people attended the opening. The invited guests dined in the Grand Ballroom and danced to the music of Harry James.

The hotel-casino was something never before seen in Reno. The building was twenty-six stories high and contained 1,015 hotel rooms. Construction cost $150 million. In addition to a gambling area the size of two football fields, there were two movie theaters, seven restaurants, the two-thousand-seat Ziegfeld Theater with the largest stage in the world, five indoor tennis courts, a pro shop with a staff of two teaching professionals, three outdoor tennis courts, a fifty-lane bowling center open twenty-four hours a day, a race and sports book, and a jai alai fronton. The arcade level featured more than forty shops, a wedding chapel, and a branch of the First Interstate Bank of Nevada.

Dean Martin was the opening act in the

Ziegfeld Theater. The long-awaited extravaganza *Hello, Hollywood, Hello* opened on June 1, 1978, and played to full houses for years.

In January 1979 Jack Pieper announced his resignation as president and general manager of the MGM Hotel-Casino. He was replaced by Barry Brunet, who had been with the MGM Corporation since 1958 and had been chairman of the board of the Reno MGM since 1976.

In November 1979 the Reno City Council approved MGM's plans for a twenty-seven-story, 982-room expansion tower. Construction began in 1980 and was concluded in 1981. Upon completion, the facility had 2,001 hotel rooms.

In March 1980 Glen Neely was promoted from casino manager to senior vice-president. The casino manager position was taken by Larry Sommerfield.

In April 1986 the Bally Manufacturing Corporation purchased the MGM Hotel-Casinos in Las Vegas and Reno for $587 million. In October 1990 Bally was unable to make the interest payments on the bonds used to finance the casino's purchase, and in November 1991 Bally filed for bankruptcy.

In May 1992 Harvey's Wagon Wheel, Inc., announced an agreement to buy Bally's Hotel-Casino for $70 million, but a few days later the Hilton Hotel Corporation offered to buy Bally's for $73 million. On June 15, 1992, Bally's was auctioned off in a bankruptcy sale held in Camden, New Jersey. The winning bid was $83 million from the Hilton Hotel Corporation. Hilton immediately vowed to spend more than $100 million upgrading the property and turning it into a themed-destination resort.

Currently the property is operating as the Reno Hilton.

Nev. St. Journal, 7 Oct. 75, 11 Nov. 75, 18 Nov. 75, 21 Nov. 75 (photo), 29 Apr. 76, 23 July 76, 25 Dec. 77 (adv.), 24 Mar. 78, 30 Apr. 78 (photos), 2 May 78, 4 May 78 (photos), 2 June 78, 12 Jan. 79, 11 Apr. 79, 4 Oct. 79, 14 Nov. 79 (photos), 16 Jan. 80 (photos), 17 Mar. 80, 18 Mar. 80, 17 June 92.

MILLER, WILLIAM W. "BILL"

Bill Miller, a former New Jersey restaurant operator who had previously been li-

censed at the Dunes and the Sahara Hotels in Las Vegas, was okayed to purchase the Riverside Hotel for $5 million in November 1960. He purchased the property from a group headed by Dr. Robert Franks.

Miller operated the property until June 1962, when he sold the Riverside to Raymond Specter.

Nev. St. Journal, 22 Nov. 60, 14 June 62.

MINER'S TAVERN

128 East Commercial Row; licensed from June 1949 to May 1958 for 21, slots, craps, poker, and keno.

The Miner's Tavern was another casino that was more a bar than a casino. Located in an area that was often called "skid row," the Miner's Tavern catered to less-affluent local residents.

Several people had gaming licenses during its short tenure. In 1949 J. P. Gabrielli was licensed for one 21 game, and in 1952 he was joined on the license by Margaret Sarzotti. On April 28, 1953, John Bender was licensed for ten slot machines, one craps game, one 21 game, and one poker game. Also licensed with Bender was Robert Haugen. In April 1954 Paul Tyler and

Tony Hopper were licensed for gaming, and the club featured western music and dancing. In 1954 Paul Tyler was licensed for a racehorse keno game. In 1956 the Miner's Tavern's licensees were Paul Tyler (20 percent), William Gong (40 percent), and Elmer Lew (20 percent). They were licensed for one craps game, one 21 game, and a $10,000-limit keno game. Licensed as a partner in 1957 was Weldon Bryan.

The business closed in 1958. The site is now part of Harrah's parking garage.

Nev. St. Journal, 25 May 49, 12 Sept. 52, 28 Apr. 53, 10 May 53, 9 June 53, 30 June 53, 28 May 54 (adv.), 18 May 56, 20 June 56, 5 Aug. 56 (adv.), 23 Sept. 56, 5 June 57.

MING'S CAFÉ

246 Lake Street; licensed in 1954 for slots only.

This business was located at the former site of the longtime Reno nightspot the Colombo. Ming's Café was licensed for slots in August 1954 by Dea Him Ming and Thomas Non. They operated the property until 1956. At that time, it became known as the King's Café.

Currently, the site is a parking lot.

Nev. St. Journal, 10 Aug. 54, 26 Aug. 54.

Interior of the Mint Club in 1942. Note the one-man craps table, commonly referred to as a tub. Courtesy of the Joe "Luke" Lukanish family.

The Mint Club in 1942. Photo taken from the Lincoln Alley entrance looking toward Virginia Street. Note the keno counter on the right. Co-owner Joe "Luke" Lukanish is in the left corner of the picture wearing a white shirt and necktie. Courtesy of the Joe "Luke" Lukanish family.

MINT

210 North Virginia Street; licensed from July 1941 to August 1942 for slots, 21, craps, roulette, keno, big-six, pan, and a football pool.

The Mint was located at the former site of the Block N Club. It was opened by Dick Kolbus, a former athletic star at the University of Nevada. Kolbus, who had also been associated with the Block N, and his partner, Joe "Luke" Lukanish, signed a five-year lease with Joe and Victor Saturno on June 21, 1941, and opened the club on the following July 1.

In February 1942 Kolbus and Lukanish subleased a portion of the property to Bill Harrah. Harrah's portion had the address of 214 North Virginia Street and had eighteen front feet on Virginia Street.

Dick Kolbus entered the military service shortly after the lease was signed, and the Mint closed in August 1942.

In 1946, when the lease between Kolbus-Lukanish and the Saturnos expired, Bill Harrah leased the property. On June 20, 1946, he opened his first full casino at the former location of the Mint.

The site is now part of Harrah's.

Reno City Directory, 1941, 1942.

MINT CLUB

246 Lake Street; licensed from November 1958 to May 1960 for slots, 21, craps, keno, and poker.

This property was located on the former site of the longtime Reno landmark the Colombo Hotel, although the business operating immediately prior at the address was King's Café.

In November 1958 the State of Nevada licensed Al Figoni, Elmo Sarboraria, and Norbert Michalski at the Mint for five games and twenty-four slot machines. Figoni was the operator of the A-1 Supply Company on Second Street, Michalski was a former operator of coin machines in Chicago, and Sarboraria was the operator of the Lido Hotel in Reno. They each invested $22,500 and announced that they would spend $30,000 remodeling the property.

The property offered various types of entertainment. When the Mint first opened, it advertised free jam sessions for all casino employees, especially musicians, several times during the week. In 1959 and 1960 it offered "exotic and seductive dancers." The club became a late-night hangout for many casino employees and for tourists who ventured away from the established casinos on Virginia Street.

In the spring of 1960, the business closed, but it reopened in October 1960 as the China Mint. The former location of the Mint Club is today a parking lot.

Nev. St. Journal, 25 Nov. 58, 27 Nov. 58 (adv.), 3 Dec. 58 (adv.), 15 July 59 (adv.).

MOANA SPRINGS BAR

246 West Moana Lane; licensed from July 29, 1944, to April 1, 1947, for 21 and craps.

The Moana Bar was located next to the Moana Hot Springs Swimming Pool. It was more a bar than a casino, and the table games were there only as an adjunct to the bar.

Currently the former location of the Moana Springs Bar is part of the City of Reno's Moana Swimming Pool complex.

Reno City Telephone Directory, 1945 (yellow pages adv.).

MOHAWK BAR

229 East Second Street; licensed from May 17, 1941, to June 1, 1943, for keno, 21, and craps.

The Mohawk was a small bar that was licensed for a 21 game and a craps game during World War II. The site is now a parking lot.

MONACO CLUB

2700 South Virginia Street; never licensed.

In April 1962 the proprietor of the Monaco Club, Wallace Meacham, was denied an application for a gaming license for a bingo game and twenty slots. In June 1962 the Monaco opened under the management of Ken Kendall and Robert Harmon. In September 1962 Jeff Brophy and Sylvan Green took over as proprietors of the Monaco.

In September 1963 the property became a restaurant called the Chinese Pagoda, with the renowned Chinese chef T. F. Gee as proprietor.

Currently at the former location of the Monaco Club is the Roger Dunn Golf Shop.

Nev. St. Journal, 17 Apr. 62, 1 June 62, 5 Aug. 62, 18 Sept. 62, 25 Sept. 63.

MONARCH CAFÉ

225 North Virginia Street; licensed in 1946 for slots only.

The Monarch Café catered to a working-class clientele. In the 1930s and much of the 1940s and 1950s, most downtown casinos did not have eating facilities, so casino workers as well as patrons had to leave the casino in order to eat. The Monarch's location made it a natural choice for such individuals.

Manuel Gavallos was licensed to have slot machines in the Monarch.

Currently at the former site of the Monarch Club is the Horseshoe Jewelry and Loan Store.

Nev. St. Journal, 23 July 46.

MONEY TREE

211 North Virginia Street; licensed from July 1, 1969, to December 17, 1982, as a full casino.

On November 6, 1968, Charles Mapes announced plans for a two-story casino to be constructed on Virginia Street a few yards north of Second Street. The casino, Mapes said, would have five hundred slot machines, a full pit, and a keno game on the first floor, and a 150-seat restaurant on the second floor. The operation would employ two hundred people and would open about July 1, 1969. Demolition of the existing buildings on the site, which housed a jewelry store, a fashion shop, and a western apparel shop, was already under way even as the announcement was made. Walker Boudin was the contractor, and Raymond Hellman was the architect.

On June 18, 1969, Charles Mapes and Gloria Mapes Walker appeared before the Nevada Gaming Control Board and applied to be licensed for 50 percent each of the Money Tree Casino. As described in the license application, the casino would have ten table games and 325 slot machines. Many of the slots would be built into two bars in the casino, recessed into the bar in front of each seat. This business was one of the first in Reno to feature bar slots. The two-story casino would have a 184-seat restaurant on the second floor. The name (Money Tree) was derived from

a silver-colored metal tree that would stand just inside the front entrance of the casino.

On June 28, Charles Mapes and his sister, Gloria Walker, were given final approval by the state. They were licensed for one roulette game, two craps games, six 21 games, one keno game, and 325 slot machines. The Money Tree opened, as scheduled, at 5:00 P.M. on July 1.

In October 1969 Steve Campbell, Don Fontana, Julius Pozzi, and Larry Finn were licensed as key employees of the Money Tree. All were longtime gaming veterans and worked as shift managers at the Money Tree.

Many of the personnel of the Mapes Hotel and the Money Tree worked at both locations. This often resulted in some people working part of a shift at the Money Tree and part of the same shift at the Mapes. Sometimes an employee might work part of his forty-hour workweek at one location and the rest in the other location. Management teams also worked together between the two casinos. Mapes employed many longtime gaming figures, such as Chuck Webster, Jim Hunter, Larry Semenza, Herb Grellman, Joe Piscevich, George Karagosian, and others, in the two casinos.

In July 1974 Pat Mooney was named general manager. Mooney at the time had almost thirty years of experience in the gaming business, having worked in executive positions at Harrah's, the Cal-Neva Lodge, and other casinos.

In October 1974 Deering Dixon, a local gaming figure, was named casino manager of the Money Tree. Dixon had almost forty years of gaming experience, having previously worked at the Waldorf, Harrah's, the Mapes, and several other casinos.

On November 22, 1975, Charles Mapes announced plans for the expansion of the Money Tree. He planned to lease the air space over Fulton Alley from the city, thereby joining the property on Virginia Street with the site bounded by Sierra Street on the east, Second Street on the south, Fulton Alley on the west, and the Ace Motel on the north. By joining the two properties, Mapes would not have to license the expansion property. Neither would he have to build hotel rooms on the property. City ordinances at the time forbade the issuance of a gaming license to hotel-casinos with fewer than one hundred rooms (the so-called red-line law), or to casinos in the downtown area with no rooms.

Almost a year later, the City Council voted to lease Mapes the air rights over Fulton Alley, allowing him to proceed with his plans to expand the Money Tree.

Another year later, in October 1977, demolition began on buildings in the expansion area. They included the Crest Theatre, the Carlton Hotel, Hamilton Opticians, and the Baby Doll Topless Lounge (formerly the Flame Room). The property was owned by the Faretto family and the Whiddett family.

In January 1978 Charles Mapes unveiled his final plans for his new Money Tree expansion. The two-story, 43,500-square-foot structure would include three restaurants and a show lounge on the second floor, with a disco in the basement area. The outside of the building was to be covered by a sign composed largely (70 percent) of mirrors. Mapes did not plan for any parking for his expansion, nor did he plan any housing for his employees.

The new Money Tree opened at 12:01 A.M. on Saturday morning, July 1, 1978. Opening at exactly the same time were the Circus Circus Casino and the Reno Sahara. The sudden proliferation of Reno hotel-casinos in 1978 sent several businesses into financial trouble. Within a few months, there had been an approximate one-third increase in gaming devices, but the customer base had not increased at the same rate. Casinos lacking sufficient cash reserves to weather the crisis soon found themselves experiencing financial difficulties. The Money Tree was one of them.

On January 7, 1980, the new wing on Sierra and Second Streets was closed, and at least one hundred people lost their jobs. By July the Mapeses' financial situation had not improved, and First National Bank of Nevada (later First Interstate Bank and currently Wells Fargo) filed notice that it intended to foreclose on six loans that

listed the Mapes Hotel and the Money Tree as collateral. The Mapes Corporation was given thirty-five days to make up $1.5 million in back payments.

In late July the pit area in the Money Tree was closed, putting twenty employees out of work. Only the slots and the bar remained open.

The deadline for back payments passed without any payments being made. In September the First National Bank brought in a Southern California consulting firm, Jaeger Industries, to manage both the Mapes Hotel and the Money Tree. In November 1980 the Mapes Corporation filed a Chapter 11 bankruptcy reorganization plan allowing it to pay off creditors over an extended period of time.

In May 1981 the Money Tree expansion reopened, and the Money Tree began operating all its facilities. John Brevick, former general manager of the Cal-Neva, was brought in to oversee the business. He managed the casino for almost one and a half years and reportedly made a profit of $750,000, all of which was sent to the Mapes Hotel to try and keep that property open. Brevick's employment came to an end in late 1982. Shortly after he left on December 17, 1982, both the Mapes and the Money Tree were closed.

The closure of the two properties resulted in at least five hundred employees being put out of work. Besides two banks being owed about $16 million, employees were owed around $73,000 and unsecured creditors were owed around $880,000. The Mapes was closed quietly, but at the Money Tree it was a different story. Silvio Petricciani, general manager of the properties, made the announcement to angry employees, and his speech was drowned out by employees shouting and demanding their paychecks. Petricciani did his best to explain the situation and prevent a riot. The facility was completely closed down by 6:30 P.M. and never again opened as the Money Tree.

In 1984 Philip and Mary Schwab purchased the property and announced that they were going to reopen the casino and name it the Players. They hired former

Harrah's executives Pat France and Lee De-Lauer to organize and operate the casino for them. When it became obvious that the Schwabs were going to have trouble getting a gaming license, they withdrew their application in 1985 and then defaulted on their loan in November 1986. The property reverted back to Eureka Savings and Loan, and the Players never opened.

In 1987 the property was purchased by the Ramada Corporation, and on June 19, 1987, a theme casino, Eddie's Fabulous 50's, opened. Eddie's closed due to a lack of profitability on August 1, 1989.

Currently the site is being operated as Guidici's Virginia Street Gambler on the Virginia Street side and as Eddie's Fabulous 50's (under new ownership) on the Sierra Street side.

Nev. St. Journal, 6 Nov. 68, 17 June 69, 24 June 69, 28 June 69, 1 July 69 (adv.), 2 July 69 (photo), 10 Oct. 69, 21 July 74 (photo), 11 Oct. 74, 22 Nov. 75, 31 Oct. 76, 19 Oct. 77, 16 Jan. 78, 14 Apr. 78 (photo), 1 July 78, 18 Jan. 80 (photo), 2 July 80, 6 Aug. 80, 12 Aug. 80, 22 Sept. 80, 1 Oct. 80, 14 Nov. 80, 15 May 81, 18 Dec. 82.

MONFREY, JOHN

John Monfrey came to Reno from San Antonio, Texas, where he had been a prominent local businessman and sports promoter. He purchased 30 percent of the Holiday Hotel-Casino on Mill Street in June 1967 for $165,000. His partners were Tom Moore and Austin Hemphill. In May 1968 he sold his percentage of the Holiday Hotel to Ebe Cox.

Nev. St. Journal, 23 June 67, 27 July 67, 14 May 70.

MONTE CARLO

218 Sierra Street (located in the Ames Hotel); licensed from July 1 to December 1938 for 21, craps, and roulette.

The Monte Carlo was a cocktail lounge located in the Ames Hotel, which later became the Carlton Hotel. More a bar, lounge, and dance-floor property than a casino, the games of chance were there as an adjunct to the bar.

Managed by Jim Countryman and Buzz White, the Monte Carlo was taken over by new management and changed its name to the Ames Hotel Cocktail Lounge early in 1939.

The site is now part of Eddie's Fabulous 50's.

Nev. St. Journal, 2 July 38 (adv.), 1 Oct. 38 (articles and adv.), 23 Nov. 38, 1 Apr. 39 (adv.).

MONTE CARLO

216 North Virginia; licensed from June 19 to December 31, 1931, for a full casino.

When the Monte Carlo opened in June 1931, it had an extremely varied casino. It was licensed for one hazard game, one roulette game, one big-six wheel, two craps games, two 21 games, one draw poker game, one stud poker game, one pan game, one klondike game, and one chemin-de-fer game.

The casino opened at 7:00 P.M. on June 20, 1931. Advertised as "Reno's Casino Deluxe for ladies and gentlemen," the casino featured entertainment by Jane Jones, Mel Calish, and George Lloyd, with the music of Earl Wright and his orchestra for the patrons' dancing pleasure.

In October a new type of keno (bingo) game called "darte" was introduced. However, the new game was not enough to keep the casino open, and it closed in December 1931.

The former location of the Monte Carlo Club is now part of Harrah's Club.

Nev. St. Journal, 20 June 31, 10 Oct. 31 (adv.).

MONTE CARLO CASINO

1010 East Sixth Street (inside the Holiday Inn); licensed in 1975 as a full casino.

On March 1, 1974, the Holiday Inn on Sixth Street opened its guest rooms. Although the casino was expected to begin operation later the same year, it did not open until March 1975. The casino was licensed to the T. K. Corporation, which consisted of Bob Klaich, John Tillis, Lou Benetti, and Don Eamelli. The 2,125-square-foot casino opened with three 21 games and sixty slot machines.

In April 1976 a major expansion was completed. Two thousand invited guests came to a grand-opening party at 5:30 P.M., with an estimated fifteen hundred more

guests at the opening for the general public three hours later.

In a license revision in 1976 the Gaming Commission approved John Hammond, a part-owner of the Holiday Inn, for 70 percent of the casino; Bob Klaich, a native of East Ely, Nevada, and for a number of years the comptroller of Harolds Club, for 15 percent of the casino; and John Tillis, formerly employed at the Riverside, Harolds Club, and Rod's Shy Clown, for 15 percent.

The Monte Carlo was a separate company from the Holiday Inn. Hammond owned the property and the Holiday Inn, but there was no corporate connection.

In May 1977 Norm Brown was licensed as a shift manager along with William Price. Brown later became casino manager of the Monte Carlo and remained in that position until ownership changed hands in 1994.

Tragedy struck the Monte Carlo in April 1978 when a single-engine plane carrying John Tillis, co-owner and general manager, crashed and Tillis was killed. Tillis, a native of West Virginia, was forty-six years old at the time of his death.

Klaich, Hammond, and Tillis's heirs continued to operate the Monte Carlo until 1994. At that time, Klaich died and Hammond turned the operation of the casino over to a management company.

The Diamond Casino is currently operating at the former site of the Monte Carlo Casino.

Nev. St. Journal, 2 Mar. 74, 27 Feb. 75, 15 Aug. 75, 13 Nov. 75, 2 Apr. 76 (photo), 25 June 76, 12 May 77, 13 Jan. 78, 30 Apr. 78, 17 Jan. 80.

MONTE CARLO

One and one-half miles from downtown Reno on South Virginia Street; licensed from July 1 through December 1937 for 21, craps, and roulette.

The Monte Carlo opened on July 1, 1937, and was licensed for gaming for only six months. It was operated by Albert and Carlos Casali and catered to locals, especially off-duty casino employees.

Nev. St. Journal, 30 June 37 (adv.).

MONTICELLI, PETER AND IRMA

The Monticellis were licensed at the Blue Bird Club on East Second Street in the late 1930s and early 1940s. In July 1945 they were licensed at the New Blue Bird Club on West Commercial Row. They lost their license in April 1949, when the Blue Bird was closed by the health department.

The Blue Bird was destroyed by fire in 1949. It was reopened in 1951 by Gene Rovetti and named the Haymarket Club.

Nev. St. Journal, 13 July 45, 20 Jan. 48, 1 July 48, 25 Jan. 49, 2 Apr. 49, 6 Apr. 49, 7 June 49, 2 June 51.

MOONEY, PATRICK "PAT"

Pat Mooney was born in Tonopah, Nevada, on July 16, 1918, and came to Reno in 1925. He worked for almost thirty-five years in executive positions for Harrah's, the Mapes Hotel, the Mapes Money Tree, the Cal-Neva Lodge, the Holiday Hotel, the Horseshoe Club, and the Primadonna. He was also licensed as a 3.4-percent owner of the Horseshoe Club in 1957 and retained ownership there until 1967. In 1974 Mooney was named general manager of the Mapes Money Tree on North Virginia Street.

On December 11, 1979, Pat Mooney died in a Reno hospital. He was employed as the controller of the Mapes Hotel at the time of his death.

Nev. St. Journal, 24 May 57, 21 July 74 (photo), 12 Dec. 79 (obit.).

MOORE, TOM

Tom Moore, who was born in Eddie, Texas, in 1902, came to Reno in 1967 from San Antonio, where he had many holdings in real estate and oil wells.

Moore purchased one-third of the Holiday Hotel on Mill Street, along with John Monfrey and Austin Hemphill, in June 1967. His portion of the purchase price was $165,000.

Moore was very active in sports and sports-related activities. It was during his regime that the Holiday expanded its marketing program with events such as the Mug Hunt, the famous Holiday-sponsored golf tournament. Many sports celebrities, such as Dizzy Dean and Joe DiMaggio, made the Holiday their home when they visited Reno.

Tom Moore divested himself of his holdings in the Holiday Hotel in September 1970, selling out to Al Ferrarri and Len McIntosh.

Nev. St. Journal, 23 June 67, 27 July 67, 10 Sept. 70.

MR. C'S

Corner of Arlington Avenue and Third Street; licensed from April 1, 1981, to 1983 for a full casino.

Mr. C's was the name given to an area in the Sands Plaza. The reason for the name change was to honor the memory of Peter Cladianos Sr. Mr. C's was later incorporated into the Sands Regency Hotel.

Nev. St. Journal, 1 Apr. 81.

MUNLEY, CHARLES "RED"

Red Munley worked as a pit boss, shift manager, and casino manager in several casinos in Reno from the 1930s to the 1960s. In the 1930s he was a shift manager at the Palace Club. He also worked as a shift manager and casino manager at the Mapes for twelve years in the late 1940s and early 1950s. In 1959 and 1960 Munley worked for his nephew, Emmett Munley—who was casino manager—as a pit boss at the Riverside Hotel. Both the Munleys resigned when the Riverside was purchased by William Miller.

Nev. St. Journal, 5 Nov. 38.

MUNLEY, EMMETT

Munley was the first chief investigator of the Nevada Gaming Control Board when the position was created in the 1950s.

In 1960 Munley was casino manager of the Riverside but was forced to resign when the Riverside was sold to William Miller. In 1961 Munley and Paul Elcano were licensed as partners in the M&E Coin Company.

Nev. St. Journal, 28 Feb. 61.

MURRAY'S CLUB

230 North Virginia Street; licensed from June 1942 through 1952 for slots, roulette, and 21.

The site of Murray's Club was previously a clothing store owned by Phillip Jacobs, a well-known Reno clothier. Upon Jacobs's retirement, his son Murray took possession of the property and continued to operate the business as a clothing store until 1942. At that time he turned the property into a liquor store with a few slot machines. In 1944 Jacobs leased the eastern portion (the portion fronting on Lincoln Alley) to Bill Harrah, who opened a bar named the Blackout Bar.

In June 1944 Jacobs turned his liquor store into a bar and cocktail lounge. He named it Murray's Club and was licensed for eleven slot machines and one 21 game. It was advertised as "Reno's newest gathering place," and the night of its grand opening featured Art Kinney at the piano bar.

In January 1945 Jacobs once again licensed one 21 game but increased his slot machines to a total of sixteen. In July 1945 a roulette game was added to the license along with the 21 game and the sixteen slots. Eventually Jacobs licensed sixty slot machines and three table games.

In 1952 Jacobs sold his business to the Nevada Club for $50,000. He retained ownership of the property itself, which he leased to the Nevada Club, with a renewable option, for five years at $25,000 a year. The property was immediately incorporated into the Nevada Club, where it has remained. The lease was renewed in 1957 and remained in effect until Jacobs sold the property to the Nevada Club owners in 1996.

The former site of Murray's Club now comprises the northern eighteen feet of the Nevada Club.

Nev. St. Journal, 5 May 42, 27 May 44 (adv.), 23 Jan. 45, 27 June 45, 16 Apr. 52.

N

NEELY, GLEN

Glen Neely was born in Jerome, Arizona, on August 6, 1923. After serving in the military during World War II, he was asked to come to Reno to play for the nationally known Harolds Club softball team and to work in the club during the off-season.

Neely played softball and worked at Harolds Club from 1947 to 1949. In 1949 he left Harolds Club to work for the Picadilly Club. He remained there for three years prior to going to Las Vegas to work in the Golden Nugget.

While in Las Vegas, Neely worked twelve years at the Golden Nugget, was a shift manager at the Hacienda Hotel-Casino, casino manager of the Four Queens Casino, and general manager of the Silver Slipper Casino. In the 1970s he moved to the North Shore of Lake Tahoe and was employed by the Hyatt Hotel-Casino. In 1977 he opened the Cal-Neva Lodge for Kirk Kerkorian.

When Kerkorian opened the MGM Hotel-Casino in Reno in 1978, Neely was appointed casino manager of what was at that time the largest casino in Reno. He remained in that position until 1980, when he was appointed senior vice-president of casino gaming. In 1986, when the MGM Hotel-Casino was sold to Bally's, Neely stayed on as vice-president of casino gaming until his retirement in September 1988.

Glen Neely is currently living in Reno.

Nev. St. Journal, 16 Jan. 80.

NELSON, ROY

Roy Nelson was born in Sioux City, Iowa, in 1902. He worked in several illegal gambling houses in Iowa and the Midwest before coming to Reno in 1941. His first job in Reno was at the Bank Club. He later worked at Harolds Club in the early 1940s before becoming part-owner of the Reno Club in Douglas Alley in 1945 and operating it until 1946. He also worked at the Club Cal-Neva when it was operated by Jim Contratto.

During his gaming career, Nelson owned and/or operated the games at the Town House in the early 1950s and at the Waldorf Club, along with Harold Walters, in the middle 1950s. He also worked at the Mapes Hotel-Casino for ten years and at the Riverside for five years. He was a shift manager at the Horseshoe Club and at Lawton's Casino, and when the Holiday Hotel on Mill Street opened gambling, he was one of the three original shift managers.

Nelson, who was also active in real estate in the Reno area, retired completely from gaming in 1978.

Nev. St. Journal, 19 June 52; 1 Aug. 57.

NELSON, WARREN

Warren Nelson was born in Great Falls, Montana, on January 19, 1913. He came to Reno in 1936 to work at the Palace Club, where he had been hired to help open the first racehorse keno game in Reno. He worked at the Palace Club from 1936 to 1942, learning all facets of the gaming business. In 1942 he enlisted in the Marine Corps. After receiving his discharge, Nelson worked for Harrah's Club from 1946 to 1948 as manager of the club. He is said to have created the first casino credit office in Reno and was instrumental in installing the first catwalk system for casino surveillance.

After leaving Harrah's, Nelson was a co-owner and operator of the Waldorf Club from 1948 to 1949. When he left the Waldorf, he was employed at the Mapes Hotel-Casino from 1949 to 1953. In 1953 he was licensed as one of the thirteen owners of the Palace Club. He remained as one of the co-owners of the Palace Club until 1962.

In 1962 Nelson, along with Leon Nightingale, Jack Douglass, Ad Tolen, John Cavanaugh Sr., and Howard Farris, opened what was to become one of the most successful clubs in Nevada gaming history, the Club Cal-Neva. Nelson maintained a hands-on style of management at the Cal-

Neva for many years, and his expertise was instrumental in the Cal-Neva's success.

During Nelson's gaming career, he was also licensed at the Tahoe Palace (Plaza), the Cal-Neva Lodge, the Maxim in Las Vegas, and the Comstock Hotel-Casino.

Warren Nelson is now retired and living in Reno.

Warren Nelson, *Always Bet on the Butcher: Warren Nelson and Casino Gaming, 1930s–1980s* (Reno: University of Nevada Oral History Program, 1994); Meyer Berger, "The Gay Gamblers of Reno," *Saturday Evening Post,* 10 July 1948, 26; *Nev. St. Journal,* 11 Dec. 53, 21 Mar. 69, 1 Feb. 78.

NEVADA BAR

1002 East Fourth Street; licensed from October 10, 1944, to October 1, 1946, for roulette and keno (bingo).

The Nevada Bar was a local bar that operated a roulette wheel and a bingo game. The site is now the parking lot for Ray Heating Products, Inc.

NEVADA CLUB

224 North Virginia Street; licensed from March 22, 1946, to January 1998 as a full casino.

In April 1941 Harry and Ed Robbins opened a casino called Robbin's Nevada Club. They operated the business by themselves until March 22, 1946, when they became partners with Dan Sullivan, Ruby Mathis, Mert Wertheimer, and Lincoln Fitzgerald. In a short time Mathis and Wertheimer left the operation. Sullivan and Ed Robbins stayed on with Fitzgerald, and in 1952 the trio did away with their partnership and formed a corporation. Dan Sullivan stayed with the corporation until his death in 1956, and Fitzgerald bought out Ed Robbins the same year.

A grand opening to celebrate the new management began at 7:00 P.M. on March 22, 1946. An ad proclaimed that the "New Nevada Club" was featuring a new bar, a new keno game, and gambling games of all kinds. Twenty table games were licensed by the newly remodeled club. A racehorse book was added the next year.

On August 10, 1946, Dan Sullivan and Lincoln Fitzgerald were named in a fugitive-from-justice case. They were charged with bribing public officials in Macomb County,

The Reno Rodeo parade heading south on Virginia Street in the mid-1940s. Note the signs and/or partial signs of the Nevada Club, Murray's Club, the Reno Club, Harolds Club, and the California Club. Courtesy of Neal Cobb.

Michigan, on several dates between August 1, 1940, and August 1, 1946. They were also charged with running illegal gambling in Macomb County from August 1, 1940, to June 23, 1946. For the next sixteen months, Fitzgerald and Sullivan engaged in legal maneuvering aimed at fighting extradition. In January 1948 the maneuvering came to an end, and they were both jailed without bail. Sullivan listed his occupation as general manager of the Nevada Club, and Fitzgerald stated that he was casino manager of the Nevada Club.

In August 1948 Sullivan and Fitzgerald were sent to Michigan to face the illegal gambling charges (the bribery charges had been dropped). They were found guilty and fined a total of $52,000. After paying the fine, they were released, and they returned to Reno to continue operating the Nevada Club.

Misfortune continued to plague Fitzgerald. On November 18, 1949, he was shot twice from ambush at his home on 123 Mark Twain Drive. The attack occurred at 11:43 P.M. as he was leaving to go to the Nevada Club. Fitzgerald, who was fifty-seven at the time of the shooting, lingered on the brink of death for several days, and doctors said only his will to live kept him alive. He eventually recovered, but not until April 20, 1950, was he released from Washoe Medical Center. Fitzgerald remained somewhat crippled for the rest of his life, and he went into semiseclusion for the next several years. The assailant was never found.

Also in April 1952 the Nevada Club entered into a five-year lease (which was extended and continued until Jacobs sold the property to the Nevada Club in 1996) with Murray Jacobs for the use of the Jacobs Building at 230 North Virginia Street (immediately adjoining the Nevada Club). The business (the Jackpot Arcade) was purchased for $50,000, and the lease payment was $25,000 a year. The building, which had a front footage of 17 feet and extended 140 feet east to Lincoln Alley, was renamed the Nevada Club Annex.

Early in the history of the Nevada Club, Lincoln Fitzgerald introduced a feature that gained the Nevada Club a great deal of publicity and a great deal of business. It was the Monte Carlo wheel, a roulette wheel that had only one zero instead of the usual double zero, and a double layout. The single zero noticeably added to a player's chances of winning. It was an extremely popular game with all roulette players, especially system players. The wheel stayed in use until the Nevada Club was sold to the Lincoln Management Group.

The Nevada Club was one of the first casinos to install a restaurant on its property. Its fine food and reasonable prices, along with its famous pies and desserts, made the Nevada Club a popular place to eat and gamble.

Business continued to grow. In April 1955 the Nevada Club was licensed for 100 more slots (making a total of 631 slot machines), four more 21 games, and two more craps games.

In October 1955 the Nevada Club introduced the new four-reel Buckaroo slot machines, which were manufactured by the Jennings Company. Many of them were still in use in the Nevada Club when it closed in 1998. They were advertised as the first machines with "no lemons or other blanks." A player could win $5,000 with a $1 bet.

The Nevada Club was also famous for the way it paid jackpots. The absence of hoppers in those days prevented the machines from dropping the total amount of a large payout, so most casinos hand-paid the customer with currency. The Nevada Club machines dropped twenty coins when a jackpot hit, and the balance of the payout, in coins, was prepackaged in a brown paper bag bearing the Nevada Club logo and handed to the winner. Naturally, with all those coins instantly available to them, many customers played their winnings right back into the machines.

The single-coin slot machines in the Nevada Club were very popular with local players. During the 1950s and 1960s, the Nevada Club had as much local slot play as any casino in town.

In August 1957 the Nevada Club and Lincoln Fitzgerald extended their holdings to Lake Tahoe when they purchased the Biltmore Club on the North Shore for $421,000 and renamed the property the Nevada Lodge.

In the 1960s Fitzgerald started buying

up property on West Commercial Row and Virginia Street. This property became the site of Fitzgeralds Casino-Hotel, which opened in 1976.

The Nevada Club had previously purchased property at 200 North Center Street and planned to open a casino there, but illness prevented Lincoln Fitzgerald from going ahead with his plans.

The Nevada Club was always a well-illuminated, unpretentious, simple casino. It was, however, one of the first—if not the first—to have a restaurant on the property. Free of any gimmicks, the casino never offered any type of entertainment.

The club was also noted for its many longtime employees. Fitzgerald, known as "Fitz" or "Boss" to his employees, was a firm, strict disciplinarian. An employee did not leave the club for any reason during the eight-hour working shift and did not fraternize with any employee of the opposite sex. Those who transgressed were immediately terminated. Also, Fitzgerald personally interviewed every prospective employee. The Nevada Club had a pay scale different from any other casino in town. Fitzgerald liberally rewarded employees who stayed with him, both in hourly wages and in bonuses. However, employees were forbidden to tell anyone how much they earned. Divulging wages was another reason for termination. However, it was well known around the downtown casinos that "Fitz was good pay."

Some of the many longtime employees at the Nevada Club included Mark DeSautel, Oscar Dykes, Emma "Ma" Baker, James Erwin, Dan Fagan, Wilford Nolan, Charles Kossol, Vern Peterson, Emmett Shea, Ed Beatty, and many more.

Lincoln Fitzgerald died in 1981. His widow, Meta, along with her brother, Carlton Konarske, operated the Nevada Club until December 31, 1986. At that time, the Lincoln Management Group took over management of the business and leased the property with an option to buy. The option was exercised, and on January 1, 1987, Lincoln Management closed the property but reopened it one month later. The new owners maintained much of the atmosphere and appearance of the early-day Nevada Club.

On November 20, 1997, the Fitzgerald Gaming Corporation (the former Lincoln Management Group) announced that it had sold the Nevada Club to a yet-to-be-announced new owner. The casino closed earlier than expected on December 28, 1997. It never reopened. *(See Addendum 1)*

Nev. St. Journal, 22 Mar. 46 (adv.), 10 Aug. 46, 27–28 Jan. 48, 12 Aug. 48, 13 Aug. 48, 25 Sept. 48, 19 Nov. 49, 20 Nov. 49, 1 Mar. 52, 16 Apr. 52, 19 Oct. 52, 27 Apr. 55, 8 Oct. 55 (adv.), 26 July 56, 11 June 57, 29 Aug. 57, 20 Sept. 57, 8 Nov. 64, 10 Sept. 70, 15 Dec. 70, 25 June 76, 23 July 76, 31 Dec. 86.

NEVADA ROULETTE

140 North Virginia Street; licensed from June 10 to October 1, 1931, for roulette.

The Nevada Roulette Club was licensed for one roulette game in the early days of legalized gaming. The site is now occupied by the Virginian Hotel-Casino.

NEVADA TURF CLUB

34 East Commercial Row (also 34 East Douglas Alley); licensed from 1946 to 1956 for 21, roulette, slots, pan, poker, keno, and race book.

Joe Hornstein was licensed by the city for a race book in December 1945. He opened the establishment in January 1946. Table games were added soon after the opening. Also involved in the operation and ownership of the Nevada Turf Club while Joe Hornstein was the owner were Henry and George Hornstein, Charles Smith, Frank King, and James Smitten.

On February 28, 1955, Joe Hornstein announced that he had closed the Nevada Turf Club. He was scheduled for a state hearing on March 1, 1955, regarding the revocation of his license for accepting out-of-state bets.

The business remained closed until February 1956. At that time, Howard Farris was licensed at the property. He closed the casino later that same year.

The former location of the Nevada Turf Club is now part of Harolds Club.

NEW CAPITOL CLUB

208 Lincoln Alley; licensed in 1932 for slots and craps.

Tim Martinez was the proprietor of the New Capitol Club, a business that was more a bar than a casino. The site is now part of Harrah's Club.

Nev. St. Journal, 8 Apr. 33.

NEW CHINA CLUB

260 Lake Street; licensed from August 1952 to December 31, 1971.

The New China Club was formerly known as the Palm Club. In 1952 Bill Fong was granted a bar license at the location, and in August he applied for a gaming license. Fong was a Chinese businessman from Oakland, California.

His spokesperson was local realtor Helen Penny. In Fong's application, he stated that he wanted a club that would cater to Asian and African American customers. He admitted that he had been arrested several times in California for operating a Chinese lottery but that he had served all the time that he had been sentenced to serve. He also stated that he and his wife had $32,000 in total assets and that they would employ only experienced dealers. Fong was granted a license and opened with one craps game, one 21 game, and one keno game.

In 1952 and 1953 the casino showed good growth, and Fong opened another 21 game, ten slot machines, and a chuck-a-luck game. In 1954 Bill Fong took in his brother, Yee Fong, as an equal partner. In 1955 another 21 game was added. In 1956 Fong added another keno game to the New China Club, making his casino one of the first to have two keno games in one property.

In September 1958 Fong announced the first of two major marketing events. Jesse Owens, famous sports figure and a gold-medal winner in the 1936 Olympics, was scheduled to participate in the first annual New China Club's Keno Queen contest. At 9:00 P.M. on Friday, September 26, twelve Keno Queen contestants were honored at a reception in the New China Club. On Saturday a parade formed at Lake Street and Commercial Row and continued from there down Virginia Street to California Avenue. The twelve queen contestants, each dressed in a formal gown, rode in convertibles. Jesse Owens was the parade marshall. On Sunday at noon in the New China Club, Jesse Owens crowned the first

Keno Queen, Mrs. Ruby Roberts of Oakland, California.

In October 1958 the second big marketing event of the year was introduced when the New China Club announced that starting on December 1, the "World's First Craps Contest" would begin. The grand prize was to be a pair of oversized gold dice, studded with diamonds, plus $1,500 in cash. The contest would include monthly prizes, and the finals were to be held in May 1959. The prize would be awarded to the player shooting the most consecutive passes.

In 1959 Bill Fong inaugurated a scholarship program similar to one that Raymond I. Smith had started many years earlier. Fong's plan was to send two high-school graduates to the University of Nevada. The first two recipients of the scholarships were Don Hunt of Hawthorne and Betty Jones of Las Vegas.

In 1960 Bill Fong announced another major publicity gimmick. He sponsored a golf tournament with former heavyweight boxing champion Joe Louis as co-host and tournament director. The tournament, which garnered nationwide publicity for Bill Fong and the New China Club, was a huge success.

In 1966 Fong introduced the game of fan-tan to the New China Club. It proved to be very popular with Asian customers, and in 1967 he added another Oriental game, pai-gow.

In 1970 Allen Wu and Elvin Wu, half-brothers of Bill Fong, were licensed for 13 percent each of the New China Club.

On December 31, 1971, Bill Fong allowed the gaming license at the New China Club to expire, and the business closed. In June 1971 he had announced plans for a new high-rise hotel-casino on the site, but he never followed through with his plan.

In December 1972 Bill Fong went into business at the El Cortez Hotel, where he opened a bar and a Chinese restaurant.

The building that housed the New China Club was razed in the 1980s. The site is currently a parking lot.

Nev. St. Journal, 30 Apr. 52, 6 Aug. 52, 7 Aug. 52, 17 Oct. 52, 27 Jan. 53, 28 Apr. 54, 16 June 54, 10 Aug. 54, 27 Apr. 55, 10 May 56, 26 Sept. 58, 27 Sept. 58 (adv.), 28 Sept. 58 (photo), 3 Oct. 58 (photo), 5 Oct. 58 (adv.), 1 Sept. 59, 20 Sept. 59, 14 Apr. 60 (photo), 20 Oct. 60, 22 Oct. 60, 24 Dec. 61 (photo), 16 Oct. 62, 15 Nov. 66, 31 Mar. 67, 24 May 67, 8 Oct. 67 (photo), 13 Aug. 70, 10 Apr. 71 (photo), 12 Jan. 72, 3 Dec. 72.

NEW KENO CLUB
232 North Virginia Street
See Keno Club.

NEW STAR CLUB
141 Lake Street; licensed from 1932 to 1944 for 21, craps, and keno.

Originally opened as the Star Club in 1931, the New Star Club opened in 1932. It was owned by Walter Tun and was located at the corner of Lake and Second Streets. The New Star Club was another gambling business owned and operated by Asians. It was a popular spot that catered mostly to Asian and African American customers.

The former location of the New Star Club is now a parking lot.

Nev. St. Journal, 10 Sept. 37 (adv.).

NEW STAR KENO CLUB
142 East Second Street; licensed in 1947 and 1948 for 21, craps, slots, and roulette.

The New Star Keno Club, sometimes known as the New Star Club, operated for two years as a bar and small casino on East Second Street. The site is now part of the Hampton Inn on the corner of Lake and Second Streets.

Nev. St. Journal, 6 Mar. 48, 15 June 48.

NEW YORK CLUB
224 North Center Street; licensed from May 1931 to June 1935 for 21, craps, roulette, faro, big-six, and hazard.

In 1931 the New York Club was one of the most glamorous nightspots in downtown Reno. It featured the most elaborate entertainment in connection with gambling of any club in the downtown area. Two of the early managers of the New York Club were Larry Potter and Eddie Shields, who took over on November 20, 1931.

The club catered to the female trade. Everything was done to attract sophisticated local ladies, and the club also catered to women in town "for the cure," as the six-week waiting period for divorce was called.

Jack Dempsey, former heavyweight boxing champion, was a frequent visitor at the New York Club, and it was well patronized by movie stars when they came to town.

The club had one of the largest downtown neon signs in the 1930s. The sign said THE ROYAL FLUSH and served to advertise the poker games, which were said to be some of the biggest in town.

On opening night, the New York Club featured two roulette wheels, two 21 games, two craps games, one hazard game, one big-six wheel, and one faro game.

Center Street in the 1930s, 1940s, and early 1950s was the focal point of nightclubs and gambling, and the New York Club was one of the first to exploit the combination of entertainment, dancing, drinking, and gambling. Revues were the most popular form of entertainment at the New York Club, and Tommy Leonard was featured as the master of ceremonies. Jack Ryan's orchestra furnished the dancing music, and "a bevy of beautiful dancing girls were there for your entertainment and enjoyment."

In 1935 the property was purchased by the Greyhound Bus Company, and a bus depot was opened at the location. The site of the New York Club is now part of Harrah's Casino on Center Street.

Nev. St. Journal, 17 May 31 (adv.), 4 Oct. 31, 24 Dec. 31 (adv.), 15 Jan. 32 (adv.), 17 Jan. 32, 20 Mar. 35; Reno Personal Service Bureau publication (1931).

NEW YORK CLUB
218 Sierra Street; licensed February to April 1947 for 21 only.

The New York Club was actually the name given to a lounge area inside the Carlton Hotel. It had a 21 game only. The location is now part of the Eddie's Fabulous 50's property.

Nev. St. Journal, 8 Feb. 47 (adv.).

NIGHTINGALE, LEON
Leon Nightingale came to Reno from Oakland in 1947 and took over the operation of Leon & Eddie's, a popular bar on East Second Street. His partner was Eddie Silva, and they were licensed for three slot machines and one 21 game.

With that small beginning, Nightingale started his business career in Reno. He sold Leon & Eddie's in 1955 and became a co-owner of the Club Cal-Neva—for the first time. He sold his interest in the Cal-Neva in 1957 and bought the Stein Restaurant. He sold the Stein in 1964, but in the meantime he had purchased the Waldorf Club in 1959, the Tahoe Palace (Plaza) in 1960, and in 1962, along with Warren Nelson, Howard Farris, Jack Douglass, Ad Tolen, and John Cavanaugh Sr., he became a co-owner of the Club Cal-Neva—for the second time. Nightingale was also licensed as a co-owner of the Cal-Neva Lodge at Lake Tahoe in 1967, the Maxim Hotel in Las Vegas in 1977, and the Comstock Hotel-Casino on West Second Street in 1978.

Nightingale was a noted philanthropist and generous supporter of the local arts and the University of Nevada. The construction of UNR's Nightingale Hall, said to be northern Nevada's finest concert facility, was made possible through a generous contribution from the Nightingale family. He received UNR's Distinguished Nevadan Award in 1986 and was granted honorary alumnus status by the UNR Alumni Association.

Leon Nightingale died on October 21, 1990, at the Stanford Medical Center in Palo Alto, California, of complications from heart surgery.

Nev. St. Journal, 26 Mar. 47, 26 Jan. 56, 1 Feb. 64 (photo), 21 Mar. 69, 26 Apr. 77, 1 Feb. 78, 22 Oct. 90 (obit.).

NORMANDY CLUB

196 Airport Road (now called Gentry Way); licensed from February 1946 to 1950 for slots, 21, craps, and roulette.

The Normandy Club was opened by Nick and Eddie Sahati in February 1946. It offered slot machines, 21, craps, and roulette, and featured dancing, dining, and a floor show.

In August 1946 the Normandy headlined the DeCastro Sisters from Havana, Cuba. The DeCastros later became nationally known when one of their songs, "Teach Me Tonight," reached the top ten.

The Normandy was located a few miles south of town and attracted mostly locals out on the town and late-night casino workers who wanted to get away from downtown. In 1946 the Sahati brothers ran an ad with an unusual offer: "You call the taxi—we pay the fare."

The Sahatis closed the Normandy in December 1948. In July 1949 they were sued by the owners of the property, William and Violet Wells, who contended that they has signed a five-year lease with Nick and Eddie Sahati and that in December 1948 the Sahatis transferred the lease to Denny and Rose Wood without the Wellses' approval. No rent had been paid to the Wellses, and the club had been closed for some time at the time of the suit.

In November 1949 William Bostwick and Roy Johnson leased the Normandy from the Wellses. In March 1950 the Wellses sued Bostwick and Johnson, claiming that the rent was not paid in February or March, the property was locked up, and they did not have a key to get into the property.

Madge Howard and Bud Hower reopened the Normandy in April 1950, but it closed again later in the year. It never reopened.

Many nightclubs and bars have operated at the location since the closure. The site is currently occupied by a bar called Tiger Tom's.

Nev. St. Journal, 2 Feb. 46 (adv.), 28 July 46 (adv.), 10 Oct. 46, 28 July 49, 12 Mar. 50, 29 Apr. 50, 8 Aug. 66, 13 Dec. 66; Reno Telephone Directory, 1946 (yellow pages adv.).

NORTHERN CLUB

207 North Center Street; licensed from 1931 to 1941 for a full casino.

One of the first casinos to open in 1931, the Northern was located on the ground floor of the Commercial Hotel. It was owned by Felix Turillas Sr. and John Etchebarren. On April 24, 1931, in what is believed to be the first ad in a Reno newspaper for a casino, the Northern was advertised as offering "beautifully appointed club room equipment with an atmosphere of gorgeous surroundings."

Turillas, who had operated gaming in Reno prior to its becoming legalized, had a great deal of experience in gambling. When the Northern Club opened, there were two craps games, one hazard game, one faro game, two 21 games, one big-six

The Reno Rodeo parade heading south on Center Street in the late 1930s. Note the sign for the Northern Club, one of the first casinos licensed in Reno. Courtesy of Neal Cobb.

wheel, one pan game, one stud poker game, and three slot machines waiting to be played. Turillas believed that he knew what people wanted, and he tried to give it to them. In May 1936 he put in a $4,000-limit keno (bingo) game.

The Northern operated until December 1940, when it was sold to Jack Fugit and reopened as the Barn. It later became the Bonanza Club, and then Harrah's Bingo Club. The site of the Northern Club is now a part of Harrah's on the west side of North Center Street.

Nev. St. Journal, 24 Apr. 31 (adv.), 17 May 31 (adv.), 29 May 32, 28 May 36; Reno Personal Service Bureau publication (1931).

NUGGET
233 North Virginia Street; licensed for the year 1953 for slots, 21, craps, and big-six.

The Nugget was opened in 1953 at the former location of the Picadilly Club. It was owned by a group of investors headed by John Hickok, a local realtor, and was licensed for slots, craps, 21, and a big-six wheel.

The Nugget was sold to Dick Graves and Jim Kelly in late 1953. Graves sold his share of the Nugget to Kelly in 1955, and in 1990 Kelly's Nugget was sold to Jackpot Enterprises.

The property is once again known as the Nugget, after being known as Jim Kelly's Nugget for many years. It is currently owned and operated by Eric "Rick" Heaney.

Nev. St. Journal, 23 May 53 (adv.), 19 Aug. 53, 22 Oct. 53 (adv.), 20 Jan. 54, 26 Jan. 54.

OAK ROOM

236 and 240 North Center Street; licensed from 1953 to 1973 for slots and 21.

The Oak Room was a bar and cocktail lounge located in the same building as the Greyhound Bus Depot.

In its nearly twenty years of existence, there were several licensees at the location. C. T. Inskeep was the first licensee; he had Joe Caulk, Emmett Shea, and Mrs. B. H. Hicks as partners. In 1954 Heber Mechan and John Selvige were licensed, and in 1963 they had thirty slot machines, one 21 game, and one poker game in the Oak Room. A Mr. Dean was licensed in 1969 and 1970, and then Al Figoni, president of the A-1 Supply Company, was licensed at the property. In July 1971 Figoni was denied permission to add two 21 games because of "unsuitable supervisory enforcement of the pit," indicating at the very least "inadequate supervisory control."

In January 1972 Si Redd was approved for a license to install thirty-six slots in the Oak Room. Si Redd was president and director and 100-percent owner of the A-1 Supply Company. George Vucanovich was the secretary-treasurer and director of the company. No table games were licensed. In April 1972, A-1 Supply added seventy more slots to the Oak Room license.

In September 1973 Harrah's Club announced that it was taking over the Greyhound Bus Depot property, and the Oak Room was closed. Harrah's later (1975) opened its Sports Casino in that space.

The former location of the Oak Room is still a part of Harrah's Sports Casino.

Nev. St. Journal, 15 Apr. 54, 7 May 54, 9 Sept. 54, 15 July 63, 15 July 71, 13 Jan. 72, 18 Apr. 72.

OASIS BAR AND GRILL

1295 East Second Street; licensed from January 1957 to December 1958 for slots and 21.

The Oasis was located about twelve blocks from downtown. It was a neighborhood bar where a customer could get a drink and a sandwich and, if he wished, could play a slot machine or a few hands of 21. Fred Aoyama was the licensee.

At the former location of the Oasis Bar and Grill there is now a topless bar called Black Velvet.

Nev. St. Journal, 21 Dec. 57.

O'BRIEN'S CORNER

136 North Center Street; never licensed.

In August 1952 Sam O'Brien applied to re-open the much tossed-about premises at 136 North Center Street. The location had housed several gaming casinos in the previous few years—the Bar of Music, Buddy Baer's, and Freddy's Lair. However, it had been closed for several months. The license was denied, but the business did open as a bar in September. It closed early in 1953 and reopened as the Trade Winds.

The former location of O'Brien's is now part of the Cal-Neva parking garage on the east side of Center Street.

Nev. St. Journal, 27 Aug. 52, 9 Sept. 52.

O'DOWD, EDDIE

Eddie O'Dowd was the casino manager of the Riverside Hotel-Casino in the mid-1950s when it was owned by the Wertheimer brothers, Ruby Mathis, and Baldy West.

OHIO CLUB

21 East Douglas Alley; licensed from November 1958 to February 1966 for 21, poker, pan, and faro.

The Ohio Club was a bar located at a site that has housed bars and gambling ever since Reno was founded. The first legal casino at the location was the Douville Club, and the business that immediately preceded the Ohio Club was the Blue Chip Card Room.

Harry Auger, Robert McCartney, George Disney, and Walter Solon were the original licensees at the Ohio Club. In August 1965, Johnnie Russo, a local boxing promoter, was licensed to bankroll one poker and one pan game for a $2,500 investment.

The former location of the Ohio Club is now part of Harolds Club.

Nev. St. Journal, 25 Nov. 58, 6 Aug. 65, 17 Aug. 65.

OLD CATHAY CLUB

222 Lake Street; licensed from September 1956 to June 1957 for 21, craps, and keno.

A casino that catered to Asian customers, the Old Cathay Club was licensed to Harry Chon. In April 1957 the Nevada Gaming Control Board accused Chon of abandoning his license to other interests, making misrepresentations, and using improper methods of operation. He was ordered to show cause why his license should not be revoked. In May 1957 Chon's gaming license was revoked. The club had then been closed for several weeks.

In June 1957 George Chinn applied for a license at the location but was denied. He had planned to rename the business the California Club.

The site had formerly been occupied by the Happy Buddha. It is now a parking lot.

Nev. St. Journal, 11 Apr. 57, 24 May 57, 27 June 57.

OLD RENO CLUB

44 West Commercial Row; licensed since 1973 for 21, slots, and keno.

Located at the former site of the Town House and Zimba's, the Old Reno Club has been a popular spot with locals and tourists alike for over twenty years. Nothing is fancy or glamorous in the Old Reno. The theme of the decor is the Old West. The walls are covered with arrowhead collections, barbed wire, old guns, and other memorabilia of the pioneer days.

Over the years, the Old Reno has offered a keno game and a small 21 pit; however, the main emphasis has always been on slot machines. Slots of all kinds, even penny-progressive machines, have always been the main drawing card.

Old Reno currently has only slot machines. It has always been owned and operated by Eb Cox and his family, and it is still doing business at its original location.

Nev. St. Journal, 4 May 92 (photo).

Pictured at the Riverside Hotel casino in 1935 are (l. to r.) Swede Oleson, Nick Abelman, and Max Baer, heavyweight boxer. Courtesy of William Pettite.

OLESON, ALBERT "SWEDE"

Albert "Swede" Oleson was also known as "Little Swede," to distinguish him from his brother, Ed "Big Swede" Oleson. Born in Berkeley, California, on May 17, 1909, Oleson came to Reno in 1945 and worked in several casinos, including the Bank Club, the Palace Club, and the Riverside, before going to work for Harrah's at Lake Tahoe in 1956.

He worked in Harrah's until he semi-retired in the 1970s. In later years he worked as an advisor and troubleshooter at the Crystal Bay Club at Lake Tahoe and at other casinos in the Lake Tahoe and Carson City areas before completely retiring in 1984. Known for his joviality and sense of humor, Oleson epitomized the pit boss of the '40s and '50s who had great knowledge of all the games and could protect the house's money with the best of them.

Swede died on January 13, 1995. He had spent the last ten years of his life in Big Pine, California.

OLESON, EDWARD "SWEDE"

Edward Oleson was born in Berkeley, California, on November 12, 1904. He came to Reno in 1931. Oleson, known as "Swede" or sometimes as "Big Swede," to distinguish him from his younger brother, Al, worked as a dealer and/or boss in several Reno clubs during his long career. He was casino manager of the Riverside Hotel in the 1930s and also worked at the Palace Club and the Town House during that decade. In the 1940s he was co-owner of the Stork Club on West Second Street. In the 1950s he worked as a pit boss at the Golden-Bank Casino.

In 1963 Oleson was working at the Holiday Hotel-Casino when he suffered a heart attack and died while he was on shift.

Nev. St. Journal, 26 Oct. 35, 19 Dec. 36, 1 Mar. 50, 7 Sept. 55, 13 Apr. 63 (obit.).

116 CLUB

116 North Center Street; licensed from May 1941 to 1955 for slots, 21, and roulette.

The 116 Club opened on December 30, 1939, at the former site of the Alpine Club. The owners were Andre Duque and Leon Indhart. The walls of the newly decorated club were covered with western murals painted by well-known local artist Cletus Fisher.

In 1941 the club was purchased by Willi Brueckner, Marcel Peters, and K. D. Dalrymple. They were licensed for slots, 21, and roulette in May of that year.

The 116 Club was famous for its restaurant, and the gaming was there mainly as a convenience for the customers (not to say that the gaming devices didn't make money for the owners). Brueckner and Peters were two culinary veterans of the best nightspots, and Dalrymple managed the bar.

In 1952 "Dal" Dalrymple left the partnership, and in 1954 the state licensed Willi Brueckner and Marcel Peters for 10 percent each and John Gabrielli for 80 percent of the 116 Club.

The 116 closed in April 1955 when Brueckner and his partners were unable to renew the lease with the owners of the Pearson-Cafferata Building. The business later reopened as the Stein Hof-Brau and operated until 1985. The site of the 116 Club is now part of the Club Cal-Neva parking garage on the east side of Center Street.

Nev. St. Journal, 30 Dec. 39 (article and adv.), 8 Oct. 42, 1 Aug. 46, 15 Apr. 52, 30 Apr. 52, 10 Aug. 54, 1 May 55; Reno City Directory, 1942.

ONSLOW HOTEL

133 North Virginia Street; licensed from June 1977 to October 1989 for a full casino.

In November 1975 the Reno news media announced that Conrad Priess, Jose Gastanaga, Eugene Gastanaga, Everett Brunzell, and Tania Maloff had joined together and planned to build a multimillion-dollar hotel-casino on the site of the old Hilp's Drugstore. Construction of the sixteen-story, 182-room facility, tentatively named the Kit Carson Hotel, was scheduled to start in January 1976 and was to be completed in one year. The hotel was to be built on a 140-by-75-foot lot. The architect was David Jacobson Jr., and the contractor was Brunzell Construction.

On May 3, 1976, groundbreaking ceremonies were held for the Onslow (formerly the Kit Carson) Hotel. The name was changed to Onslow to honor longtime Reno resident Onslow Dodd. An informed source said that the owners were given a substantial discount on the price of the property if they agreed to name the hotel in Dodd's memory.

Final gaming approval was given to the Onslow and its owners on June 18, 1977. The Onslow was licensed for thirteen table games, one keno game, and three hundred slot machines. The hotel was scheduled to open on July 1, 1977, but because of construction problems it didn't actually open until September 5, 1977. The following were the licensees: Tania Maloff, Eugene Gastanaga, and Conrad Priess were licensed for 23.4 percent each; Everett Brunzell, 13.4 percent; James R. Parker Sr., 6.1 percent; and several relatives for a small percentage each. James Mack was announced as hotel manager, James Parker Jr. was named general manager and keno manager, LaVerl Kimpton was named pit manager, and Jimmy Gore was the slot manager.

When the Onslow opened, most of the 182 hotel rooms were still under construction. However, by mid-September the hotel was completely ready for business.

The Onslow executives touted their second-floor supper club as a revival of the dine-and-dance era in Reno. Guests could choose from a Continental menu and dance to the music of Lenny Herman and his orchestra. The second floor also housed a twenty-four-hour coffee shop, and the third floor had banquet and convention facilities for three hundred people.

The Onslow Hotel-Casino had several general managers and several casino managers in its thirteen-year existence. Among the general managers were James Parker Jr., Ron Erickson, Steve Simon, Jim Mack, Don Trimble, Jim Calhoun, and Frank Perrone. Some of the assistant general managers and/or casino managers were LaVerl Kimpton, Dean Rittenmeyer, Bob Hicks, David Britton, and Ken Barrenchea.

On July 22, 1989, the owners of the Onslow announced that they would cease operations on September 30. Although the prospective new owners were slated to remodel the 182-room hotel and reopen it in 1990 as a time-share operation with gaming, about three hundred employees would lose their jobs when the property closed. The expected sale never came about, and on July 31, 1990, the First Western Savings Association foreclosed on the shut-down operation. Everett Brunzell, one of the three principal owners of the Onslow, said the property went "busted" because "timing was bad and the debt service was pretty heavy."

After almost two years of legal maneuvering and bargaining, the Riverboat Hotel-Casino bought the property in the spring of 1992. The rooms were reconditioned and opened in 1993, and the new owners announced plans for a hotel tower, but it was never built. The Riverboat itself closed in November 1998. The ground level of the building (the former casino area) is currently being operated as a retail store, and the hotel rooms are leased to and operated by the Club Cal-Neva.

Nev. St. Journal, 12 Nov. 75 (photo), 4 May 76, 9 June 77, 18 June 77, 14 Aug. 77 (photo), 31 Aug. 77 (photo), 29 Apr. 79 (photo), 3 June 79, 19 Aug. 79 (photo), 6 Mar. 81 (photo), 22 July 89, 1 Aug. 90, 17 May 92.

OPEN DOOR (JOHNNY'S)
565 West Moana Lane; licensed from 1951 to 1955 for roulette, 21, craps, and slots.

The Open Door was established by John Ross and his wife, Vera, in March 1951. The business was intended primarily as a restaurant, but it naturally followed that a few slots and gaming tables would be added. Ross had several partners in the four-plus years that the Open Door was in operation, and most of them were well versed in the business of gaming. Some of his partners included Walter Parman, George Carr Jr., George Redican, George Evans, Walter Kerr, Harry Lauritson, and Charles Smith.

In 1955 Ross sold the business to a group headed by Frances and James Hammond. They renamed the property the Supper Club and operated it until it burned in 1959. The site is currently occupied by the Yen Ching Restaurant.

Nev. St. Journal, 22 Sept. 55.

ORLICH, DAN
Dan Orlich was born in Chisholm, Minnesota, in 1925 and attended Northwestern University before joining the Marine Corps in 1943. After his discharge in 1946, he attended Northwestern for one more year before transferring to the University of Nevada. Orlich played both basketball and football at the university, and his accomplishments earned him a spot in the school's Athletic Hall of Fame. Upon graduation, Orlich played three seasons of professional football with the Green Bay Packers before returning to Reno permanently in 1952.

He was hired by Harolds Club and worked in a variety of positions. He started out as a bouncer and eventually became casino manager. In June 1971, almost a year after Harolds Club was sold to the Hughes Corporation, Orlich resigned his position, and one year later he went to work at Harrah's Club. He remained there for fifteen years, advancing to the position of vice-president of special casino programs before retiring in 1986.

Orlich, a big man in many ways, stood six feet, five inches tall and weighed 225 pounds in his prime. An accomplished trapshooter, he was selected to the All-American Trapshooting Team twenty-one times and is a member of the Trapshooting Hall of Fame.

Dan Orlich, an All-American trap shooter for many years, worked in top management for both Harrah's and Harolds Club. Courtesy of Dan Orlich.

Dan Orlich is now retired and lives in Reno.

Nev. St. Journal, 30 June 71; *Reno Evening Gazette,* 16 Feb. 83 (photo), 31 Dec. 86.

OVERLAND BAR

242 North Center Street; licensed from December 20, 1933, to December 1, 1948, for 21, roulette, and pan.

The bar area of the Overland Hotel was licensed in 1933 for one roulette game only. In the first few years of legal gambling in Reno, roulette was one of the most popular table games in town, and it was not unusual for a bar to license a roulette table.

The Overland Bar leased out the gaming concessions to several people over the years, and at various times other games were added to the license. It is believed that R. E. Taffee was the last individual to be licensed at the Overland Bar. The Overland Hotel was purchased by Pick Hobson in 1959, and from that time on, Hobson was licensed for all the gaming in the building.

The former location of the Overland Bar is now part of Harrah's parking garage.

Nev. St. Journal, 6 Apr. 33, 28 Dec. 45.

OVERLAND HOTEL

102 East Commercial Row or 238 North Center Street (corner of Commercial Row and Center Street); licensed from April to July 1931 for 21 and roulette, then licensed from April 1960 to April 1977 for a full casino.

The Overland Hotel was built in 1916 by the Dromiack family and remained in their possession until it was purchased by Pick Hobson in 1959. Gaming was licensed for three months by W. D. McKnight in 1931, then no one was licensed in the Overland until Pick Hobson was licensed in 1960. However, there was gaming for a time in the bar area.

When Hobson purchased the Overland, he remodeled the period hotel, refurbished the rooms, and added air conditioning. He opened the entire street floor to his gaming operation and introduced an early-Comstock decor. There was red-plush wallpaper, walnut paneling, and huge chandeliers. More than twenty life-size oil portraits of early western outlaws and gunfighters, including Jesse James, Wild Bill Hickok, Wes Hardin, and others, adorned the walls. Pick titled his collection of paintings "Gunfighters of the Old West." The original marble staircase remained in the lobby and led overnight guests to the upstairs rooms.

Hobson was first licensed for seven 21 games, a craps game, a roulette game, a keno game, and slots. In 1970 he acquired the adjoining Cosmo Club. In 1975 the Cosmo Club was closed to make room for a possible Overland expansion.

Also in 1975 Hobson put together a management team for the Overland Hotel, the Gold Club, and the Topaz Lodge (all properties that he owned). The following were the members of the management team: Craig Soper, Anthony Gabriel, Steve Gurasevich, Robert Hawkins, J. J. Page Jr., Richard Sturdivant, and George Miller.

On March 30, 1977, newspapers announced that Harrah's had leased the Overland. The Overland was scheduled to close on May 1. The 140-room hotel had 480 people on the payroll. The Overland closed the very next day in the early morning hours. The closure came as a surprise to most of the employees. General manager Craig Soper said there was no choice but to close the hotel-casino after the article in the previous day's paper.

In June 1977 demolition of the property began in preparation for construction of Harrah's 450-space off-street parking facility. In March 1978, Harrah's purchased the Riverside Hotel from Jessie Beck and traded it to Hobson for the Overland Hotel. It was a good arrangement for all parties, because Jessie Beck wanted to get out of the gaming business, Pick Hobson wanted to get back into gaming, and Bill Harrah was able to acquire the key piece of property that he needed in order to build an off-street parking facility for his Center Street expansion.

The former location of the Overland Hotel is now part of Harrah's parking facility on North Center Street.

Raymond Sawyer, *Reno: Where the Gamblers Go!* (Reno: Sawston Publishing Company, 1976); *Nev. St. Journal,* 6 Apr. 60, 14 June 68, 30 Aug. 68, 20 Dec. 74, 11 Sept. 75, 30 Mar. 77 (photo), 31 Mar. 77, 7 June 77 (photo), 10 Mar. 78.

OWL CLUB

142 East Commercial Row; licensed from March 1931 to January 1, 1938, for slots, craps, roulette, poker, pan, and faro.

The Owl Club, owned by Dan Shoemaker, was the first location in Nevada to be granted a gaming license when gaming became legal in 1931. Shoemaker had owned the Owl Club since coming to Reno in 1917, and he had operated poker games there for several years. When gaming became legal in 1931, he added casino games. His first license was for one roulette game, one craps game, one 21 game, one stud poker game, one draw poker game, one pan game, and four slot machines (two nickel, one dime, and one quarter machine).

Dan Shoemaker died in October 1932 at the age of forty-two. The club was taken over for a short time by J. P. Brown and E. Ross, but late in 1933 it was purchased by Alex Nystrom and Joe Beloso. The site is now part of Harrah's Club parking garage.

Nev. St. Journal, 27 Mar. 31, 6 Apr. 33, 27 July 54; Sawyer, *Reno: Where the Gamblers Go!*; Reno City Directory, 1941.

P

PADILLA, JOSEPH

Joe Padilla came to Reno from the San Francisco Bay area in 1953. He was licensed, along with twelve other investors, at the Palace Club from December 1953 to June 1964. He was also a licensee at the Colony Club in Reno from 1956 to 1974 and at the El Morocco in Las Vegas from 1959 to 1961.

The original Colony Club was on Virginia Street. When the location was purchased by Harolds Club in 1964, Padilla and his partners reopened the Colony Club at the corner of Center Street and Commercial Row.

Nev. St. Journal, 11 Dec. 53, 20 June 56, 26 Feb. 59, 8 June 61, 9 Dec. 64, 20 Jan. 67.

PALACE CLUB

46 East Commercial Row; licensed as the Palace Cigar Store in June 1931 for one craps game; licensed as the Palace Bar in January 1934; licensed from June 1934 to September 28, 1979, as a full casino.

The Palace Club property was purchased by John Petricciani in 1924, although for many years he did not operate a business there himself. He leased the property to various businesses, including a department store, a soft-drink parlor, and a barber shop. He also leased the second floor of the building to Bill Graham and Jim McKay, who used the location for their Bank Palace Club from 1931 through 1933.

John Petricciani operated a craps game in the Palace for one month (June 1931). It was licensed as the Palace Cigar Store. He left the casino business when he rented his property to Graham and McKay, but he maintained a slot-machine route that he had operated for many years in Reno. It was because of this slot route that Petricciani was often called "Slot Machine Johnny." In 1934 he got back into the casino

business when he licensed the Palace Bar for one roulette game and one 21 game. In 1935 he changed the name on the license to the Palace Club and was licensed for two craps games, two faro games, two roulette games, one 21 game, one stud poker game, and six slot machines.

An interesting aside is the following quote from the *Nevada State Journal* of April 22, 1935: "Silvio Petricciani is nominated as the best craps dealer in town" (Silvio was John's son).

On April 26, 1936, the following ad ran in the *Nevada State Journal:* "The Palace Club presents Reno's newest sensation, Race horse Keno—Today and everyday. Post time twelve noon." This same ad ran every day for several weeks.

Racehorse keno, known today as simply keno, has played an important role in Reno gaming history. During keno's peak popularity from the early 1940s through the early 1980s, it was a large revenue producer for many casinos and an important tax contributor to the State of Nevada. The Palace Club was noted for bringing keno to a place of prominence in Reno and for refining and polishing the game. Originally, keno was the name of the game known today as bingo. To differentiate keno from bingo and because Chinese lottery (the game that keno is patterned after) was illegal, John Petricciani and Peter Merialdo had to convince the governor of Nevada that racehorse keno was a "banking game" and was played with a mechanical device (a keno goose). They convinced the governor, and so the Palace Club was able to license the game.

On May 7, 1936, the Palace Club placed this ad in the *Nevada State Journal:* "The Palace Club is in their second sensational week of Race Horse Keno, the game that has taken Reno by storm. First post time is 10:00 A.M.—Races every twenty minutes until 2:00 A.M. Saturdays until 4:00 A.M."

By the first of June, the Palace Club had extended the keno limit to $500 and was operating the game twenty-four hours a day. Francis Lyden of Butte, Montana, was in charge of the keno game, and his three keno shift bosses, all from Great Falls, Montana, were Clyde "Sugar Plum" Bitt-

ner, Jack "MacTavish" Mullen, and Warren "Swede" Nelson. Also among those coming down from Montana to work the keno game were Jim Brady, Ken Watkins, John Morse, Tom Cavanaugh, Jim Crowley, James Kalley, Jim Shay, and Dick Trinastich.

John Petricciani believed in leasing out some of the gambling in the Palace. In 1935 Virgil Smith came from Lovelock to operate the poker games, and in 1937 Wayne Martin, also from Lovelock, and Brownie Paretti leased the poker and pan games.

In January 1936 Billy Jordan was named manager of the Palace gaming tables. By 1937 the Palace had increased its casino space to 7,000 square feet and had one craps game, six 21 games, one roulette game, two faro games, and 150 slot machines to go along with its successful keno game.

In June 1943, with his son Sil (Silvio) in the military service, John Petricciani leased the Palace Club for five years to Ernie Primm, Joe Hall, Archie Sneed, Jim Contratto, all of Southern California, and Elmer "Baldy" West of Reno. West was a floor manager at the Palace and took over as manager. Sneed, Hall, Primm, and Contratto each put up $35,000; West's contributions were to be in the form of services. The five men were also given a five-year lease option, which they renewed in 1948. Contratto sold his interest in October 1943, a few months after the lease was signed.

In July 1943 a full-page ad in the *Nevada State Journal* announced that "for the first time, we have lady clerks [dealers] and many new men clerks." World War II was creating a shortage of male workers in all industries, and the gaming business was no exception. For many years, none of the clubs had hired female dealers, but after the Smith family began the practice in Harolds Club, some other clubs followed. In November 1943 the Palace Club placed the following ad in the help-wanted section: "The Palace Club is offering young women 21 to 25 years of age the chance to learn how to deal all games and earn up to $90 a week."

In June 1948 a full-page ad in the *Nevada State Journal* reproduced a letter from the Pace Slot Machine Company addressed to

Elmer West, thanking the Palace for an order of fifty-two Pace slot machines (with a payout to the customers of 95.75 percent). This and similar advertisements ran throughout July, August, and September 1948.

On October 31, 1951, Ernie Primm filed a suit alleging that Elmer West's "wild temper and dictatorial policies rendered the Palace Club's four way partnership ineffectual." Judge A. J. Maestretti named Clayton Phillips, former Reno police chief, as receiver to operate the Palace. A few weeks later, in mid-November, Elmer West and Archie Sneed bought out Ernie Primm and Joe Hall, and the litigation was ended.

The lease held by West and Sneed was due to expire on June 1, 1953, and as early as July 1952 three men—Walter "Big Bill" Pechart, David Kessell, and Walter Parman—filed an application with the Nevada Gaming Commission to be licensed at the Palace. The three men were former associates of Elmer "Bones" Remmer, a well-known California and Nevada gambler.

After two months of delays and deferments, the state gave preliminary approval to Pechart, Kessell, and Parman on September 30, 1952. However, in May 1953 the state denied them a license.

On May 26 Walter Parman, who claimed to have a valid lease at the Palace, filed for a gaming license. He sought licenses for 150 slots, eight 21 games, two craps games, two roulette games, one poker game, one pan game, and one keno game. The same day, Brad Hewins, who also claimed to have a valid lease at the Palace, filed for a gaming license. He wanted licensing for 175 slots, ten 21 games, three craps games, one pan game, one poker game, one roulette game, and one keno game.

In June the lease held by West and Sneed expired, and the Palace Club was closed, throwing two hundred people out of work. Both Parman and Hewins were still claiming that they had signed leases. On July 19 Judge Wines ruled that Brad Hewins would be awarded the lease. Walter Parman appealed the decision, but Wines rejected the appeal.

On July 22, 1953, the Palace opened at 6:00 P.M. with 175 slot machines, seven 21 games, three craps games, one pan game, one poker game, one roulette game, and one keno game. The license fee was $21,800, and the owner percentages were as follows: Brad Hewins, 87 percent; Lou Iacometti, 5 percent; Jack Guffey, 2 percent; and Louis Rosasco, 6 percent.

On November 10, 1953, the ownership of the Palace Club changed dramatically when Brad Hewins sold his percentage and the City of Reno licensed the following request: the stockholders listed would hold 99 of the 100 shares then outstanding. The proposed partners and the amounts of stock held were given as follows: Jack Guffey, 5 shares; Warren Nelson, 4 shares; Joe Hornstein, 25 shares; Cliff Grady, 5 shares; Louis Rosasco, 10 shares; Louis Iacometti, 10 shares; Howard Farris, 11 shares; Frank Cohen, 8 shares; Joe Padilla, 2 shares; Bernard Vignaux, 4 shares; Jack Austin, 4 shares; Harry Weitz, 7 shares; and William Weitz, 4 shares. All were Reno residents except Padilla, Vignaux, and William Weitz, who were from San Francisco, and Austin, who was from San Jose.

On December 10, 1953, the Palace was licensed for 175 slot machines, three craps games, one roulette game, six 21 games, one keno game, and two pan games. Howard Farris, Jack Guffey, and Harry Weitz were licensed as shift managers.

The Palace Club proved to be extremely profitable for the next several years, and the only ownership changes occurred when Warren Nelson and Howard Farris left to buy into the new Club Cal-Neva; when Frank Cohen died and his shares were taken over by his widow, Clara; when Cliff Grady died and his estate was licensed; and when William Weitz was killed in an automobile accident and his brother Harry took over his percentage.

In 1964, when the lease expired, a group that had owned the property and building for many years applied for the gaming license at the Palace. The group was composed of the following: Silvio and John Petricciani, sons of John Petricciani, and their two sisters, Clorinda Delich of Las Vegas and Marietta Carli. They were each licensed for 25 percent of the operation, and Sam Delich was approved as a corporate officer with no investment. The group was given final approval on May 19, on the condition that they put up a $370,000 bankroll.

The first thing Sil Petricciani did when he took over was to clean up the club. He gave it a full face-lift and put up a big, beautiful new sign on the outside of the building. He also put in a new restaurant with good food for reasonable prices. His chef was Bill Stevens, who had many years of experience. His good food brought lots of business to the Palace.

In November 1964 the Petricciani group sold 13 percent of the operation to three employees of the Palace Club, Larry Russo, Mike Garfinkle, and Sam D'Andea. In 1965, 5 percent of the club was sold to Carl Weeks for $15,000.

In the late 1970s the Gaming Commission licensed Russell Oberlander, Carl Weeks, Don Dennis, Lonnie Snyder, and Jim Burrows as shift managers at the Palace Club.

On September 28, 1979, Sil Petricciani broke the news to his 281 employees that the club had been sold to Harrah's Club for a price that wasn't disclosed, other than that the amount was in "six figures." Harrah's Club had been seeking the property for several months, but it wasn't until the Palace's co-owner, Sam Delich, told Petricciani that he was no longer able to work because of back surgery that they decided to sell. Sil, who was sixty-two, said he was too old to run the business by himself. Harrah's declined to comment on when it would reopen the club.

The Palace never reopened, and the building was soon demolished. The site is now a parking lot.

Nev. St. Journal, 15 Sept. 35, 8 Apr. 36, 26 Apr. 36 (adv.), 7 May 36 (adv.), 30 May 36, 6 June 36, 6 Feb. 37, 18 May 37 (adv.), 25 Dec. 37 (adv.), 31 Dec. 37, 5 Nov. 38, 10 June 43, 12 June 43, 3 July 43 (adv.), 20 Nov. 43 (adv.), 28 Jan. 44, 20 Oct. 44 (adv.), 24 Nov. 45, 1 Jan. 46 (adv.), 20 Mar. 46, 16 Aug. 47, 17 June 48 (adv.), 31 Oct. 51, 10 Nov. 51, 17 Nov. 51, 24 July 52, 7 Aug. 52, 11 Sept. 52, 30 Sept. 52, 9 May 53, 26 May 53, 10 June 53, 19 July 53, 21 July 53, 23 July 53, 17 Sept. 53, 30 Oct. 53, 10 Nov. 53, 11 Dec. 53, 28 Apr. 54, 10 Jan. 56 (adv.), 19 Feb. 57, 22 Mar. 57, 16 Apr. 64, 8 May 64, 20 May

64, 22 July 64 (photo), 7 Nov. 64, 12 June 65 (photo), 10 Dec. 65, 25 May 70, 19 Nov. 76, 16 Dec. 77, 17 Feb. 78, 22 Sept. 78, 29 Sept. 79 (photo); Reno City Directory, 1942.

PALM CLUB (ALSO KNOWN AS THE PALM SALOON AND THE PALM CAFE)

260 Lake Street; licensed for slots and 21 from 1931 to 1935.

The Palm Club was at one time or another a bar, a coffee shop, and a gathering place for Asians and African Americans. Gambling was conducted on a hit-or-miss basis. Bill Fong purchased the property in 1952 and operated his casino, the New China Club, at the location.

Currently the site is part of a parking lot.

Nev. St. Journal, 30 Apr. 52.

PALOMAR CLUB

On the Verdi Highway; licensed from January 1 to July 1, 1946, for 21, craps, and roulette.

Nothing more is known of this establishment.

PANELLI, BILL

Bill Panelli was born in Dayton, Nevada, on September 23, 1902. He was a prize

fighter in his youth. In the 1930s he worked at the Bank Club and the Palace Club, where he dealt hazard, roulette, craps, and faro bank. Many considered him one of the best faro bank dealers in Reno. He was an absolute perfectionist in everything he did, and this trait placed him above others in his profession.

In 1946, when Bill Harrah opened his first casino on Virginia Street, Bill Panelli was one of the first employees hired. In Bill Harrah's oral history, he remarks that Bill Panelli "smiled once a year" and that his nickname for Panelli was "Joe Deadpan." Harrah also called Panelli "one of his favorite pit bosses."

Bill Panelli died on March 10, 1965.

PARKER, JAMES "REGGIE" OR "ARKIE"

Reggie Parker was born in Russellville, Arkansas, on February 18, 1921. He came to Reno in 1944 to play football for the University of Nevada. After his football days were over, he served in the merchant marine until the end of World War II. Upon returning to civilian life, Parker went to work at the Palace Club as a bouncer (security guard) and later learned the game of keno.

After working as a keno shift manager at the Palace Club and the Overland Hotel, he was licensed as a co-owner and keno manager of the Silver Spur Casino on Virginia Street when it opened in 1967. In 1969 Parker became general manager of the Silver Spur and remained in that position until retiring to Arkansas in 1980. He retained his interests in the Silver Spur until the casino was sold in 1981. Parker was also one of the original owners of the Onslow Hotel on Virginia Street, from 1977 to 1981.

Reggie, or Arkie, as he was often called, was noted in the gaming industry for giving young people a chance to work in his department or in his casino while they were furthering their education at the University of Nevada. Several teachers, attorneys, doctors, and professional men completed their educations while working for him.

Parker retired in 1980 to return to his native Arkansas. He died there on November 17, 1994.

Nev. St. Journal, 9 June 77.

PARMAN, WALTER

Walter Parman was born in Seattle on September 26, 1898, and came to Reno in 1931. Parman was one of the premier gamblers in Nevada during the first fifty years of legalized gaming. He was an owner, operator, and manager during his career and was highly respected in all three major gambling markets in the state—Reno, Lake Tahoe, and Las Vegas.

Parman was a manager in the Bank Club in the 1930s and early 1940s. Leaving the Bank Club, he was owner and manager of the Tahoe Village on the South Shore of Lake Tahoe in the late 1940s, a partner in Johnny's Open Door in 1951, and a partner, with Cliff Kehl, at the Circle R-B Lodge on West Fourth Street from 1951 to 1953. In 1953 Parman purchased the California Club in Las Vegas but sold his interest in 1954. He also worked at the Stardust Casino while he was in Las Vegas. In 1958 owner Newt Crumley named Parman casino manager of the Holiday Hotel-Casino on Mill Street.

In 1961 Parman returned to Las Vegas and was licensed as a co-owner of the El

Bill Panelli with his son, Rick. Panelli is wearing a Harrah's uniform shirt with "Harrah's Club" embroidered over the right pocket and "Bill" over the left pocket. Courtesy of Rick Panelli.

Morocco. He also worked at the Riverside and the Mapes Hotels and finished his career working at the MGM Hotel-Casino in Reno.

Parman passed away February 4, 1990, at his Sun Valley, Nevada, residence.

Nev. St. Journal, 8 May 51, 29 July 51, 12 Nov. 53, 16 June 54, 1 July 54, 23 July 54, 11 Sept. 58, 8 June 61, 9 Apr. 74, 4 Feb. 90 (obit.).

PASTIME CLUB

116 East Commercial Row (1929–1944); 246 Sierra Street (1944–1948); licensed from 1931 to 1948 for 21, craps, poker, and pan.

Bruno Pagni opened the Pastime Club in 1929 and put in a 21 game and a poker game in May 1931. In June he added a craps game, and in June 1934 he added a pan game. In the mid-1930s the Pastime Club operated with slots only, then in 1942 the club was licensed for a poker game and a 21 game.

In June 1944 the Pastime Club moved to 246 Sierra Street. The Sierra Street location was licensed for a 21 game, slots, and poker.

The former Commercial Row location of the Pastime Club is now part of Harrah's parking garage, and the Sierra Street location is part of the Flamingo Hilton.

Nev. St. Journal, 5 Aug. 39 (adv.), 16 June 42, 9 June 44, 15 Oct. 47.

PEAVINE CLUB

219 Peavine Street (now called Evans Avenue); licensed from 1941 to 1947 for slots, craps, and 21.

The Peavine Club was owned by Harry Wright during the early 1940s. It catered to African Americans. During World War II, many African Americans were stationed at the Reno (Stead) Army Air Base and at the Herlong Ammunition Depot. The Peavine Club was one of the few clubs or casinos where they were welcomed. Nevada casinos were segregated until civil rights legislation was enacted in the early 1960s, and prior to that time African Americans were admitted to very few casinos, regardless of whether or not they were in military service. If they entered a segregated casino, they were asked to leave, and if they did not leave, they were forcefully ejected.

In December 1944 Walter Ector, a craps dealer at the Peavine Club, shot Joe Jones after Jones accused Ector of using phony dice. In September 1945 John Berton, an African American soldier from Herlong, was shot by Harry Wright, the sixty-seven-year-old proprietor of the Peavine Club.

Shortly after that incident, the Peavine Club was sold to Bill Bailey, an African American businessman who owned and operated several bars, clubs, and cabarets that catered to the African American trade. Bailey was licensed for one 21 game, one craps game, and six slot machines. He operated the Peavine Club until 1947, when the building was condemned and the site was turned into a parking lot.

The site is still a parking lot. It is located across the street from the Reno Fire Station on Evans Avenue, just north of East Second Street.

Nev. St. Journal, 17 Dec. 44, 23 Jan. 45, 4 Sept. 45.

PECHART, WALTER "BIG BILL"

Bill Pechart was born in Bingham City, Utah, on January 14, 1892. As a young man, he moved to Chico, California, and became associated with David Kessell. They set up gambling operations in Martinez, San Pablo, El Cerrito, and Chico before World War II and operated illegally all during the war and into the late 1940s.

In 1952 Pechart and Kessell attempted to buy into the Palace Club. Pechart, however, withdrew his application before the state could complete its investigation, and Kessel was denied a license.

In March 1955 Charles Mapes hired Pechart "to watch his money." Mapes had leased the Mapes Casino to a group headed by Bernie Einstoss, and he evidently felt that he wasn't getting a good count on the profits, which the lease stipulated were to be shared on an equal basis. Pechart was hired for a salary of $35 a day plus $1,000 a month in expenses, and he was given a suite in the hotel.

In May 1955 the state removed the Einstoss group from the license, and Charles Mapes became the only licensee. The state made Mapes's licensing subject to the termination of Pechart as an employee and

further stated that Pechart was not to be granted access to the casino pits or counting rooms. Gaming officials objected to Pechart's presence on the property for several reasons: his gambling connections in Contra Costa County, California, and his association with David Kessel; his involvement in a Las Vegas shooting during the boom days of the Boulder (Hoover) Dam construction; and his citation for contempt by the Kefauver Committee investigating organized crime involvement in the Nevada gaming industry (in 1950 Pechart had been called before the Kefauver Committee and had refused to answer questions about his associations with the crime world).

The state later relented and allowed Pechart to be employed as a credit manager in the Mapes, but he was still not allowed to enter the pit area or the counting rooms. In 1963 the authorities relented further and allowed Pechart to serve as casino manager.

On September 25, 1965, Bill Pechart died of a heart attack while on duty as casino manager of the Mapes.

Nev. St. Journal, 4 Feb. 55, 2 Mar. 55, 23 May 55, 24 May 55, 20 Mar. 63, 26 Sept. 65 (obit.).

PEPPERMILL

2707 South Virginia Street; licensed since 1980 for a full casino.

In November 1967 former Lake Tahoe land developers Bill Paganetti and Nate Carsalli opened a cocktail lounge called the Mouse House on Oddie Boulevard. They were already the owners of Topper's Steak House in Reno's Keystone Square. Over the next two years, Paganetti and Carsalli opened two more restaurants known as the Sir Loin Steak Houses. In December 1969 they opened a third Sir Loin Steak House, which later became known as Leonardo's.

Their next major move came in 1971, when Paganetti and Carsalli joined motel owner Fred Hill to construct a new restaurant and lounge on the property of Hill & Son's Motel at 2701 South Virginia Street. The property opened in the spring of 1971 and was known as the Peppermill Restaurant and Lounge.

In May 1980 the Peppermill was approved for 2,200 square feet of gaming space. The casino addition housed 130 slots and four 21 games. The expansion continued in October 1980, giving the property a total of 429 hotel rooms. The Peppermill also added 11,000 square feet of casino space at that time.

The Peppermill has never stopped expanding. More casino space, a convention area, and a buffet restaurant opened in 1983; the first tower, more casino and convention space, an expanded buffet, and the Le Moulin gourmet restaurant opened in 1988. In 1991 another major expansion brought the casino space up to 36,000 square feet and added another parking lot on the north side of the property and another restaurant.

The Peppermill shunned the trend for theme casinos and focused instead on creating a first-class, full-service resort hotel-casino without gimmicks. Peter Wilday, the noted architect, is given much of the credit for the building's beautiful interior and exterior. The customer is truly the king or queen at the Peppermill, and the business's extraordinary treatment of its patrons has had a great deal to do with its success. Phil Bryant, general manager for a time, did a great deal to lead the Peppermill through its expansion years. Also, as in any successful operation, the leadership that came from owners Bill Paganetti, Nate Carsalli, and the Seeno family—Albert Sr., Albert Jr., and Tom—contributed to the continued growth of the Peppermill.

The Peppermill is still "on the go." On November 10, 1994, the Reno City Council approved more expansion plans for the popular casino. A $100-million project—to be completed by the year 2000—will include twin towers connecting to the west edge of the existing tower, boosting its rooms from 632 to more than 1,400. Plans also include two more parking garages, a swimming pool, more restaurants, and an enlarged casino area.

Nev. St. Journal, 27 Nov. 67 (photo), 10 Jan. 69, 13 July 69, 14 Dec. 69, 9 May 80, 13 May 80, 8 Oct. 80, 28 Oct. 80.

The flamboyant George "Frenchy" Perry (r.) pictured with Nick Abelman in 1939. Courtesy of William Pettite.

PERRY, GEORGE "FRENCHY"

George Perry operated games in several locations around Reno in the 1930s, 1940s, and the early 1950s. From 1941 to 1944 Perry, along with Jack Blackman, operated the games at the popular Town House on West First Street. In the mid-1940s Perry, along with Phil Curti, operated the Tropics on North Center Street. In 1947 they converted the nightspot to a bowling alley.

Perry was also a part-owner of the Bar of Music in 1950. In 1951, after the Bar of Music location had changed its name to Freddy's Lair, Perry applied for, but was denied, a license by the newly created Nevada State Tax Commission headed by Robbins Cahill. The ruling effectively ended Perry's career in gaming.

Nev. St. Journal, 18 Jan. 47.

PETRICCIANI, JOHN "SLOT MACHINE JOHNNY"

John Petricciani was born in Tuscany, Italy, in 1888 and came to Reno in 1915. He purchased the Palace Club property in 1924, but for many years he did not operate the businesses located there. He did operate the Louvre Bar on Commercial Row in a partnership with Joe Elcano in the early 1930s, and later he became a partner of Bert Baroni in a slot-machine route. It was while he was running the slot route that he became known as "Slot Machine Johnny." He also owned several other downtown properties, including the Traveler's Hotel.

John leased the Palace Club to Bill Graham and James McKay in 1931, but in 1934 he took over operation of the Palace and was licensed for two table games. The next year he added eight table games and six slot machines to the license. In 1936 he made gambling history when he introduced the game of keno, as we now know it, to the state of Nevada.

Petricciani was a great host and was known by many as "the best boss in town." He was liked by everyone and always had a big smile and a hello for anyone he met. He was also a sharp dresser who was generous almost to a fault, donating heavily to many charities and seldom hesitating to help individuals down on their luck.

He retained ownership of the Palace Club property until his death but ceased operating the club in 1943 when his son, Sil, entered the military service. At that time he leased the club to a group headed by Elmer "Baldy" West.

John Petricciani passed away on May 9, 1955, in San Francisco.

Nev. St. Journal, 26 Feb. 38, 10 May 55 (obit.).

PETRICCIANI, SILVIO "SIL"

Sil Petricciani was born in Reno on December 1, 1917. He grew up in the gaming industry, because his father, John, was the owner of the Palace Club and also operated a large slot route in the Reno area. Sil went to work in the Palace in 1934 and soon became one of the top dice dealers in Reno.

When Sil entered military service during World War II, his father leased out the Palace Club. The Palace was still leased out when Sil returned from the service, so he went to work with his brother-in-law, Pick Hobson, at Shorty's Club in Sparks. When Shorty's was sold, Sil went to the Frontier Club as graveyard-shift manager, then later worked at the Riverside Hotel-Casino before going to Las Vegas in 1948. In Las Vegas Sil worked at the El Rancho, the Fremont, and the Stardust in top-level management positions.

In 1964 Sil returned to Reno to take over operation of the Palace Club. The facility, he recalled later, "was dirty, filthy and smelled." He completely remodeled, painted, and cleaned up the building and created an entirely new image in the longtime casino. Sil operated the Palace Club from 1964 until he sold the property to Harrah's Club in September 1979.

After selling the Palace Club, Sil returned to the gaming business as general manager of the Shy Clown. Later he was general manager of the Horseshoe Club, the Mapes Hotel, the Money Tree, and George Benny's planned but never-opened River Palace.

Sil is a likable, popular individual and is highly regarded in the gaming industry. He is also notably civic-minded and has served on the Board of Trustees of the Reno Air Races and on the Board of Directors of the Reno Airport. Currently he is retired in Reno, but he remains active in several civic organizations.

Nev. St. Journal, 22 Apr. 38, 14 Apr. 64, 29 Sept. 79, 17 Feb. 81; Silvio Petricciani, "The Evolution of Gaming in Nevada: The Twenties to the Eighties" (Reno: University of Nevada Oral History Program, 1982).

PETTITE, FRANCIS "FRAN"

Fran Pettite was born in 1915 in Fenton, Iowa. He came to Reno in 1937 and was associated for many years with his aunt and uncle, Nick and June Abelman, at the Riverside Hotel, the Waldorf Club, the Stateline Club at Lake Tahoe, and the Christmas Tree on the Mount Rose Highway. Pettite also worked at the Pershing Hotel in Lovelock and was employed for many years as a pit supervisor and shift manager at the Mapes Hotel and as a pit supervisor at Harrah's Club and at the Ponderosa Hotel-Casino.

Pettite is retired and lives in Reno.

PICADILLY

233 North Virginia; licensed from July 1946 to 1952 for slots, pan, poker, and roulette.

The Picadilly, when it opened on July 2,

Fran Pettite pictured in 1946 in front of the Tahoe Village on Lake Tahoe's South Shore. Courtesy of William Pettite.

Interior view of the Picadilly. One of the many co-owners, Oly Glusovich, is standing at the far end of the bar. Note the motto across the top of the bar and the many copper mugs hanging on the back bar. Courtesy of Neal Cobb.

1946, was owned by Leon Harbert, Bill Hoover, and George "Mick" Mixson. Mixson owned 70 percent, and Harbert and Hoover owned the remaining 30 percent. The Picadilly was located at the former site of the Virginia Bar.

The Picadilly was decorated to resemble an English pub, and the back bar was covered with red bricks reminiscent of Old England. Its slogan was "A Bit of Old England, right here in Reno," and written in large letters on the wall behind the bar was the following: "Dear Soul from Kindly Goblets Take a Sip, T'will Curb The Pensive Tear—Tis Not as Sweet as Woman's Lips, But, ah, Tis More Sincere."

The Picadilly was famous for its Moscow Mules, a drink made with vodka and tonic water with a sprig of mint and served in copper mugs. Regular customers had their personalized mugs on display and always available on the back bar. During the six years the Picadilly was open, several people owned a percentage of the club. They included the previously mentioned Mixson, Harbert, and Hoover, as well as Oly Glusovich, Emmett Sullivan, Doug Busey, John Hickok, W. M. Leeper, C. W.

Hoyt, Bob Armstrong, Jack Douglass, and Joseph McAulay. Another well-known Renoite, Louis Rosasco, was a manager and host at the Picadilly in the summer of 1952.

The Picadilly was sold late in 1952 to a group headed by Reno realtor John Hickok and was renamed the Nugget. In late 1953 the property was sold to Dick Graves and Jim Kelly. It operated for many years as Jim Kelly's Nugget. It is currently operating as the Nugget Casino.

Nev. St. Journal, 2 July 46 (adv.), 8 Feb. 47 (adv.), 27 Mar. 48 (adv. and photos), 22 Sept. 50, 16 Nov. 50, 14 Dec. 50, 10 Apr. 51 (adv.), 8 May 51, 30 Oct. 51, 29 June 52 (adv.), 7 Sept. 52.

PICK'S CLUB

220 North Virginia Street; licensed from December 1943 to 1945 for slots, 21, craps, and roulette.

Pick's Club was opened in December 1943 by Pick Hobson. The location had been the site of several clubs and bars over the previous years. Hobson operated the club until 1945, when he and his brother, Joe Hobson, along with other investors, opened the Frontier Club at the same location.

The Frontier Club was sold to Harrah's

Club in November 1956. The site is now part of the north end of Harrah's on Virginia Street.

Reno Telephone Directory, 1944 (yellow pages adv.); Reno City Directory, 1944; *Nev. St. Journal,* 23 Jan. 45.

PIEPER, JACK

Jack Pieper, a native of St. Louis, Missouri, began his gaming career as a dealer in the Cal-Neva Club in Reno in 1949. The next year he moved to Las Vegas. In Las Vegas he worked for eighteen years at the Golden Nugget, rising to the position of casino manager. He left the Golden Nugget in 1968 to become managing director of the Silver Slipper.

In 1970 Pieper returned to Reno as manager of Harolds Club shortly after the club was purchased by the Hughes Corporation. In 1972 he was transferred to the Frontier Club in Las Vegas and was named general manager of that property.

Pieper left the Frontier Club in 1976 to return to Reno as president of the MGM Hotel-Casino, which had not yet opened. He was the force behind planning and organizing the largest casino (at that time) ever opened in Reno. Pieper served as president of the MGM until January 1979, when he resigned to become president and general manager of the Holiday Hotel-Casino on Mill Street. In August 1980 Pieper resigned to return to Las Vegas. He died there on August 1, 1999.

Nev. St. Journal, 24 June 72, 13 Jan. 76 (photo), 27 June 76 (photo), 27 Jan. 79, 30 Aug. 80; 4 Aug. 99 (obit.).

PIONEER INN

221 South Virginia Street; licensed since 1972 for a full casino.

The Pioneer Inn opened in August 1968 with 162 rooms and no gaming. John Lazovich was the general manager, and the property featured a gourmet dining room known as the Iron Sword Restaurant. The original partners in the venture were Don Carano, John Lazovich, Ray Poncia Jr., Jack Lyons, Bob McDonald, and Thomas "Spike" Wilson. Within a few years of the opening, Wilson and McDonald had left the corporation, and Jack Lyons was killed in a motorcycle accident.

In April 1972 the Pioneer Inn installed sixty-five slot machines, and John Lazovich, Don Carano, and Ray Poncia Sr. were licensed for one-third each of the operation. Table games were introduced in 1974, and two of the first casino managers were Bill Nance and Charles Kruse. Later casino managers included Gary Carano, Herb Grellman, and Guy Archer.

In 1969 the owners of the Pioneer signed a twenty-year lease with Denny's Restaurant to operate a coffee shop at the location. In 1989 the Pioneer opened its own restaurant.

The first general manager of the Pioneer was John Lazovich. He was followed by Pat Allison, Roberto Crawford, and Les Clavir. At the present time, the Pioneer is co-managed by Guy Archer, who was hired in 1979, and Earl Howsley.

The Pioneer Inn has maintained a quiet, low-key operation over the years, and there are several longtime employees, including pit supervisor Yvonne "Todd" Davis, who have been employed by the Pioneer for over twenty years.

The Pioneer Inn is still located at its original site. It has expanded over the years and currently has 252 hotel rooms, a coffee shop, the Iron Sword Restaurant, a keno game, 320 slots, and a ten-table pit area.

Nev. St. Journal, 25 Aug. 68 (photo), 13 Apr. 72, 21 Apr. 72, 13 Sept. 74, 21 Nov. 75, 21 May 77.

PIPER, RICHARD "DICK"

Dick Piper was born in Medford, Massachusetts, on March 12, 1926. He enlisted in the U.S. Navy in 1943 and served in the submarine service until receiving his discharge in 1946. Piper came to Reno in 1948. His first job was as a shill and nickel-wrapper at the Palace Club for Baldy West. He learned to deal all the table games, and he worked at the Palace until 1953. When West's lease expired, he moved on to the Golden-Bank Casino.

In 1957 Piper was hired by Harvey's Wagon Wheel on the South Shore of Lake Tahoe. He started there as a pit boss and eventually became casino manager. Leav-

ing Lake Tahoe in 1962, Piper went to Ely, where he was co-owner of the Bank Club and the Hotel Nevada. He stayed in Ely until 1968.

After taking a year off from gaming, Piper returned to Nevada and in June 1969 opened the King's Castle at Incline Village, Lake Tahoe, for Nate Jacobsen. After one year, he returned to Ely and purchased and operated the Mustang Club there until 1974. From 1974 to 1977 Piper was casino manager at the King 8 Casino in Las Vegas. From 1978 to 1981 Piper worked as a pit supervisor at the Club Cal-Neva and the Comstock Hotel-Casino. From 1981 to 1982 he was employed as manager of the Gold Dust East and the Gold Dust West casinos. In 1982 Piper was hired as general manager of the Crystal Bay Club on the North Shore of Lake Tahoe. He eventually became a co-owner, and since retiring from the job of general manager of the club, he remains on its board of directors. In June 1996 Piper was named general manager of the Holiday Hotel in Reno. He maintained that position until the property was closed in November 1998.

Piper and his wife, Diannia, are also the owners of Piper's Casino in Silver Springs. Diannia is general manager of that operation.

PLAYER'S CASINO
211 South Virginia Street; never licensed.

See Money Tree.

PLAZA CLUB
320 Sierra Street; licensed from June 15, 1931, through 1932 for chuck-a-luck only.

Owned by O. Nannini, the Plaza Club was a bar that had a chuck-a-luck game for eighteen months in the early 1930s. The site is now part of the Flamingo Hilton Hotel.

Nev. St. Journal, 8 Apr. 32.

PONCIA, JERRY

Jerry Poncia, a Reno native, attended Reno High School with his longtime associate Don Carano. Their first casino partnership was at the Pioneer Inn on South Virginia Street in 1968, and they remain co-owners of that operation. Poncia is also

co-owner of the Eldorado Hotel-Casino on North Virginia Street.

Poncia, an architect by profession, designed and supervised the first four expansions of the Eldorado Hotel-Casino.

Nev. St. Journal, 28 May 92.

PONDEROSA HOTEL-CASINO
515 South Virginia Street; licensed intermittently since 1966, sometimes as a full casino, sometimes for slots only.

In October 1965 the newly formed P and G Hotel Corporation announced that it planned to build a $1.64-million hotel-casino at the corner of California Avenue and Virginia Street. The proposed 165-room hotel was designed by Frank Merrill, and the architect was Jerry Poncia. The P and G Corporation was originally composed of Conrad Priess and three members of the Gastanaga family, Eugene and Jose of Reno and Segundo "Jake" of Winnemucca. The Gastanagas were the principal owners of the Eagle Thrifty Stores.

Construction of the hotel-casino began in December 1965 when the Codding and Wetzel Ski Center was torn down to make room for the new building. By October 1966 the Ponderosa was nearing completion, and the cost of the hotel had risen to over $3 million. Also in October, Conrad Priess, president of the P and G Corporation, announced that Kurt Kerber, former manager of the Riverside Hotel, had been appointed manager of the Ponderosa.

On November 30, 1966, the Ponderosa opened its doors to the public and proudly displayed its many luxury features. Included among the amenities were color televisions in all of the hotel's 165 guest rooms. The decor was early Spanish-American. The hotel offered year-round individual room control of heat or air conditioning, the 112-seat Bonanza Room for formal dining, a 260-seat coffee shop, a lounge seating 116, five executive suites, five bridal suites, and several other facilities.

The opening entertainment at the Ponderosa featured Ray Sawyer, popular Reno organist, in the lounge, and Lenny Herman and his orchestra for dancing. Key personnel employed at the opening of the Ponderosa included Armand d'Amico, executive chef, and Ellis Baldwin, bar manager.

On December 20, 1966, the state licensed a six-man group at the Ponderosa for forty slots and two electronic 21 games. The group had invested $350,000 to open gaming. The six men and their percentages were: Lawrence Tripp, a retired Southern California lawyer who moved to Reno in 1959, the major investor, investing $150,000 for 42.9 percent (he had also held interests in the El Rancho in Las Vegas and the Bonanza in Reno); Conrad Priess, owner and manager of the Red Carpet Motor Lodge, $50,000 for 14.2 percent; Everett Brunzell, a Reno contractor, $50,000 for 14.2 percent; and Eugene, Jose, and Segundo "Jake" Gastanaga, owners of Eagle Thrifty Stores, $33,333 for 9.5 percent each.

In April 1967 the Ponderosa was licensed for five table games, one dice game, one roulette game, and three 21 games. The casino opened on May 4, 1967. Decorator Paul Burton had the honor of making the first bet in the casino. The opening ceremony was held up for a short time when it was discovered that the bankroll for the pit was locked up in the safe, with the key to the safe locked inside. Conrad Priess and Larry Tripp hurried to a downtown bank to borrow a new bankroll. After that, all went well.

In December 1967 the Ponderosa celebrated its first anniversary. At that time, the casino had eighty slot machines, four keno machines, one roulette game, one craps game, and four 21 games. Kelly Black, former longtime Harolds Club employee, was casino manager.

After a three-year, sometimes stormy relationship, Priess, Brunzell, and the Gastanagas parted with Larry Tripp. On December 11, 1969, the state approved Tripp's buyout of his five partners' combined 57 percent of the operation for $1.1 million. In 1970 Larry Tripp was licensed as president, secretary-treasurer, and director of the Ponderosa. Art Green was the new casino manager. In the next few years, Larry Tripp's wife, Kathy, became more and more involved in the operation of the

hotel-casino, and in October 1974 the state licensed Kathy Tripp for 46 percent of the operation.

In August 1979 the Nevada Gaming Control Board announced that the Ponderosa had violated dozens of gaming regulations, and a hearing was set for October 18 to seek a license revocation and a $300,000 fine against the Ponderosa. The meeting resulted in a $95,000 fine against the property and a warning that if the owners did not improve their accounting system by June 1980, the hotel-casino would be closed.

In October 1980 Nevada Gaming Control Board member Jack Stratton said that because of several accounting violations the Ponderosa might be closed by the following month. Stratton was right. On November 23, 1980, the Gaming Commission closed the casino portion of the Ponderosa for failing to furnish two of the three audits that the Commission had directed them to make available at their meeting that day. The Commission felt that the Tripps had purposely failed to comply with its request. Kathy Tripp announced that the hotel and restaurant portions of the Ponderosa would remain open. However, in a short time the property was closed.

During the 1980s several owners were licensed at the Ponderosa. George Prock was licensed from 1982 to 1988, and Josh Ketcham was licensed from 1989 to 1990. Ketcham is noted for operating the Ponderosa as the world's first totally nonsmoking casino.

Currently the Ponderosa is open for business at the same location and is owned and operated by the family of the late Joe Keshmiri. There are slot machines on the property but no table games.

Nev. St. Journal, 7 Oct. 65, 1 Dec. 65 (photo), 18 Oct. 66 (photo), 3 Nov. 66, 27 Nov. 66 (photos), 2 Dec. 66 (photo), 21 Dec. 66, 30 and 31 Dec. 66 (adv.), 5 Jan. 67 (adv.), 23 Mar. 67, 20 Apr. 67, 5 May 67 (adv.), 6 May 67 (photo), 14 Dec. 67 (photo), 11 Dec. 69, 14 May 70, 8 Feb. 71, 24 Feb. 71, 15 Nov. 71, 25 May 73, 11 Oct. 74, 8 Apr. 79, 25 Aug. 79, 19 Oct. 79, 25 Oct. 79, 16 Oct. 80, 24 Nov. 80, 2 Mar. 89.

POOR PETE'S

275 North Virginia Street; licensed from April 9, 1963, to October 30, 1964, for slots and 21.

Peter Perinati, a novelty and vending machine operator from Sacramento, applied for a gaming license in March 1963. He wanted to invest $50,000 for a 100-percent interest in a casino to be known as Poor Pete's. Perinati, forty-three, had leased a concrete building located between the Southern Pacific railroad tracks and Commercial Row on the west side of Virginia Street. He planned to open his casino in mid-June with twenty slots and one 21 game, and he would employ about twenty-five people.

On March 19 the Gaming Control Board recommended denial, without prejudice, because of the proposed casino's location—six feet from the railroad tracks. However, the denial was overturned at the Board meeting the next day, and the casino opened in August 1963.

Peter Perinati died in February 1964. Ronald Darney was granted a temporary gaming license as administrator of the estate of Peter Perinati.

Poor Pete's was closed in October 1964 and reopened in 1965 as the Whistle Stop. In later years the Gem Casino operated at the location for several years. The site of Poor Pete's is now occupied by Fitzgeralds' personnel office.

Nev. St. Journal, 6 Mar. 63, 19 Mar. 63, 30 Mar. 63, 15 May 63, 17 Aug. 63 (adv.), 18 Feb. 64, 19 Feb. 64, 30 Oct. 64.

POWERS, JAMES

James Powers was a co-owner of the California Club on North Virginia Street in 1946 when the name was changed to the Colony Club. He sold out of the Colony Club in June 1956. In August 1956 Powers was one of thirteen people licensed at the Horseshoe Club on North Virginia Street. He was licensed as a co-owner of the El Morocco Club in Las Vegas in 1961.

In 1967 Powers and his associates sold the Horseshoe Club to the Mason family.

Nev. St. Journal, 25 Feb. 50, 28 May 54 (adv.), 20 June 56, 24 Aug. 56, 8 June 61.

PRESTON, ROBERT AND MILDRED

Robert Preston was a 50-percent owner of the Waldorf Club when he died in 1932 at the age of fifty-nine. He had opened the Waldorf Club in 1910 in the old Clay-Peters Building. The Waldorf Club was moved to 142 North Virginia Street in 1929, and Preston took in Charles Brenda as his partner.

When Preston died, his widow, Mildred, inherited 50 percent of the Waldorf. Because of this legacy, Mildred Preston is considered by many to be the first female casino owner in Nevada.

Mildred Preston and Charles Brenda operated the casino until selling it to Joseph and Solomon Bulasky in 1938.

Nev. St. Journal, 20 Dec. 32 (obit.).

PRIESS, CONRAD

Conrad Priess, a real-estate developer and investor, came to Reno from Montana in the 1950s. His first casino investment was in 1966, in the Ponderosa Hotel-Casino on South Virginia Street. In 1969 Priess sold his percentage in the Ponderosa to Larry Tripp.

Priess later became a co-owner of the Silver Spur Casino, the Tahoe Plaza (Palace), and the Onslow Hotel-Casino. He is currently a co-owner of the Crystal Bay Club and the Tahoe Biltmore Hotel-Casino. Both are located on the North Shore of Lake Tahoe.

Nev. St. Journal, 5 May 60, 3 Nov. 66, 20 June 68, 11 Dec. 69, 9 June 77.

PRIMM, ERNEST J.

Ernie Primm was born in Multon, Texas, in 1908. In the early 1940s he was the founder, owner, and operator of the Monterey Club and the Rainbow Club—cardrooms in the Southern California town of Gardena. He came to Reno in 1943 and was one of four partners in the Palace Club from 1943 to 1951. In 1951 Primm and Baldy West had a disagreement, and Primm sold his percentage of the club.

In 1951 Primm triggered the earliest controversy concerning the expansion of gaming in downtown Reno when he tried to open the Primadonna Club on the west side of Virginia Street. Primm fought for four years to get the City Council to permit gaming on the west side of Virginia Street. He went to court and lost both in district court and in the Nevada Supreme Court. But when the results of the 1955 election changed the makeup of the City Council, Primm finally got his gaming license.

The Primadonna, when it opened July 1, 1955, was the first major casino on the west side of Virginia Street. It was soon joined by the Horseshoe Club.

Primm again sparked controversy in 1961 when he tried to expand the Primadonna across Sierra Street. After he spent several months fighting with the City Council and Mayor Bud Baker, the Council approved the expansion in December 1961.

Primm was noted for individuality in his operation as well as in his casino decor. The many bold colors and almost gaudy decorations that were such a part of his casino were unique to the Primadonna. The decorations that will probably be most remembered were the huge statues of showgirls that overlooked both Virginia and Sierra Streets. The showgirl statues that Primm placed on the marquee of the Primadonna in July 1964 had an average height of twenty feet, and the girl in the center was thirty-five feet tall. In 1970 Primm added five more statues on the Sierra Street side of the Primadonna.

In the mid-1960s Primm started buying up property on both sides of Sierra Street as well as property along Douglas Alley and Second Street. By November 1968 he was the largest single owner of contiguous property in downtown Reno.

In 1974 Primm sold the Primadonna and all of his Reno property to the Del Webb Corporation for $5.5 million. He did retain possession of another casino, Whiskey Pete's, located in Jean, Nevada.

Ernie Primm died on August 16, 1981, of pneumonia at a hospital in Newport Beach, California.

Nev. St. Journal, 12 June 43, 17 Nov. 51, 21 May 52, 18 Aug. 81 (obit.), 21 Aug. 81 (editorial).

PRIMADONNA CLUB

241 North Virginia Street; licensed since July 1, 1955, mostly as a full casino.

To tell the story of the Primadonna, it is first necessary to recount the history of the Golden Gate Club. In the summer of 1951, Ernie Primm took a lease on the property located at 241 North Virginia Street. On September 30 he began evicting the tenants. The property had housed the Victory Coffee Shop earlier in the year, and at the time of the eviction, the Morgan Smith Jewelers and the Lincoln Apartments were located on the site.

On October 9, 1951, Ernie Primm filed for gaming licenses for thirty slots, two roulette games, two craps games, and four 21 games. He filed his application under the name of the Golden Gate Club. Two weeks later, the City Council denied Primm's application, stating that it did not want gambling on the west side of Virginia Street.

On February 7, 1952, Ernie Primm was granted a restaurant license for the Cafe Primadonna but was again denied a gaming license. In June 1952 Primm filed a lawsuit against the city, but he lost his suit. Ever persistent, Primm again applied to the state for a gaming license and appealed the court's decision. The state deferred action on the application, and in January 1953 the Nevada Supreme Court ruled against Primm, stating the opinion that the City Council had the right to deny him a gaming license.

Primm never gave up his licensing attempts, and finally, on June 28, 1955, he was licensed for four 21 games and forty-nine slots. The casino was the first licensed on the west side of Virginia Street and was named the Primadonna Club. It opened on July 1, 1955.

The specifics of Primm's business deal were spelled out during his license hearing. Primm was to spend $30,000 to remodel the building, and he was required to put up $75,000 for a bankroll. His lease was for fifty years and called for $2,000 a month in 1955, $3,000 a month in 1956, and $3,500 a month for the next forty-seven years.

Ernie Primm opened his Primadonna

Ernie Primm's Club Primadonna on the west side of Virginia Street, ca. 1957. Courtesy of Neal Cobb.

Club at 6:00 P.M. on July 1, 1955. Ray Sawyer, "Nevada's most popular organist," furnished the music on opening night. Two weeks later, the Primadonna was approved for one craps game, one more 21 game, and twenty more slots.

After a "short summer," the Primadonna closed for remodeling on November 23. The slots, cocktail lounge, and bar remained open. Also closed during that period were the Golden Hotel and the Club Cal-Neva. On December 18, Primm closed the entire club for "alterations." These closings and partial closings forced the Gaming Control Board to take action. In 1956 the Board ruled that casinos that closed down in the winter months, putting hundreds of people out of work, and then opened again in the spring when business and weather got better, could not reopen without going through the entire licensing process. This ruling was an effective deterrent to casinos closing down during the slow winter months.

The only casino grandfathered, in that it was allowed to close in the winter and reopen without being relicensed, was Jim Kelly's Nugget on the North Shore of Lake Tahoe.

The Primadonna reopened on Friday, April 20, 1956. Shortly thereafter, it added twenty more slot machines.

The club continued to expand during the next few years. In January 1959 the Primadonna management announced that the top two floors of the building would be removed as part of a plan to house the casino, bar, restaurant, and slot-machine arcade in one open expanse. The club remained open and in full operation during the remodeling.

In June 1961 the Regional Planning Commission approved Ernie Primm for gambling on Sierra Street, an area hitherto closed to gaming operations. The issue had been debated for several weeks, and there was a two-hour discussion the night the vote was taken. The motion passed 8–2. However, the City Council still had to approve Primm's request, and on August 15 the Council voted 4–3 to deny him the privilege of opening gambling on Sierra

Street. The next week Primm announced plans to build a large restaurant and coffee shop on Sierra Street.

In December 1961, in a major policy change, the City Council agreed to the expansion of the gambling zone to include both sides of Sierra Street between Commercial Row and Second Street. This change, which had been contested for months, allowed Ernie Primm to expand the Primadonna. Immediately after the ruling, Primm resumed construction of his multimillion-dollar theater-restaurant on Sierra Street.

The Primadonna opened a new showroom on the second floor of its new $2-million addition on June 14, 1963. The opening act was a lavish revue titled *Paree, Ooo, La La!* The adults-only revue offered three shows nightly—10:00 P.M., midnight, and 2:00 A.M.

In July 1964 the Primadonna placed five showgirl statues on its marquee. The average height of the showgirls was twenty feet, but the girl in the middle was thirty-five feet tall.

In November 1965 Primm made another major purchase when he bought the old Sears Roebuck Building at 215 South Sierra Street. The transaction gave Primm control, through title or lease, to property a block and a half in width. His North Virginia Street property (the Primadonna Club) extended southward from Douglas Alley and continued westward, the width of the club, to Sierra Street. Now, with his latest purchase, Primm's property crossed Sierra Street to the west side and included an L-shaped parcel of land nearly two city lots in size. A lot and a half fronted Sierra Street, and at the rear, along the north-south alley, the property extended from West Douglas Alley to West Second Street.

In November 1965 Allen Roberts Sr. gave his son, Allen Roberts Jr., 1.9 percent of the Primadonna. That left Roberts Sr., who was general manager of the Primadonna, with 2.86 percent of the club and Ernie Primm owning the remaining 95.2 percent.

In June 1968 Ernie Primm purchased the Pickett Hotel, formerly the William Tell

House, at 245 North Sierra Street. Primm, who paid $400,000 for the property, said he was buying it as a future investment and that he was betting on the future of Reno. He continued his buying binge in November 1968 when he purchased the northwest corner of Sierra and Second Streets for $600,000. This purchase made Primm the largest single owner of contiguous property in downtown Reno. He did not reveal his plans for the property, but he did not rule out the possibility of building a hotel.

In June 1969 Ernie Primm began demolition on his proposed hotel site between Second Street and Douglas Alley on Sierra Street. He announced that "plans are under way for an 800 room hotel which should be ready in two years." He also said that he planned to rebuild the Primadonna, and that "we're going to put a new sign out by the Sierra Street entrance, similar to the one on Virginia Street." True to his word, Primm added a little Virginia Street glamour to his Sierra Street entrance when, in January 1970, he added new signs and five towering showgirl statues to his Sierra Street marquee.

Some well-known gaming personalities who worked at the Primadonna were Allen Roberts Sr., George Piazza, Bill Troye, Hardy Brafford, and Herb Grellman. In the last few years of Ernie Primm's Primadonna, Primm's son, Gary, was vice-president of the operation.

On January 28, 1974, Ernie Primm sold all of his properties to the Del Webb Corporation. On March 1 the Del Webb Corporation applied to the Gaming Control Board for permission to consummate the purchase of the Primadonna—then licensed with thirty table games and eight hundred slot machines—for $5.5 million. Ernie Primm was listed as sole owner, and the $5.5-million selling price included all of Primm's prime downtown property as well as the casino. The sale and transaction were approved on March 21, 1974, and on April 1, 1974, the club was opened as Del Webb's Primadonna.

Phil Arce was named the first president and general manager of Del Webb's Primadonna. One year later, Al Gomes was named general manager, and two years later the position was taken over by Leo Lewis on an interim basis. He was replaced by Tom Aro.

On July 1, 1978, the Del Webb Sahara Reno opened on Sierra Street. By May 1979 the giant hotel-casino was "quietly swallowing up" its sister property, Del Webb's Primadonna. The first signs of the impending transformation came when the famous statues of the chorus girls were taken down from their North Virginia Street perch and replaced by a "Del Webb's Sahara Reno" sign. The two casinos, already linked by a walkway across Sierra Street, were put under the same management and operated as a single property.

The property remained under the management of the Sahara Reno until December 31, 1981, when the Sahara Reno sold all its Reno property to the Hilton Hotel Corporation. The former original Primadonna location became known as the Virginia Street Casino and later as Paco's. Both clubs were managed by the Hilton Corporation. The property is still operating under the direction of the Hilton Corporation and is part of the Flamingo Hilton.

Nev. St. Journal, 21 May 52, 18 June 52, 21 June 52, 24 Mar. 53, 21 Nov. 54 (photo), 28 June 55, 1 July 55 (adv.), 12 July 55, 23 Nov. 55, 18 Dec. 55, 19 Apr. 56 (adv.), 24 July 56, 1 Mar. 57, 22 Mar. 57 (adv.), 4 June 57 (adv.), 16 Oct. 58 (photo), 9 Jan. 59, 8 Sept. 60, 28 June 61, 15 Aug. 61, 22 Aug. 61, 8 Sept. 61, 11 Dec. 61, 12 Dec. 61, 14 June 63, 20 Nov. 65, 30 Nov. 65, 6 June 68, 8 June 68, 4 Oct. 68, 15 Nov. 68, 18 Jan. 69, 20 June 69 (photo), 28 Jan. 70 (photo), 15 Oct. 70, 15 Sept. 72, 14 Dec. 72, 21 Apr. 73, 28 July 73 (obit.), 29 Jan. 74, 1 Mar. 74, 22 Mar. 74, 1 Apr. 74, 5 Apr. 54 (adv.), 10 May 74, 16 Nov. 74 (photo), 20 Mar. 75, 25 Apr. 75, 23 July 76, 5 Oct. 77, 11 Dec. 77 (photo), 9 July 78, 11 May 79 (photo), 13 June 79 (photo), 3 Oct. 79 (adv.).

PUBLIC CLUB

233 Lake Street; licensed from 1932 to August 1933 as the Public Club; licensed in 1933 and 1934 as Crane's; licensed from February 1, 1935, to July 1, 1937, as the Public Club.

The Public Club was licensed by J. B. Crane in 1932 for a craps game and a keno (bingo) game. In 1933 the business became known as Crane's. In 1935 Woo Sing took over the location and added a 21 game to go along with the craps game and the bingo game. The Public Club catered mostly to Asians and other minority groups.

In June 1937 the County Licensing Board revoked the license of the Public Club because narcotics were found on the property, and the business was closed. Currently at the site of the Public Club is the Santa Fe Basque Hotel and Restaurant.

Nev. St. Journal, 6 June 37.

RAINBOW CLUB

146 North Center Street; licensed for slots, keno (bingo), and tango from August 22, 1939, to 1941.

The Rainbow Club was opened at the former site of Don's Drug Store by a group of investors from Long Beach, California. The grand opening of the Rainbow Bingo Salon was held on August 26, 1939, and the new club advertised three bingo cards for ten cents.

In October 1939 the Rainbow Club advertised a nightly cash drawing award of $100 to be given away at 11:30 P.M. During the next few months, the Club Fortune, Harrah's Heart Tango, and the Rainbow Club ran ads almost daily, each club trying to outdo the others by raising the amount of the cash prize drawings and increasing the frequency of drawings. For example, the Club Fortune gave away as much as $150 at some of its free cash drawings. The Rainbow's prizes peaked at $100 in November, and Harrah's Heart Tango's cash prizes peaked at $75. Then suddenly the war was over.

The Long Beach group sold the Rainbow Club to Grace Nerone in February 1940. She appointed a Mr. Prosser as her club manager. On February 7, 1940, the following ad ran in the *Nevada State Journal*: "The Rainbow Bingo Salon will open on Saturday, February 10th at 7:30 P.M. All $50 games are ten cents a card." Within a few weeks, the "bingo war" was once again going full blast. The Club Fortune advertised free cash

drawings of $125, while Harrah's Heart Tango was advertising "No games less than $4.00 and all cards are two for five cents. Free cash drawings for $75 at 11:30 P.M." These competitive cash drawings, inexpensive bingo cards, and higher-prize games continued on through the spring and early summer. Bob Ring stated in his oral history that the Rainbow Club "with their unlimited finances almost busted Bill Harrah and forced him out of the business."

Finally, the "second bingo war" came to an end in the fall of 1940, and the Rainbow Club closed later that same year. It reopened in February 1941 under new management but closed after a few months.

Currently, the Cameo Super Pawn Shop occupies the former location of the Rainbow Club.

Robert A. Ring, "Recollections of Life in California, Nevada Gaming, and Reno and Lake Tahoe Civic Affairs," unpublished oral history, University of Nevada Oral History Program, 1973; *Nev. St. Journal*, 26 Aug. 39 (adv.), 12 Oct. 39, 7 Feb. 40 (adv.), 24 Feb. 40 (adv.), 5 Mar. 40, 5 Feb. 41.

RAINBOW GARDENS

Located at an unknown address on South Virginia Street (Highway 395 South); licensed from May 22 to August 31, 1931, for 21, craps, and roulette.

The Rainbow Gardens was licensed for only three months in the summer of 1931. The exact location and address are unknown to the author, but the club was located just north of the Reno Hot Springs.

RANCHO BAR

3310 South Virginia Street; licensed in 1943 and 1944 for poker only; licensed again from July 1, 1948, to September 30, 1950, for slots, 21, and roulette.

Swede Collet operated a cardroom at this location in 1943 and 1944. The room was called Swede and Jack's.

The Rancho Bar was licensed from July 1, 1948, to September 30, 1950, for slots, 21 and roulette. It was licensed again in October 1954 by Francisco Licini.

Currently at the former location of the Rancho Bar there is a bar called Carl's.

Nev. St. Journal, 6 June 44, 13 Oct. 54.

RED FOX

3155 Kietzke Lane; licensed in 1964 for one 21 game.

In July 1964 the state licensed George Harding for one 21 game at the Red Fox Bar. He invested $2,000. The site is currently occupied by the "R" Bar.

Nev. St. Journal, 22 July 64.

REEF

567 West Fourth Street; licensed from February 28, 1974, to November 4, 1975, for slots, 21, and craps; licensed from May 1, 1978, to April 19, 1979, for slots, 21, and craps.

The Reef Hotel opened in January 1974. The property was owned by Ernest and Nellie Collins. The Collinses leased the gaming to Joe and Paul Elcano, who were licensed by the state as the operators of the Reef.

In December 1974 Lane Fleisher, Marshall Davis, Neil Davis, and Lou Benetti purchased the Reef from Ernest Collins. In March 1975 Benetti, Fleisher, and Stein were licensed for one-third each of the Reef.

In January 1976 the ownership merry-go-round continued as the Reef, now once again owned by Ernest Collins and managed by the Matson-Tyson Investment Company, went on the auction block on January 15. Collins had repurchased the hotel-casino in September 1975. Union Federal Savings and Loan took possession of the Reef with a winning bid of $1,586,872. In March 1976 the Imperial Corporation, owned by Hoshang Shariff and Isaac Poura, took over the operation of the Reef. They opened only the hotel rooms and the coffee shop, but did apply for a gaming license. The Reef operated as a slots-only establishment with Bally Manufacturing licensed as the operator until May 1978. At that time, Isaac Poura was licensed by the Gaming Commission. The Gaming Control Board had recommended denial of the application, but the Gaming Commission approved Poura for a six-month probationary license. Six months later, the conditional licensing was continued.

In March 1979 the Gaming Control Board recommended that Isaac Poura be required to close his 21 game because he was having major problems with his creditors. The Board also recommended that he be allowed to leave in his sixty slot machines. The Gaming Commission disagreed, and on March 22, 1979, the Reef was put out of business when its license was revoked.

The Reef property reopened as the Golden Resort Hotel-Casino on July 1, 1980, with slots and 21 games, but it closed May 29, 1981. The property next reopened in 1984 as the Pearl. It operated as the Pearl until 1988. In 1989 it reopened as Cheers. The property is currently operating as Howard Johnson's Great American Hotel-Casino. There are slot machines on the property, but no table games.

Nev. St. Journal, 18 Oct. 73, 6 Dec. 74, 3 Mar. 75, 13 Jan. 76, 16 Jan. 76, 24 Apr. 76, 19 Feb. 77, 12 May 77, 3 Jan. 78, 16 Mar. 78, 21 Apr. 78, 28 Oct. 78, 16 Mar. 79, 23 Mar. 79.

RENNIE, CHARLES

Charles Rennie was the owner, builder, and first operator of the Town House, located at 39 West First Street. It was a popular bar, restaurant, casino, and cabaret from 1932 to 1955.

In June 1935 Rennie opened the opulent Country Club Casino on South Plumas Street. He was president, general manager, and operator of the property, and the facility was the most elaborate operation in Reno up to that time. After the Country Club operation was up and running, Rennie returned to the Town House to devote his full time to that club.

The Country Club was destroyed by fire in 1936. Shortly afterward, the Town House went into receivership. Rennie's business reputation was destroyed when both the Country Club and the Town House went out of business. The demise of the two clubs signaled the end of Rennie's career as a casino and nightclub operator in Reno.

Nev. St. Journal, 26 June 35, 9 Aug. 50.

RENO BAR

209 East Second Street; licensed in June 1937 for one 21 game only.

The Reno Bar was licensed for one 21 game on June 25, 1937. The property was basically a bar, and the 21 game was licensed only once. The site is now a parking lot.

RENO CASINO

14–16 East Commercial Row; licensed from April 1944 to October 1947.

This address was the site of several gaming businesses over the years, including Bill Harrah's short-lived (1938) Plaza Tango Club. The Reno Casino was the largest of several casinos that operated at this location. It opened at the peak of World War II. At that time it was very difficult to find experienced dealers, as the following preopening help-wanted ad will attest: "The Reno Casino, invites applications from ladies 21 to 31, as well as disabled war veterans, who are willing to learn to deal various games. Up to $90 a week."

The Reno Casino, owned and operated by Dan Stewart, opened on April 1, 1944. On the casino floor were three 21 games, two craps games, one roulette game, one chuck-a-luck game, and twenty-one slots. During the next few months, the Reno Casino ran a heavy (for that era) ad campaign. Ads ran almost daily, stressing the fact that the casino was next door to the well-known Wine House and only a few steps away from the Reno arch, and that it had a full casino and offered a $5,000-limit racehorse keno game. The casino was advertised as "The Club with a Pledge" and offered "Fair Play and a Square Deal to Everyone." The club also advertised that its dice tables had a limit of $100, but that limits could be raised with management approval.

In November 1945 the management of the casino was taken over by the Benningfield brothers, Virgil and Newell. In 1946 M. J. Gallo took over operation of the property, and in 1947 Dewey Richards was licensed for a dice game and an electric roulette wheel. The property was sold to Joe Snyder in October 1947. Snyder renamed it the Rolo Casino.

The former location of the Reno Club is now part of Harolds Club.

Reno City Directory, 1944; *Nev. St. Journal,* 1 Mar. 44 (classified adv.), 8 Mar. 44 (adv.), 1 Apr. 44 (adv.), 28 May 44 (adv.), 24 June 44 (adv.), 30 June 44 (adv. and photo), 1 Aug. 45, 10 Oct. 45, 31 Oct. 45 (adv.), 27 Nov. 45, 14 Mar. 46 (adv.), 1 Apr. 46 (adv.), 4 Jan. 47 (adv.), 5 June 47.

RENO CLUB

232 North Virginia Street; licensed from 1931 to 1934.

242 North Virginia Street; licensed from 1934 to 1942 for bingo only.

The Reno Club, Inc., formerly Rovetti's, opened on July 4, 1931. It featured a deluxe gaming casino and a new type of keno (bingo) game called tango. Its ad read: "Come enjoy pleasure with a profit." The Reno Club is thought to be the first club in Nevada licensed for a bingo game.

In November 1931 the City Council demanded that the license of the Reno Club be revoked because the club was operated by Japanese aliens. A special committee decided that it must be settled in court whether the owners of the Reno Club—Frank Furuta, Fred Aoyama, Oshira Yamagishi, and the late A. W. Shaw—were in violation of the alien gaming law. The case was settled out of court on November 28, 1931, when Frank Furuta produced his birth certificate, which indicated that he was born in Oakland, California, on April 17, 1905. Furuta had borrowed $1,500 from Yamagishi, but the loan had been repaid. Furuta was proved to be the majority owner, and two other minority owners, Grant and Beery, were American citizens.

In 1934 the property at 242 North Virginia Street was renamed the Heart Tango Club and leased to Ed Howe. The property was owned by Mark Yori and managed by Tom Smith.

The Reno Club, now owned solely by Fred Aoyama and Fred Yamagishi, moved its operation to 232 North Virginia Street. The club operated bingo games only, no table games. Early in January 1942, hatred and animosity against people of Japanese ancestry in the aftermath of Japan's attack on Pearl Harbor caused the Reno Club, operated by Fred Aoyama and Fred Yamagishi, to go out of business. A few months later Bill Harrah took over the lease and operated the property until 1948.

In July 1947 Harrah was sued by the Reno Club, Inc., owned by Fred Aoyama. Aoyama claimed that the lease Harrah had signed in 1942 was good for only one year and that he must vacate the property. Aoyama won, and Harrah was ordered to vacate. Fred Aoyama then sold the lease to James O'Keefe. Then, in a lawsuit that took five years to settle, O'Keefe sued Harrah for back lease payments. O'Keefe asked for $133,632. In a settlement reached on May 25, 1952, Harrah was ordered to pay $8,155.

The site is now part of Harolds Club.

Nev. St. Journal, 4 July 31, 13 Sept. 31 (adv.), 24 Nov. 31, 25 Nov. 31, 28 Nov. 31, 24 Dec. 39 (adv.), 7 July 47, 12 Feb. 48, 14 Feb. 48, 17 Feb. 48, 25 May 52.

RENO CLUB

32 West Douglas Alley; licensed from April 14 to August 30, 1931, for one 21 game.

The Reno Club was a bar licensed for one 21 game for five months in 1931. When gaming became legal in March 1931, many small bars and clubs put in gambling games, only to take them out soon after. Many of the one- or two-table game operations discovered that the revenue generated did not warrant the expense of taxes and labor.

Currently the former location of the Reno Club is part of Fitzgeralds Casino-Hotel.

RENO HOT SPRINGS

15001 South Virginia Street; never licensed.

From the 1920s to the 1960s there was a public swimming area located at what was known as the Reno Hot Springs. There were many amenities, such as food and beverage concessions, bath houses, and dressing rooms. In June 1931 manager John Canson announced the completion of a 30-by-60-foot building to house a gaming casino. The casino was to be located just north and west of the large swimming pool. No record is found of gaming ever being licensed at the Reno Hot Springs Resort. The area has been closed for many years.

Nev. St. Journal, 27 June 31.

RENO RACING ASSOCIATION

Located at the Washoe County Fairgrounds near Wells Avenue; licensed from June to September 1931 for roulette, 21, craps, and big-six.

The Reno Racing Association was the name given to a group licensed to operate a casino at the Washoe County Fairgrounds in the summer of 1931. The casino, called Jack Dempsey's Casino, was open during the horse-racing season at the county fairgrounds and was of course open for the Max Baer–Paulino Uzcuduno fight. An article in the *Reno Evening Gazette* of July 1, 1931, stated that "The race track opened with eight races. Nine thousand people attended opening day races and there were twenty gambling games on the property." Bill Graham, Jim McKay, and possibly Ray Kindle were partners along with Jack Dempsey in the summertime operation.

RENO RAMADA HOTEL-CASINO

200 East Sixth Street (corner of Sixth and Lake Streets); licensed from July 24, 1980, to September 30, 1989, for a full casino.

Construction of the Reno Ramada started in March 1979, and on July 2, 1980, the $8-million, seven-story hotel was opened to hotel and restaurant customers only. It offered 150 rooms and a twenty-four-hour restaurant, the Gaming Table. The 4,000-square-foot casino opened a few weeks later, on July 26, with seven 21 games, one craps game, one roulette game, one keno game, and two hundred slot machines. The state licensed Seely Mudd II of Los Angeles and Elsie Mudd Marvin of Monterey, California, to hold 59.4 percent and 39.6 percent respectively in the Ramada Inn. John McClure, general manager, was licensed for 1 percent.

In December 1980 construction began on an expansion of the Ramada. When completed in May 1981, the hotel-casino had added four more floors and 91 more rooms, giving the hotel a total of 241 rooms.

On August 3, 1989, general manager Richard Cooley announced that the Reno Ramada would shut down all table and keno games and a number of slot machines on September 30 as part of a major renovation and remodeling program. On August 6, 1996, the hotel closed. On January 21, 1997, the hotel was sold to a Las Vegas–based investment company, Reno Hotel LLC, headed by Shawn Scott, for $4.1 million. In May 1998 Scott sold the Ramada Plaza to the MTR Gaming Group, Inc., of Chester, West Virginia. It was renamed Speakeasy's Hotel-Casino, and Bruce Dewing was named general manager. There are currently no table games on the property.

Nev. St. Journal, 10 Feb. 76, 29 May 80 (photo), 3 July 80, 17 July 80, 5 Dec. 80.

RENO RANCHO (BOB NEEMAN'S)

9400 West Fourth Street; licensed from May to July 1944 for slots, 21, craps, and roulette.

See Lawton's.

RENO TURF CLUB

Locations at 16 East Second Street, 275 North Virginia Street, 12 East Commercial Row, and currently 280 North Center Street; licensed since 1946 for slots, sports betting, and 21.

The Reno Turf Club was licensed for sports betting, 21, and slots, but its main emphasis was always on sports betting and especially horse-race wagering. Some of the licensees over the years included, but were not limited to, Frankie Frost, William Stremmel, T. Byrens, Hugh Rauhut, Joe Adelman, North Swanson, and Richard Drake.

The Reno Turf Club is still operating at 280 North Center Street.

Nev. St. Journal, 13 Jan. 48, 24 Jan. 48, 10 Feb. 48, 30 Oct. 51, 14 Nov. 51, 4 Feb. 55, 28 Nov. 56, 18 Dec. 56.

RESNICK, CHARLES

Charles Resnick was one of the original owners, along with Sanford Adler, Morris Brodsky, and Louis Mayberg, of the Club Cal-Neva. The quartet purchased the former Club Fortune property from Jack Sullivan, James McKay, and Bill Graham in November 1948 for $350,000 and sold it to a group headed by Dr. Robert Franks and James Contratto in November 1955.

REX CLUB

16–18 East Douglas Alley; licensed from April 1931 to April 1941 for slots, 21, craps, and roulette.

The Rex Club was famous for a shooting incident that occurred there in June 1931. William Graham, a colorful figure in Nevada gaming history who later served six years in a federal penitentiary, shot and killed F. R. "Blackie" McCracken on the morning of June 4, 1931. Graham and McCracken had engaged in a fistfight prior to the shooting, and when McCracken returned to the Rex Club with a .45-caliber automatic he fired two shots, hitting Graham in the arm with one of the shots. Graham fired three shots, the third shot hitting McCracken in the heart and killing him instantly. At the time of the shooting, McCracken was licensed to operate a poker game and a craps game at the Bank Palace Club at 46 East Commercial Row, which was owned by Bill Graham and James McKay.

A coroner's jury convened the day of the shooting ruled that Graham had fired in self-defense. He was exonerated of all blame in McCracken's death.

The Rex Club had operated as an illegal "bootleg joint" prior to the legalization of gambling. When gambling was made legal, the Rex Club was one of the twenty-one original applicants for licenses. The club paid a total of $450 in fees for one craps game, one 21 game, and one roulette game.

The Rex was operated in its early years by Carl Sather; however, the consortium of Bill Graham, Jim McKay, and Tex Hall had controlling interest in the club before the legalization of gaming and for the first few years afterward. Graham and McKay, along with Tex Hall, sold the Rex in late 1935.

The Rex, like so many small clubs in and around Reno in the early days, had several owners and managers during the 1930s. Among them were Pat O'Brien, who was one of the original owners in 1929 and who operated the Rex again in 1936; Phil Blume; and Bill Fox. Both Fox and Blume were managers in the late 1930s.

In April 1941 the Rex was taken over by Fred Saunders and Earl Fuselier. They renamed the property the 333 Club. The site is now part of the Harolds Club property.

Nev. St. Journal, 1 Apr. 31, 5 June 31 (photos), 6 June 31, 30 June 35 (adv.), 11 Aug. 35 (adv.), 19 Dec. 36, 5 Mar. 38 (adv.), 17 June 38, 18 Apr. 41 (adv.).

RICHARDS, JOHN "JACK"

Jack Richards, born in San Jose, California, on February 7, 1902, came to Reno in the early 1940s. He was a co-owner of the Colony Club on North Virginia Street from the late 1940s until 1964, when it was sold to Harolds Club. In November 1964 Richards was licensed for 10 percent of the Riverside Hotel. However, a year later, in November 1965, he sold his interest. He was also licensed as a 25-percent owner of the Plantation Club in Sparks in 1976.

Richards passed away on January 9, 1979.

Nev. St. Journal, 28 May 54 (adv.), 20 June 56, 18 Nov. 64, 27 Aug. 76, 13 Jan. 79 (obit.).

RICHTER, BERNARD "RICK"

In February 1965 Bernie Richter was licensed as the assistant to the president of the Riverside Hotel and as a 12.5-percent owner of the property. His percentage cost him $50,000. The following November, he became a 34-percent owner. Richter's father was Sam Gordon, who owned and operated seven Sam's Hofbrau restaurants. Richter had helped his father design, build, and operate the popular eating establishments.

Bernie Richter was one of the licensees when the Riverside was closed on cheating charges in September 1967.

Nev. St. Journal, 24 Dec. 64, 21 Feb. 65 (photo), 17 Sept. 67.

RICK'S RESORT

West of Reno on the Verdi Road (now known as Mayberry Road)

Built in the early 1900s by Rick DeBernardi, the resort was located on the old Verdi Road. It was the training quarters of Jack Johnson, who defeated Jim Jeffries in Reno on July 4, 1910, for the heavyweight championship of the world. With the coming of Prohibition, the resort went into decline. In the late 1920s it was taken over by Bill Graham and Jim McKay, who renovated it and renamed it the Willows. It became the most exclusive gambling house and speakeasy in all Nevada. The business was destroyed by fire in 1932, during another refurbishing project.

Nev. St. Journal, 8 June 69 (photo).

RIDDICK, BERT

Bert Riddick, a native of New York City, came to Goldfield in 1907. He was a partner with well-known gamblers Nick Abelman and Steve Pavlovich in several operations in Reno and Lake Tahoe as well as in Tonopah. The major casinos Reddick was associated with were the Stateline Club on the South Shore of Lake Tahoe in the early 1940s, the Ship and Bottle on Center Street in Reno from 1931 to 1935, and the Riverside Casino from 1934 to 1949.

Bert Riddick passed away in 1957 at the age of sixty-seven.

RING, ROBERT SR. "BOB"

Bob Ring, born in St. Louis, Missouri, on March 15, 1913, came to Reno from Southern California in August 1938. Bill Harrah, who had first met Ring in Venice, California, in 1937, wanted Bob to manage his newly opened bingo parlor. Their association would last until their deaths. Ring was Harrah's closest confidant, and he served as best man at several of Harrah's weddings.

Bill Harrah, in his oral history, talked about his own ability and willingness to delegate authority and stated that Ring was most often on the receiving end of the delegating. "He took over when he got here and did an admirable job right from day one," Harrah recalled. "Bob and I worked together perfectly all those years." Harrah also called Ring his "alter ego." Although Ring always credited Harrah with the vision that made the operation grow, it was Ring's determination and attention to detail that made Harrah's ideas reality.

As operations expanded over the years, Ring's titles and focus changed many times, from supervising daily operations to sitting in the president's chair. However, his real claim to fame was his friendly, honest service to Harrah's employees, to the community, and to the state of Nevada.

By 1978 Ring and Harrah had built the operation into the largest gaming company in the world, and Ring became the most experienced gaming executive in the nation. To quote Rollan Melton, "Harrah's genius lay in his vision and his keen knack of getting things done through others. He was fortunate to have had Robert Ring, who had an orderly mind, a beautiful personality and a humane streak that endeared him to two generations of employees." In 1980 Bob Ring was appointed vice-chairman, emeritus, of Harrah's Club. He continued in that capacity until his death on March 25, 1992.

At that time, two of Ring's longtime employees, Lloyd Dyer, former Harrah's president, and Holmes Hendricksen, longtime vice-president of entertainment for Harrah's, made statements that said a great deal about Bob Ring. Dyer said, "I never met a man who didn't like Bob Ring." Hendricksen added that, "Other than Bill Harrah, Bob Ring was the person most responsible for Harrah's success." Ring was one of the most influential and powerful men who ever worked in gaming, and he epitomized the personality and business astuteness that enabled the gaming industry to survive and grow in Nevada.

Reno Gazette Journal, 26 Mar 92 (obit.); William F. Harrah, "My Recollections of the Hotel-Casino Industry, and as an Auto Collecting Enthusiast," unpublished oral history, University of Nevada Oral History Program, 1980; *Nev. St. Journal,* 5 Mar. 80, 3 May 87.

RINGSIDE

19 East Douglas Alley; licensed from 1965 to 1972 for 21, poker, and slots.

The Ringside was another club that was more a bar than a casino. It was located where several other clubs had been licensed through the years, including Roy's Bar, Bob's Saloon, the Cherokee, and others. The property was known as the Maverick prior to being renamed the Ringside. Sam Sarlo was the licensee from 1965 until 1970. In 1970 John Russo, a local fight promoter and former football player for St. Mary's College in California, was licensed at the Ringside. Russo operated the Ringside until 1972.

The former location of the Ringside is now part of Harolds Club.

RIO NEVA CLUB

On Mayberry Road; never licensed.

The Rio Neva Club (or Ranch) opened on June 20, 1931. It advertised that it featured a casino, horseback riding, and cottages for rent. It was located on the Mayberry Ranch, five miles west of Reno on the Truckee River at the foot of the Sierra Nevada. The property was once the home of former governor John Sparks.

No record has been found of any legalized gaming at the Rio Neva resort.

Nev. St. Journal, 19 June 31 (adv.), 20 June 31 (article and adv.).

RITZ BAR

8 East Commercial Row; licensed from August 1, 1934, to July 1, 1936, for pan only.

The Ritz Bar was located in the Ritz Hotel. It was owned by C. F. Stevens, Victor Partipilo, and Fred Rosenberg from August 1934 until January 1935. In 1935 Partipilo sold his percentage to J. J. Shannon.

The Ritz Bar closed in July 1936. The site is now part of the Harolds Club property.

Nev. St. Journal, 13 Aug. 31, 29 Apr. 34, 15 Jan. 35.

RIVER HOUSE

9400 West Fourth Street; licensed from January to December 1942 for 21, slots, craps, and roulette.

See Laughton's (Lawton's) Hot Springs.

RIVER INN

9400 West Fourth Street; operated from 1972 to 1979.

See Holiday Spa.

RIVERSIDE HOTEL-CASINO

17 South Virginia Street; licensed from 1931 to 1988 as a full casino.

The Riverside Hotel is located on the original site of the Lake House, built in 1870 by Myron Lake, founder of the settlement of Lake's Crossing. William Thompson purchased the Lake House, a three-story barn-like structure, in 1880 and renamed it the Riverside—a name that was to have a significant place in Reno history.

In 1896 Thompson sold the hotel to Harry Gosse, who subsequently replaced the wooden building with a 110-room, three-story brick structure with ornate towers and moved the Lake House onto the rear of the property. On March 15, 1922, Gosse's Riverside was destroyed in a disastrous fire.

The property stood vacant until 1925, when Gosse sold it to George Wingfield.

Wingfield rebuilt the property and opened what is now known as the Virginia Street section in 1927. When gaming was legalized in 1931, Wingfield was licensed from 1931 until December 27, 1933. At that time, he leased a portion of the hotel to Nick Abelman, Steve Pavlovich, and Bert Riddick. They named the area the Riverside Buffet and offered a dining and bar area as well as a roulette wheel, a 21 game, and a hazard game. In December 1935 Abelman, Pavlovich, and Riddick announced that they would introduce supper dancing at their Riverside Buffet.

In the years ahead, more table games were added. Abelman and Riddick operated the gaming on a month-to-month rental basis for fifteen years.

In April 1949 the Abelman group left the Riverside, and George Wingfield leased the gaming area to Mert Wertheimer. Wertheimer was licensed for one 21 game, one craps game, one roulette game, and ten slots. On May 7, the date of Wertheimer's grand opening at the Riverside, he was quoted as follows: "We have left some of the old and added much that is new."

In September 1949 construction began on an addition to the Riverside, which was to be erected just west of the existing structure. The addition, which was not finished until August 1950, consisted of eighty-four rooms, a swimming pool, a theater-restaurant, a dance floor, and a banquet area. The addition cost $1.5 million, and the swimming pool was the first to be built in a Reno hotel.

Mert Wertheimer made the Riverside famous for featuring big-name entertainers. His opening act on July 1, 1950, was the well-known headliner Ted Lewis. In August 1951, Frank Sinatra was the headliner, and over the next several years just about every big-name entertainer in America played the Riverside showroom. The Riverside, the Mapes, and the Golden competed with each other to present the top acts in show business, to the extent that during the forties, fifties, and sixties Reno was known as the entertainment capital of the world.

In August 1951 Lou Wertheimer, Mert's brother, was licensed as a partner at the Riverside. The property was also licensed for 105 slots, four craps games, two roulette games, and ten 21 games. In July 1954 the Riverside completed a three-story addition that cost $500,000 and doubled the number of hotel rooms.

On December 17, 1955, George Wingfield sold the Riverside to Lou and Mert Wertheimer, Baldy West, and Ruby Mathis for $4,010,000. The property was then six stories high and had two hundred hotel rooms. Prior to this time, the Wertheimer brothers had leased the Riverside gaming area but had not owned the hotel. The new group immediately named Lee Frankovich as hotel manager. Frankovich had previously been employed as hotel manager of the Commercial Hotel in Elko and for the last year had worked for Harrah's Club.

In January 1958 the Crummer Corporation of Reno purchased the Riverside for a price estimated to be between $4 and $5 million. The Wertheimer group was given a ten-year lease on the casino, bars, restaurants, and entertainment. The Crummer group would operate the hotel only. Five months after leasing the Riverside, Lou Wertheimer died, and two months later Mert Wertheimer also died. The two deaths effectively ended the group operation, and in August 1958 Virgil Smith took over the lease. Smith's corporate officers were his wife, Nelva, and his longtime attorney, Clark Guild Jr.

September 1958 saw the end of a longtime relationship. The Bill Clifford Orchestra, which had performed at the Riverside for seven years, was replaced by the Eddie Fitzpatrick Orchestra. Fitzpatrick had been at the Mapes for ten years but left when Charles Mapes ended entertainment in the famous Mapes Sky Room.

In December 1959 Virgil Smith bought the Riverside for $5 million from the Crummer Corporation, after having leased the property for sixteen months. In January 1960 Smith sold 49 percent of the hotel to Harold Munley, Dr. Robert Franks, Sam Leavy, and Jack Douglass, and in February Smith announced that he would sell his remaining interest to his four partners. In April 1960 the sale was approved by the Gaming Commission, and Virgil Smith was completely out of the Riverside. Although there were obvious policy differences between Smith and his partners, the pressure of operating the hotel-casino had been a strain on Smith's health and he felt it best for him to leave the Riverside.

The new owners and their percentages, as of April 1960, were: Dr. Robert Franks, 44 percent; Harold Munley, 14 percent; Jack Douglass, 14 percent; Sam Leavy, 6 percent; and the corporation, 22 percent.

In September 1960 the Riverside was sold for the third time in less than a year. Each sale was for "around five million." The new owner was Bill Miller, a former investor in the Last Frontier Casino in Las Vegas. The sellers were Franks, Munley, and Leavy. Jack Douglass had sold his percentage a few weeks earlier.

In November 1960 the Gaming Commission okayed Miller, former licensee at the Last Frontier, the Sahara, and the Dunes, for 95 percent of the Riverside, with Franks retaining the remaining 5 percent.

In January 1961 Gerald Layne, the Riverside casino manager, disappeared after leaving Reno with several thousand dollars on his person. He was headed for a high-stakes poker game in Placerville. His abandoned car was later found in the Harrah's Tahoe parking lot, but Layne was never found.

During the next few months, Frank Cunardi and Roy Denhart were licensed for small percentages of the Riverside, and E. F. McGarry and Gene Young were licensed for a percentage of the keno game.

While under Bill Miller's ownership, the Riverside introduced a female impersonator show that caused such an uproar that the Reno City Council passed an anti-impersonation ordinance.

In June 1962 Miller, who had owned the Riverside since November 1960, sold his interest to Raymond Specter for "over five million dollars." Specter was a former director and principal stockholder of Hazel Bishop, Inc., a cosmetic firm in New York City. After taking over the Riverside, Specter obtained a $2.75-million loan from the Central States, Southeast, and Southwest pension funds of Jimmy Hoffa's Teamsters Union. With the loan he retired the hotel's obligations to the Crummer Corporation and the Wingfield interest. Specter had to issue a deed of trust to the pension fund with the hotel real estate as security for the loan, which called for monthly payments of $20,625.

On December 20, 1962, the Riverside was closed and the corporation filed for bankruptcy. Three hundred and twenty-five employees were put out of work five days before Christmas, without their final paychecks. In explaining the closure, a hotel executive said, "We simply ran out of money. A payment of $35,000 was due yesterday and we didn't have the money."

In February 1963 the Hughes Porter Corporation of Nevada purchased the Riverside for $3.5 million. In July Hughes Porter leased the property to a ten-man corporation known as Riverside Incorporated. The corporation was composed of Jack Streeter, Calvin "Red" Swift, Leonard Wykoff, Don Hall, John Sanford, Jack Sommers, Ferdie Sievers, Richard Fraser, James Ensign, and Neil Johnson.

On July 25, 1963, the Riverside reopened with two hundred slots, two craps games, one roulette game, and eight 21 games. Jack Sommers was hotel manager and John Sanford casino manager.

In June 1964 Lee DeLauer was approved by the Gaming Commission to become general manager of the Riverside Inc. Corporation and to sublease the hotel, food, and bar operation. The Riverside Corporation already operated the casino. DeLauer brought in a new management team consisting entirely of Reno people. The department managers whom he hired, who together had over two hundred years of Reno residency, were Bill Goupil, casino manager; Bill Campbell, casino supervisor; William "Bull" DeMarco, casino supervisor; Jim Jeffers, purchasing; Dee Garrett, credit manager; Jake Sigwart, keno manager; and Neil Brooks, comptroller. DeLauer, who owned 25 percent of the corporation, had as his partners Leonard Wykoff, L. A. Dickinson, Neil Johnson, James Ensign, Don Hall, Calvin "Red" Swift, Richard Fraser, and Ferdie Sievers.

After a short time, it became obvious that the reorganization of the Riverside wasn't going to work. In November 1964 the Gaming Commission approved Bernie Einstoss, John Richards, and Andrew Desimone to purchase the Riverside. Ed Olsen, chairman of the Gaming Commission, said, "The Riverside has many financial problems, its chances of surviving the winter without new capital are pretty slim." In December James Lloyd Sr. and Bernie Richter also bought an interest in the Riverside. The new arrangement provided for Einstoss to own 50 percent with Richter, Lloyd, Desimone, and Richards each owning 12.5 percent.

In November 1965 Richter bought Richards's share of the Riverside, and in February 1966 Lloyd bought Bernie Einstoss out of the Riverside. This arrangement made Lloyd a 50-percent owner, Richter a 34-percent owner, and Desimone a 16-percent owner.

The gambling at the Riverside was closed on September 16, 1967, after gaming agents confiscated crooked dice from the craps table. On September 26, 1967, Newell Hancock was named trustee to manage the Riverside and keep it operating. The showroom and the gambling were closed, but the restaurant, bar, and hotel rooms remained open.

On December 29, 1967, the Gaming Commission revoked the corporate license of the Riverside as well as the individual licenses of James Lloyd Sr., Bernie Richter, and Andy Desimone. The Commission did allow Lloyd to keep his $100,000 investment in his slot-route operation, the A-1 Novelty Company.

On February 5, 1968, the Riverside closed completely. The hotel had been sold the day before, at auction, to the Teamsters Union Pension Fund for $1.9 million. The bid was actually nothing more than a paper transaction, because the Teamsters already held a first deed of trust on the property for $2,745,000. Second and third deeds of trust were held by Hughes Porter and the Reno Riverside Hotel, Inc. On September 5, the Riverside was sold for $3 million to three southern businessmen, Winfield Moon of Birmingham, Alabama, and Jake Clegg and Jim Saccomanno of Houston, Texas.

The hotel was not reopened until May 16, 1969, and it opened without gambling. It was closed again on November 3, this time by the Internal Revenue Service, which was owed $46,283 in back taxes by the hotel corporation for the quarter ending September 30, 1969. On November 19, 1969, Robert Berry, an attorney for a New York corporation, Bonafide Productions, Inc., presented a check for $84,500 to the IRS to settle the claim against the Riverside. The corporation had no plans to open the hotel.

In May 1970 Texas land developer William Phares purchased the Riverside for $3 million. He was licensed for two craps tables, one roulette game, eleven 21 games, one keno game, and two hundred slots. He was scheduled to open the hotel-casino on July 4.

On July 3, Phares was killed in an automobile accident. One week later, on July 10, 1970, it was announced that the Riverside would go on the auction block again, because Phares's death prevented the sale from closing. The Teamsters Union Pension Fund—for the second time—bought back the 186-room hotel on October 7. Its bid of $1.8 million was the only one made.

On January 6, 1971, Jessie Beck purchased the Riverside for "an amount in excess of three million dollars." She announced that she expected to spend more than $1 million renovating the building. In February 1971 the Jessie Beck Corporation was licensed for one hundred slots, nine table games, and one keno game.

The Riverside reopened on April 1, 1971, with Arthur Allen as hotel manager; Jim Hunter, formerly of Harolds Club, as director of public relations; Don McDonnell as casino manager; Augie Landucci as assistant casino manager; and William Salas, Gene Mattson, and Art Aloiau as shift managers. Some of the people who were licensed as shift managers in the coming years included Kelly Black, Clark Brown, Chuck Clifford, Keith Jones, Mary Delaplaine, and Connie Paris.

In March 1978 the Riverside was sold to Harrah's Club as part of a three-way real estate deal with Overland Inc. and Jessie Beck. Harrah's purchased the Riverside in order to trade it to the Overland (Pick Hobson) for that firm's old hotel-casino at the corner of Center Street and Commercial Row. The Overland site, on which Harrah's had taken a long-term lease in March 1977, would become the site of Harrah's multimillion-dollar expansion.

On April 21, 1978, the Gaming Commission okayed Pick Hobson to take over the Riverside and licensed J. J. Page as general manager, Robert Hawkins as casino manager, and Richard Sturdivant, Anthony Gabriel, and Steve Gurasevich as vice-presidents and directors.

In November 1986 Pick Hobson, faced with a debt service of over $4.6 million and a decreasing market share, filed for bankruptcy. A little over a month later, on December 30, 1986, Hobson closed the casino. He was able to keep the restaurant and the hotel rooms operating until November 1, 1987, when he had to close down because operating expenses exceeded the business's revenue. On November 25, 1987, Hobson turned over the hotel and other property to the Valley Bank of Nevada. The action left nearly three hundred other creditors owed about $1.4 million.

On June 20, 1989, a Canadian investment group headed by Peter Ng, a Canadian businessman, purchased the Riverside from Valley Bank of Nevada for an undisclosed price. Despite talk of plans for improvements and development of the Riverside, Ng did nothing with the property.

Finally, in 1997, after years of bargaining and negotiation with Ng, the City of Reno took possession of the Riverside. On November 14, 1997, demolition crews began to tear down the newer section of the Riverside Hotel, which had been built in 1951, leaving the older portion, which was built in 1927, untouched for the time being. On February 25, 1998, the Reno City Council gave the final approval to a contract with Oliver McMillan, a San Diego developer, to renovate the Riverside and turn the property into artists' lofts, restaurants, and shops.

Nev. St. Journal, 14 Dec. 35, 29 Mar. 42 (adv.), 2

Apr. 49, 5 Apr. 49, 27 Apr. 49, 7 May 49, 1 Sept. 49, 25 Mar. 50, 30 June 50, 11 Aug. 51 (adv.), 30 Aug. 51, 18 July 54, 17 Dec. 55 (photos), 3 Jan. 56, 12 Jan. 56, 19 Jan. 56 (photos), 15 May 56, 11 June 57, 21 Jan. 58, 20 May 58, 22 July 58, 20 Aug. 58, 23 Sept. 58, 25 Sept. 58, 30 Sept. 58, 15 Oct. 58 (photo), 10 Dec. 59, 25 Dec. 59, 3 Jan. 60, 7 Jan. 60, 21 Jan. 60, 24 Feb. 60, 27 Feb. 60, 2 Mar. 60, 20 Apr. 60, 7 July 60, 21 Sept. 60, 29 Sept. 60, 3 Nov. 60, 22 Nov. 60, 28 Dec. 60, 4 Jan. 61, 5 Jan. 61, 10 Jan. 61, 17 Feb. 61 (photo), 22 Feb. 61, 11 Apr. 61, 26 Apr. 61, 21 June 61, 9 Nov. 61, 25 Nov. 61, 6 Dec. 61, 16 Mar. 62, 8 June 62, 14 June 62, 20 June 62, 23 Aug. 62, 24 Aug. 62, 24 Sept. 62 (photo), 16 Oct. 62, 25 Oct. 62, 25 Nov. 62, 29 Nov. 62, 21 Dec. 62, 22 Dec. 62, 1 Jan. 63, 26 Jan. 63, 21 Feb. 63, 3 July 63, 15 July 63, 17 July 63, 25 July 63 (photos and adv.), 22 Oct. 63, 25 Apr. 64, 5 June 64, 12 June 64 (photo), 16 June 64, 26 July 64 (photo and adv.), 14 Nov. 64, 17 Nov. 64, 24 Dec. 64, 19 Jan. 65, 17 Feb. 65, 21 Feb. 65 (photo), 17 Nov. 65, 24 Dec. 65, 7 Jan. 66, 16 Feb. 66, 2 May 66, 17 Sept. 67, 18 Sept. 67, 19 Sept. 67, 21 Sept. 67, 26 Sept. 67, 29 Dec. 67, 4 Feb. 68, 17 July 68 (photos), 18 July 68, 7 Sept. 68, 13 Dec. 68, 22 Apr. 69, 30 May 69, 23 Sept. 69, 4 Nov. 69, 19 Nov. 69, 6 June 70, 19 June 70, 2 July 70, 3 July 70, 10 July 70, 8 Oct. 70, 11 Dec. 70, 5 Jan. 71, 6 Jan. 71 (photo), 8 Jan. 71, 29 Jan. 71, 15 Feb. 71, 19 Feb. 71, 4 Mar. 71 (photos), 30 Mar. 71, 1 Apr. 71 (photos), 7 July 71, 19 Aug. 71, 2 Apr. 72 (adv. and photos), 24 Aug. 73, 21 July 75 (photo), 16 Sept. 76, 21 Jan. 77, 13 Jan. 78, 10 Mar. 78, 13 Apr. 78, 31 Dec. 86.

ROARING CAMP

128 Lake Street; licensed from June 1, 1946, to February 1949 for slots, 21, craps, roulette, and big-six.

The Roaring Camp, also known as Stagg's Roaring Camp, opened on June 1, 1946, and housed what was probably the largest collection of western memorabilia in the western United States. It featured over two thousand guns, including Tom Mix's personal gun collection, a "prairie schooner," a host of old-time carriages, hundreds of artifacts of all kinds related to western life, and dozens of mechanical pianos, player pianos, and organs of all kinds.

At the bar, patrons sat astride authentic saddles while enjoying their drinks and perhaps waiting to eat in the restaurant, which was operated by local favorite Ramona and featured the best Mexican food in town.

Unfortunately, during its short life of less than three years, the Roaring Camp was plagued with problems in the gaming end of the business. Raymond Stagg was the principal owner of the establishment, but he frequently leased the gaming to other people, and he had trouble with some of them. In June 1946 Bill Bush and Manuel Fleisher were licensed as operators of a mechanical horse-race game, but a month later Stagg and his partner, R. J. Forwood, kicked them out of the Roaring Camp. Bush and Fleisher then sued Stagg and Forwood for $15,840 in punitive damages. The lawsuit was settled in October, when Judge McKnight ruled that the plaintiffs, Bush and Fleisher, had tampered with the racehorse game they were leasing and operating in a room at the rear of the Roaring Camp. Since tampering with any gambling game was prohibited by state law, the judge ruled that the game was being conducted in an illegal manner, which gave the proprietors the right to break the lease and remove Bush and Fleisher from the business.

On December 4, 1947, Murl Hell, a dealer at the Roaring Camp, was arrested for dealing a 21 game with marked cards. The accused was employed by Virgil Benning-field, who had the gambling concession at that time. Cheating charges against Hell were finally dismissed on January 23, 1949, after several witnesses, including Ken Clever, a dealer at the Christmas Tree Restaurant, proved that the cheating charge was a frame-up perpetrated by a disgruntled customer.

On December 31, 1947, Ray Stagg was licensed for twenty-two slot machines at the Roaring Camp, but no table games were licensed.

Customer charges against the business came up again on July 24, 1948, when Ray Stagg was charged with operating a "plugged slot machine." During an inspection, machines were found with a piece of metal riveted to the third reel to prevent them from paying jackpots or the three-bells payoff. Stagg was bound over for trial. The case was not resolved until April 1949, when cheating charges against Stagg were dismissed. It had been determined that a former employee had rigged the slots without Stagg's knowledge.

On February 19, 1949, local newspapers announced that Ray Stagg had sold the Roaring Camp to Raymond I. "Pappy" Smith of Harolds Club for $300,000. Stagg

Jerry Cobb (r.), photographer and radio personality, and a friend sitting on bar stools (real saddles) at Stagg's Roaring Camp. Courtesy of Neal Cobb and the Nevada Historical Society.

went to work for Harolds Club as a public-relations person and traveled all over the United States promoting Harolds Club. He signed a ten-year contract that paid him $15,000 a year.

Harolds Club opened the Roaring Camp on Saturday, April 2, 1949. Harolds operated the Roaring Camp until late in the year, then it closed the club. The Smiths eventually transported all Stagg's memorabilia to Harolds Club and placed the collection in a section of the club that they appropriately named the Roaring Camp Room. For years, all or portions of the one-of-a-kind collection were displayed in Harolds Club and were considered a famous piece of Reno history. After Harolds Club was sold, first to the Summa Corporation and later to the Fitzgerald Group, the collection was always "in harm's way." In December 1993 the collection was sold to the Butterfield and Butterfield Auction House for an undisclosed sum. An auction was held on May 31, and by June 1, 1994, the famous collection was no more.

The site of Stagg's Roaring Camp Room at the corner of Lake and Second Streets is now occupied by the Long Neck Bar and Grill.

Reno Telephone Directory, 1945; *Nev. St. Journal,* 3 June 46, 4 June 46, 25 June 46, 3 Aug. 46, 23 Oct. 46, 24 Oct. 46, 20 July 47 (adv.), 4 Dec. 47, 30 Dec. 47, 23 Jan. 48, 24 July 48, 6 Aug. 48, 6 Oct. 48, 20 Feb. 49, 16 Mar. 49, 31 Mar. 49 (adv.), 7 Apr. 49; *Reno Gazette-Journal,* 29 May 94.

ROBBINS, HARRY AND ED

Harry and Ed Robbins were a father-and-son team who opened the Nevada Club on Virginia Street in 1941. They operated the mostly bingo and slot club by themselves until 1946, when they entered into a partnership with Dan Sullivan, Lincoln Fitzgerald, Ruby Mathis, and Mert Wertheimer.

In 1952 a new corporation agreement was set up, and Fitzgerald took complete control of the Nevada Club.

ROBBIN'S NEVADA CLUB

224 North Virginia Street; licensed from April 1941 to March 1946 as a full casino.

Robbin's Nevada Club was opened in April 1941 by Harry and Eddie Robbins at the former site of Langley's Tango Club. The location originally operated as a penny-roulette parlor. It was open from 11:00 A.M. to 3:00 A.M. daily and was advertised as the "largest exclusive roulette parlor in the state of Nevada." In August, the Robbinses added 21, craps, and slots, and in April 1942 they added a bingo game. Bingo was popular in Reno in the 1940s, and by May 1944 the Robbinses were featuring bingo for ten cents a card, with a minimum prize of $6 per game.

In January 1945 Robbin's Nevada Club was licensed for ten 21 games, four roulette games, one faro game, and one racehorse keno game. In February 1946 the table-game licenses were increased to cover a total of twenty games.

The next month, the Robbins family joined forces with Dan Sullivan, Lincoln Fitzgerald, Mert Wertheimer, and Ruby Mathis to form a partnership. The Robbins name was dropped, and the property was known from then on as the Nevada Club.

The property closed in December 1997. It remains closed. *(See Addendum 1)*

Nev. St. Journal, 20 June 41 (adv.), 3 July 41 (adv.), 4 July 41 (adv.), 28 Aug. 41 (adv.), 9 Nov. 41 (adv.) 30 Apr. 42 (adv.), 5 May 42, 7 May 44 (adv.), 1 Nov. 44 (adv.), 15 Feb. 46, 13 Mar. 46, 17 June 47, 15 Oct. 47, 13 May 64; Reno City Directory, 1941; Reno City Directory, 1942; Reno Telephone Directory, 1945 (adv.).

ROBERTS, ALLEN SR.

Allen Roberts Sr. was licensed as general manager and 4.7-percent owner of the Primadonna Club in September 1961. He continued as general manager until he retired in 1971 and returned to the town of his birth, Genevieve, Missouri. He died there two years later, in July 1973, at the age of seventy-three.

Nev. St. Journal, 13 Mar. 46, 20 Sept. 61, 28 July 73 (obit.).

ROLO CASINO

14–16 East Commercial Row; licensed from November 1947 to April 1950 for slots, 21, craps, roulette, poker, and a horse book.

In October 1947 Joe Snyder purchased the Rolo Club from M. J. Gallo. Snyder was licensed for one craps game, one roulette game, one poker game, and fourteen slots when he first opened the casino. He later added a 21 game and a horse-race book under the direction of Elwood Haggerty.

In 1950 Snyder sold the property to Harry Weitz and Irving Schneider. They licensed the property as the Sierra Turf Club in April 1950. The site is now part of Harolds Club.

Nev. St. Journal, 30 Nov. 47 (adv.), 20 Jan. 48, 16 Mar. 48 (adv.), 12 Jan. 49, 13 Sept. 49, 11 Jan. 50.

ROSASCO, LOUIS

Louis Rosasco, a native of Reno, was born on February 7, 1903. He began his musical career in his hometown but soon was a featured accordion player on the West Coast theater circuit. In 1927 he led his own orchestra in the Senator Hotel in Sacramento. In 1931 he returned to Reno, along with Byron Curlee, and opened the Coconut Ballroom on North Virginia Street.

During the 1930s Rosasco appeared in many nightclubs, cabarets, and casinos in and around the Reno area. He was known as someone who knew no strangers and liked everyone he met. A large man who loved to dress in brown clothing, he was always jovial and trying to make friends out of strangers.

In the 1930s he became a co-owner of the Cedars, a popular Reno nightclub, and

Louis Rosasco, bar manager of the Palace Club, in 1957. Courtesy of Jan Rosasco Savage.

in 1944 he became manager of the Club Fortune (now known as the Club Cal-Neva) at that time the most popular night-spot, cabaret, and casino in downtown Reno. In 1945 he was co-owner, along with Cam Mottino, of Louie and Cam's on West 2nd Street. In 1952 he was the manager and host of the popular downtown spot, the Picadilly. In 1953, Rosasco, along with twelve others, was licensed as a co-owner of the Palace Club. Three years later he was licensed as co-owner of the Tahoe Plaza (Palace) Club on the South Shore of Lake Tahoe.

Rosasco belonged to a time in Reno when smaller clubs were often owned by people who had expertise in certain areas of a casino. For example, a pit man or a keno man might be sold a percentage of a club and be expected to run that particular department. Rosasco became a part-owner of a casino because of his knowledge and ability to run a food and/or beverage department. When Rosasco became co-owner and manager of the bar department at the Palace Club, liquor sales in the casino soared.

Rosasco died in 1968 at age sixty-four. However, his legacy continues. His daughter, Jan Savage, has been an entertainer in the Reno–Lake Tahoe area for several years, and his grandsons, Tony Savage and Ron Savage, are both well known for their musical talents, not only in Reno but throughout the country.

Nev. St. Journal, 17 Dec. 31, 1 Sept. 45 (adv.), 29 June 52, 11 Dec. 53, 20 June 56; Raymond Sawyer, *Reno, Where the Gamblers Go!* (Reno: Sawston Publishing Company, 1976).

ROSS, JOHN

John Ross, born on May 31, 1900, in Fairmount, Virginia, came to Nevada in 1932. He and his wife, Alice, built and opened the Christmas Tree in 1946 as a bar, and in 1947 they added a restaurant. Gaming was usually evident at the Christmas Tree, but Ross always leased out the tables. Ross also was owner and/or operator of the Mount Rose Lodge, the Riverfront, and the Sunflower. He was also licensed at the Cedars and Johnny's Open Door.

Ross passed away on April 30, 1974, in Incline Village.

Nev. St. Journal, 3 Feb. 55, 1 Mar. 74, 30 Apr. 74 (obit.).

ROULETTE CLUB

244 North Virginia Street; licensed in 1935.

In the Reno City Directory of 1935 there was a listing for a Roulette Club located at 244 North Virginia Street. This is the only available information about this establishment. The La Rue Club was licensed at this location in March 1935.

The site is now part of Harolds Club.

ROVETTI, GENE

Gene Rovetti, who was born in Italy in 1891, came to Reno in 1900. He was widely known as a nightclub owner. His best-known resort was the Cedars, which was located at 1585 South Virginia Street and was a popular nightclub of the Prohibition era and the early 1940s. Rovetti also owned the Blue Bird Club on Commercial Row, which later became the Haymarket Club, and he was co-owner of the Rovetti Brothers Grocery Store, which occupied the present site of Harolds Club. Other clubs in which Rovetti had an interest included the Topper, a cocktail lounge on Sierra Street; and Lawton's Club at Lawton's Hot Springs.

Rovetti died on September 14, 1960, at his home at 1625 Lakeside Drive.

Nev. St. Journal, 16 Dec. 36, 26 July 45, 15 Sept. 60 (obit.).

ROY'S COCKTAIL LOUNGE (ROY'S BAR)

19 East Douglas Alley; licensed in 1961 for 21 only.

Roy's was originally a bar located in Douglas Alley and owned by Earl Roberts. In early November 1961 Roberts applied for a gaming license for a $10-limit 21 game. His application was originally deferred, but the license was granted on November 21, 1961. On June 26, 1962, Roberts was licensed for a poker game.

In September 1962 the Reno City Council allowed Earl Roberts to change the name of Roy's Cocktail Lounge to Maverick's Saloon. The property operated as

Maverick's Saloon until 1965. The site is now part of Harolds Club.

Nev. St. Journal, 9 Nov. 61, 10 Nov. 61, 21 Nov. 61, 27 Sept. 62.

RUGGERIO, VAL

Val Ruggerio was first granted a gaming license at the Christmas Tree on the Mount Rose Highway from September 1963 to February 1964. In February 1966 Ruggerio, along with Eugene Belluomini, was licensed at Val's Club, located at 333 North Second Street. He was also licensed as casino manager and 5-percent owner of the King's Inn on West Third Street in January 1975.

Ruggerio is still involved in gaming. Currently, he heads a tour group that brings gamblers to Reno.

Nev. St. Journal, 3 Feb. 66, 21 Apr. 66, 4 Jan. 75.

S.P. CLUB

136 East Commercial Row; licensed from November 1, 1965, to April 1, 1969, for poker, pan, slots, and 21.

The S.P. Club was a bar that had some card tables and a few slot machines in the rear of the building. It was located at an address that for many years was home to cardrooms and/or bars. The site is now part of the Harrah's Club parking garage.

SAGEBRUSH CLUB

129 East Douglas Alley; licensed from April 3 to June 30, 1931, for slots and 21.

The Sagebrush Club was a small bar that was licensed for one 21 game and five slot machines for three months during the first days of legalized gaming in 1931. The site is currently part of Harrah's parking garage.

SAGEHEN CLUB

1099 South Virginia Street; licensed from April to December 31, 1945, for 21 only.

The Sagehen Club was a small bar that catered to locals. It was licensed for one 21 game for approximately eight months in 1945. The site is now occupied by the 1099 Club.

SAHARA RENO

255 North Sierra Street; licensed from July 1, 1978, to December 29, 1981, as a full casino.

Early in November 1976 the Del Webb Corporation announced that it would start construction of a seventeen-story, 440-room hotel as soon as the City of Reno gave its approval. Webb's spokesman estimated that the cost of the facility would be between $50 million and $75 million. Construction began in April 1977, and in December the Del Webb Corporation announced that it was expanding the project, which was still under construction, to twenty stories and 610 hotel rooms.

The Sahara Reno property, which also included the Del Webb Primadonna property on Virginia Street, opened on July 1, 1978. Doyle Mathia, a former longtime employee of Harrah's Club, was the first vice-president and general manager of the Sahara Reno. His assistant was Vlad Chuhlantseff. Managing the casino was Ted Kelty, another former Harrah's employee, and in charge of the keno department was Vart Markarian. The casino area opened with nine hundred slot machines, sixty-four 21 games, seven poker games, two mini-baccarat games, four roulette games, two big-six wheels, and one keno game. Natalie Cole was the opening act in the Sahara Showroom.

Early in 1979 the Primadonna property on Virginia Street was quietly swallowed up by its larger relative, the Sahara Reno, and the Primadonna image began to be phased out. The first and most noticeable change came when the famous "Primadonna Dollies" showgirl statues were removed from the marquee on Virginia Street and replaced with Sahara Reno signs.

Also in 1979 the Sahara Reno added three new Oriental games, pai-gow, sic-bo, and fan-tan, in a move designed to capture the Asian trade from the San Francisco Bay Area.

In June 1980 Doyle Mathia announced at the stockholders' annual meeting that in 1978 and 1979 the property had lost money. However, in 1979 new marketing techniques, streamlined hotel operations, a bingo game, four Broadway stage productions (including *The Music Man* and *Annie*), and expanded transportation efforts in Northern California had "turned things around," and the hotel-casino books were now in the black.

Mathia's optimistic comments at the stockholders' meeting failed to stop rumors that the property was for sale. The Sahara Reno continued to be plagued by labor troubles and management turnover. In the first thirty months that the hotel-casino was open, the property had three general managers and five casino managers, and in addition Del Webb's casino division had gone through three chief executive officers in less than four years.

Problems continued to multiply at the Sahara Reno, and in late 1981 the rumors of an impending sale were put to rest when it was announced that the Hilton Corporation would assume ownership of the Sahara Reno on December 29, 1981. The purchase price was $34.5 million (one half of what the property was appraised for less than six months earlier).

The property is now operating as the Reno Flamingo Hilton.

Nev. St. Journal, 6 Nov. 76 (photo), 12 Apr. 77, 11 Oct. 77 (photo), 8 Dec. 77, 14 Mar. 78, 25 June 78, 1 July 78, 11 Mar. 79, 11 May 79, 13 June 79 (photo), 3 Oct. 79, 7 June 80, 31 Aug. 80. 21 Sept. 80 (photo), 23 Dec. 81.

SAHATI, EDDIE

Eddie Sahati was called the "ultimate gambler" by Harold Smith Sr. of Harolds Club. Smith said, "Nothing else, not even beautiful women, could stir such a passion in him. Nothing else compared to gambling." Sahati was known to play craps for hours. Harolds Club furnished a stool for him at the craps table and brought him food and drink, and he would play for as long as forty-eight hours without sleep.

In his prime, Eddie Sahati was a large man, six feet tall and weighing 215 pounds. He had straight black hair that he combed straight back. He dressed like a fashion plate and spoke softly, never raising his voice.

In the mid-1940s, Sahati was only in his thirties and already a millionaire. He had made his money starting with illegal race books in the San Francisco area. In 1945 he and his brother Nick purchased the Stateline Club at the south end of Lake Tahoe. With that purchase, Eddie branched into nightclub and casino operations. In 1946 the Sahati brothers acquired the Normandy Club on Airport Road in Reno to go along with their Stateline Club.

The Normandy Club was not a financial success for the Sahatis, and they soon divested themselves of the property. However, the Sahati family retained possession of the (then) seasonal Stateline Club until they leased it to Harrah's Club in 1957. They sold the property to Harrah's Club in 1958.

Eddie Sahati (in dark suit) pictured in Sahati's Stateline Country Club in the late 1940s. Jerry Mesorobian is the dealer. Sahati's Stateline Country Club was later purchased by Harrah's. Courtesy of Sharkey Begovich.

Eddie Sahati was a narcotics addict. Whether he became addicted because of his long hours of gaming, because of his association with other addicts, or because he used pain-killers to control the pain brought on by stomach cancer—which eventually killed him—is not known. In March 1952 Eddie Sahati, along with twenty-two others in Nevada and the Bay Area, was arrested on narcotic charges. In April he pleaded guilty to trafficking in narcotics, and on May 8, 1952, he was sentenced to two years in a federal prison.

On May 25, 1952, it was revealed that Sahati had stomach cancer and would be released from the prison hospital at Fort Worth, Texas. He died in a San Francisco hospital on November 11, 1952, at the age of forty-one.

Harold Smith Sr., *I Want to Quit Winners,* with John Wesley Noble (Englewood Cliffs, N.J.: Prentice Hall, Inc., 1961); *Nev. St. Journal,* 27 May 45, 26 Feb. 46, 8 Mar. 52, 9 Mar. 52 (photo), 11 Apr. 52, 25 May 52, 28 June 52, 12 Nov. 52 (obit.).

SAHATI, NICK

Nick Sahati and his brother Eddie owned the Stateline Club at Lake Tahoe and the Normandy Club in Reno. When Eddie died in 1952, Nick continued to operate the Stateline Club.

The Sahati brothers divested themselves of the Normandy Club after two years (in 1948), but the Stateline Country Club proved to be a real winner. Purchasing the property in 1945, they operated it on a seasonal basis (usually from Memorial Day weekend to Labor Day weekend) until 1957, when they leased it to Harrah's Club. In 1958 they sold the Stateline to Harrah's for over $1 million.

Nick Sahati, like his brother Eddie, gambled heavily. At six feet tall and weighing more than two hundred pounds, he was a domineering figure at a dice table. He usually stood at the end of the table next to the dealer, and his theatrics, bad language, and abusive treatment of dealers and customers who "shot him out of his money" made him an unpopular customer. He was actually barred from playing in some casinos because of his offensive behavior and also because he was such a heavy player, sometimes winning tens of thousands of dollars during his play. He was the opposite of his brother Eddie, who was quiet and refined. Nick was often belligerent and obnoxious—but only when he was gambling.

Two traits the Sahati brothers shared were that they could both stay at a dice table for hours—sometime days—at a time, and they both loved, and lived, to gamble.

Nev. St. Journal, 27 May 45, 2 Feb. 46, 28 Sept. 58.

SANDS REGENCY (ALSO KNOWN AS SANDS HOTEL-CASINO, SANDS MOTOR INN, MR. C'S, AND SANDS PLAZA)

345 North Arlington Avenue; licensed from 1965 to 1969 for slots only; licensed since 1970 as a full casino.

In 1932 Peter Cladianos Sr. bought five slot machines. With this purchase, the Cladianos family found itself in the gaming business. Thirty-three years later, Pete's oldest son, Pete Jr., and his daughter, Katherene, entered the hospitality business with the purchase of the seventy-nine-unit Sands Motel in 1965. The Sands Motel had three slot machines in it, and that was the beginning of what today is one of the largest hotel-casino properties in northern Nevada.

The Sands Motor Inn applied for unlimited gambling in 1969. By then, the Cladianos family had added 24 hotel rooms to the business, giving them a total of 103, enough to qualify for a gaming license outside the "red line." In March 1970 the Sands was given final approval to install 415 slots. In May 1970 the Sands Motor Inn celebrated its grand opening. Along with 415 slots, it featured a Denny's Coffee Shop, a cocktail lounge, and underground parking. In July 1972 the Cladianos family added one 21 game to go along with their slot operation. It wasn't until 1976 that five more 21 games were added to the license, and one year later, in 1977, the owners added a $25,000-limit keno game.

In May 1978 construction began on a thirteen-story, $4.25-million expansion that became known as the Regency Tower. The addition was completed in 1979 and added three hundred more rooms, an enlarged casino, and new restaurants to the Sands property.

On April 1, 1981, the Sands opened Mr. C's Casino. This was really not a new casino, simply a new name for the casino area that had for ten years been known as the Sands Plaza. The casino was named Mr. C's as a tribute to Peter Cladianos Sr. Tom Piculas, Mr. C's general manager, also said it was named to give the casino an identity separate from the other casino space at the opposite end of the Sands building.

The next expansion came in 1983, when the Sands modified its name to the Sands Regency and brought its room total to 688 with the addition of the Empress Tower, dedicated to the memory of Mr. and Mrs. Peter Cladianos Sr.

Through the years, as the Sands continued to expand its facilities, Peter Cladianos Jr. maintained a definite hands-on style of management and was completely involved in the operation. He surrounded himself with top men in the hotel and gaming industry. Some of the many talented individuals who were associated with the Sands over the years include Maurice Sheppard, former Harrah's president, who served on the Sands board of directors; Jack Stratton, former member of the Nevada Gaming Control Board, who also served on the board of directors; Jon Bengston, who served as treasurer and director of the Sands; Jerry LaCroix, the Sands's longtime casino manager; Bruce Dewing, who held many positions at the Sands; Phil Gravino, who worked as shift manager and casino manager; and Steve Hopkins, longtime pit supervisor.

In 1985 the Sands Regency became a publicly held company, traded nationally as an over-the-counter stock. In the late 1980s, *Forbes* magazine rated the Sands one of the two hundred best-managed small companies in the country. By the early 1990s, the Sands was ranked twelfth in revenue in northern Nevada and fifth in profitability.

In 1988 the Sands announced plans for a six-year, $50-million expansion that would eventually add nearly five hundred hotel rooms to the property.

In November 1997 Peter Caldianos Jr. announced that the Sands Regency would be sold to a Las Vegas–based gaming company headed by Shawn Scott. However, in December 1997 Cladianos reported that the sale had fallen through. In May 1999

the Cladianos family announced that the Sapphire Gaming LLC, a division of the Hertz Group of Los Angeles, had purchased the family's 45 percent of the operation. The Sands Regency property currently consists of five buildings, including three hotel towers, located between Arlington Avenue and Ralston Street. Facilities include 938 rooms, 30,000 square feet of casino space, one thousand slots, twenty-four table games, and over one thousand employees.

Nev. St. Journal, 23 Sept. 69, 6 Jan. 70, 20 Mar. 70, 24 May 70, 22 July 72, 25 June 76, 21 May 77, 9 May 78 (photo), 21 July 78, 19 Dec. 80, 1 Apr. 81, 27 May 81 (adv.), 13 May 92; *Reno Gazette-Journal,* 3 Dec. 87, 22 May 99.

SANFORD, JOHN

In 1936 John Sanford went to work in the Palace Club as a cashier. He later learned to deal and became a pit boss, a shift manager in several casinos, and a casino manager in the Holiday Hotel-Casino, the Waldorf Club, and the Riverside Hotel-Casino.

Nev. St. Journal, 13 June 36, 1 Aug. 47, 11 Feb. 48, 8 Oct. 54, 25 July 63.

SARLO, SAM

Sam Sarlo, who was born in Steubenville, Ohio, in 1915, came to Reno in 1959. After working as a pit boss for a few years, he was licensed in 1966 for two poker games at Zimba's Card Room in Douglas Alley. In 1969 he moved Zimba's to 44 West Commercial Row and was licensed for fifty slots, a poker game, a pan game, and six 21 games.

Sam Sarlo passed away on May 30, 1974, at fifty-eight.

Nev. St. Journal, 19 May 66, 1 Nov. 69, 17 Dec. 69, 1 June 74 (obit.).

SATURNO, VICTOR AND JOE

The Saturno brothers, Joe and Victor, owned and operated several small cafes, bars, and restaurants in Reno in the 1930s and the 1940s. However, their biggest claim to fame may have been the fact that they were the gentlemen who sold Bill Harrah the land and building at 210–214 North Virginia Street. This property, which had housed the Mint Club, was the location

where, in June 1946, Bill Harrah opened his first full casino.

715 CLUB

715 South Virginia Street; no record found of licensing.

The *Nevada State Journal* of February 25, 1971, ran an ad stating that the 715 Bar was to open on March 1, 1971. The club was to have been operated by John Andriola and Perry Andreas and was to have "full tables and gaming." However, no other record of gaming at this location has been found.

SHADOWS

9825 South Virginia Street; licensed in the 1930s and 1940s for 21 only.

The Shadows was a supper house and nightclub located south of downtown. It was popular with local customers. Licensed for one 21 game in the late 1930s and early 1940s, the business became known as the Trader's in 1957. The site is now the office of Mobile Home Realty.

SHADOWS SUPPER CLUB

5560 South Virginia Street; licensed from January 1, 1961, to October 25, 1962, for slots and 21.

The Shadows Supper Club was a fashionable restaurant located a few miles south of downtown Reno. Benjamin Barnica was licensed for slot machines only in January 1961, and the following September he was licensed for a 21 game.

The club closed in October 1962. The last business to operate there was the Chinese Tea House, which closed in 1995. The property was razed in 1998, and the site of the Shadows Supper Club is now a vacant lot.

Nev. St. Journal, 8 Sept. 61, 20 Sept. 61.

SHEALEY (SHEELY), FRANK

Frank Shealey was a co-owner (along with Dick Todd) of the Silver Dollar Club on Center Street in 1944. In August 1944 he was arrested for stealing ten cases of whiskey and for accepting a stolen dollar slot machine from Bill Harrah's Blackout Bar. In his oral history, Bill Harrah states that Shealey looked the part of a crossroader, "husky looking and well built, he dressed well, wore cowboy clothes and had a slight drawl."

Reno police chief Harry Fletcher testified in a hearing that the Silver Dollar Club was a "hoodlum joint" and a hangout for ex-cons. Fletcher also testified that most of the trouble there started when Dick Todd took in Frank Shealey as a partner.

The gaming license at the Silver Dollar Club was revoked on September 30, 1944. In December Shealey was found guilty of accepting stolen property, and in September 1945 he was sentenced to jail.

In April 1947 it was reported that Shealey had died mysteriously shortly after being released from jail. The following October, Shealey's jewelry was auctioned off to pay his final hospital and burial expenses.

Nev. St. Journal, 23 Aug. 44, 16 Sept. 44, 6 Dec. 44, 30 Mar. 45, 28 Sept. 45, 25 Apr. 47, 18 Oct. 47.

SHEEHAN, JOHN

John Sheehan was born in Butte, Montana, on September 1, 1914. He came to Reno in 1938. Sheehan worked for Harrah's and the Nevada Club prior to being hired by the Sparks (Ascuaga's) Nugget. He worked at the Nugget for twenty-three years and served as one of the casino's five club managers in the 1970s.

Sheehan passed away in March 1980.

Nev. St. Journal, 19 May 80 (obit. and photo).

SHEPPARD, M. F.

Maurice Francis Sheppard was born in Longmont, Colorado, on May 24, 1917. He moved to Reno at an early age and attended Reno schools, graduating from the University of Nevada with a degree in biology and economics. He served in the Air Force during World War II.

After receiving his discharge from military service, Sheppard went to work for Harrah's Club as a cashier-accountant in 1946. He rose steadily through the company to become office manager, controller, and assistant to the president. In 1969 he replaced Bob Ring as president of Harrah's and served in that position until resigning because of poor health in June 1975.

Sheppard is credited with developing the "daily report" (sometimes called the

Maurice F. "Shep" Sheppard, longtime employee of Harrah's Club and president of Harrah's from 1969 to 1975. Courtesy of Mrs. Audrey Sheppard.

"day book"), which is still used today in most gaming businesses to help management determine the actual approximate daily profit (or loss) of a casino. It shows the amount of money dropped in the pit, keno, and slots, the payouts of those departments, and the net win to the casino, as well as revenue from nongaming areas such as the bar and restaurant. It actually produces a mini-profit (or loss) statement for the preceding day. Bill Harrah demanded it daily, and it was usually the first thing he wanted to see when he came into the club.

It has been said that when Sheppard was president of Harrah's and Lloyd Dyer was executive vice-president, the club had the best management team in its history.

After resigning as president, Sheppard stayed with Harrah's as a vice-president of community relations until 1982. He later served on the board of directors of the Sands Regency Corporation. In 1982 he became associated with the Prospector's Club and remained with that organization until retiring in 1996.

Shep, as he was known among friends and employees, served on a number of

community and state boards, including the Reno Chamber of Commerce board of directors. He was a member of the Governor's Gaming Task Force and helped form the Northern Nevada Gaming Industry Association. Sheppard passed away on June 4, 1997.

Nev. St. Journal, 11 June 75; Leon Mandel, *William Fisk Harrah: The Life and Times of a Gambling Magnate* (Garden City, N.Y.: Doubleday and Company, 1982).

SHERWOOD, HARRY

Harry Sherwood came to Reno from San Francisco in 1946. In July of that year, Sherwood, along with Joe Skoff, purchased the Bar of Music on Center Street for $150,000. The following December, Sherwood and Skoff traded the Bar of Music to Denny and C. M. Woods and Fred Wilkins for the Tahoe Village Casino on the South Shore of Lake Tahoe.

On September 17, 1947, Harry Sherwood was shot by his then-partner, Louie Strauss. First accounts of the shooting in local newspapers treated it as just another local homicide. Then it was revealed that Sherwood was a one-time partner of Tony Stralla, a well-known West Coast gambling figure, and Strauss was the notorious "Russian Louie" of eastern gangland fame. On October 4, 1947, Sherwood died of his wounds. Strauss was arrested and later convicted of murder.

Nev. St. Journal, 11 July 46, 13 Dec. 46, 17 Sept. 47, 5 Oct. 47.

SHIM SHAM CLUB
No address

The only available data is that the *Nevada State Journal* of September 9, 1950, stated that the Tax Commission had granted a gaming license to John and Alice Walters at the Shim Sham Club.

Nev. St. Journal, 9 Sept. 50.

SHIP AND BOTTLE CLUB
222 North Center Street; licensed from March 31, 1932, to 1940 for slots, 21, and roulette.

The Ship and Bottle Club was opened in March 1932 by Nick Abelman, Steve Pavlo-

Nick Abelman in front of his club, the Ship and Bottle, 1932. Courtesy of William Pettite.

vich, and Bert Riddick. It was downtown Reno's first ornate club and rivaled the famous Willows Resort as a gathering place for Reno's night life. The building was fronted with a replica of a ship's prow, complete with a jackstaff. The club was a replica of a popular English pub of the same name.

The Ship, as the club was commonly known, featured some of the best entertainment available in Reno at the time. It was also a favorite with wealthy divorcees and celebrities like Barbara Hutton and Doris Duke, then two of the richest women in America, as well as boxing champ Max Baer and actress Mary Pickford.

The club opened with one roulette wheel and one 21 game. It featured "refined gambling," and a large collection of antiques adorned the walls. One such antique was a ship's clock that had once adorned the captain's quarters of an old sailing ship.

The club was in business from 1932 until late 1940, and some of the entertainers who appeared there included Harry Abell, Martha Beale, Bobby Leahey, Paula Jory with the Della Quadri Orchestra, Patsy McDonald, "The Cutest Little Nudist" (who appeared in the magic mirror dance), Jackie Sherman, Babe Maester, and many more.

The Ship and Bottle had almost as many owners as it did entertainers. Abelman, Pavlovich, and Riddick, who opened the club in 1932, sold it to J. C. Winters in 1935. Cliff Grady and Charles Flynn owned the Ship from December 1935 until July 1936. At that time, Grady sold his percentage to Francis Rudy and Bruce Sheehey. In October 1936 Eddie Hambleton and Owen Short bought the Ship and Bottle. They sold out on December 31, 1938, to Johnny Rayburn and Fred Reiselt. In 1940 Frank Boisseau, Frank Shealey, and John Liedloff were the proprietors of the Ship and Bottle. The club closed late in 1940.

In February 1941 the property reopened as the 222 Club. The site is now part of Harrah's Sports Casino on the east side of Center Street.

Nev. St. Journal, 7 Nov. 33 (adv.), 17 Feb. 34, 28 Nov. 34 (adv.), 15 Jan. 35, 18 Oct. 35 (adv.), 21 Dec. 35 (adv.), 13 June 36, 1 July 36 (adv.), 17 Oct. 36, 12 Jan. 39, 18 Mar. 39, 25 Aug. 40 (adv.); Reno City Directory, 1940.

SHOEMAKER, DAN

Dan Shoemaker came to Reno from Buffalo, New York, in 1917. He purchased the Owl Club on Commercial Row shortly after arriving in town. When gaming became legal in 1931, Shoemaker's Owl Club was issued the first gaming license in Reno.

Shoemaker died at forty-two in October 1932, after a short illness caused by a sinus infection. His death created a pall over Commercial Row and Center Street. Shoemaker reputedly made a fortune in Reno but gave most of it away. He is said to have helped hundreds of men from all walks of life when they were in need.

Nev. St. Journal, 2 Oct. 32 (obit.).

SHORT, HARRY

Harry Short was licensed at the Bar of Music, along with George Johnson and Sam Erlich, in 1946, and licensed at the Villa Sierra, along with Mike Sherdon, in April 1947.

Short was also an orchestra leader. His group performed frequently at his and other nightclubs and cabarets in Reno.

Nev. St. Journal, 11 July 46, 22 Apr. 47, 29 July 51.

SHOW CASE CASINO
143 West Third Street; licensed from March to September 1976.

The Show Case Casino was a small bar that was licensed for one 21 game and five slots in 1976. Currently at this location is a bar called Molly Malone's.

SIERRA BAR
243 Sierra Street; licensed from June 16 to August 31, 1936, for one 21 game.

The Sierra Bar was a small bar that was licensed for a 21 game for a few months in 1936. The site is now part of the Flamingo Hilton.

SIERRA CLUB
232 North Virginia Street; never licensed.

On October 23, 1951, Nick Sahati applied to the City of Reno for a gaming license for a casino to be known as the Sierra Club. The application was for one hundred slots, two roulette games, two craps games, six 21 games, and a bar. Sahati was joined on the application by Nick Abelman, who was to be president of the parent company— the Sierra Investment Company—Charles O'Keefe, who was to be vice-president of the company, and Evelyn Barrett, who was to be secretary-treasurer.

At the time, the property was owned by Harolds Club, but Nick Sahati planned to lease the location.

On July 26, 1951, the state granted a gaming license to the Sierra Investment Company, and on October 30, 1951, the state approved Nick Abelman and Nick Sahati as licensees. However, on November 17, 1951, the Sierra Investment Company withdrew its application, and in 1952 the location was opened as part of an expansion of Harolds Club.

The address is still part of the Harolds Club property.

Nev. St. Journal, 23 Oct. 51, 30 Oct. 51, 17 Nov. 51.

SIERRA TURF CLUB

14 East Commercial Row; licensed as a race book only from 1950 to 1967.

The Sierra Turf Club was opened as a race book in April 1950 by Harry Weitz and Irving Schneider. In September 1951 James and Charles O'Keefe became additional partners, and shortly thereafter they took over as sole owners. They operated the Sierra Turf Club until their lease expired in June 1967. The O'Keefes then opened the Nevada Turf Club, which was located at 34 East Commercial Row.

The site of the Sierra Turf Club is now part of Harolds Club.

Nev. St. Journal, 1 Mar. 50, 14 Apr. 50, 26 Apr. 50 (adv.), 12 Sept. 51, 8 June 62, 11 Jan. 66.

SIGG, JEAN

Jean Sigg was born in Switzerland in 1897 and came to Reno as a young man. He was one of the most famous chefs in Reno between 1930 and the 1960s. He was chef at the Tavern when it opened in 1932, and the restaurant there became famous nationwide. In later years he was chef at the Riverside Hotel, the Willows on Mayberry Road, the Willows on South Virginia, the Cal-Neva Lodge at Lake Tahoe, and the Club Fortune. When a club owner wanted the best in his restaurant, he always tried to hire Jean Sigg.

On October 3, 1973, Jean Sigg passed away in a Susanville, California, hospital.

Nev. St. Journal, 8 Dec. 32, 5 Dec. 36, 4 Oct. 73 (obit.).

SILVER DOLLAR CLUB

261–265 North Virginia Street; licensed from June 24, 1959, to December 1974 as a full casino.

The Silver Dollar Club was licensed by the State of Nevada on March 26, 1959. However, the Reno City Council was divided over the issue of allowing another casino without hotel rooms to be opened on the west side of Virginia Street and deferred its licensing of the casino. Finally, on June 23, the Council voted 4–3 for the licensing of five table games and fifty slots.

The major owners were George Piazza, who owned 51 percent of the casino, and Fred Vonderahe. Other owners included Ambrose Russo, Ray Capurro, Cap Van Cittar, Joe Lischke, and Saul Freedman.

In April 1960 Vince Harley purchased the club and applied for a gaming license. He was granted a license on May 18 for seventy-four slots, one dice game, five 21 games, and one roulette game. In the spring of 1961, Harley began an expansion program at the Silver Dollar Club. A grand opening for the enlarged and completely remodeled Silver Dollar Club was held on May 19, 1961. The newly expanded casino occupied all the space formerly used by the smaller Silver Dollar Club at 261 North Virginia Street.

Owner-operator Vincent "Jerry" Harley estimated the cost of remodeling and enlarging, plus the cost of new equipment, at more than $150,000. He said the new casino would utilize 3,000 additional square feet of gaming area. The front and side of the new club were all glass with a curved marquee. The underside of the marquee consisted of colored lucite sections, and the lighting required ten thousand watts of power. The new operation featured a roulette wheel, a craps table, six 21 games, and 150 slots. Harley named Ray Gibberson as casino manager, and Bud Sorenson, Ray Capurro, and Saul Freedman as shift managers.

The Silver Dollar closed in December 1963. Shortly thereafter, the property was purchased by Lincoln Fitzgerald, owner of the Nevada Club. In May 1965 Fitzgerald and his brother-in-law, Carlton Konarske, were licensed to operate three table games and 125 slots in the Silver Dollar Club. Later, a craps game, a big-six wheel, and a keno game were added.

In December 1974 the Silver Dollar was demolished to make way for the construction of Fitzgeralds Casino-Hotel. The site is now part of Fitzgeralds Casino-Hotel.

Nev. St. Journal, 19 Mar. 59, 26 Mar. 59, 26 May 59, 24 June 59, 25 June 59, 19 July 59 (adv.), 6 Apr. 60, 12 Apr. 61, 14 May 61, 19 May 61 (adv.), 31 Oct. 61, 8 Nov. 64, 8 Jan. 65, 7 May 65, 19 May 65, 18 Feb. 67, 18 Dec. 74.

SILVER DOLLAR CLUB

202 North Center Street; licensed from October 25, 1934, to October 1, 1944, for 21, craps, roulette, and slots.

The Silver Dollar Club was opened by Eddie Hambleton in October 1934. It was actually a small bar and opened with only one roulette game. A 21 game was added in November 1935.

In October 1936 Hambleton sold the Silver Dollar to Frank Manda and Dick Todd. They added a 21 game in 1938 and a craps game in November 1942.

In January 1944 Frank Shealey replaced Frank Manda as Dick Todd's partner. The following August, Shealey was arrested for stealing ten cases of whiskey and for accepting a dollar slot machine that had been stolen from Bill Harrah's Blackout Bar. The following September 13, during a Reno City Council hearing on the possible revocation of the licenses of the Silver Dollar Club, Reno Chief of Police Harry Fletcher called the Silver Dollar Club a "hoodlum joint" and a hangout for ex-convicts. He also testified that most of the troubles there started when Dick Todd took in Frank Shealey as a partner. On September 15, the City Council ruled that the Silver Dollar's license would be revoked at midnight on September 30. Besides the two charges pending against Shealey, there had been several complaints from people who said they had been cheated at gambling by a "dice switch."

Frank Shealey was later found guilty of receiving stolen property and was sentenced to one year in jail. In April 1947 he died mysteriously in his Los Angeles hotel room. In October his jewelry was auctioned off for $2,600 to pay his final hospital and burial expenses.

In February 1945 the Clover Club opened at the former location of the Silver Dollar Club. The site is now part of Harrah's Sports Casino on Center Street.

Nov. St. Journal, 20 Nov. 35 (adv.), 17 Oct. 36, 24 Oct. 36, 3 Oct. 41, 23 Aug. 44, 12 Sept. 44, 16 Sept. 44, 10 Oct. 44, 24 Oct. 44, 6 Dec. 44, 25 Apr. 47 (obit.).

SILVER SLIPPER

1410 East Fourth Street; licensed from April 2, 1931, to early 1937, then again from late 1937 to December 1941 for roulette, craps, 21, and slots.

The Silver Slipper was an elegant dinner house originally owned and operated by

Felix Turillas. It operated as a dinner house and speakeasy prior to legalized gaming, and it was one of the first clubs to be licensed when gaming became legal in 1931.

The Silver Slipper had previously operated as the Idlewild Club and was located near the site of the 1910 heavyweight championship boxing match between Jack Johnson and Jim Jeffries. Located on the front of the building was a huge neon Silver Slipper sign.

After Turillas left the Silver Slipper to devote his full attention to his Northern Club in downtown Reno, the Silver Slipper had several owner-managers. They included Ed Ruschburg, Cy Andrini, and A. Benetti.

In June 1936 Fred Jauregi, manager of the Silver Slipper, announced that the club would feature something new for the entertainment of its patrons—pig races. The pig races proved to be a popular draw, and pig racing was held for several weeks.

The Silver Slipper closed in 1936 and reopened as the Black Derby in April 1937. The Black Derby closed a few months after opening. The property reopened in 1937 as the Silver Slipper and continued to operate until the fall of 1941. At that time it closed and was opened on December 10, 1941, as the Sphynx.

The building was completely destroyed by fire in January 1943. Currently near the former location of the Silver Slipper is a marker denoting the site of the Johnson-Jeffries fight. The actual former location of the Silver Slipper is the parking lot between the Ponderosa Lodge and the Los Compadres Restaurant.

Nev. St. Journal, 20 Feb. 31 (adv.), 21 Mar. 31 (adv.), 25 Apr. 31, 1 Oct. 31, 24 Dec. 31 (adv.), 3 Jan. 32 (adv.), 12 Oct. 34, 12 Dec. 34, 21 Dec. 34, 15 Jan. 35, 14 Mar. 35, 23 June 36 (adv.), 18 July 36, 3 Apr. 37, 1 July 41 (adv.), 20 Sept. 41 (adv.).

SILVER SPUR CASINO

221 North Virginia Street; licensed from July 1, 1968, to December 31, 1981, as a full casino.

On June 19, 1968, the Nevada Gaming Control Board recommended that seven men put up more than $300,000 to open the

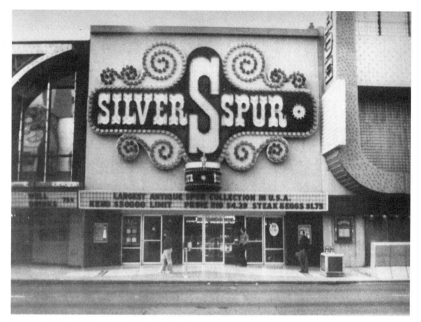

The Silver Spur Casino, 1981. Author's collection.

Silver Spur Casino on "casino row" next to the Horseshoe Club at 221 North Virginia Street. The percentages as recommended were: Fred Cavendish, 12 percent; William Hamilton, 5 percent; Jose Gastanaga, 14 percent; Everett Brunzell, 10 percent; Tom Mullis, 10 percent; James Parker, 6 percent; and Charles Stepro, 2 percent. The Board deferred action on the applications of Conrad Priess for 20 percent, Sasha Maloff for 10 percent, and John Gojack for 11 percent. Two days later, the Gaming Commission approved eight men for licensing at the Silver Spur. It refused to license Sasha Maloff, a Lake Tahoe–Reno land promoter, because of what it deemed his unsuitable finances.

During the session, Conrad Priess's application for 20 percent was postponed to allow more time for investigation of his finances. Priess denied that he was in financial trouble, but the Commission said that it needed more time to check its information.

Both the Gaming Board and the Gaming Commission closely questioned John Gojack, a former Midwest labor leader, as to whether he had ever headed a pro-Communist union. Gojack was at that time in

the bank marketing field and denied that his union was ever a Communist organization. He claimed that he had tried to keep his union politically independent and not let it fall into either the Republican or the Democratic Party. The Board eventually voted 2 to 1 to give Gojack a license. Keith Campbell opposed the bid on the grounds that Gojack's "background is not acceptable." However, Board member Wayne Pearson said the Board "could not afford to judge an applicant on his political beliefs." The five-member Commission's vote was unanimous for Gojack's approval.

It wasn't until July 31 that Conrad Priess was given final approval by the Commission to invest $100,000 for 20 percent of the Silver Spur. The Commission apologized for any embarrassment that the delay may have caused Priess.

The Silver Spur opened at 6:00 on July 1, 1968. A silver spur worn by actor Audie Murphy in the motion picture *Billy the Kid* was used for the ribbon-cutting ceremony opening the casino. The four-day opening festivities featured the entertainment of a western group, the Bob Day Trio. During the celebration, all standard bar drinks were priced at twenty-five cents. Fresh orchids were flown in from Hawaii and presented to women attending the celebration.

The Silver Spur facilities covered two stories above the street level, with restrooms, employee lounges, a kitchen, and executive offices in the basement. The casino proper and the restaurant were on ground level.

In the casino, a plush atmosphere reminiscent of the mid-nineteenth-century elegance of Nevada hotels was carried out in furnishings designed by Dohrman Company, which also designed the restaurant and offices. The feeling of the Old West permeated the casino from floor to ceiling. Carpets were custom-made of wool and nylon with black and gold accents framing silver spurs set in a deep red field. The design was repeated every eighteen inches in the pattern. Burlap flocked with a red velvet damask design covered the walls between massive mirrors and dark wood paneling. Custom-designed chandeliers with authentic silver spurs, hung from the ceiling with leather straps and buckles suspended from bronze chains and rings, completed the period evocation of early western gambling halls.

The general manager of the Silver Spur on opening night was Fred Cavendish. In addition to Cavendish, Silver Spur executives were Charlie Stepro, casino manager; Bill Hamilton, pit manager; James "Reggie" Parker, keno manager; and Clyde Keeling, slot manager.

Casino games included a $25,000-limit keno game, five 21 games, one roulette game, one craps game, and 150 slot machines.

In 1969 it became very obvious that the Silver Spur had to expand. The entire casino plus the keno game, the restaurant, and all the slots were on the first floor, and all facets of the operation were too crowded. Construction began early in 1969. By June, the "Top of the Spur" was opened, providing the casino with an additional 5,000 square feet of space. The restaurant was moved to the second floor, along with a bar and a spacious keno lounge. The area was known as the Virginia City Parlor. Moving these facilities allowed the pit area

and the keno game on the first floor to expand dramatically.

In 1969 the Silver Spur purchased several paintings of seminude girls for display in the Virginia City Parlor. The paintings were tastefully done, and copies of several of them were used by the casino in its marketing program. Calendars, menus, and brochures all featured the "Virginia City Girls."

In 1971 the Silver Spur purchased one of the world's largest antique spur collections. There were more than forty spurs in the collection, which included, along with the western spurs, spurs from more than a dozen countries, the oldest set from Germany, dating back to the thirteenth century. Also included were camel spurs from Morocco, Spanish spurs from the sixteenth and seventeenth centuries, Mexican spurs from the eighteenth century, and many more. Over the years, additional spurs were added to the collection, and when the casino was sold in 1981 there were more than eighty sets of spurs on the walls.

In the early 1970s the Silver Spur Casino began the tradition of awarding genuine silver spurs to the eight winners of the major categories at the annual Reno Rodeo.

The Silver Spur was known as a great place to work, and there was little turnover among the employees. There was also very little change in management. During the more than thirteen years the casino was open, there were only three general managers—Fred Cavendish, James Parker, and Dwayne Kling. Some of the casino managers of the Silver Spur were Ray Gibberson, Harry Bay, Norm Brown, Kent Buchanan, Dwayne Kling, and Steve Gerlach. Pit supervisors and shift managers included Dan Becan, Jim Lewis, Steve Hopkins, LaVerl Kimpton, Joe Devers, Ron Bryant, and George Ardans.

The keno game at the Silver Spur was often rated the best in Reno. Some of the people employed in the keno game included James Parker Jr., John Tyler, Norm Nelson, John Whitehead, Don Trimble, Ken Barrenchea, Bill Scott, John Riordan, Chuck Thomas, Rod Jones, Cliff Hogan, and Gordon Drendel.

In 1979 James Parker retired as general manager of the Silver Spur to return to his native state of Arkansas. Dwayne Kling, a part-owner of the Silver Spur who had been employed there since 1971, was named the new general manager of the club.

On December 31, 1981, the Silver Spur was sold to the Mason Corporation, doing business as the Horseshoe Club, for $4 million. The transaction became final at midnight. The owners at the time of the sale were Conrad Priess, Everett Brunzell, Jose Gastanaga, John Gojack, James Parker, Charles Stepro, and Dwayne Kling.

In 1988 the Horseshoe closed, and the Silver Spur reverted to its former owners, but they never reopened it. Instead, they sold the business to Bob Cashell, who had purchased the Horseshoe out of bankruptcy earlier in the year. Cashell operated the Silver Spur portion of the building as part of his Horseshoe Club until he closed it in 1995.

The former location of the Silver Spur is now occupied by the Silver Spur Gift Shop.

Nev. St. Journal, 4 Apr. 67, 20 June 68, 22 June 68, 30 June 68 (adv. and photos), 1 July 68 (adv. and photos), 31 July 68, 12 June 69 (adv.), 1 July 69 (adv. and photos), 28 June 70 (photo), 19 Aug. 79 (photo).

SILVER TANGO PARLOR
124 North Center Street; licensed from March 21 to July 31, 1937, for tango (bingo) and slots.

The Silver Tango Parlor was opened on March 21, 1937, by Mary Leslie and C. H. Majors. When it opened, it was considered one of the largest and most modern tango parlors in Reno. It is unknown why it closed after operating for only a little more than three months.

Bill Harrah leased the property in October. This was Harrah's first business in Reno.

The site is now part of the Cal-Neva parking garage on Center Street.

Nev. St. Journal, 22 Mar. 37 (adv.).

SKELLY, HARRY
Harry Skelly was born in Brooklyn, New York, in 1902 and came to Reno in 1942. He

was co-owner and general manager of the Bonanza Club on North Center Street in the early 1940s.

Skelly died on November 28, 1980.

Nev. St. Journal, 29 Nov. 80 (obit.).

SLOT-ROUTE OPERATORS

In the early days of Reno gambling, there were many business establishments such as bars, drugstores, nightclubs, restaurants, and sundry stores that had slot machines on the premises. However, the owners of the businesses, in most cases, did not own the slot machines.

The slot machines were owned by individuals who formed companies to buy the machines and place them in various locations. Sometimes the slot-route operators paid a flat rate for "renting" space in a business, but in most cases the operator and the business owner split the profits from the machines on a percentage basis agreed to by both parties.

On April 1, 1931, the Washoe County sheriff delivered hundreds of licenses for hundreds of machines, 161 to two slot-route operators alone.

Some route operators even placed their machines in licensed casinos, such as the Bank Club or the Palace Club, when casino owners were unable to acquire enough slot machines to fill their floor space. Slot machines were difficult to purchase in the 1930s, 1940s, and 1950s, when there were no major suppliers as there are now.

Some slot-route operators eventually became major players in the casino industry. The most notable was Jack Douglass, owner or co-owner at various times of the Club Cal-Neva, the Riverside Hotel, the Comstock Hotel, and others. Douglass was one of the most energetic slot-route operators in Nevada. When he worked out of Tonopah in the early 1930s, he sought locations for his slot machines, pinball machines, and jukeboxes in Goldfield, Silver Peak, Hawthorne, Fallon, and Reno. After Douglass and Louie Benetti, who was business rival Angelo Benetti's brother, founded the Reno-based Nevada Novelty Company in the mid-1930s and acquired the central

and southern Nevada distributorship for the Mills Novelty Company's gambling and amusement devices, they placed or sold machines from that company, and others, all around the state. Their route included Austin, Elko, Battle Mountain, Eureka, Goldfield, and even Las Vegas.

Other casino owners or operators who had slot-route beginnings or connections included, but were not limited to, Pete Cladianos Sr. and Pete Cladianos Jr., John Petricciani, James Lloyd Sr., Paul Elcano, Louis Iacometti, Al Figoni, and Si Redd.

Some of the other slot-route companies in the early years included, but were not limited to, the Angelo Benetti Novelty Company; the A-1 Novelty Company; the Lovejoy Distributing Company, originally owned by Earl Lovejoy, which after Lovejoy's death became the Rex Distributing Company, owned by Joe Williamson; the Reno Vending Company; the Nevada Coin Machine Company; the Beecher Novelty Company; Sierra Novelty, owned by Paul Elcano and Stan Smith; the Reno Vending Company, owned by Wallace Trefey; and H. G. Buckley's Race Horse Machines.

In the 1970s and 1980s major corporations such as Bally Distributing, Jackpot Enterprises, CARDA, and Sircoma (which became International Game Technology) became the major suppliers to casinos and in some cases, such as Jackpot Enterprises, became casino owners.

The profiles of the slot-route operators have changed over the years. However, they were a very important part of gambling in its early years and still remain an important part of Nevada's biggest industry.

SMILANICK, GEORGE

Smilanick was born in Chicago in April 1906, moved to Ely, Nevada, when he was six years old, and moved to Reno in 1937. He worked in Harrah's as a dealer and as a pit boss, at the Golden Bank as a casino manager when the Golden was owned by the Tomerlin brothers, and at the Mapes as a shift manager.

Very active in politics, Smilanick ran for lieutenant governor of Nevada on the Democratic ticket in 1954.

He died in Reno on November 21, 1973.

Nev. St. Journal, 1 Dec. 55, 22 Nov. 73 (obit.).

SMITH, HAROLD JR.

Harold Smith Jr. was born on August 5, 1932, in Willows, California. He was named Raymond I. Smith after his grandfather, but later in life he went to court to change his name to Harold Smith Jr. He came to Reno with his family in 1935 and attended elementary and junior high schools in Reno, then went to San Rafael Military School for his high school education. During the summer months, he returned to Reno and worked in the Harolds Club slot-machine repair shop. He served in the Coast Guard from 1951 to 1954, and when he turned twenty-one, he went to work in Harolds Club and learned all aspects of the family business. His grandfather began grooming him eventually to take over the management of the business.

Smith had a flamboyant manner and an outgoing personality. He was a flashy, self-assured young man who exuded confidence, traveled in the best circles, and maintained a high profile in the community and in the club. For several years, he carried on a highly visible relationship with entertainer Kay Starr. She was older than he, and even for Reno in the 1950s it was almost scandalous that this young man was having such a relationship with an older woman.

Some of Harold Jr.'s activities upset his father and grandfather, and on several occasions he was exiled or shunted out of the club and sometimes even out of Reno or out of the entire state. However, his family always eventually relented and eventually welcomed him home again.

Harold Jr. had sharp, distinctive features and eyes that could be described as nothing but sparkling. He could be sarcastic and biting, but he had a way with people—especially women—that won them over immediately. When he entered a room, he immediately dominated the gathering.

It was always assumed that he was the heir apparent to the family-run Harolds Club, but when his grandfather, Raymond

The Harold Smith Sr. family, ca. 1944. Left to right: Dorothy, Harold Jr., June, Joan, and Harold Sr. Courtesy of Neal Cobb.

I. "Pappy" Smith died, things changed. Harold Sr. announced that he did not want to run the club without Pappy, and in 1970 Harold Jr. watched the club pass out of family ownership.

In 1971 Harold Jr. made headlines when he signed an agreement to operate a casino in Sveti Stefan on the Adriatic Sea in Yugoslavia. After a year and a half, the Yugoslavian government forced Smith and his associates out of the country. He spent the next several years living in Europe. When Smith returned to the U.S. in 1975, he was a changed man. He was a more mature, gentler, quieter person.

By 1978 he was deeply in debt and behind on child support payments to the mother of his five children. To expedite settlement of his mother's estate and allow her property to go to his sisters, Smith declared bankruptcy. He remarked that "I've had it all, and I've been busted—flat ass broke. That gives you a unique perspective." He went to work as a pit supervisor at the Club Cal-Neva in 1979 and worked

there until 1987, then for another period just prior to his death in 1992.

To have to work as a pit supervisor after having been manager of the largest casino in the world, knowing the people he had known, and living the life that he had lived, showed tremendous character and resolve. Many people came by to see him, and some came to ridicule him. People who had been envious of him in the past were glad to see him "get his comeuppance." However Smith really felt about his circumstances, he always carried himself like a gentleman.

Harold Jr. spent the last sixteen years of his life married to Phyliss Devore Smith, a former 21 dealer in Harolds Club and other casinos. Although he had been a heavy drinker and gambler in his early days, he didn't have a drink in the last fourteen years of his life, and the extent of his gambling was limited to playing in private card games for inconsequential amounts of money.

When Harold Jr. was diagnosed with

cancer and the treatments he was receiving in the United States weren't helping, he decided to try a cancer clinic in Germany. The effort was not a success. On May 8, 1992, the young man (fifty-nine) who had once had it all passed away in the town of Badsteben, Germany.

One of the songs played at Harold's memorial service was the Frank Sinatra tune "My Way." That song said it all. His entire life he had done things his way, even to the end.

Nev. St. Journal, 20 Aug. 89, 15 May 92, 28 May 92 (obit.).

SMITH, HAROLD SR.

Harold Smith Sr. was born in Denver on February 23, 1910. He came to Reno in 1935 after running bingo games and games of chance in several states, including California. Along with his brother, Raymond A. Smith, Harold Sr. opened Harolds Club on February 23, 1935. A short time later, Harold's father, Raymond I. Smith, came on board as general manager of the new club.

Harold Sr. worked hard to get the club on its feet and is seldom given the credit he deserves. He spent long hours in the club during the early years and was very instrumental in its growth. Harold Sr., along with his father, Raymond I. Smith, brought gambling out of dark back rooms, put it out in the open, and made it more acceptable to society. Raymond I. Smith is always said to have been the tough-minded, shrewd genius who carefully planned the club's growth, and Harold is usually pictured as the drinking, gambling, "cowboying" member of the family.

This is true to an extent, but Harold Smith Sr. was also the only knowledgeable gambler in the family. It was he who actually ran the casino gaming and developed and trained most of the dealers and bosses in the early days. He hand-picked most of the bosses. It was also Harold Sr. who knew the cheaters and their methods and took measures to ensure the security of the club.

Harold Sr. worked and played hard. In his autobiography (written in conjunction with John Wesley Noble), *I Want to Quit*

Left to right: Raymond I. Smith, Mrs. Harold Smith Sr. (Lois Morris Smith), and Harold Smith Sr., pictured at a California racetrack, ca. 1954. Courtesy of Neal Cobb and the Nevada Historical Society.

Winners, he revealed much about his personal life and his philosophy of life. Harold Sr. loved to gamble, he loved to drink, and he loved women. He was married for the first time to Dorothy McPherson in 1931. That marriage ended in divorce in 1947, and one month after the divorce was final he married Lois Morris. That marriage also ended in divorce, and he was to marry one more time before he died.

Harold's father, Raymond I. Smith, died in 1967, and in 1970 Harold sold the club to the Howard Hughes Corporation. He was quoted as saying, "My Pappy and I were partners, and when I lost my daddy, I couldn't run Harolds Club." Harold Sr. spent most of the rest of his life in seclusion. He usually wore old clothing and frequently walked through town unrecognized. He passed away in his Reno home on October 21, 1985.

Reno Gazette-Journal, 23 Oct. 85 (obit. and photo).

SMITH, MERT

Mert Smith was hired as a craps dealer at Harrah's in Reno in 1955. He rapidly rose through the ranks, and in 1966 he was appointed director of gaming. That promotion put him in charge of all of Harrah's gaming operations, both in Reno and in Lake Tahoe. In 1971 Smith was named vice-president and general manager of Harrah's Reno, and in 1978 he was named vice-president of Harrah's Atlantic City and helped guide Harrah's entry into Atlantic City gaming.

On March 29, 1980, Smith resigned from Harrah's. On April 19, it was announced that he was joining the Del Webb Corporation as executive vice-president of the Sahara Hotel-Casino operation.

Mert Smith now lives in Las Vegas.

Nev. St. Journal, 5 Sept. 66, 29 Mar. 80 (photo), 19 Apr. 80.

SMITH, RAYMOND A.

Raymond A. Smith was born in South Burlington, Vermont, on July 3, 1907. He came to Reno in 1935 with his younger brother,

Harold. Raymond was part-owner and one of the founders of Harolds Club. A diffident man, less flamboyant and less in the public eye than his brother, Harold, and his father, Raymond I. "Pappy" Smith, Raymond A. is credited with having coined the name of the family casino in his brother's behalf. Throughout his career, he was more involved in the financial side of the business than in the gambling aspect of the casino.

Smith was very active in community affairs (as were all the Smiths) and organizations. Some of his activities included the Knights of Columbus, Elks Lodge 597, and Darrell Dunkel Post #1 American Legion. He was a colonel in the Civil Air Patrol, a member of the Bowler's Hall of Fame, and was involved in many other groups. His generosity was legendary around Reno, as several additions to St. Mary's Hospital testify. A quiet, very unassuming individual, Raymond A. Smith was blessed with a multitude of friends.

He died on June 6, 1993, in a Reno care center.

Reno Gazette-Journal, 8 June 93 (obit.); Harry Spencer, "Memories of the Silent Smith," 9 June 93.

SMITH, RAYMOND I. "PAPPY"

Raymond I. Smith was born on April 30, 1887, on a farm near Addison, Vermont. After operating carnival concessions, bingo games, and games of chance throughout the United States, he came to Reno in 1935 to help his two sons, Harold Sr. and Raymond A., operate Harolds Club.

Smith was without a doubt the most influential person ever to appear on the northern Nevada gambling scene. The only person close to Pappy in having an influence on the development of Reno casino gambling would be Bill Harrah. Pappy was the first person to bring gambling out of the back rooms and put it out in the open for everyone to see and patronize. He pioneered a number of Nevada gambling innovations. He was the first to hire women dealers, and he led in the field of casino promotions with his "Harolds Club or Bust" signs that appeared throughout the United States. He established one of the greatest gun collections of all times, financed a series of books about Nevada's early history, and was a leader in the drive to develop a four-lane interstate highway over the Sierra. He is also credited with installing the first casino credit office and the first casino "eye in the sky" (or surveillance) system—although some old-timers will tell you that Bill Harrah deserves credit for both. He sponsored fireworks displays on the Fourth of July and scholarships that sent hundreds of high-school graduates to the University of Nevada. He was honored by nearly every service club in western Nevada. He was also the motivating force in the establish of Harolds Trapshooting Club, the nation's second largest gun club.

Pappy Smith was frugal in his personal life style and adamantly opposed to drinking and smoking. His family had a difficult time convincing him that Harolds Club needed a bar to keep up with the competition. He never gambled at casino games, and his only card playing consisted of private bridge games.

He was a favorite with customers and employees alike. He spent untold thousands of hours in Harolds Club, and his employees loved him because he was always there on the floor, working with them. The customers also loved him, because he was determined that people have fun in his club and that they get "an honest shake." He liked to go through the club doubling customers' bets, a practice he began in 1939, often simply giving money away or dealing a hand guaranteed to make the customer a winner. He was almost always dressed in shirtsleeves, with an Indian-bead tie and bright red suspenders. He looked like a typical country bumpkin, and many people tried to take advantage of him, but they were only fooling themselves.

His son Harold Sr. said that his father felt that "hard work was the key to life's problems." Hard work certainly solved lots of Pappy's problems. He lived a long, full life and was active in the club almost to the end of his life.

Pappy Smith died on May 24, 1967, of

Raymond I. Smith, ca. 1944, pictured in front of Harolds Club. Courtesy of Neal Cobb.

complications from cancer. His funeral was held on Memorial Day weekend, and of course, Harolds Club was *not* closed down for the services. Pappy wouldn't have allowed it.

Nev. St. Journal, 25 May 67 (obit.), 28 May 67, 20 Aug. 89; Harold Smith Sr., with John Wesley Noble, *I Want to Quit Winners* (Englewood Cliffs, N.J.: Prentice-Hall, 1961).

SMITH, VIRGIL

Virgil Smith was born in Winnemucca on December 29, 1909, and spent his youth in Lovelock. He came to Reno in the early 1930s. He had worked in grocery stores as a young man but came to Reno to work at the Palace Club. Smith loved to play cards and was especially fond of poker. John Petricciani of the Palace Club leased his card games to Smith, and this was the beginning of a method of operation by Smith that proved very successful. Over the next several years, Smith acquired concessions all over town. A concession was then (in the 1930s and 1940s) a common practice of outside ownership of games within casinos, bars, restaurants, and clubs. Smith's idea was to form a chain of gambling games all through the Reno area, modeled on grocery chains such as Safeway and Skaggs.

The operators of Harolds Club (l. to r.), Harold Smith Sr., Raymond I. "Pappy" Smith, and Raymond A. Smith. Courtesy of Neal Cobb.

Virgil Smith (r.), pictured with Jack Dempsey, was a highly respected and well-liked person in the early days of the gaming industry. Courtesy of Mrs. Virgil (Nelva) Smith.

Left to right: Bill Harrah, Virgil Smith, Hugh Rahut, and Wayne Martin. Courtesy of Mrs. Virgil (Nelva) Smith.

In the 1930s, Smith owned the roulette wheels in the Golden Hotel, the Villa Sierra, and the Villa Roma. He also operated the games at Belle Livingstone's Cowshed and the Cedars. He later managed the games at Colbrandt's Flamingo Club and eventually purchased the club; was a partner with Bill Williams, Bill Harrah, Wayne Martin, and Ralph Austin at John's Bar in the 1940s; controlled the games at Leon & Eddie's; was licensed for the slot arcade in the Frontier Club in the late 1940s; owned a roulette table in the Golden Gulch (located in the Golden Hotel) in 1947; was licensed for the games at the Colony Club in 1950; was licensed at Johnny's Open Door in 1951; and was a partner with Bill Harrah at the Christmas Tree and the Sky Tavern in the 1940s.

Virgil Smith was probably Bill Harrah's best friend in the 1930s, '40s, and '50s. They met when Smith was running Colbrandt's Flamingo. They both liked to drink and gamble, and they frequented many clubs in Reno, especially the Bank Club, the Palace Club, and the Club Fortune. During the early years (the 1930s and '40s), Smith often bailed Bill Harrah out of trouble

when Harrah's cash got a little low. When Harrah opened his first major casino in 1946, Virgil Smith lent him $25,000 to help get the club open.

In September 1958 Virgil Smith leased the casino operation at the Riverside Hotel from the Crummer Corporation. Smith, who was a friend of Crummer's, went to the Riverside to ask if he could lease space for one roulette table. A short time later, Smith found himself leasing the entire casino, and a little over a year later, in December 1959, Smith purchased the Riverside from the Crummer Corporation for $5 million.

The next month, in January 1960, Smith sold 49 percent of the Riverside, and in April 1960 he totally divested himself of his holdings in the Riverside. He retired from gaming in 1961.

For the next several years, Smith busied himself with his many real-estate holdings in Lovelock and Reno—when he wasn't enjoying himself playing poker at the Peppermill, Harrah's Club, or any of a half-dozen other local spots. Smith was also owner of the Cavalier Motor Lodge and he, along with Norman Biltz, Thomas Dant, and Bill Stremmel, developed properties on and around Kietzke and Moana Lanes and where the Atlantis Hotel, the Sierra Marketplace, and Independence Square now stand.

Promissory note from Bill Harrah to Virgil Smith, dated two months prior to the opening of Harrah's first full casino. Courtesy of Mrs. Virgil (Nelva) Smith.

He was active in the American Legion, the Reno Chamber of Commerce, and the Elks, and he was a director, president, and charter member of the Prospector's Club. He also belonged to many other fraternal and civic organizations.

"Smitty" was one of the most popular and well-liked individuals ever associated with the gaming industry. He always had a smile and a kind word for everyone he met. He died in Reno on July 16, 1995.

Mandel, *William Fisk Harrah*; *Nev. St. Journal,* 1 Oct. 46, 14 Apr. 50, 29 July 51, 20 Aug. 58, 15 Oct. 58 (photo), 10 Dec. 59, 3 Jan. 60, 20 Apr. 60, 18 May 67; *Reno Gazette-Journal,* 18 Jul. 95 (obit. and photo).

SNEED, ARCHIE

Archie Sneed, who was born in 1901, was a co-owner of the Palace Club, along with Ernie Primm, Baldy West, and Joe Hall from 1943 to 1953.

SNOOKER CLUB

224 North Virginia Street; licensed for poker and pan in August 1939.

The Snooker Club featured pool, pan, poker, and snooker at its location on Virginia Street. Roy "Dutch" Williams was the proprietor. The club's slogan was "Where Men are Men and Women are Scarce."

The location became Langley's Tango in 1940 and Robbin's Nevada Club in 1941. Currently the site of the Snooker Club is part of the Nevada Club.

Nev. St. Journal, 12 Aug. 39 (adv.).

SNYDER, JOE
"BACK LINE JOE"

Joe Snyder was known as "Back Line Joe" because he never played anything on the dice table except the back line (betting against the dice). He was born in Baltimore in 1893. He was involved in illegal gambling in Baltimore, and when it got a little too "hot" there he headed for Nevada. He arrived in Reno in 1942, and because of his previous connections with friends of Bill Graham and James McKay, he immediately went to work as a pit boss in the Bank Club.

Snyder later worked summers at the Tahoe Village Casino on the South Shore of Lake Tahoe. In 1948 and 1949 he owned and operated the Rolo Club on Commercial Row, and in 1951 he was manager of the Frisco Club on North Center Street.

Snyder suffered a heart attack while working in the catwalk of Harvey's Wagon Wheel and died on June 28, 1957.

Snyder's son, Joe, also worked in the gaming industry. His first job was as a dealer at the Tahoe Village Casino. Most of his almost fifty-year casino career was spent as a pit supervisor.

Nev. St. Journal, 24 Aug. 51.

SOURDOUGH CLUB

8 West Commercial Row; licensed from September 1, 1956, to June 1, 1957, for poker only.

The Sourdough Club was a poker club owned by Chester Jackson and Earl Forayter. The Gold Trail Club, another poker

Action on a craps table at the Bank Club in 1948. Joe Snyder Sr. is the pit boss and Joe Merhar the dealer. Note that the racks are almost completely filled with silver dollars. Courtesy of Joe Snyder Jr.

club, had previously been located at the site. The Sourdough Club closed in June 1957. The site is now part of Fitzgeralds Casino-Hotel.

Nev. St. Journal, 27 July 56, 18 Sept. 56 (adv.).

SOUTH VIRGINIA BAR

1695 South Virginia Street; licensed from October 26, 1943, to March 31, 1949, for 21 only.

The South Virginia Bar was operated by Gene and Lou Munn. They had a 21 game that they leased to Shirley Johnson from 1943 to 1949. The site is now occupied by Bricks Restaurant.

Nev. St. Journal, 10 Sept. 44 (adv.).

SPECTER, RAYMOND

Raymond Specter was the owner of the Riverside Hotel from June until December 1962. He had made millions as a public-relations and advertising executive. He took the Hazel Bishop Company (a cosmetics manufacturer) from a net worth of $34,000 to a $30-million empire. He was also the producer of *This Is Your Life*, one of the most popular early television programs.

In June 1962 Specter made what he considered a real-estate investment when he made a loan to the Riverside. He had never been to Reno and had never seen the Riverside, and he had no intention of engaging in the hotel-casino's management. However, after he had added substantially to the original loan, he was forced to take over the hotel and casino. Eventually Specter invested $5 million in the property.

A little more than six months later, on December 20, 1962, the Riverside filed for bankruptcy and was closed by the Northern Nevada Board of Trade. The inventory was auctioned off, and Specter's brief fling in Reno ended on a sour note.

Nev. St. Journal, 14 June 62, 25 Nov. 62, 21 Dec. 62.

SPHYNX

1410 East Fourth Street; licensed from December 10, 1941, to 1943 for 21, craps, and roulette.

The Sphynx was opened by Fred Lewis on December 10, 1941. On opening night the nightclub featured the music of Joe Carter and his band and offered three floor shows.

It opened with one 21 game and one roulette game. In 1942 a craps game was added to the license.

The popular nightclub was formerly known as the Silver Slipper. It was one of the oldest nightclubs in the area and was a favorite of many Renoites.

In the short time the Sphynx was open, it had several owners and/or managers. They included Fred Lewis, Larry Brady, George Hilliard, and Phil Tringali.

Early in December 1942, the owners, George Hilliard and Phil Tringali, closed the club after wartime gas rationing had caused a drastic decrease in business. On January 1, 1943, the one-story brick building housing the Sphynx was completely destroyed by fire.

Currently near the site of the Sphynx is a marker denoting the location of the Jack Johnson–Jim Jeffries heavyweight championship boxing match on July 4, 1910. The actual location of the Sphynx is the parking lot between the Ponderosa Lodge and the Los Compadres Restaurant.

Nev. St. Journal, 10 Dec. 41 (adv.), 26 Apr. 42 (adv.), 3 June 42 (adv.), 15 Aug. 42, 2 Jan. 43.

SPORTS CENTER

21 East Douglas Alley; licensed in 1966 and 1967 for race and sports book only.

In February 1966 John Russo was licensed at the Sports Center for a race and sports book. The club was formerly known as the Ohio Club, and John Russo had also headed that operation.

In January 1967 Amelio Mongelli applied to the Gaming Commission to invest $5,000 in the Sports Center. He was denied a license because of "unsuitable prior operations." The business closed soon after the denial. The site is now part of Harolds Club.

Nev. St. Journal, 16 Feb. 66, 19 Jan. 67, 18 Feb. 67.

STAGG, RAYMOND

Raymond Stagg was the owner of Stagg's Roaring Camp, located at 128 Lake Street. He opened the club in 1945 and operated it until 1949, when he sold it to Raymond I. Smith of Harolds Club.

Stagg put together a collection of west-

ern memorabilia unrivaled in the western United States. The collection included over two thousand guns, many of them unique. It was considered the most comprehensive exhibit of western frontier weapons ever assembled. Stagg also displayed early amusement devices, including cards, dice, faro, fan-tan boards, and mechanical orchestras, as well as newspapers, mining claims, and other documents relating to early Nevada.

In the gambling section of the club, Stagg operated as many as twenty-two slot machines, along with craps, 21, and roulette games.

In February 1949 Stagg sold the Roaring Camp to Harolds Club for $300,000. The Smith family operated the club for a short time in 1949 before closing it and moving Stagg's memorabilia collection to the second floor of Harolds Club, in an area that they named the Roaring Camp Room.

After Smith purchased Stagg's Roaring Camp, the two men entered into a ten-year work contract. Stagg was paid $15,000 a year to promote Harolds Club. He traveled throughout the U.S. in a truck built to resemble a covered wagon, and he always dressed in a fringed buckskin outfit. His hair was gray and worn long, giving him the appearance of a mountain man. This marketing ploy, tied in with the "Harolds Club or Bust" theme, resulted in tens of thousands of people coming to Reno and Harolds Club.

STAG INN

265 North Virginia Street; licensed from 1933 to 1960 for slots, 21, roulette, faro, poker, and craps.

The Stag Inn was a bar with a few slots and occasionally a table game or a poker game. During the nearly thirty years the Stag was licensed, some of the licensees were Santino Oppio, Romano Benedetti, Bert Biancone, and Ken Caldwell.

The Stag Inn closed in 1960, and the property was purchased by Lincoln Fitzgerald. The site is now part of Fitzgeralds Casino-Hotel.

Nev. St. Journal, 19 June 37, 15 June 48, 29 June 48, 2 July 54, 14 July 54, 26 Oct. 54.

Downtown Reno in 1946. Note the New Stag Inn on the right, current site of Fitzgeralds Casino-Hotel, and the California Club on the left, current site of the Harolds Club property. Courtesy of the Nevada Historical Society.

STAR CLUB

141 Lake Street; licensed from June 19, 1931, to 1932 for slots, craps, and 21.

The Star Club operated from 1931 to 1932, and the New Star Club operated at the same location from 1932 to 1944. There were several changes in management and ownership over the years. The Star Club always catered to Asian customers and never had more than one or two table games and a few slots.

The site is now a parking lot.

STATE CLUB

7 East Douglas Alley and 43 East Douglas Alley; licensed from April 31, 1931, to March 31, 1932.

The State Club was a bar in Douglas Alley that was licensed for a roulette game. The site is now part of the Harolds Club property.

Nev. St. Journal, 3 July 31 (adv.).

STENGLER'S DUTCH GARDEN

Moana Lane

See Dutch Garden.

STEPRO, CHARLES

Charles Stepro, a native of Louisville, Kentucky, came to Reno in 1947 after serving with the Marine Air Corps in World War II. After working in various casinos, including the Horseshoe and the Primadonna, Stepro became a co-owner of the Silver Spur Casino when it opened in 1967. He later worked at the Holiday Hotel-Casino for several years as a shift manager and was appointed casino manager in 1980. Charlie, as he was known, was a personable, well-liked individual who was popular with customers and employees alike.

Nev. St. Journal, 31 Aug. 80 (photo).

STILLIAN, DOMINICK

Dominick Stillian was born in Ohio on February 13, 1913. He came to Reno in 1936 and was employed at the Palace Club and the Bank Club in the early 1930s and the 1940s.

In 1957 Stillian was licensed as casino manager of the Golden Hotel, and in 1963 he was licensed for 4 percent of the Golden Hotel-Casino. The Tomerlin brothers, James and William, were licensed for the other 96 percent. He stayed on as casino manager of the Golden until it was sold to Harrah's Club in 1966.

Stillian died in a Reno hospital on May 5, 1976. The World War II veteran was sixty-three at the time of his death.

Nev. St. Journal, 7 Dec. 55, 22 Mar. 57, 16 Jan. 59, 19 June 63, 5 May 76 (obit.).

STILLIAN, ROCCO "ROCKY"

Rocky Stillian was born in Ohio in July 1919. He came to Reno in 1938 and was employed at the Palace Club. Over the years, he worked as a pit boss at several casinos, including the Bank Club, the Oak Room on Center Street, and the Sahara Reno, where he was working when he died in June 1980.

Nev. St. Journal, 5 Nov. 38, 15 July 71, 29 June 80 (obit.).

STONE, GEORGE

In 1944 George Stone was licensed as co-owner, along with Howard McMullen, of the Dear Head Lodge on Virginia Street. In 1947 he was licensed as a co-owner of the Cedars on Virginia Street.

STORK CLUB

16 West Second Street; licensed from February 28, 1947, to 1950 for 21, craps, and slots.

The Stork Club opened on February 28, 1947, as a bar with gambling. The three proprietors, Bill Wirts, Bill Dixon, and Edward "Swede" Oleson, had all been associated with the gaming industry in Reno in other casinos and would all remain in the industry for many years to come. They had purchased the property, formerly known as John's Bar (or John's Club), from Howard McMullen, Virgil Smith, and Bill Williams earlier in the month.

The club closed late in 1950, and in June 1951 the Nevada Board of Trade held a public auction to dispose of its fixtures and equipment. The auction was necessary to pay the business's creditors. Owners at the time were Oleson and M. W. Moore.

The former location of the Stork Club is currently occupied by the Pioneer Gift Shop.

Nev. St. Journal, 28 Feb. 47 (adv.), 22 Aug. 47 (adv.), 28 Apr. 48, 11 Jan. 50, 13 June 51.

STRIP

Located four miles out of town on South Virginia Street; licensed in 1948.

The Strip was a bar and nightclub located south of town, originally opened in 1947 by A. R. McAphee, Robert Stellon, and George Brazil. It was purchased in December 1947 by Joe Griffith and Robert Rose. On May 27, 1948, it was taken over by Tom Nickola and George Smith (no relation to the Harolds Club Smiths).

On January 6, 1949, Jack Nolan, who had recently purchased the Strip from Mrs. Jean Filtzer, was granted a cabaret license. An ad in the *Nevada State Journal* of June 8, 1950, announced that the Strip, featuring the finest floor show in Reno, was having its grand opening that night. The ad also invited everyone to visit the club's gaming room.

The Strip's exact address and date of closure are not known.

Nev. St. Journal, 29 Aug. 47 (adv.), 6 Nov. 47, 7 Dec. 47, 25 May 48, 6 Jan. 49, 14 Apr. 49, 8 June 50 (adv.).

SULLIVAN, DAN

Dan Sullivan was born in St. Louis, Missouri, in 1889. He came to Reno with Lincoln Fitzgerald from Macomb County, Michigan, in 1945.

In 1946, shortly after coming to Reno, Sullivan and Fitzgerald became partners in the Nevada Club, along with the Robbins family. In 1948 Sullivan and Fitzgerald were extradited to Macomb County, Michigan, to face charges of bribery and conducting illegal gambling. They pleaded guilty to conducting illegal gambling but were found innocent of bribery. They were fined a total of $52,000. They returned to Reno and resumed operating the Nevada Club. Dan Sullivan was general manager of the Nevada Club, while Fitzgerald was the casino manager.

Dan Sullivan died on September 9, 1956. Even though he suffered from a kidney ailment and was under a nurse's care, he had gone to work daily until the day before he died.

Nev. St. Journal, 11 Sept. 56 (obit.).

SULLIVAN, HOWARD "HOWDY"

Howdy Sullivan came to Reno from Virginia City in the 1920s. He was employed by the Tavern on West Fourth Street. When the Tavern opened in 1932 he was a host and a greeter. Soon afterward, Sullivan was named casino manager. He held that position until 1937.

Nev. St. Journal, 16 Dec. 36.

SULLIVAN, JACK

Born Jack Scarlett in Canada in 1879, Sullivan came to Tonopah in 1906. There he took up professional boxing and used the name Sullivan. He came to Reno from Ely in the 1920s with Tex Hall. Shortly after coming to Reno, Sullivan went to work for Bill Graham and James McKay in various locations around Reno, including the Willows, the Bank Club, and the Rex Club.

Graham and McKay sold Sullivan one-third of the Bank Club in 1939 when they were sentenced to prison for mail fraud. Sullivan and Harry Bond were supposed to watch over Graham and McKay's interests in the Bank Club while they were in prison.

In 1950 Sullivan attempted to sell his one-third interest in the Bank Club to Joseph Stacher. However, the state refused to license Stacher, so Sullivan's percentage was purchased by Graham and McKay.

Sullivan was a large man with a brusque manner and an intimidating personality. He usually had a cigar in his mouth. When he was in the Bank Club, he seldom missed anything that was happening. He discovered that if he sat on a tall stool between the faro tables he could see every game in the house by utilizing mirrors placed strategically around the casino.

Jack Sullivan died on April 24, 1951.

Mandel, *William Fisk Harrah*; *Nev. St. Journal,* 25 Apr. 51 (obit.).

SUNDOWNER HOTEL-CASINO

450 North Arlington Avenue; licensed since July 1975 for a full casino.

The Sundowner Hotel-Casino opened in the summer of 1975 as a Quality Inn Hotel. The $6-million, eleven-story, 249-room hotel was at that time the largest hotel in Reno under one roof. Frank Sorce was the first casino manager, and Hector Herrera the first hotel manager. The Sundowner was (and still is) owned by George Karadanis and Robert Maloff. The casino was licensed for seven table games, one keno game, and two hundred slots on July 25, 1975. In October 1976 Chuck Clifford was licensed as casino manager and director of gaming. He is still working in the same position.

The Sundowner has operated under the same ownership and the same top-level management since opening over twenty years ago. This has led to steady growth over the years.

Some of the pit supervisors who worked at the Sundowner include Dean Rittenmeyer, Jim Wilbur, Oddie Carpenter, Ray Bruner, Owen Alfritz, Lee Crawford, and Augie Landucci.

In the early 1980s a hotel tower was added. The expansion brought the total number of hotel rooms to just over six hundred. Today there are sixteen 21 games, two craps games, one roulette game, and over one thousand slot machines licensed at the Sundowner.

The Sundowner is still operating at its original location on the corner of Arlington Avenue and West Fourth Street.

Nev. St. Journal, 16 May 75, 19 June 75, 27 June 75, 17 July 75, 26 July 75, 11 Sept. 75, 16 Sept. 76, 13 Oct. 76.

SUNFLOWER CLUB

9825 South Virginia Street; licensed from May 17, 1949, to August 31, 1950, for slots, 21, craps, and roulette.

The Sunflower Club was a supper club with fine dining, dancing, and entertainment, located about seven miles south of town. Other restaurants, such as the Shadows, had operated at that address prior to the Sunflower's opening, and other restaurants, such as the Trader's, would later do business at the same location.

The State of Nevada licensed a group consisting of Echo Leonetti, Phillip and Lorraine Kinzell, Donald and Alta Moore, and Aaron and Josephine Holt on April 14, 1950. The casino failed to renew its license in September 1950, however, and in May 1951 the business reopened as Echo's Club with some of the same licensees—Echo Leonetti, and Phillip and Lorraine Kinzel.

The site of the Sunflower Club is currently occupied by the Mobile Home Realty sales office.

Nev. St. Journal, 14 Apr. 50, 8 June 50 (adv.).

SUPPER CLUB

565 West Moana Lane; licensed from October 1955 to April 1959 for slots and 21.

The Supper Club opened in October 1955 at the former site of Johnny's Open Door. It was a basically a gourmet restaurant with a bar and a small dance floor, one of those spots where Renoites went for a nice dinner and an evening of dancing and relaxation. Glen Rolfson, popular Reno entertainer, appeared there frequently. Clubs such as the Supper Club always had a few slots and a table game or two to provide amusement for their patrons and to produce some extra revenue for the proprietors.

The original owners of the Supper Club were Charles (Jack) Smith, Frances and J. P. Hammond, George Evans Jr., and James Mask. There were several owners and managers over the years, although the Hammonds or the Hammonds' estate and Jim Mask always had a piece of the action. Some of the other owners included George Redican, Edith Fritchie, Byron Wilbur, Cliff Lightner, and Tom Lawson.

The Supper Club suffered $75,000 worth of damage in an early-morning fire on April 28, 1959, and it never reopened. The site is currently occupied by the Yen Ching Restaurant.

Nev. St. Journal, 22 Sept. 55, 26 Oct. 55, 13 Nov. 55 (adv.), 20 Apr. 56, 19 May 56, 3 Oct. 56 (adv.), 20 Sept. 57, 19 Oct. 57, 22 Nov. 57, 27 Feb. 58 (adv.), 27 Apr. 58, 31 Oct. 58 (adv.), 25 Nov. 58, 18 Dec. 58, 29 Apr. 59.

SWEDE'S

333 East Second Street; licensed from April 16, 1963, to February 19, 1965, for slots and 21.

Swede's was a small club with a bar and a small restaurant that featured pizza. In April 1963 Harold Peterson and Opal Graham applied for a gaming license at Swede's. The Nevada Gaming Control Board recommended denial. A few days later, the Gaming Commission okayed Opal Graham to be licensed for six slot machines, but only if she dissolved her partnership with Peterson. In July 1963 a 21 game was added to the license at what was then called Swede's Pete-zza.

The club closed in February 1965 and re-

opened a year later as Val's. The site is now a parking lot.

Nev. St. Journal, 16 Apr. 63, 17 Apr. 63, 15 July 63, 19 Feb. 65, 3 Feb. 66, 21 Apr. 66.

SWING CLUB

220 North Virginia Street; licensed from May 29 to July 1, 1940, for one 21 game.

The Swing Club was located at a site that housed several clubs and bars over the years. It later became Pick's Club and then the Frontier Club. The site is now part of Harrah's Club on Virginia Street.

TAMARACK BAR

13101 South Virginia Street; licensed in 1952.

On June 18, 1952, the State Tax Commission approved Benny Petronzi and Brownie Paretti for a gaming license.

The property is currently operating with slot machines but no gaming tables.

Nev. St. Journal, 18 June 52.

TANGO CLUB

242 North Virginia Street; licensed in the 1930s for keno (bingo) only.

Located next to Harolds Club, the Tango Club ran a bingo operation in the mid-1930s. The site is now part of the Harolds Club property.

TAVERN

1801 West Fourth Street; licensed from December 1932 to May 1941 for 21, craps, slots, and roulette.

Built in the 1920s and meeting with varying success under numerous managements and under such names as the Log Cabin and Hutton's Hut, the Tavern was remodeled and improved and was tentatively scheduled to open on October 31, 1932. The worst financial blow ever suffered in the state occurred on October 29, 1932, when every bank in the state—except three—closed its doors as a consequence of the general economic collapse of the Depression. Under these circumstances, the Tavern did not open as planned. However, on December 8, the Tavern, "Reno's Smartest Night Club," did open its doors with dancing, entertainment, dining, and gaming.

The original owners of the Tavern were George Coppersmith, George King, George Nelson, and Jack Clark. The general manager was Fay Baker, and working in the casino as floor men and managers were Howdy Sullivan, Ed Rich, Terry Terrano, and Ed Ward.

The Tavern featured the Tavern Music Makers for its patrons' dancing and listening pleasure. Heading up the restaurant was Chef Jean Sigg, formerly of the Willows and the Club Cal-Neva at Lake Tahoe. The club gained national recognition for its fine cuisine and refined appointments. Famous entertainers such as Lionel Hampton and Nick Stuart appeared at the Tavern, and nightly radio broadcasts originated there. In fact, the Tavern constructed its own broadcast control room to eliminate the difficulties of remote broadcasting. The first worldwide broadcast from Nevada originated from the Tavern in 1935.

In 1937 there was a shake-up in the management of the Tavern when Ed Rich took control of the gaming and Fay Baker left to become part-owner of the Town House in downtown Reno.

Starting in 1938, the fortunes of the Tavern took a turn for the worse. Within less than two years, the Tavern was operated first by Barney Newman and Herman Landres, then by Ernie Crofton, and finally by James Carey and Morrie Treiber. Eventually it was taken over by creditors, and in November 1939 all assets of the Tavern, including six roulette tables, several slot machines, and various gaming tables, were sold at a public auction.

On November 20, 1939, Victor Portopilo and his wife announced that they would reopen the Tavern on Thanksgiving Day. Jean Sigg was to return as the executive chef, and once again the Tavern would feature fine dining, entertainment, and gaming.

The Tavern prospered until May 4, 1941, when a devastating fire did $100,000 worth of damage. The building and most of the contents were completely destroyed. The property never again operated as a nightclub. Instead, Portopilo and his partner, Brownie Paretti, opened the El Tavern Auto Court and Coffee Shop at the former location of the Tavern.

In January 1947 the El Tavern was purchased by Harry Bond and William Parker, who operated slot machines at the location for a short time but had no table games. In June 1954 the El Tavern Auto Court was sold by Bond and Parker to Charles Moore Jr. and C. C. Payne for an amount "in excess of $500,000." The site is currently occupied by the El Tavern Motel.

Nev. St. Journal, 8 Dec. 32 (article and adv.), 4 Oct. 35 (adv.), 16 Dec. 36 (photo), 6 Jan. 37, 21 Mar. 37, 1 Apr. 37, 21 May 38 (photo), 26 Aug. 38, 29 Aug. 38, 3 Oct. 38, 23 Nov. 38 (adv.), 30 June 39, 14 Nov. 39, 20 Nov. 39, 3 May 41 (adv.), 5 May 41 (photos), 25 Jan. 47, 30 Dec. 47, 3 June 54.

THORNE, GLEN

Glen Thorne was born in American Falls, Idaho, in 1915 and came to Reno in 1926. After serving in the 767th Tank Battalion during World War II, Thorne was employed at the Mapes Hotel. He was named casino manager in 1957 and worked in various supervisory positions at the Mapes for more than twenty-two years.

Glen Thorne passed away in Reno on March 3, 1993.

Reno Gazette-Journal, 4 Mar. 93 (obit.).

THORNTON, WILLIAM R.

William Thornton was born in Reno on February 24, 1934. He attended Reno schools and was attending the University of Nevada when the Korean War began. Thornton interrupted his education to enlist in the Air Force. After his discharge, he returned to the University of Nevada, graduating in 1958. He also attended the University of Arizona and later received a law degree from the George Washington University Law School.

Thornton began practicing law with the firm of Guild, Busey, and Guild. He was later associated with other law firms and with various partners, including Nevada's current attorney general, Frankie Sue Del Pappa.

In 1959 he married Barbara Cavanaugh, whose family was invested in the Club Cal-Neva, and in 1964 he was retained as counselor for the Club Cal-Neva. When his father-in-law, John Cavanaugh Sr., was killed in an automobile accident in 1973, Thornton became a part-owner of the Club Cal-Neva and was the family representative on the board of directors. He was also named a corporate officer of the organization.

In 1981 Thornton conceived the idea of a

"Fifty Years of Gaming" celebration, and he served as chairman of the event, which was held at the MGM Hotel-Casino in March of that year. The observance commemorated the first half century of legal gaming in Nevada and honored several gaming pioneers.

Over the years, Thornton and his wife have been extremely active in the Reno community, and in recent years he has been president of the Reno-Sparks Chamber of Commerce, vice-president of the Reno Tourism Committee, chairman of the UNR Foundation, and has held many other offices relating to the betterment of northern Nevada. In 1998, the William Thornton family donated 180 acres of land adjoining the Rancho San Rafael Park to the city of Reno. The land, which includes the area where the large white *N* is located, will be used for the future expansion of the park.

Thornton currently serves as chairman of the board of the Cal-Neva Club, and the Thornton family holds 28 percent of the stock of the corporation.

Nev. St. Journal, 1 Feb. 78.

395 CLUB

9825 South Virginia Street; licensed in August 1955.

The 395 Club was formerly known as Echo's Club and the Sunflower Club and was later to become the Trader's. In August 1955 the state approved John Fahey, Morgan Dale, David Anderson, and R. W. Tretton for 25 percent each of the 395 Club. They paid $160,000 for the club and put up $50,000 for the bankroll. The Trader's opened at this address in 1956.

The former location of the 395 Club is currently occupied by the sales office of Mobile Home Realty.

Nev. St. Journal, 28 July 55, 26 Aug. 55.

TIVOLI BAR

20 East Commercial Row; licensed from February 20, 1935, to July 1, 1942, for 21 and poker.

The Tivoli was a small bar located on Commercial Row in the same area as many other small bars and cardrooms. The site is now part of Harolds Club.

TOBIN, PHILLIP

Phil Tobin was born in Portland, Oregon, in 1901. Born Phil Lorenzen, he was adopted by his stepfather, C. L. Tobin, a Winnemucca banker and rancher, when he was nine years old.

Tobin, often called the "father of gambling," was the legislator who introduced the bill to legalize gambling in Nevada. His position was that gambling was too common to ignore and was untaxed to boot. He presented the bill on February 13, 1931, and the two opposing sides of the question debated for almost a month. Despite opposition from groups concerned about the impact of legalized gambling on public morals, the bill enjoyed the support of gambling interests and of financier George Wingfield and other businessmen. Finally, on March 9, the assembly passed the bill 24 to 11, and eight days later the state senate approved it 13 to 3. Two days after senate passage, on March 19, 1931, Governor Fred Balzar signed the bill into law.

Under the new law, card games were taxed $25 a month and slot machines $10 a month. One-quarter of the new gaming income went to the state treasury, and three-quarters to the county treasuries. Cheating was made illegal, as was gambling by minors.

Phil Tobin passed away on December 8, 1976.

Nev. St. Journal, 9 Sept. 76 (obit.); *Nevada Magazine,* Mar./Apr. 1981.

TOLEN, ADRIAN "AD"

Ad Tolen was born on March 15, 1911, in Naco, Arizona, and began his gaming career in Mexico at age seventeen. He came to Reno in 1938, and his first job was as a roulette dealer at the Club Fortune at Second and Center Streets (the future location of the Club Cal-Neva). He later worked at the Palace Club and at the Primadonna.

As a wheel dealer, Tolen was in such demand that casinos let him use his personal checks when he dealt the wheel. His own checks were a necessity because Tolen was color-blind. He was an honest and reliable worker, qualities that paid off for him as he rose from the trenches to become part of

ownership teams in five different casinos—the Bonanza Club in the middle 1940s, the Tahoe Palace in the middle 1950s, the Club Cal-Neva in Reno from 1962 to his death, the Cal-Neva Lodge at Lake Tahoe in the late 1960s, and the Comstock Hotel-Casino in the 1970s.

Ad Tolen passed away in 1992.

Nev. St. Journal, 25 July 56, 29 Mar. 62, 21 Mar. 69, 1 Feb. 78.

TOMERLIN, WILLIAM AND JAMES

In February 1954 William and James Tomerlin purchased the Golden Hotel for $3.5 million from Frank Hofues, who had paid $6 million for the hotel only two years earlier. The purchase had no effect on the long-term gaming lease held by Bill Graham and John Drew. However, in November 1955 the Tomerlins paid Graham and Drew $425,000 for the remaining seventeen years of their lease. They took over operation of the casino on December 1, 1955.

On April 3, 1962, the Golden Hotel was completely destroyed by fire. In June preliminary work began on construction of what was to be called Tomerlin's New Golden Hotel. In June 1963 the Tomerlins were licensed for 48 percent each of the New Golden, and their casino manager, Dominick Stillian, was licensed for 4 percent. The New Golden Hotel opened at 7:00 P.M. on July 3, 1963.

On March 29, 1966, newspapers announced that the Tomerlins had sold the New Golden Hotel to Harrah's. The facility closed the same day, and three hundred employees were put out of work.

The Tomerlin brothers were never again associated with gambling in the Reno area.

Nev. St. Journal, 4 Feb. 61 (photo), 13 Nov. 78 (obit.).

TOM'S CARD ROOM

120 East Commercial Row; licensed from November 9, 1965, to 1966 for poker only.

Located at an address long a home to bars, small casinos, and cardrooms, Tom's Card Room featured a bar and poker tables and catered mainly to local customers. The site is now part of Harrah's parking garage.

TONOPAH CLUB

1402 South Virginia Street; licensed in December 1945 for roulette and 21.

On December 27, 1945, the Reno City Council licensed John Morgan for one roulette game and one 21 game at the Tonopah Club at 1402 South Virginia Street. There is no record of state licensing at this location. The site is now a vacant lot next to Miguel's Mexican Restaurant.

Nev. St. Journal, 28 Dec. 45.

TOWN CLUB

44 West Commercial Row; licensed in 1972 and 1973 for slots and 21.

The Town Club was opened in December 1972 by Elbert Cox and his 50-percent partner, Cy Lopp. Cox was licensed as president of the corporation and Lopp as secretary-treasurer. The club opened at the former location of Zimba's Club. It was originally licensed for sixty slot machines and no table games, but a 21 game was licensed a few months after the club opened.

In 1973 the name of the business was changed to the Old Reno Club. It is still operating under that name at the same address.

Nev. St. Journal, 14 Dec. 72, 13 Sept. 74, 18 Oct. 74.

TOWN HOUSE

39 West First Street; licensed from October 5, 1932, to September 2, 1955, for 21, craps, slots, and roulette.

The Town House was built in 1932 by Charles Rennie, who was also its first operator. Another casino, the Deauville, which opened in 1931, was located in the basement area of the Town House. When the Deauville closed, the large basement area was used for dancing and small parties, and the ground level of the Town House contained the restaurant, bar, and gaming area. Rennie, who later opened the opulent Country Club on Plumas Avenue, had as his partners Louie Marymount and Chester Condon.

In the first few years of operation, the club was also known as the Dude Ranch Town House. One of its early slogans was, "You may have your country home, but make this your Town House."

After the Country Club burned down in 1936, Rennie was unable to keep the Town House operating and it went into receivership in 1937. A public auction was held in November, with the money received going to pay off the Town House's many creditors.

The club reopened in December 1937 with Fay Baker and Tom Brown as the new owners and operators. Baker and Brown had both been in Reno for many years and were well known to what was called the "sporting crowd" around town. They featured a French menu, but their decor was rustic western. The walls looked like those of a log cabin and featured equine murals. The dude-ranch theme was extended to the logo—a rear view of two young women sitting on bar stools. Standing between them was a cowboy, and the caption was, "The Riding Lesson." In 1939 Fay Baker left the Town House, and Leon Indhart and Tom Brown took over the operation.

In January 1940 the controlling interest in the Town House was sold to Monaei Lindley. She had been a Reno resident for two years and was the owner of the Shadow Dude Ranch. Russ Bixby was named club manager. George Perry and Jelly Jack Blackman took over the Town House in 1941 and operated it for over three years. In February 1945 Lou Vallin purchased the club and named Jim Turpin club manager. The next few years were probably the highest peak of financial success for the Town House. Business flourished after the war and continued until the big hotels began to lure away free-spending customers with floor shows and larger facilities.

In January 1948 Lou Vallin lost his gaming license. As a result, he also lost the lease. Taking over the property in April 1948 were Jim Metrovich, Jack Duffy, and John Achuff. As chef, they hired longtime Reno favorite T. F. Gee, whose name alone meant a flourishing business for any restaurant with which he was associated. The new owners were licensed for one craps game, one 21 game, and eight slots.

In November 1949 the ownership was restructured, and Ernie DeLoe and Jim Metrovich assumed the remainder of a three-year lease. Jack Duffy and John Achuff left the Town House to pursue other interests.

In less than a year—August 1950—the club closed and the owners filed for bankruptcy. The liquidation of assets was put in the hands of Glen Meyers, head of the Nevada Board of Trade.

In January 1951 the Town House reopened. Robert Hunt and Al Vario were partners in the operation, and Roy Nelson was given a license to operate the gaming tables. Over the next few years, there was a multitude of owners and managers. In April 1951 the full list of owners included Harold Walters, Art Miller, Robert Hunt, Joe Viano, Silvio Vario, Al Vario, and Roy Nelson. They were banded together in a corporation known as the Nevada Enterprise. In August 1951 Al Vario was licensed for seven slots, one roulette game, one craps game, and one 21 game.

In 1952 Harold Walters and Roy Nelson left the corporation, and in 1953 William Riordan and Charles Brown were added. Also, in July 1953, Carl Amante was licensed by the state for 31 percent of the Town House with an investment of $14,000. In 1954 Amante became sole owner.

On September 2, 1955, the Town House was destroyed by fire. In August the landlord, Mark Yori, had served Carl Amante with an eviction notice effective January 1, 1956. Yori planned to have the premises razed to make way for the construction of a J.C. Penney store.

On December 16, 1955, a trial began in federal court over the fire in the Town House. Two insurance companies had refused to pay claims, charging that the fire was a result of arson. On December 21 the court ruled that the insurance companies did not have to pay the claims. The court also accused Amante of deliberately burning the property.

The J.C. Penney store operated for over twenty years at the former site of the Town House. The site is now occupied by a craft mall.

Nev. St. Journal, 6 Apr. 33, 7 May 33 (adv.), 15 Jan. 35, 20 Nov. 37 (adv.), 16 Dec. 37 (adv.), 15 Nov. 38, 26 Apr. 39 (adv.), 20 Sept. 39 (adv.), 12 Jan. 40, 23 Feb. 45, 3 Mar. 45, 8 Feb. 47 (adv.), 19 Feb. 47 (adv.), 24 Jan. 48, 24 Feb. 48, 9 Apr. 48 (adv.), 24 July 48, 1 Jan. 49 (adv.), 11 Jan. 49, 1 Mar. 49, 22 Sept. 49, 2 Nov. 49 (article and adv.), 9 Aug. 50 (photo), 23 Jan. 51, 1 Mar. 51, 11 Mar. 51 (adv.),

28 Mar. 51, 25 Apr. 51, 30 Aug. 51, 12 Dec. 51, 27 Jan. 52, 29 Oct. 52 (adv.), 24 Mar. 53, 9 July 53, 14 Apr. 54, 23 Dec. 54 (photo), 27 Apr. 55, 3 Sept. 55, 17 Dec. 55, 22 Dec. 59; Harrah, "My Recollections"; Reno Telephone Directory, 1945.

TRADER'S

9825 South Virginia Street; licensed from August 1 to December 1957 for 21 only.

The Trader's was a bar and restaurant located about seven miles south of downtown Reno. Several other nightclubs and casinos, including Echo's Club and the Shadows, had previously operated at this location. In November 1956 the Gaming Control Board recommended the approval of R. W. Tretton and William Lee to invest $5,000 to operate a 21 game there. The state approved the application for the 21 game on August 1, 1957. The license was not renewed for 1958.

The former location of the Trader's is the site of the sales office of Mobile Home Realty.

Nev. St. Journal, 19 Sept. 56, 28 Nov. 56, 23 July 57.

TRADE WINDS

136 North Center Street; never licensed.

The Trade Winds was located at the former site of many nightclubs, including the Bar of Music, Freddy's Lair, and Buddy Baer's. In March 1953 Harry Karns applied for a gaming license but final approval was never given. The following November, the Trade Winds closed. Russ "Candy" Hall, who was later to become entertainment director of Harrah's Tahoe, reopened the club as Candy's Trade Winds. He obtained a cabaret license only, with no gaming.

The site is now part of the Cal-Neva parking garage.

Nev. St. Journal, 24 Mar. 53, 13 May 53, 6 Oct. 53 (adv.), 24 Nov. 53, 6 Apr. 60.

TRIPP, LARRY

Larry Tripp was born in Salt Lake City on December 4, 1894. He came to Reno in 1940. Prior to coming to Reno, Tripp lived in Las Vegas, where he helped to open the El Rancho Hotel and the Last Frontier Hotel.

In Reno, Tripp, a retired Southern California lawyer, was a real-estate developer and promoter as well as a casino owner. One of his major projects was the University Foothills development.

Tripp was a co-owner of the Barn, a nightclub and casino on North Center Street, in 1943. When the Barn was renamed the Bonanza Club, Tripp remained a co-owner of the property until he and his partners sold it in 1947. He was also one of the original owners of the Ponderosa Hotel-Casino at 715 South Virginia Street. In 1966 Tripp invested $150,000 for 42.9 percent of the operation. He retained ownership, along with his wife, Kathy, until 1980, when the casino was closed by the Gaming Commission for accounting violations.

Larry Tripp passed away in 1989.

Nev. St. Journal, 3 Nov. 66.

TROPICS

130 North Center Street; licensed from July 1944 to July 1946 for 21, craps, roulette, and big-six.

In May 1944, the Tropics, formerly known as the Dog House, opened its doors. Completely redecorated in a South Sea Islands theme, the Tropics had palm trees, grass shacks, hula girls, and a Hawaiian atmosphere. Dick McIntire and his string band were there on opening night to furnish music. The Tropics featured Chinese food, tropical drinks, hula dancing, and even travelogue motion pictures of the South Sea Islands.

When the Tropics first opened, it was owned by Phil Curti and Al Hoffman. However, Hoffman soon became terminally ill, and shortly after the Tropics opened he sold his portion of the property to George "Frenchy" Perry. In January 1947 Phil Curti and George Perry announced that the Tropics would close on February 4 and be converted to a bowling alley.

The site of the Tropics is now part of the Cal-Neva parking garage.

Nev. St. Journal, 10 May 44 (article and adv.), 2 Aug. 44, 8 Mar. 46 (adv.), 10 Mar. 46, 8 Jan. 47, 27 Sept. 66, 4 Feb. 67.

TROUNDAY, ROGER

Roger Trounday was born in Reno in 1934 and raised in Smith Valley. He attended Reno High School and was the recipient of a Harolds Club Scholarship, which stipulated that he was not to go into gambling clubs at any time during his college career. Trounday was a star athlete in basketball and baseball at both Reno High and the University of Nevada, as well as student-body president at both schools.

From 1956 to 1971 he worked as a teacher, coach, vice-principal, and principal at various schools in Washoe County. In 1971 Governor Mike O'Callaghan selected Trounday as state director of the Department of Human Resources.

In 1977 Trounday replaced Phil Hannifan as chairman of the Gaming Control Board. After doing an excellent job for almost three years, he resigned to become chief executive officer of Caesars Tahoe in January 1980. In 1983 Trounday left Lake Tahoe to become managing partner of the Red Garter Casino in Wendover. In 1987 he was named operations officer of Ascuaga's Nugget. He is still active in that position.

Nev. St. Journal, 29 Jan. 80.

TURF CLUB

South Virginia Street

On August 6, 1948, the bar and gaming licenses of the Turf Club were transferred from Jack Douglass to Rick Benedetti and Lou Bevilacqua. Also on that date the property's name was changed to the Play Room.

No other information about this business has been found.

Nev. St. Journal, 6 Aug. 48.

TURILLAS, FELIX SR.

In 1919 Felix Turillas Sr. built a hotel at East Fourth and Evans Streets called the Español. In 1923 he leased the Commercial Hotel at 207 North Center Street and placed several card games in the lobby. This was his first attempt at running a gambling establishment. In 1925 he bought the resort at Lawton's Hot Springs, where he operated illegal gambling. Because he operated gaming prior to its being legalized in 1931, when it did become legal he was one of the first operators to get into action. He was licensed at Lawton's Hot Springs on April 7, 1931, for one craps game, one 21 game, one roulette game, and seven slots. One month later he was licensed for ten table games and three slot machines at the Northern Club, which was located in the Commercial Hotel and was owned by Turillas.

In the mid-1930s Turillas divested himself of the operation at Lawton's but was licensed at the Silver Slipper on East Fourth Street for a few years. He operated the Northern Club through 1940. At that time he sold the Northern and moved to Lovelock, where he was licensed for gambling at the Big Meadows. In 1952 the Gaming Commission closed the gambling at the Big Meadows. It has never been restored.

On August 7, 1956, Felix Turillas Sr. died of a skull fracture and a brain hemorrhage after an altercation in the Riverside Hotel. It was the night of the wedding of one of his daughters, and the wedding party was celebrating in the showroom when another patron complained of the noise the party was making. In the altercation that followed, Turillas fell and injured himself. He was sixty-seven at the time of his death. The other patron was cleared of any liability.

Nev. St. Journal, 4 July 31, 29 Oct. 52, 8 Aug. 56 (obit.).

TUX CLUB

1303 East Fourth Street; licensed from April 18, 1955, to March 22, 1964, for slots, 21, and craps.

The Tux Club was located in a building that has housed many small clubs, bars, and restaurants over the years. The owners and operators of the Tux were Charles "Ed" Keeney Sr. and Bill McGowan. The Tux had a bar and a small restaurant and specialized in Mexican food.

In 1961 Lew Moreno applied for a license for 50 percent of the 21 game in the Tux but was denied. In 1963 Charles Keeney Jr. was licensed for 50 percent of the Tux. He purchased his percentage from his father, Charles Keeney Sr., for $20,000.

The Tux closed in March 1964 and reopened a short time later as the Copper Club. The site is currently occupied by a bar known as Dilligas Saloon.

Nev. St. Journal, 2 May 58 (adv.), 5 Sept. 58, 17 Jan. 59, 17 Oct. 61 (adv.), 9 Nov. 61, 8 May 63.

TWO J'S

No address or opening and closing dates are available.

On November 26, 1955, the state okayed a gaming license for Annie Bartolini at the Two J's. No other information about this establishment is available.

Nev. St. Journal, 26 Nov. 55.

222 CLUB

222 North Center Street; licensed from February 3, 1941, to October 1944, then from June 10, 1947, to January 23, 1949, for slots, 21, craps, and roulette.

The 222 Club was first opened by Jack Fisher, a prominent sportsman, longtime friend of Jack Dempsey, and a famous horse-racing judge and impresario. Fisher came to Reno to retire but instead found himself opening a new business.

Fisher opened the 222 Club at the former location of the Ship and Bottle Club on February 3, 1941. The interior of the club was decorated in a warm, cheery style with a fireplace in the rear of the room. The fireplace was said to have been transported to Reno in the "early days" and was reputed to have once been in Simón Bolívar's castle. Also in the club was a famous old ship's clock that was taken from the wreck of the *Mary Hatch* in the year 1821. In the ads that Fisher ran in the *Nevada State Journal,* he printed the following quote: "Blest be that spot, where cheerful guests retire to pause from toil, and trim their evening fire." To go along with the "evening fire," Fisher added four different entertainment acts, including "The Girl in the Mirror," one roulette game, one 21 game, and (a few months later) a craps game.

Sometime in 1942 or 1943 Fisher sold the 222 Club to Cliff Judd and Blanche Dupuis. They sold the club to Al Hoffman and Frank Mercer on October 10, 1944, and the property's name was changed to the La Fiesta Club on October 27, 1944. The property operated as the La Fiesta until June 1947.

Early in 1947 A. K. Sekt attempted to open the property as the Grid Iron Club, but the sale was never completed.

On June 5, 1947, William Barrett was granted a gaming license at the "new" 222 Club for six slots, one 21 game, and one craps game.

In January 1948, under the first ruling of the newly created Nevada Tax Board (headed by Robbins Cahill), F. J. Esswein was denied a license at 222 North Center Street. He had proposed to buy the 222 Club and change its name to the Dunes.

In January 1949 the City of Reno refused to renew the gaming license at the 222 Club. The application was made by William Barrett, but the reason for the denial was that Lois Maury, wife of co-owner Oscar "Lee" Maury, had recently been arrested for possession of narcotics. In April the city once again denied Barrett a license for a 21 game but did license him and the 222 Club for six slot machines.

Warren Wilson, former owner of the Inferno Club, took possession of the 222 Club in July 1949 but was never licensed for gaming there. Ernest Zottola bought the 222 Club in December 1949. On January 5, 1950, the 222 Club—owned by Zottola and managed by William Barrett—was destroyed by fire. In April 1950 the building was condemned and razed.

The site of the 222 Club is now part of Harrah's Sport Casino on the east side of Center Street.

Nev. St. Journal, 31 Jan. 41 (advs. and photos), 4 May 41 (adv.), 4 July 41 (adv.), 10 Oct. 44, 27 Oct. 44 (adv.), 5 June 47, 10 June 47 (adv.), 9 Dec. 47, 6 Jan. 48, 7 Mar. 48, 14 Nov. 48 (adv.), 25 Jan. 49, 12 Feb. 49, 4 Mar. 49, 12 Apr. 49, 31 May 49, 31 July 49 (adv.), 15 Nov. 49, 24 Dec. 49, 29 Dec. 49, 6 Jan. 50, 12 Apr. 50, 24 Jan. 53, 28 Mar. 53.

U

U.S. 40 TAVERN

640 East Fourth Street; licensed from March 12, 1946, to June 1, 1948, for slots and 21.

The U.S. 40 Tavern, named because of its location on the former U.S. Highway 40, was licensed for one 21 game in March 1946. Oscar Hewitt was the licensee. The club was located next to a motel and was more a bar than a casino. The U.S. 40 Tavern (not to be confused with the Tavern on West Fourth Street) featured entertainment and dining as well as a 21 game.

In August 1948 Eli Moran and Eli Borrin purchased the Tavern. They sold it to Elmer Avansino in 1951. Avansino licensed the U.S. 40 Tavern for thirty-five slot machines, one roulette game, one craps game, and one 21 game.

In 1967 the U.S. 40 Tavern was sold, and the name was changed to the Carnival Room. The site is now called the Highway 40 Motel.

Nev. St. Journal, 16 Feb. 46 (adv.), 13 Mar. 46, 14 July 46 (adv.), 24 Aug. 48, 12 June 51, 5 Mar. 67 (adv.).

UNITED CLUB ROOM

27 East Douglas Alley; licensed from May 10, 1962, to October 21, 1964, for slots, 21, and poker.

The United Club Room was owned equally by Gen Wong and Tom Wong. Tom Wong had at various times owned many cardrooms in Reno and other locations in northern Nevada. The site is now part of Harolds Club.

Nev. St. Journal, 20 Feb. 62.

V

VAGABOND CLUB

127 West Second Street; never licensed.

On November 25, 1952, the City of Reno licensed Marshall Wardall for one 21 game and one craps game. On December 24 Wardall withdrew his application for a gaming license from the State of Nevada and was therefore never licensed.

The site of the Vagabond Club is now part of the Flamingo Hilton Hotel.

Nev. St. Journal, 25 Nov. 52, 24 Dec. 52.

VALLIN, LOU

Lou Vallin was the owner of the Town House at 43 West First Street from 1945 to 1948. In 1948, when the Nevada Tax Board headed by Robbins Cahill was formed, one of its first official actions was to revoke Lou Vallin's gaming license. The loss of his license resulted in Vallin also losing the lease on the Town House, effectively putting him out of business.

VAL'S CLUB

333 East Second Street; licensed from April 2, 1966, to November 13, 1967, for slots and 21.

In February 1966 Val Ruggerio and Eugene Belluomini (also known as Gene Bell) applied to reopen Swede's Club, which had closed in 1965 because of financial difficulties. Ruggerio and Belluomini wanted to invest $25,000 to finance one 21 game and five slot machines. The club was to be named Val's. Ruggerio had previously held gaming licenses at the Christmas Tree and at the El Morocco in Las Vegas (and would later be licensed at the King's Inn).

Val's Club was licensed and opened in April 1966. It operated until November 1967. The site is now a vacant lot.

Nev. St. Journal, 3 Feb. 66, 21 Apr. 66, 13 Nov. 67.

VICTORY LODGE

South Virginia Street; licensed from May 23 to December 1942 for 21 only.

No other information available.

VIGNAUX, BERNARD

Bernard Vignaux, originally from San Francisco, was a 5-percent owner of the Palace Club from December 1953 until May 1964.

Nev. St. Journal, 11 Dec. 53.

VILLA ROMA

4201 West Fourth Street; licensed from January 24 to December 1959 for slots, 21, and roulette.

The Villa Roma was a fine Italian restaurant on West Fourth Street (also known as Highway 40). It featured dancing, dining, and entertainment as well as gaming. Frank Dodge, Gordon Burnett, and Joe Carlos, who were previously licensed at the Eagle Club in Yerington, were the licensees at the Villa Roma. They operated slot machines as well as roulette and 21 games.

Currently located at the former site of the Villa Roma is a popular restaurant known as the Glory Hole.

Nev. St. Journal, 15 Jan. 59, 21 Jan. 59, 27 Feb. 59 (adv.).

VILLA SIERRA

4245 West Fourth Street; licensed from December 1941 to 1952 for slots, 21, craps, roulette, and poker.

The Villa Sierra was a popular local nightclub and restaurant located on the outskirts of town. It had quite a varied history. Opened in 1941, it closed shortly thereafter, possibly because of the many shortages created in the early days of World War II. It was reopened in September 1944 by Earl McCracken. In 1944 and early 1945, John Harden and Ed Burgess were partners in the operation, until Harden committed suicide in February 1945. In May 1945 Bill and Alice Dixon reopened the property and named it Reno Chicken Hut. In 1946 Joe Anselmo took over the property and reopened it as the Villa Sierra.

Harry Short and Mike Sherdon took control of the property in 1947. Harry Short was also a bandleader, and his band was the main entertainment for several

years in the late 1940s and early 1950s. At one time or another, Harry Short also had as partners Rudy Pollack, Mel Wilder, and Joe Anselmo.

The last person to be licensed for gaming at the Villa Sierra was Don Eamelli in 1952.

Currently at the former location of the Villa Sierra is Johnny's Ristorante Italiano.

Nev. St. Journal, 13 Dec. 41 (adv.), 7 Sept. 44, 4 Feb. 45, 16 May 45, 17 July 46 (adv.), 1 Aug. 46 (adv.), 22 Apr. 47, 8 July 47 (adv.), 25 Apr. 48 (adv.), 19 Oct. 49 (adv.), 8 May 51, 29 July 51, 2 Dec. 52, 1 Mar. 65; Reno Telephone Directory, 1946.

VIRGINIA BAR

233 North Virginia Street; licensed from 1941 to 1945 for 21, craps, roulette, and slots.

The Virginia Bar was a favorite meeting place for many off-duty casino workers, and Bill Harrah was a regular customer. The first game licensed there was a roulette table. In the years ahead, the bar was also licensed for slots, a 21 game, and a craps game.

The Virginia Bar closed in early 1946 and was reopened as the Picadilly Club in July 1946. The site is now part of the Nugget Casino.

Nev. St. Journal, 13 Dec. 41 (adv.), 10 Jan. 46, 2 July 46.

VIRGINIAN HOTEL

241 North Virginia Street and the corner of North Sierra and Plaza; never licensed.

Ernie Primm, who was at one time the largest property owner in downtown Reno and who owned the Primadonna Casino for many years, never owned a hotel in Reno, but twice he announced that he would build a hotel and name it the Virginian.

On June 23, 1954, Primm announced that he had plans to build a $2-million hotel at 241 North Virginia Street, to be called the Virginian Hotel. The hotel would be eight stories high and have 108 rooms. However, ground was never broken for the structure. On October 19, 1977, Primm announced plans for an $11-million, fourteen-story hotel, to be called the Virginian Hotel-Casino, to be located at the corner of North Sierra and Plaza Streets. He said the hotel would have 216 rooms and two and one-half levels of parking, and that it would be completed within two years. Again, ground was never broken.

Currently there is a Virginian Hotel-Casino located at 140 North Virginia Street. It was owned by the Karadanis family for many years and was sold to the Best Gaming Corporation in 1998. It is currently being leased to the Club Cal-Neva. This business has no connection with the Primm projects. It closed in July 1997, but it re-opened in 1999. *(See Addendum 3).*

Nev. St. Journal, 23 June 54, 19 Oct. 77.

VOSS, DARL

Darl Voss, a navy veteran of World War II, was hired by Harolds Club shortly after his discharge from the service and remained there until 1971. He was later employed as the manager of Barney's Club at Lake Tahoe, and was both casino manager and general manager of the Gold Dust East in the 1980s. After leaving the Gold Dust East, he returned to Harolds Club and remained there until his retirement.

In the 1940s and the early 1950s, when Voss was dealing at Harolds Club, he was known as an outstanding roulette dealer. Many roulette dealers in the fifties, sixties, and seventies attributed their skills to Voss's help. Voss was a shift manager at Harolds Club for many years and is remembered fondly by dozens of former dealers as their favorite boss.

Darl Voss is now retired and lives in Reno.

Nev. St. Journal, 20 Apr. 80.

W

WAGON WHEEL BAR

136 East Commercial Row; licensed from November 27, 1945, to 1950 for slots and 21.

116 East Commercial Row; licensed from April 26, 1956, to December 13, 1960, for slots and 21.

The Wagon Wheel Bar was located in what was then known as Reno's skid row. Patrons of the Wagon Wheel were mainly the unemployed, the homeless, and minority groups. Don Backus was granted a gaming license at this location for slots and 21 in 1945. In March 1950 the Wagon Wheel Bar was cited for using a marked 21 deck, and on April 11 the Reno City Council closed the business. In June 1952, Judge A. J. Maestretti ordered Don Backus to vacate the premises. Backus had been operating without a legitimate lease, was "disturbing the peace," and was operating a 21 game without a license.

Gaming was licensed again at the Wagon Wheel's new location at 136 East Commercial Row in April 1956. In December 1960, after a rash of incidents involving the sale of liquor to minors and several fistfights and knife fights, the Reno City Council once again closed the Wagon Wheel. It was reopened in the 1960s, but there was no table gaming.

The site is now part of Harrah's Club parking garage.

Nev. St. Journal, 27 Nov. 45, 4 Mar. 49, 30 Mar. 50, 11 Apr. 50, 8 June 50, 17 Apr. 51, 13 June 52, 13 Dec. 60, 28 Dec. 60.

WALDORF CLUB

142 North Virginia Street; licensed from April 1931 to November 30, 1956, for slots, poker, faro, pan, roulette, craps, hazard, chuck-a-luck, and 21; licensed for slots only in 1957.

The Waldorf Club was opened by Robert Preston in the Clay-Peters Building in 1910. In 1929 Preston and his partner, Charles Brenda, moved the Waldorf next door to 142 North Virginia Street. In April 1931 the Waldorf was licensed for five slot machines, and over the next few months various table games were added to the license. Through the years and under various owners, the Waldorf was licensed for just about every gambling game played in the Reno area.

Robert Preston died in December 1932. Because his widow, Mildred Preston, inherited his share of the Waldorf, she became the first female casino owner in Northern Nevada. Mildred Preston and Charles Brenda operated the Waldorf until they sold it to Joseph and Solomon Bulasky in 1938. The Bulaskys owned the business but leased out the casino to Jake and George Hagenson.

In October 1939 the Waldorf was sold to Arthur Nelson and Glen Whiddett. Jake and George Hagenson continued to operate the casino. Besides the casino, the Waldorf featured a smoke shop, a sandwich bar, its famous Coca-Cola soft drinks, and a barber shop. The Waldorf's building was owned by Charles Richards, but Nelson and Whiddett operated the business for the next ten years.

On October 1, 1948, the Waldorf was sold to Warren Nelson and Howard Farris. At the time of the sale, the business was licensed for one pan game, one roulette game, and one 21 game. Nelson and Farris operated the Waldorf until April 1, 1949. At that time, Farris left the partnership. Nick Abelman took over 75 percent of the business, and Warren Nelson retained the other 25 percent interest.

The Abelman-Nelson partnership never worked well, and it wasn't long until Warren Nelson left the Waldorf. In January 1950 Nick Ableman was licensed for one roulette game, one 21 game, and six slot machines.

In September 1951 Harold and Anna Walters and Roy Nelson were licensed for gaming at the Waldorf. Originally, Nick Abelman was supposed to divest himself of any interest in the Waldorf, but this did not come about. The new partnership licensed the club for twenty-five slot machines, one craps game, and one roulette game.

Nick Abelman, pictured in 1946. Courtesy of William Pettite.

In November 1951 the Waldorf was licensed by three new stockholders: Roy Black, I. L. Lawlor, and Bernie Ivener. The following were listed as corporate officers of the Waldorf: Harold Walters, president; Anna Walters, vice-president; and Roy Nelson, secretary-treasurer. The grand opening of "Reno's oldest and newest landmark" was held on November 28, 1951. Harold Walters announced that Reno's famous chef Jean Sigg would oversee the restaurant, Frenchy DuPouy would be the bar manager, and Eddie Starr and Rommele would be featured at the piano bar.

Nick Abelman died on December 15, 1951, and in March 1952, Abelman's widow, June—representing Abelman's estate—and Al Bisignano were licensed as new partners in the Waldorf. During the next four years, there were several changes in the gaming license of the Waldorf. First, Roy Nelson sold his percentage to Harold Walters in June 1952. Then in 1953 Phyliss Matthews, Al Vario, Mark Yori Jr., and Peter Amante were added to the license. Al Vario was deleted from the license in late 1953. In July 1954 James Hammond was licensed as a partner in the Waldorf, and the club was licensed for fifteen slots, two 21 games, and a roulette game. Changes were also made in management, as Andre Simetys was named chef and John Sanford became manager of the club.

On July 7, 1956, the state cited the Waldorf for improper operation of a 21 game. The Waldorf's president, Harold Walters, denied the charges, but on July 31, 1956, the Gaming Control Board recommended that the Waldorf have its gaming and slot licenses revoked. The next day the Gaming Commission concurred. The listed owners at the time of the recommendation were Harold and Anna Walters, J. R. Lawlor, June Abelman (representing the estate of Nick Abelman), James Hammond, and Edward Thomas.

On August 4 the Waldorf obtained a temporary restraining order preventing the state from closing it down until the state supreme court ruled on the closure. But before the supreme court heard the case, the Waldorf closed of its own accord. On November 29, 1956, after the graveyard shift, the doors were closed and fifty-five employees were put out of work. Business had gone steadily downhill since July when the state took legal action to close the club's gaming. President Walters stated that "he regretted closing, but business doesn't warrant staying open." The casino was operating two 21 games, twenty slots, a bar, and a restaurant at the time of closure.

In March 1957 James Hammond was licensed for twenty slots at the Waldorf. However, the club was soon sold again, this time to John Nash, who in turn leased it to Eddie Andary. Andary reopened the club on March 12, 1958, as Andary's, a dinner house that did not have gaming. Glen Rolfson entertained at the organ.

Andary's soon went out of business, and the property was closed again until Leon Nightingale and Frank Harris opened it in 1959. Nightingale and Harris sold the property to Jack and Georgia Young in June 1959. The Youngs, along with John Edgecomb, operated the Waldorf as a bar and restaurant, without gaming. They were famous for their prime-rib dinners, and the place was a late-night hangout for many local musicians and casino workers in the 1960s and early 1970s. Jack Joseph, a local disc jockey, played

records and hosted entertainment and local personalities until the wee hours of the morning during that period.

The Youngs sold the property to the Club Cal-Neva in 1979. The doors of the Waldorf closed for the last time on July 28, 1979. The site is now part of the Club Cal-Neva.

Nev. St. Journal, 3 May 31 (adv.), 6 Apr. 33, 5 Aug. 39 (adv.), 15 Oct. 39, 25 Sept. 48, 3 Oct. 48 (adv.), 30 Mar. 49, 3 June 49 (adv.), 11 Jan. 50, 30 Aug. 51, 7 Sept. 51, 15 Sept. 51, 23 Oct. 51, 14 Nov. 51, 28 Nov. 51 (adv.), 4 Dec. 51, 16 Dec. 51, 1 Mar. 52, 24 June 52, 26 Nov. 52 (adv.), 18 June 53, 24 Nov. 53 (adv.), 25 Nov. 53, 20 Jan. 54, 7 July 54, 16 July 54, 8 Oct. 54 (adv.), 7 July 56, 31 July 56, 1 Aug. 56, 4 Aug. 56, 11 Aug. 56, 15 Aug. 56, 18 Oct. 56, 30 Nov. 56, 15 Feb. 57, 22 Mar. 57, 21 July 57, 12 Jan. 58, 11 Mar. 58, 16 Jan. 59, 20 July 59, 22 July 79.

WALKER, JACK

Jack Walker came to Reno in 1955 and had several managerial jobs in various casinos around the Reno area. In March 1963 he was appointed casino manager of the Holiday Hotel-Casino. Walker, whose son, Wayne, was a professional football player, was instrumental in making the Holiday the center of a multitude of sports-oriented marketing programs.

Nev. St. Journal, 16 Mar. 63 (photo).

WANDER INN

220 North Virginia Street; licensed from April 1, 1936, to May 13, 1937, for one 21 game.

The Wander Inn opened originally at 135 North Virginia Street in December 1934. It moved to 220 North Virginia Street in 1935. Owned by Victor Portopilo, it opened as a sandwich shop but later evolved into a nightclub and cabaret.

The address was home to several small clubs during the 1930s and 1940s. This was also the location of the Frontier Club from 1946 to 1956. The site is now part of Harrah's Club on Virginia Street.

Nev. St. Journal, 11 Dec. 34, 18 Jan. 35 (adv.).

WASHOE CAFE (WASHOE CLUB OR WASHOE BAR)

32–34 East Commercial Row; licensed from June to December 1931 for craps and 21.

The Washoe Cafe was located on East Commercial Row with entrances on both Commercial Row and Douglas Alley. It was located in an area where several small clubs, bars, and cardrooms operated during the early years of Reno gaming. The former location of the Washoe Cafe is now part of Harolds Club.

WATERMAN, SANFORD

Sanford Waterman headed a group of investors who launched the original Cal-Neva in 1947. The same group also owned the Cal-Neva Lodge at Lake Tahoe. In 1955 Waterman's group sold the Cal-Neva to a group headed by James Contratto and Dr. Robert Franks.

Waterman spent the remainder of his gaming career in Las Vegas, where he was associated with the Sands Hotel and, at the time of his death in April 1977, with Caesars Palace, where he was vice-president and casino manager.

Nev. St. Journal, 31 May 70 (biog.), 5 Apr. 77 (obit.).

WEBSTER, CHARLES "CHUCK"

Chuck Webster was born in Canada on July 2, 1909, and moved to Minot, North Dakota, at an early age. He came to Reno in the late 1930s and was hired by Harolds Club in 1940. Except for time in military service during World War II, he was employed there continuously until 1970. Over six feet tall and always impeccably dressed, Chuck had a smile for everyone and was one of the most popular casino shift managers who ever worked at Harolds Club.

Shortly after Harolds Club was sold to the Hughes Corporation in 1970, Webster went to work for the Mapes Corporation. He worked in both the Mapes Hotel and the Mapes Money Tree Casino until his retirement in the 1980s.

Webster passed away on April 23, 1986.

WEITZ, HARRY

Harry Weitz was born in Russia on October 30, 1904, and came to the United States as a young man. He first came to Reno in 1936.

Weitz was licensed as co-owner of the Sierra Turf Club in 1950. He was later licensed for 11 percent of the Palace Club from 1953 to May 1964, and he was also licensed as one of the three shift managers at the Palace. In 1956 Weitz was licensed as a co-owner of the Tahoe Palace (or Plaza) on the South Shore of Lake Tahoe.

Harry Weitz was well liked by most of his employees. One reason for his popularity was that he believed in giving cash (usually "under the table") to his employees if the club or a particular shift had won some money. He explained away his generosity by saying, "It wasn't that I was such a nice guy. I just wanted to keep them honest."

Harry Weitz died in a rest home in Reno on January 29, 1991.

Nev. St. Journal, 14 Apr. 50, 20 June 56.

WEITZ, WILLIAM

William Weitz was born in St. Louis, Missouri, and came to Reno via San Francisco in 1953. He was a 4-percent owner of the Palace Club from 1953 until he was killed in an automobile accident sixteen miles south of Tonopah in March 1959. His brother, Harry, was also a co-owner of the Palace.

Nev. St. Journal, 11 Dec. 53, 31 Mar. 59 (obit.).

WERTHEIMER, LOU

Lou Wertheimer was born in Cheboygan, Michigan, in 1889. He and his brothers, Al, Lionel, and Mert, operated casinos in Detroit and Florida before Lou headed west to Palm Springs, California, in the 1930s. In Palm Springs he was associated with the famous Clover Club, the Colonial Club, and the Dunes. The gambling clubs in Palm Springs were wide open in the thirties, forties, and fifties, and movie stars like George Raft and others frequented them. Many dealers and pit bosses traveled a circuit, going from Lake Tahoe in the summer to Palm Springs in the winter, with stops in-between at places such as Hot Springs, Arkansas.

Wertheimer came to Reno in 1944 and was a co-owner of the Bonanza Club on North Center Street from 1944 to 1947. In 1947, when the Mapes Hotel opened its casino, Lou Wertheimer was one of four partners who leased the gaming from Charles Mapes, the others being Bernie Einstoss, Frank Grannis, and Leo Kind.

In December 1955 Lou and his brother, Mert Wertheimer, along with Baldy West and Ruby Mathis, purchased the Riverside Hotel from George Wingfield for $4 million. The Wertheimer brothers had been leasing the casino since 1950. In January 1958 they sold the Riverside to the Crummer Corporation but took a ten-year lease on the casino, bars, restaurants, and entertainment. Crummer would run the hotel only.

On May 20, 1958, Lou Wertheimer died in a Hollywood hospital after a long illness.

Nev. St. Journal, 12 Jan. 56, 21 Jan. 58, 20 May 58 (obit.).

WERTHEIMER, MERT

Mert Wertheimer was born in Cheboygan, Michigan, in 1884. He survived the gangland gaming rivalries of Detroit to become one of Nevada's best-known gaming figures. In the late 1920s in Detroit, he headed the Chesterfield Syndicate, which controlled various gaming operations in the Detroit area. After Detroit authorities cracked down on gambling in the 1930s, Wertheimer and many of his associates moved to Florida. Their biggest operation there was the Royal Palms Casino in Miami. After coming to Reno in 1946, Wertheimer was prominent in the move to set up more rigid state controls on gaming. One of his most famous comments was, "The thing I like about it here is that you don't have to pay anyone off."

In his first business venture in 1946, he entered a short-term partnership with former Chesterfield Syndicate members Lincoln Fitzgerald and Dan Sullivan at the Nevada Club. In May 1949 Wertheimer leased the gambling at the Riverside, taking over from Nick Abelman and Bert Riddick. His partners were Ruby Mathis and Baldy West. He was joined in 1951 by his brother, Lou.

In December 1955 the Wertheimers, along with Baldy West and Ruby Mathis, purchased the Riverside Hotel from George Wingfield for $4 million. In January 1958 the same group sold the Riverside to the Crum-

mer Corporation for a price estimated to be between $4 and $5 million. However, they took a ten-year lease on the casino, bar, restaurant, and entertainment.

Mert Wertheimer was the first to introduce big-name entertainment in a nightclub atmosphere to the Reno area on a regular basis. The first big-name entertainer to appear at the Riverside was Ted Lewis in July 1950. In August 1951 the headline performer was Frank Sinatra. During the Wertheimer era, just about every big name in the entertainment industry, including Sammy Davis Jr., Nat "King" Cole, Patti Page, Kay Starr, and many more, appeared at the Riverside.

Ironically, within a few months from the time they entered into their lease arrangement with the Crummer Corporation, both Wertheimers died. Lou died on May 20, 1958, and two months later, on July 20, Mert died of leukemia in a Hollywood hospital.

Nev. St. Journal, 5 Apr. 49, 12 Jan. 56, 21 Jan. 58, 22 July 58 (obit.).

WEST, ELMER "BALDY"

Elmer West came to Reno in the mid-1920s. He became associated with Bill Graham and James McKay soon after his arrival, and he worked for them in the late 1920s and the early 1930s at the Willows, the Rex Club, and the Idlewild Club, among others.

In 1936 West operated the gambling at the famous but short-lived Country Club on Plumas Avenue. The Country Club was razed by fire after being in operation less than a year. For the next several years, West worked for Graham and McKay at the Bank Club.

In 1943 West, along with Ernie Primm, James Contratto, Joe Hall, and Archie Sneed, leased the Palace Club for ten years. As a testimony to West's management skill, the other owners invested $35,000 each, but West's contribution was in the form of services. Contratto sold his interests a few months after the agreement took effect, and in 1951 West and Sneed bought out Hall and Primm and operated the club until their lease expired in June 1953.

Baldy West was a co-owner and manager at the Riverside Hotel for a short time in the middle 1950s before leaving to open the Horseshoe Casino on North Virginia Street. The Horseshoe opened in November 1956 with thirteen owners. West was licensed as president and major owner (31 percent) of the casino. He sold his holdings in the Horseshoe in January 1958.

West left active gaming for several years, but after his wife died in 1970 he went back to work at the Holiday Hotel-Casino and was working there when he passed away on November 16, 1973. He was seventy-one at the time of his death.

Nev. St. Journal, 10 June 53, 28 Apr. 55, 12 Jan. 56, 25 Oct. 56, 3 Jan. 58, 18 Nov. 73 (obit.).

WEST INDIES CLUB

5560 South Virginia Street; licensed from September 1945 to 1954 for 21 and slots.

The West Indies Club opened on July 27, 1944, as a restaurant featuring Chinese and American food. It wasn't until 1945 that a 21 game was licensed there.

In October 1948 the operator of the gaming at the West Indies was Newell Benningfield. He also dealt the 21 game. On the night of October 25, a man named Leonard Wolff entered the club at 3:30 A.M. with a female companion (the wife of writer John Steinbeck, who was in Reno for a divorce), and they both gambled for six hours. He played as much as $500 a hand on the 21 game and played as many as six or seven hands at a time, while she played the dollar slot machines. At the conclusion of Wolff's play, he had lost $86,000. He wrote checks to cover his losses in the amounts of $7,000, $29,000, and $50,000. However, he signed them without using his middle initial. Wolff then took Mrs. Steinbeck back to her room. A few hours later, he was found dead in his parked car near the Mount Rose Highway. The cause of death was a gunshot wound to his head. His death was believed to have been suicide, but it was never proved.

When Benningfield took Wolff's checks to the bank, the bank refused to cash them because the middle initial was missing from the signature. In February 1949 Benningfield filed a claim against Wolff's estate for the $86,000 he had won from Wolff in

October. In April Judge McKnight ruled that Benningfield could not collect on Wolff's checks. Benningfield appealed the decision to the Nevada Supreme Court, and on January 18, 1950, the court made a final ruling upholding Judge McKnight's decision.

Benningfield, in the meantime, had sold the West Indies to F. A. Palmer in July 1949. Palmer in turn sold the property to John, Peggy, and Bill Rhodes in 1951. In March 1951 Raymond "Bud" Dutcher was named manager of the West Indies, and in May 1951 Bud Dutcher, his wife, Gloria, and Charles Lindstrom were granted gaming licenses.

On January 1, 1953, tragedy struck down Bud Dutcher. He was at Dixie's Log Cabin on Gentry Way when he and Lee Maury became involved in an altercation. Maury shot Dutcher and wounded him fatally. Maury was eventually convicted of second-degree murder.

The West Indies was closed in 1954 when Raymond I. Smith of Harolds Club purchased the two parcels of land where the West Indies was located. The business later reopened, and over the years several restaurants and bars operated there. The building was razed in 1998. The empty lot is about twenty yards south of the northeast corner of Meadowood Mall Way and South Virginia Street.

Nev. St. Journal, 27 July 44 (adv.), 19 Apr. 46, 4 May 46 (adv.), 26 Oct. 48, 6 Nov. 48, 16 Feb. 49, 23 Apr. 49, 10 May 49, 6 July 49, 18 Jan. 50, 10 Mar. 51, 8 May 51, 1 Sept. 51 (adv.), 12 Jan. 53, 12 June 54.

WHEEL CLUB

146 North Center Street; licensed from February 16, 1944, to November 1945 for 21, craps, and roulette.

Jack Hoyt and John Coffee Jr. opened the Wheel Club on the southeast corner of Second and Center Streets on February 16, 1944. The Wheel Club featured penny roulette, blackjack, and 21. It was one of the last clubs to deal a penny roulette game.

The Wheel Club was located in what was then known as the Lyons Building. On November 13, 1945, a fire in the Lyons Building

did so much damage to the Wheel Club that it was closed and never reopened. The site is now occupied by the Cameo Super Pawn Shop.

Nev. St. Journal, 15 Feb. 44 (adv.), 17 Mar. 44 (adv.), 28 Mar. 44, 29 May 45, 14 Nov. 45, 25 Sept. 57; Reno City Directory, 1944.

WHISTLE STOP

275 North Virginia Street; licensed from July 1, 1965, to March 11, 1966, for slots and 21.

The Whistle Stop opened on July 1, 1965, at the former location of Poor Pete's. William Epperson and Furnifold Dale were the licensees, and they were approved for sixty-nine slots and one 21 game. The Whistle Stop advertised itself as "Reno's only authentic go-go discotek."

The Whistle Stop closed in 1966. The personnel office of Fitzgeralds Casino-Hotel now occupies the site.

Nev. St. Journal, 11 June 65, 23 June 65, 29 June 65 (adv.), 2 July 65.

WHITE HORSE BAR

6295 South Virginia Street; licensed in 1946 and 1947 for one 21 game only; licensed again in 1956 and 1957.

The White Horse Bar was located south of the city limits and was basically a bar that offered the convenience of a 21 game and slots to a primarily local clientele. Fred Saunders was the gaming licensee in 1956 and 1957. The gaming was closed in April 1957.

The site is part of the Shopko parking lot.

WILD BILL HICKOK'S GOLDEN GULCH

34 East Second Street; licensed in 1964 for eighteen slots and two table games.

On April 14, 1964, the Reno City Council invoked the controversial red-line law to limit a gaming license for Hickok's Golden Gulch. John Hickok had applied for forty-eight slots, a chuck-a-luck game, and a wheel of fortune, but he was granted only eighteen slots and two table games.

The Golden Gulch opened on May 1, 1964, advertising itself as "The Biggest Little Club in the Biggest Little City." Currently the former location of Hickok's Golden Gulch is part of the Club Cal-Neva.

Nev. St. Journal, 14 Apr. 64, 1 May 64 (adv.).

WILLIAMS, INGRAM "BILL"

Bill Williams was born in Georgia in 1896 and came to Reno via Los Angeles in the late 1930s. He was a friend and associate of Bill Harrah and Virgil Smith, and the three of them were partners in several leased gaming concessions in the late 1930s and early 1940s, including John's Bar on West Second Street and the Christmas Tree on the Mount Rose Highway. In 1958 Williams was named casino manager of the Holiday Hotel-Casino, and in January 1960 he was licensed as casino manager of the Riverside Hotel-Casino.

Bill Williams passed away in 1992.

Nev. St. Journal, 16 May 58, 21 Jan. 60, 3 Oct. 64; Reno Gazette-Journal, 8 Jan. 92.

WILLOWS

Located on the Old Verdi Road (currently Mayberry Road); licensed from April 31, 1931, to June 14, 1932, for 21 and roulette.

The Willows was originally owned by Rick DeBernardi and called Rick's Resort. Built in the early 1900s, it was a popular roadhouse. It gained fame when the location was used as the training quarters for Jack Johnson, who defeated Jim Jeffries in the 1910 heavyweight title fight held in Reno.

With the coming of Prohibition in the 1920s, the Willows closed its doors, and in 1922 James McKay and Bill Graham purchased it from Rick DeBernardi for $40,000. McKay, Graham, and their associates spent $160,000 on renovations and improvements.

Tex Hall, one of Graham and McKay's associates, was instrumental in the remodeling and decorating. He spent thousands of dollars on machines that stamped out the delicate metal filigree work that adorned the hundreds of lights in the Willows and on the grounds surrounding the plush casino and dinner house. The entrance was approached along an avenue of colored lights. The interior was divided into four areas—the Blue Room, where the popular pianist and manager, George Hart,

held court; the restaurant area; the dancing area; and the Chinese Room, where gambling was conducted. The Chinese Room was decorated with Chinese red and blue lacquer on the walls, ceiling, and fixtures. Soft lights shimmered on gold tablecloths and upholstery and on silk draperies.

The Willows was a Reno landmark with a nationwide reputation for its gaiety, hospitality, beauty, and opulence. It catered not only to the more exclusive gamblers and fun-seekers in the western United States but also to the many women from the East who were in Reno seeking a divorce. A Saturday night in the Blue Room often resembled the premiere of an important motion picture. Men dressed in tuxedos and women in evening gowns would enter the room, and George Hart kept the crowd informed as to what was going on in the club. "Mrs. John Doe is now entering the room," he would chant. "She is dressed in a lacy black silk, cut low at the neck, and she is wearing a corsage of violets." Then Hart would take his seat at the piano and paraphrase a popular song, substituting the real names of persons intended to be complimented. Frequently in his introductions Hart volunteered the information that the person introduced was in Reno "to take the cure" (to get a divorce).

The Willows operated as a speakeasy and gambling operation long before gaming was legalized in 1931. When gambling was made legal, it became easier for clubs such as the Willows to operate.

Disaster struck the Willows on June 14, 1932. A fire that originated in the furnace room in the basement of the resort leaped through the wooden structure and destroyed it in less than two hours. The club had been closed for remodeling and was expected to reopen in a few days. James McKay, head of the closed corporation that owned the Willows, announced that they would probably build a new Willows at the same location. But the facility was never rebuilt.

A housing development now covers the area where the Willows formerly stood. The exact location would be the northwest corner of Sherwood Road and Mayberry Road.

Sawyer, Reno, Where the Gamblers Go!; New York Times, 23 Mar. 31 (photo), 1 Nov. 31 (photos); Nev. St. Journal, 17 May 31 (adv.), 15 June 32; Kansas City Star, 26 Apr. 31.

WILLOWS

South Virginia Street; licensed from April 1953 to May 16, 1956, for craps and 21.

The Willows was a dinner house that opened in May 1953 at the former location of Ray's Dinner House, 1.3 miles south of Gentry Way. It was owned and operated by Walt and Nell Daly, who were licensed for one 21 game and one craps game. Well-known Reno host Leon Harbert operated the bar. In 1955 William Quier was licensed by the state to operate one 21 game at the Willows.

The former location of the Willows is now a vacant lot near the intersection of South Virginia Street and McCarran Boulevard.

Nev. St. Journal, 15 Apr. 53, 6 May 53 (photo), 15 May 53 (adv.), 30 June 55.

WINE HOUSE

16–18 East Commercial Row; licensed from April 6, 1931, to July 25, 1960, for slots, 21, craps, roulette, pan, faro, and big-six.

The Wine House was located on East Commercial Row and had entrances on both Douglas Alley and Commercial Row. It was a bar and restaurant as well as a gambling house. Opened by Eli Francovich in 1874, the property was owned by the Francovich family until 1971. The Wine House probably had more gambling games in the years prior to 1931 than it did afterward. In the early 1900s there were three levels of gaming in the establishment, and during the teens and twenties there was gaming of all sorts—including cock-fighting—conducted in the high-ceilinged building.

When gaming was legalized in 1931, the Wine House was one of the first places to be licensed. Its first licensed games were pan, craps, 21, roulette, faro, and a big-six wheel. In August it added a racehorse pool. In October the owners leased space for a faro game to George Allen, and in 1938 they leased space for a faro game to W. E. Buzzard. In 1936 they added a racehorse keno game and also featured wire services from every major-league baseball park in the United States.

The gaming aspects of the Wine House diminished as the years went by. In the last thirteen years of the club's existence, gaming became almost nonexistent as the owners focused on their restaurant.

The property was sold to Harolds Club in 1961 and was used for many years as the break room (recreation area and locker room) for Harolds Club employees. The building was razed in the 1970s to make room for an expansion of Harolds Club. The site is still part of Harolds Club.

Nev. St. Journal, 25 June 36 (adv.), 17 Sept. 39 (adv.), 23 Jan. 45.

WINMOR CLUB
146 North Center Street; licensed in January 1946.

The Winmor Club was licensed by A. F. Winters in January 1946 at the former location of the Wheel Club, which had been severely damaged by a fire in November 1945 and never reopened. The site is now occupied by the Cameo Super Pawn Shop.

Nev. St. Journal, 16 Jan. 46.

WRIGHT, HARRY
Harry Wright, who was born in Missouri in 1875, is believed to be the first African-American to own a gambling casino in Reno. He came to the Reno-Sparks area in 1939 and was licensed as the owner-operator of the Peavine Club in the early 1940s.

At the time of Wright's death in January 1946, he was still active in the operation of the Peavine Club.

YAMAGISHI, OSHIRA, FRED AND Y.

The Yamagishi brothers went into a partnership with Fred Aoyama in the Reno Club in 1931. Aoyoma and Frank Furuta had opened the Reno Club in July 1931 at 232 North Virginia Street. It is believed to be the first licensed bingo game in Nevada.

When war with Japan was declared in December 1941, the Yamagishis and Aoyama were forced to close their business. Bill Harrah leased the location in 1942 and used it to operate Harrah's Bingo Club. After the war the Yamagishis and Aoyama wanted to take back their property, but Harrah refused to give up his lease. In February 1948 the court ruled in favor of Aoyama and the Yamagishis, and Harrah was forced to vacate.

The Yamagishis and Aoyama never opened or operated the property again. In 1948 Harolds Club expanded to include the property at 232 North Virginia Street.

Nev. St. Journal, 16 July 47.

YUKON CLUB

136 East Commercial Row; licensed from January 20, 1954, to June 30, 1959, for craps, 21, keno, slots, and poker.

On January 20, 1954, the State of Nevada licensed J. H. and Harry McMahon and Emerson Wilson for one 21 game, one keno game, and one craps game at the Yukon Club. The business catered mainly to African Americans. In the 1950s the Yukon Club was one of the few Reno casinos that welcomed minority customers. The Yukon Club was located in what was then considered the skid row part of town, where several other small clubs and bars had been licensed at the same location during the early years of legalized gaming in Reno.

On October 10, 1955, the Nevada Gaming Control Board held a hearing concerning the Yukon Club's allegedly falsifying and concealing information about the club's owners. The Board accused owners John and Henry McMahon and Emerson Wilson of concealing the fact that George Chinn held an interest in the club. Chinn had reportedly put up a considerable amount of money to bankroll the blackjack, craps, and keno games. Gaming was halted at the club, and the license was revoked on October 27, 1955.

In October 1956 John Singer, Leverett Bishop, and James Popper were denied a gaming license at the Yukon Club because of Singer's background. The club was to have been named the Singer Club.

The Yukon Club was not licensed again until December 1956, when owner Harry McMahon was licensed for four slot machines.

The club closed in 1959 and was later opened as the S.P. Club. The site is now part of Harrah's parking garage.

Nev. St. Journal, 11 Dec. 53, 20 Jan. 54, 26 Jan. 54, 18 Nov. 54, 28 Sept. 55, 11 Oct. 55, 27 Oct. 55, 26 Oct. 56, 28 Nov. 56, 18 Dec. 56.

Z

ZAKARDI, JOSEPH

Joe Zakardi was a casino executive at Reno's Horseshoe Club in the late 1960s and early 1970s. He was later a casino manager at Barney's Club on the South Shore of Lake Tahoe and casino manager of the Cal-Neva Lodge on the North Shore of Lake Tahoe. In the 1980s he was casino manager of the MGM Hotel-Casino in Reno. When the MGM was sold to Bally's, Zakardi retired from the gaming industry.

Nev. St. Journal, 10 Sept. 70.

ZEMANSKY, JOSEPH

Joe Zemansky was born in Sacramento and came to Reno in 1937. Before that

Joe and Sadie Zemansky. The Zemanskys owned and operated the Club Fortune from 1937 to 1947. Courtesy of Eric "Rick" Heaney.

time, he had managed heavyweight champion Jack Johnson, owned a chain of jewelry stores, and was one of a group that owned and operated the famous Aguascalientes Resort in Mexico. He took over as owner and manager of the Club Fortune in October 1937. Both Zemansky and his wife, Sadie, were involved in the operation of the Club Fortune and were active in civic and community affairs in Reno.

The Club Fortune was one of Reno's finest and most widely known nightclubs and casinos from 1937 until it closed in January 1947. Zemansky owned the club until the lease expired and he was forced to close.

Joe Zemansky passed away on January 12, 1953, while visiting relatives in San Bernadino, California.

Nev. St. Journal, 7 July 71.

ZIMBA'S CARD ROOM
19 East Douglas Alley; licensed from May 19, 1966, to July 11, 1969, for poker and slots.

ZIMBA'S CASINO
44 West Commercial Row; licensed from December 17, 1969, to August 16, 1972, for slots, 21, craps, roulette, and poker.

Sam Sarlo, a former pit boss who moved to Reno from Steubenville, Ohio, was licensed for two poker games at Zimba's Card Room in Douglas Alley in May 1966. In October 1969 Sarlo left his Douglas Alley location to open a casino at 44 West Commercial Row.

In December 1969 the state approved Zimba's for licensing, but only on a six-month probationary basis. Sam Sarlo was licensed for 70 percent, Paul Richards for 30 percent, and Joe Sarlo as an officer with no percentage. The club opened with fifty slot machines, one poker game, and one pan game. In May 1970 Michael DePeano was added to the license, and six table games were also added to the license.

On April 25, 1972, Paul Richards, a 30-percent owner, filed to put Zimba's into receivership. A week earlier, the Nevada Gaming Control Board had asked that Zimba's be closed for failure to report $70,818 in revenue and for not reporting

$81,727 in loans. The Board asked that the casino be fined $30,000 plus interest and be required to pay back-taxes and penalties. In his petition, Richards stated that the 70-percent owner, Sam Sarlo, would not allow him any say in management and that he had filed for receivership to protect his reputation.

It wasn't until August 10 that the state approved John Ross as court-appointed receiver and Benny Hill, former partner in the Horseshoe Club, as casino manager.

Zimba's was closed soon after it went into receivership, and in December 1972 the property was purchased by Elbert Cox and Cy Lopp, who reopened the business and named it the Town Club. The site of Zimba's Casino is currently occupied by the Old Reno Club.

Nev. St. Journal, 6 May 66, 19 May 66, 1 Oct. 69, 13 Nov. 69, 11 Dec. 69, 17 Dec. 69, 21 May 70, 28 June 70 (photo), 25 Apr. 72, 11 Aug. 72, 14 Dec. 72.

ADDENDA

ADDENDUM 1

On June 18, 1999, Steve Yarrow, senior vice-president and general manager of Harrah's Reno, announced that Harrah's had purchased the entire Harolds Club and Nevada Club properties. Harrah's planned to expand into the site with added casino attractions and amenities.

The Harolds Club property included a dozen narrow parcels stretched along Virginia Street, Douglas Alley, and Commercial Row.

Terms of the sale were not made public, but documents from the Fitzgeralds Gaming Corporation indicated that the Nevada Club was sold for $3.8 million. There were no estimates available of the price paid for Harolds Club. However, in 1995 Fitzgeralds sold Harolds for $8.9 million to an out-of-town buyer who then fell into bankruptcy.

On July 28, 1999, Steve Yarrow announced plans to raze the Harolds Club and Nevada Club buildings. Asbestos removal was to begin on August 9, and demolition was expected to begin on September 20 and end October 18. Yarrow did not reveal Harrah's plans for the expansion, but he hinted that the result would be a "spectacular" addition to Reno and would take two to three years to complete.

Reno Gazette-Journal, 19 June 99, 7 July 99, 28 July 99.

ADDENDUM 2

In June 1999, the agreement between the City of Reno and the Oliver McMillan group was terminated. As of August 1999, there were no definite plans for the future of the Mapes Hotel.

ADDENDUM 3

On April 13, 1999, the Club Cal-Neva announced that it would reopen the Virginian Hotel-Casino and lease it with an option to buy. On April 20, 1999, the Cal-Neva announced that it would reopen the Riverboat Hotel-Casino. It has purchased the east hotel tower and retail space connected to the property and has a lease with an option to buy the west tower and the rest of the property.

On May 27, 1999, the Virginian opened for gaming with 126 hotel rooms. The Riverboat opened on June 18 with 126 rooms, giving the Cal-Neva a total of 422 hotel rooms. Both properties are known as the Club Cal-Neva's Virginian. The casino area of the Riverboat has not been reopened.

Reno Gazette-Journal, 11 May 99, 28 May 99.

APPENDIX

Note: The following maps, which are not drawn to scale, indicate the general location of the casinos and gaming establishments mentioned in this book.

The numbers indicated on each map are keyed to the *first* number in each entry on the facing page. The *boldface* numbers refer to the numbered street address. Following each address is a chronological list of the gaming establishments in business at that location during the period covered by this book.

MAP 1: DOWNTOWN RENO, NORTH-SOUTH STREETS

North Virginia Street

1. **133** Onslow Hotel (1977–1989).
2. **136** Lee's Hofbrau House (1969).
3. **140** Nevada Roulette (1931).
4. **142** Waldorf Club (1929–1979).
5. **147** Colbrandt's Flamingo Club (1935–1957); Coral Reef (1957).
6. **210–214** Block N (1931–1941); Mint (1941–1942); Harrah's (1946–present).
7. **211** Henry's Club (1945); Money Tree (1969–1982).
8. **216** Heart Club (1932–1933); Heart Tango Club [1] (1933–1934); Monte Carlo (1937).
9. **220** Bungalow Club (1931); Wander Inn (1936–1937); C&M Club (1940); Swing Club (1940); Pick's Club (1943–1945); Frontier Club (1946–1956).
10. **221** Silver Spur Casino (1968–1981).
11. **224** Snooker Club (1939); Langley's Tango (1940); Robbin's Nevada Club (1941–1946); Nevada Club (1946–1998).
12. **225** Monarch Cafe (1946–1956).
13. **229** Horseshoe Club (1956–1996).
14. **230** Fascination Club (1930); Murray's Club (1942–1947).
15. **230½** Blackout Bar (1943–1945).
16. **232** Keno Club (1931); New Keno Club (1932); Reno Club (1934–1942); Harrah's Reno Club (1942–1948); Sierra Club (1951; never licensed); Harolds Club (1952 to present).
17. **233** Virginia Bar (1942–1945); Picadilly (1946–1952); Nugget (1953); Jim Kelly's Nugget (1955–1990).
18. **236** Harolds Club (1935 to present).
19. **238** Ace of Spades (1934); Elite Tango Club (1935).
20. **241** Golden Gate (1951; never licensed); Primadonna Club (1955–1978).
21. **242** Heart Tango [2] (1934–1938); Tango Club (1939).
22. **244** La Rue Club (1935); Roulette Club (1935).
23. **254** California Club (1946); Colony Club (1946–1964); Harolds Club (1964 to present).
24. **255** Fitzgeralds Casino-Hotel (1976 to present).
25. **261–265** Silver Dollar Club (1959–1974).
26. **265** Stag Inn (1933–1960).
27. **268** Bud(weiser) Bar (1936); Acme Bar (1943–1944).
28. **275** Reno Turf Club (1956–1960); Poor Pete's (1963–1964); Whistle Stop (1965–1966); Gem Casino (1977–1978, 1987–1988).
29. **342** Arena Cigar Store (1931).
30. **345** Eldorado Hotel-Casino (1973 to present).
31. **361** Leo's Den (1972; never licensed); Grotto Bar (1954).

North Center Street

32. **116** Alpine Club (1930–1931, 1932–1939); Majestic Club (1931–1932); 116 Club (1939–1955).
33. **124** Harrah's Club Bingo (1937).
34. **130** Jokereno Club (1931–1932); Dog House (1935–1944); Tropics (1944–1946).
35. **136** Bar of Music (1946–1951); Buddy Baer's (1950–1951); Freddy's Lair (1951; never licensed); Beery's Night Club (1952; never licensed); O'Brien's (1952–1953; never licensed); Trade Winds (1953; never licensed).
36. **146** Wheel Club (1944–1945); Winmor Club (1946).
37. **190** Center Club (1948–1949).
38. **202** Silver Dollar Club (1934–1944); Clover Club (1945–1957).
39. **207** Commercial Hotel (1920s–1950s); Northern Club (1931–1941); Barn (1941–1944); Bonanza Club (1944–1951); Frisco Club (1951–1952); Harrah's Bingo (1952–1962).
40. **208** Elite Turf Club (1957–1961).
41. **219** Golden Gulch (licensed in Golden Hotel in 1947 and 1948); Golden Bank (licensed in the Golden Hotel from 1953 to 1962).
42. **222** Ship and Bottle Club (1932–1940); 222 Club (1941–1944, 1947–1950); La Fiesta (1944–1947); Grid Iron Club (1947; licensed but never opened); Dunes (1948; never licensed).
43. **224** New York Club (1931–1935).
44. **226½** Comstock Club (1932–1935); Inferno Club (1936–1945).
45. **227** Brunswick Club (1931–1946).
46. **228** Center Club (1931); Central Club (1931–1932).
47. **231** Jackpot Arcade (1945–1951).
48. **234** Bright Spot (1961–1965).
49. **238** Overland Hotel (1916–1977); California Club (1931–1932).
50. **239** Bank Club (1931–1952).
51. **240** Oak Room (1953–1973).
52. **242** Overland Bar (1933–1948).
53. **280** Colony Turf Club (1967–1976); Reno Turf Club (1976 to present).

Lake Street

54. **111** Don Lee Club (1931).
55. **128** Stagg's Roaring Camp (1946–1949).
56. **133** Henry Club (1931–1932).
57. **141** Star Club (1931–1932); New Star Club (1932–1944).
58. **150** Bill's Corner Bar (1965–1966).
59. **222** Lido Club (1956, 1962–1964); Old Cathay Club (1956–1957); California Club (1957; never licensed); Happy Buddha (1958–1960).
60. **227** Club of All Nations (1942).
61. **233** Public Club (1932–1933, 1935–1937); Crane's (1933–1935).
62. **238** Toscano Hotel (1920s to 1960s).
63. **246** Colombo Hotel & Colombo Cafe (1920s to middle 1960s); Ming's Cafe (1954–1956); King's Cafe (1956–1957; never licensed); Mint Club (1958–1960); China Mint (1960–1963); Basin Street Club (1964–1966).
64. **260** Palm Club (1931–1935); Palm Cafe (1935–1952); New China Club (1952–1971).

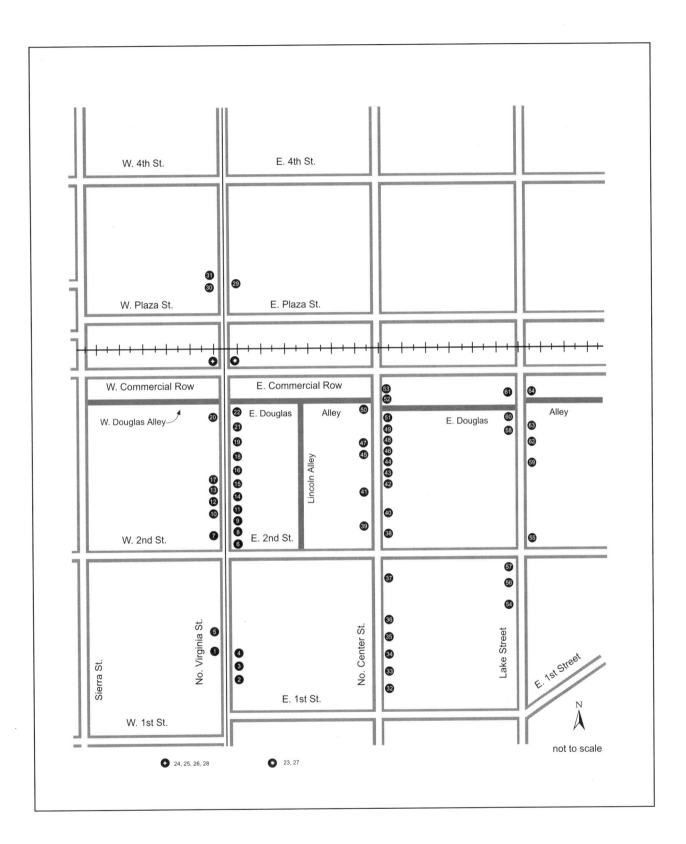

W. 4th St.

E. 4th St.

W. Plaza St.

E. Plaza St.

W. Commercial Row

E. Commercial Row

W. Douglas Alley

E. Douglas   Alley

E. Douglas   Alley

Lincoln Alley

W. 2nd St.

E. 2nd St.

Sierra St.

No. Virginia St.

No. Center St.

Lake Street

E. 1st Street

W. 1st St.

E. 1st St.

N

not to scale

24, 25, 26, 28   23, 27

MAP 2: DOWNTOWN RENO, EAST–WEST STREETS AND ALLEYS (E–W & N–S)

West Commercial Row

❶ **8** Gold Trail Club (1956); Sourdough Club (1956–1957).
❷ **10** Blue Bird Club (1945–1949); Haymarket Club (1951–1953).
❸ **44** Zimba's Casino (1969–1972); Town Club (1972–1973); Old Reno Club (1973 to present).

East Commercial Row

❹ **2** Elite Cigar Store (1931).
❺ **6** L & A Club (1931–1932); Commercial Bar (1944); Delano Club (1945–1946).
❻ **8** Ritz Bar (1934–1936).
❼ **12** Reno Turf (1960–1974).
❽ **14** Art's Darto (1937); Rolo Casino (1947–1950); Plaza Tango (Harrah's) (1938); Sierra Turf Club (1950–1967); and **14-16** Reno Casino (1944–1947).
❾ **16** Wine House (early 1900s to 1960).
❿ **20** Tivoli Bar (1935–1942).
⓫ **22** Louvre (1931–1939); Martin's (1940).
⓬ **32–34** Washoe Club (1931); Washoe Bar (1932); Washoe Cafe (1932–1933).
⓭ **34** Nevada Turf Club (1946–1956).
⓮ **46** Palace Club (1920s to 1979).
⓯ **116** Pastime Club (1929–1944); Wagon Wheel Bar (1956–1960).
⓰ **120** Casino Cigar Store (1931–1932); Tom's Card Room (1965–1966).
⓱ **124** Casino Bar (1942); Depot Bar (1944); Inferno Club (1945); Depot Bar (1946).
⓲ **128** Depot Club (1931–1935); Miner's Tavern (1949–1958).
⓳ **136** Wagon Wheel Bar (1945–1950); Yukon Club (1954-1959); S.P. Club (1965–1969).
⓴ **140** Cosmo Club (1956–1974).
㉑ **142** Owl Club (1931–1938).
㉒ **150** Corner Bar (1937–1945).

East Douglas Alley

㉓ **7** State Club (1931–1932).
㉔ **10** Alley Club (1938).
㉕ **16–18** Rex Club (1931–1941).
㉖ **19** Cherokee Club (1947–1948); Roy's Bar (1961–1962); Maverick (1962–1965); Bob's Saloon (1965–1966); Zimba's Card Room (1966–1969); Ringside (1970–1972).
㉗ **21** Douville Club (1931–1933); Menlo Card Room (1957–1958); Blue Chip Card Room (1958–1959); Ohio Club (1959–1966); Sports Center (1966–1967).
㉘ **27** United Club Room (1962–1964).
㉙ **29½** Hollywood Club (1931).
㉚ **123½** Casino Club (1931).
㉛ **129** Sagebrush Club (1931).
㉜ **218** Dixie's Social Club (1943–1948).
㉝ **219** Elite Club (1949–1952).
㉞ **221** Harlem Club (1948–1968); Soul Club (1968–1977).

Lincoln Alley

㉟ **208** New Capitol Club (1932).
㊱ **231** Blackout Bar (1943–1946).

West Second Street

㊲ **16** John's Bar (1937–1947); Stork Club (1947–1950); Esquire Club (1951–1952).
㊳ **26** Blondy's Bar (1944–1945); Merry-Go-Round Bar (1946–1956).
㊴ **34** Gold Dust East (1976–1983).
㊵ **127** Vagabond Club (1952; never licensed).

East Second Street

㊶ **12** Louie's Rendevous (1935–1938); Leon & Eddie's (1938–1958).
㊷ **16** Reno Turf (1946–1956).
㊸ **31** Grand Buffet (1935–1960).
㊹ **34** Hickok's Golden Gulch (1964).
㊺ **38** Club Cal-Neva (1948 to present).
㊻ **40** Club Fortune (1937–1947).
㊼ **43** Capitol Bar (1931–1948).
㊽ **102** Bingo Center (1948–1949).
㊾ **121** Lucky Club (1936–1944).
㊿ **125** Lucky Club (1931–1936).
(51) **132** Blue Bird Club (1941–1945).
(52) **135** Jim's Bar (1948–1949).
(53) **139** Alturas Club (1931–1944); Alturas Bar (1944–1946).
(54) **142** New Star Keno Club (1947–1948).
(55) **209** Reno Bar (1937).
(56) **229** Mohawk Bar (1941–1943).
(57) **333** Swede's (1963–1965); Val's (1966–1967).

West First Street

(58) **39** Town House (1932–1955).
(59) **43** Deauville Club (1931–1933).

North Virginia Street

(60) **1** Mapes Hotel-Casino (1947–1982).

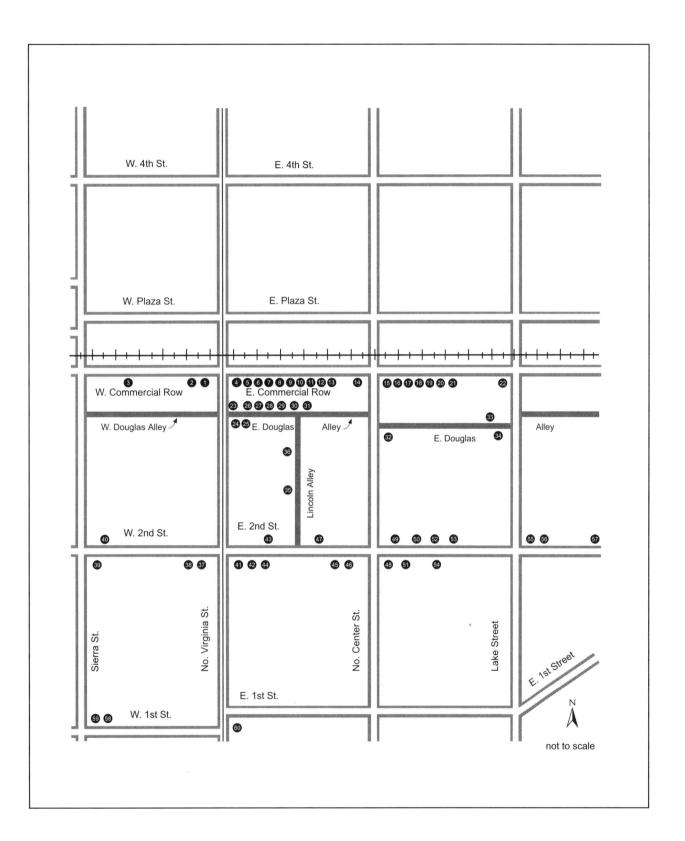

W. 4th St.

E. 4th St.

W. Plaza St.

E. Plaza St.

W. Commercial Row

E. Commercial Row

W. Douglas Alley

E. Douglas

Alley

Lincoln Alley

E. Douglas

Alley

W. 2nd St.

E. 2nd St.

Sierra St.

No. Virginia St.

No. Center St.

Lake Street

E. 1st Street

E. 1st St.

W. 1st St.

N

not to scale

MAP 3: DOWNTOWN RENO

North Arlington Avenue

① **250** Colonial Motor Inn (1966 to present).

② **345** Sands Motor Inn, Sands Hotel-Casino, Mr. C's, Sands Plaza, and Sands Regency (1965 to present).

③ **450** Sundowner Hotel-Casino (1975 to present).

West Second Street

④ **200** Comstock Hotel-Casino (1978 to present).

⑤ **239** El Cortez Hotel (1931 to present).

North Sierra Street

⑥ **218** Ames (1936–1938); Monte Carlo (1938); Carlton Hotel and Bar (1943–1946, 1948–1952); New York Club (1947).

⑦ **243** Sierra Bar (1936).

⑧ **246** Pastime Club (1944–1948).

⑨ **255** Sahara Reno (1978–1981); Flamingo Hilton (1981 to present).

⑩ **320** Plaza Club (1931–1932).

⑪ **500** Circus Circus Hotel-Casino (1978 to present).

West Third Street

⑫ **143** Fan Tan Club (1967); Show Case Casino (1976).

East Sixth Street

⑬ **200** Reno Ramada (1980–1989).

North Virginia Street

⑭ **1** Mapes Hotel-Casino (1947–1982).

South Virginia Street

⑮ **17** Riverside Hotel-Casino (1931–1988).

⑯ **142** Hub (1932).

⑰ **221** Pioneer Inn (1968 to present).

⑱ **325** Charlie's Cocktail Lounge (1941–1952); Bob's Cocktail Lounge (1952–1953).

⑲ **515** Ponderosa Hotel-Casino (1966 to present).

Mill Street

⑳ **111** Holiday Hotel-Casino (1956 to present).

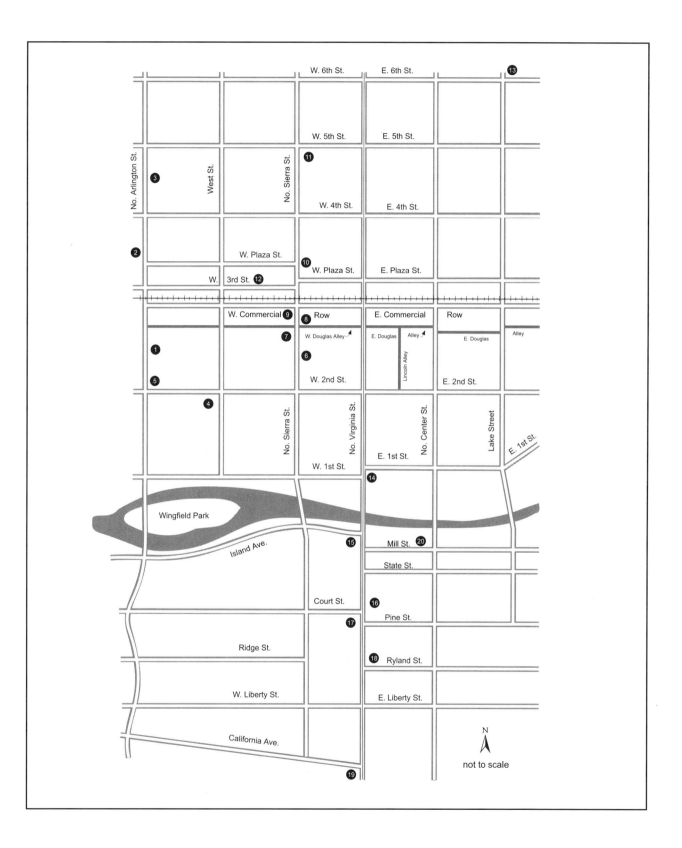

MAP 4: EAST RENO

East Fourth Street

1. **560** Barboot Club (1965).
2. **640** U.S. 40 Tavern (1946–1948).
3. **1002** Nevada Bar (1944–1946).
4. **1303** Tux Club (1955–1964); Copper Club (1964–1965).
5. **1410** Idlewild Club (1920s); Silver Slipper (1931–1937, 1937–1941); Black Derby (1937); Sphynx (1941–1943).
6. **1601** Half Way House (1940s to present).

East Sixth Street

7. **1010** Monte Carlo Casino (1975–1995).

Peavine (now Evans) Street

8. **219** Peavine Club (1941–1947).

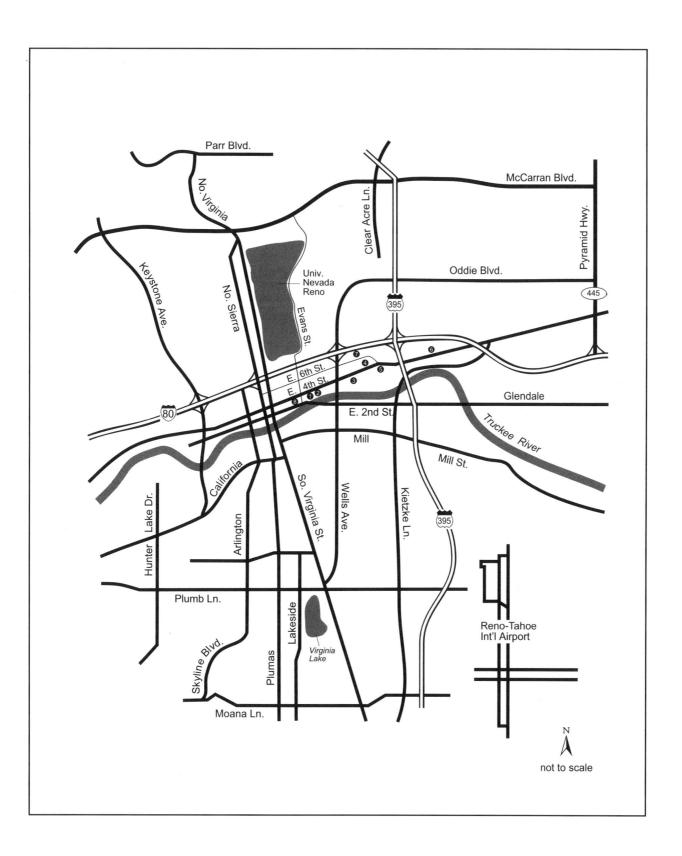

① **715** 715 Club (1971).

② **1099** Sagehen Club (1945).

③ **1402** Tonopah Club (1945).

④ **1585** Cedars (1932–1938, 1940–1947); La Hacienda (1939).

⑤ **1695** South Virginia Bar (1943–1948); Alibi Club (1948–1954).

⑥ **2250** Doll House (1955–1960).

⑦ **2295** Belle Livingstone's Cowshed (1931–1937).

⑧ **2400** Mac's Club (1950–1960, 1961–1963); Jarrard's (1960).

⑨ **2600** Deer Head Lodge (1944–1951); Jolly Jolly Club (1953–1954).

⑩ **2700** Monaco (1961–1963; never licensed).

⑪ **2707** Peppermill (1971 to present).

⑫ **2955** Eugene's (1944–1953).

⑬ **2999** El Morocco (1947).

⑭ **3310** Rancho Bar (1943–1954); El Rancho (1954–1956).

⑮ **3501** Big Hat (1947–1971).

⑯ **3800** Golden Road (1972–1980).

Airport Road (Gentry Way)

⑰ **140** Desert Club (1953); Guy's Rancho Bar (1955).

⑱ **196** Normandy Club (1946–1950); Desert Club (1954–1955).

⑲ **596** Log Cabin (1943–1947); Dixie's Log Cabin (1949–1954).

Kietzke Lane

⑳ **3155** Red Fox (1964).

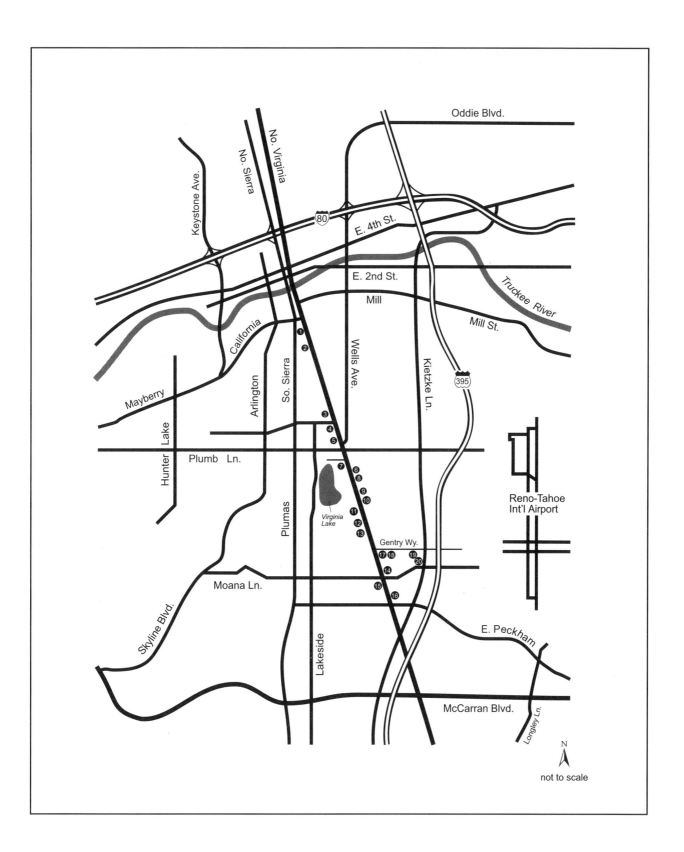

West Interstate 80

① **7 miles w of Reno** Bill & Effie's (1956–1972); Boomtown Casino (1972 to present).

Mayberry Drive

② **NW corner of Sherwood and Mayberry** Willows, formerly Rick's Resort (1931–1932).

Vine Street

③ **444** Gold Dust West Casino (1977 to present).

West Fourth Street

④ **567** Reef (1974–1979); Golden Resort (1980–1981).
⑤ **1801** Tavern (1932–1941).
⑥ **2205** Circle R-B (1951–1962).
⑦ **4201** Villa Roma (1950s to early 1960s).
⑧ **4245** Hutton's Hut (1930s); Villa Sierra (1941–1945, 1946–1953); Reno Chicken Hut (1945–1946).
⑨ **9400** Lawton's (Laughton's) (1880s to 1962. Several casinos operated in Lawton's from 1931 until it was sold in 1962 and renamed the Holiday Lodge); Holiday Lodge (1962–1971); River Inn (1972–1979); Holiday Spa (operated in the River Inn 1971–1979); River Palace (1981 to present; never opened, never licensed).

North Virginia Street

⑩ **4700** Branding Iron (1952–1954); Bodie Mike's Branding Iron (1954–1957).
⑪ **4720** Bonanza Square Casino (1973–1976); Bonanza Casino (1976 to present).

East Fourth Street

⑫ **1601** Half Way House (Club) (1940s to present).

East Second Street

⑬ **1295** Oasis Bar and Grill (1957–1958).
⑭ **2500** MGM Hotel-Casino (1978–1986); Bally's Hotel (1986–1992); Reno Hilton (1992 to present).

South Plumas Avenue

⑮ **NW corner of Moana Lane** Country Club (1935–1936).

West Moana Lane

⑯ **246** Moana Springs Bar (1944–1947).
⑰ **565** Stengler's Dutch Garden (1945–1946); Dutch Garden (1946); Great Dane (1946); Dutch Garden (1946–1948); (Johnny's) Open Door (1951–1955); Supper Club (1955–1959).

East Peckham Lane

⑱ **865** Beatrice Kay Guest Ranch (1956).

South Virginia Street

⑲ **4250** Li'l Red Barn (1953–1958); Liberty Belle (1958 to present).
⑳ **5560** Shadows Supper Club (1961–1962).
㉑ **6295** White Horse Bar (1946–1947, 1956–1957).
㉒ **6405** Heidelburg (1931–1935); Del Monte (1936).
㉓ **9825** Shadows (late 1930s to early 1940s); Sunflower Club (1949–1950); Echo's Club (1951); 395 Club (1955); Trader's (1956–1957).
㉔ **13101** Tamarack Bar (1952 to present).
㉕ **15001** Reno Hot Springs (never licensed).
㉖ **23005** Jubilee Club (1953–1978).

Mount Rose Highway

㉗ Mesa (1948–1959); Lancer (1959–1971).
㉘ **23900** Christmas Tree (1946 to present).

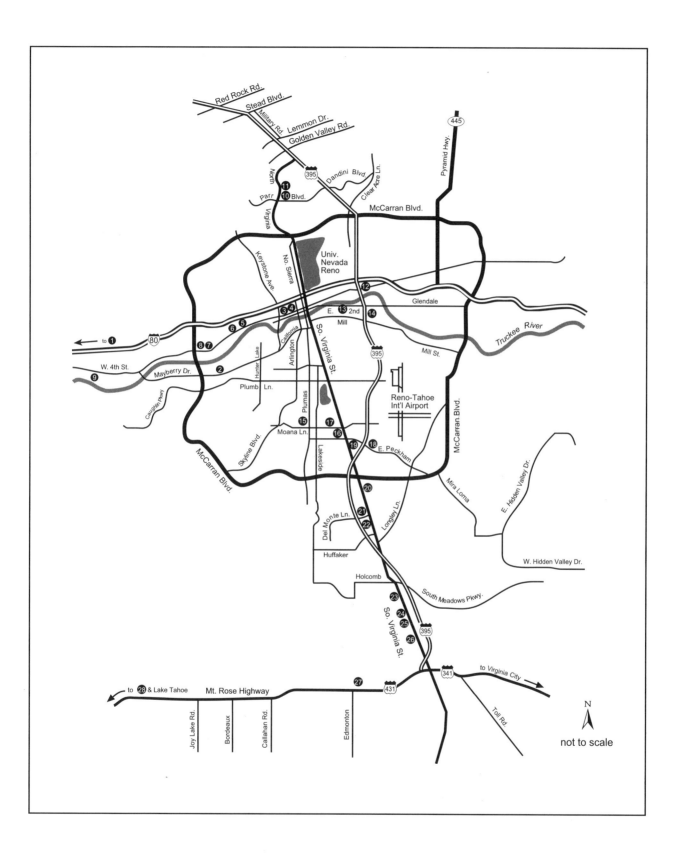

Ace. (1) The highest-ranking card in most card games. (2) The one-spot on a die. (3) A $1 bill.

Ace-Deuced. Died, passed away.

Acey-Deucey. A variation of the game of backgammon.

Ada from Decatur. In craps, slang for the point of 8.

Agent. A person who works in collusion with a crooked casino dealer to cheat the house. Also known as an "A."

Baccarat. Baccarat, under its earlier name, baccara, first made its appearance in America in 1911, and by 1912 several of New York City's illegal gambling clubs featured baccara tables. The game disappeared from the American scene a few years later when the structurally similar blackjack was introduced. It wasn't until the late 1950s that baccarat again became popular in Nevada casinos. The game is dealt from an eight-deck shoe, with the player's hand and the banker's hand each given two cards alternately. To win at baccarat, a player has to select the winning hand between the player's hand and the banker's hand. The object of the game is to get as close to 9 as possible. Ties are a standoff. Face cards, 10s, and any combination of cards totaling 10 have 0 value. If the player's hand is 0, 1, 2, 3, 4, or 5, it automatically receives a hit card. On any other total, the player stands. The bank's play depends on the player's outcome. The following is the "Third-Card Rule":

BANK HAS	DRAWS WHEN GIVING
3	1, 2, 3, 4, 5, 6, 7, 9, 10
4	2, 3, 4, 5, 6, 7
5	4, 5, 6, 7
6	6, 7
7	Stands
8, 9	Stands

If the player takes no card, the banker must draw on 0 through 5 or stand on 6 through 9.

All player bets are paid at even money. Ties are paid off 8 to 1. Bank bets are also paid at even money, but a 5-percent commission is charged.

Back Line (Betting the). In craps, betting that the dice won't pass (i.e., win).

Back to Back. Two cards of the same denomination consisting of the hole card and the top card. Frequently used expression when the dealer has a 10-point value card showing and the same value card in the hole.

Barber Pole. To bet a stack of chips that are different colors and different denominations. A practice frowned on by dealers and casinos because the chips must be separated by the dealer when the bet is made.

Barboot (also known as Barboutie and Barbout). An even-money dice game where the house makes its money by taking a percentage of the money wagered. Has only been licensed in the State of Nevada on one or two occasions.

Beef. A complaint, fight, or argument.

Benjie. A $100 bill.

Bet. Any wager made on the outcome of an event.

Bevels or Beveled Dice. Crooked dice with one or more sides slightly rounded, rather than flat, so that the dice tend to roll off the rounded surface more often than the flat surface.

Big Dick. In craps, slang for the number 10.

Big Eight. On a craps table, a space where the player can make a wager that the dice will roll an 8 before they roll a 7. The wager pays even money.

Big Red. In craps, slang for the number 7.

Big Six. On a craps table, a space where the player can make a wager that the dice will roll a 6 before they roll a 7. The wager pays even money.

Big-Six Wheel. A giant, upright wheel—about five feet in diameter and eight feet tall—that stands on a pedestal behind the layout. Around the rim of the wheel are 54 spaces with individual pictures of three dice, each bearing different combinations. The players put their money on one or more numbers on the layout, and the dealer spins the wheel in a clockwise direction. Nails projecting from the outer edge of the wheel's rim separate the spaces and pass under a leather paddle at the top of the wheel. When the wheel comes to a stop, the section in which the paddle rests is the winning combination. The betting, layout, and payoffs are the same as in the game of chuck-a-luck.

The layout bears the numbers 1, 2, 3, 4, 5, and 6. Players place their bets on one or more of the layout numbers. After the wheel stops, if a player's number appears on one die, he gets paid even money; if his number appears on two dice, he gets paid off at 2 to 1; and if all three dice bear his number, he gets paid off at 3 to 1.

Big-six wheels were common in the early days of Nevada gambling. However, the game's strong percentage against the player (the house percentage is over 22 percent) brought about its demise. There are currently no big-six wheels licensed in Nevada.

Bird Cage. A wire cage used in the games of over-and-under-7 and chuck-a-luck. The cage contains the dice used in the operation of the games.

Black and Whites. Dealers.

Blackjack. (1) Two cards with a total point value of 21—an ace and a 10, jack, queen, or king. (2) *See* Twenty-One.

Bleeder. A pit boss who worries and agonizes about money lost by the casino. Sometimes called a "sweater."

Blow. To lose money.

Bottom Dealer. A cheating dealer who deals cards from the bottom of the deck.

Box Cars. In craps, a pair of 6s on the dice for a total of 12.

Boxman. A person who sits on a low chair located directly behind the drop box at a dice table. The boxman observes all action on the craps table and verifies all payoffs and money transactions. The boxman also verifies the authenticity and denomination of bills handed in for change and, in the early days of gaming, put the bills in the drop box.

Break In. A new dealer.

Breaking Card. A hit card that will cause the player or the dealer to go over twenty-one.

Break the Deck. To shuffle the deck. When the deck is rich in aces or 10-count cards, the pit boss will sometimes tell the dealer to "break the deck" so that the player does not have an advantage. Breaking the deck is a preventative measure that casinos take against card counters.

Bubble and Peek. The name given to the action performed by a cheating "seconds dealer" when he is getting a peek at his top card. He will save his top card and keep dealing the second card until he finds a use for his top card.

Bullet. An ace.

Burn Card. The card taken from the top of a newly shuffled deck and discarded or placed at the bottom of the deck.

Busted. (1) When a 21 player's total card count exceeds 21. (2) When a player or the house loses all their money, they are "busted."

Busters. In craps, a pair of "tops" (misspotted dice). Tops are made in various combinations that make only certain numbers. They are called busters because one combination will bust up another combination.

Bust-Out Man. A dice mechanic who specializes in switching crooked dice in and out of a craps game.

C and E. In a craps game, slang for a bet where the player splits his wager on the 11 and (any) craps.

Call Bet. To make a bet without putting up any money. Seldom accepted in a casino. Most craps layouts have "no call bets accepted" printed on them.

Carpet Joint. In the early days of gambling, when few casinos had carpets, a carpet joint was a luxurious casino. *See also* Sawdust Joint.

Case. In faro, the abacus-type counting board on which a record is kept of the cards used in the deal and whether they won or lost.

Case Bet. (1) The bet made with a player's last remaining money. (2) The last bet. (3) A bet made in faro when three cards of one denomination are gone. Naturally, only one card of the denomination remains, so it is an even bet as to whether the remaining card will be a winner or a loser.

Case Card. The last undealt card of any denomination—for example, the last king in the deck.

Case Keeper. In faro, the employee who operates the case during the game.

Case the Deck. Keep track of which cards have been dealt out of the deck and which cards remain in the deck.

Casino Host. Someone who greets players, especially high-rollers; tracks their play; provides them with complimentary meals, show tickets, and hotel rooms; takes care of their needs; buys gifts for the player and/or his family; and in general sees that all good players are recognized.

Casino Manager. The person in charge of the gaming operation of a casino.

Catwalk. The ramps above a casino where casino security personnel walk to look at the action in the casino. They are concealed by one-way mirrors. Sometimes called the "peek" or the "eye in the sky." Nowadays, casino action is observed by electronic surveillance systems, and catwalks are seldom used by security personnel.

Check Racker. A casino employee who works at a roulette table along with the roulette dealer. A racker helps pick up the roulette checks (chips), helps rack them, and helps with the payoffs. A check racker is usually an employee in training to become a dealer.

Checks. *See* Chips.

Chemin-de-Fer. An ancient game, sometimes called "shimmy," first developed in France in the 1400s. It was introduced to America in Florida, shortly after World War I, and was a very popular game in the plush Florida casinos during the 1940s. Chemin-de-fer was introduced to Nevada in 1958 at the Star Dust Hotel-Casino in Las Vegas. It was soon available at many other Strip casinos, but it never became as popular as the very similar game of baccarat. Chemin-de-fer is similar to baccarat, with the major exception being that the casino operators take no risk, since the players bet against each other. The operators make their money by taking a 5-percent cut out of the player's winning bet. The object of the game is to win by holding a combination of two or three cards totaling 9 or as close as possible to 9, or to a two-digit number ending in 9. When the total of the cards is a two-digit number, only the latter digit has any value. For example, a 6 and a 4 (10) would count as 0, or a 10 and a 5 (15) would count as 5. The ace is the lowest-ranking card and has a point value of 1. Kings, queens, and jacks have a value of 10; all other cards have their numerical face values. If, after the first two cards are dealt, neither the player or the banker has an 8 or a 9, the many complicated rules of the game determine if the player and/or the banker stands or draws another card, and the winning and losing bets are settled at that time. If the banker wins, he retains the deal; if he loses, the deal passes to the player to his right and the game continues.

Chips. A token, usually made of a mixture of clay and vinyl or a mixture of brass and plastic, used for betting purposes instead of currency or coin. Chips come in various denominations, and their color is mandated by the Gaming Control Board. One-dollar chips, although many casinos use metal tokens for dollars, must be blue; $5 chips must be red; $25 chips must be green; and $100 chips must be black.

Chuck-A-Luck (or Bird Cage). A game quite popular in the early days of legalized gambling but not currently licensed in Nevada. The equipment and rules are as follows: Three two-inch dice are tumbled in a wire cage shaped like an hourglass. The slim waist of the cage is encircled by a metal band connected to an axle on which the cage turns. The three dice tumble from end to end of the cage when it is spun, then come to rest on one of the drumlike coverings at the end of the cage. The layout bears the numbers 1, 2, 3, 4, 5, 6. Players place their bets on one or more of the layout numbers. After the cage is spun and the dice come to rest, if a player's number appears on one die, he gets even money; if his number appears on two dice, he gets paid off at 2 to 1; and if his number appears on all three dice, the payoff is 3 to 1.

Clerk. A dealer.

Clock. (1) To count or keep track of the amount of money wagered at a given table or game. (2) To keep a record of the numbers that have come up on a roulette game or on a dice game.

Cold Deck. A deck of cards that has been illegally and secretly arranged in a certain order. The deck is then switched for the deck currently in play, either by the dealer and his agent, or by an outside cheater.

Come-Out Roll. The initial roll of the dice when a dice shooter is trying to establish a point.

Comp. Slang for *complimentary.* "Comps" are given to regular players and high-rollers as a "reward" for their patronage. The "rewards" can be in the form of meals, drinks, hotel rooms, showroom tickets, or any other amenity that a casino has to offer.

Cooler. *See* Cold Deck.

Copper. (1) *noun:* In faro, a small six-sided chip put on a bet to signify that a player is betting that the card will be a loser. (2) *verb:* In faro, to put the copper on a bet.

Court Card. A jack, queen, or king.

Cowboy. (1) A fast and reckless gambler. (2) To act wild and irresponsibly.

Craps. A game that has been played, in one form or another, for over two thousand years. It first became popular in the United States in the 1800s, especially in New Orleans and along the Mississippi River. In 1907 John Winn developed the first craps layout that allowed a player to bet whether the dice would "win" or "lose." Within a few years, the Winn layout, and variations of it, were used throughout the United States in the many illegal craps games being operated in most major cities. The popularity of craps continued to grow, and during World War II tens of thousands of servicemen played the game anywhere and anytime they could. From 1945 to the late 1960s, craps was the most popular casino game. In the 1960s, after Dr. Thorp's book on card-counting became a best-seller, more and more 21 games were licensed, and today craps runs a distant second in popularity to 21.

Craps is played with two dice and any number of players. To begin the game, a player, called the "shooter," throws the dice. His first roll of the dice is called the "come-out roll." If, on the come-out roll, the shooter throws a natural (a 7 or an 11), it is a winning decision called a "pass"; a craps (a 2, 3, or 12) is a losing decision called a "miss-out." If the shooter throws a 4, 5, 6, 8, 9, or 10, that number becomes his point and he continues rolling the dice until he either throws his point again, which is a winning decision (a pass), or he throws a 7, which is a losing decision (a miss-out). When a player misses out on a point, the dice pass to the next player on his left. The dice continue on around the table in a clockwise direction. On the come-out roll of the dice, the players may bet that the dice will pass or miss-out. They may also bet on any other combination on the layout. After the first roll, the players may bet that the next roll of the dice will be a winning decision (a come bet) or a losing decision (a don't-come bet), and they may continue to do so until the shooter's point is made or missed.

Along with the come and don't-come bets, other bets that can be made at any time by any of the players at the table include: (1) *One-roll bets.* As the name implies, these bets are good for one roll only and include the "horn," which is a method of covering the numbers 2, 3, 11, or 12 with one wager; any craps (covers the numbers 2, 3, and 12); individual bets on 2, 3, 7, 11, or 12, or any hard-way numbers. The field is also a one-roll bet, and it consists of the numbers 2, 3, 4, 9, 10, 11, and 12. If any of these numbers is rolled, the player wins. If 2 is rolled, the player is paid double, and if 12 is rolled, the player is paid three times his bet. (2) *Place Bets.* These are bets that the player may place on certain specific numbers. The numbers 4 and 10 pay odds of 9 to 5, the numbers 5 and 9 pay odds of 7 to 5, and the numbers 6 and 8 pay odds of 7 to 6. Place bets can be made at any time and can be taken off or called off at any time. (3) *Big-Six and Big-Eight Bets.* These are bets made on a section of the layout marked with a red 6 and a red 8. The player is betting that a 6 or an 8 will be rolled before a 7 is rolled. Winners are paid at even money. (4) *Hard-Way Bets.* These are bets that a player makes when he is betting that a specific number (4, 6, 8, or 10) will be thrown with two double numbers. The player loses if the number is made any other way than with doubles (for example, 5 and 5 or 4 and 4), or if a 7 is rolled.

Credit. (1) When a table has an excess of chips, a procedure is initiated by the pit boss to return the excess to the cashier's cage. (2) The amount of money that a casino will extend to a player in order for the player to gamble. Credit can be either in the form of markers or in check-cashing privileges.

Credit Manager. The individual who determines the amount of credit that a casino will extend to a player and who is responsible for operating the credit office. His decisions on credit will be given final approval by the casino manager and/or the general manager.

Counter (Card-Counter). A player who tracks the cards that have been played in order to gain an advantage by knowing which cards have been played and which remain in the deck.

Count Room. Rooms where the money collected from table games and slot machines is counted. The room where the currency from the pit drop-boxes is counted is called the "soft-count room."

The room where coins from the drop-boxes or buckets located beneath the slot machines is counted is called the "hard-count room."

Crap Out. In a craps game, to roll a 2, 3, or 12 on the come-out roll. A crap-out is a loser for the front line and a winner or a stand-off for the back line. The expression is sometimes used erroneously when a shooter rolls a 7 and misses out.

Crimp. (1) Bending cards so that a deck can be cut at a certain place or so that a player can identify a card by its bend. (2) The name of the bend.

Crossroader. Any cheater who attempts to beat (illegally) any type of gambling game.

Daub. (1) A paste or fluid used in marking the backs of cards so a cheater can distinguish one card from another. Different daubs are concocted for use on the backs of red decks and blue decks. (2) The act of applying the daub.

Dauber. An individual applying "daub" to the cards.

Deuce. (1) A die with two spots. (2) A $2 bill. (3) Any two-spot card.

Deuce Dealing. A method of cheating in which a crooked dealer deals the second card from the top of the deck when he appears to be—and should be—dealing the card on the top of the deck. *See* Seconds Dealing.

Dice Bowl. In craps, the container in front of the boxman containing the dice not in use.

Dolly. The marker used to indicate the winning number on a roulette table.

Double Sawbuck. A $20 bill.

Drag Down. To reduce the size of a wager on the next bet or to take the winnings and leave only the original bet on the table.

Drilling. A method of cheating a slot machine where the cheat drills a hole in the side of the machine and inserts a wire that trips the payoff mechanism. This method of cheating has been almost entirely eliminated by the installation of antitheft devices in modern slot machines.

Drop. (1) The cash used to purchase chips or tokens at a casino table game and "dropped" through a slot into the box located beneath the table. (2) The coins taken out of a slot machine by the casino.

Drop Box. The removable, locked container located under a casino pit game that holds the money used by players to purchase tokens and chips for the game.

Drop Buckets. The containers located under slot machines that catch any overflow of coins that have been fed into the machines.

Dry or Dry-Holed. Expression used to describe a player who has lost his money and is "busted."

Dummy Up. Keep quiet.

Dump the Tray. In the early days of gaming, illegally losing money to a confederate (an agent). Today, the term means simply that the dealer has lost a great deal of money to a player.

Early Out or E.O. What happens when a dealer gets off work early or gets the last break of the shift, enabling him to leave work before the majority of other employees on the same shift.

Easy-Way. In craps, when the shooter makes a 4, 6, 8, or 10 any way except in pairs. For example, an easy-way 8 would be 6–2 or 5–3, while a pair of 4s would be a hard-way 8.

Edge Work. A deck of cards marked with a slight bevel drawn on certain points of each card between the design and the edge of the card. A bevel mark high up might indicate an ace, lower down a king, etc.

Eighter (Ada) from Decatur. In craps, slang for the number 8.

Eight, Skate, and Donate. In craps, slang for the number 8.

Eighty-Six (86). (1) To throw someone out of the building or gaming area. (2) To cut someone off from drinking. (3) To bar someone from entering a casino or gaming area.

Eye in the Sky. (1) Slang for the person working in a casino security observation area. (2) The area over a casino floor that is used as an observation area. Nowadays, the "eye in the sky" function is performed by electronic surveillance cameras; however, there are usually one or more people working in the surveillance area to oversee the cameras, monitors, and video tapes.

Face Card. A king, queen, or jack in a deck of cards.

Fade. In craps, matching or covering the amount of money wagered by the shooter. The term is used in private craps games only, not in bank craps.

False Cut. A cut that leaves the deck or part of the deck in its original location.

Faro. A game that originated in France in the seventeenth century and was first known as Pharaoh or Pharoo. It entered the United States by way of New Orleans in the eighteenth century, and shortly after the Louisiana Purchase (1803) became the most widely played gambling-house game in the country. It was not until the early twentieth century that it was surpassed in popularity by the game of craps.

Faro is played with a standard fifty-two-card deck. The deck is shuffled, cut, and placed face-up in an open-top box called the dealing box. The faro dealer removes the top card, laying it face-up a short distance from the dealing box to start a pile to which all the winning cards will be added. The dealer then removes another card from the top of the deck, placing that one face-up alongside the dealing box. The third card in the deck, remaining on top of the deck in the dealing box, has now been exposed and identified. The second and third cards in the deck, unknown when the full deck was placed in the dealing box, form the first turn, or pair of cards on which betting can be done. In all, twenty-five pairs of cards are worked from the deck; the final card, because it can't be paired with another, is discarded and does not figure in the betting. The card remaining in the dealing box is considered the winner, and the card drawn from the box is the loser.

The common bet in faro is whether the card the player bets on is a winner or a loser. To bet the card is a winner, the player simply places his bet on the card; if he is betting that it will be a loser, he places a "copper" (a small six-sided black chip) on the bet. Bets can also be made on the high or low card in the turn. There are actually ninety-seven ways that bets can be made. This number is arrived at because of various splits and combinations of cards that are available for the player.

A case-keeper manipulates an abacus-type counting board with beads (called a case) that shows which denominations and how many of them have already been removed from the dealing box or exposed on top of it. This makes it easier for a player to follow the action and progress of the game at any time. A player must pay careful attention to the case if he is to play the game to his best advantage.

Many players think that faro is an even-money bet for the house. However, no single house-percentage figure can be given for the entire game. The house percentage varies at each stage of the game, depending on how many denominations of the card a player is betting on have been disposed of and how many cards remain in the box. The casino's actual earnings are low because few customers bet until at least three cards of any denomination have been disposed of—thereby raising their chances of winning. Faro reaches its climax on the twenty-fifth or final turn. There are several ways a player can bet the final turn, depending on the cards left in the box. When the denomination of all three cards in the final turn is different, a player can "call the turn" and take a chance on naming both the winner and the loser in the turn, with the probability of one chance in six of being correct. This bet pays 4 to 1.

Few casinos still offer faro. The game is not attractive to the house because of its low percentage and the fact that it often costs more to operate than it takes in. Players don't care for it because most of the payoffs are even money and because the game demands concentration and patience. Casinos and players alike currently demand fast-action games with high payoffs.

Fat. A person with a lot of money.

Fever. In craps, slang for the number 5.

Field. In craps, that portion of the layout that covers betting on the numbers 2, 3, 4, 9, 10, 11, and 12.

Fills. Replacement money for table-game trays or slot-machine hoppers. Each table and slot machine starts operation with a fixed amount of money. When that amount is reduced to a certain level, it must be replenished to its original level by making a "fill."

Fill Slip. A form, in triplicate, signed by a pit boss or slot supervisor, a security guard, and a cashier, stating that a certain amount of chips and/or tokens is being delivered to a table game or a slot machine. The three copies of a fill slip are disbursed as follows: one goes to the table game or slot machine, one stays with the casino cashier, and one stays in the fill-machine box.

First Base. In a 21 game, the player closest to the dealer's left, the first position.

Flash. When a dealer exposes the top card or the hole card to a player, thereby enabling the player to know whether to hit or stand.

Flat Bet. A wager that is paid, when won, with the same amount as bet. An even-money bet.

Flat Passers. Dice shaved on various sides so that the numbers rolled most frequently are 4, 5, 9, and 10. Those numbers are passing or winning numbers.

Flats (or Flat Dice). Crooked dice that have been shaved so that they are slightly brick-shaped.

Flat Store. A casino that cheats its customers, usually by operating rigged games or by using altered equipment, such as dice.

Flop. In hold-'em poker, the turning up, by the dealer, of three common cards in the center of the table.

Foreign Chips. In a casino, a chip from another casino.

Frets. The metal partitions that separate each of the thirty-eight numbered sections of a roulette wheel.

Front Line. In craps, the area on the layout for making the initial bet before a shooter begins a new sequence of rolls. It is also known as the pass line.

Front Money. Cash deposited in the cashier's cage or "put up front" by a high-stakes player. This deposit allows the player to be granted credit while playing.

Gaff. To alter or rig any gambling equipment with the intent of cheating the customer.

Gaming Commission (Nevada). Created in 1959, its primary job is licensing. This group grants or denies gaming licenses, and it can revoke, suspend, or condition licenses of existing gambling operations. Although the Gaming Commission acts on the recommendations of the Gaming Control Board, the Commission's action is independent of the Gaming Control Board. The Gaming Commission has the power to hold disciplinary hearings and to set regulations that gaming establishments must follow to the letter.

The Gaming Commission is made up of five part-time members appointed by the governor for staggered four-year terms. No more than three members can be of the same political party, no more than two from the same occupational area, and none can have a financial interest in any gaming establishment.

Gaming Control Board (Nevada). A three-member state board, created in 1955, that investigates all applicants for major licensing and has the responsibility of enforcing all the gaming laws and regulations of the State of Nevada. Its agents have peace-officer authority to appear unannounced to examine any gaming premises. They also have the authority to seize equipment and supplies and to examine and audit the papers, books, and records of any gaming establishment in the state of Nevada.

The three members are appointed to four-year terms by the governor. Each member is required to have specific expertise in an aspect of the gaming industry. The chairman must have at least five years of administrative experience; a second member must have five years of experience as a certified public accountant and be an expert in corporate financing and auditing; and the third member must have full training and experience in law enforcement or law.

George. A player who bets money for a dealer and/or gives money to a dealer as a "toke" or tip. Also known as a "live one."

Go for the Money. To cheat, in any manner, in order to "win" money from a player.

Goose. In bingo or keno, the plastic, metal, or, formerly, wooden container that holds all the balls to be drawn in the calling of the game.

Grind. To play conservatively, betting small amounts of money; to play to make a profit, slowly but surely.

Grind Joint. A casino that caters to low-limit players, shuns high-rollers, and attempts to make a profit from volume play rather than from high-limit players.

Gross Gaming Revenue. In a casino, the total of all money won, prior to expenses.

Hand In. In a casino, a tip given directly to a dealer rather than the player making a bet for the dealer.

Hand Mucker. A cheater who illegally puts cards in and takes other cards out of a card game in order to give himself a winning hand.

Hand Mucking. A method of illegally introducing a card (or cards) into a game, usually a 21 game, but it can also be done in other card games. The cheater exchanges a secreted card (or cards) for the card (or cards) he was dealt and thereby creates a winning hand for himself.

Hand Pay. When a casino employee pays a customer—by hand—the money that has been won at a slot machine.

Hard Way. In craps, the numbers 4, 6, 8, and 10 can be made the easy way or the hard way. Hard-way numbers are made with two duplicate numbers, such as two 2s, two 3s, two 4s, or two 5s.

Hazard. One of the first games to be legalized by the State of Nevada in 1931, hazard is estimated to be at least seven hundred years old. Hazard lost its popularity after the introduction of 21 (or blackjack), and there are currently no hazard games licensed in Nevada. Hazard is played with three dice and is similar to

chuck-a-luck. The layout bears the numbers 1, 2, 3, 4, 5, and 6, and a player may place his bet on one or more of the layout numbers. The layout also allows for twenty-five other wagers, including betting on "raffles," a bet that any *specific* three of a kind (three aces, or three deuces, etc.) will appear; any "raffle," a bet that *any* three of a kind will appear; a low bet, a bet that the total count on the dice will be 10 or below; a high bet, a bet that the total count on the dice will be 11 or more; or an odd-and-even bet, a bet that the total count on the dice will add up to an even or odd number. A player may also bet that he can pick the exact winning number of the total count, such as 4, 5, 6, 7, and so on, up to and including 17. After all bets have been placed, the "bird cage" containing the three dice is "flopped," and the winning and losing wagers are settled.

High-Low Bet. In craps, a one-roll bet made on the numbers 2 and 12. If either number is rolled, the bet is a winner.

High-Roller. A high-limit bettor and big-spender.

Hock. In faro, the last card in the dealing box.

Hold. The amount of money that a gaming device or a casino wins, or keeps, out of the amount of money wagered by a player.

Hold Check. A postdated check that a casino accepts from a player and holds until the player has a chance to deposit money in his account to cover the check.

Hold Out. A cheating practice when a player palms one or more cards that he will put back in the game at an appropriate time. Comparable to hand-mucking, when a player illegally runs cards in and out of a game.

Hole Card. In 21, the card dealt face-down to the dealer; in poker, any cards that are not exposed.

Hop Bet. A one-roll bet on any combination of the dice. Two pairs, such as 6–6, 4–4, 5–5, etc., pay 30 to 1. Other combinations such as 1–2, 1–3, 1–4, etc., pay 15 to 1.

Hopper. The part of a slot machine that holds the coins. When a player wins at a

slot machine, the winning coins come out of the hopper.

Horn Bet. In craps, a one-roll bet that enables a player to win if the numbers 2, 3, 11, or 12 are rolled.

Huckeley-Buck. (1) Busy and hectic. (2) A way of gambling that is fast, loose, and reckless.

In. As in, how much a player is "in" the game. For example, a player who has purchased $5,000 worth of chips is "in" $5,000.

Insurance Bet. When a player in a 21 game bets that the dealer has a natural blackjack. The bet is made when the dealer is showing an ace as his top card. A winning bet is paid 3 to 2.

Jimmy Hicks. In craps, slang for the number 6.

Jonah. A person whose presence is thought to bring bad luck.

Juice. (1) A connection or an "in" that gives someone an advantage or an edge. For example, "I've got 'juice' with Bill; he can get me a job at the Sands." (2) Payoff or protection money paid by an illegal operation to a law-enforcement agency so the operation will be allowed to continue.

Juice Dealer. The operator of a craps table or roulette wheel that uses electricity to control the dice or the movement of the wheel.

Juice Joint. A gambling establishment devoted to cheating, especially by means of electromagnetically controlled dice tables or roulette wheels.

Keno. (1) One of the first games to be legalized by the State of Nevada in March 1931. The original keno game was played in 1931 just as bingo is played today, except that there was no "free play" on the center square. The word *keno* is derived from *quine,* meaning five, and in the original form of the game, the first player to get five beans, or markers, in a row was the winner and announced it by shouting "quine" or "keno." During the 1920s, and even today, many social organizations played keno for fund-raising purposes. They sometimes called the game *beano* or *bingo,* rather than keno, because keno was then associated with "hard gambling." Because the general public was more familiar with the name *keno* than it was with *bingo,* the word *keno* was used when gaming was legalized in 1931. The name *tango* was also given to the game we now know as bingo. Neither keno nor tango should be confused with the current game of keno, that was first legalized in 1936 and known then—and for many years thereafter—as racehorse keno.

(2) A game patterned after the ancient Chinese lottery that was renamed *racehorse keno* and legalized in 1936. The game was generally known as racehorse keno until around 1960. The first legal racehorse keno game was opened in the Palace Club in Reno in May 1936. To begin a racehorse keno game, a player marks his choice of numbers and the amount of money he wishes to wager on the next game on a numbered ticket, then gives his ticket to the keno writer. The player may choose any amount of numbers from 1 to 80. The amount of money he may wager depends on the casino's limit. The keno writer makes a duplicate copy of the player's selection and gives it the player. The original ticket is kept by the keno writer, and all payoffs are based on the numbers marked on the original ticket. The game is played with eighty numbered balls in a container. The player wins or loses his wager by how many of the numbers he has selected match the numbers on the balls that have been randomly selected from the container. There are literally thousands of payoffs possible in a keno game, and some of the payoffs can be very high. A player can win $50,000 by wagering as little as $2. Keno, once a very popular game, today generates only a small percentage of a casino's revenue and is not played at all in several states where gambling is legal. Reasons cited for the decline of the game include the slowness of the game, a lack of interest among younger players, the high percentage of the game (the house wins approximately 26 to 28 percent of all money wagered), and the large jackpots paid by slot machines and video poker that make the smaller keno payoffs less attractive.

Key Employee. A casino employee, or a part-owner of a casino, who is empowered to make major decisions about the operation of the casino. The State of Nevada normally requires all key employees to be licensed.

Key Man. An employee in the slot-machine department who is authorized to unlock slot machines, make minor repairs, and pay jackpots. A key man works on the casino floor, as opposed to a slot mechanic, who usually works in the slot-repair shop.

Ladder Man. A casino employee who sits on an elevated stand overlooking the casino action. In the early days of gaming, the ladder man's duty was to watch for dealers' errors and to catch anyone trying to cheat at faro, baccarat, chemin-de-fer, and craps.

Lammer. A small disk put on a table indicating that money is owed to that table by a player, or to show that money was removed from a table. Also used to designate the value of chips or checks in play on a roulette table.

Laydown (Make a). To make a bet.

Layout. The printed felt surface on a gaming table that shows the different wagers available and provides spaces where players can place their bets so that the dealers can deal the game in a proper and efficient manner.

Lid It, or Put a Lid on It. What a pit boss says when he wants the dealer to close a table.

Little Joe or Little Joe from Kokomo. In craps, slang for the number 4.

Live One. A player with money, or a player who gives "tokes" (tips) to dealers.

Loads. Illegal dice that have weights placed in them to make certain numbers roll more often than they should.

Lump (or Lumpie). An inept, clumsy dealer.

Mallard. Slang for a $100 bill.

Marker. (1) An IOU from a player to the casino. (2) A coin placed on a roulette chip on the wheel to indicate the denomination of the chip the customer is playing.

Martingale System. A system of betting in which the amount of the bet is doubled after a loss.

Mechanic. A term used to describe a dealer who manipulates the tools of the trade (i.e., dice, cards, etc.) in an illegal manner in order to alter the outcome of a gambling game.

Midnight. In craps, slang for the number 12.

Misspots. Any dice that have the incorrect number of spots. They are used by cheaters—on either side of the table—to illegally alter the outcome of a dice game.

Money Plays. Words shouted out by a dealer when a customer is betting currency.

Monte Carlo Wheel. A roulette wheel with one 0, as opposed to the American wheel, which has a 0 and a 00.

Muck. To palm a card illegally for use later in a game.

Nailed. Caught cheating. For example, "I nailed him pressing his bet."

Natural. In 21, an ace and a 10-count card. In craps, a 7 or an 11 on the come-out roll.

Nina Ross (The Buckin' Hoss). In craps, slang for the number 9.

Ninety Days (in the County Jail). In craps, slang for the number 9.

Nut. The daily operating expenses of a gaming establishment.

Odds. The ratio of unfavorable chances to favorable chances.

One-Roll Bet. In craps, a bet that is decided on the next roll of the dice.

P.C. Slang for *percentage.*

Paddle. (1) The device used by a dealer to force paper money through a slot in the gaming table into the drop box. (2) A device on a big-six wheel, or any carnival wheel, that projects above the rim of the wheel and after the wheel has been spun and comes to a stop, indicates the winning number.

Paint Card. A picture card (i.e., a king, queen, or jack).

Panguingui (or Pan). A game similar to rummy, played with six decks of cards. Seldom played in casinos in recent years.

Paper. (1) Marked cards. (2) A check or other negotiable document.

Paperhanger. Someone who writes bad checks.

Parlay. A system of betting in which the gambler, after a win, risks the entire stake on the next bet.

Pass. In craps, a winning decision for the craps shooter when he either throws a 7 or an 11 on the first roll, or repeats the point before he throws a 7.

Passers. In craps, altered dice on which the number 7 is rarely rolled, thus allowing the shooter to make many passes.

Pass Line. A space on the craps table where a player places his bet when he is betting that the dice will win.

Past Post. The act of placing a bet after a decision has already been made. It can pertain to any game, but the expression originated with bettors making bets on horse races after the race had been run and the winner was already determined. Post time is when the horses leave the post and the race begins. Therefore, past post means making a bet after the action is over. Past posting is most commonly done on crap tables and roulette tables when a cheater diverts the attention of the dealer while his confederate places a bet on the winning number or area.

Peek. (1) To secretly look at the top card of the deck. (2) An area (usually above the table games) where a casino employee can secretly observe the games and look for any irregularities from either the players or the employees. Sometimes called "the eye in the sky," or the "catwalk."

Percentage. The edge, or advantage, enjoyed by the house and often called the house advantage. It is obtained by paying less than the true odds of the game.

Pinch a Bet. To illegally take money or chips away from a bet after it is evident that the bet has been lost.

Pit Boss. A casino employee who supervises a gaming area. He, or she, is stationed in the pit area and watches the games, writes out fill and credit slips, corrects errors made by dealers or players, and watches for cheating by dealers and/or players.

Plunger. A person who acts hastily or recklessly, especially a rash gambler or speculator.

Point. The number rolled by the shooter on the first roll of the dice—other than a 7, 11, 2, 3, or 12. This number (4, 5, 6, 8, 9, or 10) becomes the "point," and the shooter must roll this number again before he rolls a 7. If a 7 comes up before his point, regardless of how many times he rolls, he wins.

Pole. Also called "stick." In craps, the wooden canelike implement used to retrieve the dice and return them to the shooter.

Power of the Pen (The). Slang for the authority given to a casino employee who has the right to sign for complimentary drinks, meals, or rooms.

Pressing a Bet. The illegal act of adding to a bet after it has been won but not yet been paid.

Puck. The round marker used to identify the point in action at the craps table.

Push. (1) In blackjack or 21, when the player and the dealer have the same point total. (2) A tie or a stand-off.

Quarter Chip. A $25 chip.

Rack. (1) A box, case, or tray with open grooves used to keep game chips stacked in an orderly fashion. (2) In roulette, to pick up checks and stack them in their proper location.

Rail. On a craps table, the raised side of the table, often grooved with troughs for holding chips.

Rathole. To put money or chips into a pocket while still gambling. Done to prevent the dealer or other players from knowing how much money the "ratholer" has in his position.

Readers. Marked cards.

Red Dog. Red dog is played with a standard deck of fifty-two cards. The player is dealt five cards, and the object of the game is for the player to hold a card, in the same suit, of a higher rank than the card that the dealer turns over from his deck. For example, if a jack of clubs is turned up by the dealer, the player must have a queen, king, or ace of clubs in order to win. Winning bets are paid even money.

Red-Line Law. A Reno city ordinance, originally enacted in the 1940s, intended to confine unlimited gaming within a small downtown area. In 1970 a new ordinance was passed that allowed unlimited gaming anywhere in the City of Reno but required that the license be issued in conjunction with one hundred or more hotel rooms.

Rhythm System. A former method of cheating a slot machine that involved manipulating the slot-machine handle, reels, and clock. The timing of pulling the handle could result in bringing up winning combinations on the payline of the slot machine. No mechanical gimmicks were needed because the manipulation was done through the expertise of the cheater. Modern prevention methods have eliminated this method of cheating.

Rig. To gaff or make crooked. A "rigged" game is a crooked game.

Right Bettor. (1) In craps, a player who bets the dice to win. (2) A front-line player.

Roll the Deck. *See* Turn the Deck.

Roulette. The traditional glamour game of the casino industry, roulette is at least 350 years old. It was played in France and throughout Europe and Asia as early as the middle 1600s. Roulette was introduced to the United States in the late 1700s. It was one of the original games made legal by the Nevada Gaming Act of 1931. Currently, the only difference between the European roulette wheel and the American wheel is that the American wheel has a 0 and a 00, and the European wheel has only the 0. The payoffs are the same on both wheels, so it follows that the European wheel offers better odds to the player.

Along with the 0 and the 00, the roulette wheel has thirty-six numbers. The numbers are alternately colored red and black, and the 0 and the 00 are green.

The layout is marked accordingly, with additional areas for betting red or black (an even-money payoff); odd or even (even money); the first or second 18 numbers (even money); the columns (2 to 1); and the first, second, or third dozen (2 to 1). Bets on single numbers, including 0 and 00, pay 35 to 1, on two numbers 17 to 1, on three numbers 11 to 1, on four numbers 8 to 1, on five numbers 6 to 1, and on six numbers 5 to 1. Players place their bets on the layout while the dealer spins a small white ball in the opposite direction from the spinning wheel. Bets may be made until the ball is about to leave its track. At that time, the dealer signals no more bets. Where the ball falls and comes to rest between any two metal partitions of the wheel becomes the winning number. The dealer announces the number and the color, as well as pointing out the winning number on the layout. He then collects all losing bets and pays off all the winning wagers, starting with the even-money bets and paying the 35 to 1 bets last.

Rounder. (1) An individual who goes around from casino to casino drinking, gambling, and in general socializing with his friends and other casino employees. (2) An individual who goes to as many casinos as possible, in as short a time as possible, in order to establish credit, cash checks, and bilk casinos out of money by cashing nonnegotiable checks.

Rounder's Slang. Slang that substitutes rhyming words for common words. It originated in nineteenth-century England and was very popular in the bars and casinos of Reno in the thirties and forties. Some examples of rounder's slang: Near and Far—A bar. Tall and Slender—The bartender. Joe Goss—The boss. Once or Twice—Ice. Elephant's Trunk—A drunk. Bread and Water—Your daughter. Moan and Groan—The telephone. Fiddle and Flute—A suit. Apron String—A ring. North and South—Your mouth. Rats and Mice—Pair of dice. Bees and Honey—Money. Heel and Toe—On the go. Rattle and Jar—A

car. Twist and Twirl—A girl. Ones and Twos—Your shoes. Simple Simon—A diamond. Wires and Cable—A table. Shovel and Broom—Your room.

Sand. To mark the edges of playing cards with sandpaper. The location of the sanded area tells the cheater the denomination of the card. For example, sanded areas on the top of the card might mean a high card, on the middle of the card might mean a 7, 8, or 9, etc.

Sawbuck. A $10 bill.

Sawdust Joint. A plain, unpretentious casino. The expression comes from the late 1800s when gaming establishments had sawdust or even dirt floors.

Score. To win a large amount of money.

Second Dealing. A method of cheating where the crooked dealer deals the second card from the top of the deck when he appears to be—and should be—dealing the top card. *See* Deuce Dealing.

Seven-and-a-Half. One of the original games specifically mentioned in the bill legalizing gambling in Nevada that was passed in March 1931. Believed to be the direct forerunner of present-day blackjack, seven-and-a-half has the same basic structure as blackjack or 21. The seven-and-a-half deck contains only forty cards, the 8s, 9s, and 10s being absent. Court cards each count one-half, and others count their numerical value. The king of diamonds is wild and may have any value. The object of the game is to get as close to 7 and one-half as possible, without going over. When a player draws cards totaling 8 or more, he busts—as he does when going over 21 in blackjack—and he loses his wager.

Shading. A method of marking cards by delicately shading their backs with a diluted solution of marking ink the same color as the ink printed on the back of the cards.

Shapes. Dice whose shapes have been altered in some way so that they are no longer perfect cubes.

Shill. A casino employee who plays house money and pretends to be a player in order to attract business and get a game going. Shills are seldom used nowadays

in pit games but are frequently used in poker games.

Shimmy. Slang for the game of chemin-de-fer.

Shoe. A card-dealing box employed in baccarat, chemin-de-fer, and 21 games when multiple decks are used.

Shooter. In any dice game, the player who rolls the dice.

Single Deck. In 21, a game in which only one deck of cards is used, as distinct from games in which double or multiple decks are used.

Six-Ace Flats. Cheating dice that have had their 6 and 1 sides shaved down so that 6 and 1 come up more often than they would on square dice, and therefore produce more 7s.

Skinny Dugan. In craps, slang for the number 7.

Sleeper. Money or a bet left on the table or layout, which has been forgotten by a player.

Snake Bet. In roulette, a wager on twelve contiguous numbers on the layout, usually the same color, starting at red 1 and ending at red 34.

Snake Eyes. In craps, slang for the number 2.

Snap. A 21 game.

Snapper. A natural blackjack (an ace and a face card or a 10).

Snowballs. In craps, misspotted dice showing only the numbers 4, 5, and 6. Cheaters sneak them into play and then make a bet in the field. The dice are called snowballs because the spots are white, and when they roll down the table they show mostly white and very little red.

Soda. In faro, the exposed top card in the deck when the full deck is placed in the dealing box.

Soft 17. A combination of cards, including an ace, totaling 17, that can be hit with a 10-count card without breaking the hand.

Split Store. A casino where the dealers' tokes (tips) are pooled and divided equally at the end of a shift or a twenty-four-hour period.

Spooning. A method of cheating a slot machine by inserting a spoon-shaped device through the payout opening into the payout mechanism and thereby causing coins to drop out. A description of a "spoon" in an article in the *Reno Evening Gazette* of August 8, 1948, described a "spoon" as a small, flat piece of celluloid with three small holes bored in it with a curved screwdriver shaft. Recent improvements in slot-machine security devices make this method of cheating impossible.

Square. Honest. Can pertain to gaming equipment, an individual, or a casino.

Stacked Deck. A deck that has been secretly pre-arranged in such a manner that the cheater who arranged the deck will win all wagers.

Stand. In 21, to play the cards you have been dealt.

Stand Off. (1) No decision, a tie. (2) In craps, a casino may "bar 12 or bar 2," which means that if the barred number is rolled, the back-line player does not win or lose and the result is a stand-off.

Stick Man. The person in the craps table crew who uses the stick to retrieve and/or push the dice to the player who is shooting the dice.

Stiff. (1) A player's or dealer's hand that can be broken by a hit card. (2) A player who does not give tips or "tokes" to dealers.

Store. Slang for a gambling casino. Thought to have been brought into common usage by Harold Smith Sr., because "store" was originally a slang term for any carnival game, and Smith began his gaming career in the carnival business.

Strippers. A deck of cards whose edges have been trimmed, making some cards either narrower or shorter than others, thereby enabling a cheater to "read" the cards.

Stripping. Shuffling a deck of cards by pulling small packets from the top and placing them at the bottom of the pack, usually with a rapid motion.

Stuck. The amount a player has lost, or is losing, on a game.

Sub or Submarine. A pocket-like piece of cloth worn under a dealer's pants. Dishonest dealers slip chips or tokens into their subs when no one is looking.

Suits. Pit bosses.

Surrender. In 21, a provision that allows a player to retire from a hand after the first two cards are dealt. In giving up his hand, the player normally surrenders half his wager.

Sweat. To agonize or worry about money lost by the casino.

Sweater (also known as a Bleeder). A pit supervisor who becomes angry when players win too much or too often.

Swing. To steal money.

Switch Man. A person who puts altered or illegal dice or cards in a game.

Take a Bath. To lose heavily.

Take a Shot. To make a cheating move.

Take Off. To steal, cheat, or in some way take money from someone dishonestly.

Tango. Early name for the game of bingo. In the 1930s, the games of tango, bingo, and keno were all the same game. Many early bingo parlors were known as tango clubs (or parlors). Bill Harrah's first bingo game in Reno was known as the Plaza Tango, and he later operated another bingo parlor called Harrah's Heart Tango. The name comes from the Spanish word *tengo*, which means *I have it*. In the early 1930s, when a player had five winning numbers in a row, instead of shouting "bingo," he would shout "tengo." *Tengo* eventually evolved into *tango*, and that is how the game came to be called tango. By the early 1940s, the names keno and tango were no longer used in conjunction with bingo games.

Tap Out. To go broke.

Texas Sunflowers. In craps, a hard 10 (two 5s).

Third Base. The last position in a 21 game. The last player to receive his cards.

Tiger (Bucking the). The tiger was the traditional symbol for a faro game, and "bucking the tiger" meant playing faro. Today it is used to refer to gambling on any game or event.

Tips. Side money given by players to dealers to bring them luck, to show their appreciation at winning, or simply "to share the wealth." Commonly called "tokes."

Tokens. Metal coins used as dollars in table games or as coins of various denominations in slot machines.

Tokes. Slang for tips. Short for tokens of appreciation—money given to dealers by players. *See* Tips.

Tops. Crooked dice. Usually dice on which the number of pips on each side have been altered.

Tops and Bottoms. Crooked dice that bear only three different numbers on each die. Also called tops, T's, misspots, and busters.

Track. (1) To keep a count of the money wagered on a game. (2) To keep a record of the amount of action a customer gives a casino. This information is used to determine the amount of complimentary benefits, such as food, drinks, and hotel or showroom privileges, that a player is offered.

Trey. (1) In cards, a card ranked third in any suit. (2) In craps, the side of a die with three spots.

Trims. Crooked cards that have been trimmed in such a manner that a cheat can "read" them.

Tub. A small craps table that can be operated by one person.

Turn the Deck (or Roll the Deck). A method of cheating at 21 that occurs when a dishonest dealer picks up exposed cards on the layout in a predetermined pattern, puts them under the deck with their backs down, and then, after the dealer's agent has made his bets, turns the deck over and deals out the cards. When properly executed, this method of collusion cannot lose. This method of cheating is the main reason why most 21 games now employ discard racks.

Twenty-One (or Blackjack). One of the most popular casino table games. The object of the game is for the player to draw cards that total 21 or come closer to 21 than those held by the dealer. A king, queen, and jack count 10; other cards count at their face value, except the ace, which counts as 1 or 11, as the player or the dealer decides. The game begins when the dealer delivers two cards, face down, to each player. The dealer's first card faces up, the second faces down. An ace with any 10, jack, queen, or king is a "blackjack." The player must turn that hand over immediately, and the dealer will pay the bet 3 to 2, unless the dealer also has a blackjack, in which case the hand is a "push" or tie, and neither the player nor the dealer wins. If the player does not have a blackjack, he has the option of asking for more cards (taking a hit). A player may take as many "hits" as he wants, but if his card total goes over 21, he is busted (or broke) and must turn over his cards, and his wager is lost. If the player does not want any cards other than the two originally dealt to him, he stands (does not take any more cards).

After all players are satisfied with their hands, the dealer turns his down card face-up and stands or draws more cards as he chooses. The dealer must draw to any count up to and including 16, and he must stand on 17, except a soft 17. A soft 17 is any combination of cards containing an ace, but not a 10, that totals 7 or 17. At the end of his play, the dealer pays off players who have a higher count than his with an amount equal to the bet they placed, and he collects the bets placed by players showing a lesser count. If a player and the dealer have the same count, it is considered a push or a tie, and no one wins or loses. If the dealer goes over 21, he pays each remaining player an amount equal to his bet.

Up Jumped the Devil. In craps, an expression used when the shooter rolls a 7 rather than his point.

Vigorish (or Vig). The percentage taken by the house on certain bets in baccarat, craps, and chemin-de-fer. The amount is usually 5 percent.

Wave. (1) To bend the edge of a card so that a cheater can "read" the cards. (2) The bend itself.

Wrong Bettor. In craps, the player who bets against the dice, a back-line player, a don't player. The opposite of a right bettor.

Yard. A $100 bill.
Yo. In craps, short for the number 11.
Yoleven. In craps, the number 11.

Zuke (or Zook). A tip or a toke given to a dealer.

BIBLIOGRAPHY

MANUSCRIPTS

Washoe County, Nevada. County Gaming Records, 1931–1945. Washoe County Records Center, Reno, Nevada.

INTERVIEWS

Cox, Elbert. Interview by author. Reno, Nevada. 7 September 1995.

Dixon, Deering. Interview by author. Reno, Nevada. 19 March 1997.

Dyer, Lloyd. Interview by author. Reno, Nevada. 18 March 1997.

Hobson, H. R. "Pick." Interview by author. Reno, Nevada. 7 September 1979.

Neely, Glen. Interview by author (by telephone). Reno, Nevada. 12 March 1995.

Orlich, Dan. Interview by author. Reno, Nevada. 4 March 1997.

Parker, James R. "Arky." Interview by author. Cotter, Arkansas. 10 October 1997.

Sheppard, Maurice. Interview by author. Reno, Nevada. 18 March 1997.

Smith, Virgil. Interview by author. Reno, Nevada. 12 August 1994.

Weitz, Harry. Interview by author. Reno, Nevada. 12 May 1982.

ORAL HISTORIES

Harrah, William F. "My Recollections of the Hotel-Casino Industry, and as an Auto Collecting Enthusiast." 1980. University of Nevada Oral History Program, Reno, Nevada.

Petricciani, Silvio. "The Evolution of Gaming in Nevada: The Twenties to the Eighties." 1982. University of Nevada Oral History Program, Reno, Nevada.

Ring, Robert A. "Recollections of Life in California, Nevada Gaming, and Reno and Lake Tahoe Civic Affairs." 1973. University of Nevada Oral History Program, Reno, Nevada.

BOOKS

Douglass, Jack, as told to William A. Douglass. *Tap Dancing on Ice*. Reno: University of Nevada Oral History Program, 1996.

Fuller, Harvey J. *Index of Nevada Gaming Establishments*. Minden, Nev.: The Coin Company, 1992.

Lewis, Oscar. *Sagebrush Casinos*. Garden City, N.Y.: Doubleday and Company, 1953.

Mandel, Leon. *William Fisk Harrah: The Life and Times of a Gambling Magnate*. Garden City, N.Y.: Doubleday and Company, 1982.

Nelson, Warren. *Always Bet on the Butcher: Warren Nelson and Casino Gaming, 1930s–1980s*. Reno: University of Nevada Oral History Program, 1994.

Sawyer, Raymond. *Reno: Where the Gamblers Go!* Reno: Sawston Publishing Company, 1976.

Schrader, Larry. *Reno, Round the Clock: The True Story of America's Gambling Mecca*. New York: Exposition Press, 1954.

Smith, Harold S., Sr., with John Wesley Noble. *I Want to Quit Winners*. Englewood Cliffs, N.J.: Prentice Hall, Inc., 1961.

Thackrey, Ted, Jr. *Gambling Secrets of Nick the Greek*. Chicago: Rand McNally & Company, 1968.

Van Tassel, Bethel Holmes. *Wood Chips to Game Chips: Casinos and People at North Lake Tahoe*. N.p.: Bethel Holmes Van Tassel, 1985.

ARTICLES

Berger, Meyer. "The Gay Gamblers of Reno." *Saturday Evening Post,* 10 July 1948: 22–78.

Butterfield, Roger. "Harolds Club." *Life,* 15 October 1945: 116–31.

Donovan, Richard. "How to Run a Gambling Casino." *Collier's,* 31 January 1953: 11–14.

Perry, George Sessions. "Reno." *Saturday Evening Post,* 5 July 1952: 24–72.

Wernick, Robert. "The World's Biggest Gambler." *Saturday Evening Post,* 13 February 1965: 22–23.

MISCELLANEOUS PRINTED MATERIALS

Nevada Magazine, Special Gaming Issue, March/April 1981.

NEWSPAPERS

Nevada State Journal. 1931–1985.

New York Times. 1931–1938.

Reno Evening Gazette. 1931–1965.

Reno Gazette Journal. 1985–1997.

INDEX